A·N·N·U·A·L E·D·I·T·I·O·N·S

Child Growth and Development

00/01

Seventh Edition

Editors

Ellen N. Junn
California State University, Fullerton

Ellen Junn is a professor of child and adolescent studies and director of the Faculty Development Center at California State University, Fullerton. She received a B.S. in experimental psychology from the University of Michigan and her M.A. and Ph.D. in cognitive and developmental psychology from Princeton University. In addition to her work on educational equity issues, Dr. Junn's research and publications focus on developments in children's conceptions regarding adult social relationships and on college teaching effectiveness.

Chris J. Boyatzis
Bucknell University

Chris Boyatzis is an assistant professor of psychology at Bucknell University. He received a B.A. in psychology from Boston University and his M.A. and Ph.D. in developmental psychology from Brandeis University. Many of his research interests lie at the intersection of social and cognitive development in early childhood. Dr. Boyatzis has published research on children's nonverbal behavior and social status, media effects on children, symbolic development, and play and art. He has also written on the use of literature and film to teach developmental psychology.

Dushkin/McGraw-Hill
Sluice Dock, Guilford, Connecticut 06437

Visit us on the Internet
http://www.dushkin.com/annualeditions/

Credits

1. Conception to Birth
Unit photo—Courtesy of Middlesex (Connecticut) Hospital.
2. Cognition, Language, and Learning
Unit photo—United Nations photo by Shelley Rotner.
3. Social and Emotional Development
Unit photo—© 2000 by PhotoDisc, Inc.
4. Parenting and Family Issues
Unit photo—© 2000 by Cleo Freelance Photography.
5. Cultural and Societal Influences
Unit photo—© 2000 by Cleo Freelance Photography.

Copyright

Cataloging in Publication Data
Main entry under title: Annual Editions: Child Growth and Development. 2000/2001.
    1. Child psychology—Periodicals. I. Junn, Ellen N., *comp.* II. Boyatzis, Chris J., *comp.*
III. Title: Child growth and development.
ISBN 0-07-236525-0   155.4'.05   ISSN 1075-5217

© 2000 by Dushkin/McGraw-Hill, Guilford, CT 06437, A Division of The McGraw-Hill Companies.

Seventh Edition

Cover image © 2000 PhotoDisc, Inc.

Printed in the United States of America   1234567890BAHBAH543210   Printed on Recycled Paper

Members of the Advisory Board are instrumental in the final selection of articles for each edition of ANNUAL EDITIONS. Their review of articles for content, level, currentness, and appropriateness provides critical direction to the editor and staff. We think that you will find their careful consideration well reflected in this volume.

Editors/Advisory Board

Staff

To the Reader

In publishing ANNUAL EDITIONS we recognize the enormous role played by the magazines, newspapers, and journals of the public press in providing current, first-rate educational information in a broad spectrum of interest areas. Many of these articles are appropriate for students, researchers, and professionals seeking accurate, current material to help bridge the gap between principles and theories and the real world. These articles, however, become more useful for study when those of lasting value are carefully collected, organized, indexed, and reproduced in a low-cost format, which provides easy and permanent access when the material is needed. That is the role played by ANNUAL EDITIONS.

New to ANNUAL EDITIONS is the inclusion of related World Wide Web sites. These sites have been selected by our editorial staff to represent some of the best resources found on the World Wide Web today. Through our carefully developed topic guide, we have linked these Web resources to the articles covered in this ANNUAL EDITIONS reader. We think that you will find this volume useful, and we hope that you will take a moment to visit us on the Web at *http://www.dushkin.com* to tell us what you think.

We are delighted to welcome you to this seventh volume of *Annual Editions: Child Growth and Development 00/01*. The amazing sequence of events of prenatal development that lead to the birth of a baby is an awe-inspiring process. Perhaps more intriguing is the question of what the future may hold for this newly arrived baby—for instance, will this child become a doctor, a lawyer, an artist, a beggar, or a thief? Although philosophers and prominent thinkers such as Charles Darwin and Sigmund Freud have long speculated about the importance of infancy on subsequent development, not until the 1960s did the scientific study of infants and young children flourish. Since then, research and theory in infancy and childhood have exploded, resulting in a wealth of new knowledge about child development.

Past accounts of infants and young children as passive, homogeneous organisms have been replaced with investigations aimed at studying infants and young children at a "microlevel"—as active individuals with many inborn competencies, who are capable of shaping their own environment—as well as at a "macrolevel," by considering the larger context surrounding the child. In short, children are not "blank slates," and development does not take place in a vacuum; children arrive with many skills and grow up in a complex web of social, historical, political, economic, and cultural spheres.

As was the case for previous editions, we hope to achieve at least four major goals with this volume. First, we hope to present you with the latest research and thinking to help you better appreciate the complex interactions that characterize human development in infancy and childhood. Second, in light of the feedback we received on previous editions, we have placed greater emphasis on important contemporary issues and challenges, exploring topics such as understanding development in the context of current societal and cultural influences. Third, attention is given to articles that also discuss effective, practical applications. Finally, we hope that this anthology will serve as a catalyst to help students become more effective future professionals and parents.

To achieve these objectives, we carefully selected articles from a variety of sources, including scholarly research journals and texts as well as semiprofessional journals and popular publications. Every selection was scrutinized for readability, interest level, relevance, and currency. In addition, we listened to the valuable input and advice from members of our advisory board, consisting of faculty from a range of institutions of higher education, including community and liberal arts colleges as well as research and teaching universities. We are most grateful to the advisory board as well as to the excellent editorial staff of Dushkin/McGraw-Hill Publishers.

Annual Editions: Child Growth and Development 00/01 is organized into five major units. Unit 1 focuses on conception, prenatal development, and childbirth. Unit 2 presents information regarding developments in cognition, language, and learning. Unit 3 focuses on social and emotional development. Unit 4 is devoted to parenting and family issues such as child care issues, divorce and marital transitions, and parenting and discipline. Finally, unit 5 focuses on larger cultural and societal influences (such as the influence of popular culture and violent media on children, after-school care, and international child labor) and on special challenges (such as poverty, childhood victimization and abuse, resilience, and children with attention deficits).

Instructors for large lecture courses may wish to adopt this anthology as a supplement to a basic text, whereas instructors for smaller sections might also find the readings effective for promoting student presentations or for stimulating discussions and applications. Whatever format is utilized, it is our hope that the instructor and the students will find the readings interesting, illuminating, and provocative.

As the title indicates, *Annual Editions: Child Growth and Development* is by definition a volume that undergoes continual review and revision. Thus, we welcome and encourage your comments and suggestions for future editions of this volume. Simply fill out and return the comment card found at the end of this book. Best wishes, and we look forward to hearing from you!

Ellen N. Junn
Editor

Chris J. Boyatzis
Editor

Contents

To the Reader   iv
Topic Guide   2
◎ Selected World Wide Web Sites   4

Overview   6

1. **Politics of Biology,** Wray Herbert, *U.S. News & World*   8
   Report, April 21, 1997.
   This interesting article highlights the **nature vs. nurture debate**
   and addresses research on the roles of **genes and experience**
   in shaping mental illness, violence, sexual orientation, and alcoholism. Wray Herbert shows how **psychological research** both
   contributes to and reflects the trends in broader societal values
   about the roles of biology and environment in human behavior.

2. **Multiplying the Risks,** Geoffrey Cowley and Karen Springen,   13
   Newsweek, December 1, 1997.
   Due to the rise of **fertility drugs and reproductive technologies,** multiple births—twins, triplets, etc.—have quadrupled since
   the 1970s. This brief article reviews what can be done to control
   the effects of fertility drugs and to reduce the **risk of multiple
   births** with its attendant problems.

3. **Designer Babies,** Sharon Begley, *Newsweek,* November   14
   9, 1998.
   Technological advances offer the potential for prenatal **"gene
   therapy"** to cure a child's inherited disease even before birth.
   This article describes how such procedures would be done, and
   the **ethical dilemmas** they raise.

4. **Hope for 'Snow Babies,'** Sharon Begley, *Newsweek,*   16
   September 29, 1997.
   Though once believed to be doomed, **babies born to crack
   cocaine users are not severely impaired emotionally or
   cognitively.** The effects of cocaine, or of any drug, on a fetus
   are neither predictable nor simple.

Overview   18

A. **EARLY COGNITIVE AND PHYSICAL DEVELOPMENT**

5. **Fertile Minds,** J. Madeleine Nash, *Time,* February 3,   20
   1997.
   This article explains the **development of neurons and synapses,** the connections between brain cells. Research on vision,
   motor development, language, and emotion demonstrates that
   **both nature and experience in early childhood play im-
   portant roles** in shaping brain development.

UNIT 1

Conception to Birth

Four articles discuss the
development of the child from
the prenatal state to birth.

UNIT 2

Cognition, Language, and Learning

Nine selections consider the growth
of children's cognitive and language
abilities and their experiences in
the learning process in school.

The concepts in bold italics are developed in the article. For further expansion please refer to the Topic Guide and the Index.

v

6. **What Do We Know from Brain Research?** Pat Wolfe   **25**
    and Ron Brandt, *Educational Leadership,* November 1998.
    This article discusses four major findings from *brain develop-*
    ment research: the *importance of experience and envi-*
    ronment in early brain development, *the malleability of IQ,*
    "sensitive periods," and the role of *emotion.*

7. **Evolution and Developmental Sex Differences,**   **29**
    David C. Geary, *Current Directions in Psychological Science,*
    August 1999.
    David Geary uses an *evolutionary framework and Dar-*
    winian principles to predict and understand *sex differences*
    in childhood in behaviors such as social development,
    play, and sexual selection. The influence of *culture* is also
    considered.

8. **Baby Talk,** Shannon Brownlee, *U.S. News & World Report,*   **33**
    June 15, 1998.
    Shannon Brownlee offers new evidence on how *children's brains*
    are designed for language acquisition. She reports on new
    views of how children *decode patterns* and engage in *"fast*
    mapping" while interpreting their linguistic environment.

9. **Effects of Sleep Position on Infant Motor Develop-**   **40**
    ment, Beth Ellen Davis, Rachel Y. Moon, Hari C. Sachs,
    and Mary C. Ottolini, *Pediatrics,* Volume 102, 1998.
    To reduce the risks of SIDS (Sudden Infant Death Syndrome), most
    parents now put their babies to sleep on their backs. But is the
    physical development of babies influenced by their sleep position?
    This article presents evidence that *babies reach motor devel-*
    opment milestones earlier if they sleep in a prone (on
    their stomach) position.

10. **Categories in Young Children's Thinking,** Susan A.   **47**
    Gelman, *Young Children,* January 1998.
    This review of research by several prominent developmentalists de-
    scribes how *children's thinking about the world is*
    strongly influenced by the categories that they are able to
    create and use. Children's thinking is also discussed in terms of
    the child's ability to *distinguish appearance from reality,* to
    understand the orderliness and naturalness of *biological growth,*
    and to use *words and names* as a guide for making inferences.

The concepts in bold italics are developed in the article. For further expansion please refer to the Topic Guide and the Index.

11. **Why Children Talk to Themselves,** Laura E. Berk,   54
Scientific American, November 1994.
Young children often talk to themselves. Laura Berk analyzes this
behavior from different theoretical perspectives, especially those of
Vygotsky and **Piaget,** and discusses research showing that ***private talk promotes self-control and new skills.***

B. LEARNING IN SCHOOL

12. **How Asian Teachers Polish Each Lesson to Per-**   59
fection, James W. Stigler and Harold W. Stevenson,
American Educator, Spring 1991.
The authors' research on **math education in China, Japan,
and the United States** reveals **significant cultural differences in the values, practices, and expectations of both
teachers and students.** However, due to cultural differences,
adoption of Asian teaching techniques in the United States would
not necessarily result in similar benefits to children in our culture.

13. **"Ready, READ!"** Nicholas Lemann, *The Atlantic Monthly,*   72
November 1998.
Nicholas Lemann analyzes the **problems of failing public
education;** he contrasts the tradition of **autonomy for schools
and teachers** with new approaches such as **charter schools**
and **standardized curriculum and control by outsiders,**
which appear to work.

Overview   80

A. THE CHILD'S FEELINGS: EMOTIONAL DEVELOPMENT

14. **Early Experience and Emotional Development:**   82
The Emergence of Wariness of Heights, Joseph J.
Campos, Bennett I. Bertenthal, and Rosanne Kermoian, *Psychological Science,* January 1992.
How do we become afraid of heights? Are we born with that fear
or do we learn it through life experiences? This article by prominent
researchers describes careful **experiments designed to determine whether babies are born with a fear of heights
or if they acquire it** only after they begin to crawl and to
experience moving around in the world.

15. **Babies, Bonds, and Brains,** Karen Wright, *Discover,*   86
October 1997.
***How does early experience shape our temperaments
and personalities?*** Karen Wright reviews research on monkeys
and humans that helps us understand the **complex links between behavior and early environment, biology, and
personality.**.

UNIT 3

Social and Emotional Development

Eight articles follow a child's
emotional development into
the larger social world.

The concepts in bold italics are developed in the article. For further expansion please refer to the Topic Guide and the Index.

16. **How Kids Mourn,** Jerry Adler, *Newsweek,* September 22, 1997.   **90**
    Coping with the ***death of a parent*** is a lifelong process. Even if grief cannot be eliminated, a ***child's mourning a deceased parent can be ameliorated by open discussion*** rather than by denial and distraction.

B. *ENTRY INTO THE SOCIAL WORLD: PEERS, PLAY, AND POPULARITY*

17. **The EQ Factor,** Nancy Gibbs, *Time,* October 2, 1995.   **92**
    Recent brain research suggests that emotions, not the traditional IQ rating, may be ***the true measure of human intelligence.*** Nancy Gibbs examines this latest trend in the assessment of human ability to cope successfully with challenges.

18. **Children without Friends,** Janis R. Bullock, *Childhood Education,* Winter 1992.   **97**
    According to research, ***having friends is crucial for normal development.*** Janis Bullock describes the ***sociometric status*** of different kinds of children—the ***popular, rejected,*** and ***neglected***—and the implications of not having friends. Suggestions are given for teachers to identify and help children who are without friends.

19. **Teacher Response to Superhero Play: To Ban or Not to Ban?** Brenda J. Boyd, *Childhood Education,* Fall 1997.   **102**
    Children's superhero play is often linked to ***aggression,*** which would be a cause of concern. Brenda Boyd reviews research on teachers' perceptions of children's play and aggression, and argues that superhero play is actually ***associated with children's friendships and social development.***

20. **Assisting Toddlers & Caregivers During Conflict Resolutions: Interactions That Promote Socialization,** Denise A. Da Ros and Beverly A. Kovach, *Childhood Education,* Fall 1998.   **106**
    Conflicts that arise between adults can be uncomfortable, but ***when conflict occurs between young children,*** the issues are even more complex.

21. **Gender Segregation among Children: Understanding the "Cootie Phenomenon,"** Kimberly K. Powlishta, *Young Children,* May 1995.   **112**
    Gender segregation—boys playing with boys, girls with girls— is common in childhood. Kim Powlishta describes research on the origins and consequences of this social phenomenon, explains the impact of an "us versus them" mentality, and suggests ways to reduce gender segregation.

The concepts in bold italics are developed in the article. For further expansion please refer to the Topic Guide and the Index.

Overview   120

22. **Where Will the Baby Sleep? Attitudes and Prac-   122
tices of New and Experienced Parents Regarding
Cosleeping with Their Newborn Infants,** Helen L.
Ball, Elaine Hooker, and Peter J. Kelly, *American Anthro-
pologist,* March 1999.
This research addresses **cosleeping, the practice of babies
sleeping with their parents for all or part of the night.
Parents' attitudes** are investigated as are the **benefits of
cosleeping for parents and babies.**

23. **What Matters? What Does Not? Five Perspec-   131
tives on the Association between Marital Transitions and Children's Adjustment,** E. Mavis
Hetherington, Margaret Bridges, and Glendessa M. Insabella, *American Psychologist,* February 1998.
This review of research addresses **children's adjustment to divorce, life in stepfamilies, and relations to stepparents.**
The authors also discuss children's characteristics that influence their
adjustments to their parents' divorces and remarriages.

24. **Boys Will Be Boys,** Barbara Kantrowitz and Claudia   149
Kalb, *Newsweek,* May 11, 1998.
This article shows how recent concern over girls' well-being may
have led to a neglect of the **challenges and crisis points in
boys' development.** The **influence of parents, especially
fathers,** is emphasized as crucial for helping boys develop
optimally.

25. **Father Love and Child Development: History and   152
Current Evidence,** Ronald P. Rohner, *Current Directions
in Psychological Science,* October 1998.
Mothers' behavior has long been the emphasis of child development research, but how are fathers important to their children's
development? This article describes research on the **influence of
fathers on children's development,** and it discusses **the cultural construction of fatherhood in America.**

26. **The Moral Development of Children,** William   156
Damon, *Scientific American,* August 1999.
William Damon, a prominent development psychologist, discusses
the **origins of morality,** the **universality of values,** and the
**key role parents play in promoting their children's
moral development.**

27. **Playing with God,** Tracy Cochran, *Parabola,* Summer   163
1999.
This first-hand account by a mother provides an **intimate look
at one family's discussions about religion, science, and
God.** The essay helps us appreciate **children's active role in
their own spiritual socialization,** and how parents and children influence each other through such discussions.

UNIT 4

Parenting and Family Issues

Six articles assess the latest
implications of child development
with regard to attachment, marital
transitions, day care, and discipline.

The concepts in bold italics are developed in the article. For further expansion please refer to the Topic Guide and the Index.

ix

UNIT 5

Cultural and Societal Influences

Eight selections examine the impact that society and culture have on the development of the child.

Overview   166

A. SOCIAL ISSUES

28. **Buried Alive,** David Denby, *The New Yorker,* July 15,   168
    1996.
    In a thoughtful essay, David Denby argues that ***today's youth
    are buried by "an avalanche of crud" from popular
    culture***—television, films, toys, and video and computer games.
    Denby offers many novel ideas about the impression this culture
    may leave on ***children's character and on their views of
    reality.***

29. **It's 4:00 p.m. Do You Know Where Your Children   176
    Are?** Jonathan Alter, *Newsweek,* April 27, 1998.
    Due to parents' work demands and school schedules, there are
    now ***17 million parents looking for after-school care*** for
    their children. Research suggests that ***the most dangerous time
    of day for children is from 2 to 8 p.m.,*** as children without
    after-school supervision appear to be more likely to have poorer
    grades and to engage in problem behaviors.

30. **Of Power Rangers and V-Chips,** Chris J. Boyatzis,   180
    Young Children, November 1997.
    Chris Boyatzis describes recent ***legislative and technological
    changes*** that could affect the role of television in children's lives.
    He reviews research to demonstrate why we should be concerned
    about ***television violence.*** Suggestions are also offered for better
    television management by parents in the home.

B. SPECIAL CHALLENGES

31. **The Effects of Poverty on Children,** Jeanne Brooks-Gunn   186
    and Greg J. Duncan, *The Future of Children,* Summer/Fall
    1997.
    In recent years, ***one in five American children has lived
    below the poverty level.*** This article offers detailed research
    findings on the ***relationship between poverty and chil-
    dren's outcomes in physical, emotional, cognitive, and
    school achievement*** development.

32. **Victimization of Children,** David Finkelhor and Jennifer   201
    Dziuba-Leatherman, *American Psychologist,* March 1994.
    This eye-opening article presents statistics showing that children are
    more prone to victimization than are adults. ***Victimology of
    childhood*** falls into three broad categories—***pandemic victimi-
    zation*** (assault by siblings, parents, peers), ***acute victimization***
    (physical abuse), and ***extraordinary victimization*** (homicide).
    The authors call for more research and theory on childhood victi-
    mology, using a developmental perspective.

33. Resilience in Development, Emmy E. Werner, *Current* **212**
Directions in Psychological Science, June 1995.
Many of the studies that focused on children and youths who overcame great odds have been relatively short-term. Emmy Werner
discusses a study that analyzes ***child resiliency and development over a period of three decades.***

34. Creating False Memories, Elizabeth F. Loftus, *Scientific* **215**
American, September 1997.
Elizabeth Loftus, a prominent scientist in the study of memory development, describes research that demonstrates how ***suggestion
and imagination can create memories of events that
did not occur.*** This work helps us understand how vulnerable
our memory is to distortion and fabrication.

35. Escaping from the Darkness, Howard Chua-Eoan, **221**
Time, May 31, 1999.
Approximately ***500,000 to 1 million American children
and youth take prescription antidepressants.*** This article
discusses children's depression, what parents and schools can do
about it, and the potential long-term risks of antidepressant drugs
for children.

Index   **225**
Article Review Form   **228**
Article Rating Form   **229**

The concepts in bold italics are developed in the article. For further expansion please refer to the Topic Guide and the Index.

Topic Guide

This topic guide suggests how the selections and World Wide Web sites found in the next section of this book relate to topics of traditional concern to students and professionals who study infant and child development. It is useful for locating interrelated articles and Web sites for reading and research. The guide is arranged alphabetically according to topic.

The relevant Web sites, which are numbered and annotated on pages 4 and 5, are easily identified by the Web icon (◉) under the topic articles. By linking the articles and the Web sites by topic, this ANNUAL EDITIONS reader becomes a powerful learning and research tool.

TOPIC AREA	TREATED IN	TOPIC AREA	TREATED IN
Aggression/ Violence	1. Politics of Biology 7. Evolution and Developmental Sex Differences 18. Children without Friends 19. Teacher Response to Superhero Play 20. Assisting Toddlers & Caregivers 24. Boys Will Be Boys 30. Of Power Rangers and V-Chips 32. Victimization of Children ◉ *4, 14, 18, 19, 24, 27, 32*		4. Hope for 'Snow Babies' 35. Escaping from the Darkness ◉ *3, 4, 19, 27*
		Economic Issues/Poverty	31. Effects of Poverty on Children ◉ *11, 28, 29, 31*
Attachment	16. How Kids Mourn 23. What Matters? What Does Not? 25. Father Love and Child Development ◉ *17, 20, 22, 23, 24, 25*	**Emotional Development**	1. Politics of Biology 4. Hope for 'Snow Babies' 7. Evolution and Developmental Sex Differences 11. Why Children Talk to Themselves 14. Early Experience and Emotional Development 16. How Kids Mourn 17. EQ Factor 18. Children without Friends 22. Where Will the Baby Sleep? 23. What Matters? What Does Not? 25. Father Love and Child Development 26. Moral Development of Children 27. Playing with God 33. Resilience in Development 35. Escaping from the Darkness ◉ *4, 6, 14, 15, 16, 17, 18, 19, 21, 24, 25, 26*
Birth and Birth Defects/ Reproduction/ Teratogens	2. Multiplying the Risks 3. Designer Babies 4. Hope for 'Snow Babies' ◉ *5, 7, 19, 22*		
Brain and Physical Development	4. Hope for 'Snow Babies' 5. Fertile Minds 6. What Do We Know from Brain Research? 9. Effects of Sleep Position on Infant Motor Development 14. Early Experience and Emotional Development ◉ *5, 7, 13, 15, 18*		
		Family/ Parenting	7. Evolution and Developmental Sex Differences 16. How Kids Mourn 22. Where Will the Baby Sleep? 23. What Matters? What Does Not? 24. Boys Will Be Boys 25. Father Love and Child Development 26. Moral Development of Children 27. Playing with God 28. Buried Alive 29. It's 4:00 p.m. Do You Know Where Your Children Are? 30. Of Power Rangers and V-Chips 32. Victimization of Children 33. Resilience in Development 35. Escaping from the Darkness ◉ *19, 20, 21, 22, 23, 24, 25, 26*
Child Abuse	4. Hope for 'Snow Babies' 5. Fertile Minds 32. Victimization of Children ◉ *7, 9, 11, 13*		
Cognitive Development	4. Hope for 'Snow Babies' 6. What Do We Know from Brain Research? 10. Categories in Young Children's Thinking 11. Why Children Talk to Themselves 12. How Asian Teachers Polish Each Lesson to Perfection ◉ *7, 9, 10, 11, 13*		
		Gender Issues/ Sexual Orientation	1. Politics of Biology 7. Evolution and Developmental Sex Differences 21. Gender Segregation among Children ◉ *7, 19, 23*
Creativity	28. Buried Alive		
Cross-Cultural Issues	7. Evolution and Developmental Sex Differences 12. How Asian Teachers Polish Each Lesson to Perfection. 22. Where Will the Baby Sleep? ◉ *31*	**High Risk Infants/ Children**	3. Designer Babies 4. Hope for 'Snow Babies' 18. Children without Friends 23. What Matters? What Does Not? 32. Victimization of Children 33. Resilience in Development 35. Escaping from the Darkness ◉ *14, 24, 25, 26, 27, 28, 29, 30, 31, 32*
Discipline	26. Moral Development of Children		
Divorce/ Stepparents	23. What Matters? What Does Not? ◉ *19, 20, 22, 23, 24, 25, 26*		
Drug Use/Abuse	1. Politics of Biology		

TOPIC AREA	TREATED IN	TOPIC AREA	TREATED IN
Infant Development	5. Fertile Minds 6. What Do We Know from Brain Research? 9. Effects of Sleep Position on Infant Motor Development 10. Categories in Young Children's Thinking 14. Early Experience and Emotional Development 22. Where Will the Baby Sleep? ☺ *5, 6, 7, 9, 10, 11, 13*		19. Teacher Response to Superhero Play 20. Assisting Toddlers & Caregivers 21. Gender Segregation among Children 26. The Moral Development of Children 29. It's 4:00 p.m. Do You Know Where Your Children Are? ☺ *17, 18, 19*
Intelligence	5. Fertile Minds 6. What Do We Know from Brain Research? 11. Why Children Talk to Themselves 17. EQ Factor ☺ *8, 9, 10, 11, 12, 13*	**Personality Development**	1. Politics of Biology 17. EQ Factor 18. Children without Friends 23. What Matters? What Does Not? 24. Boys Will Be Boys 26. Moral Development of Children 28. Buried Alive 31. Effects of Poverty on Children 33. Resilience in Development ☺ *4, 7, 9, 16, 18, 24, 25, 26, 27, 28, 29, 31*
Language Development	6. What Do We Know from Brain Research? 8. Baby Talk 11. Why Children Talk to Themselves ☺ *7, 13*	**Physical Development**	5. Fertile Minds 6. What Do We Know from Brain Research? 9. Effects of Sleep Position on Infant Motor Development 31. Effects of Poverty on Children ☺ *3, 5, 6, 9, 17, 29, 31*
Learning/ Literacy	5. Fertile Minds 6. What Do We Know from Brain Research? 12. How Asian Teachers Polish Each Lesson to Perfection 13. Ready, READ! 21. Gender Segregation among Children 29. It's 4:00 p.m. Do You Know Where Your Children Are? 31. Effects of Poverty on Children ☺ *8, 9, 10, 11, 12, 13*	**Prenatal Development and Diagnosis**	2. Multiplying the Risks 3. Designer Babies 4. Hope for 'Snow Babies' ☺ *7*
		Preschoolers/ Toddlers	8. Baby Talk 10. Categories in Young Children's Thinking 18. Children without Friends 19. Teacher Response to Superhero Play 20. Assisting Toddlers & Caregivers 21. Gender Segregation among Children ☺ *7, 15, 17, 19, 20, 21, 23*
Memory	5. Fertile Minds 34. Creating False Memories ☺ *5, 7*		
Mental Illness	1. Politics of Biology 23. What Matters? What Does Not? 32. Victimization of Children 35. Escaping from the Darkness ☺ *14, 15, 16, 19, 24, 25, 26, 27, 28, 30, 32*	**Public Policy/ Government and Development**	1. Politics of Biology 29. It's 4:00 p.m. Do You Know Where Your Children Are? 30. Of Power Rangers and V-Chips 31. Effects of Poverty on Children ☺ *2, 4, 6*
Moral Development	26. Moral Development of Children ☺ *21, 22, 23, 24, 25, 26*	**Resilience**	29. It's 4:00 p.m. Do You Know Where Your Children Are? 33. Resilience in Development ☺ *19, 21, 22, 23, 24, 27*
Nature/Nurture Issues	1. Politics of Biology 3. Designer Babies 5. Fertile Minds 6. What Do We Know from Brain Research? 7. Evolution and Developmental Sex Differences 8. Baby Talk 14. Early Experience and Emotional Development 15. Babies, Bonds, and Brains 22. Where Will the Baby Sleep? ☺ *4, 7, 11, 13, 16, 18*	**Socialization**	7. Evolution and Developmental Sex Differences 18. Children without Friends 20. Assisting Toddlers & Caregivers 21. Gender Segregation among Children 24. Boys Will Be Boys 26. Moral Development of Children 28. Buried Alive 29. It's 4:00 p.m. Do You Know Where Your Children Are? ☺ *4, 5, 13, 27*
Peers/Social Skills	7. Evolution and Developmental Sex Differences 17. EQ Factor 18. Children without Friends		

● AE: Child Growth and Development

The following World Wide Web sites have been carefully researched and selected to support the articles found in this reader. If you are interested in learning more about specific topics found in this book, these Web sites are a good place to start. The sites are cross-referenced by number and appear in the topic guide on the previous two pages. Also, you can link to these Web sites through our DUSHKIN ONLINE support site at *http://www.dushkin.com/online/*.

The following sites were available at the time of publication. Visit our Web site—we update DUSHKIN ONLINE regularly to reflect any changes.

General Sources

1. American Academy of Pediatrics
http://www.aap.org
This organization provides data for optimal physical, mental, and social health for all children.

2. CYFERNet
http://www.cyfernet.mes.umn.edu
The Children, Youth, and Families Education Research Network is sponsored by the Cooperative Extension Service and USDA's Cooperative State Research Education and Extension Service. This site provides practical research-based information in areas including health, child care, family strengths, science, and technology·

3. KidsHealth at the AMA
http://www.ama-assn.org/KidsHealth/
This site was developed to help parents find reliable children's health information. Click on the topic bars: Baby's Development, Nutrition, Pediatric News, Safety and Accident Prevention, and Childhood Infections.

4. National Institute of Child Health and Human Development
http://www.nichd.nih.gov
The NICHD conducts and supports research on the reproductive, neurobiological, developmental, and behavioral processes that determine and maintain the health of children, adults, families, and populations.

Conception to Birth

5. Babyworld
http://www.babyworld.com
Extensive information on caring for infants can be found at this site. There are also links to numerous other related sites.

6. Children's Nutrition Research Center (CNRC)
http://www.bcm.tmc.edu/cnrc/
CNRC, one of six USDA/ARS (Agricultural Research Service) facilities, is dedicated to defining the nutrient needs of healthy children, from conception through adolescence, and pregnant and nursing mothers. The *Nutrition and Your Child* newsletter is of general interest and can be accessed from this site.

7. Zero to Three: National Center for Infants, Toddlers, and Families
http://www.zerotothree.org
This national organization is dedicated solely to infants, toddlers, and their families. It is headed by recognized experts in the field and provides technical assistance to communities, states, and the federal government. The site provides information that the organization gathers and disseminates through its publications.

Cognition, Language, and Learning

8. Educational Resources Information Center (ERIC)
http://www.ed.gov/pubs/pubdb.html
This Web site is sponsored by the U.S. Department of Education and will lead to numerous documents related to elementary and early childhood education, as well as other curriculum topics and issues.

9. I Am Your Child
http://iamyourchild.org
Information regarding early childhood development is provided on this site. Resources for parents and caregivers are provided.

10. National Association for the Education of Young Children (NAEYC)
http://www.naeyc.org
The National Association for the Education of Young Children provides a useful link from its home page to a "parent information" site.

11. Results of NICHD Study of Early Child Care
http://156.40.88.3/publications/pubs/ early_child_care.htm
This study indicates that the quality of child care for very young children does matter for their cognitive development and their use of language. Quality child care also leads to better mother-child interaction, the study finds.

12. Vandergrift's Children's Literature Page
http://www.scils.rutgers.edu/special/kay/childlit.html
This site provides information about children's literature and links to a variety of resources related to literacy for children.

13. Project Zero
http://pzweb.harvard.edu
Harvard Project Zero, a research group at the Harvard Graduate School of Education, has investigated the development of learning processes in children and adults for 30 years. Today, Project Zero is building on this research to help create communities of reflective, independent learners; to enhance deep understanding within disciplines; and to promote critical and creative thinking. Project Zero's mission is to understand and enhance learning, thinking, and creativity in the arts and other disciplines for individuals and institutions.

Social and Emotional Development

14. Counseling for Children
http://montgomery-al.com/cfc/index.htm
This site discusses parents' questions about child counseling: What children would benefit? How is counseling of children different from that of adults? What about testing? It also offers a toy guide, homework hints, how to foster creativity, and a discussion of the power of play.

15. Help Children Work with Feelings
http://www.aha4kids.com/index.html
New multimedia materials that deal with emotional intelligence are available at this Web site.

16. Max Planck Institute for Psychological Research
http://www.mpipf-muenchen.mpg.de/BCD/bcd_e.htm
Several behavioral and cognitive development research projects are available on this site.

17. National Child Care Information Center (NCCIC)
http://www.nccic.org
Information about a variety of topics related to child care and development is available on this site. Links to the *Child Care Bulletin,* which can be read online, and to the ERIC database of online and library-based resources are available.

18. Serendip
http://serendip.brynmawr.edu/serendip/
Organized into five subject areas (brain and behavior, complex systems, genes and behavior, science and culture, and science education), Serendip contains interactive exhibits, articles, links to other resources, and a forum area for comments and discussion.

Parenting and Family Issues

19. Facts for Families
http://www.aacap.org/publications/factsfam/index.htm
The American Academy of Child and Adolescent Psychiatry here provides concise, up-to-date information on issues that affect teenagers and their families. Fifty-six fact sheets include issues concerning teenagers, such as coping with life, sad feelings, inability to sleep, getting involved with drugs, or not getting along with family and friends.

20. Families and Work Institute
http://www.familiesandworkinst.org
Resources from the Families and Work Institute, which conducts policy research on issues related to the changing workforce and operates a national clearinghouse on work and family life, are provided.

21. The National Academy for Child Development
http://www.nacd.org
This international organization is dedicated to helping children and adults reach their full potential. Its home page presents links to various programs, research, and resources in topics related to the family and society.

22. National Council on Family Relations
http://www.ncfr.com
This NCFR home page will lead you to articles, research, and a lot of other resources on important issues in family relations, such as stepfamilies, couples, and divorce.

23. The National Parent Information Network (NPIN)
http://ericps.ed.uiuc.edu/npin/
The National Parent Information Network contains resources related to many of the controversial issues faced by parents raising children in contemporary society. In addition to articles and resources, discussion groups are also available.

24. Parenting and Families
http://www.cyfc.umn.edu/Parenting/parentlink.html
The University of Minnesota's Children, Youth, and Family Consortium site will lead you to many organizations and other resources related to divorce, single parenting, and stepfamilies, as well as to information about other topics of interest into the study of children's development and the family.

25. Parentsplace.com: Single Parenting
http://www.parentsplace.com/family/singleparent/
This resource focuses on issues concerning single parents and their children. Although the articles range from parenting children from infancy through adolescence, most of the articles deal with middle childhood.

26. Stepfamily Association of America
http://www.stepfam.org
This Web site is dedicated to educating and supporting stepfamilies and to creating a positive family image.

Cultural and Societal Influences

27. Ask NOAH About: Mental Health
http://www.noah.cuny.edu/illness/mentalhealth/mental.html
This enormous resource contains information about child and adolescent family problems, mental conditions and disorders, suicide prevention, and much more, all organized in a "clickable" outline form.

28. Association to Benefit Children (ABC)
http://www.a-b-c.org
ABC presents a network of programs that includes child advocacy, education for disabled children, care for HIV-positive children, employment, housing, foster care, and day care.

29. Children Now
http://www.childrennow.org
Children Now focuses on improving conditions for children who are poor or at risk. Articles include information on education, influence of media, health, and security.

30. Council for Exceptional Children
http://www.cec.sped.org
This is the home page for the Council for Exceptional Children, a large professional organization that is dedicated to improving education for children with exceptionalities, students with disabilities, and/or the gifted child. It leads to the ERIC Clearinghouse on disabilities and gifted education and the National Clearinghouse for Professions in Special Education.

31. National Black Child Development Institute
http://www.nbcdi.org
Resources for improving the quality of life for African American children through public education programs are provided at this site.

32. Prevent Child Abuse America
http://www.preventchildabuse.org/fs.html
Dedicated to their child abuse prevention efforts, PCAA's site provides fact sheets and reports that include statistics, a public opinion poll, a 50-state survey, and other resources materials.

We highly recommend that you review our Web site for expanded information and our other product lines. We are continually updating and adding links to our Web site in order to offer you the most usable and useful information that will support and expand the value of your Annual Editions. You can reach us at: http://www.dushkin.com/annualeditions/.

www.dushkin.com/online/

Unit Selections

1. **Politics of Biology,** Wray Herbert
2. **Multiplying the Risks,** Geoffrey Cowley and Karen Springen
3. **Designer Babies,** Sharon Begley
4. **Hope for 'Snow Babies,'** Sharon Begley

Key Points to Consider

❖ Where do you stand on the nature/nurture issue? Does it comfort you—or unsettle you—to know that the genes you inherited influence your mental health or sexual orientation, and so on? Given the information in the article "Politics of Biology," how would you respond to someone who claimed that a person's mental health or sexual orientation is "determined" by their genes?

❖ How would you balance the personal wish for a child and the expense and ethical complications of available reproductive technology? Assuming that new procedures continue to be developed, what options might be available to parents in the future?

❖ What ethical dilemmas arise if couples were given the option to genetically engineer their babies, whether it be to cure the baby from a potential disease, or for eye or hair color? What other issues arise if this genetic engineering were available only to those who could afford medical intervention?

 **Links** | **www.dushkin.com/online/**

5. **Babyworld**
   http://www.babyworld.com
6. **Children's Nutrition Research Center (CNRC)**
   http://www.bcm.tmc.edu/cnrc/
7. **Zero to Three: National Center for Infants, Toddlers, and Families**
   http://www.zerotothree.org

These sites are annotated on pages 4 and 5.

Our understanding of conception and prenatal development is not what it used to be. We are now witness to dramatic changes in reproductive technology. Advances in this new "prenatal science" include fertility treatments for couples who have difficulty conceiving and a host of prenatal diagnostic tests, such as amniocentesis and alpha-fetoprotein testing, which assess the well-being of the fetus as well as detect genetic or chromosomal problems. These technological developments result in both benefits and risks that are discussed in the article "Multiplying the Risks."

Perhaps the oldest debate in the study of human development is the "nature versus nurture" question. Scientists have moved beyond thinking of development as due to either genetics *or* environment, now recognizing that nature *and* nurture interact to shape us. Each human is a biological organism, and each is surrounded, from the moment of conception, by environmental forces. According to "Politics of Biology," recent research highlights the contributions of genes and experience in influencing mental illness, violence, sexual orientation, and alcoholism. This selection is especially valuable because it helps the reader appreciate that findings from the nature/nurture

debate both contribute to and reflect the trends of broader societal values and may in turn have ethical, political, legal, and societal consequences.

Students of child development should realize that the classic nature/nurture controversy applies as much to prenatal development as to other stages of childhood. While prenatal development is largely the result of the unfolding of an individual's genetic blueprint, the fetus is also in an environment within the mother's womb. The author of the article, "Designer Babies" takes the concept of genetic influences on development to the next step and asks, given additional modern genetic techniques, should we consider the option of genetically altering a baby's potential diseases, using gene therapy, in order to create the dream baby?

No matter what the genetic potential however, the fetus still remains vulnerable to teratogens, hazards from the maternal and external environment that interfere with normal prenatal development. We are learning a great deal more about potential harm to the developing fetus due to increasing rates of maternal use of illegal drugs. For example, the deleterious effects of prenatal exposure to cocaine on babies is discussed in "Hope for 'Snow Babies.' "

Conception to Birth

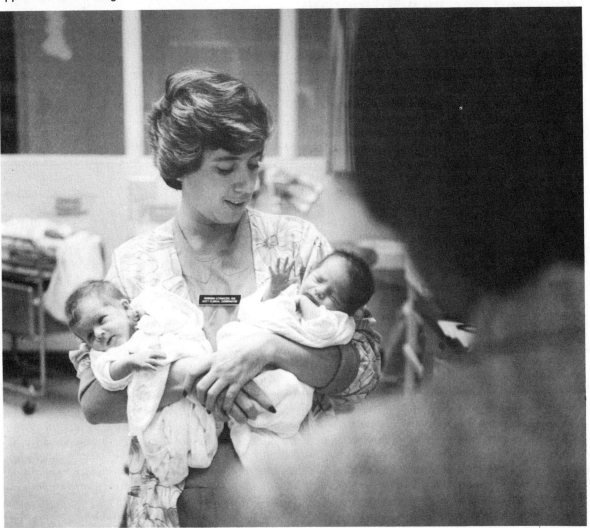

POLITICS OF BIOLOGY

How the nature vs. nurture debate shapes public policy—and our view of ourselves

BY WRAY HERBERT

Laurie Flynn uses the technology of neuroscience to light up the brains of Washington lawmakers. As executive director of the National Alliance for the Mentally Ill, she marshals everything from cost analysis to moral pleading to make the case for laws banning discrimination against people with mental illness. But her most powerful advocacy tool by far is the PET scan. She takes a collection of these colorful brain images up to Capitol Hill to put on a show, giving lawmakers a window on a "broken" brain in action. "When they see that it's not some imaginary, fuzzy problem, but a real physical condition, then they get it: 'Oh, it's in the brain'."

The view of mental illness as a brain disease has been crucial to the effort to destigmatize illnesses such as schizophrenia and depression. But it's just one example of a much broader biologizing of American culture that's been going on for more than a decade. For both po-

litical and scientific reasons—and it's often impossible to disentangle the two—everything from criminality to addictive disorders to sexual orientation is seen today less as a matter of choice than of genetic destiny. Even basic personality is looking more and more like a genetic legacy. Nearly every week there is a report of a new gene for one trait or another. Novelty seeking, religiosity, shyness, the tendency to divorce, and even happiness (or the lack of it) are among the traits that may result in part from a gene, according to new research.

This cultural shift has political and personal implications. On the personal level, a belief in the power of genes necessarily diminishes the potency of such personal qualities as will, capacity to choose, and sense of responsibility for those choices—if it's in your genes, you're not accountable. It allows the alcoholic, for example, to treat himself as a helpless victim of his biology rather

than as a willful agent with control of his own behavior. Genetic determinism can free victims and their families of guilt—or lock them in their suffering.

On the political level, biological determinism now colors all sorts of public-policy debates on issues such as gay rights, health care, juvenile justice, and welfare reform. The effort to dismantle social programs is fueled by the belief that government interventions (the nurturing side in the nature-nurture debate) don't work very well—and the corollary idea that society can't make up for every unfortunate citizen's bad luck. It's probably no coincidence that the biologizing of culture has accompanied the country's shift to the political right, since conservatives traditionally are more dubious about human perfectability than are liberals. As Northeastern University psychologist Leon Kamin notes, the simplest way to discover someone's political leanings is to ask his or her view on genetics.

Even so, genetic determinism can have paradoxical consequences at times, leading to disdain rather than sympathy for the disadvantaged, and marginalization rather than inclusion. Cultural critics are beginning to sort out the unpredictable politics of biology, focusing on four traits: violence, mental illness, alcoholism, and sexual orientation.

The nature of violence. To get a sense of just how thorough—and how politicized—the biologizing of culture has been, just look at the issue of urban gang violence as it is framed today. A few years ago, Frederick Goodwin, then director of the government's top mental health agency, was orchestrating the so-called Federal Violence Initiative to identify inner-city kids at biological risk for criminal violence, with the goal of intervening with drug treatments for what are presumed to be nervous-system aberrations. Goodwin got himself fired for comparing aggressive young males with primates in the jungle, and the violence initiative died in the resulting furor. But even to be proposing such a biomedical approach to criminal justice shows how far the intellectual pendulum has swung toward biology.

The eugenics movement of the 1930s was fueled at least in part by a desire to get rid of habitual criminals, and many attempts have been made over the years to identify genetic roots for aggression, violence, and criminality. A 1965 study, for instance, found that imprisoned criminals were more likely

As with many psychopathologies, criminal aggression is difficult to define precisely for research. Indeed, crime and alcohol abuse are so entangled that it's often difficult to know whether genetic markers are associated with drinking, criminality—or something else entirely, like a personality trait. A 1993 National Research Council study, for example, reported strong evidence of genetic influence on antisocial personality disorder, but it also noted that many genes are probably involved. Getting from those unknown genes to an actual act of vandalism or assault—or a life of barbaric violence—requires at this point a monstrous leap of faith.

Yet it's a leap that many are willing to make. When geneticist Xandra Breakefield reported a possible genetic link to violent crime a few years ago, she immediately started receiving phone inquiries from attorneys representing clients in prison; they were hoping that such genetic findings might absolve their clients of culpability for their acts.

Mutations and emotions. Just two decades ago, the National Institute of Mental Health was funding studies of economic recession, unemployment, and urban ills as possible contributors to serious emotional disturbance. A whole branch of psychiatry known as "social psychiatry" was dedicated to helping the mentally ill by rooting out such pathogens as poverty and racism. There is no longer much evidence of these sensibilities at work today. NIMH now focuses its

tating emotional and mental disorder was caused by cold and distant mothering, itself the result of the mother's unconscious wish that her child had never been born. A nationwide lobbying effort was launched to combat such unfounded mother blaming, and 20 years later that artifact of the Freudian era is entirely discredited. It's widely accepted today that psychotic disorders are brain disorders, probably with genetic roots.

But this neurogenetic victory may be double edged. For example, family and consumer groups have argued convincingly that schizophrenia is a brain disease like epilepsy, one piece of evidence being that it is treatable with powerful antipsychotic drugs. Managed-care companies, however, have seized upon the disease model, and now will rarely authorize anything but drug treatment; it's efficient, and justified by the arguments of biological psychiatry. The American Psychiatric Association just this month issued elaborate guidelines for treating schizophrenia, including not only drugs but an array of psychosocial services—services the insurance industry is highly unlikely to pay for.

The search for genes for severe mental disorders has been inconclusive. Years of studies of families, adoptees, and twins separated at birth suggest that both schizophrenia and manic-depressive illness run in families. But if that family pattern is the result of genes, it's clearly very complicated, because most of the siblings of schizophrenics (in-

VIOLENCE. How can an act of vandalism or a bank robbery be rooted in DNA? There are a lot of choices involved in living a life of crime.

than other people to have an extra Y chromosome (and therefore more male genes). The evidence linking this chromosomal aberration to crime was skimpy and tenuous, but politics often runs ahead of the evidence: Soon after, a Boston hospital actually started screening babies for the defect, the idea being to intervene early with counseling should personality problems become apparent. The screening was halted when further study showed that XYY men, while slightly less intelligent, were not unusually aggressive.

studies almost exclusively on brain research and on the genetic underpinnings of emotional illnesses.

The decision to reorder the federal research portfolio was both scientific and political. Major advances in neuroscience methods opened up research that wasn't possible a generation ago, and that research has paid off in drugs that very effectively treat some disorders. But there was also a concerted political campaign to reinterpret mental illness. A generation ago, the leading theory about schizophrenia was that this devas-

cluding half of identical twins, who have the same genes) don't develop the disorder. Behavioral geneticists suspect that several genes may underlie the illness, and that some environmental stress—perhaps a virus or birth complications—also might be required to trigger the disorder.

On several occasions in the past, researchers have reported "linkages" between serious mental illness and a particular stretch of DNA. A well-known study of the Amish, for example, claimed a link between manic-depression and an aberration on chromosome 11. But none of these findings has held up when other researchers attempted to replicate them.

Even if one accepts that there are genetic roots for serious delusional illnesses, critics are concerned about the biologizing of the rest of psychiatric illness. Therapists report that patients come in asking for drugs, claiming to be victims of unfortunate biology. In one case, a patient claimed he could "feel his neurons misfiring"; it's an impossibility, but the anecdote speaks to the thorough saturation of the culture with biology.

Some psychiatrists are pulling back from the strict biological model of mental illness. Psychiatrist Keith Russell Ablow has reintroduced the idea of "character" into his practice, telling depressed patients that they have the responsibility and capacity to pull themselves out of their illness. Weakness of character, as Ablow sees it, allows mental illness to grow. Such sentiment is highly controversial within psychiatry, where to suggest that patients might be responsible for some of their own suffering is taboo.

Besotted genes. The best that can be said about research on the genetics of alcoholism is that it's inconclusive, but that hasn't stopped people from using genetic arguments for political purposes. The disease model for alcoholism is practically a secular religion in this country, embraced by psychiatry, most

ently; or they may have inherited a certain personality type that's prone to risk-taking or stimulus-seeking. While studies of family pedigrees and adoptees have on occasion indicated a familial pattern for a particular form of alcoholism (early-onset disorder in men, for example), just as often they reveal no pattern. This shouldn't be all that surprising, given the difficulty of defining alcoholism. Some researchers identify alcoholics by their drunk-driving record, while others focus on withdrawal symptoms or daily consumption. This is what geneticists call a "dirty phenotype"; people drink too much in so many different ways that the trait itself is hard to define, so family patterns are all over the place, and often contradictory.

Given these methodological problems, researchers have been trying to locate an actual gene (or genes) that might be involved in alcoholism. A 1990 study reported that a severe form of the disorder (most of the subjects in the study had cirrhosis of the liver) was linked to a gene that codes for a chemical receptor for the neurotransmitter dopamine. The researchers even developed and patented a test for the genetic mutation, but subsequent attempts to confirm the dopamine connection have failed.

The issues of choice and responsibility come up again and again in discussions of alcoholism and other addictive disorders. Even if scientists were to

character flaw, many are concerned that the widely accepted disease model of alcoholism actually provides people with an excuse for their destructive behavior. As psychologist Stanton Peele argues: "Indoctrinating young people with the view that they are likely to become alcoholics may take them there more quickly than any inherited reaction to alcohol would have."

Synapses of desire. It would be a mistake to focus only on biological explanations of psychopathology; the cultural shift is much broader than that. A generation ago, the gay community was at war with organized psychiatry, arguing (successfully) that sexual orientation was a lifestyle choice and ought to be deleted from the manual of disorders. Recently the same community was celebrating new evidence that homosexuality is a biological (and perhaps genetic) trait, not a choice at all.

Three lines of evidence support the idea of a genetic basis for homosexuality, none of them conclusive. A study of twins and adopted siblings found that about half of identical twins of homosexual men were themselves gay, compared with 22 percent of fraternal twins and 11 percent of adoptees; a similar pattern was found among women. While such a pattern is consistent with some kind of genetic loading for sexual orientation, critics contend it also could be explained by the very similar experiences many twins share. And, of course,

MENTAL ILLNESS. Are psychiatric disorders diseases? The answer influences everything from insurance coverage to new research funding.

treatment clinics, and (perhaps most important) by Alcoholics Anonymous. What this means is that those seeking help for excessive drinking are told they have a disease (though the exact nature of the disease is unknown), that it's probably a genetic condition, and that the only treatment is abstinence.

But the evidence is not strong enough to support these claims. There are several theories of how genes might lead to excessive drinking. A genetic insensitivity to alcohol, for example, might cause certain people to drink more; or alcoholics might metabolize alcohol differ-

identify a gene (or genes) that create a susceptibility to alcoholism, it's hard to know what this genetic "loading" would mean. It certainly wouldn't lead to alcoholism in a culture that didn't condone drinking—among the Amish, for example—so it's not deterministic in a strict sense. Even in a culture where drinking is common, there are clearly a lot of complicated choices involved in living an alcoholic life; it's difficult to make the leap from DNA to those choices. While few would want to return to the time when heavy drinking was condemned as strictly a moral failing or

half the identical twins did not become gay—which by definition means something other than genes must be involved.

A well-publicized 1991 study reported a distinctive anatomical feature in gay men. Simon LeVay autopsied the brains of homosexual men and heterosexual men and women and found that a certain nucleus in the hypothalamus was more than twice as large in heterosexual men as in gay men or heterosexual women. Although LeVay couldn't explain how this neurological difference might translate into homosexuality, he speculates that the nucleus is somehow related to sexual orientation. The hypothalamus is known to be involved in sexual response.

The only study so far to report an actual genetic connection to homosexuality is a 1993 study by Dean Hamer, a National Institutes of Health biologist who identified a genetic marker on the X chromosome in 75 percent of gay brothers. The functional significance of this piece of DNA is unknown, and subsequent research has not succeeded in duplicating Hamer's results.

Homosexuality represents a bit of a paradox when it comes to the intertwined issues of choice and determinism. When Hamer reported his genetic findings, many in the gay community celebrated, believing that society would be more tolerant of behavior rooted in biology and DNA rather than choice. LeVay, himself openly gay, says he undertook his research with the explicit agenda of furthering the gay cause. And Hamer testified as an expert witness in an important gay-rights case in Colorado where, in a strange twist, liberals found themselves arguing the deterministic position, while conservatives insisted that homosexuality is a choice. The argument of gay-rights advocates was that biological status conveyed legal status—and protection under the law.

History's warning. But history suggests otherwise, according to biologist and historian Garland Allen. During the eugenics movement of the 1920s and 1930s, both in the United States and

blemindedness," pauperism, and mental illness. The ultimate outcome of the eugenics craze in Europe is well known; homosexuals were not given extra sympathy or protection in the Third Reich's passion to purify genetic stock.

Allen is concerned about the possibility of a "new eugenics" movement, though he notes that it wouldn't be called that or take the same form. It would more likely take the form of rationing health care for the unfortunate. The economic and social conditions today resemble conditions that provided fertile ground for eugenics between the wars, he argues; moreover, in Allen's view, California's Proposition 187 recalls the keen competition for limited resources (and the resulting animosity toward immigrants) of the '20s. Further, Allen is quick to remind us that eugenics was not a marginal, bigoted movement in either Europe or the United States; it was a Progressive program, designed to harness science in the service of reducing suffering and misfortune and to help make society more efficient.

These concerns are probably justified, but there are also some signs that we may be on the crest of another important cultural shift. More and more experts, including dedicated biologists, sense that the power of genetics has been oversold and that a correction is needed. What's more, there's a glimmer of evidence that the typical American may not be buying it entirely. According to a recent *U.S. News*/Bozell poll,* less

no role whatsoever in homosexuality, and a similar percentage think heredity is irrelevant to drug addiction and criminality. Across the board, most believe that people's lives are shaped by the choices they make.

These numbers can be interpreted in different ways. It may be that neurogenetic determinism has become the "religion of the intellectual class," as one critic argues, but that it never really caught the imagination of the typical American. Or we may be witnessing a kind of cultural self-correction, in which after a period of infatuation with neuroscience and genetics the public is becoming disenchanted, or perhaps even anxious about the kinds of social control that critics describe.

Whatever's going on, it's clear that this new mistrust of genetic power is consonant with what science is now beginning to show. Indeed, the very expression "gene for" is misleading, according to philosopher Philip Kitcher, author of *The Lives to Come*. Kitcher critiques what he calls "gene talk," a simplistic shorthand for talking about genetic advances that has led to the widespread misunderstanding of DNA's real powers. He suggests that public discourse may need to include more scientific jargon—not a lot, but some—so as not to oversimplify the complexity of the gene-environment interaction. For example, when geneticists say they've found a gene for a particular trait, what they mean is that people carrying a cer-

ALCOHOLISM. Heredity might be involved in some kinds of alcoholism. But no gene can make you buy a bottle of Scotch, pour a glass, and toss it down.

Europe, society became less, not more, tolerant of human variation and misfortune. Based on racial theories that held Eastern Europeans to be genetically inferior to Anglo-Saxon stock, Congress passed (and Calvin Coolidge signed) a 1924 law to restrict immigration, and by 1940 more than 30 states had laws permitting forced sterilization of people suffering from such conditions as "fee-

than 1 American in 5 believes that genes play a major role in controlling behavior; three quarters cite environment and society as the more powerful shapers of our lives. Whether the behavior under question is a disorder like addiction, mental illness, or violence, or a trait like homosexuality, most believe that heredity plays some role, but not a primary one. Indeed, 40 percent think genes play

tain "allele"—a variation in a stretch of DNA that normally codes for a certain protein—will develop the given trait in a standard environment. The last few words—"in a standard environment"— are very important, because what scientists are *not saying* is that a given allele will necessarily lead to that trait in every environment. Indeed, there is mounting evidence that a particular allele will not

---

U.S. News/Bozell poll of 1,000 adults conducted by KRC Research Feb. 6–9, 1997. Margin of error: plus or minus 3.1 percent.

produce the same result if the environment changes significantly; that is to say, the environment has a strong influence on whether and how a gene gets "expressed."

It's hard to emphasize too much what a radical rethinking of the nature-nurture debate this represents. When most people think about heredity, they still think in terms of classical Mendelian genetics: one gene, one trait. But for most complex human behaviors, this is far from the reality that recent research is revealing. A more accurate view very likely involves many different genes, some of which control other genes, and many of which are controlled by signals from the environment. To complicate matters further, the environment is very complicated in itself, ranging from the things we typically lump under nurture (parenting, family dynamics, schooling, safe housing) to biological encounters like viruses and birth complications, even biochemical events within cells.

The relative contributions of genes and the environment are not additive, as in such-and-such a percentage of nature, such-and-such a percentage of experience; that's the old view, no longer credited. Nor is it true that full genetic expression happens once, around birth, after which we take our genetic legacy into the world to see how far it gets us. Genes produce proteins throughout the lifespan, in many different environ-

loading that gives some people a susceptibility—for schizophrenia, for instance, or for aggression. But the development of the behavior or pathology requires more, what National Institute of Mental Health Director Stephen Hyman calls an environmental "second hit." This second hit operates, counterintuitively, through the genes themselves to "sculpt" the brain. So with depression, for example, it appears as though a bad experience in the world—for example, a devastating loss—can actually create chemical changes in the body that affect certain genes, which in turn affect certain brain proteins that make a person more susceptible to depression in the future. Nature or nurture? Similarly, Hyman's own work has shown that exposure to addictive substances can lead to biochemical changes at the genetic and molecular levels that commandeer brain circuits involving volition—and thus undermine the very motivation needed to take charge of one's destructive behavior. So the choice to experiment with drugs or alcohol may, in certain people, create the biological substrate of the addictive disorder. The distinction between biology and experience begins to lose its edge.

Nurturing potentials. Just as bad experiences can turn on certain vulnerability genes, rich and challenging experiences have the power to enhance life, again acting through the genes.

gist Urie Bronfenbrenner. Everything from lively conversation to games to the reading of stories can potentially get a gene to turn on and create a protein that may become a neuronal receptor or messenger chemical involved in thinking or mood. "No genetic potential can become reality," says Bronfenbrenner, "unless the relationship between the organism and its environment is such that it is *permitted* to be expressed." Unfortunately, as he details in his new book, *The State of Americans,* the circumstances in which many American children are living are becoming more impoverished year by year.

If there's a refrain among geneticists working today, it's this: The harder we work to demonstrate the power of heredity, the harder it is to escape the potency of experience. It's a bit paradoxical, because in a sense we end up once again with the old pre-1950s paradigm, but arrived at with infinitely more-sophisticated tools: Yes, the way to intervene in human lives and improve them, to ameliorate mental illness, addictions, and criminal behavior, is to enrich impoverished environments, to improve conditions in the family and society. What's changed is that the argument is coming not from left-leaning sociologists, but from those most intimate with the workings of the human genome. The goal of psychosocial interventions is optimal gene expression.

HOMOSEXUALITY. Gay-rights advocates once argued that homosexuality was a matter of lifestyle choice. Now they stress genes and destiny.

ments, or they don't produce those proteins, depending on how rich or harsh or impoverished those environments are. The interaction is so thoroughly dynamic and enduring that, as psychologist William Greenough says, "To ask what's more important, nature or nurture, is like asking what's more important to a rectangle, its length or its width."

The emerging view of nature-nurture is that many complicated behaviors probably have some measure of genetic

Greenough has shown in rat studies that by providing cages full of toys and complex structures that are continually rearranged—"the animal equivalent of Head Start"—he can increase the number of synapses in the rats brains by 25 percent and blood flow by 85 percent. Talent and intelligence appear extraordinarily malleable.

Child-development experts refer to the life circumstances that enhance (or undermine) gene expression as "proximal processes" a term coined by psycholo-

So assume for a minute that there is a cluster of genes somehow associated with youthful violence. The kid who carries those genes might inhabit a world of loving parents, regular nutritious meals, lots of books, safe schools. Or his world might be a world of peeling paint and gunshots around the corner. In which environment would those genes be likely to manufacture the biochemical underpinnings of criminality? Or for that matter, the proteins and synapses of happiness?

Multiplying the Risks

More group births mean more preemies and, often, more problems

BOBBI AND KENNY MCCAUGHEY SEEM thrilled to have seven new babies in tow, and last week's headlines show the world is happy for them. But amid the hoopla, it's worth keeping in mind that multiple birth is rarely a joyous accident. It's a growing health crisis. Driven by the aggressive use of fertility drugs and reproductive technology, the annual number of multiple births has quadrupled since the 1970s. The trouble is, kids born in groups are almost always born prematurely. And though intensive-care units can often keep them alive, the medical consequences can be devastating. As Dr. Peter Heyl of Eastern Virginia Medical School observes. "The human uterus is not meant to carry litters."

Under normal conditions, it almost never does. Women's hormonal rhythms are choreographed to ensure that the ovaries release one—and only one—fertile egg every month. Early in the menstrual cycle, a drop in circulating estrogen and progesterone prompts the body to release other hormones (GRF, FSH and LH). When stimulated by those hormones, egg-bearing sacs, or follicles, within the ovaries start to swell. After a week or so, a follicle will mature to the point where it's ready to release its egg into the fallopian tube for fertilization. But before doing that, it spurts estrogen into the bloodstream—shutting down the cascade of ovulation hormones and halting the growth of other follicles.

Fertility treatments can easily disrupt that arrangement. When supercharged by a drug like Pergonal or Metrodin (the treatment McCaughey received), a woman's ovaries can release as many as 40 eggs in one cycle. Doctors may extract them for in vitro fertilization (IVF) or leave them to be fertilized naturally. Though multiple births are rare under normal conditions, a third of all IVF pregnancies, and up to 20 percent of those achieved with fertility drugs, involve two or more babies.

That wouldn't be a problem if humans had the carrying capacity of, say, cats. But they don't. Women carrying multiple fetuses risk anemia, hypertension and labor complications that can require Caesarean delivery. And their babies are often born prematurely. On average, each additional fetus shortens the usual 40-week gestation period by three and one-half weeks. A pair of twins born at 36 weeks may do fine. But as the number of fetuses increases, the kids' gestation times and birth weights decline.

So do their health prospects. Even if they're born alive, triplets, quadruplets and quintuplets are 12 times more likely than other babies to die within a year. Many suffer from respiratory and digestive problems. They're also prone to a range of neurological disorders, including blindness, cerebral palsy and mental retardation. Until a fetus reaches about 36 weeks, its developing brain maintains a delicate cell factory known as the germinal matrix. The matrix normally finishes its job before a child is born. But if it's still active at the time of delivery, normal fluctuations in blood pressure can cause a hemorrhage that not only stalls neuron production but injuries existing brain tissue. By selectively reducing the number of fetuses in a woman's womb—i.e., killing two of four quadruplets by lethal injection—a specialist can avert such problems. But couples can't always stomach that prospect, so doctors are often left struggling to postpone a dangerous delivery as long as possible.

These crises are not inevitable. After giving a woman fertility drugs, specialists can use imaging tests to monitor the behavior of her ovaries. If the tests show that numerous eggs have been released, the doctors can advise against sex or sperm injections and try a lower dose on the next cycle. And in newly adopted guidelines, the American Society for Reproductive Medicine agrees that IVF specialists should limit the number of viable embryos they place in patients' wombs. But fertility clinics are unregulated, and as long as their clients demand success at any cost, the boom in multiple births is likely to continue. Would-be parents should realize that more is not always merrier.

GEOFFREY COWLEY and KAREN SPRINGEN

When Fertility Drugs Work Too Well

Women's hormonal rhythms normally ensure production of just one viable egg every month. By forcing the release of numerous eggs at once, fertility drugs raise the chance of multiple birth.

The Normal Ovary

Under ordinary conditions, an ovary is the size of a grape. Inside there are fluid-filled sacs called follicles, each housing an egg, or ovum. During normal ovulation, one follicle matures, releasing its egg for fertilization in the fallopian tube.

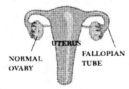

NORMAL OVARY · UTERUS · FALLOPIAN TUBE

The Ovary on Drugs

Fertility drugs jump-start follicle development, increasing the likelihood that more than one follicle will release a fertile egg. Drug treatment can make the ovaries swell up to 10 times their normal volume—roughly the size of a grapefruit.

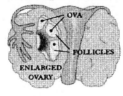

OVA · FOLLICLES · ENLARGED OVARY

Multiple Birth

The human uterus isn't designed to hold numerous fetuses. When it is forced to, the crowding causes early delivery. The consequences for babies can range from brain damage to death.

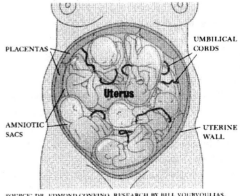

PLACENTAS · UMBILICAL CORDS · Uterus · AMNIOTIC SACS · UTERINE WALL

SOURCE: DR. EDMOND CONFINO. RESEARCH BY BILL VOURVOULIAS, ILLUSTRATION BY STANFORD KAY—NEWSWEEK

Designer Babies

Scientists say that, with gene therapy, they may soon be able to cure a child's inherited disease before he is even born. But should they be allowed to create kids with made-to-order traits? BY SHARON BEGLEY

IT IS ONLY A MATTER OF TIME. ONE DAY— a day probably no more distant than the first wedding anniversary of a couple who are now teenage sweethearts—a man and a woman will walk into an in vitro fertilization clinic and make scientific history. Their problem won't be infertility, the reason couples now choose IVF. Rather, they will be desperate for a very special child, a child who will elude a family curse. To create their dream child, doctors will fertilize a few of the woman's eggs with her husband's sperm, as IVF clinics do today. But then they will inject an artificial human chromosome, carrying made-to-order genes like pearls on a string, into the fertilized egg. One of the genes will carry instructions ordering cells to commit suicide (graphic). Then the doctors will place the embryo into the woman's uterus. If her baby is a boy, when he becomes an old man he, like his father and grandfather before him, will develop prostate cancer. But the cell-suicide gene will make his prostate cells self-destruct. The man, unlike his ancestors, will not die of the cancer. And since the gene that the doctors gave him copied itself into every cell of his body, including his sperm, his sons will beat prostate cancer, too.

Genetic engineers are preparing to cross what has long been an ethical Rubicon. Since 1990, gene therapy has meant slipping a healthy gene into the cells of one organ of a patient suffering from a genetic disease. Soon, it may mean something much more momentous: altering a fertilized egg so that genes in all of a person's cells, including eggs or sperm, also carry a gene that scientists, not

parents, bequeathed them. When the pioneers of gene therapy first requested government approval for their experiments in 1987, they vowed they would *never* alter patients' eggs or sperm. That was then. This is now. One of those pioneers, Dr. W. French Anderson of the University of Southern California, recently put the National Institutes of Health on notice. Within two or three years, he said, he would ask approval to use gene therapy on a fetus that has been diagnosed with a deadly inherited disease. The therapy would cure the fetus before it is born. But the introduced genes, though targeted at only blood or immune-system cells, might inadvertently slip into the child's egg (or sperm) cells, too. If that happens, the genetic change would affect that child's children unto the nth generation. "Life would enter a new phase," says biophysicist Gregory Stock of

UCLA, "one in which we seize control of our own evolution."

Judging by the 70 pages of public comments NIH has received since Anderson submitted his proposal in September, the overwhelming majority of scientists and ethicists weighing in oppose gene therapy that changes the "germline" (eggs and sperm). But the opposition could be a boulevard wide and paper thin. "There is a great divide in the bioethics community over whether we should be opening up this Pandora's box," says science-policy scholar Sheldon Krimsky of Tufts University. Many bioethicists are sympathetic to using germline therapy to shield a child from a family disposition to cancer, or atherosclerosis or other illnesses with a strong genetic component. As James Watson, president of the Cold Spring Harbor Laboratory and codiscoverer of the double-helical structure of DNA, said at a recent UCLA conference, "We might as well do what we finally can to take the threat of Alzheimer's or breast cancer away from a family." But something else is suddenly making it OK to discuss the once forbidden possibility of germline engineering: molecular biologists now think they have clever ways to circumvent ethical concerns that engulf this sci-fi idea.

There may be ways, for instance, to design a baby's genes without violating the principle of informed consent. This is the belief that no one's genes—not even an embryo's—should be altered without his or her permission. Presumably few people would object to being spared a fatal disease. But what about genes for personality

Pruning the Family Tree

Recent experiments suggest genetic engineering of human embryos could one day provide an early cure for inherited diseases.

An egg is fertilized. One gene that kills prostate cells, and one that triggers this gene, are added.

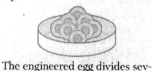

The engineered egg divides several times. This pre-embryo is implanted in the woman's uterus.

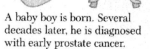

A baby boy is born. Several decades later, he is diagnosed with early prostate cancer.

An injection activates the cell-killing gene. All the prostate cells die; the man does not.

SOURCE: JOHN CAMPBELL, UCLA. DIAGRAM BY CHRISTOPH BLUMRICH — NEWSWEEK

traits, like risk-taking or being neurotic? If you like today's blame game—it's *Mom's fault* that you inherited her temper—you'll love tomorrow's: she intentionally stuck you with that personality quirk. But the child of tomorrow might have the final word about his genes, says UCLA geneticist John Campbell. The designer gene for, say, patience could be paired with an on-off switch, he says. The child would have to take a drug to activate the patience gene. Free to accept or reject the drug, he retains informed consent over his genetic endowment.

There may also be ways to make an end run around the worry that it is wrong to monkey with human evolution. Researchers are experimenting with tricks to make the introduced gene self-destruct in cells that become eggs or sperm. That would confine the tinkering to one generation. Then, if it became clear that eliminating genes for, say, mental illness also erased genes for creativity, that loss would not become a permanent part of man's genetic blueprint. (Of course, preventing the new gene's transmission to future generations would also defeat the hope of permanently lopping off a diseased branch from a family tree.) In experiments with animals, geneticist Mario Capecchi of the University of Utah has designed a string of genes flanked by the molecular version of scissors. The scissors are activated by an enzyme that would be made only in the cells that become eggs or sperm. Once activated, the genetic scissors snip out the introduced gene and, presto, it is not passed along to future generations. "What I worry about," says Capecchi, "is that if we start messing around with [eggs and sperm], at some point—since this is a human enterprise—we're going to make a mistake. You want a way to undo that mistake. And since what may seem terrific now may seem naive in 20 years, you want a way to make the genetic change reversible."

There is no easy technological fix for another ethical worry, however: with germline engineering only society's "haves" will control their genetic traits. It isn't hard to foresee a day like that painted in last year's film "Gattaca," where only the wealthy can afford to genetically engineer their children with such "killer applications" as intelligence, beauty, long life or health. "If you are going to disadvantage even further those who are already disadvantaged," says bioethicist Ruth Macklin of Albert Einstein College of Medicine, "then that does raise serious concerns." But perhaps not enough to keep designer babies solely in Hollywood's imagination. For one thing, genetic therapy as done today (treating one organ of one child or adult) has been a bitter disappointment. "With the exception of a few anecdotal cases," says USC's Anderson, "there is no evidence of a gene-therapy protocol that helps." But germline therapy might actually be easier. Doctors would not have to insinuate the new gene into millions of lung cells in, say, a cystic fibrosis patient. They could manipulate only a single cell—the fertilized egg—and still have the gene reach every cell of the person who develops from that egg.

How soon might we design our children? The necessary pieces are quickly falling into place. The first artificial human chromosome was created last year. By 2003 the Human Genome Project will have decoded all 3 billion chemical letters that spell out our 70,000 or so genes. Animal experiments designed to show that the process will not create horrible mutants are under way. No law prohibits germline engineering. Although NIH now refuses to even consider funding proposals for it, the rules are being updated. And where there is a way, there will almost surely be a will: none of us, says USC's Anderson, "wants to pass on to our children lethal genes if we can prevent it—that's what's going to drive this." At the UCLA symposium on germline engineering, two thirds of the audience supported it. Few would argue against using the technique to eradicate a disease that has plagued a family for generations. As Tuft's Krimsky says, "We know where to start." The harder question is this: do we know where to stop?

Hope for 'Snow Babies'

A mother's cocaine use may not doom her child after all

BY SHARON BEGLEY

THE EPIDEMIC OF CRACK COCAINE HAD just hit the inner cities in the mid-1980s when pediatricians and hospital nursery workers began reporting truly harrowing observations: babies born to women who had used cocaine while pregnant were not like other infants. They were underweight. They trembled. As newborns they were as rigid as plastic dolls. They cried inconsolably, seeming to recoil from hugs or touches and startled at the slightest sound. As they approached school age, it seemed that many could not sit still or focus, even on activities they enjoyed. For schools and for society, warned the press and the legions of anti-drug crusaders, cocaine babies would be a lost generation.

Well, scientists have found this generation. The snow babies, it seems, are neither the emotional and cognitive cripples that many predicted—nor the perfectly normal kids that biological revisionists have lately been claiming. Last week, at a landmark conference in Washington convened by the New York Academy of Sciences, more than three dozen neurologists, pediatricians and other researchers presented studies suggesting that the effects of cocaine on a fetus are far from simple, let alone predictable. They depend not only on such obvious things as how much of the drug the mother took and when but also on what sort of environment the baby grows up in. Although studies on large numbers of school-age children are only beginning, research on toddlers suggests that "most cocaine-exposed children do very well," says Dr. Barry Kosofsky of Har-

vard Medical School, co-chair of the conference. "Cocaine is not a sledgehammer to the fetal brain."

But neither is it a prenatal vitamin. Experiments show that rats, rabbits and monkeys exposed to cocaine in utero are profoundly messed up. Their brains develop abnormally. Neurons are too long or too short. "Receptors" to which brain chemicals attach are too many or too few or too sensitive. The animals' behavior reflects these aberrations: they typically act impulsively, have trouble learning and can't block out extraneous sights and sounds when learning a task. The challenge, obviously, is to figure out why the human and animal data tell such an "on the one hand, on the other hand" story it takes a human octopus to keep it all straight.

One reason cocaine-exposed children do not seem to be faring worse may reflect how human studies are done. To get a clean result, scientists must compare children who are as similar as possible on every measure except the one being studied—cocaine exposure. It is a fact of life, and thus of science, that the women and children who wind up in these studies are not the wealthy Wall Street traders sniffing a line at the end of a hard day. Instead they are poor, and often single, and the home they bring their baby to can be chaotic. These children have so many strikes against them that adding cocaine to the mix may not hurt them much more. Or as Prof. Barry Lester of Brown University puts it, "If you grow up in such a lousy environment, things are so bad al-

ready that cocaine exposure doesn't make much difference." That may be the case in a study at Philadelphia's Albert Einstein Medical Center. At the age of 4, cocaine-exposed kids score 70 on IQ tests; their peers in the impoverished neighborhood score 82. The U.S. average is 90 to 109.

Studies of coke-exposed children may also be looking for the wrong thing. "It is possible that what is being tested are not areas where these children are most vulnerable," says Lester. In tests at Einstein, for instance, cocaine-exposed children figure out the locks and secret compartments in a box holding little toys. And at the University of Illinois, Dr. Ira Chasnoff finds in his study of 170 children that the coke-exposed ones had roughly the same IQ scores at the age of 6 as those whose mothers were clean. But children take IQ tests, and do puzzles for scientists, in quiet rooms with few distractions. All the animal data suggest that the brain systems most damaged by cocaine are those that control attention and, especially, screen out irrelevant sights and sounds. "The children do fine in a quiet room by themselves," says neuroscientist Pat Levitt of the University of Pittsburgh. "But there is no question they have alterations in their brain structure and function which, while not keeping them from learning a task in isolation, could well hurt them in real life."

Real life is the classroom as multimedia madhouse, with posters covering every wall and kiddie art dangling from lights. It is not clear how cocaine-exposed children will fare in such environments. Of the 119 studies on how cocaine affects a child's development, reports Lester, only six have followed the children beyond the age of 3. One is already setting off alarm bells. A pilot study at Wayne State University in Detroit finds that teachers rated 27 cocaine-exposed 6-year-olds as having significantly more trouble paying attention than 75 non-exposed children (the teachers did not know who was who).

There is little debate that distractibility hinders learning. That's why thousands of parents put their hyperactive children on Ritalin. And that's why cocaine-exposed children who seem to be OK now may fare worse as they make their way through school. Dr. Gideon Koren of Toronto's Hospital for Sick Children is following 47 cocaine-exposed children who were adopted as infants. Their new families "can't tell the difference" between these children and others,

says Koren. But he can. When the children were 3 years old, their language skills were developing a little more slowly than that of nonexposed children; there were no IQ differences. But at the ages of 5 and 6, an IQ gap of 10 points has opened up. The older the children get, says Koren, "the more likely there will be [cognitive] differences" compared with other kids. "These must be biological differences."

It's too soon to draw final conclusions. Clearly the legions of crack babies have not burned out as badly as was feared, but the damage assessment is continuing. Most likely, the effects of cocaine are real but small. How starkly those effects show up depends, argues Kosofsky, on myriad factors, including the environment in which the child is raised. In Toronto, Koren's cocaine-exposed kids have, at the ages of 5 and 6, lower IQ scores than their otherwise healthy siblings. But their average score of 106 is still more than 20 points higher than typical

scores of children raised in disadvantaged homes.

There will be plenty of time for further study. Even though the crisis has left the front pages, every year at least 40,000 babies are born to women who took cocaine while pregnant, according to a 1995 estimate by the National Institute on Drug Abuse. For years these children have been demonized and written off. But as the results of studies show, few are beyond the help that a loving and stress-free home can provide. As last week's conference broke up, scientists who spend their nights tracking neurotransmitters and their days running underfunded clinics for cocaine-exposed kids raised a very different question: is labeling these babies "hopeless and lost" just a handy excuse to avoid helping them and their mothers?

With MARY HAGER *in Washington*

Unit 2

Unit Selections

Early Cognitive and Physical Development

5. **Fertile Minds,** J. Madeleine Nash
6. **What Do We Know from Brain Research?** Pat Wolfe and Ron Brandt
7. **Evolution and Developmental Sex Differences,** David C. Geary
8. **Baby Talk,** Shannon Brownlee
9. **Effects of Sleep Position on Infant Motor Development,** Beth Ellen Davis, Rachel Y. Moon, Hari C. Sachs, and Mary C. Ottolini
10. **Categories in Young Children's Thinking,** Susan A. Gelman
11. **Why Children Talk to Themselves,** Laura E. Berk

Learning in School

12. **How Asian Teachers Polish Each Lesson to Perfection,** James W. Stigler and Harold W. Stevenson
13. **"Ready, READ!"** Nicholas Lemann

Key Points to Consider

❖ Given that infants are more cognitively competent than once thought, what do you think about accelerated, formalized efforts to speed up infants' cognitive skills? What advantages or disadvantages do you envision for infants who are exposed to teaching and drilling at early ages? Do you think that there are "critical periods" in the very early years of development that will forever determine later cognitive growth? If you were a parent; would you expose your infant to classical music or mathematics? Why or why not?

❖ If sex differences between boys and girls are based on evolutionary principles, should we still teach boys to be less aggressive or girls to be more independent? If girls and boys suffer inequities or disadvantages because of their sex differences in behavior, then what role should society or culture play, even if these differences may have evolutionary roots?

❖ Parents wait expectantly for the moment when their infant utters his or her first word. And from that moment on, language development unfolds at an amazing pace. Based on the readings, as a parent or teacher, what would you do to facilitate a child's linguistic development?

❖ How would you rate American versus Asian teachers in terms of their ability to help children learn? What things would you change about our educational system? Why is it that parents from these two cultures have such different values and expectations of teachers and education? What would your expectations be?

❖ The debate on when and how to teach children to read effectively is a controversial one. Where do you stand? Should outside authorities be able to force schools to use a prescribed, standardized reading curriculum or should schools be permitted local autonomy? Should these policies be mandated equally for all students, even for those for whom English is not their first language?

 **Links** ## www.dushkin.com/online/

8. **Educational Resources Information Center (ERIC)**
   http://www.ed.gov/pubs/pubdb.html

9. **I Am Your Child**
   http://iamyourchild.org

10. **National Association for the Education of Young Children (NAEYC)**
    http://www.naeyc.org

11. **Results of NICHD Study of Early Child Care**
    http://156.40.88.3/publications/pubs/early_child_care.htm

12. **Vandergrift's Children's Literature Page**
    http://www.scils.rutgers.edu/special/kay/childlit.html

13. **Project Zero**
    http://pzweb.harvard.edu

These sites are annotated on pages 4 and 5

We have come a long way from the days when the characterization of cognition of infants and young children included phrases like "tabula rasa" and "booming, buzzing confusion." Infants and young children are no longer viewed by researchers as blank slates, passively waiting to be filled up with knowledge. Today, experts in child development are calling for a reformulation of assumptions about children's cognitive abilities, as well as calling for reforms in the ways we teach children in our schools. Hence, the articles in the first subsection highlight some of the new knowledge of the cognitive abilities of infants and young children.

Recent brain development research indicates that babies possess a number of impressive abilities. The essays "Fertile Minds" and "Categories in Young Children's Thinking" describe how scientists are discovering, by employing ingenious experimental techniques, that infants possess many heretofore unrealized skills that are heavily influenced by both nature and early experiences. "What Do We Know from Brain Research?" presents data from recent studies showing that specific cognitive skills are influenced powerfully by the complex interaction of both environment and heredity.

What accounts for sex differences between boys and girls? Are boys and girls programmed by their genes to behave in certain ways or are these behavioral differences the result of socialization and culture? The author of "Evolution and Developmental Sex Differences" argues that an evolutionary perspective along with cultural factors may help to explain some of these differences.

The word "infant" is derived from Latin, meaning "without speech." "Baby Talk" discusses the remarkable new research on the precursors to early language acquisition in infancy and continued linguistic developments in early childhood. This research demonstrates that although the human brain is wired for language, it is exquisitely responsive to the language environment. Once young children have begun to talk, they often talk out their thoughts out loud. In "Why Children Talk to Themselves," the author shows how this private speech behavior actually helps young children's language development, self-control, and mastery of new linguistic skills.

Recently, pediatricians have been advising parents of infants to put their babies to sleep on their backs in order to reduce the risk of Sudden Infant Death Syndrome or SIDS. The article "Effects

of Sleep Position on Infant Motor Development" discusses some new research showing that infants who sleep on their backs may reach motor development milestones less quickly than babies who sleep on their stomachs.

As Erik Erikson noted, from about age 6 to 12 years, children enter the period of "industry versus inferiority" and become preoccupied with learning the tools of their culture. In our culture, these tools are the "three R's"—learning to read, write, and do arithmetic in school. Thus, the second subsection of this unit addresses developments in school-age children.

"How Asian Teachers Polish Each Lesson to Perfection" presents very interesting cultural differences in attitudes and practices regarding education and teaching practices in the United States versus Asia. These articles offer much food for thought for those who believe that the United States should change its educational values and practices.

Learning to read is a significant cognitive achievement for young children in school. In "Ready, READ!" the author reviews the problems that public schools face in teaching young children to read and offers new approaches such as charter schools and a fundamental shift in focus to a standardized reading curriculum that is controlled by outsiders.

FERTILE MINDS

From birth, a baby's brain cells proliferate wildly,
making connections that may shape a lifetime of experience.
The first three years are critical

By J. MADELEINE NASH

RAT-A-TAT-TAT. RAT-A-TAT-TAT. RAT-A-tat-tat. If scientists could eavesdrop on the brain of a human embryo 10, maybe 12 weeks after conception, they would hear an astonishing racket. Inside the womb, long before light first strikes the retina of the eye or the earliest dreamy images flicker through the cortex, nerve cells in the developing brain crackle with purposeful activity. Like teenagers with telephones, cells in one neighborhood of the brain are calling friends in another, and these cells are calling their friends, and they keep calling one another over and over again, "almost," says neurobiologist Carla Shatz of the University of California, Berkeley, "as if they were autodialing."

But these neurons—as the long, wiry cells that carry electrical messages through the nervous system and the brain are called—are not transmitting signals in scattershot fashion. That would produce a featureless static, the sort of noise picked up by a radio tuned between stations. On the contrary, evidence is growing that the staccato bursts of electricity that form those distinctive rat-a-tat-tats arise from coordinated waves of neural activity, and that those pulsing waves, like currents shifting sand on the ocean floor, actually change the shape of the brain, carving mental circuits into patterns that over time will enable the newborn infant to perceive a father's voice, a mother's touch, a shiny mobile twirling over the crib.

Of all the discoveries that have poured out of neuroscience labs in recent years, the finding that the electrical activity of brain cells changes the physical structure of the brain is perhaps the most breathtaking. For the rhythmic firing of neurons is no longer assumed to be a by-product of building the brain but essential to the process, and it begins, scientists have established, well before birth. A brain is not a computer. Nature does not cobble it together, then turn it on. No, the brain begins working long before it is finished. And the same processes that wire the brain before birth, neuroscientists are finding, also drive the explosion of learning that occurs immediately afterward.

At birth a baby's brain contains 100 billion neurons, roughly as many nerve cells as there are stars in the Milky Way. Also in place are a trillion glial cells, named after the Greek word for glue, which form a kind of honeycomb that protects and nourishes the neurons. But while the brain contains virtually all the nerve cells it will ever have, the pattern of wiring between them has yet to stabilize. Up to this point, says Shatz, "what the brain has done is lay out circuits that are its best guess about what's required for vision, for language, for whatever." And now it is up to neural activity—no longer spontaneous, but driven by a flood of sensory experiences—to take this rough blueprint and progressively refine it.

During the first years of life, the brain undergoes a series of extraordinary changes. Starting shortly after birth, a baby's brain, in a display of biological exuberance, produces trillions more connections between neurons than it can possibly use. Then, through a process that resembles Darwinian competition, the brain eliminates connections, or synapses, that are seldom or never used. The excess synapses in a child's brain undergo a draconian pruning, starting around the age of 10 or earlier, leaving behind a mind whose patterns of emotion and thought are, for better or worse, unique.

Deprived of a stimulating environment, a child's brain suffers. Researchers at Baylor College of Medicine, for example, have found that children who don't play much or are rarely touched develop brains 20% to 30% smaller than normal for their age. Laboratory animals provide another provocative parallel. Not only do young rats reared in toy-strewn cages exhibit more complex behavior than rats confined to sterile, uninteresting boxes, researchers at the University of Illinois at Urbana-Champaign have found, but the brains of these rats contain as many as 25% more synapses per neuron. Rich experiences, in other words, really do produce rich brains.

The new insights into brain development are more than just interesting science. They have profound implications for parents and policymakers. In an age when mothers and fathers are increasingly pressed for time—and may already be feeling guilty about how many hours they spend away from their children—the results coming out of the labs are likely to increase concerns about leaving very young children in the care of others. For the data underscore the importance of

   From *Time*, February 3, 1997, pp. 48-56. © 1997 by Time Inc. Magazine Company. Reprinted by permission.

hands-on parenting, of finding the time to cuddle a baby, talk with a toddler and provide infants with stimulating experiences.

The new insights have begun to infuse new passion into the political debate over early education and day care. There is an urgent need, say child-development experts, for preschool programs designed to boost the brain power of youngsters born into impoverished rural and inner-city households. Without such programs, they warn, the current drive to curtail welfare costs by pushing mothers with infants and toddlers into the work force may well backfire. "There is a time scale to brain development, and the most important year is the first," notes Frank Newman, president of the Education Commission of the States. By the age of three, a child who is neglected or abused bears marks that, if not indelible, are exceedingly difficult to erase.

But the new research offers hope as well. Scientists have found that the brain during the first years of life is so malleable that very young children who suffer strokes or injuries that wipe out an entire hemisphere can still mature into highly functional adults. Moreover, it is becoming increasingly clear that well-designed preschool programs can help many children overcome glaring deficits in their home environment. With appropriate therapy, say researchers, even serious disorders like dyslexia may be treatable. While inherited problems may place certain children at greater risk than others, says Dr. Harry Chugani, a pediatric neurologist at Wayne State University in Detroit, that is no excuse for ignoring the environment's power to remodel the brain. "We may not do much to change what happens before birth, but we can change what happens after a baby is born," he observes.

Strong evidence that activity changes the brain began accumulating in the 1970s. But only recently have researchers had tools powerful enough to reveal the precise mechanisms by which those changes are brought about. Neural activity triggers a biochemical cascade that reaches all the way to the nucleus of cells and the coils of DNA that encode specific genes. In fact, two of the genes affected by neural activity in embryonic fruit flies, neurobiologist Corey Goodman and his colleagues at Berkeley reported late last year, are identical to those that other studies have linked to learning and memory. How thrilling, exclaims Goodman, how intellectually satisfying that the snippets of DNA that embryos use to build their brains are the very same ones that will later allow adult organisms to process and store new information.

As researchers explore the once hidden links between brain activity and brain structure, they are beginning to construct a sturdy bridge over the chasm that previously separated genes from the environment. Experts now agree that a baby does not come into

Wiring Vision

WHAT'S GOING ON Babies can see at birth, but not in fine-grained detail. They have not yet acquired the knack of focusing both eyes on a single object or developed more sophisticated visual skills like depth perception. they also lack hand-eye coordination.
WHAT PARENTS CAN DO There is no need to buy high-contrast black-and-white toys to stimulate vision. But regular eye exams, starting as early as two weeks of age, can detect problems that, if left uncorrected, can cause a weak or unused eye to lose its functional connections to the brain.
WINDOW OF LEARNING Unless it is exercised early on, the visual system will not develop.

AGE (in years)	Birth 1	2	3	4	5	6	7	8	9	10
Visual acuity										
Binocular vision										

the world as a genetically preprogrammed automaton or a blank slate at the mercy of the environment, but arrives as something much more interesting. For this reason the debate that engaged countless generations of philosophers—whether nature or nurture calls the shots—no longer interests most scientists. They are much too busy chronicling the myriad ways in which genes and the environment interact. "It's not a competition," says Dr. Stanley Greenspan, a psychiatrist at George Washington University. "It's a dance."

THE IMPORTANCE OF GENES

THAT DANCE BEGINS AT AROUND THE THIRD week of gestation, when a thin layer of cells in the developing embryo performs an origami-like trick, folding inward to give rise to a fluid-filled cylinder known as the neural tube. As cells in the neural tube proliferate at the astonishing rate of 250,000 a minute, the brain and spinal cord assemble themselves in a series of tightly choreographed steps. Nature is the dominant partner during this phase of development, but nurture plays a vital supportive role. Changes in the environment of the womb—whether caused by maternal malnutrition, drug abuse or a viral infection—can wreck the clockwork precision of the neural assembly line. Some forms of epilepsy, mental retardation, autism and schizophrenia appear to be the results of developmental processes gone awry.

But what awes scientists who study the brain, what still stuns them, is not that things occasionally go wrong in the devel-

oping brain but that so much of the time they go right. This is all the more remarkable, says Berkeley's Shatz, as the central nervous system of an embryo is not a miniature of the adult system but more like a tadpole that gives rise to a frog. Among other things, the cells produced in the neural tube must migrate to distant locations and accurately lay down the connections that link one part of the brain to another. In addition, the embryonic brain must construct a variety of temporary structures, including the neural tube, that will, like a tadpole's tail, eventually disappear.

What biochemical magic underlies this incredible metamorphosis? The instructions programmed into the genes, of course. Scientists have recently discovered, for instance, that a gene nicknamed "sonic hedgehog" (after the popular video game Sonic the Hedgehog) determines the fate of neurons in the spinal cord and the brain. Like a strong scent carried by the wind, the protein encoded by the hedgehog gene (so called because in its absence, fruit-fly embryos sprout a coat of prickles) diffuses outward from the cells that produce it, becoming fainter and fainter. Columbia University neurobiologist Thomas Jessell has found that it takes middling concentrations of this potent morphing factor to produce a motor neuron and lower concentrations to make an interneuron (a cell that relays signals to other neurons, instead of to muscle fibers, as motor neurons do).

Scientists are also beginning to identify some of the genes that guide neurons in their long migrations. Consider the problem faced by neurons destined to become part of the cerebral cortex. Because they arise relatively late in the development of the mammalian brain, billions of these cells must push and shove their way through dense colonies established by earlier migrants. "It's as if the entire population of the East Coast decided to move en masse to the West Coast," marvels Yale University neuroscientist Dr. Pasko Rakic, and marched through Cleveland, Chicago and Denver to get there.

But of all the problems the growing nervous system must solve, the most daunting is posed by the wiring itself. After birth, when the number of connections explodes, each of the brain's billions of neurons will forge links to thousands of others. First they must spin out a web of wire-like fibers known as axons (which transmit signals) and dendrites (which receive them). The objective is to form a synapse, the gap-like structure over which the axon of one neuron beams a signal to the dendrites of another. Before this can happen, axons and dendrites must almost touch. And while the short, bushy dendrites don't have to travel very far, axons—the heavy-duty cables of the nervous system—must traverse distances that are the microscopic equivalent of miles.

What guides an axon on its incredible voyage is a "growth cone," a creepy, crawly sprout that looks something like an amoeba. Scientists have known about growth cones since the turn of the century. What they didn't know until recently was that growth cones come equipped with the molecular equivalent of sonar and radar. Just as instruments in a submarine or airplane scan the environment for signals, so molecules arrayed on the surface of growth cones search their surroundings for the presence of certain proteins. Some of these proteins, it turns out, are attractants that pull the growth cones toward them, while others are repellents that push them away.

THE FIRST STIRRINGS

UP TO THIS POINT, GENES HAVE CONTROLLED the unfolding of the brain. As soon as axons make their first connections, however, the nerves begin to fire, and what they do starts to matter more and more. In essence, say scientists, the developing nervous system has strung the equivalent of telephone trunk lines between the right neighborhoods in the right cities. Now it has to sort out which wires belong to which house, a problem that cannot be solved by genes alone for reasons that boil down to simple arithmetic. Eventually, Berkeley's Goodman estimates, a human brain must forge quadrillions of connections. But there are only 100,000 genes in human DNA. Even though half these genes—some 50,000—appear to be dedicated to constructing and maintaining the nervous system, he observes, that's not enough to specify more than a tiny fraction of the connections required by a fully functioning brain.

In adult mammals, for example, the axons that connect the brain's visual system arrange themselves in striking layers and columns that reflect the division between the left eye and the right. But these axons start out as scrambled as a bowl of spaghetti, according to Michael Stryker, chairman of the physiology department at the University of California at San Francisco. What sorts out the mess, scientists have established, is neural activity. In a series of experiments viewed as classics by scientists in the field, Berkeley's Shatz chemically blocked neural activity in embryonic cats. The result? The axons that connect neurons in the retina of the eye to the brain never formed the left eye–right eye geometry needed to support vision.

But no recent finding has intrigued researchers more than the results reported in October by Corey Goodman and his Berkeley colleagues. In studying a deceptively simple problem—how axons from motor neurons in the fly's central nerve cord establish connections with muscle cells in its limbs—the Berkeley researchers made an

Wiring Feelings

WHAT'S GOING ON Among the first circuits the brain constructs are those that govern the emotions. Beginning around two months of age, the distress and contentment experienced by newborns start to evolve into more complex feelings: joy and sadness, envy and empathy, pride and shame.
WHAT PARENTS CAN DO Loving care provides a baby's brain with the right kind of emotional stimulation. Neglecting a baby can produce brainwave patterns that dampen happy feelings. Abuse can produce heightened anxiety and abnormal stress responses.
WINDOW OF LEARNING Emotions develop in layers, each more complex than the last.

AGE (in years)	Birth	1	2	3	4	5	6	7	8	9	10
Stress Response	▢	▢	▢	▢	▢						
Empathy, Envy			▢	▢	▢	▢	▢	▢	▢	▢	▢

unexpected discovery. They knew there was a gene that keeps bundles of axons together as they race toward their muscle-cell targets. What they discovered was that the electrical activity produced by neurons inhibited this gene, dramatically increasing the number of connections the axons made. Even more intriguing, the signals amplified the activity of a second gene—a gene called CREB.

The discovery of the CREB amplifier, more than any other, links the developmental processes that occur before birth to those that continue long after. For the twin processes of memory and learning in adult animals, Columbia University neurophysiologist Eric Kandel has shown, rely on the CREB molecule. When Kandel blocked the activity of CREB in giant snails, their brains changed in ways that suggested that they could still learn but could remember what they learned for only a short period of time. Without CREB, it seems, snails—and by extension, more developed animals like humans—can form no long-term memories. And without long-term memories, it is hard to imagine that infant brains could ever master more than rudimentary skills. "Nurture is important," says Kandel. "But nurture works through nature."

EXPERIENCE KICKS IN

WHEN A BABY IS BORN, IT CAN SEE AND HEAR and smell and respond to touch, but only dimly. The brain stem, a primitive region that controls vital functions like heartbeat and breathing, has completed its wiring. Elsewhere the connections between neurons are wispy and weak. But over the first few months of life, the brain's higher centers ex-

plode with new synapses. And as dendrites and axons swell with buds and branches like trees in spring, metabolism soars. By the age of two, a child's brain contains twice as many synapses and consumes twice as much energy as the brain of a normal adult.

University of Chicago pediatric neurologist Dr. Peter Huttenlocher has chronicled this extraordinary epoch in brain development by autopsying the brains of infants and young children who have died unexpectedly. The number of synapses in one layer of the visual cortex, Huttenlocher reports, rises from around 2,500 per neuron at birth to as many as 18,000 about six months later. Other regions of the cortex score similarly spectacular increases but on slightly different schedules. And while these microscopic connections between nerve fibers continue to form throughout life, they reach their highest average densities (15,000 synapses per neuron) at around the age of two and remain at that level until the age of 10 or 11.

This profusion of connections lends the growing brain exceptional flexibility and resilience. Consider the case of 13-year-old Brandi Binder, who developed such severe epilepsy that surgeons at UCLA had to remove the entire right side of her cortex when she was six. Binder lost virtually all the control she had established over muscles on the left side of her body, the side controlled by the right side of the brain. Yet today, after years of therapy ranging from leg lifts to math and music drills, Binder is an A student at the Holmes Middle School in Colorado Springs, Colorado. She loves music, math and art—skills usually associated with the right half of the brain. And while Binder's recuperation is not 100%—for example, she has never regained the use of her left arm—it comes close. Says UCLA pediatric neurologist Dr. Donald Shields: "If there's a way to compensate, the developing brain will find it."

What wires a child's brain, say neuroscientists—or rewires it after physical trauma—is repeated experience. Each time a baby tries to touch a tantalizing object or gazes intently at a face or listens to a lullaby, tiny bursts of electricity shoot through the brain, knitting neurons into circuits as well defined as those etched onto silicon chips. The results are those behavioral mileposts that never cease to delight and awe parents. Around the age of two months, for example, the motor-control centers of the brain develop to the point that infants can suddenly reach out and grab a nearby object. Around the age of four months, the cortex begins to refine the connections needed for depth perception and binocular vision. And around the age of 12 months, the speech centers of the brain are poised to produce what is perhaps the most magical moment of childhood: the first word that marks the flowering of language.

When the brain does not receive the right information—or shuts it out—the result can be devastating. Some children who display early signs of autism, for example, retreat from the world because they are hypersensitive to sensory stimulation, others because their senses are underactive and provide them with too little information. To be effective, then, says George Washington University's Greenspan, treatment must target the underlying condition, protecting some children from disorienting noises and lights, providing others with attention-grabbing stimulation. But when parents and therapists collaborate in an intensive effort to reach these abnormal brains, writes Greenspan in a new book, *The Growth of the Mind* (Addison-Wesley, 1997), three-year-olds who begin the descent into the autistic's limited universe can sometimes be snatched back.

Indeed, parents are the brain's first and most important teachers. Among other things, they appear to help babies learn by adopting the rhythmic, high-pitched speaking style known as Parentese. When speaking to babies, Stanford University psychologist Anne Fernald has found, mothers and fathers from many cultures change their speech patterns in the same peculiar ways. "They put their faces very close to the child," she reports. "They use shorter utterances, and they speak in an unusually melodious fashion." The heart rate of infants increases while listening to Parentese, even Parentese delivered in a foreign language. Moreover, Fernald says, Parentese appears to hasten the process of connecting words to the objects they denote. Twelve-month-olds, directed to "look at the ball" in Parentese, direct their eyes to the correct picture more frequently than when the instruction is delivered in normal English.

In some ways the exaggerated, vowel-rich sounds of Parentese appear to resemble the choice morsels fed to hatchlings by adult birds. The University of Washington's Patricia Kuhl and her colleagues have conditioned dozens of newborns to turn their heads when they detect the *ee* sound emitted by American parents, vs. the *eu* favored by doting Swedes. Very young babies, says Kuhl, invariably perceive slight variations in pronunciation as totally different sounds. But by the age of six months, American babies no longer react when they hear variants of *ee,* and Swedish babies have become impervious to differences in *eu.* "It's as though their brains have formed little magnets," says Kuhl, "and all the sounds in the vicinity are swept in."

TUNED TO DANGER

EVEN MORE FUNDAMENTAL, SAYS DR. BRUCE Perry of Baylor College of Medicine in Houston, is the role parents play in setting

Wiring Language

WHAT'S GOING ON Even before birth, an infant is tuning into the melody of its mother's voice. Over the next six years, its brain will set up the circuitry needed to decipher—and reproduce—the lyrics. A six-month-old can recognize the vowel sounds that are the basic building blocks of speech.
WHAT PARENTS CAN DO Talking to a baby a lot, researchers have found, significantly speeds up the process of learning new words. The high-pitched, singsong speech style known as Parentese helps babies connect objects with words.
WINDOW OF LEARNING Language skills are sharpest early on but grow throughout life.

AGE (in years)	Birth	1	2	3	4	5	6	7	8	9	10
Recognition of speech											
Vocabulary											

up the neural circuitry that helps children regulate their responses to stress. Children who are physically abused early in life, he observes, develop brains that are exquisitely tuned to danger. At the slightest threat, their hearts race, their stress hormones surge and their brains anxiously track the nonverbal cues that might signal the next attack. Because the brain develops in sequence, with more primitive structures stabilizing their connections first, early abuse is particularly damaging. Says Perry: "Experience is the chief architect of the brain." And because these early experiences of stress form a kind of template around which later brain development is organized, the changes they create are all the more pervasive.

Emotional deprivation early in life has a similar effect. For six years University of Washington psychologist Geraldine Dawson and her colleagues have monitored the brain-wave patterns of children born to mothers who were diagnosed as suffering from depression. As infants, these children showed markedly reduced activity in the left frontal lobe, an area of the brain that serves as a center for joy and other lighthearted emotions. Even more telling, the patterns of brain activity displayed by these children closely tracked the ups and downs of their mother's depression. At the age of three, children whose mothers were more severely depressed or whose depression lasted longer continued to show abnormally low readings.

Strikingly, not all the children born to depressed mothers develop these aberrant brain-wave patterns, Dawson has found. What accounts for the difference appears to be the emotional tone of the exchanges be-

tween mother and child. By scrutinizing hours of videotape that show depressed mothers interacting with their babies, Dawson has attempted to identify the links between maternal behavior and children's brains. She found that mothers who were disengaged, irritable or impatient had babies with sad brains. But depressed mothers who managed to rise above their melancholy, lavishing their babies with attention and indulging in playful games, had children with brain activity of a considerably more cheerful cast.

When is it too late to repair the damage wrought by physical and emotional abuse or neglect? For a time, at least, a child's brain is extremely forgiving. If a mother snaps out of her depression before her child is a year old, Dawson has found, brain activity in the left frontal lobe quickly picks up. However, the ability to rebound declines markedly as a child grows older. Many scientists believe that in the first few years of childhood there are a number of critical or sensitive periods, or "windows," when the brain demands certain types of input in order to create or stabilize certain long-lasting structures.

For example, children who are born with a cataract will become permanently blind in that eye if the clouded lens is not promptly removed. Why? The brain's visual centers require sensory stimulus—in this case the stimulus provided by light hitting the retina of the eye—to maintain their still tentative connections. More controversially, many linguists believe that language skills unfold according to a strict, biologically defined timetable. Children, in their view, resemble certain species of birds that cannot master their song unless they hear it sung at an early age. In zebra finches the window for acquiring the appropriate song opens 25 to 30 days after hatching and shuts some 50 days later.

WINDOWS OF OPPORTUNITY

WITH A FEW EXCEPTIONS, THE WINDOWS OF opportunity in the human brain do not close quite so abruptly. There appears to be a series of windows for developing language. The window for acquiring syntax may close as early as five or six years of age, while the window for adding new words may never close. The ability to learn a second language is highest between birth and the age of six, then undergoes a steady and inexorable decline. Many adults still manage to learn new languages, but usually only after great struggle.

The brain's greatest growth spurt, neuroscientists have now confirmed, draws to a close around the age of 10, when the balance between synapse creation and atrophy abruptly shifts. Over the next several years, the brain will ruthlessly destroy its weakest synapses, preserving only those that have been magically transformed by experience. This magic, once again, seems to be encoded in the genes. The ephemeral bursts of electricity that travel through the brain, creating everything from visual images and pleasurable sensations to dark dreams and wild thoughts, ensure the survival of synapses by stimulating genes that promote the release of powerful growth factors and suppressing genes that encode for synapse-destroying enzymes.

By the end of adolescence, around the age of 18, the brain has declined in plasticity but increased in power. Talents and latent tendencies that have been nurtured are ready to blossom. The experiences that drive neural activity, says Yale's Rakic, are like a sculptor's chisel or a dressmaker's shears, conjuring up form from a lump of stone or a length of cloth. The presence of extra material expands the range of possibilities, but cutting away the extraneous is what makes art. "It is the overproduction of synaptic connections followed by their loss that leads to patterns in the brain," says neuroscientist William Greenough of the University of Illinois at Urbana-Champaign. Potential for greatness may be encoded in the genes, but whether that potential is realized as a gift for mathematics, say, or a brilliant criminal mind depends on patterns etched by experience in those critical early years.

Wiring Movement

WHAT'S GOING ON At birth babies can move their limbs, but in a jerky, uncontrolled fashion. Over the next four years, the brain progressively refines the circuits for reaching, grabbing, sitting, crawling, walking and running.

WHAT PARENTS CAN DO Give babies as much freedom to explore as safety permits. Just reaching for an object helps the brain develop hand-eye coordination. As soon as children are ready for them, activities like drawing and playing a violin or piano encourage the development of fine motor skills.

WINDOW OF LEARNING Motor-skill development moves from gross to increasingly fine.

Psychiatrists and educators have long recognized the value of early experience. But their observations have until now been largely anecdotal. What's so exciting, says

Matthew Melmed, executive director of Zero to Three, a nonprofit organization devoted to highlighting the importance of the first three years of life, is that modern neuroscience is providing the hard, quantifiable evidence that was missing earlier. "Because you can see the results under a microscope or in a PET scan," he observes, "it's become that much more convincing."

What lessons can be drawn from the new findings? Among other things, it is clear that foreign languages should be taught in elementary school, if not before. That remedial education may be more effective at the age of three or four than at nine or 10. That good, affordable day care is not a luxury or a fringe benefit for welfare mothers and working parents but essential brain food for the next generation. For while new synapses continue to form throughout life, and even adults continually refurbish their minds through reading and learning, never again will the brain be able to master new skills so readily or rebound from setbacks so easily.

Rat-a-tat-tat. Rat-a-tat-tat. Rat-a-tat-tat. Just last week, in the U.S. alone, some 77,000 newborns began the miraculous process of wiring their brains for a lifetime of learning. If parents and policymakers don't pay attention to the conditions under which this delicate process takes place, we will all suffer the consequences—starting around the year 2010.

What Do We Know from Brain Research?

The recent explosion of neuroscientific research has the exciting potential to increase our understanding of teaching and learning. But it's up to educators to carefully interpret what brain science means for classroom practice.

Pat Wolfe and Ron Brandt

In July 1989, following a congressional resolution, President Bush officially proclaimed the 1990s the "Decade of the Brain." And indeed in the past nine years, we have seen an unprecedented explosion of information on how the human brain works. Thousands of research projects, books, magazine cover stories, and television specials regale us with new facts and figures, colorful PET scans, and at times, suspiciously simple ways to improve our memories, prevent Alzheimer's, and make our babies geniuses.

Our knowledge of brain functioning has been revolutionized. And many of the new findings have changed medical practice. We have a much better understanding of mental illnesses and the drugs that ameliorate them. Treatment for tumors, seizures, and other brain diseases and disorders has become much more successful.

But what about the educational applications of these new findings? Have we learned enough to incorporate neuroscientific findings into our schools? Is it possible that the Decade of the Brain will usher in the Decade of Education?

Interpreting Brain Research for Classroom Practice

Brain science is a burgeoning new field, and we have learned more about the brain in the past 5 years than in the past 100 years. Nearly 90 percent of all the neuroscientists who have ever lived are alive today. Nearly every major university now has interdisciplinary brain research teams.

But almost all scientists are wary of offering prescriptions for using their research in schools. Joseph LeDoux from New York University and author of *The Emotional Brain* (1996) says, "There are no quick fixes. These ideas are very easy to sell to the public, but it's too easy to take them beyond their actual basis in science." Susan Fitzpatrick, a neuroscientist at the McDonnell Foundation, says scientists don't have a lot to tell educators at this point. She warns,

> Anything that people would say right now has a good chance of not being true two years from now because the understanding is so rudimentary and people are looking at things at such a simplistic level. (1995, p. 24)

Researchers especially caution educators to resist the temptation to adopt policies on the basis of a single study or to use neuroscience as a promotional tool for a pet program. Much work needs to be done before the results of scientific studies can be taken into the classroom. The reluctance of scientists to sanction a quick marriage between neuroscience and education makes sense. Brain research does not—and may never—tell us specifically what we should do in a classroom. At this point it does not "prove" that a particular strategy will increase student understanding. That is not currently the purpose of neuroscience research. Its purpose is to learn how the brain functions. Neuroscience is a field of study separate from the field of education, and it is unrealistic to expect brain research to lead directly to pedagogy. So how do we use the current findings?

We need to critically read and analyze the research in order to separate the wheat from the chaff. If educators do not develop a functional understanding of the brain and its processes, we will be vulnerable to pseudoscientific fads, inappropriate generalizations, and dubious programs.

Then, with our knowledge of educational practice, we must determine if and how brain research informs

A child's brain at birth has all the brain cells, or neurons, that it will ever have.

From *Educational Leadership,* November 1998, pp. 8-13. Reprinted with permission of the Association for Supervision and Curriculum Development. © 1998 by ASCD. All rights reserved.

that practice. Educators have a vast background of knowledge about teaching and learning. This knowledge has been gained from educational research, cognitive science, and long experience. Given this knowledge base, educators are in the best position to know how the research does—or does not—supplement, explain, or validate current practices.

Although we must be cautious about many neuroscientific findings, a few are quite well established. Some validate what good educators have always done. Others are causing us to take a closer look at educational practice.

Finding One

The brain changes physiologically as a result of experience. The environment in which a brain operates determines to a large degree the functioning ability of that brain.

Researchers agree that at birth, humans do not yet possess a fully operational brain. The brain that eventually takes shape is the result of interaction between the individual's genetic inheritance and everything he or she experi-

for some time that with a few specialized exceptions, a child's brain at birth has all the brain cells, or neurons, that it will ever have. Unlike tissue in most other organs, neurons do not regenerate, so researchers assumed that the brain you had at birth was the brain you were stuck with for life.

However, Marian Diamond and her colleagues at the University of California at Berkeley pioneered research in the mid-1960s showing that brain structures are modified by the environment (Diamond & Hopson, 1998). Her research established the concept of neural plasticity—the brain's amazing ability to constantly change its structure and function in response to external experiences. A further finding that should please us all is that dendrites, the connections between brain cells, can grow at any age. Researchers have found this to be true in humans as well as in animals. Contrary to folk wisdom, a healthy older person is not necessarily the victim of progressive nerve cell loss and diminishing memory and cognitive abilities.

next, and then work on their emotional development. An enriched environment addresses multiple aspects of development simultaneously.

3. The brain is essentially curious, and it must be to survive. It constantly seeks connections between the new and the known. Learning is a process of active construction by the learner, and an enriched environment gives students the opportunity to relate what they are learning to what they already know. As noted educator Phil Schlechty says, "Students must do the work of learning."

4. The brain is innately social and collaborative. Although the processing takes place in our students' individual brains, their learning is enhanced when the environment provides them with the opportunity to discuss their thinking out loud, to bounce their ideas off their peers, and to produce collaborative work.

Finding Two

IQ is not fixed at birth.

This second finding is closely linked to the first. Craig Ramey, a University of Alabama psychologist, took on the daunting task of showing that what Diamond did with rats, he could do with children. His striking research (Ramey & Ramey, 1996) proved that an intervention program for impoverished children could prevent children from having low IQs and mental retardation.

Ramey has directed studies of early educational intervention involving thousands of children at dozens of research centers. The best programs, which started with children as young as six weeks and mostly younger than four months, showed that they could raise the infants' scores on intelligence tests by 15 to 30 percent. It is important to note that although IQ tests may be useful artifacts, intelligence is probably much more multifaceted. Every brain differs, and the subtle range of organizational, physiological, and chemical variations ensures a remarkably wide spectrum of cognitive, behavioral, and emotional capabilities.

> ## Babies don't talk one week, tie their shoes the next, and then work on their emotional development.

ences. Ronald Kotulak, in his book *Inside the Brain* (1996), uses the metaphor of a banquet to explain the relationship between genes and the environment.

The brain gobbles up the external environment through its sensory system and then reassembles the digested world in the form of trillions of connections which are constantly growing or dying, becoming stronger or weaker depending on the richness of the banquet. (p. 4)

The environment affects how genes work, and genes determine how the environment is interpreted. This is a relatively new understanding. It wasn't too many years ago that scientists thought the brain was immutable or fixed at birth. Scientists had known

So our environment, including the classroom environment, is not a neutral place. We educators are either growing dendrites or letting them wither and die. The trick is to determine what constitutes an enriched environment. A few facts about the brain's natural proclivities will assist us in making these determinations.

1. The brain has not evolved to its present condition by taking in meaningless data; an enriched environment gives students the opportunity to make sense out of what they are learning, what some call the opportunity to "make meaning."

2. The brain develops in an integrated fashion over time. Babies don't talk one week, tie their shoes the

Finding Three

Some abilities are acquired more easily during certain sensitive periods, or "windows of opportunity."

At birth, a child's cerebral cortex has all the neurons that it will ever have. In fact, in utero, the brain produces an overabundance of neurons, nearly twice as many as it will need. Beginning at about 28 weeks of prenatal development, a massive pruning of neurons begins, resulting in the loss of one-third to one-half of these elements. (So we lose up to half our brain cells before we're born.) While the brain is pruning away excess neurons, a tremendous increase in dendrites adds substantially to the surface area available for synapses, the functional connections among cells. At the fastest rate, connections are built at the incredible speed of 3 billion a second. During the period from birth to age 10, the number of synaptic connections continues to rise rapidly, then begins to drop and continues to decline slowly into adult life.

Much credit for these insights into the developing brain must be given to Harry Chugani and Michael Phelps at the UCLA School of Medicine. Phelps co-invented the imaging technique called Positron Emission Tomography (PET), which visually depicts the brain's energy use. Using PET scans, Chugani has averaged the energy use of brains at various ages. His findings suggest that a child's peak learning years occur just as all those synapses are forming (1996). Chugani states that not only does the child's brain overdevelop during the early years, but that during these years, it also has a remarkable ability to adapt and reorganize. It appears to develop some capacities with more ease at this time than in the years after puberty. These stages once called "critical periods" are more accurately described as "sensitive periods" or "windows of opportunity."

Probably the prime example of a window is vision. Lack of visual stimulation at birth, such as that which occurs with blindness or cataracts, causes the brain cells designed

Brain Fact
Enriching the Environment

Marian Diamond and her team of researchers at the University of California at Berkeley have been studying the impact of enriched and impoverished environments on the brains of rats. Diamond believes that enriched environments unmistakably influence the brain's growth and learning. An enriched environment for children, Diamond says,

■ Includes a steady source of positive emotional support;

■ Provides a nutritious diet with enough protein, vitamins, minerals, and calories;

■ Stimulates all the senses (but not necessarily all at once!);

■ Has an atmosphere free of undue pressure and stress but suffused with a degree of pleasurable intensity;

■ Presents a series of novel challenges that are neither too easy nor too difficult for the child at his or her stage of development;

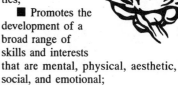

■ Allows social interaction for a significant percentage of activities;

■ Promotes the development of a broad range of skills and interests that are mental, physical, aesthetic, social, and emotional;

■ Gives the child an opportunity to choose many of his or her efforts and to modify them;

■ Provides an enjoyable atmosphere that promotes exploration and the fun of learning;

■ Allows the child to be an active participant rather than a passive observer.

Diamond, M., & Hopson, J. (1998). *Magic trees of the mind: How to nurture your child's intelligence, creativity, and healthy emotions from birth through adolescence* (pp. 107–108). New York: Dutton.

to interpret vision to atrophy or be diverted to other tasks. If sight is not restored by age 3, the child will be forever blind. . . . Similarly, the critical period for learning spoken language is totally lost by about age 10. If a child is born deaf, the 50,000 neural pathways that would normally activate the auditory cells remain silent, and the sound of the human voice, essential for learning language, can't get through. Finally, as the child grows older, the cells atrophy and the ability to learn spoken language is lost.

Not all windows close as tightly as those for vision and language development. Although learning a second language also depends on the stimulation of the neurons for the sounds of that language, an adult certainly can learn a second language and learn to speak it quite well. However, it is much more difficult to learn a foreign language after age 10 or so, and the language will probably be spoken with an accent. We might say that learning a

second language is not a window that slams shut—it just becomes harder to open.

The implications of the findings regarding early visual, auditory, motor, cognitive, and emotional development are enormous. Indeed, in many places work has already begun to enrich prenatal and early childhood environments. One example is the application of the research with premature infants. Premature babies who are regularly touched in their incubators gain weight at twice the rate of those who are not touched. Preemies whose parents visit them regularly vocalize twice as much in the third week as babies who are visited infrequently or not at all.

The research findings on early development are in stark contrast with the current situation in society.

■ An estimated 12 percent of infants born in this country suffer significant reduction of their cognitive ability as a result of preterm birth; maternal smoking, alcohol use, or drug use in pregnancy; maternal and infant malnutrition; and postbirth lead poisoning or child abuse (Newman & Buka, 1997). Many of these factors could be eliminated with education programs for parents (or future parents). Twenty-five percent of all pregnant women receive no prenatal care.

■ The early years, which are most crucial for learning, receive the least

> **The brain is essentially curious, and it must be to survive.**

emphasis in federal, state, and local programs. We spend at least seven times more on the elderly than we do on children from birth to age 5.

■ About half of all children in the United States are in full-time day care within the first year. Yet many day care centers not only are underfunded, but they are also staffed by untrained, low-paid workers and have too high an adult/child ratio. (Thirty-eight states do not require family child care providers to have *any* training prior to serving children.)

■ Our present system generally waits until children fall behind in school, then places them in special education programs. With intense early intervention, we could reverse or prevent some adverse effects. It is possible that the billions of dollars spent on special education services might be better spent on early intervention.

Finding Four
Learning is strongly influenced by emotion.

The role of emotion in learning has received a good deal of press in the past few years. Daniel Goleman's *Emotional Intelligence* (1995) and Joseph LeDoux's *The Emotional Brain* (1996) have been instrumental in increasing our understanding of emotion.

Emotion plays a dual role in human learning. First, it plays a positive role in that the stronger the emotion

connected with an experience, the stronger the memory of that experience. Chemicals in the brain send a message to the rest of the brain: "This information is important. Remember it." Thus, when we are able to add emotional input into learning experiences to make them more meaningful and exciting, the brain deems the information more important and retention is increased.

In contrast, LeDoux has pointed out that if the emotion is too strong (for example, the situation is perceived by the learner to be threatening), then learning is decreased. Whether you call this "downshifting" or decreasing the efficiency of the rational thinking cortex of the brain, it is a concept with many implications for teaching and learning.

Expect More Findings
On the horizon are many more studies that may have implications for the education of the human brain from birth through old age. Current research areas include these:

■ The role of nutrition in brain functioning

■ How brain chemicals affect mood, personality, and behavior

■ The connection between the mind/brain and the body

Rather than passively wait for research findings that might be useful, educators should help direct the search to better understand how the brain learns. James McGaugh of the University of California at Irvine has suggested that we educators need to be more proactive and tell the scientists, "Here's what we need to know. How can you help us?"

Should the Decade of the Brain lead to an enlightened Decade of Education? Eventually, yes. Along with cognitive research and the knowledge base we already have, findings from the neurosciences can provide us with important insights into how children learn. They can direct us as we seek to enrich the school experience for all children—the gifted, the creative, the

learning disabled, the dyslexic, the average students, and all the children whose capabilities are not captured by IQ or other conventional measures. We can help parents and other caregivers understand the effects of maternal nutrition and prenatal drug and alcohol use and the role of early interaction and enriched environments. Brain research can also offer valuable guidance to policymakers and school administrators as they strive to focus their priorities.

Does what we are learning about the brain matter? It must, because our children matter.

References
Chugani, H. T. (1996). *Functional maturation of the brain.* Paper presented at the Third Annual Brain Symposium, Berkeley, California.

Diamond, M., & Hopson, J. (1998). *Magic trees of the mind: How to nurture your child's intelligence, creativity, and healthy emotions from birth through adolescence.* New York: Penguin Putnam.

Fitzpatrick, S. (1995, November). Smart brains: Neuroscientists explain the mystery of what makes us human. *American School Board Journal.*

Goleman, D. (1995). *Emotional intelligence: Why it can matter more than IQ.* New York: Bantam.

Kotulak, R. (1996). *Inside the brain: Revolutionary discoveries of how the mind works.* Kansas City, MO: Andrews & McMeely.

LeDoux, J. (1996). *The emotional brain: The mysterious underpinnings of emotional life.* New York: Simon & Schuster.

Newman, L., & Buka, S. L. (1997). *Every child a learner: Reducing risks of learning impairment during pregnancy and infancy.* Denver, CO: Education Commission of the States.

Ramey, C. T., & Ramey, S. L. (1996). *At risk does not mean doomed.* National Health/Education Consortium Occasional Paper #4. Paper presented at the meeting of the American Association of Science, February 1996.

Pat Wolfe is an independent educational consultant. She can be reached at 555 Randolph St., Napa, CA 94559 (e-mail: wolfe@napanet.net).

Ron Brandt is Editor Emeritus of *Educational Leadership* and an independent educational consultant. He may be reached at 1104 Woodcliff Dr., Alexandria, VA 22308-1058 (e-mail:ronbrandt@erols.com).

Evolution and Developmental Sex Differences

David C. Geary[1]
Department of Psychology, University of Missouri at Columbia, Columbia, Missouri

Abstract

From an evolutionary perspective, childhood is the portion of the life span during which individuals practice and refine those competencies that facilitate survival and reproduction in adulthood. Although the skeletal structure of these competencies appears to be inherent, social interaction and play flesh them out during childhood so that they are adapted to local conditions. Darwin's principles of sexual selection, including male-male competition over mates and female choice of mating partners, successfully explain the acquisition and expression of reproduction competencies in hundreds of species. When this perspective is applied to humans, it predicts sex differences that are, in fact, found in the childhood activities of boys and girls and that reflect sex differences in reproductive strategies in adulthood. A few of these differences are described, along with cultural factors that modify their expression. The article closes with a brief discussion of the social and scientific implications.

Keywords

sex differences; sexual selection; development; childhood; culture

Sex differences are inherently interesting to the scientist and layperson alike. They always have been and always will be. Although the existence of such differences has been debated in the past, the scientific issue today concerns the source of these differences. The prevailing view in psychology is that most sex differences result from children's adoption of gender roles, roles that reflect society-wide differences in daily activities of men and women (Eagly, 1987). The goal here is not to provide a review or appraisal of this position, but rather to offer an alternative view of developmental sex differences, a view based on the principles of evolution (Darwin, 1871).

From an evolutionary perspective, cultural and ecological factors are expected to influence the expression of developmental sex differences, and a few of these influences are described in the final section. Before they are discussed, though, a basic evolutionary framework for understanding sex differences in general and developmental sex differences in particular is provided in the first section, and the second provides a few examples of the usefulness of this approach for understanding human developmental sex differences.

EVOLUTION AND DEVELOPMENT

Sexual Selection

One of Darwin's (1871) seminal contributions was the observation that evolutionary pressures often differ for males and females and that many of these differences center around the dynamics of reproduction. These pressures are termed sexual selection and typically result from males competing with one another for social status, resources, or territory—whatever is needed to attract mates—and from females' choice of mating partners (Andersson, 1994). Although the dynamics of male-male competition can vary across species and social and ecological conditions, one common result is the evolution of physical (see Fig. 1), cognitive, and behavioral sex differences. Females' choice of mates has been studied most extensively in birds, although it is also evident in insects, fish, reptiles, and mammals, including humans (Andersson, 1994; Buss, 1994). Females typically choose mates on the basis of indicators of physical, genetic, or behavioral fitness, that is, on the basis of traits that signal a benefit to them (e.g., provisioning) or their offspring (e.g., good genes). One example of the evolutionary result of female choice is shown in Figure 2; the long and symmetric tail feathers of the male hummingbird are an indicator of his physical and genetic health.

Male-male competition and female choice are most evident in species in which males devote most of their reproductive energies to attracting mates, and females provide most or all of the parental care (Trivers, 1972), a pattern found in nearly 97% of mammalian species (Clutton-Brock, 1991). As is the case with other mammals, women throughout the world invest more time and resources in the well-being of their children than men do (Geary, 1998). Nonetheless, many men do provide some investment in the well-being of their children, unlike most other mammalian males. Paternal care, in turn, results in female-female competition and

From *Current Directions in Psychological Science,* August 1999, pp. 115-120. © 1999 by the American Psychological Society.
Reprinted by permission of Cambridge University Press.

male choice of mates, along with male-male competition and female choice of mates.

The sex difference in the level of parental investment, along with other features (see Geary, 1998), results in differences in the nature of male-male versus female-female competition, and in the criteria used in mate choice (Geary, 1998). Throughout the world, men compete with one another for the control of culturally prized resources (e.g., status, money, or cows), and they often do so through physical contests (Keeley, 1996). Women compete with one another by means of relational aggression. They gossip, shun, and backbite their competitors (Crick, Casas, & Mosher, 1997). Both men and women want intelligent and cooperative spouses, but women more than men focus on the cultural success (e.g., control of money or cows) of suitors and men more than women focus on physical attractiveness (indicators of fertility; Buss, 1994).

Development

Biologists study development by documenting species' life history and by discerning the function of childhood. Life history refers to the typical ages associated with developmental milestones, such as age of weaning and length of childhood. The function of childhood is to refine the competencies that will be needed to survive and reproduce in adulthood (Mayr, 1974). It appears that many cognitive and behavioral systems are initially skeletal in structure—the basic framework is inborn—but are fleshed out as juveniles play, explore the environment, and interact socially (Gelman, 1990). Fleshing out these competencies results in the refinement of those skills needed to survive and reproduce in the local ecology and social group.

Developmental sex differences are expected to the degree that reproductive demands differ for male and females in adulthood. In species in which male-male competition is more intense than female-female competition, the juvenile period is longer for males than for females. Male satin bowerbirds *(Ptilonorhynchus violaceus),* for instance, mature many years after females have matured. Although there is some physical competition, males largely compete behaviorally, through the construction of complex stick structures called bowers. (Females make their mate choices, in part, on the basis of the complexity of these bowers.) During development, "young males spend a great deal of time observing older males at their bower, and practice bower building and display behaviors when the owner is absent from the bower site" (Collis & Borgia,

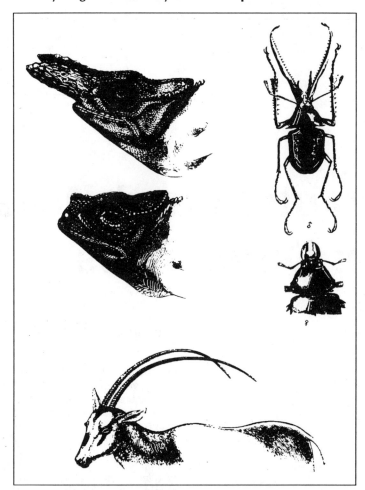

Fig. 1. Examples of sexually selected characteristics used in physical male-male competition. The pair in the upper left are the male (top) and female (bottom) of the *Chamaeleon bifurcus*; the pair in the upper right are the male and female of the beetle *Chiasognathus grantii*; at the bottom is a male *Oryx leucoryx*, a species of antelope (females do not have horns). From Darwin (1871, Vol. II, p. 35; Vol. I, p. 377; and Vol. II, p. 251, respectively). These exaggerated male characteristics are used in male-on-male aggression. For instance, two male *Oryx leucoryx* will compete by kneeling in front of each other, each then trying to maneuver the points of his horns under the body of his competitor. "If one succeeds in doing this, he suddenly springs up, throwing up his head at the same time, and can thus wound or perhaps even transfix his antagonist" (Darwin, 1871, Vol. II, pp. 251–252).

1992, p. 422). Young males also engage in play fighting, which provides the experience needed for dominance-related encounters in adulthood. Thus, delayed maturation and associated play allow for the refinement of those physical, cognitive, and behavioral skills associated with reproductive demands in adulthood.

HUMAN DEVELOPMENTAL SEX DIFFERENCES

Play Patterns

Play, in one form or another, is found in most mammalian species. "The con-

sensus that emerges from the scores of definitions is that play incorporates many physical components of adult behavior patterns, such as those used in aggression, but without their immediate functional consequences" (Walters, 1987, p. 360). Play provides delayed benefits because the individual practices those behaviors that are important for survival and reproduction in adulthood, as described earlier. Sex differences in play patterns are found in many species and mirror sex differences found in adulthood.

Like juveniles of other mammalian species, boys and girls exhibit sex differences in their play patterns, and these differences in play are a reflection of sex differences found in adulthood (Geary,

1998). One of the most consistently found differences is in the frequency and nature of rough-and-tumble play. Beginning at about 3 years of age, groups of boys engage in various forms of play fighting, such as wrestling, three to six times more frequently than groups of girls do. Boys also engage in group-level competitive play (e.g., football) more frequently than girls do. These patterns are found in every culture in which play has been studied, are related to prenatal exposure to male hormones, and mirror the activities associated with primitive warfare (Keeley, 1996). The one-on-one and group-level play fighting of boys can be viewed as an evolved tendency to practice the competencies that were associated with male-male competition during human evolution (Geary, 1998).

Another sex difference, this one favoring girls, is in the frequency of play parenting (e.g., doll play): Play parenting is the norm in female primates and has been shown to significantly reduce the mortality rates of their first-born offspring. Again, this sex difference is found in all cultures in which play has been studied, is related to prenatal exposure to sex hormones, and mirrors the adult sex difference in investment in children. Play parenting can thus be understood as an evolved tendency to seek out activities that will enhance later parenting skills.

Social Development

Beginning in the preschool years and extending throughout the life span, girls and boys and women and men tend to segregate themselves into same-sex groups. One result is that boys and girls grow up in different social cultures. The tendency of boys to play fight and to organize themselves into competing groups is manifested in the context of the boys' culture. Social relationships among girls, in contrast, are more consistently communal: They manifest greater empathy; more concern for the well-being of other girls; and more nurturing, intimacy, and social and emotional support. In short, the social behavior of boys is focused on achieving status and dominance and developing coalitions for competing against groups of other boys. The social behavior of girls is focused on developing and maintaining a network of personal relationships and social support. Similar sex differences have been found in our closest relative, the chimpanzee, suggesting that these are indeed evolved tendencies in humans (de Waal, 1993).

Nonetheless, girls and women can be quite competitive with one another. As noted earlier, this competition takes the

Fig. 2. Female (left) and male (right) hummingbirds (*Spathura underwoodi*). From Darwin (1871, Vol. II, p. 77). The long and symmetric tail feathers of the male appear to signal to the female that he has immune-system genes that can confer resistance to local parasites (e.g., worms). If she mates with this male, then her offspring will also be resistant to local parasites.

form of relational aggression—attempting to disrupt the personal networks that are important to girls and women—and in adulthood, it is often associated with competition over resources (e.g., job promotion) and mates. As is the case with play fighting in boys, relational aggression emerges in the preschool years for girls and appears to be especially intense during early adolescence. It is likely, although not certain, that relational aggression has been shaped by sexual selection and in childhood is practice for later female-female competition.

CULTURAL AND ECOLOGICAL INFLUENCES

If the function of childhood is to adapt inherent skeletal competencies to local conditions, then cultural and ecological factors should influence the expression of developmental sex differences (Gelman, 1990; Mayr, 1974). Although research conducted within Western countries suggests that parents do not influence children's development as strongly as many people assume, cross-cultural studies suggest that there are important socialization influences on the expression (not creation) of developmental sex differences.

Although boys throughout the world engage in one-on-one and group-level competitive play, the nature and intensity of this play varies across cultures. The play fighting of boys tends to be rougher in societies where male-on-male physical aggression is common in adulthood than in other societies. For instance, intergroup aggression occurs frequently among the Yanomamö Indians of South America, and young Yanomamö boys often play fight with clubs or bows and arrows, practices that are typically discouraged in suburban America. In such societies, boys' play fighting often involves inflicting physical pain and sometimes injury, and there are often social rules that discourage boys from expressing this pain. In other words, boys' play fighting is encouraged and channeled to increase the aggressiveness and physical endurance of boys, and decrease their sensitivity to the distress of other people. These practices prepare boys for the life-and-death male-male competition that they will experience as adults. In other societies, such as our own, boys also play fight, but this behavior is relatively subdued and symbolic, as in competitive sports.

In a study of 93 cultures, Low (1989) found that the socialization of girls and boys was systematically related to the cultures' social structures (e.g., stratified vs. nonstratified societies) and marriage systems (i.e., polygynous vs. monogamous). In nonstratified polygynous societies—where men could improve their social status and thus increase the number of women they could marry—the socialization of boys focused on fortitude, aggression, and industriousness, traits that would influence their cultural and reproductive success in adulthood. For these societies, there was a strong linear relation between the socialization of competitiveness in boys and the maximum harem size allowed within the society. The larger the maximum harem size, the more the competitiveness of boys was emphasized in parental socialization.

For girls, there was a relation between the amount of economic and political power held by women in the society and socialization practices. In societies where women could inherit property and hold political office, girls were socialized to be less obedient, more aggressive, and more achievement oriented than were girls who lived in societies in which men had control over economic and political resources. On the basis of these and other patterns, Low (1989) concluded that "there is thus some evidence that patterns of child training across cultures vary in ways predictable from evolutionary theory, differing in specifiable ways between the

sexes, and varying with group size, marriage system, and stratification" (p. 318).

CONCLUSION

From an evolutionary perspective, early biases in the ways in which boys and girls orient themselves to other people, in their play patterns, and in how they interact with and explore the wider ecology are expected, and, in fact, such biases are found (Geary, 1998). They lead girls and boys to create different cultures for themselves, and within these cultures to engage in activities that prepare them for the adult life of our ancestors. At the same time, a long childhood and the associated sensitivity to environmental influences ensure that the differences between boys and girls and men and women are not fixed, but rather are responsive to changing social and ecological conditions.

The combination of biological biases and sensitivity to early environmental conditions has important scientific and social implications. For instance, although boys and men are biologically destined to compete, this competition need not be deadly nor even physical, even if the evolutionary history of male-male competition was both physical and deadly (Keeley, 1996). One goal of psychological research, then, is to understand the social and ecological conditions that can push boys and men into deadly physical competition or to compete in ways that are socially beneficial (e.g., that lead to economic development). An evolutionary perspective on development highlights the importance of social and ecological factors in the expression of developmental sex differences and will provide an important theoretical framework for the study of the

social and psychological aspects of these differences.

Note

1. Address correspondence to David C. Geary, Department of Psychology, 210 McAlester Hall, University of Missouri, Columbia, MO 65211-2500; e-mail: gearyd @missouri.edu.

References

Andersson, M. (1994). *Sexual selection.* Princeton, NJ: Princeton University Press.

Buss, D.M. (1994). *The evolution of desire: Strategies of human mating.* New York: Basic Books.

Clutton-Brock, T.H. (1991). *The evolution of parental care.* Princeton, NJ: Princeton University Press.

Collis, K., & Borgia, G. (1992). Age-related effects of testosterone, plumage, and experience on aggression and social dominance in juvenile male satin bowerbirds *(Ptilonorhynchus violaceus). Auk, 109,* 422–434.

Crick, N.R., Casas, J.F., & Mosher, M. (1997). Relational and overt aggression in preschool. *Developmental Psychology, 33,* 579–588.

Darwin, C. (1871). *The descent of man and selection in relation to sex* (2 vols.). London: J. Murray.

de Waal, F.B.M. (1993). Sex differences in chimpanzee (and human) behavior: A matter of social values? In M. Hechter, L. Nadel, & R.E. Michod (Eds.), *The origin of values* (pp. 285–303). New York: Aldine de Gruyter.

Eagly, A.H. (1987). *Sex differences in social behavior: A social-role interpretation.* Hillsdale, NJ: Erlbaum.

Geary, D.C. (1998). *Male, female: The evolution of human sex differences.* Washington, DC: American Psychological Association.

Gelman, R. (1990). First principles organize attention to and learning about relevant data: Number and animate-inanimate distinction as examples. *Cognitive Science, 14,* 79–106.

Keeley, L.H. (1996). *War before civilization: The myth of the peaceful savage.* New York: Oxford University Press.

Low, B.S. (1989). Cross-cultural patterns in the training of children: An evolutionary perspective. *Journal of Comparative Psychology, 103,* 311–319.

Mayr, E. (1974). Behavior programs and evolutionary strategies. *American Scientist, 62,* 650–659.

Trivers, R.L. (1972). Parental investment and sexual selection. In B. Campbell (Ed.), *Sexual selection and the descent of man 1871–1971* (pp. 136–179). Chicago: Aldine Publishing.

Walters, J.R. (1987). Transition to adulthood. In B.B. Smuts, D.L. Cheney, R.M. Seyfarth, R.W. Wrangham, & T.T. Struhsaker (Eds.), *Primate societies* (pp. 358–369). Chicago: University of Chicago Press.

Recommended Reading

Buss, D.M. (1994). (See References)

Darwin, C. (1871). (See References)

Geary, D.C. (1998). (See References)

Morbeck, M.E., Galloway, A., & Zihlman, A.L. (Eds.). (1997). *The evolving female: A life-history perspective.* Princeton, NJ: Princeton University Press.

Learning language, researchers are finding, is an astonishing act of brain computation—and it's performed by people too young to tie their shoes

BY SHANNON BROWNLEE

Inside a small, dark booth, 18-month-old Karly Horn sits on her mother Terry's lap. Karly's brown curls bounce each time she turns her head to listen to a woman's recorded voice coming from one side of the booth or the other. "At the bakery, workers will be baking bread," says the voice. Karly turns to her left and listens, her face intent. "On Tuesday morning, the people have going to work," says the voice. Karly turns her head away even before the statement is finished. The lights come on as graduate student Ruth Tincoff opens the door to the booth. She gives the child's curls a pat and says, "Nice work."

Karly and her mother are taking part in an experiment at Johns Hopkins University in Baltimore, run by psycholinguist Peter Jusczyk, who has

spent 25 years probing the linguistic skills of children who have not yet begun to talk. Like most toddlers her age, Karly can utter a few dozen words at most and can string together the occasional two-word sentence, like "More juice" and "Up, Mommy." Yet as Jusczyk and his colleagues have found, she can already recognize that a sentence like "the people have going to work" is ungrammatical. By 18 months of age, most toddlers have somehow learned the rule requiring that any verb ending in *-ing* must be preceded by the verb *to be.* "If you had asked me 10 years ago if kids this young could do this," says Jusczyk, "I would have said that's crazy.

Linguists these days are reconsidering a lot of ideas they once considered crazy. Recent findings like

Jusczyk's are reshaping the prevailing model of how children acquire language. The dominant theory, put forth by Noam Chomsky, has been that children cannot possibly learn the full rules and structure of languages strictly by imitating what they hear. Instead, nature gives children a head start, wiring them from birth with the ability to acquire their parents native tongue by fitting what they hear into a preexisting template for the basic structure shared by all languages. (Similarly, kittens are thought to be hard-wired to learn how to hunt.) Language, writes Massachusetts Institute of Technology linguist Steven Pinker, "is a distinct piece of the biological makeup of our brains." Chomsky, a prominent linguist at MIT, hypothesized in the 1950s that children are endowed from birth with "universal grammar," the fundamental rules that are common to all languages, and the ability to apply these rules to the raw material of the speech they hear—without awareness of their underlying logic.

The average preschooler can't tell time, but he has already accumulated a vocabulary of thousands of words—plus (as Pinker writes in his book, *The Language Instinct*) "a tacit knowledge of grammar more sophisticated than the thickest style manual." Within a few months of birth, children have already begun memorizing words without knowing their meaning. The question that has absorbed—and sometimes divided—linguists is whether children need a special language faculty to do this or instead can infer the abstract rules of grammar from the sentences they hear, using the same mental skills that allow them to recognize faces or master arithmetic.

The debate over how much of language is already vested in a child at birth is far from settled, but new linguistic research already is transforming traditional views of how the human brain works and how language evolved. "This debate has completely changed the way we view the brain," says Elissa Newport, a psycholinguist at the University of Roch-ester in New York. Far from being an orderly, computer-like machine that methodically calculates step by step, the brain is now seen as work-ing more like a beehive, its swarm of interconnected neurons sending signals back and forth at lightning speed. An infant's brain, it turns out, is capable of taking in enormous amounts of information and finding the regular patterns contained within it. Geneticists and linguists recently have begun to challenge the common-sense assumption that intelligence and language are inextricably linked, through research on a rare genetic disorder called Williams syndrome, which can seriously impair cognition while leaving language nearly intact (box, Rare Disorder Reveals Split between Language and Thought). Increasingly sophisticated technologies such as magnetic resonance imaging are allowing researchers to watch the brain in action, revealing that language literally sculpts and reorganizes the connections within it as a child grows.

The path leading to language begins even before birth, when a developing fetus is bathed in the muffled sound of its mother's voice in the

Little polyglots. An infant's brain can perceive every possible sound in every language. By 10 months, babies have learned to screen out foreign sounds and to focus on the sounds of their native language.

WILLIAMS SYNDROME

Rare disorder reveals split between language and thought

Kristen Aerts is only 9 years old, but she can work a room like a seasoned pol. She marches into the lab of cognitive neuroscientist Ursula Bellugi, at the Salk Institute for Biological Studies in La Jolla, Calif., and greets her with a cheery, "Good morning Dr. Bellugi. How are you today?" The youngster smiles at a visitor and says, "My name is Kristen. What's yours?" She looks people in the eye when she speaks and asks questions—social skills that many adults never seem to master, much less a third grader. Yet for all her poise, Kristen has an IQ of about 79. She cannot write her address; she has trouble tying her shoes, drawing a simple picture of a bicycle, and subtracting 2 from 4; and she may never be able to live independently.

Kristen has Williams syndrome, a rare genetic disorder that affects both body and brain, giving those who have it a strange and incongruous jumble of deficits and strengths. They have diminished cognitive capacities and heart problems, and age prematurely, yet they show outgoing personalities and a flair for language. "What makes Williams syndrome so fascinating," says Bellugi, "is it shows that the domains of cognition and language are quite separate."

Genetic gap. Williams syndrome, which was first described in 1961, results when a group of genes on one copy of chromosome 7 is deleted during embryonic development. Most people with Williams resemble each other more than they do their families, with wide-set hazel eyes, upturned noses, wide mouths. They also share a peculiar set of mental impairments. Most stumble over the simplest spa-

womb. Newborn babies prefer their mothers' voices over those of their fathers or other women, and researchers recently have found that when very young babies hear a recording of their mothers' native language, they will suck more vigorously on a pacifier than when they hear a recording of another tongue.

At first, infants respond only to the prosody—the cadence, rhythm, and pitch—of their mothers' speech, not the words. But soon enough they home in on the actual sounds that are typical of their parents' language. Every language uses a different assortment of sounds, called phonemes, which combine to make syllables. (In English, for example, the consonant sound "b" and the vowel sound "a" are both phonemes, which combine for the syllable *ba*, as in *banana*.) To an adult, simply perceiving, much less pronouncing, the phonemes of a foreign language can seem impossible. In English, the p of *pat* is "aspirated," or produced with a puff of air; the p of *spot* or *tap* is unaspirated. In English, the two p's are considered the same; therefore it is hard for English speakers to recognize that in many other languages the two p's are two different phonemes. Japanese speakers have trouble distinguishing between the "l" and "r" sounds of English, since in Japanese they don't count as separate sounds.

Polyglot tots. Infants can perceive the entire range of phonemes, according to Janet Werker and Richard Tees, psychologists at the University of British Columbia in Canada. Werker and Tees found that the brains of 4-month-old babies respond to every phoneme uttered in languages as diverse as Hindi and Nthlakampx, a Northwest American Indian language containing numerous consonant combinations that can sound to a nonnative speaker like a drop of water hitting an empty bucket. By the time babies are 10 months to a year old, however, they have begun to focus on the distinctions among phonemes of their native language

Discriminating minds. Toddlers listen for bits of language like the, which signals that a noun will follow. Most 2-year-olds can understand "Find the dog," but they are stumped by "Find gub dog."

and to ignore the differences among foreign sounds. Children don't lose the ability to distinguish the sounds of a foreign language; they simply don't pay attention to them. This allows them to learn more quickly the syllables and words of their native tongue.

An infant's next step is learning to fish out individual words from

tial tasks, such as putting together a puzzle, and many cannot read or write beyond the level of a first grader.

In spite of these deficits, Bellugi has found that children with the disorder are not merely competent at language but extraordinary. Ask normal kids to name as many animals as possible in 60 seconds, and a string of barnyard and pet-store examples will tumble out. Ask children with Williams, and you'll get a menagerie of rare creatures, such as ibex, newt, yak, and weasel. People with Williams have the gift of gab, telling elaborate stories with unabashed verve and incorporating audience teasers such as "Gadzooks!" and "Lo and behold!"

This unlikely suite of skills and inadequacies initially led Bellugi to surmise that Williams might damage the right hemisphere of the brain, where spatial tasks are processed, while leaving language in the left hemisphere intact. That has not turned out to be true. People with Williams excel at recognizing faces, a job that enlists the visual and spatial-processing skills of the right hemisphere. Using functional brain imaging, a technique that shows the brain in action, Bellugi has found that both hemispheres of the brains of people with Williams are shouldering the tasks of processing language.

Bellugi and other researchers are now trying to link the outward characteristics of people with Williams to the genes they are missing and to changes in brain tissue. They have begun concentrating on the neocerebellum, a part of the brain that is enlarged in people with Williams and that may hold clues to their engaging personalities and to the evolution of language. The neocerebellum is among the brain's newest parts, appearing in human ancestors about the same time as the enlargement of the frontal cortex, the place where researchers believe rational thoughts are formulated. The neocerebellum is significantly smaller in people with autism, who are generally antisocial and poor at language, the reverse of people with Williams. This part of the brain helps make semantic connections between words, such as *sit* and *chair*, suggesting that it was needed for language to evolve.

the nonstop stream of sound that makes up ordinary speech. Finding the boundaries between words is a daunting task, because people don't pause . . . between . . . words . . . when . . . they speak. Yet children begin to note word boundaries by the time they are 8 months old, even though they have no concept of what most words mean. Last year, Jusczyk and his colleagues reported results of an experiment in which they let 8-month-old babies listen at home to recorded stories filled with unusual words, like *hornbill* and *python*. Two weeks later, the researchers tested the babies with two lists of words, one composed of words they had already heard in the stories, the other of new unusual words that weren't in the stories. The infants listened, on average, to the familiar list for a second longer than to the list of novel words.

The cadence of language is a baby's first clue to word boundaries. In most English words, the first syllable is accented. This is especially noticeable in words known in poetry as trochees—two-syllable words stressed on the first syllable—which parents repeat to young children (BA-by, DOG-gie, MOM-my). At 6 months, American babies pay equal amounts of attention to words with different stress patterns, like gi-RAFFE or TI-ger. By 9 months, however, they have heard enough of the typical first-syllable-stress pattern of English to prefer listening to trochees, a predilection that will show up later, when they start uttering their first words and mispronouncing giraffe as *raff* and banana as *nana*. At 30 months, children can easily repeat the phrase "TOM-my KISS-ed the MON-key," because it preserves the typical English pattern, but they will leave out the *the* when asked to repeat "Tommy patted the monkey." Researchers are now testing whether French babies prefer words with a second-syllable stress—words like *be-RET* or *ma-MAN*.

Decoding patterns. Most adults could not imagine making speedy progress toward memorizing words in a foreign language just by listening to somebody talk on the telephone.

That is basically what 8-month-old babies can do, according to a provocative study published in 1996 by the University of Rochester's Newport and her colleagues, Jenny Saffran

Masters of pattern. Researchers played strings of three-syllable nonsense words to 8-month-old babies for two minutes. The babies learned them by remembering how often syllables occurred together.

and Richard Aslin. They reported that babies can remember words by listening for patterns of syllables that occur together with statistical regularity.

The researchers created a miniature artificial language, which consisted of a handful of three-syllable nonsense words constructed from 11 different syllables. The babies heard a computer-generated voice repeating these words in random order in a monotone for two minutes. What they heard went something like "bidaku-padotigolabubidaku." *Bidaku*, in this case, is a word. With no cadence or pauses, the only way the babies could learn individual words was by remembering how often certain syllables were uttered together. When the researchers tested the babies a few minutes later, they found that the infants recognized pairs of syllables that had occurred together consistently on the recording, such as *bida*. They did not recognize a pair like *kupa*, which was a rarer combination that crossed the boundaries of two words. In the past, psychologists never imagined that young infants had the mental capacity to make these sorts of inferences. "We were pretty surprised we could get this result with babies, and with only brief exposure," says Newport. "Real language, of course, is

much more complicated, but the exposure is vast."

Learning words is one thing; learning the abstract rules of grammar is another. When Noam Chomsky first voiced his idea that language is hard-wired in the brain, he didn't have the benefit of the current revolution in cognitive science, which has begun to pry open the human mind with sophisticated psychological experiments and new computer models. Until recently, linguists could only parse languages and marvel at how quickly children master their abstract rules, which give every human being who can speak (or sign) the power to express an infinite number of ideas from a finite number of words.

There also are a finite number of ways that languages construct sentences. As Chomsky once put it, from a Martian's-eye view, everybody on Earth speaks a single tongue that has thousands of mutually unintelligible dialects. For instance, all people make sentences from noun phrases, like "The quick brown fox," and verb phrases, like "jumped over the fence." And virtually all of the world's 6,000 or so languages allow phrases to be moved around in a sentence to form questions, relative clauses, and passive constructions.

Statistical wizards. Chomsky posited that children were born knowing these and a handful of other basic laws of language and that they learn their parents' native tongue with the help of a "language acquisition device," preprogrammed circuits in the brain. Findings like Newport's are suggesting to some researchers that perhaps children can use statistical regularities to extract not only individual words from what they hear but also the rules for cobbling words together into sentences.

This idea is shared by computational linguists, who have designed computer models called artificial neural networks that are very simplified versions of the brain and that can "learn" some aspects of language. Artificial neural networks mimic the way that nerve cells, or neurons, inside a brain are hooked up. The result is a device that shares some basic properties with the brain and that can accomplish some linguistic feats that real children perform. For example, a neural network can make general categories out of a jumble of words coming in, just as a child learns that certain kinds of words refer to objects while others refer to actions. Nobody has to teach kids that words like *dog* and *telephone* are nouns, while *go* and *jump* are verbs; the way they use such words in sentences demonstrates that they know the difference. Neural networks also can learn some aspects of the meaning of words, and they can infer some rules of syntax, or word order. Therefore, a computer that was fed English sentences would be able to produce a phrase like "Johnny ate fish," rather than "Johnny fish ate," which is correct in Japanese. These computer models even make some of the same mistakes that real children do, says Mark Seidenberg, a computational linguist at the University of Southern California. A neural network designed by a student of Seidenberg's to learn to conjugate verbs sometimes issued sentences like "He jumped me the ball," which any parent will recognize as the kind of error that could have come from the mouths of babes.

But neural networks have yet to come close to the computation power of a toddler. Ninety percent of the sentences uttered by the average 3-year-

old are grammatically correct. The mistakes they do make are rarely random but rather the result of following the rules of grammar with excessive zeal. There is no logical reason for being able to say "I batted the ball" but not "I holded the rabbit," except that about 180 of the most commonly used English verbs are conjugated irregularly.

Yet for all of grammar's seeming illogic, toddlers' brains may be able to spot clues in the sentences they hear that help them learn grammatical rules, just as they use statistical regularities to find word boundaries. One such clue is the little bits of language called grammatical morphemes, which among other things tell a listener whether a word is being used as noun or as a verb. *The,* for instance, signals that a noun will soon follow, while the suffix *ion* also identifies a word as a noun, as in vibration. Psycholinguist LouAnn Gerken of the University of Arizona recently reported that toddlers know what grammatical morphemes signify before they actually use them. She tested this by asking 2-year-olds a series of questions in which the grammatical morphemes were replaced with other words. When asked to "Find the dog for me," for example, 85 percent of children in her study could point to the right animal in a picture. But when the question was "Find *was* dog for me," they pointed to the dog 55 percent of the

time. "Find *gub* dog for me," and it dropped to 40 percent.

Fast mapping. Children may be noticing grammatical morphemes when they are as young as 10 months and have just begun making connections between words and their definitions. Gerken recently found that infants' brain waves change when they are listening to stories in which grammatical

morphemes are replaced with other words, suggesting they begin picking up grammar even before they know what sentences mean.

Such linguistic leaps come as a baby's brain is humming with activity. Within the first few months of life, a baby's neurons will forge 1,000 trillion connections, an increase of 20-fold from birth. Neurobiologists once assumed that the wiring in a baby's brain was set at birth. After that, the brain, like legs and noses, just grew bigger. That view has been demolished, says Anne Fernald, a psycholinguist at Stanford University, "now that we can eavesdrop on the brain." Images made using the brain-scanning technique positron emission tomography have revealed, for instance, that when a baby is 8 or 9 months old, the part of the brain that stores and indexes many kinds of memory becomes fully functional. This is precisely when babies appear to be able to attach meaning to words.

Other leaps in a child's linguistic prowess also coincide with remark-

> ## Strict grammarians. Most 3-year-olds rarely make grammatical errors. When they do, the mistakes they make usually are the result of following the rules of grammar with excessive zeal.

able changes in the brain. For instance, an adult listener can recognize *eleph* as *elephant* within about 400 milliseconds, an ability called "fast mapping" that demands that the brain process speech sounds with phenomenal speed. "To understand strings of words, you have to identify individual words rapidly," says Fernald. She and her colleagues have found that around 15 months of age, a child needs more than a second to recognize even a familiar word, like *baby*. At 18 months, the child can get the picture slightly before the word is ending. At 24 months, she knows the word in a mere 600 milliseconds, as soon as the syllable *bay* has been uttered.

Fast mapping takes off at the same moment as a dramatic reorganization of the child's brain, in which language-related operations, particularly grammar, shift from both sides of the brain into the left hemisphere. Most adult brains are lopsided when it comes to language, processing grammar almost entirely in the left temporal lobe, just over the left ear. Infants and toddlers, however, treat language in both hemispheres, according to Debra Mills, at the University of California–San Diego, and Helen Neville, at the University of Oregon. Mills and Neville stuck electrodes to toddlers' heads to find that processing of words that serve special grammatical functions, such as prepositions, conjunctions, and articles, begins to shift into the left side around the end of the third year.

From then on, the two hemispheres assume different job descriptions. The right temporal lobe continues to perform spatial tasks, such as following the trajectory of a baseball and predicting where it will land. It also pays attention to the emotional information contained in the cadence and pitch of speech. Both hemispheres know the meanings of many words, but the left temporal lobe holds the key to grammar.

This division is maintained even when the language is signed, not spoken. Ursula Bellugi and Edward Klima, a wife and husband team at the Salk Institute for Biological Studies in La Jolla, Calif., recently demonstrated this fact by studying deaf people who were lifelong signers of American Sign Language and who also had suffered a stroke in specific areas of the brain. The researchers found, predictably, that signers with damage to the right hemisphere had great difficulty with tasks involving spatial perception, such as copying a drawing of a geometric pattern. What was surprising was that right hemisphere damage did not hinder their fluency in ASL, which relies on movements of the hands and body in space. It was signers with damage to the left hemisphere who found they could no longer express themselves in ASL or understand it. Some had trouble producing the specific facial expressions that convey grammatical information in ASL. It is not just speech that's being processed in the left hemisphere, says MIT's Pinker, or movements of the mouth, but abstract language.

Nobody knows why the left hemisphere got the job of processing language, but linguists are beginning to surmise that languages are constructed the way they are in part because the human brain is not infinitely capable of all kinds of computation. "We are starting to see how the universals among languages could arise out of constraints on how the brain computes and how children learn," says Johns Hopkins linguist Paul Smolensky. For instance, the vast majority of the world's languages favor syllables that end in a vowel, though English is an exception. (Think of a native Italian speaking English and adding vowels where there are none.) That's because it is easier for the auditory centers of the brain to perceive differences between consonants when they come before a vowel than when they come after. Human brains can easily recognize *pad*, *bad*, and *dad* as three different words; it is much harder to distinguish *tab*, *tap*, and *tad*. As languages around the world were evolving, they were pulled along paths that minimize ambiguity among sounds.

Birth of a language. Linguists have never had the chance to study a spoken language as it is being constructed, but they have been given the opportunity to observe a new sign language in the making in Nicaragua. When the Sandinistas came to power in 1979, they established schools where deaf people came together for the first time. Many of the pupils had never met another deaf person, and their only means of communication at first was the expressive but largely unstructured pantomime each had invented at home with their hearing families. Soon the pupils began to pool their makeshift gestures into a system that is similar to spoken pidgin, the form of communication that springs up in places where people speaking mutually unintelligible tongues come together. The next generation of deaf Nicaraguan children, says Judy Kegl, a psycholinguist at Rutgers University, in Newark, N.J., has done it one better, transforming the pidgin sign into a full-blown language complete with regular grammar. The birth of Nicaraguan sign, many linguists believe, mirrors the evolution of all languages. Without conscious effort, deaf Nicaraguan children have created a sign that is now fluid and compact, and which contains standardized rules that allow them to express abstract ideas without circumlocutions. It can indicate past and future, denote whether an action was performed once or repeatedly, and show who did what to whom, allowing its users to joke, recite poetry, and tell their life stories.

Linguists have a long road ahead of them before they can say exactly how a child goes from babbling to banter, or what the very first languages might have been like, or how the brain transforms vague thoughts into concrete words that sometimes fly out of our mouths before we can stop them. But already, some practical conclusions are falling out of the new research. For example, two recent studies show that the size of toddlers' vocabularies depends in large measure on how much their mothers talk to them. At 20 months, according to a study by Janellen Huttenlocher of the University of Chicago, the children of talkative mothers had 131 more words in their vocabularies than children whose mothers were more taciturn. By age 2, the gap had widened to 295 words.

In other words, children need input and they need it early, says Newport. Parking a toddler in front of the television won't improve vocabulary, probably because kids need real human interaction to attach meaning to words. Hearing more than one language in infancy makes it easier for a child to hear the distinctions between phonemes of more than one language later on.

Newport and other linguists have discovered in recent years that the window of opportunity for acquiring language begins to close around age 6, and the gap narrows with each additional candle on the birthday cake. Children who do not learn a language by puberty will never be fluent in any tongue. That means that profoundly deaf children should be exposed to sign language as early as possible, says Newport. If their parents are hearing, they should learn to sign. And schools might rethink the practice of waiting to teach foreign languages until kids are nearly grown and the window on native command of a second language is almost shut.

Linguists don't yet know how much of grammar children are able to absorb simply by listening. And they have only begun to parse the genes or accidents of brain wiring that might give rise, as Pinker puts it, to the poet, the raconteur, or an Alexander Haig, a Mrs. Malaprop. What is certain is that language is one of the great wonders of the natural world, and linguists are still being astonished by its complexity and its power to shape the brain. Human beings, says Kegl, "show an incredible enthusiasm for discourse." Maybe what is most innate about language is the passion to communicate.

Effects of Sleep Position on Infant Motor Development

Beth Ellen Davis, MD* ‡; Rachel Y. Moon, MD §‖; Hari C. Sachs, MD¶; and Mary C. Ottolini, MD, MPH §‖¶

ABSTRACT. *Background.* **As a result of the American Academy of Pediatrics' recommendation that healthy infants be placed on their side or back for sleep, the percentage of infants sleeping prone has decreased dramatically. With the increase in supine sleeping, pediatricians have questioned if there are differences in the rate of acquisition of early motor milestones between prone and supine sleeping infants.**

Methods. **To examine this question, we performed a prospective, practice-based study of healthy term infants. Infants were recruited before the age of 2 months. Parents were asked to record infant sleep position and awake time spent prone until 6 months of age. A developmental log was used to track milestones from birth until the infant was walking. Age of acquisition of eight motor milestones was determined, and the mean ages of milestone attainment of prone and supine sleepers were compared.**

Results. **Three hundred fifty-one infants completed the study. Prone sleepers acquired motor milestones at an earlier age than supine sleepers. There was a significant difference in the age of attainment of rolling prone to supine, tripod sitting, creeping, crawling, and pulling to stand. There was no significant difference in age when infants walked.**

Conclusions. **The pattern of early motor development is affected by sleep position. Prone sleepers attain several motor milestones earlier than supine sleepers. However, all infants achieved all milestones within the accepted normal age range. Pediatricians can use this information to reassure parents. This difference in milestone attainment is not a reason to abandon the American Academy of Pediatrics' sleep position recommendations.** *Pediatrics* 1998;102:1135–1140; *sleep position, sudden infant death syndrome, infant development, motor development.*

From the Department of Pediatrics, Uniformed Services University of the Health Sciences, Bethesda, Maryland; ‡ Department of Pediatrics, Walter Reed Army Medical Center, Washington, DC; § Department of General Pediatrics and Adolescent Medicine, Children's National Medical Center, Washington, DC;‖ Department of Pediatrics, George Washington University School of Medicine and Health Sciences, Washington, DC; and ¶ Holy Cross Hospital, Silver Spring, Maryland.
The results from this article were presented in part at the Ambulatory Pediatric Association meeting, Washington DC, May 1997.
The opinions and assertions contained herein represent the private views of the authors and are not to be construed as official or as reflecting the views of the Department of the Army, Uniformed Services University of the Health Sciences, or the Department of Defense.
Received for publication Jan 8, 1998; accepted Jun 2, 1998.
Reprint requests to (B.E.D.) Department of Pediatrics, Uniformed Services Univeristy of the Health Sciences, 4301 Jones Bridge Rd, Bethesda, MD 20814-4799

ABBREVIATIONS. AAP, American Academy of Pediatrics; SIDS, sudden infant death syndrome.

In 1992, the American Academy of Pediatrics[1] (AAP) published a recommendation that "healthy infants, when being put down for sleep, be positioned on their side or back" in an attempt to decrease the incidence of sudden infant death syndrome (SIDS). Since these recommendations and a subsequent national public education campaign, "Back to Sleep," the percentage of infants sleeping prone has decreased dramatically from 70% in 1992 to 27% in 1995.[2]

With the increase in supine sleeping, several pediatricians in our community have observed differences in the rate of acquisition of early motor milestones between prone and supine sleeping infants. This observation is consistent with data reported from other cultures where supine is the predominant sleep position for infants.[3–7] Since the sleep position recommendations, there have been no published prospective, longitudinal studies that have quantitated the association between sleep position and early motor development. Some recent studies support the observation that supine and prone sleepers may acquire milestones differently. A recent retrospective chart review demonstrated that sleep position influences the age when infants roll over.[8] In addition, Dewey et al[9] distributed questionnaires regarding development to participants in the Avon Longitudinal Study of Pregnancy and Childhood when the infants were 6 and 18 months of age. They found that prone sleepers had higher scores in gross motor, social skills, and overall development at 6 months but not at 18 months.

We conducted a prospective, longitudinal, practice-based study of healthy infants to determine the relationship between sleep position and the age of attainment of motor milestones in the first year of life. Based on our clinical observations, we hypothesized that supine sleeping would be associated with later age of attainment of certain motor milestones. Because prone positioning encourages use of upper body strength used in acquisition of many infant motor milestones, it may be that supine sleepers lag in milestone development in the first year because the upper body contributes less to daily movement than for predominantly prone positioned infants.

METHODS

This study was approved by the institutional review boards of Children's National Medical Center, Holy Cross Hospital, Walter Reed Army Medical Center, and the Uniformed Services University of the Health Sciences.

A prospective cohort of healthy infants was recruited at a community hospital nursery and in participating pediatricians' offices before the age of 1 month. Infants were eligible for participation if they were full term, healthy, and regularly seen by a pediatrician participating in the Children's Pediatric Research Network. The Children's Pediatric Research Network consists of 10 suburban private practices, 3 urban pediatric centers, and the Walter Reed Army Medical Center in the Washington, DC, area. The target population was healthy, full-term infants in the United States that represent the recent trends in changing sleep positions, well documented in the literature.[2] A total sample size of 276 was needed to demonstrate a difference of at least 1 month between the comparison groups. Because of the longitudinal design of the study and the transient nature of the population in the Washington, DC, area, we estimated 25% to 40% drop-out during the 15-month study period. A total of 400 infants comprised this convenience sample. The power of the study was 80%. Infants were excluded from entry into the study for the following reasons: 1) gestational age < 37 weeks; 2) orthopedic problems that might affect motor development (eg, torticollis, metatarsus adductus, club foot, developmental dysplasia of the hip); 3) hyperbilirubinemia requiring hospitalization; 4) any genetic or metabolic abnormalities (eg, hypothyroidism); and 5) asymmetric neurologic examinations. In addition, families who did not have a working telephone for monthly contacts were excluded.

Infants were enrolled from November 1995 to September 1996. Research assistants approached parents being discharged from a full-term nursery two weekdays and one weekend day every week during the study period who would be followed by one of the participating pediatric practices. Approximately 15% of accessible parents met exclusion criteria or chose not to enroll, mostly because of time constraints or knowledge of a relocation in the upcoming year. Parents completed an initial questionnaire regarding demographic information, birth history, and child care environment after giving informed consent. They were provided a brochure and advised on enrollment to place their infant on the side or back for sleep according to the AAP recommendation.[1]

Parents kept a sleep position log, listing the average number of hours per day that their infants spent sleeping and the percentage of time that infants slept in the prone, supine, or side position during the first week of life, and then monthly for the first 6 months of life. Sleep position was defined as the position in which the parents placed the infant for sleep. Using this definition for sleep posi-

tion has been shown to be reliable until infants begin to choose their own sleep positions at 6 to 7 months of age.[10] Furthermore, data shows that > 95% of younger infants placed in either supine or prone will wake up in the same position, and > 80% of infants placed on the side will wake up in either the side or supine position. Only 0.5% of side-lying infants will awaken prone.[11] In addition, parents recorded the percentage of time that the infant spent in the prone position while awake. Investigators were blinded to the sleep and awake positions during the study.

Parents completed an infant developmental log to track infant milestones. The developmental log included 18 sequential developmental items representing different motor skills, usually occurring at a rate of 1 to 2 acquisitions each month. This encouraged consistent parental observation of motor development between major milestone attainments. Standardized questions from the Revised Prescreening Developmental Questionnaire,[12,13] a standardized parent-answered questionnaire based on items from the Denver Developmental Screening Test were utilized, with illustrations of each milestone depicted next to the description for further clarification. The reported test-retest reliability of this type of measure is very high, as is reliability among all socioeconomic groups.[14] The selected milestones were: lifting chin from surface when prone, lifting head 45 degrees when prone, bringing hands together to midline, rolling prone to supine, grasping item within reach, rolling supine to prone, no head lag when pulled to sitting position, touching feet, sitting supported (tripod), transferring small objects between hands, sitting unsupported, getting to sitting position, working for toy, creeping (defined as pulling self along on abdomen), crawling (defined as moving on hands and knees, or hands and feet, with trunk off the ground), pulling to stand, cruising, and walking 10 to 15 steps independently. Parents recorded the age and/or date at which their infant performed the specified milestone. To ensure year-long durability and consistency of use, the developmental logs were plastic covered and magnetically mounted.

We ensured current and ongoing documentation of milestone attainment by two different methods: 1) a research assistant telephoned the families monthly to record the age of attainment of milestones and to remind parents to keep the sleep position and development logs current; and 2) independent assessment of health, growth, and development was performed by pediatricians at each well-child check, including a specific physician statement at the infant's 12-month visit stating that "this infant is healthy and neurologically normal at 12 months of age." Because the research assistant called in monthly intervals, parental compliance was very good as both predictor and outcome variables remained the same for weeks at a time. Periodic chart review was performed by one of the investigators to verify physician documentation of developmental milestones. The validity of parental report was supported by physician observation of developmental milestones. Approximately 5% of parent reports differed from physician assessment as documented in the medical record. In those rare instances, the latter was used for analysis. Infants were followed until they could walk independently for 10 or more steps.

To better compare the effects of prone and supine sleeping on development and to minimize the effect of changing sleep position with age, we identified consistently prone and supine subgroups within the cohort. These sleep positions have been reported to be the most stable (ie, infants placed prone tend to remain prone).[15] Infants were categorized as prone sleepers if they were placed in the prone sleep position > 70% of sleep time from age 1 month to 5 months. Supine sleepers were defined as those placed in the supine sleep position > 70% of sleep time from age 1 month to 5 months. Five months was chosen as the cutoff because we anticipated that some infants would begin to change sleep position spontaneously thereafter, diminishing reliability of sleep position based on parental placement. All other infants were reported to be mixed/side sleepers.

Of the 18 developmental tasks on the log, we included the 8 major motor milestones. Based on previous work by Capute et al,[16] these major motor milestones are identified as such by a high reported frequency of parental recall and traditionally occurring within a narrow range of variation. For this reason, we selected the 8 major motor milestones for analysis purposes: rolling prone to supine, rolling supine to prone, sitting supported (tripod), sitting unsupported, creeping, crawling, pulling to stand, and walking independently. Additionally, the fine motor milestone of transferring small objects between hands was chosen.

The frequency and distribution of sociodemographic variables were calculated for all participants. We determined the age of acquisition of the 8 major motor milestones for all participants, and we compared the age of acquisition of motor milestones among the subgroups by univariate analysis with the Kruskal-Wallis test. Linear regression analysis was then performed to compare the mean ages of milestone attainment between predominantly prone and supine sleepers, while controlling for possible confounders, such as infant size, gender, ethnicity, presence of siblings, and maternal education.

RESULTS

Demographic Data

Of the original 400 enrollees, 351 (87%) completed the study. Thirty-seven enrollees were lost to follow-up because of disconnected telephones, families not answering multiple telephone calls, family moves, or change to a nonparticipating pediatric practice. The remaining 12 patients developed medical conditions after enrollment which precluded further involvement in the study: congenital adrenal hyperplasia (n = 1), hypothyroidism (n = 1), conditions necessitating physical therapy referrals (n = 3), developmental hip dysplasia requiring use of Pavlik harness (n = 2), metatarsus adductus requiring casting (n = 2), and nonspecific asymmetric examinations requiring neurologic evaluation (n = 3). No cases of SIDS occurred in this cohort.

The mean birth weight of the infants was 3490 ± 41 g. Forty-nine percent of the infants were male. Sixty-eight percent were white, 20% African-American, 3% Asian-American, and 9% Hispanic, Native American, or other. Forty-two percent (n = 146) were first born, 37% (n = 130) had one sibling, and 21% had two or more siblings. The mean maternal age was 31.3 ± 5 years, with only 2% of mothers younger than 20 years old. Ninety-three percent (n = 295) of the mothers were married. The mean maternal educational level was 15.3 ± 2.6 years. Six percent (n = 20) of the mothers had < 12 years of schooling, 71% (n = 248) had received 2 to 4 years of college education, and 23% had > 16 years of education. At enrollment, 90% of parents anticipated being the primary child care provider for the first year of life.

When the infants were subcategorized according to sleep position, they were similar for maternal age, gender, race/ethnicity, and birth weight. Prone sleepers were more likely to have older siblings (mean, 1.3 vs 0.81 for supine sleepers; P = .007), and their mothers were less likely to be married (P = .007). The mothers of prone sleepers had fewer years of education (mean, 14.08 years) than mothers of supine sleepers (mean, 15.39 years; P < .0001).

Sleep Characteristics

Twelve percent (n = 42) of 1-week-old infants were placed prone for sleep, and 28% (n = 98) were placed in the supine position. The remaining 60% (n = 210) of 1-week-old infants were placed in the side-lying position. At 6 months of age, 32% (n = 112) were being placed prone and 48% (n = 168) supine for sleep. Side sleepers decreased to 20% (n = 71). Only 44% of infants consistently slept in the same position from 1 to 5 months of age. Sixteen percent of infants (n = 57) consistently slept in the prone position, and 28% (n = 97) were consistent supine sleepers. To minimize overlap effects, we used the predominantly prone and predominantly supine sleepers for comparison groups when we looked at effect of sleep position on motor milestone acquisition.

Awake Characteristics (Table 1)

All infants, regardless of sleep position, spent increasing amounts of time awake from 1 week of age to 6 months of age. Although the total awake time was similar for all of the infants, there was a significant difference

TABLE 1. Awake Characteristics of Study Infants ($n = 351$)

Infant Age	Mean Awake Time (Hours/Day)				Mean Awake Time Spent Prone (Hours/Day)			
	Supine Sleepers	Mixed/Side Sleepers	Prone Sleepers	P Value*	Supine Sleepers	Mixed/Side Sleepers	Prone Sleepers	P Value*
1 Week	7.18	6.57	6.26	.11	0.54	0.48	1.42	<.0001
1 Month	8.74	4.68	4.30	.01	0.74	0.68	1.79	<.0001
2 Months	9.47	9.12	8.99	.31	0.90	0.92	2.44	<.0001
3 Months	10.43	9.98	9.80	.15	1.18	1.31	2.92	<.0001
4 Months	10.79	10.47	10.30	.15	1.72	2.16	3.14	.0003
5 Months	11.30	10.72	10.66	.04	2.16	3.06	3.87	<.0001
6 Months	11.46	10.90	10.74	.02	2.59	3.40	3.70	.003

* Represents P value for prone sleepers versus supine sleepers.

in time spent awake in the prone position. Throughout the first 6 months of life, prone sleepers spent much more time awake in the prone position than the supine or side sleepers. For the first 3 months of life, prone sleepers were awake in the prone position more than twice the amount of time as the other groups.

Milestone Attainment (Fig 1 and Table 2)

In general, prone sleepers acquired motor milestones at an earlier age than their supine sleeping counterparts. There was a significant difference ($P < .05$) in the age of milestone attainment with the following milestones: rolling prone to supine, tripod sitting, creeping, crawling, and pulling to stand. Mixed/side sleepers, in general, attained milestones before the supine sleepers and later than the prone sleepers but because this group of sleepers represented significant variability, it was not used as a comparison group. There was no significant difference in the age at which the infants rolled supine to prone, sat unsupported, transferred objects, or walked. Twenty-three percent ($n = 81$) of the study participants never achieved the creeping milestone; 31% ($n = 30$) of the supine sleepers and 18% ($n = 10$) of the prone sleepers did not creep.

Because there was an impressive difference in the amount of prone playtime seen in the prone versus supine sleepers, we also analyzed the influence of prone playtime in the small group of supine sleepers. Increased prone playtime was significantly associated with earlier attainment of the following milestones: tripod sitting, sitting alone, crawling, and pulling to stand ($P < .05$). However, when maternal education, race, gender, birth weight, and number of older siblings was controlled for, the difference was significant only for the pull to stand milestone ($P < .01$).

DISCUSSION

The attainment of motor milestones has long been used by pediatricians and parents as an outward indicator of the progress of neurologic development during infancy, although there may be little association with general intelligence.[17] Parental perception of normalcy during the first year of life is heavily influenced by the infant's progressive attainment of motor milestones. Standardized screening tools used daily by general pediatricians stress developmental milestones that occur within a fixed age range in infants with normal development. Because delayed or skipped milestones are thought to place an infant at risk for abnormal development, identifying factors that influence the normal age range for milestone attainment is important. We found that sleep position significantly impacts early motor development.

Traditional age ranges for motor milestone attainment in the United States were developed when prone infant sleeping was the norm. As early as 1960, Holt[18] qualitatively reported that a small sample of prone sleeping American infants achieved certain milestones at an earlier age than the supine sleepers. He observed that the prone sleeping American infants tended to crawl earlier and were more advanced in their prone motor skills than would be expected of English supine sleeping infants.

Since the 1970s, there have been several reports from cultures in Asia and Europe where supine is the predominant sleep position, demonstrating later attainment of early motor milestones, such as rolling over and sitting up, than would be expected by US norms.[3–7] These findings have been sufficiently consistent in certain cultures that researchers have adapted and standardized the Denver Developmental Screening Test and the Denver II to fit the cultural norms.[3–5,19] The Asian studies specifically refer to supine positioning as a possible explanation for the differences seen in the gross motor milestones.

In this practice-based study, we prospectively followed a cohort of term, healthy infants from birth through their first year of life, using parental logs to document age of attainment of motor milestones and sleep position. To minimize recall bias, a research assistant called families each month to update the logs and to ensure accurate and current documentation. In addition, the medical records of all study infants were reviewed by one of the investigators to verify parental report and to identify any medical problems that would potentially affect motor development. We then analyzed the relationship of sleep position and age of attainment

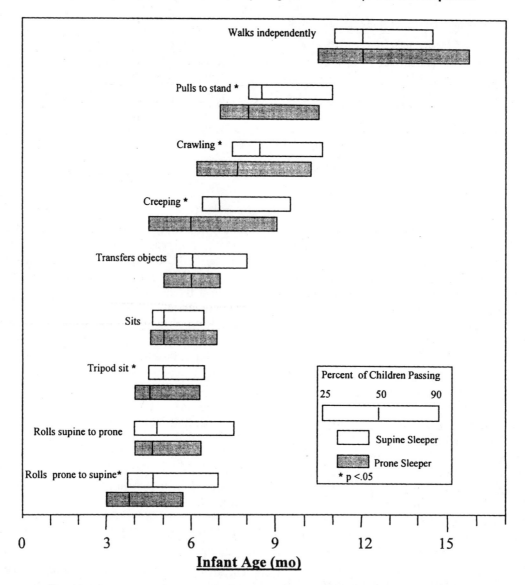

Fig. 1. Motor milestones in prone versus supine sleeping infants. This Figure represents the age range (25% to 90%) for attainment of the specified milestones for supine sleepers (white boxes) and prone sleepers (shaded boxes). The vertical line through the center of each bar represents the age at which 50% of children in that group have demonstrated the identified milestone.

of 8 major milestones (rolling to supine, rolling to prone, sitting tripod, sitting unsupported, creeping, crawling, pulling to stand, and walking).

Despite the fact that all parents were counseled on study entry to place their infants supine for sleep, 12%

of the 2-week-old infants in our study were being placed prone for sleep, and this number increased to 32% by 6 months of age. Although it is unfortunate that some of the parents in this cohort did not follow the current sleep recommendations, this is consistent with recent studies

TABLE 2. Mean Age (Months) for Milestone Acquisition

Milestone	Prone Sleepers	Mixed/Side Sleepers	Supine Sleepers	P Value* (Linear Regression)†
Rolls prone to supine	3.93 ± 1.2	4.48 ± 1.8	4.87 ± 1.33	.002 (.02)
Rolls supine to prone	4.9 ± 1.3	4.97 ± 1.9	5.0 ± 1.6	.95
Sits supported	4.7 ± 1.3	5.02 ± 1.4	5.13 ± 0.9	.003 (.03)
Sits unsupported	5.13 ± 1.1	5.17 ± 1.2	5.17 ± 1.0	.80
Transfers object	5.87 ± 1.2	5.99 ± 6.5	6.23 ± 1.1	.11
Creeps	6.07 ± 1.9	6.49 ± 1.9	7.23 ± 1.6	.0002 (.001)
Crawls	7.83 ± 2.0	8.47 ± 2.1	8.6 ± 1.7	.003 (.05)
Pulls to stand	8.1 ± 1.6	8.7 ± 1.5	8.77 ± 1.6	.01 (.04)
Walks alone	12.1 ± 2.0	12.2 ± 2.0	12.2 ± 1.7	.4

* Represents P value for prone sleepers versus supine sleepers.
† Multivariate regression analysis controlling for infant size, gender, ethnicity, presence of siblings, and maternal education.

that demonstrate that one-fourth to one-third of parents who are aware of the sleep recommendations continue to place their infants prone for sleep.[20,21]

In a retrospective study, Jantz et al,[8] determined that prone sleepers rolled over at an earlier age than nonprone sleepers but did not find significant differences in other milestones. In this and other recent studies looking at effects of sleep position,[8,9,11] an assumption was made that infant sleep position did not change during the time period. Thus, the position that parents placed infants at 1 month of age was the position used for assessment, even at 6 months of age. Our study demonstrated variability in sleep position choice during the course of the first 6 months. Despite 88% of parents placing infants in a nonprone position at 4 weeks of age, only 28% of the infants consistently slept in the supine position from 12 to 20 weeks of age. In 1973, Modlin et al[22] reported that it was difficult to predict the sleep position in 7-month-old infants by their sleep position at birth, and that only 38% of the infants in their sample had slept in the same position since birth. To ascertain more accurately the effects of sleep position, we differentiated from the large group of nonprone sleepers ($n = 265$) a smaller group of supine sleepers ($n = 97$) for comparison with the prone sleeping infants. In the predominantly supine sleepers, we found not only a significant delay in rolling prone to supine, but also significant differences between the groups for tripod sitting, creeping, crawling, and pulling to stand.

The AAP, in its most recent statement regarding infant sleep position, recommended that infants spend some time in the prone position while awake and observed.[2] In our survey, however, we discovered that many parents avoided placing their infants prone, even when the children were awake, because they were fearful of the possibility of SIDS. This is consistent with a previous report, in which 26% of parents never placed their infants prone for play.[23] We also noticed that many of the supine sleepers did not want to be placed prone while awake. When we asked parents to determine how much time their infant spent prone while awake, many parents prefaced their response with "My baby doesn't like his/her tummy!" In our study, the prone sleepers spent significantly more time prone while awake. The amount of prone playtime may be a contributing factor to the effect of supine sleeping on motor development. At the least, it seems to amplify the effect of supine sleeping, and it may be the primary factor that influences motor development. In our small sample of supine sleepers, we found that increased prone playtime did result in earlier milestone attainment. However, further, larger scale studies are indicated to determine if increased prone playtime does indeed accelerate motor development in supine sleepers.

As this study was dependent on parental reporting, the validity of these results is limited by the accuracy of the parents' responses. Although it is acknowledged that parents may have been unwilling to admit to actual sleep positions, this would have had the effect of minimizing the differences that we found in milestone acquisition. To control for potential differences in sociodemographic characteristics between prone and supine sleepers which we found and which have been reported by others,[20,24] we conducted a logistic regression analysis and found that sleep position retained a significant effect on early infant motor development. In addition, we attempted to minimize the bias introduced by parental report by also having the physicians assess the infants' developmental progress at well-child visits. When physician assessment was discrepant with parental report, the former was used in the analysis.

Whereas our study showed that most infants, regardless of sleep position, walk independently close to the time of the first birthday, the developmental progression is affected by sleep position. During infancy, supine sleepers lag behind prone sleepers in milestones that require the use of the upper trunk, specifically the upper extremities and shoulder girdle muscles: rolling prone to supine, tripod sitting, creeping, crawling, and pulling to stand. This upper-extremity muscle development occurs routinely in infants who spend time in the prone position. The milestones in which we did not find significant differences (rolling supine to prone, sitting unsupported, and walking) require less upper body strength and thus may be achievable regardless of upper-extremity muscle development. Other studies have suggested that coordination of fine-motor skills may be advanced in supine sleepers.[25] However, we found no differences between the groups when we looked at the milestone of transferring small objects from one hand to another.

Although supine sleepers attained some motor milestones as much as 1 month later than the prone sleepers, it is important to emphasize that they still attained these milestones within the accepted time range for normal. In fact, even the supine sleepers achieved milestones at ages faster than traditional means. This may be the result of increased parental vigilance and awareness of motor milestone attainment from participating in the study. It is yet unclear if there are any long-term developmental effects from sleep positioning. Because there does not seem to be a difference in attainment of walking skills or of some of the 18-month-old milestones,[9] this difference in milestone attainment may be transient. However, further studies are indicated as this generation of predominantly supine sleepers becomes older.

As more of the US population adopts supine infant sleep positioning, pediatricians need to be able to provide parental reassurance that the differences in milestone acquisition are not developmental delays, but rather are still within well-accepted normal ranges for development. It must be emphasized that this difference in developmental acquisition is not a reason for parents or pediatricians to abandon the AAP sleep recommendations. Pediatricians also need to actively incorporate the encouragement of prone play at the 2- and 4-month well-child visits to maximize development of upper-body strength.

ACKNOWLEDGMENTS

The authors would like to thank the following pediatricians in the Children's Pediatric Research Network: Valorie Anlage, MD; Louis Bland, MD; Steven Brown, MD; Angela Gadsby, MD; James Kalliongis, MD; Albert Modlin, MD; My Huong Nguyen, MD; Edward Padow, MD; Ann Werner, MD; Pamela Parker, MD; Ellen Fields, MD; Nancy Cohen, MD; Denise DeConcini, MD; Carol Miller, MD; Toby Ascherman, MD; Daniel Shapiro, MD; Jeffrey Bernstein, MD; Linda Paxton, MD; Robin Witkin, MD; Marvin Tabb, MD; Eugene Sussman, MD; Elizabeth Lubas, MD; Bonnie Zetlin, MD; Timothy Patterson, MD; Earlene Jordan, MD; Linda Williams, MD; Ivy Masserman, MD; Herbert Berkowitz, MD; James Burgin, MD; Melvin Feldman, MD; Dan Glaser, MD; Alan Gober, MD; Leonard Lefkowitz, MD; John Lowe, MD; Nancy Tang, MD; Stuart Weich, MD; Cheryl Dias, MD; Richard Hollander, MD; Larry Cohen, MD; Blair Big, MD; Robin Madden, MD; Ray Coleman, MD; Allan Coleman, MD; Viola Cheng, MD; Rosella Castro, MD; Carla Sguigna, MD; Nancy Zimmerman, PNP; and Patti Murakami, PNP. We thank Laurette Cressler and Naomi Bloom Gershon for data collection, and Bruce Sprague and Kantilal Patel, PhD, for statistical analysis. We also express appreciation to the families who participated in the study.

REFERENCES

1. American Academy of Pediatrics Task Force on Infant Positioning and SIDS. *Pediatrics.* 1992;89:1120–1126
2. American Academy of Pediatrics Task Force on Infant Positioning and SIDS. Positioning and sudden infant death syndrome (SIDS): update. *Pediatrics.* 1996;98:1216–1218
3. Ueda R. Standardization of the Denver Developmental Screening Test of Tokyo children. *Dev Med Child Neurol.* 1978;20:647–656
4. Song J, Zhu Y, Gu X. Restandardization of the Denver Developmental Screening Test for Shanghai children. *Chin Med J. (Engl).* 1982;6:95
5. Lim HC, Chan T, Yoong T. Standardization and adaptation of the Denver Developmental Screening Test (DDST) and Denver II for use in Singapore children. *Singapore Med J.* 1994;35:156–160
6. Fung KP, Lau SP. Denver developmental screening test: cultural variables. (Letter). *J. Pediatr.* 1985;106:343
7. Bryant GM, Davies KJ, Newcombe RG. The Denver Developmental Screening Test. Achievement of test items in the first year of life by Denver and Cardiff infant. *Dev Med Child Neurol.* 1974;16:475–484
8. Jantz JW, Blosser CD, Fruechting LA. A motor milestone change noted with a change in sleep position. *Arch Pediatr Adolesc Med.* 1997;151:565–568
9. Dewey C, Fleming P, Golding J, ALSPAC Study Team. Does the supine sleeping position have any adverse effects on the child? II. Development in the first 18 months. *Pediatrics* 1998;101:(1). URL: http://www.pediatrics.org/cgi/content/full/101/1/e5
10. Willinger M, Hoffman H, Scheidt PC, et al. Infant sleep position and SIDS in the United States. (Abstract). *Am J Dis Child.* 1993;147:460
11. Hunt L, Fleming P, Golding J, ALSPAC Study Team. Does the supine sleeping position have any adverse effects on the child? I. Health in the first six months. *Pediatircs.* 1997;100(1). URL: http://www.pediatrics.org/cgi/content/full/100/1/e11
12. Frankenburg W, Fandal A, Thornton S. Revision of Denver Prescreening Developmental Questionnaire. *J Pediatr.* 1987;110:653–657
13. Frankenburg W, Camp B, Van Netta P. Validity of the Denver Developmental Screening Test. *Child Dev.* 1971;42:476–482
14. Rosenbaum M, Chua-Lim C, Wilhite J, Mankad V. Applicability of the Denver Prescreening Developmental Questionnaire in a low-income population. *Pediatrics.* 1983;71:359–363
15. Kemp JS, Livne M, White DK, Arfken CL. Softness and potential to cause rebreathing: differences in bedding used by infants at high and low risk for sudden infant death syndrome. *J Pediatr.* 1998;132:234–239
16. Capute A, Shapiro B, Palmer F, Ross A, Wachtel R. Normal gross motor development: the influences of race, sex and socio-economic status. *Dev Med Child Neurol.* 1985;27:635–643
17. Capute A, Accardo P. *Developmental Disabilities in Infancy and Childhood.* Baltimore, MD: Paul H. Brookes Publishing Co; 1991
18. Holt K. Early motor development: posturally induced variations. *J Pediatr.* 1960;57:571–575
19. Bryant GM, Davies KJ, Newcombe RG. Standardization of the Denver Developmental Screening Test for Cardiff children. *Dev Med Child Neurol.* 1979;21:353–364
20. Taylor JA, Davis RL. Risk factors for the infant prone sleep position. *Arch Pediatr Adolesc Med.* 1996;150:834–837
21. Rainey D, Lawless M. Infant positioning and SIDS: acceptance of the nonprone position among clinic mothers. *Clin Pediatr.* 1994;33:322–324
22. Modlin J, Hawker A, Costello A. An investigation into the effect of sleeping position on some aspects of early development. *Dev Med Child Neurol.* 1973;15:287–292
23. Mildred J, Beard K, Dallwitz A, Unwin J. Play position is influenced by knowledge of SIDS sleep position recommendations. *J Paediatr Child Health.* 1995;31:499–502
24. Ottolini MC, Davis, BE, Patel K, Sachs HC, Moon RY. Prone sleeping despite the "Back to Sleep" campaign. Presented at the Ambulatory Pediatric Association Meeting; May 1, 1998; New Orleans, LA. Abstract
25. Francis-Williams J, Yule W. The Bayley Infant Scales of Mental and Motor Development: an exploratory study with an English sample. *Dev Med Child Neurol.* 1967;9:391–401

Categories in Young Children's Thinking

Susan A. Gelman

The world is potentially a bewildering place for young children. Every day a child's senses are bombarded by countless different sights, sounds, tastes, and smells. Furthermore, all this variety is constantly changing, since the world is not a static place: people move, voices come and go, TV images flit across the screen, and new smells waft in as meals are served. In the nineteenth century William James (1890) suggested that infants and young children are overwhelmed by all this diversity, and they experience the world as a "blooming, buzzing confusion." Over the past few decades, however, researchers have discovered that even young children are able to make sense of the world by forming categories. A *category* is any grouping of things that are different in some way. Every time children use a word, put away a toy in the toy box, recognize a person's gender, or decide that a particular food is "yucky," they are using categories to organize their experience. Simple words like "doggie," "milk," or "ball" are among children's earliest categories of the world around them.

This article will review some of the research on children's early categories. One of the most important findings from recent studies is that children can be quite sophisticated in how they group objects and think about those groupings. Children certainly do view the world somewhat differently from adults. However, the picture that emerges from recent research is that young children's categories are extremely important for guiding how they think about the world at large.

> **Researchers have consistently found that even newborns form sensible categories of simple sights, sounds, tastes, and smells. In some ways babies seem to be born knowing how to carve up the world into categories.**

Early errors

Many past studies have shown that preschool children's categories differ from those of older children or adults. One primary difference is that the preschooler is more focused on superficial properties: how things look or where they can be found. We can see this with children's earliest words. Children younger than about age two-and-a-half typically "overextend" their words by applying them in overly broad ways, such as calling any round object a ball or any four-legged animal a dog (Clark 1973). These overextension errors have been documented in children learning a variety of languages across many different cultures.

Piaget's own observations suggest that throughout early childhood children form categories that seem immature from the standpoint of an adult (Inhelder & Piaget 1964). For example, if a five-year-old is asked to sort a set of plastic shapes, he might arrange them into a picture (such as putting a triangle on top of a square to form a house) rather than place together those of the same shape (such as separating all the triangles from all the squares). Likewise, preschool children often tend to put together items that go together in a scene rather than items that are alike in more fundamental ways. For instance, if a four-year-old is given pictures of a spider, a grasshopper, and a web and is asked to "put together the ones that go

Susan A. Gelman, Ph.D., is professor of psychology at the University of Michigan. She has received awards from the American Psychological Association, the J. S. Guggenheim Foundation, and the National Science Foundation for her research on concept and language learning in children.

This is one of a regular series of Research in Review columns. The column in this issue was invited by Research in Review Editor} Carol Seefeldt, Ph.D., professor at the University of Maryland, College Park.

Illustrations © by Patti Argoff.

together," she typically will place the spider with the web (a *thematic* grouping) rather than with the grasshopper (a *taxonomic* grouping) (Smiley & Brown 1979). At this age, children also typically find it difficult to group together things in two different ways at the same time, such as realizing that someone can be *both* a boy *and* a brother (Piaget 1928; Markman 1989).

These kinds of difficulties are typical of preschool children and disappear as children get older. The same child who at age two is calling a tomato a ball will have no problem grouping it with other fruits and vegetables at age six, and may very well become a botanist as an adult! It is important to keep in mind, however, that the kinds of errors I've described above are not the only ways that young children classify. As described next, children are in some ways much more capable than these early errors would suggest.

Early abilities

One way to observe early capabilities is to study infants. In the past 20 years, researchers have devised ingenious experimental methods for gauging what infants know. Researchers measure the very simple behaviors that infants can do, such as head-turns, sucking on a pacifier, gazing, facial expressions, and even heartbeats. Using these methods, researchers have consistently found that even newborns form sensible categories of simple sights, sounds, tastes, and smells (Mehler & Fox 1985). One-month-old babies group together speech sounds in much the same way as adults do, for example, perceiving that "bay" and "day" are different sounds. Before they are six months of age, infants categorize faces and emotional expressions (happy, sad, angry). They perceive colors, objects, even kinds of animals—all well before they can even speak (Quinn, Eimas, & Rosenkrantz 1993). It seems clear, then, that simple categories are not beyond the capacity of young children. In some ways babies seem to be born knowing how to carve up the world into categories.

Perhaps even more impressive is the behavior of children who are "experts." Chi, Mervis, and their colleagues have studied young children who are exceptionally interested in a particular topic, such as dinosaurs, birds, or the game of chess. For example, one dinosaur expert who was studied at age four-and-a-half had been exposed to dinosaur information since turning three, and his parents read dinosaur books to him for an average of three hours per week (Chi & Koeske 1983). Another child became expert in identifying and naming birds and

Children younger than about age two-and-a-half typically "overextend" their words by applying them in overly broad ways, such as calling any round object a ball or any four-legged animal a dog.

could identify 118 different kinds of birds by four years of age (Johnson & Mervis 1994). The general finding from this research is that when children know a great deal about a specialized domain, their categories look remarkably like the categories one would find with older children or even adults. Age seems to present few barriers for a child who has become an expert on a certain topic. Chi, Hutchinson, and Robin (1989) studied four-year-old children who were highly knowledgeable about the domain of dinosaurs and found that their categories of dinosaurs were detailed, factually correct, and chock-full of information. These results tell us that even preschoolers can form mature categories.

We turn next to the question of how children use categories to think about information that is not immediately obvious.

Beyond the obvious

In *Beyond the Information Given*, Bruner (1973) points out that most of what we know about the world around us is not directly shown or visible. Instead, we make inferences from whatever information is available to go beyond what is most immediate. One can intuitively appreciate this point by considering a few familiar proverbs: "Don't judge a book by its cover," "Beauty is only skin deep," "Appearances can be deceiving." In real life,

Preschool children typically find it difficult to group together things in two different ways at the same time, such as realizing that someone can be both a boy and a brother.

as in proverbs, how something looks can be misleading. Consider the trick-or-treater at Halloween who looks like a witch but is really the second-grader down the street; the apple that looks luscious on the outside but is full of worms inside; the animal that flies in the sky and looks like a bird but is really a bat.

Notice that these examples involve contrasting categories: witch versus girl, edible versus inedible, bird versus bat. Much of "going beyond the information given" involves forming categories that are based on information that's neither obvious nor visible.

I would like to turn now to the question of how and when children realize that categories go beyond the obvious. I will review three areas of research evidence with preschool children: the appearance-reality distinction, the power of words, and the thinking on biological growth. The theme that will emerge is that by four years of age preschool children clearly understand that categories include nonobvious information. In the summary, I bring out the positive—and negative—implications of this understanding for young children.

The appearance-reality distinction

When do children realize that appearances can be deceiving? Past research finds that, although three-year-olds have some difficulties holding in mind the distinction between appearance and reality, these difficulties greatly subside during the preschool years. For example, some years ago deVries (1969) examined children's reactions to a docile cat wearing a dog mask. Children first saw that the cat was harmless; then the cat briefly disappeared behind a screen, reappearing a moment later with the dog mask in place. Some of the three-year-olds become quite frightened after viewing the transformation and insisted that the cat had turned into a dog. However, by age six the children typically reported that the animal wasn't really a dog; it was only a cat wearing a mask.

Flavell (1986) found a marked shift between ages three and four in how children reason about appearance-reality conflicts. He presented children with deceptive objects, such as a glass of milk taken from plain view and placed behind an orange filter. Even though children saw for themselves that the filter changed the appearance of

These are all tigers, even though they are wearing and doing different things.

the object, the three-year-olds typically insisted that appearance and reality were one and the same—for example, that the liquid looked orange and that it was "really and truly" orange juice. In contrast, the four-year-olds understood that even though the liquid looked orange, it was "really and truly" milk. Part of the difficulty for three-year-olds seems to be keeping both appearance and reality in mind at the same time.

Other researchers have found some awareness of the appearance-reality distinction at even younger ages. When children are able to view a costume change directly, even three-year-olds realize that wearing a costume doesn't affect identity (Keil 1989). So, for example, a horse wearing a zebra costume is still a horse.

In fact, by four years of age, children realize that the "insides" of an animal or object may be even more important than its "outsides" for identifying what it is. In our own work Wellman and I asked children to show us

When do children realize that appearances can be deceiving? Research finds that, although three-year-olds have some difficulties holding in mind the distinction between appearance and reality, these difficulties greatly subside during the preschool years. When appearance-reality distinctions (for example, you are still you even if you have on a mask) are complex or tricky, young children are still more likely than older children to get confused.

which items had the same outsides and which had the same insides (Gelman & Wellman 1991). By age four, children could tell us that items that were alike on the outside were not necessarily alike on the inside. For example, a piggy bank and a real pig were judged to be alike on the outside but not the inside. Conversely, a real pig and a cow were judged to be alike on the inside but not the outside. Furthermore, when we asked children what would happen if a dog, say, didn't have its blood and bones, four- and five-year-olds told us that it would no longer be a dog and would no longer bark or eat dog food. However, when we asked them what would happen if a dog didn't have its fur, they reported that it still would be a dog and still could bark. Even though children can't see an object's insides, they understand that insides can be more important than outward appearances.

One final note about the appearance-reality distinction: Although four-year-olds *can* appreciate the distinction, this does not mean that they always *do*. When appearance-reality distinctions are complex or tricky, young children still are more likely than older children to get confused. For example, early elementary school children continue to err when asked whether superficial changes affect animal identity, often reporting that operations, ingestion of pills, or injections that result in physical appearance changes also can change what an animal actually is (Keil 1989).

The power of words

Young children place great weight on the names we give to things. Piaget (1929) suggested that children at first think that names are linked to the "essence" of a category: "In learning the names of things the child at this stage believes it is doing much more." He observed that children have some difficulty recognizing that the words we assign to objects are arbitrary, and instead they attach special significance to the name itself.

More recently, research has shown that children use category names (bird, dinosaur, squirrel) as a guide to extending their knowledge and making inferences. Children tend to assume that animals with the same category name are alike in important, nonobvious ways (Gelman & Markman 1986). For example, preschool children as young as two-and-a-half years typically assume that different kinds of birds all live in nests, feed their babies the same kinds of food, and have the same kinds of bones inside. Even when we teach children biological facts that they've never heard before, three- and four-year-olds generalize these facts to other animals with the same name.

We found also that children make use of new names that they learn in the context of the research study. For example, Coley and I showed two-and-a-half-year-old children pictures of unfamiliar animals such as a pterodactyl and a leaf-insect (Gelman & Coley 1990). One group of children learned no names for these animals and tended to assume incorrect labels for them (for example, that the pterodactyl was a bird and the leaf-insect a leaf). A second group of children learned the correct category names for these animals, for example, "dinosaur" for the pterodactyl and "bug" for the leaf-insect. We then asked children various questions about the animals: whether or not the pterodactyl lived in a nest, whether or not the leaf-insect grew on a tree, and so forth. The children who had not learned the correct names typically answered the questions incorrectly, assuming that the pterodactyl lived in a nest (like other flying animals) or the leaf-insect grew on a tree. But the children who had learned the new category names made appropriate inferences based on the names. They said that the pterodactyl, like other dinosaurs, did not live in a nest, for example. Simply providing a name for the animal changed how children thought about the animal and what inferences they made.

Preschool children pay close attention to the words we apply not just to categories of animals but also to categories of people. Hearing a child labeled "boy" or "girl" has vast implications for the kinds of inferences children form (Gelman, Collman, & Maccoby 1986). Preschoolers expect that a child's behaviors, preferences,

---

Sample Generalizations Expressed in Spontaneous Talk

Some generalizations expressed by mothers

"Remember, I told you cats like balls of yarn?"

"That's a chipmunk. And they eat the acorns."

"Did you know when pigs get big, they're called hogs?"

"A wok is how people in China cook. Well, actually, a wok is how people in America cook like Chinese people."

Some generalizations expressed by children*

"That shirt's not for girls." (Ross, two years, seven months)

"Animals eat berries and they eat mushrooms." (Abe, two years, nine months)

"Indians live in Africa." (Adam, three years, three months)

"Bad guys have some guns." (Mark, three years, seven months)

*Bloom (1970), Brown (1973), Kuczaj (1976), Mac Whinney and Snow (1985, 1990), and Sachs (1983 have made their transcripts of adult-child interactions available through the Child Language Data Exchange System (CHILDES).

These are all pigs, even though they are wearing and doing different things.

goals, physical properties, and future identity can all be predicted based on whether the child is referred to as a boy or a girl. Children make such inferences even if they are thinking about a child whose appearance is atypical, such as a boy with long hair or a girl with very short hair. What is important in these cases is that an adult supplies the gender category label (boy, girl). If an adult doesn't say whether the child in question is a boy or a girl, children often have difficulty coming up with the correct classification on their own and tend instead to make inferences based on appearances. So when they meet a long-haired boy, many four-year-olds will assume that the child is a girl and plays with dolls. As soon as they hear he is a boy, however, their way of thinking about the child shifts.

Recently my colleagues and I have started to look at the kinds of generalizations children spontaneously express in their everyday talk and the kinds of generalizations that mothers express when talking with their children (Gelman et al. in press). Our focus was on statements and questions referring to an entire category rather than those referring to only a portion of a category. For example, we examined those times that children and mothers talked about mice (as a general category) rather than *some* mice, *my* mouse, or *those* mice. In other words, we wished to see when children and parents go beyond the specific context they are in to think about the category as an abstract whole. The box "Sample Generalizations Expressed in Spontaneous Talk," lists some examples.

Rodriguez and I are finding that children begin making broad generalizations about categories as early as

two-and-a-half years of age, but that these generalizations increase rather dramatically between two-and-a-half and four years. This result suggests that children may become increasingly attentive to categories during this period. We are also finding that the sorts of generalizations that both children and parents express are especially frequent for categories of people and animals (for example, in the box these categories include cats, chipmunks, pigs, girls, animals, Indians, and bad guys). Both mothers and children make many fewer generalizations about categories of inert objects such as shoes, books, chairs.

Children sometimes maintain these generalizations even in the face of conflicting information. For example, consider the conversation that I recently had with my three-and-a-half-year-old son:

Adam: Kids don't like coffee. Grown-ups do.
Me: I don't like coffee.
Adam: Yes you do! You're not a kid.

Similarly, many children express strong gender-stereotyped beliefs in the preschool years, reporting, for example, that mommies can't be doctors or that boys can't play with dolls (Liben & Signorella 1987). These category-based generalizations seem somewhat rigid and inflexible at the preschool age and are not easily overcome simply by giving the child counterevidence.

It is not yet clear whether or how the talk that children hear from others and other caregivers affects the kinds of generalizations they form. Do children who hear many generalizations tend to generalize more broadly than children who do not? Do the sorts of categories that parents and other caregivers talk about in this way affect how children think about these particular categories? For example, if a caregiver expresses many generalizations about gender categories, does this lead children to notice gender more or to make more inferences based on gender? These are important questions that await future research.

Thinking about biological growth

Caterpillars turn into butterflies, tadpoles turn into frogs, babies become adults, and acorns become oak trees. These examples of growth and metamorphosis provide an interesting arena for looking at how children un-

When children know a great deal about a specialized domain, their categories look remarkably like the categories one would find with older children or even adults.

Preschoolers expect that a child's behaviors, preferences, goals, physical properties, and future identity can all be predicted based on whether the child is referred to as a boy or a girl. Children sometimes maintain these generalizations even in the face of conflicting information. Many children express strong gender-stereotyped beliefs in the preschool years, reporting, for example, that mommies can't be doctors or that boys can't play with dolls.

derstand categories because in every case the category member undergoes dramatic change and yet in some sense remains the same.

Long before they have any detailed knowledge of biological processes children come to understand several fundamental points about growth (Rosengren et al. 1991; Hickling & Gelman 1995). Four-year-olds understand that an individual animal can change shape, color, and size over the course of growth yet still keep the same name and identity. They understand that every kind of plant comes from a specialized kind of seed; for example, apple trees come from apple sees. They understand that the growth cycle is predictable and repeating: from seed to plant to fruit to seed to plant to fruit, and so on. They recognize that growth itself comes about due to natural processes (such as sunshine and rain) and not due to artificial processes (such as human activities).

Four-year-olds also realize that nature can "win out" over nurture. For example, if four-year-old children hear about an animal that is adopted by another species and raised in this atypical environment (e.g., a cow raised by pigs), they predict that the animal will continue to grow and develop just like the birth parents (Gelman & Wellman 1991)—the cow will moo and have a straight tail when it grows up, even though it has been raised by pigs. Preschool children make similar predictions about nature-nurture conflicts with seeds (e.g., a lemon seed planted in a cornfield) or people (e.g., a baby whose birth parents and adoptive parents differ in skin color or personality traits) (Hirschfeld 1996; Springer 1996; Taylor 1996).

Taken altogether, these studies suggest that four-year-old children view growth and development as natural processes (Gelman & Kremer 1991) unfolding inside the animal or plant rather than resulting from outside influences. They expect that a great deal of how an animal or plant grows and develops is fixed at birth in the infant animal or the seed of the plant.

Children at age three know a great deal less about biological growth (Gelman & Wellman 1991; Rosengren et al. 1991; Hickling & Gelman 1995). It may be that early experiences are contributing to the changes between ages three and four. One study found that children who care for a pet goldfish at home are more knowledgeable about biology than children who do not (Inagaki 1990). However, at this point little is known about the kinds of ex-

periences that children have with growth and metamorphosis in their preschools and at home and how these experiences affect children's understanding of growth.

Summary

Children have an impressive understanding of categories by age four—they grasp the distinction between appearance and reality, they use names as a guide for making inferences, and they realize that growth is an orderly, natural process. To some extent, even two-and-a-half- and three-year-old children show some of these same early understandings. However, there are also developmental changes during the preschool period (especially between two-and-a-half and four years of age). The youngest children are apt to have more difficulties with the appearance-reality distinction, are less apt to form spontaneous generalizations using the categories that they have, and are easily confused about the growth process.

Altogether the lesson we have learned from studying children's early categories is that categories are tremendously important tools for young children and have implications for how they view the world. Like any tools, categories can be used in either useful or inappropriate ways. We have already seen some of the dangers in early categories: children sometimes take names more seriously than they should and draw overly broad generalizations based on the categories that they know. Overall, however, we view the effects of categories as mostly positive. Children make use of categories to expand their knowledge. By simply naming objects we can encourage children to notice how different items are similar and help children gain new information about the world. Furthermore, because children expect items in a category to be alike in nonobvious ways, they are able to learn about "scientific" properties (such as the insides of animals) well before kindergarten age. Both of these implications illustrate that categories are the foundation for later learning in school.

References

Bloom, L. 1970. Language development: Form and function in emerging grammars. Cambridge, MA: MIT Press.

Brown, R. W. 1973. A first language: The early stages. Cambridge, MA: Harvard University Press.

Bruner, J. S. 1973. *Beyond the information given: Studies in the psychology of knowing.* New York: Norton.

Chi, M., J. Hutchinson, & A. Robin. 1989. How inference about novel domain-related concepts can be constrained by structured knowledge. Merrill-Palmer Quarterly 35: 27–62.

Chi, M. T. H., & R. D. Koeske. 1983. Network representation of a child's dinosaur knowledge. *Developmental Psychology* 19: 29–39.

Clark, E. V. 1973. What's in a word? On the child's acquisition of semantics in his first language. In *Cognitive development and the acquisition of language,* ed. T. E. Moore. New York: Academic.

deVries, R. 1969. *Constancy of generic identity in the years three to six.* Monographs of the Society for Research in Child Development, vol. 34, no. 3, serial no. 127. Chicago: University of Chicago Press.

Flavell, J. H. 1986. The development of children's knowledge about the appearance-reality distinction. *American Psychologist* 41: 418–25.

Gelman, S. A., & J. D. Coley. 1990. The importance of knowing a dodo is a bird: Categories and inferences in 2-year-old children. *Developmental Psychology* 26: 796–804.

Gelman, S.A., J. D. Coley, K. Rosengren, E. Hartman, & T. Pappas. In press. *Beyond labeling: The role of maternal input in the acquisition of richly-structured categories.* Monographs of the Society for Research in Child Development. Chicago: University of Chicago Press.

Gelman, S. A., P. Collman, & E. E. Maccoby. 1986. Inferring properties from categories versus inferring categories from properties: The case of gender. *Child Development* 57: 396–404.

Gelman, S. A., & K. E. Kremer. 1991. Understanding natural causes: Children's explanations of how objects and their properties originate. *Child Development* 62: 396–414.

Gelman, S. A., & E. M. Markman. 1986. Categories and induction in young children. *Cognition* 23: 183–209.

Gelman, S. A., & H. M. Wellman. 1991. Insides and essences: Early understandings of the non-obvious. *Cognition* 38: 213–44.

Hickling, A. K., & S. A. Gelman. 1995. How does your garden grow? Early conceptualization of seeds and their place in plant growth cycle. *Child Development* 66: 856–76.

Hirschfeld, L. A. 1996. *Race in the making: Cognition, culture, and the child's construction of human kinds.* Cambridge, MA: MIT Press.

Inagaki, K. 1990. The effects of raising animals on children's biological knowledge. *British Journal of Developmental Psychology* 8: 119–29.

Inhelder, B., & J. Piaget. 1964. *The early growth of logic in the child.* New York: Norton.

James, W. 1890. *The principles of psychology.* New York: Dover.

Johnson, K. E., & C. B. Mervis. 1994. Microgenetic analysis of first steps in children's acquisition of expertise on shorebirds. *Developmental Psychology* 30: 418–35.

Keil, F. C. 1989. *Concepts, kinds, and cognitive development.* Cambridge, MA: MIT Press.

Kuczaj, S. 1976. -ing, -s, and -ed: A study of the acquisition of certain verb inflections. Ph.D. diss., University of Minnesota.

Liben, L. S., & M. L. Signorella, eds. 1987, *Children's gender schemata.* San Francisco: Jossey-Bass.

MacWhinney, B., & C. Snow. 1985. The Child Language Data Exchange System. *Journal of Child Language* 12: 271–95.

MacWhinney, B., & C. Snow. 1990. The Child Language Data Exchange System: An update. *Journal of Child Language* 17: 457–72.

Markman, E. M. 1989. *Categorization and naming in children: Problems of induction.* Cambridge, MA: MIT Press.

Mehler, J., & R. Fox, eds. 1985. *Neonate cognition: Beyond the blooming, buzzing confusion.* Hillsdale, NJ: Erlbaum.

Piaget, J. 1928. *Judgement and reasoning in the child.* London: Routledge & Kegan Paul.

Piaget, J. 1929. *The child's conception of the world.* London: Routledge & Kegan Paul.

Quinn, P. C., P. D. Eimas, & S. L. Rosenkrantz. 1993. Evidence for representations of perceptually similar natural categories by 3-month-old and 4-month-old infants. *Perception* 22: 463–75.

Rosengren, K. S., S. A. Gelman, C. W. Kalish, & M. McCormick, 1991. As time goes by: Children's early understanding of growth in animals. *Child Development* 62: 1302–20.

Sachs, J. 1983. Talking about the there and then: The emergence of displaced reference in parent-child discourse. In *Children's language, vol. 4,* ed. K. E. Nelson. Hillsdale, NJ: Erlbaum.

Smiley, S. S., & A. L. Brown. 1979. Conceptual preference for thematic or taxonomic relations: A nonmonotonic age trend from preschool to old age. *Journal of Experimental Child Psychology* 28: 249–57.

Springer, K. 1996. Young children's understanding of a biological basis for parent-offspring relations. *Child Development* 67: 2841–56.

Taylor, M. G. 1996. The development of children's beliefs about social and biological aspects of gender differences. *Child Development* 67: 1555–71.

Why Children Talk to Themselves

Although children are often rebuked for talking to themselves out loud, doing so helps them control their behavior and master new skills

by Laura E. Berk

A s any parent, teacher, sitter or casual observer will notice, young children talk to themselves—sometimes as much or even more than they talk to other people. Depending on the situation, this private speech (as modern psychologists call the behavior) can account for 20 to 60 percent of the remarks a child younger than 10 years makes. Many parents and educators misinterpret this chatter as a sign of disobedience, inattentiveness

LAURA E. BERK is currently a professor of psychology and Outstanding University Researcher at Illinois State University. She received her B.A. in psychology from the University of California, Berkeley, and her M.A. and Ph.D. in educational psychology from the University of Chicago. Berk has been a visiting scholar at Cornell University, at the University of California, Los Angeles, and at Stanford University, and her research has been funded by the U.S. Office of Education and the National Institute of Child Health and Human Development. She is co-editor of *Private Speech: From Social Interaction to Self-Regulation* and author of two widely distributed textbooks, *Child Development* and *Infants, Children, and Adolescents.* She has also written numerous journal articles.

or even mental instability. In fact, private speech is an essential part of cognitive development for all children. Recognition of this fact should strongly influence how both normal children and children who have trouble learning are taught.

Although private speech has presumably been around as long as language itself, the political climate in Russia in the 1930s, and the authority of a great Western cognitive theorist, prevented psychologists and educators from understanding its significance until only very recently. In Russia more than six decades ago, Lev S. Vygotsky, a prominent psychologist, first documented the importance of private speech. But at that time, the Stalinist regime systematically persecuted many intellectuals, and purges at universities and research institutes were common.

In fear, Soviet psychologists turned on one another. Some declared Vygotsky a renegade, and several of his colleagues and students split from his circle. According to the recollections of one of Vygotsky's students, the Communist party scheduled a critical "discussion" in which Vygotsky's ideas would be the major target. But in 1934, before Vygotsky could replicate and extend his preliminary studies or defend his position to the party, he died of tuberculosis. Two years later the Commu-

nist party banned his published work.

In addition to not knowing about Vygotsky, Western psychologists and educators were convinced by the eminent Swiss theorist Jean Piaget that private speech plays no positive role in normal cognitive development. In the 1920s, even before Vygotsky began his inquiries, Piaget had completed a series of seminal studies in which he carefully recorded the verbalizations of three- to seven-year-olds at the J. J. Rousseau Institute of the University of Geneva. Besides social remarks, Piaget identified three additional types of utterances that were not easily understood or clearly addressed to a listener: the children repeated syllables and sounds playfully, gave soliloquies and delivered what Piaget called collective monologues.

Piaget labeled these three types of speech egocentric, expressing his view that they sprang only from immature minds. Young children, he reasoned, engage in egocentric speech because they have difficulty imagining another's perspective. Much of their talk then is talk for themselves and serves little communicative function. Instead it merely accompanies, supplements or reinforces motor activity or takes the form of non sequiturs: one child's verbalization stimulates speech in another, but the partner is expected neither to listen nor understand. Piaget believed private speech gradually disappears as children become capable of real social interaction.

Although several preschool teachers and administrators openly questioned Piaget's ideas, he had the last word until Vygotsky's work reached the West in the 1960s. Three years after Joseph Stalin's death in 1953, Nikita S. Khrushchev criticized Stalin's "rule by terror" and announced in its place a policy that encouraged greater intellectual freedom. The 20-year ban on Vygotsky's writings came to an end. In 1962 an English translation of Vygotsky's collection of essays, *Thought and Language,* appeared in the U.S. Within less than a decade, a team led by Lawrence Kohlberg of Harvard University had compiled provocative evidence in support of Vygotsky's ideas.

In the late 1970s some American psychologists were becoming disenchanted with Piaget's theory, and at the same time, a broader range of Vygotsky's writings appeared in English. These conditions, coupled with Kohlberg's results, inspired a flurry of new investigations. Indeed, since the mid-1980s the number of studies done on private speech in the West has increased threefold. Most of these studies, including my own, corroborate Vygotsky's views.

In his papers Vygotsky described a strong link between social experience, speech and learning. According to the Russian, the aspects of reality a child is ready to master lie within what he called the zone of proximal (or potential) development. It refers to a range of tasks that the child cannot yet accomplish without guidance from an adult or more skilled peer. When a child discusses a challenging task with a mentor, that individual offers spoken direction and strategies. The child incorporates the language of those dialogues into his or her private speech and then uses it to guide independent efforts.

"The most significant moment in the course of intellectual development," Vygotsky wrote, " . . . occurs when speech and practical activity, two previously completely independent lines of development, converge." The direction of development, he argued, is not one in which social communication eventually replaces egocentric utterances, as Piaget had claimed. Instead Vygotsky proposed that early social communication precipitates private speech. He maintained that social communication gives rise to all uniquely human, higher cognitive processes. By communicating with mature members of society, children learn to master activities and think in ways that have meaning in their culture.

As the child gains mastery over his or her behavior, private speech need not occur in a fully expanded form; the self, after all, is an extremely understanding listener. Consequently, children omit words and phrases that refer to things they already know about a given situation. They state only those aspects that still seem puzzling. Once their cognitive operations become well practiced, children start to "think words" rather than saying them. Gradually, private speech becomes internalized as silent, inner speech—those conscious dialogues we hold with ourselves while thinking and acting. Nevertheless, the need to engage in private speech never disappears. Whenever we encounter unfamiliar or demanding activities in our lives, private speech resurfaces. It is a tool that helps us overcome obstacles and acquire new skills.

Currently two American research programs, my own and that of Rafael M. Diaz at Stanford University, have sought to confirm and build on Vygotsky's findings. Our respective efforts began with similar questions: Do all children use private speech? Does it help them guide their actions? And does it originate in social communication? To find out, I chose to observe children in natural settings at school; Diaz selected the laboratory.

Ruth A. Garvin, one of my graduate students, and I followed 36 low-income Appalachian five- to

Varieties of Private Speech

Egocentric Communication	Remarks directed to another that make no sense from the listener's perspective.	David says to Mark, who is sitting next to him on the rug, "It broke," without explaining what or when.
Fantasy Play	A child role-plays and talks to objects or creates sound effects for them.	Jay snaps, "Out of my way!" to a chair after he bumps into it.
Emotional Release	Comments not directed to a listener that express feelings, or those that seem to be attempts to review feelings about past events or thoughts.	Rachel is sitting at her desk with an anxious look on her face, repeating to herself, "My mom's sick, my mom's sick."
Self-Direction	A child describes the task at hand and gives himself or herself directions out loud.	Carla, while doing a page in her math book, says out loud, "Six". Then, counting on her fingers, she continues, "Seven, eight, nine, 10. It's 10, it's 10. The answer is 10."
Reading Aloud	A child read written material aloud or sounds out words.	"Sher-lock Holm-lock, Sherlock Holme," Tommy reads, leaving off the final "s" in his second, more successful attempt.
Inaudible Muttering	Utterances so quiet that an observer cannot understand them.	Angela mumbles inaudibly to herself as she works on a math problem.

10-year-olds, who attended a mission school in the mountains of eastern Kentucky. We recorded speech in the classroom, on the playground, in the halls and in the lunchroom throughout the day—paying special attention to those remarks not specifically addressed to a listener.

Our findings revealed that egocentric speech, Piaget's focus, seldom occurred. Most of the comments we heard either described or served to direct a child's actions, consistent with the assumption that self-guidance is the central function of private speech. Moreover, the children talked to themselves more often when working alone on challenging tasks and also when their teachers were not immediately available to help them. In either case, the children needed to take charge of their own behavior.

Furthermore, we found evidence suggesting that private speech develops similarly in all children and that it arises in social experience. The private speech of the Appalachian students changed as they grew older in ways that were much like those patterns Kohlberg had reported a decade and a half earlier.

Middle-class children, such as those Kohlberg observed, speak out loud to themselves with increasing frequency between four and six years of age. Then, during elementary school, their private speech takes the form of inaudible muttering. The Appalachian children moved through this same sequence but did so more slowly. At age 10, more than 40 percent of their private speech remained highly audible, whereas Kohlberg's 10-year-olds spoke out loud to themselves less than 7 percent of the time.

To explain the difference, we studied Appalachian culture and made a striking discovery. Whereas middle-class parents frequently converse with their children, Appalachian parents do so much less often. Moreover, they usually rely more on gestures than on words. If Vygotsky's theory is correct, that private speech stems from social communication, then this taciturn home environment might explain the slow development of private speech in Appalachian children.

While our Appalachian study was under way, Diaz and one of his graduate students, Marnie H. Frauenglass, videotaped 32 three- to six-year-olds in the laboratory as the youngsters matched pictures and solved puzzles. Frauenglass and Diaz also found that private speech becomes less audible with age. Yet their results, along with those of other researchers, posed serious challenges to Vygotsky's theory. First, many children emitted only a few utterances, and some none at all—seeming proof that private speech is not universal.

Another difficulty arose. If private speech facilitates self-regulation, as Vygotsky believed, then it should relate to how a child behaves while working and how well the child performs. Yet in Frauenglass and Diaz's study, children who used more private speech did worse on the tasks set before them! Other researchers had reported weak and sometimes negative associations between private speech and performance as well.

Diaz crafted some insightful explanations for these outcomes. After a close look at Vygotsky's definition of the zone of proximal development, Diaz concluded that perhaps the tasks typically given in the laboratory were not suitable for evoking private speech in all children. Some children may have been so familiar with solving puzzles and matching pictures that the cognitive operations they needed to succeed were already automatic. Other children may have found these tasks so difficult that they could not master them without help. In either case, self-guiding private speech would not be expected. Furthermore, Diaz reasoned that since private speech increases when children encounter difficulties, it would often coincide with task failure. He suggested that the beneficial impact of private speech might be delayed.

Returning to the classroom—this time, to the laboratory school at Illinois State University—I embarked on a series of studies to test these intriguing possibilities. My team of observers carefully recorded the private speech and task-related actions of 75 first to third graders as they worked alone at their desks on math problems. Their teachers considered this work to be appropriately challenging for each child. Graduate student Jennifer A. Bivens and I then followed the first graders and monitored their behavior as second and third graders.

Every child we observed talked to himself or herself—on average 60 percent of the time. Also, as in previous studies, many children whose remarks described or otherwise commented on their activity received lower scores on homework and achievement tests taken that same year. Yet private speech that was typical for a particular age predicted gains in math achievement over time. Specifically, first graders who made many self-guiding comments out loud or quietly did better at second-grade math. Likewise, second graders who often muttered to themselves grasped third-grade math more easily the following year.

Also, the relationship we noted between a child's use of private speech and his or her task-related behavior bolstered Vygotsky's hypothesis that self-guiding comments help children direct their actions. Children whose speech included a great deal of task-irrelevant wordplay or emotional expression often squirmed in their seats or chewed on or tapped their pencils against their desks.

In contrast, children who frequently made audible comments about their work used more nonverbal techniques to help them overcome difficulties, such as counting on fingers or tracking a line of text using a pencil. Finally, children who most often used quiet private speech rarely fidgeted and were highly attentive. Overall, children who progressed most rapidly from audible remarks to inner speech were more advanced in their ability to control motor activity and focus attention. The development of private speech and task-related behavior thus went hand in hand.

In a later investigation, Sarah T. Spuhl, another of my graduate students, and I attempted to witness in the laboratory the dynamic relationship Vygotsky highlighted between private speech and learning—namely, private speech diminishes as performance improves. We added a new dimension to our research as well: an exploration of how the interaction between a child and an adult can foster self-regulation through private speech.

We asked 30 four- and five-year-olds to assemble Lego pieces into a reproduction of a model. Each subject attempted the exercise in three 15-minute sessions, scheduled no more than two to four days apart. This timing permitted us to track their increasing competence. We pretested each child to ensure that the Lego tasks would be sufficiently challenging—something that had not been done before. Only novice Lego builders participated. Two weeks before the sessions began, we videotaped each mother helping her child with activities that required skills similar to those involved in Lego building, such as fitting blocks together and matching their colors and shapes.

Next we evaluated the communication between the mothers and their children as they solved problems together. According to previous research, parenting that is warm and responsive but exerts sufficient control to guide and encourage children to acquire new skills promotes competence. (Psychologists term such parenting authoritative.) In contrast, both authoritarian parenting (little warmth and high control) and permissive parenting (high warmth and little control) predict learning and adjustment problems. Based on this evidence, we thought that the authoritative style

might best capture those features of adult teaching we wished to identify.

Our results revealed that children who have authoritative mothers more often used self-guiding private speech. Among the four-year-olds, those experiencing authoritative teaching showed greater improvement in skill over the course of the three Leg-building sessions. Furthermore, we did a special statistical analysis, the outcome of which suggested that private speech mediates the relationship between authoritative parenting and task success—a finding consistent with Vygotsky's assumptions.

Unlike previous laboratory research, every child in our sample used private speech. As expected, the children's comments became more internalized over the course of the three sessions as their skill with the Lego blocks increased. And once again, private speech predicted future gains better than it did concurrent task success. In particular, children who used private speech that was appropriate for their age—audible, self-guiding utterances at age four and inaudible muttering at age five—achieved the greatest gains.

Next I turned my attention to children having serious learning and behavior problems. Many psychologists had concluded that elementary school pupils who were inattentive, impulsive or had learning disabilities suffered from deficits in using private speech. To treat these children, researchers had designed and widely implemented training programs aimed at inducing children to talk to themselves. In a typical program, children are asked to mimic a therapist acting out self-guiding private speech while performing a task. Next the therapist demonstrates lip movements only and finally asks the children to verbalize covertly.

Despite the intuitive appeal of this training, the approach most often failed. I suspected that the design of these treatments might have

been premature. The procedures were not grounded in systematic research on how children having learning and behavior problems use private speech. The spontaneous self-regulatory utterances of such children remained largely uninvestigated.

To fill this gap in our knowledge, my graduate student Michael K. Potts and I studied 19 six- to 12-year-old boys who had been clinically diagnosed with attention-deficit hyperactivity disorder (ADHD), a condition characterized by severe inattentiveness, impulsivity and overactivity. Once again, we observed private speech as the subjects worked on mathematics problems at their desks. We compared these observations to the private speech of 19 normal boys matched in age and verbal ability.

Contrary to the assumptions underlying self-instructional training, ADHD boys did not use less private speech. Instead they made substantially more audible, self-guiding remarks than did normal boys. Furthermore, we examined age-related trends and found that the only difference between the two groups was that ADHD boys made the transition from audible speech to more internalized forms at a later age.

We uncovered a possible explanation for this developmental lag. Our results implied that ADHD children's severe attention deficit prevented their private speech from gaining efficient control over their behavior. First, only in the least distractible ADHD boys did audible self-guiding speech correlate with improved attention to math assignments. Second, we tracked a subsample of ADHD subjects while they were both taking and not taking stimulant drug medication, the most widely used treatment for the disorder. (Although stimulants do not cure ADHD, a large body of evidence indicates that they boost attention and academic performance in most children who take them.) We found that this medication sharply increased the maturity of private speech in ADHD boys. And only when these children were medicated did the most mature form of private speech, inaudible muttering, relate to improved self-control.

The promising nature of these findings encouraged me to include children having learning disabilities in the research. My colleague Steven Landau joined me in observing 112 third to sixth graders working on math and English exercises at their desks. Half of the children met the Illinois state guidelines for being classified as learning disabled: their academic achievement fell substantially below what would be expected based on their intelligence. The other half served as controls. As in the ADHD study, we found that the children who had learning disabilities used more audible, self-guiding utterances and internalized their private speech at a later age than did children who did not have a disability. When we looked at a subgroup of learning disabled children who also displayed symptoms of ADHD, this trend was even more pronounced.

Research on children suffering from persistent learning difficulties vigorously supports Vygotsky's view of private speech. These children follow the same course of development as do their unaffected age mates, but impairments in their cognitive processing and ability to pay attention make academic tasks more difficult for them. This difficulty in turn complicates verbal self-regulation. Our findings suggest that training children who have learning and behavior problems to talk to themselves while performing cognitive tasks amounts to no more than invoking a skill they already possess. Furthermore, interventions that push children to move quickly toward silent self-communication may be counterproductive. While concentrating, ADHD and learning-disabled pupils show heightened dependence on audible private speech in an effort to compensate for their cognitive impairments.

How can our current knowledge of private speech guide us in teaching children who learn normally and those who have learning and behavior problems? The evidence as a whole indicates that private speech is a problem-solving tool universally available to children who grow up in rich, socially interactive environments. Several interdependent factors—the demands of a task, its social context and individual characteristics of a child—govern the extent and ease with which any one child uses self-directed speech to guide behavior. The most profitable intervention lies not in viewing private speech as a skill to be trained but rather in creating conditions that help children use private speech effectively.

When a child tries new tasks, he or she needs communicative support from an adult who is patient and encouraging and who offers the correct amount of assistance given the child's current skills. For example, when a child does not understand what an activity entails, an adult might first give the child explicit directions. Once the child realizes how these actions relate to the task's goal, the adult might offer strategies instead. Gradually, adults can withdraw this support as children begin to guide their own initiatives.

Too often, inattentive and impulsive children are denied this scaffold for learning. Because of the stressful behaviors they bring to the adult-child relationship, they are frequently targets of commands, reprimands and criticism, all of which keep them from learning how to control their own actions.

Finally, parents and teachers need to be aware of the functional value of private speech. We now know that private speech is healthy, adaptive and essential behavior and that some children need to use it more often and for a longer period than others. Still, many adults continue to regard private speech as meaningless, socially unacceptable conduct— even as a sign of mental illness. As a result, they often discourage children from talking to themselves. At home, parents can listen to their child's private speech and thus gain insight into his or her plans, goals and difficulties. Likewise, teachers can be mindful of the fact that when pupils use more private speech than is typical for their age, they may need extra support and guidance. Certainly, we have much more to discover about how children solve problems using spontaneous private speech. Nevertheless, Vygotsky's theory has greatly deepened our understanding of this phenomenon. Today it is helping us design more effective teaching methods for all children and treatments for children suffering from learning and behavior problems. One can only regret that earlier generations of psychologists and educators—and those they might have helped—did not have the advantage of Vygotsky's insights.

FURTHER READING

DEVELOPMENT OF PRIVATE SPEECH AMONG LOW-INCOME APPALACHIAN CHILDREN. Laura E. Berk and Ruth A. Garvin in *Developmental Psychology*, Vol. 20, No. 2, pages 271–286; March 1984.

A LONGITUDINAL STUDY OF THE DEVELOPMENT OF ELEMENTARY SCHOOL CHILDREN'S PRIVATE SPEECH. J. A. Bivens and L. E. Berk in *Merrill-Palmer Quarterly*, Vol. 36, No. 4, pages 443–463; October 1990.

VYGOTSKY: THE MAN AND HIS CAUSE. Guillermo Blanck in *Vygotsky and Education: Instructional Implications and Applications of Sociohistorical Psychology*. Edited by Luis C. Moll. Cambridge University Press, 1990.

DEVELOPMENT AND FUNCTIONAL SIGNIFICANCE OF PRIVATE SPEECH AMONG ATTENTION-DEFICIT HYPERACTIVITY DISORDERED AND NORMAL BOYS. Laura E. Berk and Michael K. Potts in *Journal of Abnormal Child Psychology*, Vol. 19, No. 3, pages 357–377; June 1991.

PRIVATE SPEECH: FROM SOCIAL INTERACTION TO SELF-REGULATION. Edited by Rafael M. Diaz and Laura E. Berk. Lawrence Erlbaum Associates, 1992.

PRIVATE SPEECH OF LEARNING DISABLED AND NORMALLY ACHIEVING CHILDREN IN CLASSROOM ACADEMIC AND LABORATORY CONTEXTS. Laura E. Berk and Steven Landau in *Child Development*, Vol. 64, No. 2, pages 556–571; April 1993.

HOW ASIAN TEACHERS POLISH EACH LESSON TO PERFECTION

JAMES W. STIGLER AND HAROLD W. STEVENSON

James Stigler is associate professor of psychology at the University of Chicago. He was awarded the Boyd R. McCandless Young Scientist Award from the American Psychological Association and was awarded a Guggenheim Fellowship for his work in the area of culture and mathematics learning. Harold W. Stevenson is professor of psychology and director of the University of Michigan Program in Child Development and Social Policy. He is currently president of the International Society for the Study of Behavioral Development and has spent the past two decades engaged in cross-cultural research.

This article is based on a book by Harold W. Stevenson and James Stigler, entitled The Learning Gap *(1994).*

ALTHOUGH THERE is no overall difference in intelligence, the differences in mathematical achievement of American children and their Asian counterparts are staggering.[1]

Let us look first at the results of a study we conducted in 120 classrooms in three cities: Taipei (Taiwan); Sendai (Japan); and the Minneapolis metropolitan area. First and fifth graders from representative schools in these cities were given a test of mathematics that required computation and problem solving. Among the one hundred first-graders in the three locations who received the lowest scores, fifty-eight were American children; among the one hundred lowest-scoring fifth graders, sixty-seven were American children. Among the top one hundred first graders in mathematics, there were only fifteen American children. And only one American child appeared among the top one hundred fifth graders. The highest-scoring American classroom obtained an average score lower than that of the lowest-scoring Japanese

classroom and of all but one of the twenty classrooms in Taipei. In whatever way we looked at the data, the poor performance of American children was evident.

These data are startling, but no more so than the results of a study that involved 40 first- and 40 fifth-grade classrooms in the metropolitan area of Chicago—a very representative sample of the city and the suburbs of Cook County—and twenty-two classes in each of these grades in metropolitan Beijing (China). In this study, children were given a battery of mathematics tasks that included diverse problems, such as estimating the distance between a tree and a hidden treasure on a map, deciding who won a race on the basis of data in a graph, trying to explain subtraction to visiting Martians, or calculating the sum of nineteen and forty-five. There was no area in which the American children were competitive with those from China. The Chinese children's superiority appeared in complex tasks involving the application of knowledge as well as in the routines of computation. When fifth graders were asked, for example, how many members of a stamp club with twenty-four members collected only foreign stamps if five-sixths of the members did so, 59 percent of Beijing children, but only 9 percent of the Chicago children produced the correct answer. On a computation test, only 2.2 percent of the Chinese fifth graders scored at or below the mean for their American counterparts. All of the twenty Chicago area schools had average scores on the fifth-grade geometry test that were below those of the Beijing schools. The results from all these tasks paint a bleak picture of American children's competencies in mathematics.[2]

The poor performance of American students compels us to try to understand the reasons why. We have written extensively elsewhere about the cultural differences in

Reprinted with permission from *American Educator*, Spring 1991, pp. 12–20, 43–47. © 1991 by *American Educator*, the quarterly journal of the American Federation of Teachers.

attitudes toward learning and toward the importance of effort vs. innate ability and about the substantially greater amounts of time Japanese and Chinese students devote to academic activities in general and to the study of math in particular.[3] Important as these factors are, they do not tell the whole story. For that we have to take a close look inside the classrooms of Japan, China, and the United States to see how mathematics is actually taught in the three cultures.

LESSONS NOT LECTURES

If we were asked briefly to characterize classes in Japan and China, we would say that they consist of coherent lessons that are presented in a thoughtful, relaxed, and nonauthoritarian manner. Teachers frequently rely on students as sources of information. Lessons are oriented toward problem solving rather than rote mastery of facts and procedures and utilize many different types of representational materials. The role assumed by the teacher is that of knowledgeable guide, rather than that of prime dispenser of information and arbiter of what is correct. There is frequent verbal interaction in the classroom as the teacher attempts to stimulate students to produce, explain, and evaluate solutions to problems. These characteristics contradict stereotypes held by most Westerners about Asian teaching practices. Lessons are not rote; they are not filled with drill. Teachers do not spend large amounts of time lecturing but attempt to lead the children in productive interactions and discussions. And the children are not the passive automata depicted in Western descriptions but active participants in the learning process.

We begin by discussing what we mean by the coherence of a lesson. One way to think of a lesson is by using the analogy of a story. A good story is highly organized; it has a beginning, a middle, and an end; and it follows a protagonist who meets challenges and resolves problems that arise along the way. Above all, a good story engages the readers' interest in a series of interconnected events, which are best understood in the context of the events that precede and follow it.

Such a concept of a lesson guides the organization of instruction in Asia. The curricula are defined in terms of coherent lessons, each carefully designed to fill a forty- to fifty-minute class period with sustained attention to the development of some concept or skill. Like a good story, the lesson has an introduction, a conclusion, and a consistent theme.

We can illustrate what we are talking about with this account of a fifth-grade Japanese mathematics class:

The teacher walks in carrying a large paper bag full of clinking glass. Entering the classroom with a large paper bag is highly unusual, and by the time she has placed the bag on her desk the students are regarding her with rapt attention. What's in the bag? She begins to pull items out of the bag, placing them, one-by-one, on her desk. She removes a pitcher and a vase. A beer bottle evokes laughter and surprise. She soon has six containers lined up on her desk. The children continue to watch intently, glancing back and forth at each other as they seek to understand the purpose of this display.

The teacher, looking thoughtfully at the containers, poses a question: "I wonder which one would hold the most water?" Hands go up, and the teacher calls on different students to give their guesses: "the pitcher," "the beer bottle," "the teapot." The teacher stands aside and ponders: "Some of you said one thing, others said something different. You don't agree with each other. There must be some way we can find out who is correct. How can we know who is correct?" Interest is high, and the discussion continues.

The students soon agree that to find out how much each container holds they will need to fill the containers with something. How about water? The teacher finds some buckets and sends several children out to fill them with water. When they return, the teacher says: "Not what do we do?" Again there is a discussion, and after several minutes the children decide that they will need to use a smaller container to measure how much water fits into each of the larger containers. They decide on a drinking cup, and one of the students warns that they all have to fill each cup to the same level—otherwise the measure won't be the same for all of the groups.

At this point the teacher divides the class into their groups *(han)* and gives each group one of the containers and a drinking cup. Each group fills its container, counts how many cups of water it holds, and writes the result in a notebook. When all of the groups have completed the task, the teacher calls on the leader of each group to report on the group's findings and notes the results on the blackboard. She has written the names of the containers in a column on the left and a scale from 1 to 6 along the bottom. Pitcher, 4.5 cups; vase, 3 cups; beer bottle, 1.5 cups; and so on. As each group makes its report, the teacher draws a bar representing the amount, in cups, the container holds.

Finally, the teacher returns to the question she posed at the beginning of the lesson: Which container holds the most water? She reviews how they were able to solve the problem and points out that the answer is now contained in the bar graph on the board. She then arranges the containers on the table in order according to how much they hold and writes a rank order on each container, from 1 to 6. She ends the class with a brief review of what they have done. No definitions of ordinate and abscissa, no discussion of how to make a graph preceded the example—these all became obvious in the course of the lesson, and only at the end did the teacher mention the terms that describe the horizontal and vertical axes of the graph they had made.

With one carefully crafted problem, this Japanese teacher has guided her students to discover—and most likely to remember—several important concepts. As this article unfolds, we hope to demonstrate that this example of how well-designed Asian class lessons are is not an isolated one; to the contrary, it is the norm. And as we hope to further demonstrate, excellent class lessons do not come effortlessly or magically. Asian teachers are not born great teachers; they and the lessons they develop require careful nurturing and constant refinement.

The practice of teaching in Japan and China is more uniformly perfected than it is in the United States because their system of education are structured to encourage teaching excellence to develop and flourish. Ours is not. We will take up the question of why and what can be done about this later in the piece. But first, we present a more detailed look at what Asian lessons are like.

COHERENCE BROKEN

Asian lessons almost always begin with a practical problem, such as the example we have just given, or with a word problem written on the blackboard. Asian teachers, to a much greater degree than American teachers, give coherence to their lessons by introducing the lesson with a word problem.

It is not uncommon for the Asian teacher to organize the entire lesson around the solution to this single problem. The teacher leads the children to recognize what is known and what is unknown and directs the students' attention to the critical parts of the problem. Teachers are careful to see that the problem is understood by all of the children, and even mechanics, such as mathematical computation, are presented in the context of solving a problem.

Before ending the lesson, the teacher reviews what has been learned and relates it to the problem she posed at the beginning of the lesson. American teachers are much less likely than Asian teachers to begin and end lessons in this way. For example, we found that fifth-grade teachers in Beijing spent eight times as long at the end of the class period summarizing the lessons as did those in the Chicago metropolitan area.

Now contrast the Japanese math lesson described above with a fifth-grade American mathematics classroom that we recently visited. Immediately after getting the students' attention, the teacher pointed out that today was Tuesday, "band day," and that all students in the band should go to the band room. "Those of you doing the news report today should meet over there in the corner," he continued. He then began the mathematics class with the remaining students by reviewing the solution of a computation problem that had been included in the previous day's homework. After this brief review, the teacher directed the students' attention to the blackboard, where the day's assignment had been written. From this point on, the teacher spent most of the rest of the period walking about the room monitoring the children's work, talking to individual children about questions or errors, and uttering "shushes" whenever the students began talking among themselves.

This example is typical of the American classrooms we have visited, classrooms where students spend more time in transition and less in academic activities, more time working on their own and less being instructed by

It is not uncommon for the Asian teacher to organize the entire lesson around the solution to a single problem.

the teacher; where teachers spend much of their time working with individual students and attending to matters of discipline; and where the shape of a coherent lesson is often hard to discern.

American lessons are often disrupted by irrelevant interruptions. These serve to break the continuity of the lesson and add to children's difficulty in perceiving the lessons as a coherent whole. In our American observations, the teacher interrupted the flow of the lesson with an interlude of irrelevant comments or the class was interrupted by someone else in 20 percent of all first-grade lessons and 47 percent of all fifth-grade lessons. This occurred less than 10 percent of the time at both grade levels in Sendai, Taipei, and Beijing. In fact, no interruptions of either type were recorded during the eighty hours of observation in Beijing fifth-grade classrooms. The mathematics lesson in one of the American classrooms we visited was interrupted every morning by a woman from the cafeteria who polled the children about their lunch plans and collected money from those who planned to eat the hot lunch. Interruptions, as well as inefficient transitions from one activity to another, make it difficult to sustain a coherent lesson throughout the class period.

Coherence is also disrupted when teachers shift frequently from one topic to another. This occurred often in the American classrooms we observed. The teacher might begin with a segment on measurement, then proceed to a segment on simple addition, then to a segment on telling time, and then to a second segment on addition. These segments constitute a math class, but they are hardly a coherent lesson. Such changes in topic were responsible for 21 percent of the changes in segments that we observed in American classrooms but accounted for only 4 percent of the changes in segments in Japanese classrooms.

Teachers frequently capitalize on variety as a means of capturing children's interest. This may explain why American teachers shift topics so frequently within the lesson. Asian teachers also seek variety, but they tend to introduce new activities instead of new topics. Shifts in materials do not necessarily pose a threat to coherence. For example, the coherence of a lesson does not diminish when the teacher shifts from working with numerals to working with concrete objects, if both are used to represent the same subtraction problem. Shifting the topic, on the other hand, introduces variety, but at the risk of destroying the coherence of the lesson.

No one was leading instruction 9 percent of the time in Taiwan, 26 percent in Japan, and an astonishing 51 percent of the time in the United States.

CLASSROOM ORGANIZATION

Elementary school classrooms are typically organized in one of three ways: the whole class is working as a unit; the class is divided into a number of small groups; or children work individually. In our observations, we noted when the child was receiving instruction or assistance from the teacher and when the student was working on his own. The child was considered to be receiving instruction whenever the teacher was the leader of the activity, whether it involved the whole class, a small group, or only the individual child.

Looking at the classroom in this manner led us to one of our most pronounced findings: Although the number of children in Asian classes is significantly greater than the number in American classes, Asian students received much more instruction from their teachers than American students. In Taiwan, the teacher was the leader of the child's activity 90 percent of the time, as opposed to 74 percent in Japan, and only 46 percent in the United States. No one was leading instruction 9 percent of the time in Taiwan, 26 percent in Japan, and an astonishing 51 percent of the time in the United States (see Figure 1). Even American first graders actually spent more time on their own than they did participating in an activity led by the teacher.

One of the reasons American children received less instruction is that American teachers spent 13 percent of their time in the mathematics classes not working with any students, something that happened only 6 percent of the time in Japan and 9 percent in Taiwan. (As we will see later, American teachers have to steal class time to attend to the multitude of chores involving preparation, assessment, and administration because so little non-teaching time is available for them during the day.)

A much more critical factor in the erosion of instruction time was the amount of time American teachers were involved with individuals or small groups. American children spend 10 percent of their time in small groups and 47 percent of their time working individually. Much of the 87 percent of the time American teachers were working with their students was spent with these individual students or small groups, rather than with the class as a whole. When teachers provide individual instruction, they must leave the rest of the class unattended, so instructional time for all remaining children is reduced.

Children can learn without a teacher. Nevertheless, it seems likely that they could profit from having their teacher as the leader of their activities more than half of the time they are in the classroom. It is the incredibly large amounts of time that American children are left unassisted and the effect that unattended time has on the coherence of the larger lesson that is the problem.

When children must work alone for long periods of time without guidance or reaction from the teacher, they begin to lose focus on the purpose of their activity. Asian teachers not only assign less seatwork than American teachers, they also use seatwork differently. Chinese and Japanese teachers tend to use short, frequent periods of seatwork, alternating between group discussion of problems and time for children to work problems on their own. Seatwork is thereby embedded into the lesson. After they work individually or in small groups on a problem, Asian students are called upon to present and defend the solutions they came up with. Thus, instruction, practice, and evaluation are tightly interwoven into a coherent whole. In contrast, the average length of seatwork in American fifth-grade classrooms was almost twice as long as it was in Asian classrooms. And, instead of embedding seatwork into the ongoing back and forth of the lesson, American teachers tend to relegate it to

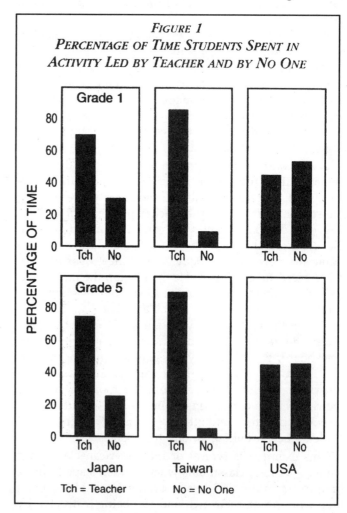

FIGURE 1
PERCENTAGE OF TIME STUDENTS SPENT IN ACTIVITY LED BY TEACHER AND BY NO ONE

one long period at the end of the class, where it becomes little more than a time for repetitious practice. In Chicago, 59 percent of all fifth-grade lessons ended with a period of seatwork, compared with 23 percent in Sendai and 14 percent in Taipei. American teachers often do not discuss the work or its connection to the goal of the lesson, or even evaluate its accuracy. Seatwork was never evaluated or discussed in 48 percent of all American fifth-grade classes we observed, compared to less than 3 percent of Japanese classes and 6 percent of Taiwan classes.

Since Asian students spend so much of their time in whole-group work, we need to say a word about that format. Whole-class instruction in the United States has gotten a somewhat bad reputation. It has become associated with too much teacher talk and too many passive, tuned-out students. But as we will see in more detail as we continue our description of Asian classrooms, whole-class instruction in Japan and China is a very lively, engaging enterprise. Asian teachers do not spend large

amounts of time lecturing. They present interesting problems; they pose provocative questions; they probe and guide. The students work hard, generating multiple approaches to a solution, explaining the rationale behind their methods, and making good use of wrong answers.

HANDLING DIVERSITY

The organization of American elementary school classrooms is based on the assumption that whole-group instruction cannot accommodate students' diverse abilities and levels of achievement; thus, large amounts of whole-class time are given up so that the teacher can work individually with students. Asian educators are more comfortable in the belief that all children, with proper effort, can take advantage of a uniform educational experience, and so they are able to focus on providing the same high-quality experience to all students. Our results suggest that American educators need to question their

HOW WE MADE SURE WE WERE LOOKING AT REPRESENTATIVE SCHOOLS

FREQUENT REPORTS on television and in books and newspapers purport to depict what happens inside Japanese and Chinese classrooms. These reports usually are based on impressions gathered during brief visits to classrooms—most likely classrooms that the visitor's contacts in Asia have preselected. As a result, it is difficult to gauge the generality of what was seen and reported. Without observing large, representative samples of schools and teachers, it is impossible to characterize the teaching practices of any culture.

The descriptions that we present are based on two large observational studies of first- and fifth-grade classrooms that we conducted in Japan, Taiwan, China, and the United States. In contrast to informal observations, the strength of formal studies such as ours is that the observations are made according to consistent rules about where, when, and what to observe.

In the first study, our observers were in classrooms for a total of over four thousand hours—over a thousand class periods in 20 first- and fifth-grade classrooms in each of three cities: Sendai, Japan; Taipei, Taiwan; and Minneapolis, Minnesota.[1] Our second study took place in two hundred classrooms, forty each in Sendai and Taipei, plus forty in Beijing, China, and eighty in the Chicago metropoli-

tan area of the United States.[2] Care was taken to choose schools that were representative. Our Chicago metropolitan area sample—the urban and suburban areas that make up Cook County—included schools that are predominantly white, black, Hispanic, and ethnically mixed; schools that draw from upper, middle, and lower socioeconomic groups; schools that are public and private; and schools that are urban and suburban.

Observers visited each classroom four times over a one- to two-week period, yielding a total of eight hundred hours of observations. The observers, who were residents of each city, wrote down as much as they could about what transpired during each mathematics class. Tape recordings made during the classes assisted the observers in filling in any missing information. These detailed narrative accounts of what transpired in the classrooms yielded even richer information than we obtained in the first study, where the observers followed predefined categories for coding behavior during the course of observations.

After the narrative records had been translated into English, we divided each observation into segments, which we defined as beginning each time there was a change in topic, materials, or activity. For example, a segment began when students put away

their textbooks and began working on a worksheet or when the teacher stopped lecturing and asked some of the students to write their solutions to a problem on the blackboard.

Both studies focused on mathematics classes rather than on classes in subjects such as reading, where cultural differences in teaching practices may be more strongly determined by the content of what is being taught. For example, it is likely that the processes of teaching and learning about the multiplication of fractions transcend cultural differences, whereas teaching children how to read Chinese characters may require different approaches from those used to teach children to read an alphabetic language.

REFERENCES

[1]Stevenson, H. W., Stigler, J. W., Lucker, G. W., Lee, S. Y., Hsu, C. C., & Kitamura, S. (1987). Classroom behavior and achievement of Japanese, Chinese, and American children. In R. Glaser (Ed.), *Advances in instructional psychology*. Hillsdale NJ: Erlbaum.
[2]Stigler, J. W., & Perry, M. (1990). Mathematics learning in Japanese, Chinese, and American classrooms. In Stigler, J. W., Shweder, R. A., & Herdt, G. (Eds.), *Cultural psychology: Essays on comparative human development*. Cambridge, Cambridge University Press. Pp. 328–356.

long-held assumption that an individualized learning experience is inherently a higher-quality, more effective experience than is a whole-class learning experience. Although it may be true that an equal amount of time with a teacher may be more effective in a one-on-one situation than in a large-group situation, we must realize that the result of individualized instruction, given realistic financial constraints, is to drastically reduce the amount of teacher instruction every child receives.

> *Tracking does not exist in Asian elementary schools. This egalitarian philosophy carries over to organization within the classroom.*

Japanese and Chinese teachers recognize individual differences among students, but they handle that diversity in a very different way. First, as we will see in more detail later, they have much greater amounts of non-teaching time than do American teachers, and part of that time is available for working with individual students. They may spend extra time with slower students or ask faster students to assist them, but they focus their lesson on teaching all children regardless of apparent differences in ability or developmental readiness. Before we discuss how they do that in a whole-group setting, we need to first address the question of whether American classrooms are more diverse than Asian ones, thus potentially rendering whole-class instruction more difficult.

Whenever we discuss our research on teaching practices, someone in the audience inevitably reminds us that Japan and China are nations with relatively homogeneous populations while the United States is the melting pot of the world. How could we expect that practices used in Asian societies could possibly be relevant for the American context, where diversity is the rule in race, ethnicity, language, and social class?

What impedes teaching is the uneven preparation of children for the academic tasks that must be accomplished. It is diversity in children's educational backgrounds, not in their social and cultural backgrounds, that poses the greatest problems in teaching. Although the United States is culturally more diverse than Japan or China, we have found no more diversity at the classroom level in the educational level of American than of Asian students. The key factor is that, in the United States, educational and cultural diversity are positively related, leading some persons to the inappropriate conclusion that it is ethnic and cultural diversity, rather than educational diversity, that leads to the difficulties faced by American teachers.

It is true, for example, that there is greater variability in mathematics achievement among American than among Japanese children, but this does not mean that the differences are evident in any particular classroom. Variability in the United States exists to a large extent across neighborhoods and schools (rather than within them). Within individual classrooms, the variability in levels of academic achievement differs little between the United States and Japan, Taiwan, or China. It is wrong to argue that diversity within classrooms is an American problem. Teachers everywhere must deal with students who vary in their knowledge and motivation.

Tracking does not exist in Asian elementary schools. Children are never separated into different classrooms according to their presumed levels of intellectual ability. This egalitarian philosophy carries over to organization within the classroom. Children are not separated into reading groups according to their ability; there is no division of the class into groups differentiated by the rate at which they proceed through their mathematics books. No children leave the classroom for special classes, such as those designed for children who have been diagnosed as having learning disabilities.

How do teachers in Asian classrooms handle diversity in students' knowledge and skills? For one thing, they typically use a variety of approaches in their teaching, allowing students who may not understand one approach the opportunity to experience other approaches to presenting the material. Periods of recitation are alternated with periods in which children work for short periods on practice problems. Explanations by the teacher are interspersed with periods in which children work with concrete materials or struggle to come up with their own solutions to problems. There is continuous change from one mode of presentation, one type of representation, and one type of teaching method to another.

Asian teaching practices thrive in the face of diversity, and some practices even depend on diversity for their effectiveness. Asking students to suggest alternative solutions to a problem, for example, works best when students have had experience in generating a variety of solutions. Incorrect solutions, which are typically dismissed by the American teacher, become topics for discussion in Asian classrooms, and all students can learn from this discussion. Thus, while American schools attempt to solve the problems of diversity by segregating children into different groups or different classrooms, and by spending large amounts of regular class time working with individual students, Asian teachers believe that the only way they can cope with the problem is by devising teaching techniques that accommodate the different interests and backgrounds of the children in their classrooms.

Asian teachers also exploit the fact that the same instruction can affect different students in different ways, something that may be overlooked by American teachers. In this sense, Asian teachers subscribe to what would be considered in the West to be a "constructivist" view of learning. According to this view, knowledge is regarded as something that must be constructed by the child rather than as a set of facts and skills that can be imparted by the teacher. Because children are engaged in their own construction of knowledge, some of the major tasks for the teacher are to pose provocative questions, to allow adequate time for reflection, and to vary teaching techniques so that they are responsive to differences in students' prior experience. Through such practices, Asian teachers are able to accommodate individual differences in learning, even though instruction is not tailored to each student.

USE OF REAL-WORLD PROBLEMS AND OBJECTS

Elementary school mathematics is often defined in terms of mathematical symbols and their manipulation; for example, children must learn the place-value system of numeration and the operations for manipulating numerals to add, subtract, multiply, and divide. In addition, children must be able to apply these symbols and operations to solving problems. In order to accomplish these goals, teachers rely primarily on two powerful tools for representing mathematics: language and the manipulation of concrete objects. How effectively teachers use these forms of representation plays a critical role in determining how well children will understand mathematics.

One common function of language is in defining terms and stating rules for performing mathematical operations. A second, broader function is the use of language as a means of connecting mathematical operations to the real world of integrating what children know about mathematics. We find that American elementary school teachers are more prone to use language to define terms and state rules than are Asian teachers, who, in their efforts to make mathematics meaningful, use language to clarify different aspects of mathematics and to integrate what children know about mathematics with the demands of real-world problems. Here is an example of what we mean by a class in which the teacher defines terms and states rules:

An American teacher announces that the lesson today concerns fractions. Fractions are defined and she names the numerator and denominator. "What do we call this?" she then asks. "And this?" After assuring herself that the children understand the meaning of the terms, she spends the rest of the lesson teaching them to apply the rules for forming fractions.

Asian teachers tend to reverse the procedure. They focus initially on interpreting and relating a real-world problem to the quantification that is necessary for a mathematical solution and then to define terms and state rules. In the following example, a third-grade teacher in Japan was also teaching a lesson that introduced the notation system for fractions.

The lesson began with the teacher posing the question of how many liters of juice (colored water) were contained in a large beaker. "More than one liter," answered on child. "One and a half liters," answered another. After several children had made guesses, the teacher suggested that they pour the juice into some one-liter beakers and see. Horizontal lines on each beaker divided it into thirds. The juice filled one beaker and part of a second. The teacher pointed out that the water came up to the first line on the second beaker—only one of the three parts was full. The procedure was repeated with a second set of beakers to illustrate the concept of one-half. After stating that there had been one and one-out-of-three liters of juice in the first big beaker and one and one-out-of-two liters in the second, the teacher wrote the fractions on the board. He continued the lesson by asking the children how to represent two parts out of three, two parts out of five, and so forth. Near the end of the period he mentioned the term "fraction" for the first time and attached names to the numerator and the denominator.

He ended the lesson by summarizing how fractions can be used to represent the parts of a whole.

In the second example, the concept of fractions emerged from a meaningful experience; in the first, it was introduced initially as an abstract concept. The terms and operations in the second example flowed naturally from the teacher's questions and discussion; in the first, language was used primarily for defining and summarizing rules. Mathematics ultimately requires abstract representation, but young children understand such representation more readily if it is derived from meaningful experience than if it results from learning definitions and rules.

Asian teachers generally are more likely than American teachers to engage their students, even very young ones, in the discussion of mathematical concepts. The kind of verbal discussion we find in American classrooms is more short-answer in nature, oriented, for example, toward clarifying the correct way to implement a computational procedure.

Teachers ask questions for different reasons in the United States and in Japan. In the United States, the purpose of a question is to get an answer. In Japan, teachers pose questions to stimulate thought. A Japanese teacher considers a question to be a poor one if it elicits an immediate answer, for this indicates that students were not challenged to think. One teacher we interviewed told us of discussions she had with her fellow teachers on how to improve teaching practices. "What do you talk about?" we wondered. "A great deal of time," she reported, "is spent talking about questions we can pose to the class—which wordings work best to get students involved in thinking and discussing the material. One good question can keep a whole class going for a long time; a bad one produces little more than a simple answer."

In one memorable example recorded by our observers, a Japanese first-grade teacher began her class by posing the question to one of her students: "Would you explain the difference between what we learned in yesterday's lesson and what you came across in preparing for to-day's lesson?" The young student thought for a long time, but then answered the question intelligently, a performance that undoubtedly enhanced his understanding of both lessons.

CONCRETE REPRESENTATIONS

Every elementary school student in Sendai possesses a "Math Set," a box of colorful, well-designed materials for teaching mathematical concepts: tiles, clock, ruler, checkerboard, colored triangles, beads, and many other attractive objects.

In Taipei, every classroom is equipped with a similar, but larger, set of such objects. In Beijing, where there is much less money available for purchasing such materials, teachers improvise with colored paper, wax fruit, plates, and other easily obtained objects. In all cases, these concrete objects are considered to be critically important tools for teaching mathematics, for it is through manipulating these objects that children can form important links between real-world problems and abstract mathematical notations.

American teachers are much less likely than Chinese or Japanese teachers to use concrete objects. At fifth grade, for example, Sendai teachers were nearly twice as likely to use concrete objects as the Chicago area teachers, and Taipei teachers were nearly five times as likely. There was also a subtle, but important, difference in the way Asian and American teachers used concrete objects. Japanese teachers, for example, use the items in the Math Set throughout the elementary school years and introduced small tiles in a high percentage of the lessons we observed in the first grade. American teachers seek variety and may use Popsicle sticks in one lesson, and in another, marbles, Cheerios, M&Ms, checkers, poker chips, or plastic animals. The American view is that objects should be varied in order to maintain children's interest. The Asian view is that using a variety of representational materials may confuse children, and thereby make it more difficult for them to use the objects for the representation and solution of mathematics problems. Having learned to add with tiles makes multiplication easier to understand when the same tiles are used.

Through the skillful use of concrete objects, teachers are able to teach elementary school children to understand and solve problems that are not introduced in American curricula until much later. An example occurred in a fourth-grade mathematics lesson we observed in Japan. The problem the teacher posed is a difficult one for fourth graders, and its solution is generally not taught in the United States until much later. This is the problem:

There are a total of thirty-eight children in Akira's class. There are six more boys than there are girls. How many boys and how many girls are in the class?

This lesson began with a discussion of the problem and with the children proposing ways to solve it. After the discussion, the teacher handed each child two strips of paper, one six units longer than the other, and told the class that the strips would be used to help them think about the problem. One slip represented the number of girls in the class and the other represented the number of boys. By lining the strips next to each other, the children could see that the degree to which the longer one protruded beyond the shorter one represented 6 boys. The procedure for solving the problem then unfolded as the teacher, through skillful questioning, led the children to the solution: The number of girls was found by taking the total of both strips, subtracting 6 to make the strips of equal length, and then dividing by 2. The number of boys could be found, of course, by adding 6 to the number of girls. With this concrete visual representation of the problem and careful guidance from the teacher, even fourth graders were able to understand the problem and its solution.

STUDENTS CONSTRUCT MULTIPLE SOLUTIONS

A common Western stereotype is that the Asian teacher is an authoritarian purveyor of information, one who expects students to listen and memorize correct answers or correct procedures rather than to construct knowledge themselves. This may or may not be an accurate description of Asian high school teachers,[4] but, as we have seen in previous examples, it does not describe the dozens of elementary school teachers that we have observed.

Chinese and Japanese teachers rely on students to generate ideas and evaluate the correctness of the ideas. The possibility that they will be called upon to state their own solution as well as to evaluate what another student has proposed keeps Asian students alert, but this technique has two other important functions. First, it engages students in the lesson, increasing their motivation by making them feel they are participants in a group process. Second, it conveys a more realistic impression of how knowledge is acquired. Mathematics, for example, is a body of knowledge that has evolved gradually through a process of argument and proof. Learning to argue about mathematical ideas is fundamental to understanding mathematics. Chinese and Japanese children begin learning these skills in the first grade; many American elementary school students are never exposed to them.

We can illustrate the way Asian teachers use students' ideas with the following example. A fifth-grade teacher in Taiwan began her mathematics lesson by calling attention to a six-sided figure she had drawn on the blackboard. She asked the students how they might go about finding the area of the shaded region. "I don't want you to tell me what the actual area is, just tell me the approach you would use to solve the problem. Think of as many different ways as you can of ways you could determine the area that I have drawn in yellow chalk." She allowed the students several minutes to work in small groups and then called upon a child from each group to describe the group's solution. After each proposal, many of which were quite complex, the teacher asked members of the other groups whether the procedure described could yield a correct answer. After several different procedures had been suggested, the teacher moved on to a second problem with a different embedded figure and repeated the process. Neither teacher nor students actually carried out a solution to the problem until all of the alternative solutions had been discussed. The lesson ended with the teacher affirming the importance of coming up with multiple solutions. "After all," she said,"we face many problems every day in the real world. We have to remember that there is not only one way we can solve each problem."

American teachers are less likely to give students opportunities to respond at such length. Although a great deal of interaction appears to occur in American classrooms—with teachers and students posing questions and giving answers—American teachers generally pose questions that are answerable with a yes or no or with a short phrase. They seek a correct answer and continue calling on students until one produces it. "Since we can't subtract 8 from 6," says an American teacher, "we have to . . . what?" Hands go up, the teacher calls on a girl who says "Borrow." "Correct," the teacher replies. This kind of interchange does not establish the student as a valid source of information, for the final arbiter of the correctness of the student's opinions is still the teacher. The situation is very different in Asian classrooms, where children are likely to be asked to explain their answers and other children are then called upon to evaluate their correctness.

Clear evidence of these differing beliefs about the roles of students and teachers appears in the observations of how teachers evaluate students' responses. The most frequent form of evaluation used by American teachers was praise, a technique that was rarely used in either Taiwan or Japan. In Japan, evaluation most frequently took the form of a discussion of children's errors.

Praise serves to cut off discussion and to highlight the teacher's role as the authority. It also encourages children to be satisfied with their performance rather than informing them about where they need improvement. Discussing errors, on the other hand, encourages argument and justification and involves students in the exciting quest of assessing the strengths and weaknesses of the various alternative solutions that have been proposed.

Why are American teachers often reluctant to encourage students to participate at greater length during mathematics lessons? One possibility is that they feel insecure about the depth of their own mathematical training. Placing more emphasis on students' explanations

necessarily requires teachers to relinquish some control over the direction the lesson will take. This can be a frightening prospect to a teacher who is unprepared to evaluate the validity of novel ideas that students inevitably propose.

USING ERRORS EFFECTIVELY

We have been struck by the different reactions of Asian and American teachers to children's errors. For Americans, errors tend to be interpreted as an indication of failure in learning the lesson. For Chinese and Japanese, they are an index of what still needs to be learned. These divergent interpretations result in very different reactions to the display of errors—embarrassment on the part of the American children, calm acceptance by Asian children. They also result in differences in the manner in which teachers utilize errors as effective means of instruction.

We visited a fifth-grade classroom in Japan the first day the teacher introduced the problem of adding fractions with unequal denominators. The problem was a simple one: adding one-third and one-half. The children were told to solve the problem and that the class would then review the different solutions.

After everyone appeared to have completed the task, the teacher called on one of the students to give his answer and to explain his solution. "The answer is two-fifths," he stated. Pointing first to the numerators and then to the denominators, he explained: "One plus one is two; three plus two is five. The answer is two-fifths." Without comment, the teacher asked another boy for his solution. "Two point one plus three point one, when changed into a fraction adds up to two-fifths." The children in the classroom looked puzzled. The teacher, unperturbed, asked a third student for her solution. "The answer is five-sixths." The student went on to explain how she had found the common denominator, changed the fractions so that each had this denominator, and then added them.

The teacher returned to the first solution. "How many of you think this solution is correct?" Most agreed that it was not. She used the opportunity to direct the children's attention to reasons why the solution was incorrect. "Which is larger, two-fifths or one-half?" The class agreed that it was one-half. "It is strange, isn't it, that you could add a number to one-half and get a number that is smaller than one-half?" She went on to explain how the procedure the child used would result in the odd situation where, when one-half was added to one-half, the answer yielded is one-half. In a similarly careful, interactive manner, she discussed how the second boy had confused fractions with decimals to come up with his surprising answer. Rather than ignoring the incorrect solutions and concentrating her attention on the correct solution, the teacher capitalized on the errors the children made in order to dispel two common misperceptions about fractions.

We have not observed American teachers responding to children's errors so inventively. Perhaps because of the strong influence of behavioristic teaching that conditions should be arranged so that the learner avoids errors and makes only a reinforceable response, American teachers place little emphasis on the constructive use of errors as a teaching technique. It seems likely, however, that learning about what is wrong may hasten children's understanding of why the correct procedures are appropriate.

WHY NOT HERE?

Few who have visited urban classrooms in Asia would disagree that the great majority of Chinese and Japanese teachers are highly skilled professionals. Their dedication is legendary; what is often not appreciated is how thoughtfully and adroitly they guide children through the vast amount of material that they must master during the six years of elementary school. We, of course, witnessed examples of excellent lessons in American classrooms. And there are of course individual differences among Asian teachers. But what has impressed us in our personal observations and in the data from our observational studies is how remarkably well most Asian teachers teach. It is the *widespread* excellence of Asian class lessons, the high level of performance of the *average* teacher, that is so stunning.

The techniques used by Chinese and Japanese teachers are not new to the teaching profession—nor are they foreign or exotic. In fact, they are the types of techniques often recommended by American educators. What the Japanese and Chinese examples demonstrate so compellingly is that when widely implemented, such practices can produce extraordinary outcomes.

Unfortunately, these techniques have not been broadly applied in the United States. Why? One reason, as we have discussed, is the Asian belief that the whole-group lesson, if done well, can be made to work for every child. With that assumption, Asian teachers can focus on the perfection of that lesson. However, even if American educators shared that belief, it would be difficult for them to achieve anything near the broad-based high quality that we observed in Asian classrooms. This is not the fault of American teachers. The fault lies with a system that prepares them inadequately and then exhausts them physically, emotionally, and intellectually while denying them the collegial interaction that every profession relies upon for the growth and refinement of its knowledge base.

The first major obstacle to the widespread development and execution of excellent lessons in America is the fact that American teachers are overworked. It is inconceivable that American teachers, by themselves, would be able to organize lively, vivid, coherent lessons under a regimen that requires that they teach hour after hour every day throughout the school year. Preparing lessons that require the discovery of knowledge and the construction of understanding takes time. Teaching them effectively requires energy. Both are in very short supply for most American teachers.

Being an elementary school teacher in the United States at the end of the twentieth century is extraordinarily difficult, and the demands made by American society exhaust even the most energetic among them. "I'm dancing as fast as I can" one teacher summarized her feelings about her job, "but with all the things that I'm supposed to do, I just can't keep up."

The full realization of how little time American teachers have when they are not directly in charge of children became clear to us during a meeting in Beijing. We were discussing the teachers' workday. When we informed the Chinese teachers that American teachers are responsible for their classes all day long, with only an hour or less outside the classroom each day, they looked incredulous. How could any teacher be expected to do a good job when there is no time outside of class to prepare and correct lessons, work with individual children, consult with other teachers, and attend to all of the matters that arise in a typical day at school! Beijing teachers teach no more than three hours a day, unless the teacher is a homeroom teacher, in which case, the total is four hours. During the first three grades, the teaching assignment includes both reading and mathematics; for the upper three grades of elementary school, teachers specialize in one of these subjects. They spend the rest of their day at school carrying out all of their other responsibilities to their students and to the school. The situation is similar in Japan. According to our estimate, Japanese elementary school teachers are in charge of classes only 60 percent of the time they are at school.

The large amounts of nonteaching time at school are available to Asian teachers because of two factors. The first concerns the number of teachers typically assigned to Asian schools. Although class sizes are considerably larger in Asia, the student-to-teacher ratio within a school does not differ greatly from that in the United States. By having more students in each class and the same number of teachers in the school, all teachers can have fewer teaching hours. Time is freed up for teachers to meet and work together on a daily basis, to prepare lessons for the next day, to work with individual children, and to attend staff meetings.

The second factor increasing the time available to Japanese and Chinese teachers at school is that they spend more hours at school each day than do American teachers. In our study, for example, teachers in Sendai and Taipei spent an average of 9.5 and 9.1 hours per day, respectively, compared to only 7.3 hours for the American teachers. Asian teachers arrive at school early and stay late, which gives them time to meet together and to work with children who need extra help. Most American teachers, in contrast, arrive at school shortly before classes begin and leave not long after they end. This does not mean a shorter work week for American teachers. What it does mean is that they must devote their evenings to working alone on the next day's lessons, further increasing their sense of isolation.

LEARNING FROM EACH OTHER

The second reason Asian class lessons are so well crafted is that there is a very systematic effort to pass on the accumulated wisdom of teaching practice to each new generation of teachers and to keep perfecting that practice by providing teachers the opportunities to continually learn from each other.

Americans often act as if good teachers are born, not made. We hear this from both teachers and parents. They seem to believe that good teaching happens if the teacher has a knack with children, gets along well with them, and keeps them reasonably attentive and enthusiastic about learning. It is a commonly accepted truism in many colleges of education that teaching is an art and that students cannot be taught how to teach.

Perhaps because of this belief, students emerge from American colleges of education with little training in how to design and teach effective lessons. It is assumed that teachers will discover this for themselves. Courses in teaching methods are designed to serve a different purpose. On the one hand, they present theories of learning and cognitive development. Although the students are able to quote the major tenents of the theorists currently in vogue, the theories remain as broad generalizations that are difficult to apply to the everyday tasks that they will face as classroom teachers. At the opposite extreme, these methods courses provide education students with lists of specific suggestions for activities and materials that are easy to use and that children should enjoy (for example, pieces of breakfast cereal make handy counters for teaching basic number facts). Teachers are faced, therefore, with information that is either too general to be applied readily or so specific that it has only limited usefulness. Because of this, American teachers complain that most of what they know had to be learned by themselves, alone, on the job.

In Asia, graduates of teacher training programs are still considered to be novices who need the guidance and support of their experienced colleagues. In the United States, training comes to a near halt after the teachers acquire their teaching certificates. American teachers may take additional coursework in the evenings or during summer vacations, or they may attend district or citywide workshops from time to time. But these opportunities are not considered to be an essential part of the American system of teacher training.

In Japan, the system of teacher training is much like an apprenticeship under the guidance of experienced col-

leagues. The teacher's first year of employment marks the beginning of a lengthy and elaborate training process. By Japanese law, beginning teachers must receive a minimum of twenty days of inservice training during their first year on the job.[5] Supervising the inservice training are master teachers, selected for their teaching ability and their willingness to assist their young colleagues. During one-year leaves of absence from their own classrooms, they observe the beginner in the classroom and offer suggestions for improvement.

In addition to this early tutelage in teaching techniques, Japanese teachers, beginners as well as seasoned teachers, are required to continually perfect their teaching skills through interaction with other teachers. One mechanism is through meetings organized by the vice principal and head teachers of their own school. These experienced professionals assume responsibility for advising and guiding their young colleagues. The head teachers organize meetings to discuss teaching techniques and to devise lesson plans and handouts. These meetings are supplemented by informal districtwide study groups and courses at municipal or prefectural education centers.[6]

A glimpse at what takes place in these study groups is provided in a conversation we recently had with a Japanese teacher. She and her colleagues spend a good deal of their time together working on lesson plans. After they finish a plan, one teacher from the group teaches the lesson to her students while the other teachers look on. Afterward, the group meets again to criticize the teacher's performance and to make suggestions for how the lesson could be improved. In her school, there is an annual "teaching fair." Teachers from other schools are invited to visit the school and observe the lessons being taught. The visitors rate the lessons, and the teacher with the best lesson is declared the winner.

In addition, national television in Japan presents programs that show how master teachers handle particular lessons or concepts. In Taiwan, such demonstrations are available on sets of videotapes that cover the whole curriculum.

Making use of lessons that have been honed over time does not mean that the Asian teacher simply mimics what she sees. As with great actors or musicians, the substance of the curriculum becomes the script or the score; the goal is to perform the role or piece as effectively and creatively as possible. Rather than executing the curriculum as a mere routine, the skilled teacher strives to perfect the presentation of each lesson. She uses the teaching techniques she has learned and imposes her own interpretation on these techniques in a manner that she thinks will interest and motivate her pupils.

Of course, teachers find it easier to share helpful tips and techniques among themselves when they are all teaching the same lesson at about the same time. The fact that Taiwan, Japan, and China each has a national curriculum that provides a common focus is a significant factor in teacher interaction. Not only do we have no national curriculum in the United States, but the curriculum may not be consistent within a city or even within a single school. American textbooks, with a spiral curriculum that repeats topics year after year and with a profusion of material about each topic, force teachers to omit some of each year's material. Even when teachers use the same textbook, their classes differ according to which topics they choose to skip and in the pace with which they proceed through the text. As a result, American teachers have less incentive than Asian teachers to share experiences with each other or to benefit from the successes and failures that others have had in teaching particular lessons.

Adding further to the sense of isolation is the fact that American teachers, unlike other professionals, do not share a common body of knowledge and experience. The courses offered at different universities and colleges vary, and even among their required courses, there is often little common content from college to college. Student teaching, the only other activity in which all budding teachers participate, is a solitary endeavor shared only with the regular classroom teacher and perhaps a few fellow student teachers.

Opportunities for Asian teachers to learn from each other are influenced, in part, by the physical arrangements of the schools. In Japanese and Chinese schools, a large room in each school is designed as a teachers' room, and each teacher is assigned a desk in this room. It is here that they spend their time away from the classroom preparing lessons, correcting students' papers, and discussing teaching techniques. American teachers, isolated in their own classrooms, find it much harder to discuss their work with colleagues. Their desk and teaching materials are in their own classrooms, and the only common space available to teachers is usually a cramped room that often houses supplies and the school's duplicating facilities, along with a few chairs and a coffee machine. Rarely do teachers have enough time in their visits to this room to engage in serious discussions of educational policy or teaching practices.

* * *

Critics argue that the problems facing the American teacher are unique and that it is futile to consider what Japanese and Chinese teaching are like in seeking solutions to educational problems in the United States. One of the frequent arguments is that the students in the typical Asian classroom share a common language and culture, are well disciplined and attentive, and are not distracted by family crises and their own personal problems, whereas the typical American teacher is often faced with a diverse, burdened, distracted group of students. To be sure, the conditions encountered by teachers differ greatly among these societies. Week after week, Ameri-

can teachers must cope with children who present them with complex, wrenching personal problems. But much of what gives American classrooms their aura of disarray and disorganization may be traced to how schools are organized and teachers are trained as well as to characteristics of the children.

It is easy to blame teachers for the problems confronting American education, and this is something that the American public is prone to do. The accusation is unfair. We cannot blame teachers when we deprive them of adequate training and yet expect that on their own they will become innovative teachers; when we cast them in the roles of surrogate parents, counselors, and psychotherapists and still expect them to be effective teachers; and when we keep them so busy in the classroom that they have little time or opportunity for professional development once they have joined the ranks of the teaching profession.

Surely the most immediate and pressing task in educating young students is to create a new type of school environment, one where great lessons are a commonplace occurrence. In order to do this, we must ask how we can institute reforms that will make it possible for American teachers to practice their profession under conditions that are as favorable for their own professional development and for the education of children as those that exist in Asia.

Note: The research described in this article has been funded by grants from the National Institute of Mental Health, the National Science Foundation, and the W. T. Grant Foundation. The research is the result of collaboration with a large group of colleagues in China, Japan, Taiwan, and the United States who have worked together for the past decade. We are indebted to each of these colleagues and are especially grateful to Shinying Lee of the University of Michigan who has been a major contributor to the research described in this article.

REFERENCES

[1]The superior academic achievement of Chinese and Japanese children sometimes leads to speculation that they are brighter than American children. This possibility has been supported in a few reports that have received attention in the popular press and in several scientific journals. What has not been reported or widely understood is that, without exception, the studies contending that differences in intelligence are responsible for differences in academic performance have failed to meet acceptable standards of scientific inquiry. In fact, studies that have reported differences in I.Q. scores between Asian and American children have been flawed conceptually and methodologically. Their major defects are nonequivalent tests used in the different locations and noncomparable samples of children.

To determine the cognitive abilities of children in the three cultures, we needed tests that were linguistically comparable and culturally unbiased. These requirements preclude reliance on tests translated from one language to another or the evaluation of children in one country on the basis of norms obtained in another country. We assembled a team with members from each of the three cultures, and they developed ten cognitive tasks falling into traditional "verbal" and "performance" categories.

The test results revealed no evidence of overall differences in the cognitive functioning of American, Chinese, and Japanese children. There was no tendency for children from any of the three cultures to achieve significantly higher average scores on all the tasks. Children in each culture had strengths and weaknesses, but by the fifth grade of elementary school, the most notable feature of children's cognitive performance was the similarity in level and variability of their scores. [Stevenson, H. W., Stigler, J. W., Lee, S. Y., Lucker, G. W., Kitamura, S., & Hsu, C. C. (1985). Cognitive performance and academic achievement of Japanese, Chinese, and American children. *Child Development, 56,* 718–734.]

[2]Stevenson, H. W. (1990). Adapting to school: Children in Beijing and Chicago. *Annual Report*. Stanford CA: Center for Advanced Study in the Behavioral Sciences. Stevenson, H. W., Lee, S., Chen, C., Lummis, M., Stigler, J., Fan, L., & Ge, F. (1990). Mathematics achievement of children in China and the United States. *Child Development,* 61, 1053–1066. Stevenson, H. W., Stigler, J. W., & Lee, S. Y. (1986). Mathematics achievement of Chinese, Japanese, and American children. *Science,* 231, 693–699. Stigler, J. W., Lee, S. Y., & Stevenson, H. W. (1990). *Mathematical knowledge.* Reston: VA: National Council of Teachers of Mathematics.

[3]Stevenson, H. W., Lee, S. Y., Chen, C., Stigler, J. W., Hsu, C. C., & Kitamura, S. (1990). Contexts of achievement. *Monographs of the Society for Research in Child Development.* Serial No. 221, 55, Nos. 1–2.

[4]Rohlen, T. P. (1983). *Japan's High Schools.* Berkeley: University of California Press.

[5]Dorfman, C. H. (Ed.) (1987). *Japanese Education Today.* Washington, D.C.: U.S. Department of Education.

[6]Ibid.

"Ready, READ!"

by NICHOLAS LEMANN

A new solution to the problem of failing public schools is emerging: takeover by outside authorities, who prescribe a standardized field-tested curriculum. This runs counter to our long-standing tradition of autonomy for local schools and teachers, but it works

MOST discussion of public education in the United States begins with the premise that big, government-run school systems no longer work. The way to provide a good education to all children, especially poor children, is to turn over control of public schools to smaller, more local, and possibly private operators—to decentralize authority. At the center of the debate is a contest between two ideas: vouchers and charter schools. Vouchers are checks from the government that are issued to parents and earmarked for education; they are redeemable at both private and public schools. Charter schools are new public schools operated by independent groups. "We must . . . bring more choice and competition into public education," President Bill Clinton said last year, in calling for the establishment of 3,000 charter schools. Both ideas address the problems in public education by walking away from them.

The rhetoric of failure is simply wrong. There are 87,000 public schools in this country, with 45 million students—a sixth of the U.S. population. Enrollment is increasing rapidly. The best measure of public schools' performance, the National Assessment of Educational Progress, has shown modest but steady overall gains since it was first administered, in 1970. One has to belong to the small but disproportionately influential subculture that interacts only with private education to believe that public education—rather than specific public schools—has failed. The total enrollment in private, nonsectarian schools where the annual tuition is more than $5,000 is about 400,000—less than one percent of public school enrollment. Catholic-school enrollment is 2.5 million. Public education is by far the largest and most important

function performed by government in this country. In no way is it in systemic crisis.

In the public schools that can fairly be described as having failed, most of which are in poor urban neighborhoods, what is actually taking place is a great and largely unremarked centralization of authority. The trend is diffuse, and its precise dimensions are difficult to limn. In at least a thousand American public schools, it is safe to say, outside control has replaced local autonomy during the 1990s. This has affected many more schools and students than has the devolution of authority through voucher programs or charter schools.

During the 1980s many states began imposing measurements of performance on their public schools, usually in the form of obligatory standardized tests in reading and math. (Bill Clinton first gained national attention by doing this in Arkansas.) In this decade, when individual schools or entire districts have persistently turned in poor scores on these tests, outside authorities have often moved in. The school systems of Chicago, Hartford, Cleveland, Baltimore, Washington, D.C., and three cities in New Jersey, among other places, are no longer under the control of the municipal school superintendent. The Pennsylvania legislature is threatening to take over Philadelphia's system. In other cities, such as San Francisco and San Antonio, the school superintendent has imposed "reconstitution" on the worst-performing schools, meaning that the entire staff has been required to reapply for employment and the school has been "redesigned."

In many of these cases, after the change in authority the schools have adopted one of about a dozen national school designs that cover such areas as governance, re-

 First published in *The Atlantic Monthly*, November 1998, pp. 92-104. © 1998 by Nicholas Lemann. Reprinted by permission.

lations with parents and the neighborhood, teaching techniques, and, especially, curriculum. Many schools that have not been taken over or reconstituted (for example, dozens of schools in Memphis and Miami) are also using these "whole school" designs. Of the three most popular—Success for All, Accelerated Schools, and the School Development Program, all designed by university professors—the first two have each been adopted by more than a thousand schools across the country, and the third by 700.

The outline emerges of a future in which schools that aren't doing their job will lose their independence and will have to adopt a standard mode of operation that has demonstrated good results. This is not what most people think of as the direction in which public education is moving. Even Clinton's constant calls for national education standards mean the setting of goals for what all students should know, not dictating the day-to-day operations of schools. If failure in the public schools is resulting not in decentralization but in the imposition of a template, then we should know it—and think about whether this is a good idea.

American public schools have never been as local as politicians claim to want them to be. In a country as big as ours it would be impractical to leave education entirely in the hands of 14,800 school boards that operate independently. So we have a strange hybrid: a system rhetorically committed to decentralization but in fact centralized in a patchwork, undeliberate way. We have national standardized tests, national teachers' unions, national textbook publishers, and national laws, regulations, and funding programs for schools. No school is free of their influence. But they influence most schools in a haphazard fashion.

The great majority of public schools muddle along fairly successfully. It is students at bad public schools who are the main losers in the patchwork system, and a consistent national standard for how to operate bad schools ought to be considered with their interests in mind.

RECENTRALIZING AUTHORITY

AT the end of the nineteenth century New York City, cobbled together out of smaller cities and towns, created the country's biggest centralized public school system. In 1969, following a long, famous, resonant battle, New York dropped centralization in favor of a policy of "community control" and created thirty-two local school boards. This was not an unqualified success, and the move back toward centralization began. In 1989 the New York State commissioner of education created a new status, called "registration review," for persistently low-performing schools, most of which

were in poor sections of New York City. The schools were under a threat of having their state registration revoked and being shut down. In 1996 the state legislature essentially rescinded community control, by giving the chancellor of New York City's schools the power to fire principals and school-board superintendents. (Chicago's school system went through much the same cycle, but faster: dramatically decentralized in 1988, recentralized in 1995.) The state commissioner kept up the saber-rattling, and in 1996 New York City's new chancellor, Rudy Crew, took direct control of nine of the worst registration-review schools—six elementary and three middle schools—in the hope of turning them around.

Fifteen percent of the registration-review schools in New York State were in a single school district—Community School District Nine, in the Bronx, the most consistently problematic school district in New York City. Its test scores have always been low, its board has twice been disbanded after the discovery of job-selling and kickback schemes, and in the most notorious incident a school principal was arrested for possession of crack cocaine.

If you drive around District Nine, which is in the collection of neighborhoods known to the outside world as the South Bronx (although it is actually in the West Bronx), you can see how the school system could have become so bad. The neighborhoods are, of course, largely poor and nonwhite, and remote from the mainstream of city life. What is really striking about them, though, is that the schools in them are the biggest buildings. Three- and four-story factory-style brick palaces, built before the Second World War, they tower over the landscape like cathedrals in medieval villages. In its heyday District Nine was a white ethnic working-class residential area; in the late 1960s and 1970s it was a burned-out, abandoned, desperately poor, all-minority area. Today it has been substantially rebuilt and repopulated with black and Hispanic immigrants. Public schools are still where the money and jobs are: the driving force of this school district has long been political patronage, not education.

The nine schools Crew took over are collectively referred to as "the Chancellor's District"; they have been operating separately for two full school years. At the beginning of the first year Crew replaced the principals of all nine schools. At the end of that year three of the schools had actually gotten worse on the crucial measure of reading scores, and only three had improved substantially. Crew replaced four of the nine new principals, and he adopted the Success for All reading program. This time the reading scores at all nine schools (and at three other schools that had been added to the district) rose significantly.

Measured by test scores, one of the worst schools in the Chancellor's District is Public School 63, in the Bronx. We'll stop there for a moment before moving on to the dramatically improved Public School 114, a short distance away. It is helpful to have a sense of what a failed school is really like.

ONE FAD ON TOP OF ANOTHER

TWO images of bad inner-city schools prevail in the wider culture: the out-of-control violent school, where weapon-toting gang members rule and teachers cower; and the underfunded school with over-crowded classrooms, peeling paint, leaking pipes, and broken heating. P.S. 63 is neither of these. To be sure, it has a lot of disciplinary problems, but it is only an elementary school. It is not overcrowded, because the surrounding neighborhood, Morrisania, hasn't been part of the revival of the Bronx and is still depopulated. Every day 240 students are bused in from other parts of the Bronx, and the average class size is twenty-three. Chancellor's District schools get extra money, so at the moment an insufficient budget is not P.S. 63's No. 1 problem. Overall, P.S. 63 seems more like a child-care facility than a school—a relatively benign and happy place, where an overall program of instruction was somehow never put in place. When I visited, the school was being run by a young woman named Gillian Williams; she was the fourth principal at P.S. 63 in six years. The New York City teachers' union has proposed to take over the school's management, and if it does, there will probably be a fifth principal, because the head of the union has all but promised publicly to fire Williams. Teacher turnover has also been high. Williams brought in eighteen new teachers, out of sixty-eight, for the 1997–1998 school year.

Control over curriculum in New York City schools has traditionally been diffuse: the state and the city set various standards and benchmarks that schools are expected to meet, although it is not clear what happens if they don't. Otherwise the schools establish their own instructional methods. Sometimes the superintendent selects the textbooks, readers, and worksheets; sometimes the principals do. During P.S. 63's first year in the Chancellor's District it was redesigned and given the name Author's Academy, to demonstrate its commitment to making students literate. The principal bought a new reading curriculum, which teachers were supposed to use to guide their students to basic literacy. The problem, Williams told me, was that the publisher didn't make good on its shipping date. All year long the curriculum materials arrived in bits and pieces, and the reading program had no structure at all. The school's reading scores dropped drastically.

The following year Williams came in as principal. On orders from the Chancellor's District she adopted the Success for All reading program, which is extremely demanding. The school also adopted a new math curricu-

lum that year and, because Williams considered Success for All to be insufficient, two other new reading programs. As a result most of the students were taking three separate and quite different reading classes every day. In third grade, for example, a student would learn one technique in the Success for All class for charting the structure of a story, based on Venn diagrams; another technique in the second reading class, based on "story maps"; and another technique in the third reading class, based on "character maps." The rest of the school day consisted of one math class and one period in the afternoon into which everything else was wedged. And this was just for the students in the main instructional program. A fifth of the school population was in special-education classes, and a fourth in "limited-English-proficient" classes. The school was a library of education vogues and special noncurricular functions.

A SCHOOL THAT WORKS

I SPENT a good deal of time recently in one of the Chancellor's District schools at the opposite (that is, better) end of the spectrum—enough time to move beyond the Potemkin-village phase of marveling at an inner-city school that works. A description of what happens there should convey what this particular way of fixing a broken school means, what the disadvantages are, and what kinds of opposition must be overcome if these schools are to succeed.

Public School 114 is in a neighborhood called Highbridge, which runs along the Hudson River behind Yankee Stadium. In its glory days, the 1920s, it was a lower-middle-class paradise populated mostly by Jews and Irish-Americans. Even Yankees could and did live proudly in the grand Art Deco apartment buildings along Jerome Avenue and the Grand Concourse; the humbler buildings on the cross streets were for cabbies and shopkeepers. P.S. 114, which was built in 1940, was considered a first-class school that put its students firmly on an upward sociological trajectory.

The neighborhood changed in the mid-1960s, when the Freedomland amusement park on the other side of the Bronx was torn down and the enormous Co-Op City apartment complex was built in its place. Whites left Highbridge for Co-Op City, and blacks moved in from Harlem, and then Puerto Ricans; the student population of P.S. 114 changed, first from all white to mostly black, and then to mostly Puerto Rican. The school's official name, which nobody uses, is Luis Llorens Torres Children's Academy, after the national poet of Puerto Rico. Today P.S. 114 is mostly Dominican. The surrounding neighborhood is populated by a polyglot ethnic working poor. It feels crowded and scruffy but safe; there aren't many empty buildings. Stores are filled with a wide variety of specialty items from the Caribbean, Africa, and Latin America. The elevated train on River Avenue rumbles by every few minutes.

P.S. 114, a large three-story building, has more than a thousand students, which is a third more than its official capacity. When the state's registration-review list was created, P.S. 114 was placed on it. The school's particular problem was that it had turned into a bilingual-education patronage machine. Students with Hispanic last names—which is to say most students—were assigned to "bilingual" classes taught in Spanish, often by non-English-speaking teachers. The school generally didn't test students or seek their parents' consent before putting them on the bilingual track, and it rarely moved anybody out of bilingual education, because that would have meant losing job slots for bilingual teachers. All of this was and is in violation of the state and city regulations governing bilingual education, but administrative supervision of P.S. 114 was so lax that the regulations weren't enforced. From 1989 to the creation of the Chancellor's District, in 1996, the school suffered no negative consequences for its extremely low reading scores—in fact, the consequences were arguably positive, because the low scores qualified it for special funding. The school adopted a popular and well-regarded reading program, Reading Recovery. But the program was only nominally implemented and didn't have much effect.

Eileen Mautschke, the current principal of P.S. 114 and a thirty-year veteran teacher and administrator in District Nine, describes the condition of the district years ago this way: "The district controlled things. There was so much corruption! Money went into the school board's pockets. Decentralization gave people control over a tremendous amount of money, and very little got down to the schools. District Nine was one of the worst offenders in that respect. There were warehouses elsewhere in the city full of supplies that didn't get to the kids."

In the first year of the Chancellor's District all the elementary schools devoted a ninety-minute period every morning—9:00 to 10:30, the meatiest part of the school day for young children—to reading instruction. Rudy Crew had made an arrangement with the teachers' union under which every school in the district would be allowed to replace half the teachers by transferring them to other schools. (The union was cooperative because it feared that if the Chancellor's District didn't work, the state would hire a private company to run the schools—one that didn't use union teachers.) The schools were told to redesign themselves.

Mautschke took over at P.S. 114 in the middle of the 1995–1996 school year, just before the creation of the Chancellor's District. After off-loading a third of the teachers and hiring new ones, most of them very young, she led the staff through a lengthy series of discussions. At the end of these P.S. 114 was divided into three mini-schools, called the Author's School, the School of Environmental Studies, and the School of World Discoverers. She began cleaning up the bilingual mess. At the end of her first full year P.S. 114's third-grade reading score—the number that had gotten it into trouble—had risen moderately.

During the first year Rudy Crew realized that the Chancellor's District, though an experiment in centralizing authority, was not centralized enough. He brought in a new superintendent, Barbara Byrd-Bennett (who, ironically, had begun her career thirty years earlier as a Harlem teacher fighting for community control), and replaced more principals. Most important, at the heavy prodding of the teachers' union, Crew adopted the Success for All reading curriculum.

THE PARRIS ISLAND APPROACH

THE inventor of Success for All is Robert E. Slavin, an education researcher at Johns Hopkins University who gives off the sweet-and-sour, casual-intense air of a perpetual graduate student. Slavin has been studying education in elementary schools for twenty-five years. In 1986 the Baltimore public school system asked him to try to figure out a way to prevent inner-city schoolchildren from falling permanently behind during their first few years in school. Slavin set up a program of tightly controlled reading instruction, which began at one school in Baltimore in the fall of 1987. The idea was to devise a system that could be transported from school to school. Although during the past decade Success for All has lost its contract with the Baltimore school system, it has grown rapidly elsewhere. By the end of this school year the Success for All organization will have a budget of $30 million and will operate in more than 1,100 schools all over the country. Among its customers are the Edison Project, which is private; the state of New Jersey; and the cities of Houston, Memphis, and Miami.

There are two reasons for Success for All's quick spread. Of all the school curricula it comes closest to guaranteeing the result that state education commissioners want: higher reading scores. Although it is quite expensive—about $70,000 per school in the first year, and $25,000 a year thereafter—the program is usually paid for by Title I, the federal compensatory-education program, so there is no direct cost to school districts. Because Title I targets schools with high percentages of children from poor families, Slavin says, "high-poverty schools can afford us, low-poverty can't." Success for All is used almost exclusively in poor schools. Most school designs offer testimonials and anecdotes to sell prospective customers on their effectiveness. Slavin has statistical comparisons of reading scores from schools that use Success for All and similar schools that don't. "There's nothing on most of these programs," he told me. "No data!

Organized research with control groups and reports every year, no matter what the data show—that just doesn't happen." The prevailing criticism of Success for All is that it is designed to produce higher scores on a couple of tests chosen by Slavin, for which the control-group schools don't train their students; the gains it produces, according to critics, are substantially limited to the first year of the program. Whether or not this is true, Slavin is right when he says that the other leading national programs for elementary schools can furnish almost no data at all on the results they produce.

It's not difficult to see why Success for All is so much quicker than the other programs to generate quantifiable benefits. The next two most popular programs for elementary schools—Accelerated Schools, devised by Henry Levin, of Stanford University; and the School Development Program, devised by James Comer, of Yale Medical School—are essentially planning and organization tools that give individual schools great latitude in choosing instructional methods. Success for All tells schools precisely what to teach and how to teach it—to the point of scripting, nearly minute by minute, every teacher's activity in every classroom every day of the year.

When a school adopts Success for All, its top administrators go for a week of intensive training at Slavin's headquarters. Then Success for All personnel come to the school to provide all the teachers with three days of training. The school must designate a full-time Success for All "facilitator" and a full-time parent "coordinator." Success for All representatives visit the school three times a year. Each student takes a Success for All reading test every eight weeks. Teachers must use a series of catch phrases and hand signals developed by Success for All. In kindergarten and first grade every piece of classroom material (readers, posters, tapes, videos, lesson plans, books—everything) is provided by the program. Afterward, Success for All's grip on what goes on in the classroom isn't quite as complete, because other companies' textbooks are incorporated. But it's still tight: at every level Slavin's programs greatly reduce teacher autonomy, through control of the curriculum. Slavin has developed curricula in math, science, and social studies. People usually describe Success for All with terms like "prescriptive," "highly structured," and "teacher-proof"; Slavin likes to use the word "relentless." One education researcher I spoke with called it "Taylorism in the classroom," after Frederick Winslow Taylor, the early-twentieth-century efficiency expert who routinized every detail of factory work.

The theoretical foundation of Success for All is supposedly cooperative learning, meaning that students are put into small groups or partnerships and help one another. This is true as far as it goes, but it fails to convey the full flavor of a Success for All classroom. The students do work in teams, but they don't work independently. Cooperative-learning sessions are frequent but strictly time-limited and task-defined. One purpose the sessions clearly serve is to keep students from drifting off during the times when the teacher is leading the whole class. A bit less obvious in the Success for All literature is that it teaches reading primarily through phonics (learning a word by decoding it, rather than deducing its meaning from context), which is not as popular as cooperative learning in the liberal education world. Students are tested, put into groups based on their skill levels, drilled in reading skills, tested again, regrouped, and drilled some more. The ones who are furthest behind receive individual tutoring. But everybody is supposed to learn to read.

A few minutes in a Success for All classroom conveys the Parris Island feeling of the program better than any general description could. It is first grade—the pivotal year. The students sit at their desks holding copies of a story called "Woo Zen." The teacher stands at the blackboard and says, "Okay, let's get ready for our shared story. Ready, read!" The students read the first page of the story loudly, in unison. The teacher says, "Okay, next page. Finger in place, ready, read!" After a few minutes of this the students have finished the story. Not missing a beat, the teacher says, "Close your books, please. Let's get ready for vocabulary." She moves to a posted handwritten sheet of words and points to herself. "My turn. Maze, haze, hazy, lazy. Your turn." She points to the class. The students shout out the words in unison: "Maze! Haze! Hazy! Lazy!"

Then the teacher announces that the students are going to do "red words"—Success for All lingo for words that students can't decode from their phonemic components. "Okay, do your first word," she says. The students call out together, "Only! O [clap] N [clap] L [clap] Y [clap]. Only!" After they've done the red words, the teacher says, "Now let's go to our meaningful sentences." The students read from a sheet, loudly and in unison, the definitions of three words, and then three sentences, each of which uses one of the words. The teacher sends the students into their cooperative-learning groups to write three sentences of their own, using each of the words. "If you work right, you'll earn work points for your work team! You clear?" Twenty voices call out, "Yes!"

RIGOR AND ROUTINE

SUCCESS for All can't work unless a school's principal and teachers cooperate. Partly for that reason, and partly to avoid having the program appear to be imposed from without (though in truth it usually is), Slavin will not sign on with a school unless 80 percent of its teachers have voted by secret ballot in favor of his program. At P.S. 114 in the spring of last year teachers twice voted it down, even though a third of the teachers were brand-new and the Chancellor's District, the union, and Eileen Mautschke were all pushing hard for Success for All. Then the principal arranged for the teachers to go on a field trip to an elementary school in Brooklyn that used Success for All. On the third and final vote the program passed.

The teachers' reluctance is understandable. Success for All takes over a school and substantially limits teachers' freedom. At P.S. 114 the Author's School, the School of Environmental Studies, and the School of World Discoverers are gone—not to mention the previous, teacher-chosen reading curriculum, which involved more student creativity and less drilling. All over the school are exhortatory posters. A veteran teacher who felt that she had accumulated wisdom over the decades about how to reach children would find that Success for All, in its insistently nice way, was now telling her that everything she thought she knew should be jettisoned in favor of lesson plans from Baltimore.

The atmosphere of the school, though, is cheerful and purposeful, not grumpy. Every morning, as the children stream in, Eileen Mautschke stands in the main hallway presiding over a scene that is impressive for not being completely chaotic: more than a thousand children, at least a third of whom don't speak English and every one of whom is poor enough to qualify for the federal free-lunch program, briefly assemble in a foyer that is far too small to hold them. Last year, when I was there, the school was phasing in uniforms; this year all the students have been asked to wear them. Mautschke, a middle-aged woman with an air of genial, slightly weary unflappability, does not have the strutting disciplinarian aspect of effective inner-city principals in the movies. If you told her that a tidal wave was about to hit P.S. 114, she would smile resignedly, say "Okay," and figure out what to do about it. But she plainly has the school under control. As she cruises the hallways during the day, she greets most of the children she passes by name.

After everyone has arrived and settled down, the hour and a half of Success for All begins. All the teachers in the school, even gym and music teachers, have been pressed into service as reading instructors, to bring down the size of the classes—not to the ideal fifteen but at least to twenty-four. Because there are forty-six reading groups and only thirty-two classrooms, groups meet in every nook and cranny: on the stage of the auditorium, in the library and the gym, in an oversized supply closet, even on the floor at the ends of hallways. It's not a scene of squalor, but it's not a scene you would encounter in a school for the children of the prosperous. P.S. 114 has been spruced up a bit since its worst days. It has the utilitarian look of a big, indestructible public facility—clayey coats of paint, clean linoleum, smudged grated windows, fluorescent lights.

P.S. 114 goes only through the fourth grade. For children that young, and for their teachers, an intensive ninety-minute morning class is so consuming that it uses up most of the school's daily energy supply, not to men-

tion its money. P.S. 114 doesn't do anything else nearly so elaborately as it does reading instruction. Administrators and parents (a parent representative helps in the school full time, without pay) must supervise the overcrowded lunchroom: teachers are exempted by their contract from that duty, to compensate for the length of the Success for All classes. Subjects such as science and social studies are relegated to shorter, later time slots. Not even math gets nearly so much time. Low reading scores got P.S. 114 into trouble with the state; thus reading instruction gets extra funds, staff, training, and time.

In addition to the hour and a half of Success for All, P.S. 114 devotes half an hour of every school day to preparation for state-required standardized reading exams. These classes are a junior version of a Stanley Kaplan or a Princeton Review course, in which students take old tests for practice, drill on vocabulary words, and learn little tricks— for example, that guessing on a question is better than giving up. The test that originally landed P.S. 114 on the state registration-review list and then in the Chancellor's District is called the DRP, for Degrees of Reading Power; it was until recently given to third-graders annually in May. The DRP is exactly the kind of test that education reformers most dislike. Children read a series of passages in which every seventh word is left blank, and pick from a multiple-choice menu a word to fill in each blank. They are being quizzed more on vocabulary than on understanding. For that reason New York State has since dropped the DRP in favor of another test. But during the time I spent at P.S. 114 enormous energy went into preparing students for the test—a test that teachers felt should not even be used, and that would in fact no longer be used in New York public schools after the end of that school year.

The fate of the entire Chancellor's District was heavily dependent on what these third-grade reading scores, which had not risen sufficiently in the district's first year, would be. The message had been forcefully communicated to the principals. As the date of the DRP approached, Mautschke and her teachers bore down with remarkable concentration. Every week the school's administrators met in a supply depository off the gym. These meetings were substantially devoted to test-prep matters. All the third-graders were given a pre-test in March. The worst performers were parceled out to the administrators, including Mautschke herself, to be given half an hour a day of one-on-one tutoring in addition to the regular test-prep class.

A leitmotif of the administrative meetings was the complaints of the school's consultant on teaching techniques, Deborah Fuhrer, about the overwhelming focus on test prep; Mautschke, without rancor but firmly, would overrule her. At the final staff meeting before the day of the test Mautschke outlined a program of concentrated memory drills on certain vocabulary words thought likely to appear on the test. Fuhrer said that this was a bad idea: it was imparting a trick, not a skill. One of the words the students would be taught was "anxiety." "This will increase their anxiety, that's all!" Fuhrer said. "What would you suggest?" Mautschke asked her evenly. "What would I suggest? Prayer. Prayer works well."

The third-graders did their vocabulary drills. When the test results came back, in June, 80.5 percent of the third-graders at P.S. 114 had scored at or above the state minimum level on the DRP. The school's scores are now above the average for all New York City public schools.

Of course, the score increase is a product of test prep, but not only that. P.S. 114's scores on the Success for All reading tests and the third-grade reading test that the state will use next year instead of the DRP (which has been given purely for diagnostic purposes for several years) also went up impressively. Last May the school was taken off the state registration-review list. On the day parents were to register their children to enter kindergarten, people started lining up outside P.S. 114 at 3:30 A.M. Later registrants had to be assigned to another school, because P.S. 114 could not accommodate anywhere near the number of students whose parents wanted them to go there. The Chancellor's District as a whole registered by far the largest rise in scores on the new reading test of any district in the city. At P.S. 114 most of the students are now learning to read. Only a few years ago that was not the case.

CONTROL WHERE IT'S NECESSARY

DRAWING lessons from inner-city education successes (and, for that matter, from failures) can be perilous. An improved school has a Rashomon aspect: the moral of the story depends on who's telling it. Whatever supposedly causes a school to turn around is bottled and exported to other schools, where it may or may not work. The successful school may sink back into desuetude in a year or two. Schools are often accumulations of shiny new reform ideas that have been jammed into the same small space and don't fit together particularly well.

Nonetheless, it seems clear that although several factors were at work in the improvement of P.S. 114, including a good new principal, a higher budget, a turnover in the teaching staff, a cooperative union, better staff training, physical improvements to the building, more parental involvement, and smaller class sizes, the key was the imposition of a tightly defined, proven reading curriculum. The most important thing in education is what the teacher does with students in the classroom. To direct that requires control of the curriculum. Structural changes, supposedly the essence of education reform, can have amazingly little effect if they do not alter what teachers actually teach. The importance of Success for All is less the particulars of how the program works than

the general idea that if one method can be proved to work better than any other, nonperforming schools should be required to use it exclusively. Given the paramount importance of reading in a student's education and later life as a citizen and worker, shouldn't we try to identify the best method of reading instruction, demonstrate its superiority, and then require it for children who aren't learning to read? This would inescapably require some centralization of authority over public education.

Airline safety offers a good analogy for what I'm suggesting. You can't fly on an airplane that has no radar or oxygen masks, because the federal government won't allow it. But you can get an unacceptable education in your local school, because so far the federal government has been reluctant to challenge local control. Vouchers and charter schools offer students a way out of bad public schools, but neither option assures decent education for all. Children with unmotivated or unsophisticated parents are left behind, in unacceptable conditions. Control of the curriculum from without—not for every public school, only for failed ones—is the way for the country to ensure a good education for every child.

Centralization is actually occurring fairly rapidly, but rhetorically it is still quite unpopular. We are generally in an anti-bureaucratic phase, and within education there is no organized, powerful force for centralization. Most politicians don't want to do the work of persuading voters that they should be taxed more in order to educate other people's children. Local school boards don't want to give up their power. Christian conservatives are afraid that centralization in the public schools will lead to liberal indoctrination. Economic conservatives want to privatize education as much as possible. Unions resist the teacher-evaluation systems that come with centralization.

From a philosophical standpoint the main force working against centralization is a progressive, humanist, anti-utilitarian view of the purpose of education. Most popular books about the education of young children—*Summerhill, Thirty-Six Children, Death at an Early Age*—take this view. Children are inherently creative, curious, and democratic: inspirational teachers and supportive schools can awaken and nurture these qualities; grim, factory-like traditional schools can extinguish them. Although progressive education rarely involves the kind of crude ideological brainwashing of which it is often accused, it does operate on an implied social critique: Education should counterbalance the commercial, regimented nature of adult working life. A school should be an arena for open discourse about values, not a job-skills training center. Schoolteachers—smart, hardworking people who aren't paid much and are rarely celebrated—are naturally drawn to the progressive view. It gives them creative latitude in the classroom and gives value to what they do.

What I encountered at P.S. 114 would deeply affront the progressive sensibility in education. Success for All turns teachers into drill instructors. The atmosphere is palpably one of preparing children to become workers. When I was there, Mautschke instituted a system of "scholar dollars," given to students for good behavior and redeemable for trinkets at the school store. The connection between what goes on in school and the economic world could hardly be clearer. And then there is the preoccupation with using children to generate test-score statistics that will propitiate state bureaucrats and keep the money flowing.

Probably the most celebrated progressive educator in the country is Deborah Meier. In 1974 Meier started a public school in East Harlem called Central Park East, which for the two decades she ran it was a remarkable success. Meier must be the only public-school principal to hold honorary degrees from Harvard and Yale and to have received a "genius grant" from the MacArthur Foundation. She recently left New York to start a public school in Boston, partly because she didn't like the direction in which the New York City schools were moving. Meier had helped to raise foundation money in order to "create a different kind of Chancellor's District," one that operated a string of schools on a progressive model of teacher and principal autonomy. But it was clear to her that Rudy Crew wasn't interested in that kind of thing.

I went to see Meier and ask what she thought of the district's adoption of Success for All. Of course she was extremely skeptical. She said it was natural that reading scores in the district were going up—the children were being taught how to do better on tests. "If kids are surrounded by grown-ups who don't have authority, who follow orders, how could they learn to question, to discuss ideas?" And, a little later in the conversation: "It's shameful that we've come to the point of test scores as the end of education. It's critical to do more for the intellectual side of the lives of disadvantaged kids, to introduce them to ideas. School's the only place they'll get that."

The hard nub of disagreement is over what the first task of schools should be—to impart intellectual curiosity or to impart a body of skills and knowledge. What would doubtless strike Meier as the worst excesses of the Chancellor's District and P.S. 114 are not, however, by-products of emphasizing skills over curiosity. They are by-products of decentralization.

True, Success for All and programs like it are the enemies of teacher autonomy. But almost every school that uses Success for All previously had a greater degree of teacher autonomy and was failing to teach its students well. Autonomy is hard to defend where it is demonstrably not working. It is also true that Success for All tilts a school toward reading instruction to the exclusion of other subjects—but if there has to be a tilt, it should be toward reading.

The real solution would be to develop a comprehensive curriculum covering all subjects and the entire school day—in other words, more centralization, not less. This is the aim of the whole-school reform movement, the chief promoter of which, a private organization called New American Schools, now has more than a thousand member schools that choose among eight designs, one of them developed by Robert Slavin. New American Schools persuades public school districts to abandon the usual impulsive way of reforming schools and adopt an all-encompassing design that has worked elsewhere. Even without committing themselves to New American Schools, however, many school districts have moved toward whole-school reform on their own.

Testing excesses are another consequence of decentralization. Every school gives tests. The problem lies in tests that are made enormously consequential even though they have nothing to do with what should go on in the classroom and can be prepared for with trick-pony exercises. If there were a nationally agreed-upon curriculum, regular classroom instruction would be the only test prep students would need.

I'm not suggesting that we impose a required curriculum on the great bulk of American public schools, which are functioning just fine on their own. I am suggesting, though, that nonperforming schools be put into the hands of higher authorities—up to and including the federal government— until they start performing. By far the best and most reliable means for turning these schools around would be to institute a prescribed curriculum that has been carefully researched and field-tested and has been proved to work.

Liberals have long dreamed of using the federal government to fix bad schools. The chief means has been the Title I program, passed in 1965, which gives more than $7 billion a year to schools in low-income areas. The money must be spent on instruction, but not on any particular kind of instruction. We are moving toward a better and more directed use of Title I funding, which now pays for nearly every operating Success for All program. Last year Congress passed a bill that sets aside $120 million of Title I funds for a variety of whole-school designs, with the idea of tilting the entire Title I program toward them if the results are promising. Many of the cities and states that have taken over bad schools have put together money from Title I and other federal education programs to pay for new curricula that are both intensive and imposed.

Changes of this kind are punitive to local school boards, principals, and teachers—but they had it coming. Students in taken-over schools aren't being punished; they're getting a genuine education, and hence a chance in life, that they would otherwise be denied. No reform that lets students abandon the public school system, or lets individual public schools redesign themselves in the absence of guidance, can possibly ensure a minimum standard of education for every American child. Only central control of the curriculum can. A decent education should be a guarantee, not an option.

Unit 3

Unit Selections

The Child's Feelings: Emotional Development

14. **Early Experience and Emotional Development: The Emergence of Wariness of Heights,** Joseph J. Campos, Bennett I. Bertenthal, and Rosanne Kermoian
15. **Babies, Bonds, and Brains,** Karen Wright
16. **How Kids Mourn,** Jerry Adler
17. **The EQ Factor,** Nancy Gibbs

Entry into the Social World: Peers, Play, and Popularity

18. **Children without Friends,** Janis R. Bullock
19. **Teacher Response to Superhero Play: To Ban or Not to Ban?** Brenda J. Boyd
20. **Assisting Toddlers & Caregivers During Conflict Resolutions: Interactions That Promote Socialization,** Denise A. Da Ros and Beverly A. Kovach
21. **Gender Segregation among Children: Understanding the "Cootie Phenomenon,"** Kimberly K. Powlishta

Key Points to Consider

❖ What are some of the ways that friends can be beneficial or harmful to a child's self-concept and self-esteem? Why is it important for children to become members of a peer group? Can you think of popular books or movies that illustrate the values of friendship and peers?

❖ Do you think you have a high EQ? What sort of emotional characteristics do you think may go into having a high EQ? Do you think personality is something that is innately given or can one's personality be changed in significant ways? If you had a child with a very introverted personality, should you try to help this child learn to become more extroverted? Why or why not?

❖ When you were a child, did you experience gender segregation—boys playing with boys, girls with girls? How might this have influenced your social and emotional development? Did your teachers encourage or discourage segregation between the sexes? What could a teacher or parent do to influence gender segregation? Recently, there is growing interest in schooling boys and girls in completely separate schools. What advantages or disadvantages might this have for boys and girls educated separately?

❖ Do you think children today experience high levels of aggression in their daily environment? Name some examples. As a parent or teacher, would you try to discourage children from acting out or playing aggressively, such as in the case of superhero play?

❖ Have you experienced a significant loss or death of a loved one as a child or as an adult? How would you help a child who has experienced this sort of profound loss?

 **Links** **www.dushkin.com/online/**

14. **Counseling for Children**
    http://montgomery-al.com/cfc/index.htm
15. **Help Children Work with Feelings**
    http://www.aha4kids.com/index.html
16. **Max Planck Institute for Psychological Research**
    http://www.mpipf-muenchen.mpg.de/BCD/bcd_e.htm
17. **National Child Care Information Center (NCCIC)**
    http://www.nccic.org
18. **Serendip**
    http://serendip.brynmawr.edu/serendip/

These sites are annotated on pages 4 and 5.

One of the truisms about our species is that we are social animals. From birth, each person's life is a constellation of relationships, from family at home to friends in the neighborhood and school. This unit addresses how children's social and emotional development is influenced by important relationships with parents, peers, and teachers.

When John Donne in 1623 wrote, "No man is an island . . . every man is . . . a part of the main," he implied that all humans are connected to each other and that these connections make us who we are. Early in this century, sociologist C. H. Cooley highlighted the importance of relationships with the phrase "looking-glass self" to describe how people tend to see themselves as a function of how others perceive them. Personality theorist Alfred Adler, also writing in the early twentieth century, claimed that personal strength derived from the quality of one's connectedness to others: The stronger the relationships, the stronger the person. The notion that a person's self-concept arises from relations with others also has roots in developmental psychology. As Jean Piaget once wrote, "There is no such thing as isolated individuals; there are only relations." The articles in this unit respect these traditions by emphasizing the theme that a child's development occurs within the context of relationships.

When most people think of children, words such as "carefree," "fun," "sheltered," and "happy" often come to mind—images of depression, sadness, and mourning are not typical. "How Kids Mourn" discusses the sobering situations faced by children who have experienced serious loss.

Having a high IQ is no guarantee of future life success. Recent research indicates that "emotional intelligence" as described in "The EQ Factor" may be a vital ingredient in determining how successful an individual becomes. This article describes how researchers are delving into how to assess and nurture children as they develop healthy and strong emotional skills and abilities.

Another major influence in the landscape of childhood is friendship. When do childhood friendships begin? Friends become increasingly important during the elementary school years. If forming strong, secure attachments with family members is an important task of early childhood, then one of the major psychological achievements of middle childhood is a move toward the peer group. Across the elementary school years, children spend ever-increasing time with peers in the neighborhood and at school. Janis Bullock, in "Children without Friends," examines children's relationships with peers and describes different kinds of children—popular, rejected, neglected. This article helps us understand that friends are clearly a developmental and psychological advantage.

An interesting characteristic of peer relations in childhood is that boys and girls do not often play together. Most of the time, boys play with boys and girls play with girls. "Gender Segregation among Children: Understanding the 'Cootie Phenomenon' " discusses research on this gender-role behavior and offers suggestions on how to reduce gender segregation.

EARLY EXPERIENCE AND EMOTIONAL DEVELOPMENT:
The Emergence of Wariness of Heights

Joseph J. Campos,[1] Bennett I. Bertenthal,[2] and Rosanne Kermoian[1]
[1]*University of California at Berkeley,* [2]*University of Virginia*

Abstract—Because of its biological adaptive value, wariness of heights is widely believed to be innate or under maturational control. In this report, we present evidence contrary to this hypothesis, and show the importance of locomotor experience for emotional development. Four studies bearing on this conclusion have shown that (1) when age is held constant, locomotor experience accounts for wariness of heights; (2) "artificial" experience locomoting in a walker generates evidence of wariness of heights; (3) an orthopedically handicapped infant tested longitudinally did not show wariness of heights so long as he had no locomotor experience; and (4) regardless of the age when infants begin to crawl, it is the duration of locomotor experience and not age that predicts avoidance of heights. These findings suggest that when infants begin to crawl, experiences generated by locomotion make possible the development of wariness of heights.

Between 6 and 10 months of age, major changes occur in fearfulness in

This research was supported by grants from the National Institutes of Health (HD-16195, HD-00695, and HD-25066) and from the John D. and Catherine T. MacArthur Foundation.

Address requests for reprints to Joseph J. Campos, Institute of Human Development, 1203 Tolman Hall, University of California at Berkeley, Berkeley, CA 94720.

the human infant. During this period, some fears are shown for the first time, and many others show a step-function increase in prevalence (Bridges, 1932; Scarr & Salapatek, 1970; Sroufe, 1979). These changes in fearfulness occur so abruptly, involve so many different elicitors, and have such biologically adaptive value that many investigators propose maturational explanations for this developmental shift (Emde, Gaensbauer, & Harmon, 1976, Kagan, Kearsley, & Zelazo, 1978). For such theorists, the development of neurophysiological structures (e.g., the frontal lobes) precedes and accounts for changes in affect.

In contrast to predominantly maturational explanations of developmental changes, Gottlieb (1983, 1991) proposed a model in which different types of experiences play an important role in developmental shifts. He emphasized that new developmental acquisitions, such as crawling, generate experiences that, in turn, create the conditions for further developmental changes. Gottlieb called such "bootstrapping" processes probabilistic epigenesis. In contrast to most current models of development transition, Gottlieb's approach stresses the possibility that, under some circumstances, psychological function may precede and account for development of neurophysiological structures.

There is evidence in the animal literature that a probabilistic epigenetic process plays a role in the development of wariness of heights. Held and Hein (1963), for instance, showed that dark-reared kittens given experience

with active self-produced locomotion in an illuminated environment showed avoidance of heights, whereas dark-reared littermates given passive experience moving in the same environment manifested no such avoidance. In these studies, despite equivalent maturational states in the two groups of kittens, the experiences made possible by correlated visuomotor responses during active locomotion proved necessary to elicit wariness of heights.

So long as they are prelocomotor, human infants, despite their visual competence and absence of visual deprivation, may be functionally equivalent to Held and Hein's passively moved kittens. Crawling may generate or refine skills sufficient for the onset of wariness of heights. These skills may include improved calibration of distances, heightened sensitivity to visually specified self-motion, more consistent coordination of visual and vestibular stimulation, and increased awareness of emotional signals from significant others (Bertenthal & Campos, 1990; Campos, Hiatt, Ramsay, Henderson, & Svejda, 1978).

There is anecdotal evidence supporting a link between locomotor experience and development of wariness of heights in human infants. Parents commonly report that there is a phase following the acquisition of locomotion when infants show no avoidance of heights, and will go over the edge of a bed or other precipice if the caretaker is not vigilant. Parents also report that this phase of apparent fearlessness is followed by one in which wariness of

From *Psychological Science*, January 1992, pp. 61–64. © 1992 by the American Psychological Society. Reprinted by permission of Cambridge University Press.

heights becomes quite intense (Campos et al., 1978).

In sum, both the kitten research and the anecdotal human evidence suggest that wariness of heights is not simply a maturational phenomenon, to be expected even in the absence of experience. From the perspective of probabilistic epigenesis, locomotor experience may operate as an organizer of emotional development, serving either to induce wariness of heights (i.e., to produce a potent emotional state that would never emerge without such experience) or to facilitate its emergence (i.e., to bring it about earlier than it otherwise would appear). The research reported here represents an attempt to determine whether locomotor experience is indeed an organizer of the emergence of wariness of heights.

Pinpointing the role of locomotion in the emergence of wariness of heights in human infants requires solution of a number of methodological problems. One is the selection of an ecologically valid paradigm for testing wariness of heights. Another is the determination of an outcome measure that can be used with both prelocomotor and locomotor infants. A third is a means of determining whether locomotion is playing a role as a correlate, an antecedent, an inducer, or a facilitator of the onset of wariness of heights.

The ecologically valid paradigm we selected for testing was the visual cliff (Walk, 1966; Walk & Gibson, 1961)—a large, safety-glass-covered table with a solid textured surface placed immediately underneath the glass on one side (the "shallow" side) and a similar surface placed some 43 in. underneath the glass on the floor below on the other side (the "deep" side).

To equate task demands for prelocomotor and locomotor infants, we measured the infants' wariness reactions while they were slowly lowered toward either the deep or the shallow side of the cliff. This descent procedure not only allowed us to assess differences in wariness reactions as a function of locomotor experience in both prelocomotor and locomotor infants but also permitted us to assess an index of depth perception, that is, a visual placing response (the extension of the arms and hands in anticipation of contact with the shallow, but not the deep, surface of the cliff [Walters, 1981]).

To assess fearfulness with an index appropriate to both pre- and postlocomoting infants, we measured heart rate (HR) responses during the 3-s period of descent onto the surface of the cliff. Prior work has shown consistently that heart rate decelerates in infants who are in a state of nonfearful attentiveness, but accelerates when infants are showing either a defensive response (Graham & Clifton, 1966) or a precry state (Campos, Emde, Gaensbauer, & Henderson, 1975).

To relate self-produced locomotion to fearfulness, we used a number of converging research operations. One was an *age-held-constant design*, contrasting the performance of infants who were locomoting with those of the same age who were not yet locomoting; the second was an analog of an experiential *enrichment* manipulation, in which infants who were otherwise incapable of crawling or creeping were tested after they had a number of hours of experience moving about voluntarily in walker devices; the third was an analog of an experiential *deprivation* manipulation, in which an infant who was orthopedically handicapped, but otherwise normal, was tested longitudinally past the usual age of onset of crawling and again after the delayed acquisition of crawling; and the fourth was a *cross-sequential lag design* aimed at teasing apart the effects of age of onset of locomotion and of duration of locomotor experience on the infant's avoidance of crossing the deep or the shallow side of the cliff to the mother.

EXPERIMENT 1: HR RESPONSES OF PRELOCOMOTOR AND LOCOMOTOR INFANTS

In the first study, a total of 92 infants, half locomoting for an average of 5 weeks, were tested at 7.3 months of age. Telemetered HR, facial expressions (taped from a camera under the deep side of the cliff), and the visual placing response were recorded. Each infant was lowered to each side of the cliff by a female experimenter, with the mother in another room.

As predicted from the work of Held and Hein (1963), locomotor infants showed evidence of wariness of heights, and prelocomotor infants did not. Only on deep trials did the HR of locomotor infants accelerate significantly from baselevels (by 5 beats/min), and differ significantly from the HR responses of prelocomotor infants. The HR responses of prelocomotor infants did not differ from baselevels on either the deep or the shallow sides. Surprisingly, facial expressions did not differentiate testing conditions, perhaps because the descent minimized the opportunity to target these expressions to social figures.

In addition, every infant tested, regardless of locomotor status, showed visual placing responses on the shallow side, and no infant showed placing responses on the deep side of the cliff. Thus, all infants showed evidence for depth perception on the deep side, but only locomotor infants showed evidence of fear-related cardiac acceleration in response to heights.

EXPERIMENT 2: ACCELERATION OF LOCOMOTOR EXPERIENCE

Although correlated, the development of locomotion and the emergence of wariness of heights may be jointly determined by a third factor that brings about both changes. Disambiguation of this possibility required a means of providing "artificial" locomotor experience to infants who were not yet able to crawl. This manipulation was achieved by providing wheeled walkers to infants and testing them after their mothers had reported at least 32 hr of voluntary forward movement in the device.

Infants who received walkers were divided into two groups: prelocomotor walkers (N = 9M, 9F, Mean Age = 224 days, Walker Experience = 47 hr of voluntary forward movement) and locomotor walkers (N = 9M, 7F, Mean Age = 222 days, Walker Experience = 32 hr). The performance of infants in these two groups was compared with the performance of age-matched subjects, also divided into two groups: prelocomotor controls (N = 9M, 9F, Mean Age = 222 days) and locomotor controls (N = 9M, 7F, Mean Age = 222 days). The average duration of crawling experience was only 5 days in the locomotor walker and the locomotor control groups. All infants were tested using the same procedure as in the prior study. No shallow trials were administered in order to minimize subject loss due to the additional testing time required for such trials.

As revealed in Figure 1, the three groups of infants with any type of locomotor experience showed evidence of cardiac acceleration, whereas the prelocomotor control infants did not. It is noteworthy that all 16 infants in the locomotor walker group (who had a "double dosage" of locomotor experience consisting of walker training and some crawling) showed HR accelerations upon descent to the cliff. Planned comparisons revealed significant differences between (1) all walker infants and all controls, (2) all spontaneously locomoting infants and prelocomotor controls, and (3) prelocomotor walkers and prelocomotor controls. These findings show that the provision of "artificial" locomotor experience may facilitate or induce wariness of heights, even for infants who otherwise have little or no crawling experience. Locomotor experience thus appears to be an antecedent of the emergence of wariness.

EXPERIMENT 3: DEPRIVATION OF LOCOMOTOR EXPERIENCE

Although Experiment 2 showed that training in locomotion accelerates the onset of wariness of heights, it is possible that this response would eventually develop even in the absence of locomotor experience. To determine whether the delayed acquisition of crawling precedes the delayed emergence of wariness of heights, we longitudinally tested an infant with a peripheral handicap to locomotion. This infant was neurologically normal and had a Bayley Developmental Quotient of 126, but was born with two congenitally dislocated hips. After an early operation, he was placed in a full body cast. The infant was tested on the visual cliff monthly between 6 and 10 months of age using the procedures described above. While the infant was in the cast, he showed no evidence of crawling. At 8.5 months of age (i.e., 1.5 months after the normative age of onset of locomotion), the cast was removed, and the infant began crawling soon afterward.

This infant showed no evidence of differential cardiac responsiveness on the deep versus shallow side of the cliff until 10 months of age, at which time his HR accelerated markedly on the deep side, and decelerated on the shallow. Although we cannot generalize from a single case study, these data provide further support for the role of self-produced locomotion as a facilitator or inducer of wariness of heights.

EXPERIMENT 4: AGE OF ONSET OF LOCOMOTION VERSUS LOCOMOTOR EXPERIENCE

In the studies described so far, HR was used as an imperfect index of wariness. However, we felt that a study using behavioral avoidance was

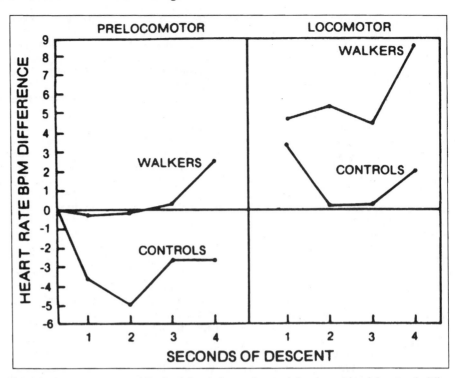

Fig. 1. Heart rate response while the infant is lowered toward the deep side of the visual cliff as a function of locomotor experience. The left panel contrasts the performance of prelocomotor infants with and without "artificial" walker experience. The right panel contrasts the performance of crawling infants with and without "artificial" walker experience. Heart rate is expressed as difference from baseline in beats/min.

needed to confirm the link between locomotor experience and wariness of heights. We thus used the locomotor crossing test on the visual cliff, in which the infant is placed on the center of the cliff, and the mother is instructed to encourage the infant to cross to her over either the deep or the shallow side. In this study, we also assessed separately the effects of age of onset of crawling (early, normative, or late) and of duration of locomotor experience (11 or 41 days), as well as their interaction, using a longitudinal design.

The results of this study demonstrated a clear effect of locomotor experience independent of the age when self-produced locomotion first appeared. This effect of experience was evident with both nominal data (the proportion of infants who avoided descending onto the deep side of the cliff on the first test trial) and interval data (the latency to descend from the center board of the visual cliff onto the deep side on deep trials minus the latency to descend onto the shallow side on shallow trials). At whatever age the infant had begun to crawl, only 30% to 50% of infants avoided the deep side after 11 days of locomotor experience. However, after 41 days of locomotor experience, avoidance increased to 60%

to 80% of infants. The latency data revealed a significant interaction of side of cliff with locomotor experience, but not a main effect of age, nor of the interaction of age with experience. The results of this study further suggest that locomotor experience paces the onset of wariness of heights.

PROCESSES UNDERLYING THE DEVELOPMENT OF WARINESS OF HEIGHTS

The pattern of findings obtained in these four studies, taken together with the animal studies by Held and Hein (1963), demonstrates a consistent relation between locomotor experience and wariness of heights. We propose the following interpretations for our findings.

We believe that crawling initially is a goal in itself, with affect solely linked to the success or failure of implementing the act of moving. Locomotion is initially not context dependent, and infants show no wariness of heights because the goal of moving is not coordinated with other goals, including the avoidance of threats. However, as a result of locomotor experience, infants acquire a sense of both the efficacy and the limitations of their own actions. Locomotion stops being an end in itself, and begins to be goal corrected and coordinated with the environmental surround. As a result, infants begin to show wariness of heights once locomotion becomes context dependent (cf. Bertenthal & Campos, 1990).

The context-dependency of the infants' actions may come about from falling and near-falling experiences that locomotion generates. Near-falls are particularly important because they are frequent, they elicit powerful emotional signals from the parent, and they set the stage for long-term retention of negative affect in such contexts.

There is still another means by which the infant can acquire a sense of wariness of depth with locomotion. While the infant moves about voluntarily, visual information specifying self-movement becomes more highly correlated with vestibular information specifying the same amount of self-movement (Bertenthal & Campos, 1990). Once expectancies related to the correlation of visual and vestibular information are formed, being lowered toward the deep side of the cliff creates a violation of the expected correlation. This violation results from the absence of visible texture near the infant when lowered toward the deep side of the cliff, relative to the shallow side. As a consequence, angular acceleration is not detected by the visual system, whereas it is detected by the vestibular system. This violation of expectation results in distress proportional to the magnitude of the violation. A test of this interpretation requires assessment of the establishment of visual-vestibular coordination as a function of locomotor experience and confirmation that wariness occurs in contexts that violate visual-vestibular coordination.

LOCOMOTOR EXPERIENCE AND OTHER EMOTIONAL CHANGES

The consequences of the development of self-produced locomotion for emotional development extend far beyond the domain of wariness of heights. Indeed, the onset of locomo-

tion generates an entirely different emotional climate in the family. For instance, as psychoanalytic theories predict (e.g., Mahler, Pine, & Bergman, 1975), the onset of locomotion brings about a burgeoning of both positive and negative affect—positive affect because of the child's new levels of self-efficacy; negative affect because of the increases in frustration resulting from thwarting of the child's goals and because of the affective resonance that comes from increased parental expressions of prohibition (Campos, Kermoian, & Zumbahlen, in press). Locomotion is also crucial for the development of attachment (Ainsworth, Blehar, Waters, & Wall, 1978; Bowlby, 1973), because it makes physical proximity to the caregiver possible. With the formation of specific attachments, locomotion increases in significance as the child becomes better able to move independently toward novel and potentially frightening environments. Infants are also more sensitive to the location of the parent, more likely to show distress upon separation, and more likely to look to the parent in ambiguous situations.

Locomotion also brings about emotional changes in the parents. These changes include the increased pride (and sometimes sorrow) that the parents experience in their child's new mobility and independence and the new levels of anger parents direct at the baby when the baby begins to encounter forbidden objects. It seems clear from the findings obtained in this line of research that new levels of functioning in one behavioral domain can generate experiences that profoundly affect other developmental domains, including affective, social, cognitive, and sensorimotor ones (Kermoian & Campos, 1988). We thus propose that theoretical orientations like probabilistic epigenesis provide a novel, heuristic, and timely perspective for the study of emotional development.

REFERENCES

Ainsworth, M. D. S., Blehar, M., Waters, E., & Wall, S. (1978). *Patterns of attachment.* Hillsdale, NJ: Erlbaum.

Bertenthal, B., & Campos, J. J. (1990). A systems approach to the organizing effects of self-produced locomotion during infancy. In C. Rovee-Collier & L. P. Lipsitt (Eds.), *Advances in infancy research* (Vol. 6, pp. 1–60). Norwood, NJ: Ablex.

Bowlby, J. (1973). *Attachment and loss: Vol. 2. Separation.* New York: Basic Books.

Bridges, K. M. (1932). Emotional development in early infancy. *Child Development, 3,* 324–341.

Campos, J. J., Emde, R. N., Gaensbauer, T. J., & Henderson, C. (1975). Cardiac and behavioral interrelationships in the reactions of infants to strangers. *Developmental Psychology, 11,* 589–601.

Campos, J. J., Hiatt, S., Ramsay, D., Henderson, C., & Svejda, M. (1978). The emergence of fear of heights. In M. Lewis & L. Rosenblum (Eds.), *The development of affect* (pp. 149–182). New York: Plenum Press.

Campos, J. J., Kermoian, R., & Zumbahlen, R. M. (in press). In N. Eisenberg (Ed.), *New directions for child development.* San Francisco: Jossey-Bass.

Emde, R. N., Gaensbauer, T. J., & Harmon, R. J. (1976). Emotional expression in infancy: A biobehavioral study. *Psychological Issues* (Vol. 10, No. 37). New York: International Universities Press.

Gottlieb, G. (1983). The psychobiological approach to developmental issues. In P. Mussen (Ed.), *Handbook of child psychology: Vol. II. Infancy and developmental psychobiology* (4th ed.) (pp. 1–26). New York: Wiley.

Gottlieb, G. (1991). Experiential canalization of behavioral development: Theory. *Developmental Psychology, 27,* 4–13.

Graham, F. K., & Clifton, R. K. (1966). Heartrate change as a component of the orienting response. *Psychological Bulletin, 65,* 305–320.

Held, R., & Hein, A. (1963). Movement-produced stimulation in the development of visually-guided behavior. *Journal of Comparative and Physiological Psychology, 56,* 872–876.

Kagan, J., Kearsley, R., & Zelazo, P. R. (1978). *Infancy: Its place in human development.* Cambridge, MA: Harvard University Press.

Kermoian, R., & Campos, J. J. (1988). Locomotor experience: A facilitator of spatial cognitive development. *Child Development, 59,* 908–917.

Mahler, M., Pine, F., & Bergman, A. (1975). *The psychological birth of the human infant.* New York: Basic Books.

Scarr, S., & Salapatek, P. (1970). Patterns of fear development during infancy. *Merrill-Palmer Quarterly, 16,* 53–90.

Sroufe, L. A. (1979). Socioemotional development. In J. Osofsky (Ed.), *Handbook of infant development* (pp. 462–516). New York: Wiley.

Walk, R. (1966). The development of depth perception in animals and human infants. *Monographs of the Society for Research in Child Development, 31*(Whole No. 5).

Walk, R., & Gibson, E. (1961). A comparative and analytical study of visual depth perception. *Psychological Monographs, 75*(15, Whole No. 5).

Walters, C. (1981). Development of the visual placing response in the human infant. *Journal of Experimental Child Psychology, 32,* 313–329.

Everybody knows a kid needs love. Now neuroscience is closing
in on just how TLC shapes a child's brain and behavior.

BABIES, BONDS, AND BRAINS

BY KAREN WRIGHT

IN TERMS OF BEHAVIORAL DEvelopment, I was something of a late bloomer. My mother reports that I slept away most of my infancy and toddlerhood, and even my adolescence was unremarkable. I didn't enter my angst-and-experimentation phase until my mid-20s, when, like a tortured teen, I blamed my parents for everything. Several years and several thousand dollars of psychotherapy later, I let my parents off the hook. I realized it couldn't all be their doing—my faults, my fears, my penchant for salty, cheese-flavored snack foods. I am not, after all, the simple product of my upbringing.

This healthy outlook threatened to come undone one recent afternoon as I stood outside the cages at the National Institutes of Health Animal Center in Poolesville, Maryland, watching Stephen Suomi's monkeys. Suomi, a primatologist at the National Institute of Child Health and Human Development, studies the effects of rearing environments on the behavior of young rhesus macaques. Fifty graduates of his program live in the center's five-acre enclosure; at the moment, they are gathered in a large chain-link cell with sawdust on the floor and monkey toys dangling from the ceiling. The arrival of human visitors stirs this cohort like dry leaves in a whirlwind, and its members quickly segregate into three factions. The boldest rush to get a cage-front view of the newcomers; a second phalanx hovers behind

them, cautious but curious; and at the far end of the cage a third group forms a simian huddle of abject fear.

These monkeys are most definitely the products of their respective upbringings. The three groups were raised in three distinct settings. The bold monkeys spent the first six months of life being shuttled between monkey play groups and individual cages (and so were used to human handling); the sensibly cautious ones were reared by their natural families, with mothers, fathers, and siblings; and the fearful monkeys grew up parentless among same-age peers, to whom they retain an abnormally strong attachment.

Suomi is keenly interested in the spectrum of behavior among his macaques—from bold and aggressive to anxious and withdrawn—for it parallels the human trait known as temperament, the fundamental cast of personality that governs our propensity for hobnobbing, taking risks, or seeking thrills. He and other researchers have found that temperament is reflected in biology as well as behavior: heart rate, immune response, stress-hormone levels, and other physiological measures can be correlated with temperamental styles in humans and monkeys alike. And despite some investigators' assertions to the contrary, Suomi's experiments imply that temperament may be largely the result of a young monkey's home life.

"The patterns have some genetic heritability," says Suomi, jangling his car keys in front of the cage to get an even more exaggerated response. "But our work shows that you can modify these tendencies quite dramatically with certain types of early experiences."

Suomi belongs to the league of scientists who are studying the role that early childhood environment plays in determining adult behavior. He and his colleagues are working a bit beyond the pale, as late-twentieth-century science seems to savor the notion of genetic determinism. But the effects of childhood environment—specifically, the "environment" supplied by parenting—are coming under renewed scrutiny now, in large part because recent neurological studies have revealed that the structure of a child's brain remains surprisingly malleable months and even years after birth. The number of connections between nerve cells in an infant's brain grow more than 20-fold in the first few months of life, for example; a two-year-old's brain contains twice as many of these connections, called synapses, as an adult's brain. Throughout early childhood, synapses multiply and are pruned away at a furious pace. Something directs this dynamic rewiring, and researchers have concluded that that something is experience.

Of course, "experience" can come in all shapes and sizes. Childhood illness and diet, for example, count as experiences, too. But there's reason to believe that a child's experience of his parents is an especially potent sculptor of the parts of the brain involved in emotion, personality, and behavior. Some studies indicate that the strength of a child's bonding with his caregivers may increase his ability to learn and to cope with stress. Others show that childhood abuse and neglect can prime the brain for a lifetime of inappropriate aggression and scattered attention.

AS THE TWENTIETH CENTURY draws to a close, more than half of America's one-year-olds are spending their days with someone other than their mothers. This historic surge in day care has coincided with a rush of reports showing that early experiences may be more critical to brain development than anyone had previously imagined. Naturally, each new bulletin tweaks the guilty fears of working parents. So far, however, the news about kids and day care is pretty good. Children in day care appear to do just fine—provided the quality of the interactions between caregiver and child is high—and good day care may even enhance their social skills and performance in school. Low-quality day care, on the other hand, may compromise a child's adjustment and academic performance.

These results are not surprising to behavioral researchers, who have long appreciated the importance of bonds between caregivers and children. "We know that little kids don't hop up and run away from lions—they don't deal directly with the world much," says Megan Gunnar, a developmental psychologist at the University of Minnesota in Minneapolis. "Their survival depends on their relationships." Hence, children are keenly attuned to the cues they receive from parents, says Gunnar, and they are especially sensitive to signs of indifference. Responsive, sensitive parents inspire trust in their children, giving rise to what behavioral scientists call secure attachment; insensitive or withdrawn parents can foster insecure attachment.

Nearly four decades of behavioral research has painted a dramatic picture of how important this attachment is to a child's emotional health. University of Wisconsin psychologist Harry Harlow's pioneering studies in the late fifties and early sixties found that monkeys reared

in total isolation developed aberrant feeding, mating, parenting, and socializing behaviors. Developmental psychologists now believe that bonding with a parent or other caregiver is as essential to a normal childhood as learning to walk and talk. In the absence of a "good mother," children will attach as best they can to whatever figure presents itself—just as Harlow's infant monkeys became virtually inseparable from the cloth-and-wire surrogates in their cages.

Stephan Suomi's simian charges are another example of how behavior can be

man beings. At the same time, turnover of norepinephrine, a chemical messenger associated with fearfulness, is unusually rapid in peer-reared monkeys. The monkeys' immune systems tend to be suppressed, while their levels of stress hormones are higher and their heart rates faster than those of mother-reared monkeys. Might these be the fruits of insecure attachment?

Megan Gunnar thinks so. Gunnar studies the relationship between attachment security and reactions to stress in human infants and toddlers. She's found

"It's not just what happens to you that counts—it's what you think happens to you. And it's difficult to figure out what a child is thinking."

warped by bonding with a maladroit mom. The timid peer-reared monkeys at the NIH center are the victims of insecure attachment; their peers didn't provide the stability and sensitivity that make for a secure bond. (Imagine what a wreck you'd be if you were raised by a twin sister.) These monkeys are anxious and inhibited, and their temperaments are reflected in their reluctance to explore strange objects, their shyness with unfamiliar peers, their low status in monkey communities, and their distress on being separated from their companions. Some peer-reared monkeys, mostly males, also have self-destructive tendencies toward impulsive behavior and aggression. They're the playground bullies, and they're often shunned by, or even kicked out of, their play groups.

Clearly, peer-rearing has unhappy consequences for an individual's social skills and ability to cope with stress. It has at least one other embarrassing side effect as well. "Every animal that's reared without a mother, no matter what its other social experience may be, turns out to be hyperoral," says Suomi. "They all suck their thumbs a lot."

Peer-rearing also leaves a distinctive stamp on the monkey's physiology. Samples of cerebrospinal fluid from Suomi's impulsive monkeys show that they grow up with lower levels of serotonin, a mood-regulating biochemical that has been linked with aggression, antisocial behavior, and depression in hu-

that stressful circumstances such as vaccinations, the presence of strangers, and separation from mom produce elevations of the stress hormone cortisol in infants. By age two, however, children with secure attachments to their mothers don't get these cortisol rushes, even when they act stressed out. Children with insecure attachment, on the other hand, continue to show elevations of cortisol. It's as if secure attachment comforts the body more than the mind.

"In the animal literature, the contact with adult conspecifics—it doesn't have to be the mom, but it needs to be somebody who acts like a mom and that the baby is familiar with—has powerful effects at blocking the activity of stress-response systems," says Gunnar. "If the attachment figure is present, and the relationship has been reliable, then some aspect of the stress response just doesn't happen."

That's a good thing, says Gunnar, because a hyperactive stress-response system can wreak havoc on the body. The racing heartbeats and suppressed immune systems that Suomi sees in peer-rearing monkeys, for example, are responses that would normally occur to help the young animal cope with a transient stress—such as being left alone while mom goes out and mates. But in peer-reared monkeys, the stress response is cranked up day in, day out, and that super-responsiveness persists into adolescence—long past the age of primate attachment. Gunnar proposes that such a skewed stress-response system can promote lasting behavioral changes by interfering with brain development. In rat pups, she points out, chronic stress is known to disturb the development of the limbic system, frontal lobes, and hippocampus, parts of the brain that are involved in fearfulness and vigilance, attention focusing, learning, and memory. Gunnar suggests that secure attachment serves as a buffer against these disturbances, while insecure attachment leaves the brain open to insults that can result in lifelong anxiety, timidity, and learning difficulties.

OF COURSE, ANXIOUS, inhibited, or impulsive behavior isn't necessarily the result of early attachment problems. The extensive work of Harvard psychologist Jerome Kagan certainly suggests that such traits can be inborn. Kagan finds that 20 percent of human infants have the behavioral and physiological signs of an inhibited temperament at just four months of age—presumably, in Kagan's view, before a child's environment would have exerted its effects. He has also found that up to 40 percent of four-month-olds have signs of a bold or fearless nature. These tendencies often mellow with time, however, so that by age four only 10 percent of children are either fearful or reckless.

Suomi finds virtually the same proportions of bold and fearful monkeys in his mother-reared troops—a fact that seems to argue for the genetic conservation of temperament. But Kagan contends that the rich inner life of the child may limit the relevance of animal studies, despite the seeming parallels in primate personalities. "It's not just what happens to you that counts—it's what you *think* happens to you," says Kagan. "And it is inordinately difficult to figure out what a child is thinking. Until we devise ways to measure what is in a child's head, we're not going to understand the child's environment."

The inner life of the child may help explain the phenomenon of so-called resilient children, those who somehow manage to rise above difficult home environments and live normal, even accomplished, lives. But these children are exceptional; it's clear that abusive or negligent parenting can have devastating effects on a child's emotional develop-

ment. All the evidence suggests that physical abuse in childhood, for example, leads to a higher risk of drug use, mood disorders, violence, and criminality in adulthood. Girls who are sexually abused are more prone to depression, panic attacks, eating disorders, drug use, and suicide. And children reared in orphanages, without any parenting at all, often develop a disturbing array of social and behavioral problems. Researchers are beginning to explore the biological mechanisms for these associations, but it's not hard to imagine the psychological ones.

"I think there are people who, for genetic reasons, are more susceptible to certain kinds of stressful stimulation," says Bruce Perry, who studies the physiology of abused and neglected children at the Baylor College of Medicine in Houston. "But even with the optimum genetic organization, trauma will create the problems we're talking about."

Many of the kids Perry sees have been exposed to domestic violence, and their unpredictable and threatening home lives, he says, can be read in both their physiology and their behavior. They seem to be in a perpetual state of arousal: their "fight or flight" response has somehow been permanently activated, and they have tense muscles, rapid heart rates, and trouble sleeping. Their stress-response systems may be irreparably altered. "These kids grow up with a neurophysiology that is perfectly adapted to survive in a chaotic, distressing environment," says Perry. "They develop this extreme hypervigilance because they never know what is going to happen next."

But the children of domestic violence are poorly adapted to life in a nonviolent world. Their vigilance can lead them to misinterpret other people's behavior and intentions, says Perry. Boys, for example, will perceive hostility and aggression in a look or an offhand remark and respond too readily in kind (think

Robert DeNiro in *Taxi Driver*). Girls are more likely to shut down or withdraw completely from even mildly threatening circumstances. In school, both boys and girls tend to tune out verbal information and become hypersensitive to nonverbal cues. They might focus more on a teacher's hand gestures, for example, than the subject he's lecturing on.

Perhaps it's not surprising that severe stress in childhood leaves both biological and behavioral scars. But researchers are learning that even less extreme emotional stressors, such as parental conflict or depression, can also have an impact

Growing up in even a mildly bad environment appears to affect your biology. The question is whether those changes can be reversed.

on kids' behavior and biology. The children of depressed mothers, for example, are at increased risk for depression themselves, and most psychologists think the risk cannot be ascribed entirely to genetics. EEG studies by psychologist Geraldine Dawson of the University of Washington in Seattle show that babies whose mothers are depressed have reduced activity in the left frontal region of the brain—the area implicated in joy, interest, and other positive emotions.

Growing up in even a mildly bad environment appears to affect your biology. The question, of course, is whether those changes can be reversed. Several lines of research suggest that they can be. Suomi, for example, has shown that even monkeys who *are born* anxious and inhibited can overcome their temperamental handicap—and even rise to the top of the dominance hierarchy in their troop—if they are raised by ultranurturing supermoms. Kagan's work confirms that mothering can alter the course of an inhibited child's development. A pioneering day-care program at the University of North Carolina at Chapel Hill has cut the incidence of mental retardation by as much as 80 percent among kids whose unstimulating home environment put them at high risk for low IQ. Dawson, too, has found that psychologically depressed mothers who manage to stay positive and engaged in caregiving can minimize the impact of their depression on their babies' brain waves. And her follow-up work revealed that, at age three, children's EEGs will return to normal if their mothers' depression lifts.

"So I wonder, how plastic is the brain?" says Dawson. "At what point in development do we start to see enduring effects as opposed to transient effects?"

The answer may be never. The new model of neural development holds that the primitive areas of the brain mature first: in the first three years of life, the regions in the cortex that govern our sensory and motor skills undergo the most dramatic restructuring, and these perceptual centers, along with instinctual ones such as the limbic system, will be strongly affected by early childhood experiences. This vulnerability is nothing to scoff at, says Robert Thatcher, a neuroscientist at the University of South Florida College of Medicine in Tampa. "The limbic system is where we live, and the cortex is basically a slave to that," he explains.

But the frontal cortex, which governs planning and decision making, and the cerebellum, a center for motor skills, are also involved in emotional development. And those parts of the brain don't get rewired until a person is five to seven years old. What's more, another major restructuring of the brain occurs between ages nine and eleven, says Thatcher. Suddenly, the brain is looking less like a sculpture in stone and more like a work in progress.

In fact, Thatcher's reading of the EEGs of adolescents and adults have revealed that some reorganization of the brain may occur about every two years from birth to death. He proposes that these reorganizations happen in response to waves of nerve growth factor that sweep across the cerebral hemispheres in two-year cycles, revamping up to one-fifth of the brain's synaptic connections at the leading edge of the wave. The idea of the traveling waves is just a theory now—but it's a theory that's making more sense to more scientists.

"The brain doesn't stop changing after three years," says Megan Gunnar. "For some things, the windows of influence are only beginning to close at that age, and for others they're only beginning to open." If Thatcher is right, the brain is, in fact, under lifelong renovation. Long-term studies are just now beginning to demonstrate that experiences later in life can redirect emotional and behavioral development, even in adulthood. Some of us—and our parents—are greatly relieved by the news.

How Kids Mourn

Dealing with death: Let children grieve, the experts say. Don't shield them from loss, but help them express their fear and anger. **BY JERRY ADLER**

THE PAIN NEVER GOES AWAY," says Geoff Lake, who is 15 now, and was 11 when his mother, Linda, died of a rare form of cancer. He is only starting to realize it, but at each crucial passage of life—graduation, marriage, the birth of children—there will be a face missing from the picture, a kiss never received, a message of joy bottled up inside, where it turns into sorrow. His sleep will be shadowed by ghosts, and the bittersweet shock of awakening back into a world from which his mother is gone forever. If he lives to be 100, with a score of descendants, some part of him will still be the boy whose mother left for the hospital one day and never came home.

A child who has lost a parent feels helpless, even if he's a future King of England; abandoned, even in a palace with a million citizens wailing at the gates. But children have ways of coping with loss, if they are allowed to mourn in their own ways. Grief can be mastered, even if it is never quite overcome, and out of the appalling dysfunction of the Windsor family, one of the few positive signs psychologists could point to was the sight of William and Harry trudging manfully behind their mother's bier, both brushing away tears during the service. "There is something very healing," says Catherine Hillman, coordinator of the Westminster Bereavement Service, "about openly sharing pain."

The death of a parent can have devastating psychological consequences, including anxiety, depression, sleep disturbances, underachievement and aggression. But so can a lot of other things, and losing a parent is actually less devastating than divorce. "We know that children tend to do better after a parental death than a divorce," says sociologist Andrew Cherlin of Johns Hopkins, "and that's a stunning statistic, because you'd think death would be harder." Historically, people have always had mechanisms for coping with the early death of a parent, a fairly common event until recently.

As late as 1900, a quarter of all American children had lost at least one parent by the age of 15. The figure today is about 6 percent. A century ago most people lived on farms and died at home, so children had a fairly intimate, routine acquaintance with death. In the genteel, antiseptic suburban culture of midcentury, death became an abstraction for most American children, something that happened on television (and, in the case of cartoon characters, was infinitely reversible). Growing up as what psychologist Therese Rando calls "the first death-free generation," Americans forgot the rituals of grief so ancient that they predate civilization itself. So the mental-health profession has had to fill the gap. In the last few decades more then 160 "bereavement centers" have opened around the country, directed at allowing children to express and channel their grief over the death of a parent or sibling. The one thing they can't do is make the grief disappear, because it never does.

If they could enroll, William and Harry would be prime candidates for bereavement counseling. Experts consider them almost a case study in risk factors for future emotional problems, with the notable exception that, unlike many other children who have lost a parent, their social and financial status is not in any jeopardy. But children who experience "multiple family transitions"—such as a death on top of Charles and Diana's acrimonious and humiliatingly public divorce—"don't do as well as children who experience just one," Cherlin warns. David Zinn, medical director of Beacon Therapeutic Center in Chicago, thinks this may be especially true if there is some casual connection, however remote, between the divorce and the death. It is not such a great leap of logic, for a child, to blame his father for the circumstances that put his mother in the back seat of a speeding car with a drunk at the wheel.

Moreover, the princes are each at an age that has been identified—by different experts—as being at particular risk when a parent dies. An adolescent, such as the 15-year-old William, is already undergoing difficult life changes, says Rabbi Earl Grollman, author of 25 books on coping with loss. "You're not only dealing with the death of a parent, you're dealing with the death of your own childhood," he says. "You thought you were beginning to know yourself, but now the road ahead is uncertain." "I think it's hardest when you're 9 to 12," says Maxine Harris, author of "The Loss That Is Forever." (Harry was just short of his 13th birthday when Diana died.) "You're not a little kid, so you feel more shy about crying or sitting on someone's lap, but you're also not an adolescent, with all the independence that comes with that."

Worse yet, in the opinions of most armchair specialists, is the famously reticent and undemonstrative temperament of the Windsor family. "The way to handle grief is to allow the expression of feelings and the sharing of sadness," declares Dr. Dennis Friedman, a psychiatrist who has written a book on the psyche of the British royal family. "This particular family doesn't allow the expression of grief.... There has been a pat-

"Can't we just fly up to heaven and get her and bring her back when God isn't looking?"

Some mourning children draw or paint, others pound a toy in frustration

tern of deprivation of love beginning with Victoria, then gathering momentum, and ending up with Charles. [The princes] are bereaved not only by the loss of a mother who was very close to them, but also for a father who is quite often unavailable to them because of his duties and temperament."

It will be hardest at night, when the routines of the day wind down and the memories crowd in. Nighttime is when 11-year-old Dennis Heaphy leaves his bedroom and pads down the hall of his home in New York's Long Island to take his place on the floor of the master bedroom. His 7-year-old sister, Catherine, is already sleeping in bed alongside their mother, Mary Beth, who lies awake with her own thoughts of Brian, the husband who died of a brain tumor last January. He was 37, a big, strong man until he got sick. Dennis remembers his father's teaching him to play basketball and the hockey games they would play in the street until 9 o'clock at night. The memories make him miss his father even more, but they are precious all the same. "My sister doesn't remember my dad so well," Dennis says. "She remembers him from when he was sick, when he would get mad at the littlest things and not act like himself. We have to help her out."

Children cling to their memories, try to fortify them against the passage of the years. "They're always afraid they're going to forget how their mother looked, what her voice sounded like, how she smelled," says Debby

Shimmel, a volunteer at the St. Francis Center in Washington. They paint their memories onto the quilts that are ubiquitous at bereavement centers, little shards of a shattered family, sharp enough to pierce the heart: "Mommy read Matty bedtime stories." "Leo and Mommy played Candyland." Or they draw their parents as angels in heaven. Envisioning what heaven is like for their dads, says Stefanie Norris of the Good Mourning program in Park Ridge, Ill., children sometimes draw a giant football stadium. At the end of each eight-week group session, children hold a memorial for their dead parents; they wear something their parent wore, or perhaps make one of their favorite dishes. This is a more concrete form of memorial than a church eulogy, and a lot more meaningful to a 7-year-old.

The other thing children can't do in church is get angry, but bereavement centers provide for that as well. The Dougy Center in Portland, Ore., the model for scores of bereavement houses around the country, includes a "splatter room," where kids throw violent sploches of paint, an innovation suggested by a child who came to the center after his father had been accidentally shot to death in his home by police. And most centers have some variation of the "volcano room," thickly padded with foam and supplied with large stuffed animals that are periodically pummeled into piles of lint. Barney is said to be the favorite of many teenagers.

This is, as it happens, almost the exact opposite of what was accepted wisdom a generation ago, when children were encouraged to get on with their lives and parents advised not to depress them with reminders of the departed. Lori Lehmann was 6 when her mother died of leukemia, 30 years ago. Lori was dropped off at a neighbor's house for the funeral, and afterward her father packed up all her mother's belongings and took down all her photographs, and no one ever talked about her. "He was so sad that you didn't feel like you could ask him about it," she remembers. Her father died himself nine years later, and now she is trying to reconstruct her parents, her mother especially, from relatives' memories. "It's the little things they tell me that I really love," she says. "Like what she cooked for dessert. I don't think my aunts realize how I cling to these things." Of course, by not talking to her, her father was sparing his own feelings as well; men of that generation didn't like to be seen crying.

And it's easy for parents to overlook the grief of young children. A child of 6, says New York psychiatrist Elliot Kranzler, is just on the cusp of mastering the four essential attributes of death: that is has a specific cause, involves the cessation of bodily function, is irreversible and is universal. Before that, children may nod solemnly when told of their father's death, and still expect him to be home for dinner. Young children process their loss a bit at a time; they may be sad for 10 minutes, then ask to go outdoors to play. And they are captives of childhood's inescapable solipsism. "It hits them over the head that they have needs to be met, and one key provider is gone," says Kranzler. "They pretty quickly tell their surviving parents to remarry." That isn't callous, merely practical on the child's part; and, of course, when the parent finally does remarry, it is one of the invariable rules of human psychology that the children will hate the new spouse. "There has not been a person I've interviewed who liked their stepparents when they were children," says Harris.

Children mourn piecemeal; they must return to it at each stage of maturity and conquer grief anew. Over the years, the sharp pang of loss turns to a dull ache, a melancholy that sets in at a certain time of year, a certain hour of the night. But every child who has lost a parent remains, in some secret part of his or her soul, a child forever frozen at a moment in time, crying out to the heedless heavens, as Geoff Lake did, when his mother died just days before his 12th birthday: "Mom, why did you die? *I had plans.*"

With PAT WINGERT *in Washington,* KAREN SPRINGEN *in Chicago,* BRAD STONE *in New York,* PATRICIA KING *in San Francisco,* CLAUDIA KALB *in Boston and* DONNA FOOTE *in London*

The EQ Factor

New brain research suggests that emotions, not IQ, may be the true measure of human intelligence

NANCY GIBBS

IT TURNS OUT THAT A SCIENTIST CAN SEE THE future by watching four-year-olds interact with a marshmallow. The researcher invites the children, one by one, into a plain room and begins the gentle torment. You can have this marshmallow right now, he says. But if you wait while I run an errand, you can have two marshmallows when I get back. And then he leaves.

Some children grab for the treat the minute he's out the door. Some last a few minutes before they give in. But others are determined to wait. They cover their eyes; they put their heads down; they sing to themselves; they try to play games or even fall asleep. When the researcher returns he gives the children their hard-earned marshmallows. And then, science waits for them to grow up.

By the time the children reach high school, something remarkable has happened. A survey of the children's parents and teachers found that those who as four-year-olds had the fortitude to hold out for the second marshmallow generally grew up to be better adjusted, more popular, adventurous, confident and dependable teenagers. The children who gave in to temptation early on were more likely to be lonely, easily frustrated and stubborn. They buckled under stress and shied away from challenges. And when some of the students in the two groups took the Scholastic Aptitude Test, the kids who held out longer scored an average of 210 points higher.

When we think of brilliance we see Einstein, deep-eyed, woolly haired, a thinking machine with skin and mismatched socks. High achievers, we imagine, were wired for greatness from birth. But then you have to wonder why, over time, natural talent seems

to ignite in some people and dim in others. This is where the marshmallows come in. It seems that the ability to delay gratification is a master skill, a triumph of the reasoning brain over the impulsive one. It is a sign, in short, of emotional intelligence. And it doesn't show up on an IQ test.

For most of this century, scientists have worshiped the hardware of the brain and the software of the mind; the messy powers of the heart were left to the poets. But cognitive theory could simply not explain the questions we wonder about most: why some people just seem to have a gift for living well; why the smartest kid in the class will probably not end up the richest; why we like some people virtually on sight and distrust others; why some people remain buoyant in the face of troubles that would sink a less resilient soul. What qualities of the mind or spirit, in short, determine who succeeds?

The phrase "emotional intelligence" was coined by Yale psychologist Peter Salovey and the University of New Hampshire's John Mayer five years ago to describe qualities like understanding one's own feelings, empathy for the feelings of others and "the regulation of emotion in a way that enhances living." Their notion is about to bound into the national conversation, handily shortened to EQ, thanks to a new book, *Emotional Intelligence* (Bantam; $23.95) by Daniel Goleman. Goleman, a Harvard psychology Ph.D. and a *New York Times* science writer with a gift for making even the chewiest scientific theories digestible to lay readers, has brought together a decade's worth of behavioral research into how the mind processes feelings. His goal, he announces on the cover, is to redefine what it means to be smart. His thesis: when it comes to predict-

ing people's success, brainpower as measured by IQ and standardized achievement tests may actually matter less than the qualities of mind once thought of as "character" before the word began to sound quaint.

At first glance, there would seem to be little that's new here to any close reader of fortune cookies. There may be no less original idea than the notion that our hearts hold dominion over our heads. "I was so angry," we say, "I couldn't think straight." Neither is it surprising that "people skills" are useful, which amounts to saying, it's good to be nice. "It's so true it's trivial," says Dr. Paul McHugh, director of psychiatry at Johns Hopkins University School of Medicine. But if it were that simple, the book would not be quite so interesting or its implications so controversial.

This is no abstract investigation. Goleman is looking for antidotes to restore "civility to our streets and caring to our communal life." He sees practical applications everywhere for how companies should decide whom to hire, how couples can increase the odds that their marriages will last, how parents should raise their children and how schools should teach them. When street gangs substitute for families and schoolyard insults end in stabbings, when more than half of marriages end in divorce, when the majority of the children murdered in this country are killed by parents and stepparents, many of whom say they were trying to discipline the child for behavior like blocking the TV or crying too much, it suggests a demand for remedial emotional education. While children are still young, Goleman argues, there is a "neurological window of opportunity" since the brain's prefrontal circuitry, which regulates how we act on

From *Time*, October 2, 1995, pp. 60–66, 68. © 1995 by Time Inc. Magazine Company. Reprinted by permission.

what we feel, probably does not mature until mid-adolescence.

And it is here the arguments will break out. Goleman's highly popularized conclusions, says McHugh, "will chill any veteran scholar of psychotherapy and any neuroscientist who worries about how his research may come to be applied." While many researchers in this relatively new field are glad to see emotional issues finally taken seriously, they fear that a notion as handy as EQ invites misuse. Goleman admits the danger of suggesting that you can assign a numerical yardstick to a person's character as well as his intellect; Goleman never even uses the phrase EQ in his book. But he (begrudgingly) approved an "unscientific" EQ test in *USA Today* with choices like "I am aware of even subtle feelings as I have them," and "I can sense the pulse of a group or relationship and state unspoken feelings."

"You don't want to take an average of your emotional skill," argues Harvard psychology professor Jerome Kagan, a pioneer in child-development research. "That's what's wrong with the concept of intelligence for mental skills too. Some people handle anger well but can't handle fear. Some people can't take joy. So each emotion has to be viewed differently."

EQ is not the opposite of IQ. Some people are blessed with a lot of both, some with little of either. What researchers have been trying to understand is how they complement each other; how one's ability to handle stress, for instance, affects the ability to concentrate and put intelligence to use. Among the ingredients for success, researchers now generally agree that IQ counts for about 20%; the rest depends on everything from class to luck to the neural pathways that have developed in the brain over millions of years of human evolution.

It is actually the neuroscientists and evolutionists who do the best job of explaining the reasons behind the most unreasonable behavior. In the past decade or so, scientists have learned enough about the brain to make judgments about where emotion comes from and why we need it. Primitive emotional responses held the keys to survival: fear drives the blood into the large muscles, making it easier to run; surprise triggers the eyebrows to rise, allowing the eyes to widen their view and gather more information about an unexpected event. Disgust wrinkles up the face and closes the nostrils to keep out foul smells.

Emotional life grows out of an area of the brain called the limbic system, specifically the amygdala, whence come delight and disgust and fear and anger. Millions of years ago, the neocortex was added on, enabling humans to plan, learn and remember. Lust grows from the limbic system; love, from the neocortex. Animals like reptiles that have no neocortex cannot experience anything like maternal love; this is why baby

snakes have to hide to avoid being eaten by their parents. Humans, with their capacity for love, will protect their offspring, allowing the brains of the young time to develop. The more connections between limbic system and the neocortex, the more emotional responses are possible.

It was scientists like Joseph LeDoux of New York University who uncovered these cerebral pathways. LeDoux's parents owned a meat market. As a boy in Louisiana, he first learned about his future specialty by cutting up cows' brains for sweetbreads. "I found them the most interesting part of the cow's anatomy," he recalls. "They were visually pleasing—lots of folds, convolutions and patterns. The cerebellum was more interesting to look at than steak." The butchers' son became a neuroscientist, and it was he who discovered the short circuit in the brain that lets emotions drive action before the intellect gets a chance to intervene.

A hiker on a mountain path, for example, sees a long, curved shape in the grass out of the corner of his eye. He leaps out of the way before he realizes it is only a stick that looks like a snake. Then he calms down; his cortex gets the message a few milliseconds after his amygdala and "regulates" its primitive response.

Without these emotional reflexes, rarely conscious but often terribly powerful, we would scarcely be able to function. "Most decisions we make have a vast number of possible outcomes, and any attempt to analyze all of them would never end," says University of Iowa neurologist Antonio Damasio, author of *Descartes' Error: Emotion, Reason and the Human Brain.* "I'd ask you to lunch tomorrow, and when the appointed time arrived, you'd still be thinking about whether you should come." What tips the balance, Damasio contends, is our unconscious assigning of emotional values to some of those choices. Whether we experience a somatic response—a gut feeling of dread or a giddy sense of elation—emotions are helping to limit the field in any choice we have to make. If the prospect of lunch with a neurologist is unnerving or distasteful, Damasio suggests, the invitee will conveniently remember a previous engagement.

When Damasio worked with patients in whom the connection between emotional brain and neocortex had been severed because of damage to the brain, he discovered how central that hidden pathway is to how we live our lives. People who had lost that linkage were just as smart and quick to reason, but their lives often fell apart nonetheless. They could not make decisions because they didn't know how they felt about their choices. They couldn't react to warnings or anger in other people. If they made a mistake, like a bad investment, they felt no regret or shame and so were bound to repeat it.

If there is a cornerstone to emotional intelligence on which most other emotional skills depend, it is a sense of self-awareness, of being smart about what we feel. A person whose day starts badly at home may be grouchy all day at work without quite knowing why. Once an emotional response comes into awareness—or, physiologically, is processed through the neocortex—the chances of handling it appropriately improve. Scientists refer to "metamood," the ability to pull back and recognize that "what I'm feeling is anger," or sorrow, or shame.

Metamood is a difficult skill because emotions so often appear in disguise. A person in mourning may know he is sad, but he may not recognize that he is also angry at the person for dying—because this seems somehow inappropriate. A parent who yells at the child who ran into the street is expressing anger at disobedience, but the degree of anger may owe more to the fear the parent feels at what could have happened.

In Goleman's analysis, self-awareness is perhaps the most crucial ability because it allows us to exercise some self-control. The idea is not to repress feeling (the reaction that has made psychoanalysts rich) but rather to do what Aristotle considered the hard work of the will. "Anyone can become angry—that is easy," he wrote in the *Nicomachean Ethics.* "But to be angry with the right person, to the right degree, at the right time, for the right purpose, and in the right way—that is not easy."

Some impulses seem to be easier to control than others. Anger, not surprisingly, is one of the hardest, perhaps because of its evolutionary value in priming people to action. Researchers believe anger usually arises out of a sense of being trespassed against—the belief that one is being robbed of what is rightfully his. The body's first response is a surge of energy, the release of a cascade of neurotransmitters called catecholamines. If a person is already aroused or under stress, the threshold for release is lower, which helps explain why people's tempers shorten during a hard day.

Scientists are not only discovering where anger comes from; they are also exposing myths about how best to handle it. Popular wisdom argues for "letting it all hang out" and having a good cathartic rant. But Goleman cites studies showing that dwelling on anger actually increases its power; the body needs a chance to process the adrenaline through exercise, relaxation techniques, a well-timed intervention or even the old admonition to count to 10.

Anxiety serves a similar useful purpose, so long as it doesn't spin out of control. Worrying is a rehearsal for danger; the act of fretting focuses the mind on a problem so it can search efficiently for solutions. The danger comes when worrying blocks thinking, becoming an end in itself or a path to resignation instead of perseverance. Over-worrying about failing increases the likelihood of failure; a salesman so concerned about his falling sales that he can't bring himself to pick up the phone guarantees that his sales will fall even further.

But why are some people better able to "snap out of it" and get on with the task at hand? Again, given sufficient self-awareness, people develop coping mechanisms. Sadness and discouragement, for instance, are "low arousal" states, and the dispirited salesman who goes out for a run is triggering a high arousal state that is incompatible with staying blue. Relaxation works better for high energy moods like anger or anxiety. Either way, the idea is to shift to a state of arousal that breaks the destructive cycle of the dominant mood.

The idea of being able to predict which salesmen are most likely to prosper was not an abstraction for Metropolitan Life, which in the mid-'80s was hiring 5,000 salespeople a year and training them at a cost of more than $30,000 each. Half quit the first year, and four out of five within four years. The reason: selling life insurance involves having the door slammed in your face over and over again. Was it possible to identify which people would be better at handling frustration and take each refusal as a challenge rather than a setback?

The head of the company approached psychologist Martin Seligman at the University of Pennsylvania and invited him to test some of his theories about the importance of optimism in people's success. When optimists fail, he has found, they attribute the failure to something they can change, not some innate weakness that they are helpless to overcome. And that confidence in their power to effect change is self-reinforcing. Seligman tracked 15,000 new workers who had taken two tests. One was the company's regular screening exam, the other Seligman's test measuring their levels of optimism. Among the new hires was a group who flunked the screening test but scored as "superoptimists" on Seligman's exam. And sure enough, they did the best of all; they outsold the pessimists in the regular group by 21% in the first year and 57% in the second. For years after that, passing Seligman's test was one way to get hired as a MetLife salesperson.

Perhaps the most visible emotional skills, the ones we recognize most readily, are the "people skills" like empathy, graciousness, the ability to read a social situation. Researchers believe that about 90% of emotional communication is nonverbal. Harvard psychologist Robert Rosenthal developed the PONS test (Profile of Nonverbal Sensitivity) to measure people's ability to read emotional

One Way to Test Your EQ

UNLIKE IQ, WHICH IS GAUGED BY THE FAMOUS STANFORD-Binet tests, EQ does not lend itself to any single numerical measure. Nor should it, say experts. Emotional intelligence is by definition a complex, multifaceted quality representing such intangibles as self-awareness, empathy, persistence and social deftness.

Some aspects of emotional intelligence, however, can be quantified. Optimism, for example, is a handy measure of a person's self-worth. According to Martin Seligman, a University of Pennsylvania psychologist, how people respond to setbacks—optimistically or pessimistically—is a fairly accurate indicator of how well they will succeed in school, in sports and in certain kinds of work. To test his theory, Seligman devised a questionnaire to screen insurance salesmen at MetLife.

In Seligman's test, job applicants were asked to imagine a hypothetical event and then choose the response (A or B) that most closely resembled their own. Some samples from his questionnaire:

You forget your spouse's (boyfriend's/girlfriend's) birthday.
A. I'm not good at remembering birthdays.
B. I was preoccupied with other things.

You owe the library $10 for an overdue book.
A. When I am really involved in what I am reading, I often forget when its due.
B. I was so involved in writing the report, I forgot to return the book.

You lose your temper with a friend.
A. He or she is always nagging me.
B. He or she was in a hostile mood.

You are penalized for returning your income-tax forms late.
A. I always put off doing my taxes.
B. I was lazy about getting my taxes done this year.

You've been feeling run-down.
A. I never get a chance to relax.
B. I was exceptionally busy this week.

A friend says something that hurts your feelings.
A. She always blurts things out without thinking of others.
B. My friend was in a bad mood and took it out on me.

You fall down a great deal while skiing.
A. Skiing is difficult.
B. The trails were icy.

You gain weight over the holidays, and you can't lose it.
A. Diets don't work in the long run.
B. The diet I tried didn't work.

Seligman found that those insurance salesman who answered with more B's than A's were better able to overcome bad sales days, recovered more easily from rejection and were less likely to quit. People with an optimistic view of life tend to treat obstacles and setbacks as temporary (and therefore surmountable). Pessimists take them personally; what others see as fleeting, localized impediments, they view as pervasive and permanent.

The most dramatic proof of his theory, says Seligman, came at the 1988 Olympic Games in Seoul, South Korea, after U.S. swimmer Matt Biondi turned in two disappointing performances in this first two races. Before the Games, Biondi had been favored to win seven golds—as Mark Spitz had done 16 years earlier. After those first two races, most commentators thought Biondi would be unable to recover from his setback. Not Seligman. He had given some members of the U.S. swim team a version of his optimism test before the races; it showed that Biondi possessed an extraordinarily upbeat attitude. Rather than losing heart after turning in a bad time, as others might, Biondi tended to respond by swimming even faster. Sure enough, Biondi bounced right back, winning five gold medals in the next five races. —*By Alice Park*

cues. He shows subjects a film of a young woman expressing feelings—anger, love, jealousy, gratitude, seduction—edited so that one or another nonverbal cue is blanked out. In some instances the face is visible but not the body, or the woman's eyes are hidden, so that viewers have to judge the feeling by subtle cues. Once again, people with higher PONS scores tend to be more successful in their work and relationships; children who score well are more popular and successful in school, even [though] their IQs are quite average.

Like other emotional skills, empathy is an innate quality that can be shaped by experience. Infants as young as three months old exhibit empathy when they get upset at the sound of another baby crying. Even very young children learn by imitation; by watching how others act when they see someone in distress, these children acquire a repertoire of sensitive responses. If, on the other hand, the feelings they begin to express are not recognized and reinforced by the adults around them, they not only cease to express those feelings but they also become less able to recognize them in themselves or others.

Empathy too can be seen as a survival skill. Bert Cohler, a University of Chicago psychologist, and Fran Stott, dean of the Erikson Institute for Advanced Study in Child Development in Chicago, have found that children from psychically damaged families frequently become hypervigilant, developing an intense attunement to their parents' moods. One child they studied, Nicholas, had a horrible habit of approaching other kids in his nursery-school class as if he were going to kiss them, then would bite them instead. The scientists went back to study videos of Nicholas at 20 months interacting with his psychotic mother and found that she had responded to his every expression of anger or independence with compulsive kisses. The researchers dubbed them "kisses of death," and their true significance was obvious to Nicholas, who arched his back in horror at her approaching lips—and passed his own rage on to his classmates years later.

Empathy also acts as a buffer to cruelty, and it is a quality conspicuously lacking in child molesters and psychopaths. Goleman cites some chilling research into brutality by Robert Hare, a psychologist at the University of British Columbia. Hare found that psychopaths, when hooked up to electrodes and told they are going to receive a shock, show none of the visceral responses that fear of pain typically triggers: rapid heartbeat, sweating and so on. How could the threat of punishment deter such people from committing crimes?

It is easy to draw the obvious lesson from these test results. How much happier would we be, how much more successful as individuals and civil as a society, if we were more alert to the importance of emotional

Square Pegs in the Oval Office?

IF A HIGH DEGREE OF EMOTIONAL INTELLIGENCE IS A PREREQUISITE FOR OUTSTANDing achievement, there ought to be no better place to find it than in the White House. It turns out, however, that not every man who reached the pinnacle of American leadership was a gleaming example of self-awareness, empathy, impulse control and all the other qualities that mark an elevated EQ.

Oliver Wendell Holmes, who knew intelligence when he saw it, judged Franklin Roosevelt "a second-class intellect, but a first-class temperament." Born and educated as an aristocrat, F.D.R. had polio and needed a wheelchair for most of his adult life. Yet, far from becoming a self-pitying wretch, he developed an unbridled optimism that served him and the country well during the Depression and World War II—this despite, or because of, what Princeton professor Fred Greenstein calls Roosevelt's "tendency toward deviousness and duplicity."

Even a first-class temperament, however, is not a sure predictor of a successful presidency. According to Duke University political scientist James David Barber, the most perfect blend of intellect and warmth of personality in a Chief Executive was the brilliant Thomas Jefferson, who "knew the importance of communication and empathy. He never lost the common touch." Richard Ellis, a professor of politics at Oregon's Willamette University who is skeptical of the whole EQ theory, cites two 19th century Presidents who did not fit the mold. "Martin Van Buren was well adjusted, balanced, empathetic and persuasive, but he was not very successful," says Ellis. "Andrew Jackson was less well adjusted, less balanced, less empathetic and was terrible at controlling his own impulses, but he transformed the presidency."

Lyndon Johnson as Senate majority leader was a brilliant practitioner of the art of political persuasion, yet failed utterly to transfer that gift to the White House. In fact, says Princeton's Greenstein, L.B.J. and Richard Nixon would be labeled "worst cases" on any EQ scale of Presidents. Each was touched with political genius, yet each met with disaster. "To some extent," says Greenstein, "this is a function of the extreme aspects of their psyches; they are the political versions of Van Gogh, who does unbelievable paintings and then cuts off his ear."

History professor William Leuchtenburg of the University of North Carolina at Chapel Hill suggests that the 20th century Presidents with perhaps the highest IQs—Wilson, Hoover and Carter—also had the most trouble connecting with their constituents. Woodrow Wilson, he says, "was very high strung [and] arrogant; he was not willing to strike any middle ground. Herbert Hoover was so locked into certain ideas that you could never convince him otherwise. Jimmy Carter is probably the most puzzling of the three. He didn't have a deficiency of temperament; in fact, he was too temperate. There was an excessive rationalization about Carter's approach."

That was never a problem for John Kennedy and Ronald Reagan. Nobody ever accused them of intellectual genius, yet both radiated qualities of leadership with an infectious confidence and openheartedness that endeared them to the nation. Whether President Clinton will be so endeared remains a puzzle. That he is a Rhodes scholar makes him certifiably brainy, but his emotional intelligence is shaky. He obviously has the knack for establishing rapport with people, but he often appears so eager to please that he looks weak. "As for controlling his impulses," says Willamette's Ellis, "Clinton is terrible." —*By Jesse Birnbaum. Reported by James Carney/Washington and Lisa H. Towle/Raleigh*

intelligence and more adept at teaching it? From kindergartens to business schools to corporations across the country, people are taking seriously the idea that a little more time spent on the "touchy-feely" skills so often derided may in fact pay rich dividends.

In the corporate world, according to personnel executives, IQ gets you hired, but EQ gets you promoted. Goleman likes

to tell of a manager at AT&T's Bell Labs, a think tank for brilliant engineers in New Jersey, who was asked to rank his top performers. They weren't the ones with the highest IQs; they were the ones whose E-mail got answered. Those workers who were good collaborators and networkers and popular with colleagues were more likely to get the cooperation they needed to reach their goals than the socially awkward, lone-wolf geniuses.

When David Campbell and others at the Center for Creative Leadership studied "derailed executives," the rising stars who flamed out, the researchers found that these executives failed most often because of "an interpersonal flaw" rather than a technical inability. Interviews with top executives in the U.S. and Europe turned up nine so-called fatal flaws, many of them classic emotional failings, such as "poor working relations," being "authoritarian" or "too ambitious" and having "conflict with upper management."

At the center's executive-leadership seminars across the country, managers come to get emotionally retooled. "This isn't sensitivity training or Sunday-supplement stuff," says Campbell. "One thing they know when they get through is what other people think of them." And the executives have an incentive to listen. Says Karen Boylston, director of the center's team-leadership group: "Customers are telling businesses, 'I don't care if every member of your staff graduated with honors from Harvard, Stanford and Wharton. I will take my business and go where I am understood and treated with respect.'"

Nowhere is the discussion of emotional intelligence more pressing than in schools, where both the stakes and the opportunities seem greatest. Instead of constant crisis intervention, or declarations of war on drug abuse or teen pregnancy or violence, it is time, Goleman argues, for preventive medicine. "Five years ago, teachers didn't want to think about this," says principal Roberta Kirshbaum of P.S. 75 in New York City. "But when kids are getting killed in high school, we have to deal with it." Five years ago, Kirshbaum's school adopted an emotional literacy program, designed to help children learn to manage anger, frustration, loneliness. Since then, fights at lunchtime have decreased from two or three a day to almost none.

Educators can point to all sorts of data to support this new direction. Students who are depressed or angry literally cannot learn. Children who have trouble being accepted by their classmates are 2 to 8 times as likely to drop out. An inability to distinguish distressing feelings or handle frustration has been linked to eating disorders in girls.

Many school administrators are completely rethinking the weight they have been giving to traditional lessons and standardized tests. Peter Relic, president of the National Association of Independent Schools, would like to junk the SAT completely. "Yes, it may cost a heck of a lot more money to assess someone's EQ rather than using a machine-scored test to measure IQ," he says. "But if we don't, then we're saying that a test score is more important to us than who a child is as a human being. That means an immense loss in terms of human potential because we've defined success too narrowly."

This warm embrace by educators has left some scientists in a bind. On one hand, says Yale psychologist Salovey, "I love the idea that we want to teach people a richer understanding of their emotional life, to help them achieve their goals." But, he adds, "what I would oppose is training conformity to social expectations." The danger is that any campaign to hone emotional skills in children will end up teaching that there is a "right" emotional response for any given situation—laugh at parades, cry at funerals, sit still at church. "You can teach self-control," says Dr. Alvin Poussaint, professor of psychiatry at Harvard Medical School. "You can teach that it's better to talk out your anger and not use violence. But is it good emotional intelligence not to challenge authority?"

SOME PSYCHOLOGISTS GO FURTHER AND challenge the very idea that emotional skills can or should be taught in any kind of formal, classroom way. Goleman's premise that children can be trained to analyze their feelings strikes Johns Hopkins' McHugh as an effort to reinvent the encounter group: "I consider that an abominable idea, an idea we have seen with adults. That failed, and now he wants to try it with children? Good grief!" He cites the description in Goleman's book of an experimental program at the Nueva Learning Center in San Francisco. In one scene, two fifth-grade boys start to argue over the rules of an exercise, and the teacher breaks in to ask them to talk about what they're feeling. "I appreciate the way you're being assertive in talking with Tucker," she says to one student. "You're not attacking." This strikes McHugh as pure folly. "The author is presuming that someone has the key to the right emotions to be taught to children. We don't even know the right emotions to be taught to adults. Do you really think a child of eight or nine really understands the difference between aggressiveness and assertiveness?"

The problem may be that there is an ingredient missing. Emotional skills, like intellectual ones, are morally neutral. Just as a genius could use his intellect either to cure cancer or engineer a deadly virus, someone with great empathic insight could use it to inspire colleagues or exploit them. Without a moral compass to guide people in how to employ their gifts, emotional intelligence can be used for good or evil. Columbia University psychologist Walter Mischel, who invented the marshmallow test and others like it, observes that the knack for delaying gratification that makes a child one marshmallow richer can help him become a better citizen or—just as easily—an even more brilliant criminal.

Given the passionate arguments that are raging over the state of moral instruction in this country, it is no wonder Goleman chose to focus more on neutral emotional skills than on the values that should govern their use. That's another book—and another debate.

—Reported by Sharon E. Epperson and Lawrence Mondi/New York, James L. Graff/Chicago and Lisa H. Towle/Raleigh

Children Without Friends

Who Are They and How Can Teachers Help?

Janis R. Bullock

This article highlights an area that should be of great concern to educators—children without friends. The author notes the serious implications of growing up friendless: "The uniqueness of peer relationships contributes to a child's normal development." Now, proven techniques of identification allow teachers and other professionals to help such children.—R. J. S.

Janis R. Bullock is Assistant Professor, Human Development and Counseling, Montana State University, Bozeman.

Children who have difficulty forming friendships and gaining acceptance among peers have received a tremendous amount of interest over the past decade. Research indicates that approximately 6 to 11 percent of elementary school-age children have no friends or receive no friendship nominations from peers (Hymel & Asher, 1977). This figure varies depending upon the assessment procedure used and it may be even higher in some subgroups. For example, children who have learning disabilities (Greshan, 1988) or are mildly retarded (Taylor, Asher & Williams, 1987) may experience even more difficulties forming social relationships. Nonetheless, many average and above-average children are without friends. Consequently, research and intervention focusing on children with peer relationship problems are becoming more extensive.

Researchers continue to seek information that may contribute to the understanding and awareness of these children. Many children who experience poor peer relations are at risk and need support. Research on the consequences of peer rejection can provide teachers with the foundation and rationale for effective intervention. Teachers working closely with children who lack friends understand the frustration such students experience during attempts to interact with peers.

The uniqueness of peer relationships contributes to a child's normal development. Unlike adult-child relationships, child-child relations are more egalitarian and involve more reciprocal interactions. These inter-actions help children achieve competency in many areas. Therefore, children who lack friends do not enjoy many important benefits of interaction. Peer relations should be viewed as necessary for a child's healthy development.

Identifying Children Without Friends

In order to determine a child's status within the peer group, researchers often use two variations of sociometric measurement techniques. These measures rely on children's perceptions of others and can identify those children who are rejected or neglected by their peer group. A widely used sociometric technique is the peer nomination method (Hymel & Rubin, 1985). In this technique, children are asked to pick from a list the names of three children with whom they like to play and three children with whom they do not like to play. In general, this procedure provides a useful means of assessing children's impact on their peers. Rejected children receive few positive nominations, while neglected children receive few positive *or* negative nominations.

The rating scale measure (Singleton & Asher, 1977), a slightly different approach, is used to assess social acceptance of preference within the peer group. Children are asked to rate each classmate on a 1-5 Likert-type scale, in response to questions about how much they like to play or work with that classmate. Rejected children receive very low overall ratings, whereas ratings of neglected children do not differ from those of average children. Although neglected children are generally liked, they very often lack friends.

Sociometric Stratus and Behaviors in Children

Once researchers were able to identify rejected and neglected children, they became interested in determining the behaviors associated with each status. Information is typically gathered on child behavior in three ways: peer reports, teacher reports and direct observation. The behaviors of the children are then correlated with sociometric status.

Peers can provide an important perspective on the behavior norms within a peer group, providing insight on areas often unavailable or unknown to adults. A common technique requires children to characterize the behavior of peers (e.g., aggressive, helpful, cooperative, shy). A variety of behaviors attributed to children by their peers are related to their sociometric status (Carlson, Lahey & Neeper, 1984; Coie, Dodge & Coppotelli, 1982; Wasik, 1987). Across age groups, peers accept children who are considered helpful, friendly, cooperative, cheerful and prosocial. Peer rejection is generally associated with aggression, disruption and fighting. Shy, quiet children lacking social involvement are often neglected.

Because of their considerable contact with children, teachers can provide a valuable perspective on children's behavior. French and Waas (1988) obtained teacher ratings on popular, rejected and neglected 2nd-and 5th-grade children. Rejected children were characterized as aggressive, hostile and task avoidant, while neglected children were described as having more school behavior problems than popular children. Coie and Dodge (1988) asked teachers to rank 1st- and 2nd-grade boys of different sociometric statuses on a variety of peer aggression items. Well-accepted and neglected children were described as the least aggressive, whereas rejected children were described as the most aggressive. Rejected children also scored low in conformity to rules and interpersonal sensitivity. In general, teacher assessments coincided with children's perceptions.

Direct observational methods also contribute to research on the assessment of peer group behavior. Trained observers unacquainted with children can provide unbiased information on discrete behaviors of children. Various studies on school-age children (Dodge, Coie & Brakke, 1982; Gottman, Gonso & Rasmussen, 1975; Ladd, 1983) show a high de-

Evidence suggests that peer rejection may be such an adverse experience that adolescents decide to leave school.

gree of consistency in outcomes. Both popular and average-status children engage in more cooperative play and social conversation than do rejected children. Rejected children show many more inappropriate behaviors than any of the other status groups. Often alone, they wander around the room and are off-task during the work period. They are also more aggressive, argumentative and likely to engage in disruptive peer interactions.

Less observational information is available on neglected children. In general, they spend more time alone and make fewer social contacts. When they do attempt to make a social contact, they are often ignored. They are characterized as being neither aggressive nor disruptive and have difficulty integrating with peers. They engage in more solitary activities than other children (Dodge, Coie & Brakke, 1982). In general, research suggests that children who are rejected and neglected display certain behaviors that may contribute to their failure to interact with peers.

Children's Status and Dropping Out of School

Children who continually experience rejection are considered to be at risk for dropping out of school. Approximately 20 percent of children who enter school do not graduate for various reasons (Weiner, 1980). A small percentage leave reluctantly, generally due to family emergencies or crises. Others do so because of frustrations related to poor social adjustment. Yet, the majority of these students are considered at least average in intelligence with the ability to graduate.

Several studies provide support for the hypothesis that peer assessments of low acceptance can predict future dropouts. Gronlund and Holmlund (1958) reported that 54 percent of low-accepted boys dropped out of school, compared to 19 percent of high-accepted boys. Among girls, the dropout figure was 35 percent for low acceptance, compared to 4 percent for high acceptance. Barclay (1966) reported that low-accepted boys and girls were two to three times more likely to drop out of school.

These early studies did not distinguish between rejected and neglected children, a more recent concern. Kupersmidt's (1983) study does address the subclassification issue. In a 6-year longitudinal study of 5th-graders, she reports the dropout rate included 30 percent of the rejected, 10 percent of the neglected, 21 percent of the average and 4 percent of the popular sample. Although differences were only marginally significant, the rejected group did show a greater dropout rate. Kupersmidt suggests that perhaps only the rejected children are at risk.

In sum, evidence suggests that many adolescents who drop out of school experience poor peer adjustments in their earlier years of school. They are more likely to drop out of school than their more accepted peers. The effects appear to be stronger for boys than girls, yet patterns are consistent regardless of gender. Evidence suggests that peer rejection may be such an adverse experience that adolescents decide to leave school (Kupersmidt, Coie & Dodge, 1990). The relationship between neglected children and dropout rates is not so clear and needs further examination.

Considerations for Teachers
Children who are rejected by their peers often report feelings of loneliness and lower levels of self-esteem. A sensitive and supportive teacher will be aware of these feelings and will attempt to assess each child's situation. Teachers can begin by careful observation of the child. While observing the child who appears to be having difficulty interacting with peers, the teacher can ask:

- Do the children in the class seem to avoid, ignore and reject the child?
- Does the child lack certain social skills necessary for successful interaction with others?
- Does the child have difficulty interpreting other peoples' cues or requests?
- Does the child have difficulty communicating with other about his/her needs and desires?
- Does the child act aggressively while interacting with others?
- Is the child disruptive in the class?

Although there are no plans that work with every child, teachers can choose from several approaches found to be successful. Teachers will need to choose strategies that best fit

the child's needs, are adaptable to the classroom and support their philosophy.

Some children are disliked by peers because they lack the skills necessary to get along with others. Researchers (Oden & Asher, 1977) have developed techniques for coaching children in social skills. Coaching involves identifying the child's problem and providing some form of direct instruction regarding strategies for use when interacting with peers.

Children can be coached on specific concepts that will contribute to more positive interactions. Concepts that were used by Oden and Asher (1977) included participation (e.g., how to get started and the impor-

> *Not having friends contributes to loneliness, low self-esteem and inability to develop social skills.*

tance of paying attention), cooperation (e.g., the importance of taking turns and sharing materials), communication (e.g., the importance of talking with others and listening) and being friendly and nice (e.g., the importance of smiling, helping and encouraging others). Coaches can assist children by:

- telling them why each concept is important to peer interaction
- asking for examples to assess children's understanding of the concept
- reinforcing the examples or providing suggestions when children have trouble finding their own examples

- discussing both positive and negative behavioral examples that are important to interactions
- trying out some of the ideas in a play situation
- assessing the situation afterward.

Some children may benefit from practice with younger age-mates. Coaching children has contributed to long-term changes in their behavior and sociometric status.

Children who have difficulty reading other children's cues may benefit by watching others who interact successfully. Low-status children can watch a variety of successful interactions on videotape or acted out by adults, other children or puppets. Studies (Gresham & Nagle, 1980; Jakibchuk & Smeraglio, 1976) indicate that low-status children exhibit an increase in positive interaction after viewing models, and the effects are maintained over time. Factors contributing to these positive outcomes seem to be:

- similarity of the model to the target child
- explicitly identifying the model's behavior to the target child
- using simple step-by-step narration to describe the purposes of the behavior (Asher, Renshaw & Hymel, 1982).

Children who act aggressively toward others are often the least liked in the classroom. Self-control training, also referred to as cognitive behavior modification, focuses on the maintenance of positive behaviors through internal cognitive control (Meichenbau, 1985). In some cases, teaching aggressive children to self-regulate their behavior has proven more effective in reducing inappropriate behaviors than external reinforcers from teachers (Bolstad & Johnson, 1972).

Researchers (Camp, Blom, Herbert & Van Doornick, 1977) have taught children to reinforce themselves directly by following a thinking-out-loud strategy that was found to reduce disruptive behaviors and increase prosocial behaviors. When using the thinking-out-loud strategy, children are trained to say to themselves, first out loud and then silently, "What is my problem? What is my plan? Am I using my plan? How did I do?" This process helps children interrupt their impulsive behavior, keeps them on task and reminds them of the necessary steps to take when carrying out their task. This training often includes social problem-solving skills, whereby children are encouraged to suggest and evaluate solutions to problems (Spivak, Platt & Shure, 1976).

Disruptiveness is another behavior often related to peer rejection. Disruptive children are often off-task and engage in inappropriate classroom behavior. The percentage of rejected children described as disruptive by peers ranges from 36 percent to 38 percent (Coie & Koeppl, 1990). Two techniques for reducing disruptive behavior in the classroom are use of reinforcement and token incentives.

Positive reinforcement, often used in connection with modeling, has produced some immediate positive outcomes (Asher, Renshaw & Hymel, 1982). The behavior of a child or group of children can be subjected to direct reinforcement. Teachers can make a point of praising socially cooperative interactions, while ignoring any undesirable interactions deemed tolerable. Specific praise of a child immediately after a desirable behavior provides the strongest results. Others studies (e.g., Gresham, 1979) used reinforcement procedures to reduce the frequency of negative social behaviors, and these effects were found to maintain over time.

The use of tokens as a reward for desirable behavior, in conjunction with positive reinforcement, tends to reduce disruptiveness and increase on-task behavior (Kazdin, 1977). In a token economy, teachers identify those behaviors deemed desirable and undesirable. When students act in a desirable manner, they are rewarded with a token of the teacher's choice. Tokens can range from a point system, plastic disks or plastic cards that can be exchanged for toys, food or other privileges. Several variations of token economies exist in schools and institutions. Descriptions of procedures, rules and additional considerations of this system can be found in Kazdin (1977).

Although token economies have shown success, they are not without their critics. This procedure focuses on the symptoms rather than the causes, and the effects of the program do not always generalize to other settings—such as home or play settings (Kazdin, 1977). In some cases, the system may not work at all. For example, Coie and Koeppl (1990) point out that children who lack basic skills or are unable to perform classroom tasks may need specific coaching in academic skills.

Communicating with parents will be especially important for teachers working with children who have difficulty interacting with peers. The increasing number of single-parent families or families with both parents working outside the home means that teachers will need to utilize a variety of approaches to maintain contact.

Options may include telephone calls, notes, letters and parent conferences. In order for children to benefit, parents need to have an understanding of their child's development and progress. Teachers can discuss their observations of the child and share what they are doing in the classroom that might also be reinforced at home. In addition, teachers can ask for parental input and suggestions. Teachers can also share information with parents on child guidance or parent discussion groups that might be available in the community.

In some cases, teachers may find that some children will need more assistance than is possible within the classroom. Not all children will respond to the techniques suggested. At some point, teachers must acknowledged the need for additional help. Teachers will need to work with the family and suggest other resources. A professional teacher will understand the importance of compiling resources and referrals that can be useful for families. This information might include services such as the school psychologist; community mental health clinics; child, family and marriage counselors; and developmental screening clinics.

Summary

A significant percentage of children are rejected or neglected during childhood. A lack of friends can put children at risk for later problems. More immediately, not having friends contributes to loneliness, low self-esteem and inability to develop social skills. Rejection or neglect by peers is a traumatic experience for some children. Research indicates that identification and intervention may help modify the negative experiences that some children encounter.

References

Asher, S., Renshaw, R., & Hymel, S. (1982). Peer relations and the development of social skills. In S. G. Moore & C. R. Cooper (Eds.), *The young child: Reviews of research*, Vol. 3, pp. 137–158. Washington, DC: NAEYC.

Barclay, J. (1966). Sociometric choices and teacher ratings as predictors of school dropout. *Journal of Social Psychology, 4*, 40–45.

Bolstad, O., & Johnson, S. (1972). Self-regulation in the modification of disruptive classroom behavior. *Journal of Applied Behavioral Analysis, 5*, 443–454.

Camp, B., Blom, G., Herbert, F., & Van Doornick, W. (1977). Think aloud: A program for developed self-control in young aggressive boys. *Journal of Abnormal Child Psychology, 5*, 157–169.

Carlson, C., Lahey, B., & Neeper, R. (1984). Peer assessment of the social behavior of accepted, rejected, and neglected children. *Journal of Abnormal Child Psychology, 12*, 189–198.

Coie, J., & Dodge, K. (1988). Multiple sources of data on social behavior and social status in the school: A cross-age comparison. *Child Development, 59*, 815–829.

Coie, J., Dodge, K, & Coppotelli, H. (1982). Continuities and changes in children's social status: A five-year longitudinal study. *Developmental Psychology, 18*, 557–570.

Coie, J., & Koeppl, G. (1990). Adapting intervention to the problems of aggressive and disruptive rejected children. In S. R. Asher & J. D. Coie (Eds.), *Peer rejection in childhood*, pp. 309–337. New York: Cambridge University Press.

Dodge, K., Coie, J., & Brakke, N. (1982). Behavior patterns of socially rejected and neglected preadolescents: The roles of social approach and aggression. *Journal of Abnormal Child Psychology, 10,* 389–410.

French, D., & Waas, G. (1985). Behavior problems of peer-neglected and peer-rejected elementary-age children: Parent and teacher perspectives. *Child Development, 56,* 246–252.

Gottman, J., Gonso, J., & Rasmussen, B. (1975). Social interaction, social competence, and friendship in children. *Child Development, 46,* 709–718.

Greshman, F. (1979). Comparison of response cost and time out in a special education setting. *Journal of Special Education, 13,* 199–208.

Greshman, F. (1988). Social competence and motivational characteristics of learning disabled students. In M. C. Laung, M. C. Reynolds & H. J. Walberg (Eds.), *Handbook of special education: Research and practice,* Vol. 2, pp. 283–302. Oxford: Pergamon.

Greshman, F., & Nagle, R. (1980). Social skills training with children: Responsiveness to modeling and coaching as a function of peer orientation. *Journal of Consulting and Clinical Psychology, 48,* 718–729.

Gronlund, N., & Holmlung, W. (1958). The value of elementary school sociometric status scores for predicting pupils' adjustment in high school. *Educational Administration and Supervision, 44,* 225–260.

Hymel, S., & Asher, S. (1977, March). *Assessment and training of isolated children's social skills.* Paper presented at the biennial meeting of the Society for Research in Child Development, New Orleans. (Eric Document Reproduction Service No. ED 136 930).

Hymel, S., & Rubin, K. (1985). Children with peer relationships and social skills problems: Conceptual, methodological, and developmental issues. In G. J. Whitehurst (Ed.), *Annals of child development,* Vol. 2, pp. 251–297. Greenwich, CT: JAI Press.

Jakibchuk, Z., & Smeraglio, V. (1976). The influence of symbolic modeling on the social behavior of preschool children with low levels of social responsiveness. *Child Development, 47,* 838–841.

Kazdin, A. (1977). *The token economy: A review and evaluation.* New York: Plenum.

Kupersmidt, J. (1983, April). Predicting delinquency and academic problems from childhood peer status. In J. D. Coie (Chair), *Strategies for identifying childhood at social risk: Longitudinal correlates and consequences.* Symposium conducted at the biennial meeting of the Society for Research in Child Development, Detroit, MI.

Kupersmidt, T., Coie, J., & Dodge, K. (1990). The role of poor peer relationships in the development of disorder. In S. R. Asher &

J. D. Coie (Eds.), *Peer rejection in childhood,* pp. 253–273. New York: Cambridge University Press.

Ladd, G. (1983). Social networks of popular, average, and rejected children in school settings. *Merrill-Palmer Quarterly, 29,* 283–308.

Meichenbaum, D. H. (1985). *Stress innoculation training.* New York: Pergamon Press.

Oden, S., & Asher, S. (1977). Coaching children in social skills for friendship making. *Child Development, 48,* 495–506.

Singleton, L., & Asher, S. (1977). Peer preferences and social interaction among third-grade children in an integrated school district. *Journal of Educational Psychology, 69,* 330–336.

Spivak, G., Platt, J., & Shure, M. (1976). *The problem-solving approach to adjustment.* San Francisco: Jossey-Bass.

Taylor, A., Asher, S., & Williams, G. (1987). The social adaptation of mainstreamed, mildly retarded children. *Child Development, 58,* 1321–1334.

Wasik, B. (1987). Sociometric measures and peer descriptions of kindergarten children: A study of reliability and validity. *Journal of Clinical Child Psychology, 16,* 218–224.

Weiner, I. P. (1980). Psychopathology in adolescence. In J. Adelson (Ed.), *Handbook of adolescent psychology,* pp. 447–471. New York: Wiley.

Teacher Response to Superhero Play: To Ban or Not To Ban?

Brenda J. Boyd

Brenda J. Boyd is Assistant Professor, Department of Human Development, Washington State University, Pullman.

Superhero play has received a great deal of attention from parents and educators in recent years. As defined here, superhero play refers to the active, physical play of children pretending to be media characters imbued with extraordinary abilities, including superhuman strength or the ability to transform themselves into superhuman entities. While some view this play as violent and aggressive, it is not so by definition.

This kind of play is a fact of life for those of us directly responsible for young children or for the training and support of those who deal with young children. A look at a bibliographic database related to early childhood (e.g., ERIC) offers ample evidence that children's involvement in superhero play is of growing concern to early childhood educators—the number of articles classified under superhero play as a subject between 1990 and 1995 is twice that found for the years 1985–1990.

Teachers of young children have become increasingly vocal opponents of superhero play, voicing concern about the behavior in their classrooms. Articles in professional publications such as *Young Children, Child Care Information Exchange* and *Childhood Education* by such authors as Bergen (1994) and Carlsson-Paige and Levin (1995) report that more and more teachers are choosing to ban superhero play from their classrooms. Newspaper articles found in the *Seattle Times* (Henderson, 1994) and the *Wall Street Journal* (Pereira, 1994) indicate that this concern has gone beyond an academic debate about child behavior. Teachers are sincerely concerned for the safety of children

> *P*erhaps teachers' sense of responsibility for children's behavior and their safety leads them to be overly sensitive to potential disruption and physical injury.

and themselves; many worry about violence as children engaged in superhero play grow older.

As a former child care provider/early educator and current teacher educator, I also have concerns about reported increases in violent and aggressive behavior in preschool classrooms. I suggest, however, that banning superhero play may not be the most effective means for dealing with children's increasing exposure to inappropriate and poor quality television programming. I will suggest that 1) we do not yet have valid data on these "increases" in classroom superhero play, 2) this behavior may play some developmental function necessary for young children's healthy growth and 3) by banning superhero play, teachers may be denying themselves a powerful opportunity to teach about values, respect, safety and living in a democratic social group.

Teacher Estimates of Play and Aggression

I begin by examining the premise that aggressive, violent superhero play is on the rise in preschool classrooms. The published reports of this increase are based on anecdotal reports from teachers (Carlsson-Paige & Levin, 1991; Jennings & Gillis-Olion, 1979; Kostelnik, Whiren & Stein, 1986) and from limited surveys of teachers of young children (Carlsson-Paige & Levin, 1995). These non-random samples are often drawn from participants at conference workshops on superhero and war play in the classroom, who may already be sensitized to and concerned about the issue of aggressive play. These reports lead us to believe that preschool children are spending the majority of their time karate chopping and pouncing on each other.

My own research, in which I collected time interval samples of preschool children's behavior, has led me to question this belief (Boyd, 1996). In one sample of a group of 3- to 5-year-old children at a laboratory preschool, I found that only 2 of 17 children exhibited superhero play during a 1-month observation period. The time spent in superhero play accounted for less than 1 percent of the 300 minutes of play observed. In a second sample, in which children in a full-day child care program were observed, only 5 percent of play time, on the average, could be classified as superhero play. In this group of 16 children, only 4 children exhibited superhero play. In both samples, boys were the

only superhero players. Furthermore, my observers and I never witnessed a child being physically hurt by another child while involved in superhero play.

Although these findings are clearly preliminary, they suggest that teacher reports of the occurrence and nature of superhero play may not be entirely objective, and may lead to an inflated estimate of this behavior. Previous research about teachers' views of aggression offers two lines of evidence to support this hypothesis.

First, evidence suggests that children and teachers have differing perspectives on "play fighting" and "aggression." In a study published in 1985, Smith and Lewis showed videotapes of play episodes to preschool children, their teacher and the assistant teacher. The children were more likely to agree with each other or with an objective observer than with their teachers in assessing behavior as play or aggression.

These results suggest that teachers rely on some perspective not shared by children to differentiate aggression and play. This perspective is reflected in the criteria teachers reportedly used for determining aggression in this study. The assistant teacher, whose assessment of behavior was least often in agreement with the children, based her remarks on her knowledge of the children's personalities, as reflected in comments such as "Well, knowing those boys, I know they can't cooperate together. Chances are it wasn't playful, it was aggressive" (Smith & Lewis, 1985, p. 180).

Second, one study (Connor, 1989) suggests that teachers' perspectives often differ not only from children's perspectives, but also from other non-teaching adults', including teachers in training. That is, teachers tend to see behavior as aggressive, rather than playful, more often than non-teachers. In this study, three preschool teachers viewed video clips of child behavior; the teachers labeled all 14 clips as examples of aggressive behavior. When the clips were shown to psychology students, however, the majority rated only two incidents as aggressive, two as play and the rest were rated differentially, depending on the viewer's gender. Men were more likely to view behavior as playful, while women more often labeled behavior as aggression. Additionally, Connor reported that preservice teachers agreed more often with female college students than with inservice teachers when rating behavior as play or aggression.

These findings suggest two points. First, some aspect of working in child care/early education may lead teachers to view play as negative behavior, in general, and as aggression in particular. Perhaps teachers' sense of responsibility for children's behavior and their safety leads them to be overly sensitive to potential disruption and physical injury. Connor's study (1989) supports this hypothesis. Teachers reported concern with the potential for injury, noting that the children "were playing too rough and someone could get hurt" (p. 217).

As I discuss superhero play with teachers, however, I find that the sense of responsibility is not only limited to concern with immediate behavior, but also includes the long-term consequences of aggressive play. I am struck by the connection teachers make between preschool play behavior and that of adolescent gangs. Early childhood educators seem to be equating young children's pretend behaviors with the actual loss of life and violence on their streets. This equation seems premature. We have too little information about the importance and/or potential harm of such fantasy play.

Second, gender socialization may also influence how teachers of young children (predominantly women) view superhero play. As Connor (1989) has suggested, women may grow up with less desire and/or opportunity to be involved in superhero and other physical play than men. This lack of involvement may lead them to be less accepting of such play. Moreover, if girls are discouraged from involvement in physical activity because they may get hurt, this may lead them to believe that rough play is dangerous and should be avoided. Taken together, the research on gender and my anecdotal information from teachers suggest that early childhood educators may be overreacting to superhero play because of their fears about an increasingly violent society, and because of gender bias about play.

The Developmental Function of Superhero Play

The possibility that superhero play may serve some developmental purpose is the essence of my second concern about banning superhero play. Early childhood educators have long held that pretend play is critical for young children's healthy emotional development. This belief has been used to defend involvement in superhero play.

Specifically, scholars suggest children have a need to resolve feelings about power and control. Some have suggested that superhero play offers a sense of power to children in a world dominated by adults, thus helping children to cope with the frustrations of limited control (Carlsson-Paige & Levin, 1990; Curry, 1971; Ritchie & Johnson, 1982; Slobin, 1976; Walder, 1976). Similarly, by

*B*y playing out scenarios focused on good and evil, children can work through feelings of anxiety and fear . . .

playing out scenarios focused on good and evil, children can work through feelings of anxiety and fear about their own safety (Peller, 1971). Additionally, such play may help children express their anger and aggression and become comfortable with these feelings, which may otherwise be frightening to the child (Carlsson-Paige & Levin, 1990; Ritchie et al., 1982).

While this theory is well-established in the child development literature, it is a weak argument for supporting the developmental function of superhero play without empirical research that directly examines its developmental relevance. Moreover, this set of hypotheses about the role of superhero play in providing emotional security is not easily tested. Other perspectives for investigating the function of superhero play, however, are available.

Although superhero play has received limited empirical attention, a related type of play, known as "rough-and-tumble play" (R & T), has been more thoroughly researched. The term "rough-and-tumble play" is commonly used to refer to children's play fighting, wrestling and chasing behaviors, from preschool through adolescence (e.g., Costabile et al., 1991; Pellegrini, 1987). I argue that superhero play is a special case of R & T and that the similarity of these types of play allows us to develop hypotheses about the potential function of superhero play. I will describe the similarities between these types of play, outline some of the hypothesized functions of R & T and consider the implications of this work for the study of superhero play.

R & T and superhero play share several characteristics. Both types of play can involve chasing, wrestling, kicking, mock battles and feigned attacks (Kostelnik et al., 1986). In addition, R & T frequently involves fantasy enactment or pretending (Smith & Connolly, 1987; Smith & Lewis, 1985), as does superhero play. Adults often confuse both R & T and superhero play with aggression (Kostelnik et al., 1986); furthermore, R & T play is often identified as pretend play in research studies (Pellegrini, 1987). Teachers' accounts of superhero play indicate that this play is routinely marked by play fighting, kicking and martial arts moves. In fact, these types of behavior seem to be the central cause for teachers' concern (Bergen, 1994; Carlsson-Paige & Levin, 1995; Henderson, 1994). These similarities suggest to me that superhero play can be conceptualized as a special case of R & T play, in which children assume the role of a superhero character.

The similarity in these types of play led researchers to examine the function of su-

perhero play. This body of research suggests that R & T play may serve some important developmental functions for young children, especially boys. R & T play serves three potential functions—specifically, affiliation, dominance and social skill facilitation (Smith & Boulton, 1990).

Affiliation. R & T play may help children form or maintain friendships. R & T's positive social nature is underscored by the presence of children laughing and smiling, and by the absence of children inflicting pain (Blurton Jones, 1972; Smith, 1982). R & T partners are consistently found to be friends (Humphreys & Smith, 1987; Smith & Lewis, 1985). While this does not directly show that R & T play builds friendships, these results nevertheless suggest that R & T play helps children develop or maintain friendships (Smith & Boulton, 1990).

Dominance. Animal researchers first used the concept of dominance to describe a hierarchical order of dominance within a species that controls access to resources such as space, food and mates (Wilson, 1975). They found that this hierarchy can reduce conflict, by clearly defining a power structure within a group (Hinde, 1974). Strayer and Strayer (1976) applied this concept to a group of children and observed a fairly stable hierarchy, with few conflicts.

Smith and Boulton (1990) suggest that through R & T play, children can maintain or improve their ranking within the hierarchy. A child can maintain her or his rank by picking worthy "opponents" who are equal in strength. Or, a child could safely improve her rank by picking a slightly stronger play partner, and suffer little if she was not successful.

Humphreys and Smith (1987) support the dominance maintenance hypothesis. When comparing class consensus rankings of 7- to 11-year-olds' strength, they found, in most cases, no consistent difference in the two participants of an R & T bout. Their findings suggest that children do select partners near to them in the dominance hierarchy.

Social Skill Facilitation. Some researchers have suggested that involvement in R & T offers children an opportunity to develop social skills, which consequently leads to successful peer interactions. Both parent-child play and peer play support this hypothesis. Parke, MacDonald and their colleagues report that children whose parents (especially fathers) engage in physical play with them are more likely to be popular with their peers (MacDonald, 1987; Parke, MacDonald, Beitel & Bhavnagri, 1987). Power and Parke (1981) argue that physical play with parents helps children learn to regulate and interpret

emotion by serving "as context for a wide range of communicative and affectively charged social interaction" (p. 160). Indeed, in one study, physical play did correlate with girls' ability to "read" facial expressions, suggesting some relationship between physical play and skill at reading social cues (Parke et al., 1987).

While the results are more numerous in terms of peer-peer R & T, they are also more mixed. Pellegrini (1988) found that children rejected by their peers were less successful than popular children at discriminating between serious fighting and R & T. In addition, for popular children, R & T served as a precursor to rule-oriented games, yet for rejected children, it led to aggression (Pellegrini, 1991). Several other researchers' findings indicate either no relation between R & T and popularity, or a negative correlation (Dodge, 1983; Ladd, 1983; Rubin, Daniels-Bierness & Hayvren, 1982). It is difficult to compare these results, however, because there is no uniform definition of R & T (Smith, 1989).

While the connection between superhero play and R & T is clearly speculative, an examination of how R & T play functions offers a measurable perspective on superhero play's possible contribution to development. The similarity between R & T and superhero play suggests that these types of play may also serve similar developmental functions. At the very least, this examination makes clear that it is premature to deny children the opportunity for involvement in superhero play. We first need to know more about the developmental implications of such a denial.

Sending Play Underground and a Lost Opportunity

This brings us to my third and final concern about banning superhero play. As other scholars of play have noted, banning has two possible effects (Carlsson-Paige & Levin, 1995). First, banning superhero play from the classroom sends children the message that they must hide their interests from adults, and that it is wrong for them to be interested in issues of power and control, good and evil, and so on. A related consequence is that teachers may lose an important opportunity to influence children's ideas about violence and the use of power, and about managing individual needs in a social community.

My concern about children's covert involvement in superhero play stems from the observation that children have always involved themselves in play about "good guys" and "bad guys." By telling children that such play is wrong or bad, we may be communicating that it is not acceptable to be interested in issues of control, nor is it acceptable to have fears about power. At the same time, we lose an opportunity to help children feel safe in a world that may be dangerous at times. While we need not

Children have always involved themselves in play about "good guys" and "bad guys."

expose children to inappropriate levels of violence, danger or fear, we should not expect that young children do not share adults' fears about violence, even if it is undeveloped. Part of the human condition is to fear and to desire mastery of that fear. Should we tell children that using a natural tool to conquer that fear, such as play, is wrong?

Second, I think that if teachers are truly concerned about exposing children to televised violence and aggression (or are concerned children will likely hear about such programming from friends anyway, even if they are not allowed to watch), are they not required to help children work through these issues in their play? When we ban superhero play (or any behavior children find interesting), we ignore a powerful opportunity for helping children learn valuable lessons in a familiar and appealing context.

Resources are available for helping teachers to use superhero play effectively in the classroom. Diane Levin (1994) has published practical suggestions for helping children to learn about establishing "peaceable" classroom communities; these ideas attend to all children's safety needs without simply banning superhero play. These suggestions can help teachers address their concerns about the children who do not like to play superheroes or who are frightened by others' superhero play. In addition, Gayle Gronlund (1992) offers interesting ideas for moving children beyond the scripted narratives they see on television, which she developed from working with her kindergarten class during the Ninja Turtle days. More recently, Julie Greenberg (1995) discussed ways to "make friends with the Power Rangers." Even when teachers decide to support superhero play in their classrooms, they may not know the best way to begin. These resources offer a starting point.

I believe that banning superhero play is not the most productive manner for dealing with our concerns about increased violence in our classrooms. Instead, educators should consider the best means for making positive use of this play; some of the resources I have described can be useful in this endeavor. Be assured that I am not advocating a free-for-all without teacher input into play. Each educator must decide, on the basis of information about their students and their needs, whether this sort of play is acceptable, at what level and with what supports in place. I encourage early childhood educators to take a broad and contextual view, as we do with all the behaviors we encounter, and to offer children the best supports we can in their daily lives.

References

Bergen, D. (1994). Should teachers permit or discourage violent play themes? *Childhood Education, 70*(5), 300–301.

Blurton Jones, N. (Ed.). (1972). *Ethological studies of child behavior* (pp. 97–129). London: Cambridge University Press.

Boyd, B. J. (1996). *Superhero play in the early childhood classroom.* Unpublished manuscript.

Carlsson-Paige, N., & Levin, D. E. (1995). Can teachers resolve the war-play dilemma? *Young Children, 50*(5), 62–63.

Carlsson-Paige, N., & Levin, D. (1991). The subversion of healthy development and play: Teachers' reactions to the Teenage Mutant Ninja Turtles. *Day Care and Early Education, 19*(2), 14–20.

Carlsson-Paige, N., & Levin, D. (1990). *Who's calling the shots? How to respond effectively to children's fascination with war play and war toys.* Philadelphia, PA: New Society Publishers.

Connor, K. (1989). Aggression: Is it in the eye of the beholder? *Play and Culture, 2,* 213–217.

Costabile, A., Smith, P. K., Matheson, L., Aston, J., Hunter, T., & Boulton, M. (1991). Cross-national comparison of how children distinguish serious and playful fighting. *Developmental Psychology, 27,* 881–887.

Curry, N. E. (1971). Five-year-old play. In N. E. Curry & S. Arnaud (Eds.), *Play: The child strives toward self-realization* (pp. 10–11). Washington, DC: National Association for the Education of Young Children.

Dodge, K. A. (1983). Behavioral antecedents of peer social status. *Child Development, 54,* 1383–1399.

Greenberg, J. (1995). Making friends with the Power Rangers. *Young Children, 50*(5), 60–61.

Gronlund, G. (1992). Coping with Ninja Turtle play in my kindergarten classroom. *Young Children, 48*(1), 21–25.

Henderson, D. (1994, December 14). No "morphing" allowed in class: Power Rangers play all the rage for kids. *The Seattle Times,* pp. A1, A21.

Hinde, R. A. (1974). *A biological basis of human social behavior.* New York: McGraw-Hill.

Humphreys, A. P., & Smith, P. K. (1987). Rough and tumble, friendship, and dominance in school children: Evidence for continuity and change with age. *Child Development, 58,* 210–212.

Jennings, C. M., & Gillis-Olion, M. (1979, November). *The impact of television cartoons on child behavior.* Paper presented at the meeting of the National Association for the Education of Young Children, Atlanta, GA.

Kostelnik, M., Whiren, A., & Stein, L. (1986). Living with He-Man: Managing superhero fantasy play. *Young Children, 41*(4), 3–9.

Ladd, G. (1983). Social networks of popular, average, and rejected children in a school setting. *Merrill-Palmer Quarterly, 29,* 283–307.

Levin, D. E. (1994). *Teaching young children in violent times: Building a peaceable classroom.* Cambridge, MA: Educators for Social Responsibility.

MacDonald, K. (1987). Parent-child physical play with rejected, neglected and popular boys. *Developmental Psychology, 23,* 705–711.

Parke, R. D., MacDonald, K. B., Beitel, A., & Bhavnagri, N. (1987). The role of the family in the development of peer relationships. In R. Peters (Ed.), *Social learning and systems approaches to marriage and the family* (pp. 17–44). New York: Bruner/Mazel.

Pellegrini, A. D. (1991). A longitudinal study of popular and rejected children's rough-and-tumble play. *Early Education and Development, 2*(3), 205–213.

Pellegrini, A. D. (1988). Elementary-school children's rough-and-tumble play and social competence. *Developmental Psychology, 24*(6), 802–806.

Pellegrini, A. D. (1987). Rough-and-tumble play: Developmental and educational significance. *Educational Psychologist, 22,* 23–43.

Peller, L. (1971). Models of children's play. In R. Herron & B. Sutton-Smith (Eds.), *Child's play* (pp. 110–125). New York: Wiley.

Pereira, J. (1994, December 7). Caution: Morphing may be hazardous to your teacher. *Wall Street Journal,* pp. A1, A8.

Power, T. G., & Parke, R. D. (1981). Play as a context for early learning. In L. M. Laosa & I. E. Sigel (Eds.), *Families as learning environments for children* (pp. 147–178). New York: Plenum.

Ritchie, K. E., & Johnson, Z. M. (1982, November). *Superman comes to preschool: Superhero TV play.* Paper presented at the meeting of the National Association for the Education of Young Children, Washington, DC.

Rubin, K. H., Daniels-Bierness, T., & Hayvren, M. (1982). Social and social-cognitive correlates of sociometric status in preschool and kindergarten children. *Canadian Journal of Behavioral Science, 14,* 338–347.

Slobin, D. (1976). The role of play in childhood. In C. Shaefer (Ed.), *Therapeutic use of child's play* (pp. 95–118). New York: Aronson.

Smith, P. K. (1989). The role of rough-and-tumble play in the development of social competence: Theoretical perspectives and empirical evidence. In B. H. Schneider, G. Attili, J. Nadel & R. P. Weissberg (Eds.), *Social competence in developmental perspective* (pp. 239–258). Dordrect: Kluwer Academic Publishers.

Smith, P. K. (1982). Does play matter? Functional and evolutionary aspects of animal and human play. *The Behavioral and Brain Sciences, 5,* 139–184.

Smith, P. K., & Boulton, M. (1990). Rough-and-tumble play, aggression, and dominance: Perceptions and behavior in children's encounters. *Human Development, 33,* 271–282.

Smith, P. K., & Connolly, K. J. (1987). *The ecology of preschool behavior.* Cambridge, England: Cambridge University Press.

Smith, P. K., & Lewis, K. (1985). Rough-and-tumble play, fighting and chasing in nursery school children. *Ethology and Sociobiology, 6,* 175–181.

Strayer, F. F., & Strayer, J. (1976). An ethological analysis of social agonism and dominance relations among preschool children. *Child Development, 47,* 980–989.

Walder, R. (1976). Psychoanalytic theory of play. In C. Shaefer (Ed.), *Therapeutic use of child's play* (pp. 79–94). New York: Aronson.

Wilson, E. O. (1975). *Sociobiology. The new synthesis.* Cambridge, MA: Belknap Press of Harvard University Press.

Article 20

**Denise A. Da Ros and
Beverly A. Kovach**

*Denise A. Da Ros is Associate Professor,
Teacher Education, Youngstown State
University, Youngstown, Ohio. Beverly
A. Kovach is R.I.E. Fellow, Montessori of*

Assisting Toddlers & Caregivers During Conflict Resolutions

Interactions That Promote Socialization

Matthew, a 15-month-old, is playing on the floor with a blue car. He appears to be peacefully exploring how he can make noise by spinning the car wheels with his fingers. Twelve-month-old Hamilton looks up from across the room to see where the noise originated. He sees Matthew spin the car wheels and creeps over for a better look. Hamilton watches Matthew momentarily and then lunges for the blue car. Before Hamilton can attempt a getaway, Matthew snatches the car back with a swift yank. Startled, Hamilton expresses his loss with a long, loud wail.

You are the caregiver who is watching the scene unfold from a distance. Do you:

● Remove the car that is causing the conflict between the two toddlers?
● Sympathetically take sides with the child you perceive to have been victimized?
● Ignore the interaction, as it is one of the numerous aggravations you learn to accept in a toddler's day?
● Move in close proximity to the situation, knowing that it has not finished playing itself out?

Conflict is common among toddlers, and many factors make it hard for caregivers to manage such conflict. McKay (1990) aptly describes the behavior of children this age:

> ...toddlers hurting each other is fairly normal behavior. It is a way they have [to express] themselves quickly, at a time when language is limited and self-control [is] difficult. Often there is no malice behind the act, and it is a way of finding out how things work. (p. 73)

The authors believe that the three most important factors that influence the outcome of toddler conflict are:

• The caregiver's beliefs about conflict and its resolution
• The caregiver's level of anxiety about toddlers and safety during conflict
• The caregiver's choices concerning interventions in toddler disputes.

The stance and position the caregiver assumes is dependent on those personal beliefs and judgments about sharing, conflict, and struggle that have formed over many years. These beliefs are now a part of a value system; hence, how caregivers resolve conflict is based on those values. Certainly, the perception of the adult who watches the toddler in conflict is heavily influenced by personal lessons learned about dealing with conflicts. Ideally, individual beliefs are not supposed to influence care, but

Many individuals are uncomfortable with conflicts that arise between adults. When conflict occurs with toddlers, the issues are even more complex.

how can they not? Logically, then, the caregiver's response to toddlers in conflict is a result of those perceptions and values. In other words: values + perceptions = behaviors + actions.

Many individuals are uncomfortable with conflicts that arise between adults. When conflict occurs with toddlers, the issues are even more complex. Usually, the level of adult anxiety during toddler conflict coincides with toddlers' rising emotions. Concerns about maintaining toddler safety in groups may cause the caregiver increased anxiety. Most adults' primary concern during a conflict is the toddlers' safety. Often, the adult wants to stop the conflict before something bad happens. The resultant anxiety can take an emotional toll on the adult. Furthermore, caregivers' assumptions that only negative things emerge during conflict may lead children to believe that their involvement in, as well as their emotional responses to, conflict are unacceptable.

The authors invite caregivers to consider toddler conflict as a natural part of life. In fact, valuable lessons can be learned through such encounters. When toddlers are allowed to go through the process of conflict, in a guided framework with an adult nearby, they can learn how to respond to life's problems. The guided framework that supports toddler's problem-solving during conflict relies on the concept of caregiver as "expert," someone who provides the ways of approaching the situation not already within the child's repertoire (Azmitia, 1988; Radziszewska & Rogoff, 1988). The authors have observed that the potential for increased socialization among toddlers grows when adults put aside their biases and do not overinvest emotionally in the outcome of toddler disputes.

Toddlers in group care, however, rarely are allowed to engage in conflict without adult interference. Instead, caregivers are more concerned with maintaining peace among toddlers (Bayer, Whaley, & May, 1995). In fact, adults not only interrupt the process, but also try to prevent toddlers from reaching resolution. By discouraging these opportunities, well-meaning adults lessen the likelihood that a toddler will develop valuable interpersonal skills.

The authors have found that adults are more uncomfortable with watching the process of conflict unfold than the toddler is while going through the conflict. If caregivers could view conflict as an opportunity for the toddlers to develop problem-solving and social skills, would they be less likely to judge harshly those children in conflict? Would they be able to adopt a more positive attitude when toddlers are engaged in a dispute?

What Is Conflict?

Webster's Collegiate Dictionary (1990) defines conflict as "a battle or opposition between two viewpoints." Resolution is the act of determining a course of intervention. In a working definition of conflict resolution, the authors include a method of intervening in a struggle that promotes socialization. Caregivers, by offering the necessary assistance, guidance, and support, could begin viewing conflicts as opportunities to teach toddlers problem-solving skills. Advocates of the problem-solving model in early childhood curriculum include Carlsson-Paige and Levin (1992), Dinwiddie (1994) and Edwards (1992). Piaget (1932/1965) viewed conflict as a critical component of development and, therefore, vital to children's construction of knowledge. "Conflict within an individual and conflict between individuals is essential in the development of the personality and the social and moral feelings that emerge from those situations" (DeVries & Zan, 1996, p. 109).

Who Is Responsible for the Process?

Caregivers of young children need to follow a consistent philosophy when intervening in conflictual situations. The literature has documented that emotional outbursts frequently occur during social situations among toddlers in group care. A study by Bayer, Whaley, and May (1995) tracked a 12-hour segment in which teachers interrupted toddler disputes on an average of once every 5.3 minutes. With this frequency of conflict, caregivers can become jaded, and so neglect to provide guidance. As a result, caregivers may lose the sensitivity necessary to observe and respond in support of the toddler's task. Consequently, the problem-solving skills that toddlers will need to become socialized are impeded. The toddler

Process of Conflict				
	POTENTIAL CONFLICT	EMERGING CONFLICT	ENGAGING CONFLICT	STRUGGLING CONFLICT	(DISENGAGING) RESOLVING CONFLICT
Toddler Behavior	Aggressive acting Child in close proximity to other children	Two toddlers in opposition over object Dissipate/escalate	Toddlers fully involved Engage in physical contact Not at maximum level	Emotionally invested in process (crying, yelling) Actively engaged in physical contact Tug-of-war Climatic Stakes are high	Win, lose or draw Emotional process is diffusing Anticipate Disengaging
Caregiver Strategies	Keenly observe More proximal	Assess at child's eye level Analyze Remain neutral Nonjudgmental	Watching and waiting Keep safe Allow natural consequences Remain neutral, attentive, focused	"I" messages; use singular pronouns Verbalize what is happening (sportscasting) Prevent hurting Available to each Keep our emotions in check Model gentleness	Provide help for them to problem-solve Available to each Do not leave scene until a toddler leaves Model gentleness Verbalize affect, emotions
	Least intrusive		LEVEL OF INTRUSIVENESS Moderate		Interactive

Figure 1

learns that conflict, and the attendant emotional responses, are not acceptable. By taking steps to remove conflict, educators compromise toddlers' authentic responses. In addition, they undermine toddlers' beginning attempts at the trial-and-error process and stifle the budding emotions that influence socialization.

Adults who work with young children often inhibit, or interact prematurely with, the toddler who is trying to learn experimentally (Bayer, Whaley, & May, 1995). How, then, is the novice toddler to become socialized? Of even greater concern are the caregivers who insist on using their own solutions to resolve the conflict, rather than allowing toddlers to try their hand at developing their own problem-solving techniques.

These adult reactions imply that children need adult intervention in disputes, and suggest that conflict is not permissible. A study by Killen and Turiel (1991) showed that in 91 percent of all interactions, an adult determined the solution for a conflict without involving the toddler. Consequently, toddlers may assume adult biases regarding conflict resolution. Moreover, adult intervention in toddler disputes may inadvertently lead to scapegoating and/or victimization.

Jason, after clutching three plastic bottles filled with colored water, temporarily distributes them to his peers; after a few minutes, he insists on collecting them. Of course, the toddlers who now possess these coveted, colorful bottles do not want to return them. Jason begins to cry as he reaches for a bottle, and he turns to his caregiver for help. The caregiver says to Jason, "That was nice of you to share the bottles with your friends; sharing makes your friends happy."

Jason was engaged in a form of play called "distributing," which is not sharing. When a toddler distributes objects, he or she still wants them. The toddler recipients, however, are reluctant to give them up. Toddlers typically will focus on their own needs and wants; egocentrism is a natural and necessary stage of development. Consequently, it is unrealistic to expect that toddlers will share.

In the above example, the caregiver expected Jason to assume the adult bias about sharing. This example illustrates an unrealistic approach to conflict resolution for toddlers. "By insisting that the child follow rules and values of others, the adult contributes to the development of an individual with a conformist mind, personality and morality" (DeVries & Zan, 1996, p. 108). Piaget (1932/ 1965) believed that adults can either promote or constrict children's ability to construct their own intelligence. Limiting adult bias during conflict may allow the construction of the child "from the child."

Typically, one out of four methods used by adults includes a judgment (Killen & Turiel, 1991). such as "We share," "That's not nice," or "Use your words." Such verbal messages compromise the child's autonomy by not allowing the toddler to take control and become a part of solving a conflict.

How Caregivers Traditionally React

The ways that caregivers intervene often do not promote resolution between children. For example, the caregiver may react by:

• *Trying To Fix the Problem.* Fixing the problem prevents toddlers from going through the resolution process. The authors believe that resolution is an integral part of socialization. For example, a well-meaning adult often will confiscate the toy or object that is causing a disturbance between two children. The message that this gives to the children—"Let me remove this ball for now, since both of you want it"—denies the children an opportunity to resolve the conflict themselves. This scenario does not support either toddler's competency and implies that an adult should be the one to work out a solution. This stance contradicts Piaget's (1932/1965) view that conflict is critical for development. By believing in a toddler's budding ability to solve some conflicts, the caregiver accepts, acknowledges, and validates the toddler's feelings. A caregiver who uses a constructivist approach *promotes* young children's autonomy in conflict by recognizing that the conflict belongs to the toddler. During situations when safety is not an issue, the constructivist caregiver refrains from taking control of the conflict away from the toddler.

• *Trying To Over-regulate the Conflict.* Some caregivers actively try to find solutions to a conflict, in the name of toddler safety. Through their words, many caregivers often redirect a situation prematurely. Johnny, for instance, takes away the red high heels that Gabrielle had been using. Gabrielle begins to shout. The caregiver moves Johnny away from the area and tells him, "Why don't you wear these brown loafers instead?" The caregiver is over-regulating the situation by finding the solution for the toddler. What would the outcome have been had the adult merely moved closer to the children and watched their interactions?

• *Trying To Promote Peace As a Solution.* Promoting peace prematurely, instead of assisting toddlers in learning negotiation skills and problem-solving approaches, can affect toddlers' socialization. Often, caregivers feel uncomfortable when toddlers are embroiled in a conflict, and they will try to resolve the problem and promote peace before it is necessary. Michael, for example, is playing quietly on the floor with Duplos. Kayla runs across the room, crossing Michael's space. He pushes. She cries out and shoves. The caregiver rushes to the scene saying, "No! Now, both of you be nice. Now hug each other." The caregiver's solution, while well-meaning, forces the toddlers to accept an adult's emotional responses and biases. It also robs the two toddlers of their own authentic responses. What would have happened if the adult had merely moved in close to the toddlers to watch their next move? Although we can only guess, it seems safe to assume that the toddlers' responses would have at least been their own, for better

or for worse. Asking toddlers to curtail their feelings has serious implications for psychosocial development. In addition, the process of teaching peaceful resolution includes helping and supporting each child's natural emotional responses.

• *Trying To Focus on a Part Instead of the Whole.* Chelsea scrapes her knee after 2-year-old Kevin pushes her on the playground. The caregiver, upon seeing blood on Chelsea's knee, rushes to her with an ice pack, and says to Kevin, "Since you pushed Chelsea and made her bleed, you need to put ice on her leg and make it better." Kevin does so with hesitation and confusion. As Chelsea continues to cry, Kevin looks fearful. Because the caregiver imposes her brand of justice, Kevin is forced to comply, albeit with conflicted feelings. Two-year-olds are not ready for lessons on empathy and such lessons are likely to fall on deaf ears. An adult can best demonstrate empathy at this stage by modeling the response, rather than forcing one from the child. Too often, well-meaning adults expect toddlers to respond in adult ways.

Prevention and Intervention

Having worked with toddlers, the authors have been exposed to many of the above scenarios, and have tried a variety of solutions. These solutions often excluded toddlers from being an active and authentic part of the problem-solving approach. We must all remember that dealing with conflict can strengthen social skills. Behaviors can be categorized into prevention and intervention strategies. Prevention strategies emphasize the adult's relations with the child, the environment, and himself or herself in ways that minimize the potential for conflict. These strategies can help prevent conflicts from flaring up. Prevention strategies are meant to alleviate problems that might arise in toddlers' social situations. The following are prevention strategies that facilitate healthy conflict resolution:

Prevention Strategies

A. Strategies related to the child and environment

• Put children in small groups, and group them by developmental compatibility
• Provide uninterrupted time on a regular basis
• Allow toddlers the freedom to move and explore
• Develop a safe and appropriate environment
• Offer opportunities to make choices
• Provide possibilities for socialization (toddlers need to experience conflict)

- Train adult caregivers to follow routines consistently
- Prevent "herding" of toddlers

B. Strategies related to adult caregiver
- Develop a keen insight when observing and monitoring interactions
- Cultivate an awareness of potential conflicts during transition times
- Develop the ability to judge the right time to intercede
- Know how to intercede
- Understand individual toddler characteristics
- Be aware of group stress factors (e.g., hungry for lunch=lower tolerance level)
- Define clear values, beliefs, and feelings around conflict and struggle (know thyself)
- Maintain a few, clear, concise house rules
- Trust the toddler's competence around conflict resolution
- Self-monitor your emotions
- Refrain from signaling the toddler to accept your biases

These prevention strategies should help adults become more effective during toddler disputes, while allowing caregivers to remain available. Intervention strategies, on the other hand, are more like active behaviors that caregivers employ for conflict resolution. They include caregiver observation and attitudes, as well as diffusion strategies to help toddlers through conflict. The caregivers' observations and attitudes are invaluable tools for influencing outcomes from the child's point of view. Ideally, the adult observes and interprets the conflict objectively. By so doing, the caregiver's behavior reflects a non-judgmental response to the unfolding struggle.

Caregivers' diffusion strategies are more active responses that allow toddlers to respond to their conflict and its resolution. These strategies require more of a caregiver than merely moving closer to the escalating social situation.

Intervention Strategies

A. Caregiver observation and attitude
- Adopt a stance to assess and analyze, rather than control
- Use a consistent philosophy and process when interacting in conflict resolution
- Remain neutral and avoid judging or taking sides
- Allow natural consequences to occur between toddlers; monitor the "struggle" in a safe environment
- Stay attentive and focused during the conflict

B. Diffusion Strategies
- Remain at the children's eye level
- Watch and wait before interceding
- Use "I" messages and proper singular pronouns
- Move closer to the conflict
- Use language that tells the toddler what you see happening
- Prevent opposing agendas between adult and toddlers from happening simultaneously
- Prevent injury by interceding quickly with both toddler parties when necessary
- Provide just enough help to allow toddlers to solve their own dilemmas
- Be available to comfort each child (squat down, remain at children's eye level, have your arms open)
- Stay at the spot until the toddler disengages from the scene
- Verbalize what you see happening
- Model gentleness to the aggressor
- Offer self, instead of objects, for comfort (e.g., your lap) if a child appears to want comfort
- Continue to verbalize what you see going on by using active, reflective listening

By implementing these intervention strategies, toddlers can safely construct their own problem-solving strategies. The following scenario depicts how these strategies were put to use. John, a 2$^{1/2}$-year-old, has been quietly playing on the floor with several wood blocks. As the caregiver passes, John states, "Look at my choo-choo train!" The adult responds, "Yes, I see." John looks down and becomes fully engrossed in his creation as the caregiver moves on.

From across the room, 2-year-old Cameron watches John building with the blocks. He moves over to John and plops down on the floor across from him. John begins to tell Cameron about his long choo-choo train as he adds more blocks to it. As John is talking, Cameron takes both his hands and messes up all the blocks. John angrily says, "Stop, Cameron!" The caregiver, observing the interaction, moves closer to the children.

John picks up the blocks and starts to build a tall structure. Cameron watches and waits. John stacks several blocks and then turns to pick up another block. Cameron sits forward and pushes the blocks, which tumble and scatter all over the floor. John angrily lunges toward Cameron. The caregiver moves in next to the children. John leaps towards Cameron, misses, and bumps his nose. John wails, "I bumped my nose." The caregiver looks into John's eyes and replies, "I know; I saw. Does your nose hurt?" "Yes!," says John, "Cameron knocked my blocks over." The caregiver responds, "I saw Cameron do that. If you don't want Cameron to knock down the blocks, you need to ask him not to." John does so. He rebuilds the blocks, and just as Cameron is about to knock them down, John beats him to the punch and knocks some of the blocks down before Cameron does. Cameron finishes the job, scattering blocks all over the floor. The two boys giggle with glee. They begin chatting together about how they made the blocks fall. The caregiver, who is there with the boys, does nothing to physically intervene. She only needed to remain nearby and make a suggestion. The ending was a happy one, and both boys seemed pleased.

This scenario is a prime example of understanding toddlers and conflict, and of how important it is that toddlers solve their own disputes in a safe environment. The caregiver should remain available to monitor, and should intervene just enough so that the toddlers can solve the problem in their own way.

This type of behavior requires a caregiver who is a skillful observer and who believes that toddlers are capable of problem-solving. It requires an understanding of both the process of conflict and of appropriate adult responses to toddlers' behavior during conflict. The caregiver in this scenario was able to respond to the situation without being either anxious or judgmental.

Figure 1 depicts caregiver strategies on a progressive continuum from least to most intrusive. The chart shows how the progress of conflict relates to the toddler's behavior during the stages of conflict. The strategies correspond to both the toddler behavior and the degree of conflict with which toddlers are involved. These strategies are helpful in determining the caregiver behavior in relation to the degree of conflict. It is amazing how moving near an escalating conflict between toddlers can dissipate the majority of situations.

Conclusion

Several implications for practice relate to the conflicts that arise with toddlers in group care situations. Some conclusions drawn from this article are:

- The ways that adults respond to children in conflict affects the toddler's authentic response.

- This model of intervention requires the adult to observe more before interacting (M. Gerber, February 14, 1979).
- It may be better for adults to wait to see if toddlers can resolve their own conflicts before stepping into the process.
- Recognize that your desire to solve the conflict may stem from your own discomfort.
- Know thyself. Identify your feelings and beliefs regarding conflict. Adult intervention relies on the stage of conflict and the toddlers' behavior during the conflict.

Toddlers will engage in conflict. It is an integral part of how they learn social skills. Adults' ways of relating and responding during toddler conflict will affect the immediate outcome of toddler problem-solving. When and how much adults should intervene, and the kinds of strategy they select, will affect the authenticity and competence of the toddlers who are in the adult's care. These choices have long-range and dramatic implications; it is time for caregivers to reflect and re-evaluate alternative ways of accepting the toddlers' involvement in their struggle for socialization.

References

Azmitia, M. (1988). Peer interaction and problem solving: When are two heads better than one? *Child Development, 59,* 87–96.

Bayer, C., Whaley, K., & May, S. (1995). Strategic assistance in toddler disputes II. Sequences and patterns of teachers' message strategies. *Early Education and Development, 6*(4), 406–432.

Carlsson-Paige, N., & Levin, D. E. (1992, March). When push comes to shove: Reconsidering children's conflicts. *Child Care Information Exchange,* 34–37.

DeVries, R., & Zan, B. (1996). A constructivist perspective on the role of the sociomoral atmosphere in promoting children's development. In C. T. Fosnet (Ed.), *Constructivism: Theory, perspectives, and practice* (pp. 103–119). New York: Teachers College Press.

Dinwiddie, S. A. (1994). The saga of Sally, Sammy, and the red pen: Facilitating children's social problem solving. *Young Children, 49*(5), 13–19.

Edwards, C. (1992, March). Creating safe places for conflict resolution to happen. *Child Care Information Exchange,* 43–45.

M. Gerber (personal communication, February 14, 1979).

Killen, M., & Tureil, E. (1991). Conflict resolution in preschool social interactions. *Early Education and Development, 2*(4), 240–255.

McKay, F. (1990). Discipline. In A. Stonehouse (Ed.), *Trusting toddlers: Planning for one-to-three year olds in child care centers* (pp. 65–78). St. Paul, MN: Redleaf Press.

Piaget, J. (1965). *The moral judgment of the child.* London: Free Press. (Original work published 1932)

Radziszewska, B., & Rogoff, B. (1988). Influence of adult and peer collaboration on the development of children's planning skills. *Developmental Psychology, 24,* 840–848.

Webster's ninth new collegiate dictionary. (1990). Springfield, MA: Merriam-Webster Inc.

Research in Review

Gender Segregation among Children: Understanding the "Cootie Phenomenon"

Kimberly K. Powlishta

One of the most striking findings during the past 20 years of research on gender-role development is that boys and girls are not nearly as different from each other as most people believe them to be. Often, commonly held stereotypes turn out to be false when investigated empirically. Even when sex differences are found, they usually represent highly overlapping distributions. Take visual-spacial skills, for example: although some studies find that boys do better in this domain than girls, the overall difference is small; furthermore, many girls do better than the average boy, and many boys do worse than the average girl. The variability within each sex is quite large relative to the difference between the sexes.

In the context of these small differences, one gender-related phenomenon stands out: virtually *all* children show preferences for playmates of their own sex. Anyone who has spent time with groups of children will recognize the following scene:

> In the lunchroom, when the two second grade tables were filling, a high-status boy walked by the inside table, which had a scattering of both boys and girls, and said loudly, "Oooo, too many girls," as he headed for a seat at the far table. The boys at the inside table picked up their trays and moved, and no other boys sat at the inside table, which the pronouncement had effectively made taboo. (Thorne 1986, 171)

Girls display a similar dislike of members of the other sex; for example, an 11-year-old told Maccoby and Jacklin that sitting next to a boy was like "being in a lower rank or peeing in your pants" (1987, 245).

Kimberly K. Powlishta, Ph.D. is an assistant professor of psychology at Northern Illinois University. Her current research focuses on individual, developmental, and contextual influences on gender segregation, social stereotyping, and intergroup processes among children.

This is one of a regular series of Research in Review columns. The column in this issue was edited by Laura E. Berk, Ph.D., Professor of Psychology at Illinois State University.

> **One of the most striking findings during the past 20 years of research on gender-role development is that boys and girls are not nearly as different from each other as most people believe them to be.**

Although the above examples involved elementary-school children, this preference for same-sex playmates, also known as *gender segregation,* actually begins much earlier. For example, in one study of preschoolers (average age = 34 months) observed during free play, 62% of the girls and 21% of the boys displayed significant gender segregation (Powlishta, Serbin, & Moller 1993). Although girls may get a head start in preference for same-sex playmates, boys soon catch up, and by the end of preschool they sometimes even show stronger same-sex preferences than do girls (LaFreniere, Strayer, & Gauthier 1984).

For children of both sexes, gender segregation increases dramatically by the elementary-school years and remains strong throughout middle childhood. Maccoby and Jacklin (1987), for instance, observed 6½-year-olds with same-sex playmates 11 times as often as with cross-sex playmates. Older children report having almost exclusively same-sex friends (e.g., Gottman & Parker 1987). Gender segregation is found in a wide variety of cultures (Edwards & Whiting 1988) and in virtually every study that has attempted to measure it, whether the children were observed in natural settings (as described above) or in more structured, experimental contexts (Powlishta in press).

The consequences of gender segregation

This separation of the sexes may have important developmental consequences. In a sense, the two sexes are

From *Young Children*, May 1995, pp. 61-69. © 1995 by the National Association of Young Children. Reprinted by permission.

raised in distinctive "cultures" Maccoby (1985) has discussed some of the ways in which the worlds of boys and girls are different: boys tend to play in larger, hierarchically organized groups; to play more in public places; and to engage in more rough play and aggression than do girls. Girls remain closer to adults than do boys, thereby receiving more exposure to an environment that promotes compliance and dependence while inhibiting independence and assertiveness (Carpenter, Huston, & Holt 1986). In this manner, gender segregation may amplify or create sex differences—differences that are not based on the individual child's interests and abilities but instead are based solely on membership in a particular social category, "male" or "female." Furthermore, the relatively little experience that boys and girls have with each other may inadequately prepare them for the adult world, which, in our society, is not nearly as segregated as are children's groups. The early lack of contact with each other may contribute to communication problems between men and women and, more generally, to promote the perception that males and females are completely different creatures: men are creatures who refuse to ask for directions when they're lost and always leave the toilet seat up; women are creatures who sob during Hallmark Card commercials and go to public restrooms in groups. These silly examples suggest a more serious problem that gender segregation may promote: reliance on stereotypes and disregard for individual differences.

Why do children choose same-sex playmates?

Despite the extensive evidence of gender segregation and the importance of its potential consequences, the reasons behind it are not well understood. Several theories have been proposed (see, for example, Maccoby 1988).

Direct socialization. The most straightforward theory holds that children segregate by sex because of pressure from adults. For example, parents may provide their children with more opportunities to play with same-sex than with cross-sex peers, while actively rewarding same-sex contact and discouraging cross-sex contact. Although such pressures may exist, they probably do not fully account for gender segregation; in fact, we see more gender segregation among children when adults are not present than when children are participating in adult-structured activities (Luria & Herzog 1985; Thorne 1986). Lockheed and Klein (1985) found greater segregation in the lunchroom than in the classroom, for example. Because children themselves are crucial for maintaining these behaviors, to understand gender segregation we need to examine the characteristics of boys and of girls.

Toy preferences. A second theory of gender segregation focuses on sex differences in toy or activity preferences. This theory states that because of socialization practices

or biological differences, boys and girls prefer different kinds of toys and activities from a very early age. When they are placed in a group setting, such as a child care center or preschool, they gravitate toward their preferred toys. As a result, boys will end up near the traditionally "masculine" toys and girls near the traditionally "feminine" toys. Gender segregation would therefore occur essentially as a by-product of this toy or activity preference. In other words, this theory holds that rather than seeking out same-sex playmates, children look for playmates with similar interests, and these playmates often turn out to be of their own sex.

Is there evidence for this theory? It is clear that sex-differentiated toy preferences emerge early in life—as early as 2 years of age (e.g., Fagot 1974; Fein et al. 1975). Young children avoid toys associated with the other sex, especially when cross-sex peers are watching (Serbin et al. 1979). Such preferences become stronger during the preschool years and are evident when children are observed in naturalistic settings or when they are presented with standard sets of toys or activities and asked to make choices from among them (e.g., Connor & Serbin 1977; Blakemore, LaRue, & Olejnik 1979; Serbin & Sprafkin 1982).

Because boys and girls prefer different toys at least as early as they begin to segregate by sex, the "toy preference" theory of gender segregation seems plausible. If the theory is accurate, then girls with the greatest preference for "feminine" toys and boys with the greatest preference for "masculine" toys should show the most gender segregation. Although there have been exceptions (Eisenberg, Tryon, & Cameron 1984), for the most part this pattern has not been upheld. For example, Powlishta, Serbin, and Moller (1993) found both gender segregation and sex-differentiated toy preferences among a group of 2½- to 3-year-olds, but the two variables were unrelated. In fact, girls with the most *masculine* toy preferences had a tendency to be the most segregated (i.e., to prefer *female* playmates). Similarly, Maccoby and Jacklin (1987) noted that their 4½-year-old research participants spent the majority of time in gender-neutral activities (e.g., on swings, in the sandbox, working on puzzles) but continued to segregate by sex. All-girl groups were seen playing on one jungle gym or swing set at the same time that all-boy groups were playing on another. It is clear, then, that gender segregation is not dependent upon sex differences in toy or activity preferences.

Sex differences in play style. A third theory of gender segregation holds that children choose playmates with general *styles* of play that are similar to their own. For example, children who like to roughhouse will find other children who like to play in this manner; children who prefer more easy-going styles will avoid the roughhousers and instead seek out more compatible playmates. To the extent that boys and girls, on the average, prefer different styles of play, this desire for play-style compatibility will lead to gender segregation. In other words, as with the sex-typed toy hypothesis, this theory states that children do not seek out same-sex playmates directly; instead, gender segregation arises as a consequence of children's choosing playmates with compatible play styles—playmates who happen to be predominantly of the same sex.

There seem to be a number of causes for self-imposed gender segregation.

There are, in fact, several ways in which typical styles of playing or interacting with others differentiates girls from boys. As noted by Maccoby (1985), boys' play tends to be rougher, with more body contact and aggression and a greater concern for leadership and dominance hierarchies. Girls tend to be more concerned with joint decisionmaking and turn taking. Their friendships tend to be more intensive, more focused on shared personal characteristics, and less focused on shared activities than are friendships between boys. Boys and girls also differ in their styles of influencing others. For example, Serbin and colleagues (1984) found that between the ages of 3 and 5, girls increase the number of polite suggestions they make when attempting to influence a play partner's behavior, whereas boys increase their frequency of direct demands and become less responsive to polite suggestions. At least partly as a function of these different styles, boys often are able to dominate mixed-sex interactions and to obtain more than their share of scarce resources (Charlesworth & LaFreniere 1983; LaFreniere & Charlesworth 1987; Powlishta & Maccoby 1990).

Do these sex differences in play or interaction style contribute to children's tendency to segregate by sex? Unfortunately, research on this topic is relatively sparse. In one recent study (Alexander & Hines 1994) using somewhat artificial stimuli, children preferred hypothetical playmates whose play styles or activities were consistent with their own sex. A study by Moller and colleagues (Moller, Powlishta, & Serbin 1990; Moller 1991) has provided some preliminary support for the play-style hypothesis, using a more naturalistic research paradigm. The researchers videotaped 2½-year-olds during free play at their nursery schools to measure their level of gender segregation and to identify each child's "best friend." Teachers also were asked to rate each child on a series of characteristics, from which four general play or interaction styles were identified: socially sensitive (e.g., doesn't give up, is verbally skilled, is not shy, doesn't accept bossiness), popular (e.g., meets new situations well, is happy, is accepted by same-sex and other-sex peers), disruptive (e.g., is restless, grabs toys, disrupts, is excitable), and adult dependent (e.g., seeks attention, maintains high proximity to teacher). Best

friends were then compared on their play styles and found to be quite similar. Because at this early age best friends were equally likely to be of the same or of the other sex, this play-style matching appears to develop earlier than full-scale gender segregation. However, when all of the children's interactions were examined (not just their interactions with best friends), early signs of gender segregation emerged. Approximately 42% of the children were observed with same-sex playmates more often than would be expected by chance. Whether a child was one of this 42% was predictable from his or her play style: among children who were not yet segregating, there were no sex differences in play style, but among segregating children, girls were rated higher in social sensitivity than were boys. These findings could be interpreted in two ways: either an emerging sex difference in play style promotes gender segregation, or the emergence of segregation causes the play styles of boys and girls to diverge. In light of the findings regarding best friends, the first explanation seems most plausible—that is, children selected best friends who had similar play styles even before they showed any preference for same-sex best friends. This pattern suggests that play-style compatibility precedes gender segregation: children seek out peers with play styles that are similar to their own; as these styles become sex-typed, play partners are increasingly likely to be of the same sex as the child.

Although more research must be done on this topic, play-style compatibility seems to be at least one factor that contributes to gender segregation. However, behavioral sex differences still cannot *fully* explain why children prefer their own sex. Children often react more positively to someone of their own sex even when they have had little or no exposure to that person's play style. For example, when provided with verbal descriptions or photographs of people they have never met, children predict that they will like same-sex individuals, select them as preferred playmates, and attribute more positive and fewer negative characteristics to them, relative to verbal descriptions or photos of the other sex (Serbin & Sprafkin 1986; Martin 1989; Powlishta in press). Children also show preferences for same-sex adults (e.g., Serbin & Sprafkin 1986), for whom the types of play styles measured by Moller and colleagues have little, if any, relevance. These findings suggest that the classification of a person as male or female may have implications for how a child will react to that person. This leads to a fourth theory of gender segregation: cognitive categorization.

Dividing the world into male and female categories. According to the cognitive categorization theory, children's tendency to categorize others on the basis of gender plays a crucial role in gender segregation. Once the child has classified the self and others in this manner, people are viewed as either "like me" or "not like me." Assuming that children have a relatively positive view of themselves (or are motivated to achieve one), the other people seen as "like me" also will be evaluated positively and thus will be seen as desirable play partners. The result is gender segregation.

Is there empirical support for this theory? Children certainly are sensitive to distinctions between males and females at a very early age. Infants as young as 5 months old can tell the difference between men and women depicted in photographs (Fagan & Singer 1979; Fagan & Shepherd 1981). By 9 to 12 months old, infants are able to match voices to these pictures (Poulin-Dubois et al. 1994). In other words, even at this early age, children have begun to form gender concepts. As children grow older, their knowledge expands and becomes more explicit. By the age of 3, most children are able to sort photographs on the basis of gender and to use gender labels for themselves and others accurately (Thompson 1975; Weinraub et al. 1984; Leinbach & Fagot 1986).

Do such abilities contribute to gender segregation? The evidence on this point is mixed. One group of researchers has found a relation between labeling ability and same-sex peer preferences (Fagot 1985; Fagot, Leinbach, & Hagan 1986), while others have not (Moller, Powlishta, & Serbin 1990). Maccoby (1988) has argued that even though children may be able to label the gender of self and others by the time they start to segregate, it is unlikely that they are efficient yet at matching the two concepts—in other words, reasoning such as "I am a girl; you are a girl; we are therefore the same" is probably too complex for a child in the beginning stages of gender segregation. Perhaps factors such as play-style compatibility more readily account for a child's initial selection of same-sex playmates. With maturity, the division of the social world into in-groups (i.e., same-sex) and out-groups (i.e., other sex) may play an increasingly important role. As a result, older children gravitate toward same-sex peers even in the absence of play-style information. Whereas young children's behavior may be governed largely by what they see other boys and girls doing, older children's behavior may be governed more by their beliefs about males and females.

Us versus them: The impact of social groups

Research evidence has shown that dividing people into in-groups and out-groups can have important consequences (see Messick & Mackie 1989 for a recent review). When random groups of adults are created, supposedly on the basis of some trivial distinction (e.g., having either over- or underestimated the number of dots in an array), participants show favoritism toward members of their own groups when allocating rewards, making ratings on traits, or evaluating group products. They also exaggerate differences between and similarities within the groups and believe that other groups are more homogeneous than their own ("those people are all just alike") (Messick & Mackie 1989). These processes may

encourage the formation and use of social stereotypes, because stereotypes are based on the notion that all members of a particular social category are alike in some way—a way that makes them distinct from other categories of people. Could these generic group processes help to explain children's attitudes toward males and females?

One study has investigated this possibility (Powlishta in press). Third- and fourth-graders watched videotaped scenes and rated each featured unfamiliar child on several characteristics. Both boys and girls perceived children of their own sex as more positive (e.g., intelligent), less negative (e.g., boring), and more likeable, similar to themselves, and varied than children of the other sex. In addition, all children in the video were viewed in a stereotype-consistent manner (i.e., boys were seen as more daring and messy than girls: girls were seen as more gentle and prone to crying than boys). In other words, the full range of intergroup phenomena previously demonstrated in laboratory studies of adults was seen in children's attitudes toward unfamiliar boys and girls.

Does this general tendency to favor members of our own groups and to see members of other groups as very different from ourselves help explain gender segregation? It seems logical that children would want to play with peers who they expect to have positive characteristics that are similar to their own. In the study described (Powlishta in press), a measure of gender segregation also was collected. Groups of classmates (two boys and two girls) were asked to complete two puzzles. Although extensive gender segregation was found, the amount of time a child spent interacting with a same-sex classmate (i.e., gender segregation) was *not* related to his or her attitudes toward the unfamiliar videotaped children.

At first, this finding seems to suggest that general attitudes toward in-groups and out-groups do not contribute to gender segregation. However, almost all groups split into same-sex pairs for the entire duration of the puzzle task. Because everyone was so highly segregated, it is not surprising that a child's degree of segregation was unrelated to his or her attitudes. There was not enough individual variability. Consistent with previous research (e.g., Maccoby & Jacklin 1987; Powlishta, Serbin, & Moller 1993), nearly all children show equally strong preferences for same-sex playmates, at least under some circumstances.

Why is gender such a salient characteristic for children? First of all, a person's gender usually is immediately apparent from visual cues; it is something we notice right away. As Allport put it, "All our experience teaches us that when things look different they usually are different. A black cloud in the sky has very different significance from a white cloud. A skunk is not a cat. Our comfort and sometimes our lives depend on learning to act differently in the face of unlike objects" (1954, 131). In addition to being perceptually salient, gender also is emphasized by our society. Furthermore, because often real differences exist between the sexes within the child's world, using these categories and their corresponding stereotypes (e.g., men mow the lawn; women vacuum) often is useful in making predictions about the behavior of males and females (Martin & Halverson 1981; Serbin, Powlishta, & Gulko 1993). All of these factors help to explain why children pay so much attention to gender.

Implications for reducing gender segregation

One advantage of knowing something about the causes of gender segregation is that such knowledge may suggest possible ways to encourage more positive interactions between boys and girls.

Should we try to reduce it?   Given that gender segregation among children is such a pervasive phenomenon, one that seems to occur naturally, without direct pressure from adults, should we attempt to reduce it? As previously noted, there are a number of reasons why lack of interaction with peers of the other sex could have negative consequences for children. Gender segregation exposes boys and girls to differing social influences—not on the basis of the individual child's interests and aptitudes but on the basis of gender alone. When boys and girls play separately, they miss out on opportunities to learn from and cooperate with each other. The maintenance of separate groups encourages an acceptance of gender stereotypes, suggesting that boys and girls are more different from each other than they really are.

Research evidence also supports the notion that boys and girls may benefit from interacting with each other. For example, Feiring and Lewis (1991) found that girls who had frequent contact with male peers at ages 3, 6, and 9 were rated as high in social competence by teachers. Although we cannot be certain that the cross-sex contact *caused* social competence to increase, the authors suggest that interacting with male friends may help girls develop social skills such as independence and assertiveness. Howes (1988) has found similar beneficial effects of cross-sex contact for boys as well as girls. In her observational study of 1- to 6-year-olds, Howes found that children with at least one cross-sex friend were more socially skilled than children who had only same-sex friends.

Breaking down the gender barriers.   These findings indicate that gender segregation may deprive children of important social opportunities. Is there anything that can be done to encourage positive interactions between boys and girls in school settings? Bianchi and Bakeman (1978) found that segregation was higher in a "traditional" than in an "open" preschool. The open preschool had deliberately set out to minimize sex typing. Its philosophy was described as follows:

The emphasis is on the individual development of each child; the goal is to respond to children on the basis of their individual behaviors, needs, and characteristics; thus, sex-stereotyped expectations about children's interests, abilities, or personalities are consciously avoided. Several aspects of school practice reflect this. For example, as often as possible, there are both male and female teachers in the classroom, and both teachers consciously engage in a wide range of activities and roles. (1978, 911)

Unfortunately, there is no way of knowing whether these characteristics led to lower levels of gender segregation. Families choosing to place their children in the "open" preschool may have differed from "traditional" school families; their children may have been less prone to segregation for any one of a variety of reasons (e.g., maternal employment, parental modeling or encouragement, etc.) regardless of their preschool experience. Nevertheless, these findings do support the notion that gender segregation is not "fixed in stone" but instead is subject to change.

Rewarding mixed-sex play.   Other, more direct attempts to manipulate gender segregation have met with only moderate success. For example, Serbin, Tonick, and Sternglanz (1977) had preschool teachers reward cross-sex play by giving positive attention (e.g., "I like the tower John and Kathy are building with the blocks"). Rates of cooperative mixed-sex play doubled when this treatment was implemented. However, gender segregation quickly reappeared when teachers returned to their normal classroom procedures. Given that children spend quite a bit of time away from adult surveillance, a teacher reinforcement approach to reducing gender segregation has limited practicality. As the results of this study demonstrated, it is difficult to have lasting effects on gender segregation through short-term efforts to influence the phenomenon directly.

Encouraging similar play styles.   Because gender segregation is not caused by direct pressure from adults but instead is instigated primarily by the children, it should not be surprising that direct teacher pressure has limited effectiveness in reducing segregation. Even though encouragement from adults can push children toward mixed-sex play, other forces pull in the opposite direction. A desire for playmates with similar play styles is one such force. If sex differences in play style drive segregation, then reducing these play-style differences may be more effective in lowering rates of gender segregation than attempting to reduce segregated play directly. Although some aspects of play style seem to be biologically determined (e.g., Hines & Kaufman 1994), socialization practices may enhance these biologically based sex differences and create additional differences, as well.

Research evidence supports the notion that teachers often interact with boys and girls differently, in ways that

There are also a number of reasons why we should not promote or accept gender segregation, but should provide opportunities for positive interactions between boys and girls.

might encourage sex differences in play or interaction style. Specifically, the treatment of girls encourages compliance and dependence, whereas the treatment of boys encourages assertiveness. Beal (1994) summarized these differences: girls receive more teacher attention when they are indoors playing quietly. When a misdeed is noted, girls typically receive only quiet reprimands from the teacher. Boys, on the other hand, are likely to receive teacher attention even when they are playing at a distance. Teachers tend to monitor boys for signs of misbehavior and to scold them publicly when it happens. Many boys seem to enjoy this public attention and thus are more likely to misbehave in the future.

It seems logical that if boys and girls were treated more similarly, sex differences in play style would decline, thus reducing gender segregation; however, such attempts are likely to meet with limited success. Although teachers often react to the same behavior differently depending on whether it was enacted by a boy or girl, they also react to actual differences between the sexes. Boys and girls behave differently long before entering school; thus, teachers reinforce lessons that have already been learned at home (Beal 1994).

Beal (1994) has summarized some of the ways in which adults in general, and parents in particular, treat boys and girls differently. When adults believe that they are playing with a boy baby, they are likely to bounce, toss, and roughhouse with the baby; when they think that the baby is a girl, they talk with her more frequently. Although there are probably more similarities than differences in the way parents treat their sons and daughters, some differences do exist. Mothers tend to hold infant daughters closer and to touch and cuddle them more than they do sons; infant sons are allowed more independence. Fathers are more likely to use a rough-and-tumble style of play with sons than with daughters, a style that is active, unpredictable, and physically stimulating. Differential parental treatment that encourages compliance on the part of girls and independence on the part of boys continues during the toddler and school-age years. Parents react positively when female toddlers follow them around the house but negatively when boys do the same thing. They worry about a boy who is too compliant. During the elementary school years, girls are granted much less independence than boys, for example, by being picked up after school and by being required to play at home rather than in public places (Beal 1994).

Such differential treatment, when coupled with potentially innate differences between the sexes, is likely to result in gender-typed play or interaction styles. It is unlikely that teachers could wipe out such differences simply by treating boys and girls similarly. However, play style is only one factor contributing to gender segregation. As noted earlier, children typically choose same-sex playmates even in the absence of information about play style. The mere fact that a person has been cognitively categorized as "like me" (same sex) or "not like me" (other sex) sets group processes in motion, whereby same-sex individuals are preferred. If we could interrupt this categorization process, gender segregation should decline.

Reducing the salience of gender. The salience of gender varies considerably from one situation to another. Deaux and Major (1987), for instance, point out that some events (e.g., watching the Miss America Pageant) may prime us to focus on the gender of other people. Although we have seen that gender is typically very salient for children, there are times when they seem able to ignore it, at least temporarily, and allow barriers between the sexes to fall. Thorne (1987) provides the following anecdotal evidence. A group of fourth-graders, who were usually quite gender segregated on the playground, came together in a mixed-sex group to defend and discuss the plight of a classmate who had been unjustly punished by a teacher. The children united on the basis of classroom membership, which temporarily became more salient than gender.

> Unfortunately, situations are often created in the classroom that emphasize gender distinctions: In a combined fourth-fifth grade classroom the teacher introduced a math game organized as girls against boys; she would write addition and subtraction problems on the board, and a member of each team would race to be the first to write the correct answer. As the teacher wrote two score-keeping columns headed 'Beastly Boys' and Gossipy Girls,' several boys yelled out, 'Noisy girls! Gruesome girls!' while some of the girls laughed. (Thorne 1987, 10)

Teachers sometimes try to manage the behavior of boys by comparing them to girls or threatening to make them work with girls. "One teacher told the girls to line up first for recess and said, 'Oh, Billy thinks he's a girl' when a boy stood up and tried to head out the door; he promptly sat down again" (Beal 1994, 141–42). In schools where children wear uniforms, all girls often wear one outfit and all boys wear another outfit. By emphasizing differences between boys and girls and similarities within each sex in these ways, the likelihood of cooperative, mixed-sex interactions is minimized.

Besides avoiding these kinds of artificial distinctions, is there anything that teachers can do to de-emphasize gender? Thorne (1986) has identified some characteristics of setting in which boys and girls are likely to interact with each other:

1. Children are engaged in an absorbing task (e.g., a group art project) that encourages cooperation and takes attention away from gender.
2. Children are not responsible for group formation, such as when the teacher has organized mixed-sex encounters.
3. Principles of grouping other than gender are invoked explicitly (e.g., by forming "hot lunch" and "cold lunch" lines, or by organizing workgroups on the basis of interests or abilities).

Research evidence has supported the contention that boys and girls interact more frequently, have more positive attitudes about each other, and acknowledge similarities between the sexes under these kinds of circumstances. For example, Lockheed (1986) asked teachers to make use of small, mixed-sex workgroups. Relative to control classrooms, children in these experimental classes engaged in more cross-sex interactions. The experimental treatment also improved boys' preference for working in mixed-age groups. However, the treatment did not influence children's perceptions of each other; children from all classes continued to rate same-sex classmates more positively than cross-sex classmates.

Another similar study was more successful at influencing children's attitudes toward individual boys and girls (Deschamps & Doise 1978). Groups of 12 children (6 boys, 6 girls) were taken into a room and seated according to gender. For half of these groups, two subgroups were created: three boys and three girls were given blue pens and labeled "the blue group"; the remaining children were given red pens and labeled "the red group." Each child then individually completed a series of paper-and-pencil games and was asked to estimate how well each of the other children did at these games. When the children had been divided into mixed-sex groups (blue versus red), they predicted that boys and girls would do equally well. When these mixed groups were not created, boys and girls believed that their own sex had done better than the other sex. So the creation of groups that cross gender boundaries and accentuate commonalities between boys and girls, especially when such groupings are made explicit (e.g., with distinct names), can be successful at reducing children's biases against the other sex.

Emphasizing attributes that boys and girls have in common can also reduce perceived differences between the sexes. In one study (Powlishta 1989), children reviewed photographs of unfamiliar boys and girls and judged the similarity of several boy-girl pairs. Pairs were seen as more similar when they were surrounded by photographs of adults and explicitly labeled as "children" than when the same pairs were surrounded by photographs of other children. In the former, more diverse context, focusing attention on a characteristic shared by boys and girls, one that distinguished then from other people (i.e., "childhood"), reduced children's tendency to view males and females as different types of creatures.

Conclusion

The previous studies suggest that gender barriers may be less rigid in diverse social contexts in which children share similarities and differences with members of both sexes. By emphasizing variability within each sex and by creating or highlighting commonalities between boys and girls, gender should become a less salient basis for social categorization. This approach argues against the formation of single-sex classes in public schools, an arrangement for which some people have recently been advocating. These advocates have argued that boys and girls have different learning styles (e.g., competitive versus cooperative), that girls receive less attention than boys and are discouraged from being assertive in mixed-sex classes, and that teachers of coeducational classes expect boys and girls to adhere to sex-typed norms (deGroot 1994). This argument overlooks the tremendous individual variability that exists within each sex, and it avoids rather than attempts to correct the problem of differential treatment of boys and girls. More importantly, creating separate classes or workgroups for each sex enhances the salience of gender and legitimizes children's gender stereotypes. It sends the message to children that gender is the most important distinction among people—more important than interests, aptitudes, achievements, values, cultural heritage, personality, etc. Given the considerable evidence that social categorization leads to stereotyping and biases against those who are viewed as different, enforcing gender segregation through single-sex classes can only aggravate the strained relations that already sometimes exist between boys and girls. Any short-term gains (e.g., easier classroom management) will be compensated for by long-term problems (e.g., encouraging males and females to be seen as more different than they really are).

Instead of encouraging or accepting gender segregation, we should provide opportunities for positive interactions between boys and girls. It does not seem likely that we can block the basic human tendency to form social categories that help us make sense of the world. However, by creating situations that require cooperation between boys and girls, and by forming groups or pointing out characteristics that unify both sexes, we may be able to discourage children from always reaching to others on the basis of their gender.

References

Alexander, G.M., & M. Hines. 1994. Gender labels and play styles: Their relative contribution to children's selection of playmates. *Child Development* 65: 869–79.
Allport, G. 1954. *The nature of prejudice.* Cambridge, MA: Addison-Wesley.

Beal, C.R. 1994. *Boys and girls: The development of gender roles.* New York: McGraw-Hill.

Bianchi, B.D., & R. Bakeman. 1978. Sex-typed affiliation preferences observed in preschoolers: Traditional and open school differences. *Child Development* 49: 910–12.

Blakemore, J.E.O., A.A. LaRue, & A.B. Olejnik. 1979. Sex appropriate toy preference and the ability to conceptualize toys as sex-role related. *Developmental Psychology* 15: 339–40.

Carpenter, C.J., A.C. Huston, & W. Holt. 1986: Modification of preschool sex-typed behaviors by participation in adult structured activities. *Sex Roles* 14: 603–15.

Charlesworth, W.R., & P. LaFreniere. 1983. Dominance, friendship, and resource utilization in preschool children's groups. *Ethology and Sociobiology* 4: 15–26.

Connor, J.M., & L.A. Serbin. 1977. Behaviorally based masculine- and feminine-activity-preference scales for preschoolers: Correlates with other classroom behaviors and cognitive tests. *Child Development* 48: 1411–16.

Deaux, K., & B. Major. 1987: Putting gender into context: An interactive model of gender-related behavior. *Psychological Review* 94: 369–89.

deGroot, G. 1994. Do single-sex classes foster better learning? *The APA Monitor*, July, 60–61.

Deschamps, J.-C., & W. Doise. 1978. Crossed category memberships in intergroup relations. In *Differentiation between social groups*, ed. H. Tajfel, 141–58. London: Academic Press.

Edwards, C.P., & B.B. Whiting. 1988. *Children of different worlds.* Cambridge, MA: Harvard University Press.

Eisenberg, N., K. Tryon, & E. Cameron. 1984. The relation of preschoolers' social interaction to their sex-typed toy choices. *Child Development* 55: 1044–50.

Fagan, J.F., III, & P.A. Shepherd. 1981. Theoretical issues in the early development of visual perception. In *Developmental disabilities in preschool children*, eds. M. Lewis & L. Taft. New York: Spectrum.

Fagan, J.F., III, & L.T. Singer. 1979. The role of simple feature differences in infants' recognition of faces. *Infant behavior and Development* 2: 39–45.

Fagot, B.I. 1974. Sex differences in toddlers' behavior and parental reaction. *Developmental Psychology* 10: 554–58.

Fagot, B.I. 1985. Changes in thinking about early sex role development. *Developmental Review* 5: 83–98.

Fagot, B.I., M.D. Leinbach, & R. Hagan. 1986. Gender labeling and the adoption of sex-typed behaviors. *Developmental Psychology* 22: 440–43.

Fein, G., D. Johnson, N. Kosson, L. Stork, & L. Wasserman. 1975. Sex stereotypes and preferences in the toy choices of 20-month-old boys and girls. *Developmental Psychology* 11: 527–28.

Feiring, C., & M. Lewis. 1991. The development of social networks from early to middle childhood: Gender differences and the relation to school competence. *Sex Roles* 25: 237–53.

Gottman, J.M., & J.G. Parker, eds. 1987. *Conversations of friends: Speculations in affective development.* New York: Cambridge University Press.

Hines, M., & F.R. Kaufman. 1994. Androgen and the development of human sex-typical behavior: Rough-and-tumble play and sex of preferred playmates in children with congenital adrenal hyperplasia (CAH). *Child Development* 65: 1042–53.

Howes, C. 1988. Same- and cross-sex friends: Implications for interaction and social skills. *Early Childhood Research Quarterly* 3: 21–37.

LaFreniere, P.J., & W.R. Charlesworth. 1987. Preschool peer status, behavior and resource utilization in a cooperative/competitive situation. *International Journal of Behavioral Development* 10: 345–58.

LaFreniere, P., F.F. Strayer, & R. Gauthier. 1984. The emergence of same-sex preferences among preschool peers. *Child Development* 55: 1958–66.

Leinbach, M.D., & B.I. Fagot. 1986. Acquisition of gender labels: A test for toddlers. *Sex Roles* 15: 655–67.

Lockheed, M.E. 1986. Reshaping the social order: The case of gender segregation. *Sex Roles* 14: 617–28.

Lockheed, M.E., & S.S. Klein. 1985. Sex equity in classroom organization and climate. In *Handbook for achieving sex equity through education*, ed. S. Klein, 189–217. Baltimore, MD: Johns Hopkins University Press.

Luria, Z., & E. Herzog. 1985. *Gender segregation across and within settings.* Paper presented at the Biennial Meeting of the Society for Research in Child Development, April, Toronto, Ontario, Canada.

Maccoby, E.E. 1985. Social groupings in childhood: Their relationship to prosocial and antisocial behavior in boys and girls. In *Development of antisocial and prosocial behavior: Theories, research and issues*, eds. D. Olweus, J. Block, & M. Radke-Yarrow. San Diego, CA: Academic Press.

Maccoby, E.E. 1988. Gender as a social category. *Developmental Psychology* 24: 755–65.

Maccoby, E.E., & C.N. Jacklin. 1987. Gender segregation in childhood. In *Advances in child development and behavior*, Vol. 20, ed. H. Reese, 239–88. New York: Academic Press.

Martin, C.L. 1989. Children's use of gender-related information in making social judgements. *Developmental Psychology* 25: 80–88.

Martin, C.L., & C.F. Halverson. 1981. A schematic processing model of sex typing and stereotyping in children. *Child Development* 52: 1119–34.

Messick, D.M., & D.M. Mackie. 1989. Intergroup relations. *Annual Review of Psychology* 40: 45–81.

Moller, L.C. 1991. *Toddler peer preferences: The role of gender awareness, sex-typed toy preferences and compatible play styles.* Ph.D. dissertation, Concordia University, Montreal, Quebec, Canada.

Moller, L.C., K.K. Powlishta, & L.A. Serbin. 1990. *Three theories of gender segregation: Cognitive consonance, sex-typed toy play, and play style compatibility.* Paper presented in the 13th Annual Conference of the Societe Quebecoise pour la Recherche en Psychologie, November, Montreal, Quebec, Canada.

Poulin-Dubois, D., L.A. Serbin, B. Kenyon, & A. Derbyshire. 1994. Infants' intermodal knowledge about gender. *Developmental Psychology* 30: 436–42.

Powlishta, K.K. 1989. *Perceived similarity and the salience of gender.* Paper presented at the Biennial Meeting of the Society for Research in Child Development, April, Kansas City, Missouri.

Powlishta, K.K. In press. Intergroup processes in childhood: Social categorization and sex-role development. *Developmental Psychology.*

Powlishta, K.K., & E.E. Maccoby. 1990. Resource utilization in mixed-sex dyads: The influence of adult presence and task type. *Sex Roles* 23: 223–40.

Powlishta, K.K., L.A. Serbin, & L.C. Moller. 1993. The stability of individual differences in gender-typing: Implications for understanding gender segregation. *Sex Roles* 29: 723–37.

Serbin, L.A., & C. Sprafkin. 1982. Measurement of sex-typed play: A comparison between laboratory and naturalistic observation procedures. *Behavioral Assessment* 4: 225–35.

Serbin, L.A., & C. Sprafkin. 1986. The salience of gender and the process of sex-typing in three- to seven-year-old children. *Child Development* 57: 1188–99.

Serbin, L.A., K. K. Powlishta, & J. Gulko. 1993. The development of sex-typing in middle childhood. *Monographs of the Society for Research in Child Development* 52(2).

Serbin, L.A., I.J. Tonick, & S.H. Sternglanz. 1977. Shaping cooperative cross-sex play. *Child Development* 48: 924–29.

Serbin, L.A., J.M. Connor, C.J. Burchardt, & C.C. Citron. 1979. Effects of peer presence on sex-typing of children's play behavior. *Journal of Experimental Child Psychology* 27: 303–09.

Serbin, L.A., C. Sprafkin, M. Elman, & A.B. Doyle. 1984. The early development of sex differentiated patterns and social influence. *Canadian Journal of Social Science* 14: 350–68.

Thompson, S.K. 1975. Gender labels and early sex role development. *Child Development* 46: 339–47.

Thorne, B. 1986. Girls and boys together, but mostly apart. In *Relationships and development*, eds. W.W. Hartup & Z. Rubin, 167–84. Hillsdale, NJ: Erlbaum.

Thorne, B. 1987. *Children and gender: Constructions of difference.* Paper presented at the conference on Theoretical Perspectives on Sexual Difference, February, Stanford University, Stanford, California.

Weinraub, M., L.P. Clemens, A. Sockloff, T. Ethridge, E. Gracely, & B. Meyers. 1984. The development of sex role stereotypes in the third year: Relationship to gender labeling, identity, sex-typed toy preference, and family characteristics. *Child Development* 55: 1493–1503.

Unit Selections

22. **Where Will the Baby Sleep? Attitudes and Practices of New and Experienced Parents Regarding Cosleeping with Their Newborn Infants,** Helen L. Ball, Elaine Hooker, and Peter J. Kelly
23. **What Matters? What Does Not? Five Perspectives on the Association between Marital Transitions and Children's Adjustment,** E. Mavis Hetherington, Margaret Bridges, and Glendessa M. Insabella
24. **Boys Will Be Boys,** Barbara Kantrowitz and Claudia Kalb
25. **Father Love and Child Development: History and Current Evidence,** Ronald P. Rohner
26. **The Moral Development of Children,** William Damon
27. **Playing with God,** Tracy Cochran

Key Points to Consider

❖ Where did you get your ideas, values, and beliefs about how a parent behaves? If you were unsure about how to respond to a particular parenting situation, whom would you consult? How do you think your own experience of parenting has affected your attitudes or possible parenting practices for your current or future children? Do you think your parents had a significant effect on your growing up? Do you think you or your child's friends will have a stronger influence on your child? Would this make you change the way you permit your children to make friends?

❖ Virtually no one has a family network that has not been touched by divorce and remarriage. Have you experienced these transitions, and what was the outcome? Since divorce and remarriage affect boys and girls differently and at different ages, how might you handle these transitions in the best interests of a child?

❖ What was your father like when you were growing up? How do you think your father may have influenced you? Do you think society today supports fathers? Why or why not? As you think about being or becoming a parent, how will you support or change your parenting style in light of these readings on fatherhood?

❖ Given the violence that we see being committed increasingly by younger youth and even children today, what solutions do you have to offer to counteract these tragic instances? Who is to blame, the parents, the children, society? Do other countries experience the same level of violence, or is this a distinctly American phenonemon? What should happen to children who have committed heinous crimes? Do you think they can be rehabilitated into responsible and moral adults? As a parent or professional working with children, what can you do to raise morally responsible children?

❖ Were you raised in a religious family? What do you remember about religion growing up, and what do you retain as an adult now? Do you think religion is a critical ingredient in family life? Why or why not? If a family chooses not to introduce formalized religion to their children, do you think that the children are being developmentally disadvantaged? Why or why not?

 **Links**   **www.dushkin.com/online/**

19. **Facts for Families**
   http://www.aacap.org/publications/ factsfam/index.htm

20. **Families and Work Institute**
   http://www.familiesandworkinst.org

21. **The National Academy for Child Development**
   http://www.nacd.org

22. **National Council on Family Relations**
   http://www.ncfr.com

23. **The National Parent Information Network (NPIN)**
   http://ericps.ed.uiuc.edu/npin/

24. **Parenting and Families**
   http://www.cyfc.umn.edu/Parenting/ parentlink.html

25. **Parentsplace.com: Single Parenting**
   http://www.parentsplace.com/family/ singleparent/

26. **Stepfamily Association of America**
   http://www.stepfam.org

These sites are annotated on pages 4 and 5.

Few people today realize that the potential freedom to *choose* parenthood—deciding whether to become a parent, deciding when to have children, or deciding how many children to have—is a development due to the advent of reliable methods of contraception and other recent sociocultural changes. Moreover, unlike any other significant job we may aspire to, few, if any, of us will receive any formal training or information about the lifelong responsibility of parenting. For most of us, our behavior is generally based on our own conscious and subconscious recollections of how we were parented as well as on our observations of the parenting practices of others around us. In fact, our society often behaves as if the mere act of producing a baby automatically confers upon the parents an innate parenting ability and as if a family's parenting practices should remain private and not be subjected to scrutiny or criticism by outsiders.

Given this climate, it is not surprising that misconceptions about many parenting practices continue to persist today. Only within the last 30 years or so have researchers turned their lenses on the scientific study of the family. Social, historical, cultural, and economic forces also have dramatically changed the face of the American family today. For example, significant numbers of children in our country will experience the divorce and/or remarriage of their parents at some point during their lifetimes. In "What Matters? What Does Not? Five Perspectives on the Association between Marital Transitions and Children's Adjustment," E. Mavis Hetherington and colleagues describe the effects of divorce and remarriage on children.

When parents bring their baby home from the hospital for the first time, what arrangements will they make for their new family member? In "Where Will the Baby Sleep?" the authors describe research on the potential benefits of parents' attitudes and practices when they chose to cosleep with their newborn infants.

Research on fathers and their influence on their children has increased dramatically in recent years. "Boys Will Be Boys" and "Father Love and Child Development: History and Current Evidence" both address the research and discuss the social construction of fatherhood in America and the important consequences that fathers have on their childen.

With alarming frequency, news reports bring us accounts of tragedies and other unspeakable acts committed increasingly now by young adults and even by children. How do children and adults learn to behave in a moral and responsible way? In "The Moral Development of Children" William Damon discusses research on the origins of morality in children and the key role that parents play in promoting their children's moral development.

Religious exposure and training is present in many families. One family's personal account of discussing religion, science, and God with their child is chronicled in "Playing with God." This account highlights the active nature of a child's own spiritual socialization and the give and take between parents and children in this process.

Parenting and Family Issues

Where Will the Baby Sleep? Attitudes and Practices of New and Experienced Parents Regarding Cosleeping with Their Newborn Infants

HELEN L. BALL
Department of Anthropology and UDSC
University of Durham
Durham DH1 3HN, England

ELAINE HOOKER
Department of Anthropology and UDSC
University of Durham
Durham DH1 3HN, England

PETER J. KELLY
Center for Health & Medical Research
University of Teesside
Middlesborough, TS1 3BA, England

An evolutionary perspective on human infant sleep physiology suggests that parent-infant cosleeping, practiced under safe conditions, might be beneficial to both mothers and infants. However, cosleeping is not part of mainstream parenting ideology in the United States or the United Kingdom, and little evidence is available to indicate whether, and under what circumstances, parents sleep with their newborn infants. We present data from an anthropological investigation into the practices and attitudes of new and experienced parents of newborn infants regarding parent-infant sleeping arrangements in a community in the northeast of England. Despite not having contemplated cosleeping prior to the birth, new parents in our sample found it to be a convenient nighttime caregiving strategy, and one which was practiced regularly. Infants slept with both their parents, some being habitual all-night cosleepers, but commonly beginning the night in a crib and sleeping with their parents for several hours following the early morning feed. [*infant sleep, newborn, cosleeping, new parents*]

An evolutionary perspective on human infant sleep physiology suggests that parent-infant cosleeping practiced under safe physical and social circumstances might provide a variety of (as yet unexplored) psychosocial and physiological benefits to both mothers and infants. For example, based on laboratory studies of mother-infant bed sharing, McKenna and colleagues have suggested that the types of physiological changes mother-infant cosleeping induces in the infant's sleep architecture, arousals, and breast-feeding patterns may help to protect some infants from SIDS (cot death), and they provide a substantial amount of physiological, behavioral, and cross-cultural evidence supporting this hypothesis (e.g., Davies 1985; McKenna 1990a, 1990b; McKenna and Mosko 1990; McKenna et al. 1994; McKenna et al. 1997; Mosko et al. 1993; Mosko et al. 1996; Mosko et al. 1997a, 1997b; Richard et al. 1996). However, cosleeping is not part of mainstream British or American parenting ideology, and issues relating to the potential benefits and risks of cosleeping are rarely addressed in antenatal classes, advice pamphlets, or publications for new parents. When cosleeping is addressed it tends to be presented as if it were a unitary phenomenon—practiced in the same manner across all cultural circumstances, for the same reasons, producing the same likely outcomes, which are typically assumed to be negative (e.g., Mitchell and Scragg 1993). McKenna (1995) argues against this perspective and discusses why cosleeping cannot be treated in binary terms (i.e., practiced or not practiced), or considered a discrete or uniform variable. Rather, he suggests, outcomes (whether benign, beneficial, or risky) will vary depending on how and why it is practiced, and whether breast-feeding is part of the cosleeping experience for infants. Furthermore, research-based data on whether, and under what circumstances, new parents decide to sleep with their newborn infants, and how they operationalize their decision, are almost nonexistent. This paper presents data from an anthropological investigation into the practices and attitudes of new and experienced parents of newborn infants regarding parent-infant sleeping arrangements. The data presented were generated as part of a community-based research project conducted in the North Tees Health District in the northeast of England. The project was designed to investigate attitudes and practices toward nighttime parenting strategies and to obtain baseline data on the prevalence of cosleeping and the circumstances under which it occurred in a sample of parents interviewed before and after their baby's birth (see Hooker and Ball 1998).

Recent generations of British and American parents have been advised by pediatric health professionals that sleeping with their babies is "wrong" (e.g., Spock and Rothenberg 1985; Sturgess 1977; Wright 1972). Until this decade it was common for pediatricians, child psychotherapists, and other "baby experts" to dismiss parent-infant cosleeping (or bed sharing) as poor parenting practice with detrimental side effects for both parents and children (e.g., Ferber 1986; Janes and Rodway 1974). Professional objections included predictions that cosleeping may foster dependency, be habit-forming (even addictive), be sexually arousing, be overstimulating, be frightening for children (who may observe their parents having sex), be harmful to the parents' relationship (if they refrain from sex), reflect poor limit setting, and contribute to sleep problems (Lozoff et al. 1984; Schachter et al. 1989). Parents were also warned that not only was cosleeping with newborns ill-advised, it was downright dangerous—25 years ago even having the baby in the same bedroom was considered a bad idea:

> May I make an earnest plea that, whenever it is possible, no new baby should sleep in the same room as his parents? There are several reasons for this, one of them is the fact that mothers are liable to be anxious and want 'to just have a look at him' all the time—or worse, to lean over and pick him up. This can be lethal because Mother is tired when she cuddles the baby and she is likely to lie down on her bed . . . and fall asleep. Babies have been suffocated that way. . . . So if you do have any other room, put the baby in it. . . . He is not going to die before the dawn just because he's alone in there! [Wright 1972: 57–58]

Recently a new wave of interest in cosleeping (also called bed sharing, or "the family bed") has prompted fresh discussion in both popular and scientific media (Jackson 1992; McKenna et al. 1993; Wright 1997). While it is often cited that most "traditional" societies, and some notable "developed" or "industrialized" ones such as Japan (Caudill and Plath 1966) and Korea (Lee 1992), practice cosleeping as the cultural norm, anecdotal evidence suggests that British and American parents who sleep with their infants/children view themselves as a

much maligned minority. Little research has actually been conducted, however, on the prevalence of cosleeping in American and Western European nations (see Rath and Okum 1995). Where such data exist they tend to either contrast cosleeping prevalence among families with different ethnic backgrounds (and hence different cultural traditions regarding childrearing) in a given community (e.g., Gantley et al. 1993; Lozoff et al. 1984; Schachter et al. 1989), or contrast prevalence of cosleeping in case-control studies of clinical and nonclinical samples from pediatric sleep disorder or psychotherapy clinics (e.g., Forbes et al. 1992; Hanks and Rebelsky 1977; Kaplan and Poznanski 1974). The result is a confusing array of literature on cosleeping that juxtaposes data on children of different ages, obfuscates cosleeping with infants (as custom or cultural practice) and cosleeping with toddlers (as a reactive attempt to address sleep problems), and confounds normal variation in parenting practice with extreme examples associated with trauma and family psychotherapy.

With an article in *Medical Anthropology* (1986) McKenna reignited interest in the cosleeping debate when he hypothesized that the behavioral and physiological relationship between a cosleeping mother and child may play a protective role in helping some infants to resist some forms of SIDS (cot death). Subsequently elaborated upon in a detailed series of articles (McKenna 1990a, 1990b; McKenna and Mosko 1990), and reinforced with experimental data (McKenna and Mosko 1993, 1994; McKenna et al. 1994; McKenna et al. 1997a, 1997b; Mosko et al. 1996; Mosko et al. 1997a, 1997b; Richard et al. 1996), these ideas have struck a chord with many parents and professionals (e.g., Davies 1994; McKenna et al. 1993; Wright 1997). McKenna drew attention to a series of positive reasons for parent-infant cosleeping (particularly in the first six months) that emerge from evolutionary, developmental, and cross-cultural perspectives. His laboratory research demonstrates that maternal sleep contact promotes infant arousals while at the same time lengthening the total amount of time infants (and sometimes mothers) sleep (Mosko et al. 1997a, 1997b), and mothers and infants who sleep together experience synchronous arousals and coordination of sleep stages. Routinely cosleeping infants sleep in a supine position to facilitate breast-feeding (McKenna et al. 1997), and breast-feeding occurs more frequently (both factors being associated with lower risk of SIDS in some studies) (McKenna et al. 1997). The argument that the normal sleep environment for healthy newborns is with their mothers receives support from the analysis of the composition of human milk—its low energy value causing infants to feed on demand throughout the day and night; comparative data from closely related primate species (great-ape infants sleep on their mothers) and cross-cultural evidence indicates that cosleeping is the species-typical pattern for humans (Blurton-Jones 1972).

A review of the academic literature prior to 1987 indicates that there was little published research about the prevalence and practice of parent-child cosleeping at that time, let alone parent-infant cosleeping. An oft-cited cross-cultural survey (Barry and Paxson 1971), reporting on the presence or absence of cosleeping as cultural "norm" in 186 societies worldwide, described 65% of the 127 societies surveyed as practicing cosleeping (for the remaining 35% infants slept in the same room, but not the same bed as the parent(s)—for a further 61 societies infants shared the parent's room, but it was unknown whether they also shared the same bed). Caudill and Plath (1966) observed that it was common practice in Japanese culture for children to share their parents' bed, this style of nighttime parenting emphasizing the nurturing aspects of Japanese family life. The observation that cosleeping was the norm in other cultures prompted Lozoff et al. (1984) to investigate the sleep practices of urban families in the United States; however, they restricted their analyses to children over six months old. In the decade since McKenna's hypothesis was published several surveys of cosleeping have been undertaken (e.g., Hayes et al. 1996; Johnson 1991; Morelli et al. 1992; Schachter et al. 1989), but again the predominant focus has been on toddlers and preschoolers, not newborns. A notable exception was an ethnographic investigation of infant care practices in Welsh and Bangladeshi families in Cardiff (Gantley et al. 1993), which found that it was customary for Bangladeshi mothers to sleep with their infants, while babies born to Welsh and English parents were sometimes placed in cots in their parents' rooms for a period of two or three months, and then encouraged (close to the peak age for SIDS) to "get used" to sleeping alone, where possible in their own rooms. The authors also observed less pressure in Bangladeshi families for babies to "sleep through the night," whereas for Welsh parents, the demands of either or both working outside the home resulted in considerable emphasis on the infant's sleeping time. In contrast to the notion of vulnerability in infants expressed by Bangladeshi families, there was among Welsh and English mothers a clear push toward encouraging babies to be independent. Gantley et al.'s descriptions of Welsh parental behavior resonate distinctly with the findings, published 30 years earlier, of the Newsons' study of infant care practices in Nottingham (Newson and Newson 1966).

Although Gantley et al. included no statistics on the frequency of cosleeping families in their sample, such data were published following a survey on infant care practices in Birmingham (Farooqi 1994). This study determined that, based on the responses of 374 mothers who completed a questionnaire issued at a large District General Hospital, 36% of Asian infants slept in their parents' bed compared with 11% of white infants. Furthermore, 33% of white infants were reported to sleep in a separate bedroom, compared with only 4% of Asians.

Given the dearth of detailed recent information regarding the behavior of parents of newborns, the present study was designed to investigate the nighttime strategies of parents with small infants in an economically depressed, postindustrial community in the northeast of England. Our particular interest was in where newborn infants slept and how parents coped with nighttime caregiving. In this paper we present and compare data on the expectations and experiences of nighttime caregiving for parents having their first baby with those of experienced parents. Other aspects of the data will be presented elsewhere (Hook et al. in press; Ball et al. n.d.).

Methods

Using a prospective study design we investigated the opinions and practices of parents regarding nighttime caregiving, before and after the birth of their infants, via semi-structured interviews and focus groups. Ethics approval was obtained from North Tees Health Authority and we contacted parents-to-be through antenatal classes, clinics, and the maternity wards at North Tees Hospital. Parents-to-be were approached personally by one of the investigators (EH), either in the antenatal ward of North Tees Hospital, or at one of the antenatal classes run by North Tees midwives and Health Visitors. The purpose of the study was explained to parents in general terms (no specific mention was made of cosleeping), and confidentiality of all information obtained was assured. If parents agreed to participate their permission was obtained on a consent form and the initial interview was conducted. At the initial interview, background data on the parents and household were obtained (e.g., ages, marital status, occupations, educational qualifications, medical problems, smoking, family composition, etc.), together with information on the current pregnancy, and parents' expectations and intentions regarding infant feeding, sleep arrangements, infant illness, and sources of parenting information. A contact number was obtained in order to arrange follow-up interviews when the infant was expected to be two to four months old. This procedure allowed us to gather data on both parents' expectations and opinions prior to the birth, and to monitor actual parental child-care practices after the birth. After sufficient time had elapsed, parents were recontacted and (if available and willing) were reinterviewed by the original interviewer. Recontact interviews were conducted with one or both parents in their own homes. At this second interview, parents were asked about the birth, feeding arrangements, sleeping arrangements, baby's environment (e.g., smoking, etc.), baby's temperament, baby's illnesses, advice received from health professionals, parents' assessment of how they were coping, changes they had instigated in infant care, and the effect of the baby on their relationship and family. All initial and recontact interviews were conducted

Table 1. Background data on participants.

	New Parents	Experienced Parents
N	23	17
Parity range	1	2–10
Boys; girls	11:12 (all singletons)	11:8 (inc. boy twins x 1, mixed twins x 1)
Delivery	16 vaginal	11 vaginal
	7 c-section	6 c-section
Mean age mother	25.2 (range 15–33)	31.2 (range 23–42)
Mean age father	27.9 (range 19–34) 2 missing	32.9 (range 24–46)
Marital status	16 married	17 married
	3 living with partner	
	3 single	
	1 living apart from partner	
Smoking	21 nonsmoking parents	14 nonsmoking parents
Mother's education	9 no postsecondary	10 no postsecondary
	14 some postsecondary	7 some postsecondary
Mean age of baby at post-natal interview	10.04 wks (range 4–25)	8.23 wks (range 3–17)

by the same researcher (EH). Written notes were made on the interview forms, then coded, entered into a spreadsheet for quantification, and written up as field notes.

Results

Sixty mothers or couples participated in intensive interviews prior to the birth of their infant and 40 participated in recontact interviews. Five original subjects declined to be reinterviewed, 14 were uncontactable (phone numbers had changed to a cable company in the interim and new numbers were unobtainable), and one couple experienced a premature stillbirth. Among the 40 families recontacted, two sets of twins had been born. For 23 of the mothers recontacted this was their first baby. Background data on the participants by parenting experience are presented in Table 1. First-time parents were, on average, five years younger than the experienced parents. 83% were married or living together, while 100% of the experienced parents were married. Two of the first-time parents were teenage mothers living with their own parents. 19% of new and 18% of experienced parents included at least one smoker. 61% of first-time mothers and 42% of experienced mothers had some postsecondary education. Approximately 30–35% of deliveries for both primiparous and multiparous mothers were by cesarean section, an unusually high percentage, probably a reflection of the fact that we recruited some mothers who were in the antenatal ward because of potential delivery complications.

The majority of both new (74%) and experienced (59%) mothers intended to try breast-feeding. None of the new parents intended to sleep with their baby (al-

though 4 thought it might happen), while over a third (35%) of experienced parents acknowledged that they would, or might, cosleep. Furthermore, 30% of new parents and 47% of experienced parents never anticipated bringing the baby into their bed for any reason. Situations imagined by parents who thought that they might do so included ease of breast-feeding, when baby was ill, and morning cuddles. New parents were significantly more fearful of perceived negative consequences of sleeping with their infants than were experienced parents. 52% of new parents rated fear of overlaying as their primary reason against cosleeping, while two sets of parents were fearful of promoting bad habits, one mother citing an example of a friend who was still sleeping with her 5-year-old daughter. Another mother commented that she had read a news report about a baby who, when sleeping with its parents, had "been nearly strangled" by becoming tangled in the mother's long hair. Among the experienced parents, 4 sets were concerned with overlaying, 1 set about promoting bad habits, and 2 about their own sleep being affected.

Despite the fact that they did not plan to sleep with their new babies, all the first-time parents planned to keep their newborns close by them at night, 100% indicating parents' bedroom, and particularly "next to parents' bed" as the place where the baby would sleep. Carry cots and Moses baskets were the most frequently cited items that infants would sleep in, although a couple of other options (cot, swinging crib) were mentioned. Parents' reasons for initially keeping the baby in their room centered around two themes: safety and security; for instance, one mother commented that she thought her baby would "feel more secure" if it slept near her. New parents anticipated that the infant would sleep in their room for only a few weeks or months. The longest estimate was of nine months—the majority of new parents, however, assumed that they would move their infant into another room at some point between one and three months of age. The parents of almost all the first-time infants (except the expectant teenage mothers) already had the infant's nursery prepared. However, most indicated that they would be flexible in their arrangements and recognized that they had to wait and see what things would be like before making any firm decisions. Several of the first-time mothers, and particularly the younger mothers, seemed to have thought very little about what they would do with their baby after it was born, seemingly having difficulty contemplating beyond labor.

When asked to reflect upon why they had chosen a particular sleeping arrangement for their infant, and where their ideas had come from, most new parents claimed to have trusted their instincts: "it was a natural decision," "it feels like the right thing to do," "feels comfortable," "more convenient." Other popular sources of ideas included family and friends and literature. Advice from parent-craft classes was cited only once as a source of ideas for where the baby could sleep. When questioned further, several new parents commented that although feeding at night had been discussed at parent-craft/antenatal classes, no mention was made of any other aspects of nighttime parenting. When we conducted focus groups at parent-craft classes, however, parents consistently volunteered "lack of sleep" as the primary negative influence the impending birth would have on their lives. Nighttime parenting was, therefore, something they anticipated with trepidation. Although parents had been asked near the beginning of the interview whether they anticipated that their baby would sleep in their bed, and all the parents expecting their first child had replied in the negative, we rephrased the question at the end of the interview and asked parents if they ever imagined bringing the baby into their bed. The answers we received were strikingly different—only 5 of the new parents were adamant that they could not imagine ever bringing their baby into their bed. Many parents anticipated bringing their baby into bed if it was ill, for breast-feeding, or to help it go to sleep, but imagined that they would return it to its crib before they fell asleep themselves. Some parents were comfortable with the idea of falling asleep with their babies, and one young father (age 19) commented that if he ever had to take care of the baby by himself at night he "would definitely feel safer if the baby was in the bed" with him.

For the experienced parents, less imagination and more retrospection was involved in planning for the present baby. All but 2 sets of experienced parents anticipated having their baby in their bedroom at night initially, and expectations of how long this would last were much greater than the expectations of the first-time parents. No experienced parents thought the infant would sleep in their room for less than four months, most anticipated six months, with a couple of families planning on one to one and a half years. Of the 2 who were not planning to have the baby in their room, 1 mother with one previous child stated that the baby would be in its own room, and she "didn't want a sound monitor either." This mother reported that her first child had slept and been fed in its nursery as soon as it came home, but that it had also been kept in intensive care for two weeks after birth and she didn't feel she had bonded with the first baby. With regard to the preparation of a nursery, few of the experienced parents had gone to the effort of preparing a special room in advance, and approximately one third anticipated that the baby would move into a sibling's room. This group of parents were evenly divided about establishing a routine and sticking rigorously to it, half generally expecting that they would follow the pattern established with their previous child(ren), the other half anticipating "playing it by ear." One experienced mother who was expecting twins commented in response to our query about her plans that she was prepared to be flexible because "you can't dictate to babies!"

When we recontacted the parents in our sample two to four months after birth, we found them pursuing a varied array of nighttime parenting strategies. New parents' expectations turned out to be (as surmised) a far cry from their later experience. Although none of the new parents anticipated bed sharing with their infants, at the postnatal interview 70% were found to be sleeping in bed with their infants at least occasionally. Of these 16 newborns and their parents, 2 habitually slept in their parents' bed all night every night, another 11 habitually slept in their parents' bed every night for part of the night, while a further 5 slept in their parents' bed occasionally (once per week or less). Although all of the new parents had envisaged that the baby would sleep in their bedroom for at least a month, at the time of the recontact interview three (13%) infants were sleeping in a separate room, one after two nights, another after one week, and the third after two weeks. The parents remarked that these infants were "too noisy," and one or more of the parents was unable to sleep with the baby in the room. The remainder of the babies were in the parents' room in either their own crib or basket, their parents' bed, or a combination of the two. The infant of one of the teenage mothers slept next to the mother's bed on weekends and next to the grandparents' during the week. This was explained by the grandmother as an arrangement to help her daughter cope with schoolwork, but was clearly resented by the daughter herself, telling her mother during the interview "she might as well be *your* baby, Mam!"

The two habitual all-night cosleepers were both breast-feeding infants, and 9 of the 11 combination cosleepers were, or had initially been, breast-fed. The 5 babies who never slept in their parents' bed were all bottle-fed from birth, and the association between breast-feeding and cosleeping for new parents was significant ($\chi^2 = 10.08$, p < 0.001). The ease of breast-feeding in bed, and its natural relationship with cosleeping, was frequently brought up by new parents during interviews: mothers remarked that they were surprised how easy they found it to breast-feed lying down—some having been shown how to do this in the hospital, particularly after a c-section delivery. New fathers occasionally initiated bringing the baby into bed, but generally it was the breast-feeding mothers who implemented this strategy, causing some new fathers a degree of concern (see Ball and Hooker et al. n.d.). One new father, whose wife had to return to hospital due to persistent bleeding after five weeks, coped with the nighttime care of his daughter by having her in bed. Generally, however, it was mothers who periodically had to cope with the new baby at night on their own (fathers on business trips, working night shifts, etc.), and they described the prevalence of all-night cosleeping as increasing at these times.

All of the habitual and combination cosleepers, and 3 out of the 5 occasional cosleepers, expressed surprise at how much easier it was to take care of their infants when they coslept. Of these 14 sets of new parents, 10 had claimed at the antenatal interview that they would not cosleep, and 3 had rejected the idea of ever bringing their baby into bed, including one couple who subsequently slept all night, every night with their newborn.

Amongst the experienced parents, 35% anticipated that they would sleep with their infants, while 59% actually did so. Two newborns were habitual all-night, every night cosleepers (in both cases parents had coslept with a previous baby), with another 3 being combination cosleepers who habitually spent part of the night in the parents' bed. Additionally, 1 of the sets of twins were regular combination cosleepers. A further 4 occasional cosleepers had slept with their parents a handful of times, or had been brought into bed when ill or unsettled. Seven sets of experienced parents told us that they had never (or "not really") let their babies sleep in their bed. All of the infants of experienced parents who were habitual or combination cosleepers were also breast-fed. One experienced father insisted that his baby went straight into his own room from birth, while another who would have preferred such an arrangement was overruled by his wife. In general, however, the experienced fathers were happy to have their babies both in their bedroom and in their bed. In one instance (the cosleeping twins) the mother had a previous child with whom she had coslept, but for the father these were his first offspring. Although he soon adjusted to having the babies sleep in the bed (alternating one asleep on his chest and one by the mother's side), for the first week he described sleeping with "one foot firmly planted on the floor" for fear of rolling on them.

Our results indicate that for both new and experienced parents in our sample cosleeping was a relatively common practice. Generally infants were brought into bed with *both* parents, but parents having to cope with the baby alone at night (both mothers and fathers) described cosleeping as a strategy they commonly employed. Many of the parents we talked to practiced regular part-night cosleeping with the infant beginning the night in a crib or cot and moving to the parents' bed sometime during the course of the night, generally between midnight and 4 a.m., and remaining there until morning. Despite preconceptions to the contrary and initial fears of overlaying, new parents who coslept considered it an effective and easy means of obtaining a good night's sleep, and experienced parents who had coslept with a previous infant were willing to repeat the practice.

Discussion

The first-time parents in our sample reinforced the findings of other researchers in reporting how ill-prepared they felt for the reality of coping with the demands of a newborn baby (e.g., Monk et al. 1996). Several parents acknowledged they found it extremely difficult to cope in the first few postnatal weeks, especially at night. Although adamant at the prenatal interview that they would not cosleep with their infant, few realized how frequently infants wake during the night, and many adopted cosleeping as part of their coping strategy. Parents with no prenatal intention to cosleep (primarily first-time parents) were found to be taking their babies into bed with them for a variety of reasons including ease of feeding, desire to monitor infant, parental need for more sleep, desire for closeness, and inability to settle baby alone.

The finding from our small sample that 70% of new, and almost 60% of experienced, parents with newborn infants were cosleepers is interesting in comparison with previous American studies. Morelli et al. (1992) reported that of 18 families who were interviewed, none of the parents slept with their newborns on a regular basis, most sharing a room temporarily, with 58% of babies sleeping in separate rooms by the age of three months. This finding contrasted with data from interviews with 14 Mayan mothers, all of whom slept in the same bed with their infant for over a year (Morelli et al. 1992). A survey of U.S. mothers of 126 older infants (from six months) and children up to four years old (Lozoff et al. 1984) determined that cosleeping was a routine and recent practice in 35% of white and 70% of black families (defining a child as a cosleeper if parent(s) and child slept more than once in the same bed together during the previous month as part of the normal family practice). Black children, particularly, were frequent all-night cosleepers. In our sample there was negligible ethnic diversity (we interviewed only one Bangladeshi family in which the mother coslept downstairs with the infant, while the father coslept upstairs with their older children). Lozoff et al. reported a suggestive trend in both black and white families for cosleeping to be increased in father-absent households, a finding which is reflected in our data with regard to temporary parental absence, but not restricted to fathers.

A further survey of cosleeping in urban Hispanic-American young children (6–48 months old) (Schachter et al. 1989), following the protocol and definitions of Lozoff et al. (1984), found frequent all-night cosleeping was significantly more common in the Hispanic-American sample than Lozoff et al.'s sample of white U.S. families (21% vs. 6%). While 25–28% of children in the age brackets 13–24, 25–36, and 37–48 months were frequent all-night cosleepers, contrary to our findings very few parents coslept with their infants under one year of age (6.7% in 6–12 mo. category). The finding that frequent all-night cosleeping was rare for infants of 6 to 12 months was consistent with the white middle-class American data and also with the Japanese data of Caudill and Plath (1966). A recent survey in rural New England (Hayes et al. 1996) of parent-infant cosleeping in a sample of 51 3–5-year-old children included retrospective questions about sleeping in infancy. Using response categories of "always," "often," and "sometimes" to classify cosleepers, and "rarely" or "never" for solitary sleepers, the authors determined that although approximately half of the children were cosleepers at ages 3 to 5, all but one of the 51 children had been placed to sleep in a separate bed in infancy. The practice of infants remaining in the parents' bed after breast-feeding was recorded in this survey but was not classified by these authors as cosleeping. This discrepancy raises an important point regarding research into cosleeping in infancy: parents often respond to questions regarding the place where their infant sleeps at night by identifying the place where *the infant starts the night*, or where the infant "is supposed to sleep." As almost any parent will confirm, newborns have rarely read the rule book and commonly fail to conform to expected patterns of behavior, particularly regarding where (and when) they "should" sleep. Thus many infants who spend large portions of the night asleep with their parents (i.e., those who start the night elsewhere but are brought into the parental bed during the night for whatever reason) fail to be identified as cosleepers unless researchers specifically ask parents if their baby is moved during the course of the night. The data presented in this paper would look remarkably different if we had taken an infant's initial nighttime sleep site as the indicator of whether or not it coslept (9% for new parents vs. 70%; 12% for experienced parents vs. 59%) and would be very similar to figures generated for white infants in Birmingham (UK) (Farooqi 1994). An illustrative case can be made from a study conducted in Toledo, Ohio (Chessare et al. 1995), that attempted to determine prevalent infant sleep positions via questionnaires issued at pediatricians' offices to parents with infants under seven months. One of the questions asked

parents to indicate where their baby slept, specifying a series of tick boxes. The results from this question indicated that 42% indicated "crib in parents' room," 6% "in parents' bed," 50% "own room," and 2% "other." Taken at face value these results indicate that only a few infants sleep in their parents' bed. Without documenting whether the baby was moved during the night, however, the results of neither this study nor that by Farooqi in Birmingham (UK) are very useful in helping us understand the prevalence or practice of parent-infant cosleeping in these communities.

The relationship observed between breast-feeding and cosleeping is an obvious one—cosleeping breast-feeding mothers are able to nurse their infants with a minimal amount of disruption, and without either of them fully waking up, a finding compatible with the reports of Mayan mothers (Morelli et al. 1992) who claimed that they generally did not notice feeding their babies in the night. Observations of cosleeping breast-feeding infants indicate that they nurse more frequently and for longer periods than breast-feeding infants who do not cosleep (McKenna et al. 1997), but nonetheless routinely cosleeping mothers sleep as much as solitary sleeping mothers and rate their sleep more positively (Mosko et al. 1996; Mosko et al. 1997b). New mothers who had discovered the ease with which they could nurse at night when cosleeping indicated that they persisted with breast-feeding for much longer periods than they might have done otherwise.

Another important finding highlighted by this research is the fact that newborn cosleepers in our sample (with both first-time and experienced parents) generally slept with both their parents. This is relevant in light of research into the physiological and behavioral correlates of cosleeping in newborns, which has thus far examined only mother-infant cosleeping (e.g., McKenna et al. 1990, 1994; Sawczenko 1997; Taylor 1997; Young 1997; although see Ball and Hooker 1997, 1998).

We conclude, from this research, that the reality of parenting a newborn infant causes first-time parents to implement nighttime caregiving strategies that they had not previously contemplated. Bringing the baby into their bed to sleep was described as an "intuitive" strategy by many new parents. In fact, many parents explained their change of opinion regarding cosleeping with their newborn because "it just felt like the right thing to do." Experienced parents, who had much more realistic expectations regarding infants and sleep, generally followed the strategies that had worked with their previous child(ren). The majority had previously coslept with other infants and sometimes harbored severe anger or resentment toward third parties (health professionals, relatives, strangers) who voiced the opinion that parents and infants should not cosleep, feeling passionately that cosleeping with their infant was "natural." Trevathan and McKenna (1994) summarized the results of 59 studies that illustrate why parent-infant sleep contact "feels like the right thing to do," ranging from the benefits of bonding and attachment, through frequent suckling, sensory cues that regulate breathing, physiological effects of touch (especially skin-to-skin contact), to the soothing effects on infants of vestibular stimulation and maternal heartbeat. Although new parents were generally unaware of the range of developmental, psychological, and physiological benefits accruing from parent-infant sleep contact, they were able to articulate that cosleeping with their newborn reduced their anxiety regarding its safety at night, soothed their infant, minimized the effect of nightfeeds on parental sleep, and enhanced their feelings of "closeness" with their baby. The results of this research indicate that, despite receiving advice to the contrary (and holding opinions to the contrary in the prenatal period), new parents in our sample experimented with a variety of infant sleeping arrangements in the first few postnatal weeks. Once they had experienced cosleeping, the benefits to both themselves and their infants became obvious, and cosleeping emerged as a regular pattern of behavior. Contrary to the opinion of Davies (1994) that cosleeping (bed sharing) is unfamiliar to the white ethnic majority of the United Kingdom, the results of this sample of new and experienced parents from the northeast of England lead us to predict that parent-infant cosleeping is a more prevalent practice in Britain than has been generally recognized.

Note

Acknowledgments. This project was funded by the University of Durham and the Centre for Health and Medical Research, University of Teesside. We are grateful for the cooperation of North Tees Area Health Trust, particularly the staff of the antenatal wards at North Tees Hospital, and all the North Tees midwives and health visitors who contributed to the study. We are particularly grateful to the parents and their newborns who participated in the research, and to colleagues whose comments improved this manuscript.

References Cited

Ball, H. L., and E. Hooker 1997 The North Tees Cosleeping Project: The First 3 Years. Paper presented at Workshop on Mother/Infant Interactions and the Effects upon Development, Morbidity and Mortality, Institute of Child Health, Bristol, U.K., June 18.—1998 What Happens to Infants Who Sleep with Their Parents? American Journal of Physical Anthropology (abstract) Suppl. 26:67.

Ball, H. L., E. Hooker, and P. J. Kelly N.d. Parent Infant Cosleeping: Fathers' Roles and Perspectives.

Barry, H., and L. M. Paxson 1971 Infancy and Early Childhood: Cross-Cultural Codes 2. Ethnology 10:466–508.

Blurton-Jones, N. G. 1972 Comparative Aspects of Mother-Child Contact. *In* Ethological Studies of Child Behaviour. N. G. Blurton-Jones, ed. Pp. 305–329. Cambridge: Cambridge University Press.

Caudill, W., and D. W. Plath 1966 Who Sleeps by Whom? Parent-Child Involvement in Urban Japanese Families. Psychiatry 29:344–366.

Chessare, J. B., C. E. Hunt, and C. Bourguignon 1995 A Community-Based Survey of Infant Sleep Position. Pediatrics 96:893–896.

Davies, D. P. 1985 Cot Death in Hong Kong: A Rare Problem? Lancet 2:1346–1349.—1994 Ethnicity and SIDS: What Have We Learnt? Early Human Development 38:215–220.

Farooqi, S. 1994 Ethnic Differences in Infant Care Practices and in the Incidence of Sudden Infant Death Syndrome in Birmingham. Early Human Development 38:209–213.

Ferber, R. 1986 Solve Your Child's Sleep Problems. New York: Simon and Schuster.

Forbes, J. F., D. S. Weiss, and R. A. Folen 1992 The Cosleeping Habits of Military Children. Military Medicine 157:196–200.

Gantley, M., D. P. Davies, and A. Murcott 1993 Sudden Infant Death Syndrome: Links with Infant Care Practices. British Medical Journal 306:16–19.

Hanks, C. C. and F. G. Rebelsky 1977 Mommy and the Midnight Visitor: A Study of Occasional Cosleeping. Psychiatry 40:277–280.

Hayes, M. J., S. M. Roberts, and R. Stowe 1996 Early Childhood Co-Sleeping: Parent-Child and Parent-Infant Nighttime Interactions. Infant Mental Health Journal 17:348–357.

Hooker, E., and H. L. Ball 1998 Parent-Infant Cosleeping: Attitudes and Practices in North Tees, England. American Journal of Physical Anthropology Suppl. 26:136.

Hooker, E., H. L. Ball, and P. J. Kelly In press Sleeping Like a Baby: Attitudes and Experiences of Cosleeping in Northeast England. Medical Anthropology.

Jackson, D. 1992 Three in a Bed. New York: Avon Books.

Janes, E., and A. Rodway 1974 The Bounty Baby Book. 10th edition. London: Bounty Services.

Johnson, C. M. 1991 Infant and Toddler Sleep: A Telephone Survey of Parents in One Community. Developmental and Behavioral Pediatrics 12:108–114.

Kaplan, S. L., and E. Poznanski 1974 Child Psychiatric Patients Who Share a Bed with a Parent. Journal of American Academy of Child Psychiatry 13:344–356.

Lee, K. 1992 Pattern of Night Waking and Crying of Korean Infants from 3 Months to 2 Years Old and Its Relation with Various Factors. Developmental and Behavioral Pediatrics 13:326–330.

Lozoff, B., A. W. Wolf, and N. S. Davis 1984 Cosleeping in Urban Families with Young Children in the United States. Pediatrics 74:171–182.

McKenna, J. J. 1986 An Anthropological Perspective: On The Sudden Infant Death Syndrome (SIDS). *Medical Anthropology* 10:8–22. —1990a Evolution and Sudden Infant Death Syndrome (SIDS): Part 1: Infant Responsivity to Parental Contact. Human Nature 1:145–177.—1990b Evolution and Sudden Infant Death Syndrome (SIDS): Part II: Why Human Infants? Human Nature 1:179–206.—1995 The Potential Benefits of Infant-Parent Cosleeping in Relation to SIDS Prevention: Overview and Critique of Epidemiological Bed-Sharing Studies with Notes on Future Research Directions. *In* SIDS: New Trends in the Nineties. Torl O. Rognum, ed. Pp. 256–265. Oslo: Scandinavian Press.

McKenna, J. J., and S. S. Mosko 1990 Evolution and Sudden Infant Death Syndrome (SIDS): Part III: Infant Arousal and Parent-Infant Co-Sleeping. Human Nature 1(3):291–330.—1993 Evolution and Infant Sleep: An Experimental Study of Infant-Parent Co-Sleeping and Its Implications for SIDS. Acta Paediatrica Supplement 389:31–36. —1994 Sleep and Arousal, Synchrony and Independence, among Mothers and Infants Sleeping Apart and Together (Same Bed): An Experiment in Evolutionary Medicine. Acta Paediatrica Supplement 397:94–102.

McKenna, J. J., S. S. Mosko, C. Dungy, and J. McAninch 1990 Sleep and Arousal Patterns of Co-Sleeping Human Mother/Infant Pairs: A Preliminary Physiological Study with Implications for the Study of Sudden Infant Death Syndrome (SIDS). American Journal of Physical Anthropology 83:331–347.

McKenna, J. J., S. S. Mosko, and C. A. Richard 1997 Bedsharing Promotes Breastfeeding. Pediatrics 100(2):214–219.

Hunt, M. B. Cetel, and J. Arpaia 1994 Experimental Studies of Infant-Parent Co-Sleeping: Mutual Physiological and Behavioral Influences and Their Relevance to SIDS. Early Human Development 38: 187–201.

McKenna, J. J., E. B. Thoman, T. F. Anders, A. Sadeh, V. L. Schechtman, and S. F. Glotzbach 1993 Infant-Parent Co-Sleeping in an Evolutionary Perspective: Implications for Understanding Infant Sleep Development and the Sudden Infant Death Syndrome. Sleep 16:263–281.

Mitchell, E. A., and R. Scragg 1993 Are Infants Sharing a Bed with Another Person at Increased Risk of Sudden Infant Death Syndrome? Sleep 16(4):387–389.

Monk, T. H., M. J. Essex, N. A. Smider, M. H. Klein, K. K. Lowe, and D. J. Kupfer 1996 The Impact of the Birth of a Baby on the Time Structure and Social Mixture of a Couple's Daily Life and Its Consequences for Well-Being. Journal of Applied Social Psychology 26:1237–1258.

Morelli, G. A., B. Rogoff, D. Oppenheim, and D. Goldsmith 1992 Cultural Variations in Infants' Sleeping Arrangements: Questions of Independence. Developmental Psychology 28(4):604–613.

Mosko, S., J. J. McKenna, M. Dickel, and L. Hunt 1993 Parent-Infant Cosleeping: The Appropriate Context for the Study of Infant Sleep and Implications for Sudden Infant Death Syndrome (SIDS) Research. Journal of Behavioral Medicine 16:589–611.

Mosko, S., C. Richard, and J. McKenna 1997a Infant Arousals during Mother-Infant Bedsharing: Implications for Infant Sleep and SIDS Research. Pediatrics 100(20):841–849.

——— 1997b Maternal Sleep and Arousals during Bedsharing with Infants. Sleep 201(2):142–150.

Mosko, S., C. Richard, J. McKenna, and S. Drummond 1996 Infant Sleep Architecture during Bedsharing and Possible Implications for SIDS. Sleep 19:677–684.

Newson, J., and E. Newson 1966 Patterns of Infant Care in an Urban Community. Middlesex, U.K.: Penguin.

Rath, F. H., and M. E. Okum 1995 Parents and Children Sleeping Together: Cosleeping Prevalence and Concerns. American Journal of Orthopsychiatry 65:411–418.

Richard, C., S. Mosko, J. McKenna, and S. Drummond 1996 Sleeping Position, Orientation, and Proximity in Bedsharing Infants and Mothers. Sleep 19:685–690.

Sawczenko, A. 1997 Observations of the Effects of Bedsharing and Maternal Actions upon Infant Night-Time Thermal Physiology and CO_2 Micro-Environment, in a Low SIDS Risk Group. Paper presented at Workshop on Mother/Infant Interactions and the Effects upon Development, Morbidity and Mortality, Institute of Child Health, Bristol, U.K., June 18.

Schachter, F. F., M. L. Fuchs, P. E. Bijur, and R. K. Stone 1989 Cosleeping and Sleep Problems in Hispanic-American Urban Young Children. Pediatrics 84:522–530.

Spock, B., and M. B. Rothenberg 1985 Dr. Spock's Baby and Child Care. New York: Pocket Books.

Sturgess, R. 1977 The Baby Book. London: Magnum Books.

Taylor, B. 1997 Preliminary Observations of a Bed-Sharing Study, Ethics and Methods of Analysis. Paper presented at Workshop on Mother/Infant Interactions and the Effects upon Development, Morbidity and Mortality, Institute of Child Health, Bristol, U.K., June 18.

Trevathan, W. R., and J. J. McKenna 1994 Evolutionary Environments of Human Birth and Infancy: Insights to Apply to Contemporary Life. Children's Environments 11:88–104.

Wright, E. 1972 The New Childhood. London: Tandem.

Wright, R. 1997 Why Johnny Can't Sleep. Time, April 14:74–75.

Young, J. 1997 Night-time Behaviour between Low SIDS Risk Infants and Their Mothers: A Longitudinal Study of Room Sharing and Bed Sharing. Paper presented at Workshop on Mother/Infant Interactions and the Effects upon Development, Morbidity and Mortality, Institute of Child Health, Bristol, U.K., June 18.

What Matters? What Does Not?

Five Perspectives on the Association Between Marital Transitions and Children's Adjustment

E. Mavis Hetherington, Margaret Bridges, and Glendessa M. Insabella
University of Virginia

This article presents an analysis of 5 views of factors that contribute to the adjustment of children in divorced families or stepfamilies. These perspectives are those that emphasize (a) individual vulnerability and risk; (b) family composition; (c) stress, including socioeconomic disadvantage; (d) parental distress; and (e) disrupted family process. It is concluded that all of these factors contribute to children's adjustment in divorced and remarried families and that a transactional model examining multiple trajectories of interacting risk and protective factors is the most fruitful in predicting the well-being of children.

In the past 30 years, there has been a significant decline in the proportion of two-parent families in first marriages and a complementary increase in the number of single-parent households and stepfamilies. These changes are the result of a rapid rise in the divorce rate that began during the 1960s (Simons, 1996) and also, to a lesser extent, of an increase in births to single mothers. Although there has been a modest decrease in the divorce rate since the late 1970s, almost one half of marriages end in divorce in the United States, and one million children experience their parents' divorce each year (U.S. Bureau of the Census, 1992). It is projected that between 50% and 60% of children born in the 1990s will live, at some point, in single-parent families, typically headed by mothers (Bumpass & Sweet, 1989; Furstenberg & Cherlin, 1991). Currently, stepfamilies make up approximately 17% of all two-parent families with children under 18 years of age (Glick, 1989).

Although the high divorce rate has been interpreted as a rejection of the institution of marriage, 75% of men and 66% of women eventually will remarry, suggesting that although people are rejecting specific marital partners, most are not rejecting marriage itself (Booth & Edwards, 1992; Bumpass, Sweet, & Castro-Martin, 1990; Cherlin & Furstenberg, 1994; Ganong & Coleman, 1994). Since the 1960s, however, the annual rate of remarriage has actually declined as the divorce rate has increased. Moreover, divorces are more frequent in remarriages and occur at a rate 10% higher than that in first marriages

(Bumpass et al., 1990; Cherlin & Furstenberg, 1994). Couples with remarried wives are almost twice as likely to divorce as are couples with remarried husbands. This association may be attributable to the 50% higher rate of dissolution in remarriages in which children from previous marriages are present (Tzeng & Mare, 1995), although the presence of children appears to be less relevant to the marital quality of African American couples (Orbuch, Veroff, & Hunter, in press). As a result of their parents' successive marital transitions, about half of all children whose parents divorce will have a stepfather within four years of parental separation, and 1 out of every 10 children will experience at least two divorces of their residential parent before turning 16 years of age (Furstenberg, 1988). These numbers underestimate the actual number of household reorganizations to which children are exposed because many couples cohabit before remarriage or cohabit as an alternative to remarriage (Bumpass & Raley, 1995; Bumpass, Sweet, & Cherlin, 1991; Cherlin & Furstenberg, 1994; Ganong & Coleman, 1994).

The national figures for marital transitions and family structure mask very different patterns among racial and ethnic groups because the social context of marriage varies across communities (Orbuch et al., in press). African American children are twice as likely as White children to experience at least one parental divorce (National Center for Health Statistics, 1988) and also are more likely to bear children out of wedlock in adolescence and adulthood (Demo & Acock, 1996; Tzeng & Mare, 1995; U.S. Bureau of the Census, 1992). In addition, African Americans and Hispanic Whites are less likely to divorce after separation and to remarry than are non-Hispanic Whites

E. Mavis Hetherington, Margaret Bridges, and Glendessa M. Insabella, Department of Psychology, University of Virginia.

Correspondence concerning this article should be addressed to E. Mavis Hetherington, Department of Psychology, University of Virginia, 102 Gilmer Hall, Charlottesville, VA 22903–2477. Electronic mail may be sent to emh2f@virginia.edu.

(Castro-Martin & Bumpass, 1989; Cherlin, 1992). Thus, in comparison with White children, more African American children spend longer periods of time in single-parent households, which often include kin and cohabiting partners.

As marriage has become a more optional, less permanent institution in contemporary American society, children in all ethnic groups are encountering stresses and adaptive challenges associated with their parents' marital transitions. Children from divorced and remarried families, in contrast to those from never-divorced families, exhibit more problem behaviors and lower psychological well-being. Little agreement exists, however, about the extent, severity, and duration of these problems because there is great diversity in children's responses to parental marital transitions (Amato & Keith, 1991a; Emery & Forehand, 1994; Hetherington, 1991b; McLanahan & Sandefur, 1994). Furthermore, although it is clear that marital dissension and dissolution, life in single-parent households, and remarriage present families and children with new experiences, risks, and resources, there is some disagreement on how these factors undermine or enhance the well-being of children.

Theoretical Perspectives on Marital Transitions and the Adjustment of Children

Five main theoretical perspectives have been proposed to explain the links between divorce and remarriage and children's adjustment. These perspectives are those emphasizing (a) individual risk and vulnerability; (b) family composition; (c) stress, including socioeconomic disadvantage; (d) parental distress; and (e) family process.

Individual Risk and Vulnerability

It has been proposed that some characteristics of parents and children may influence their exposure and vulnerability to adversity. Some adults possess characteristics (e.g., antisocial behavior) that place them at increased risk for marital discord, multiple marital transitions, and other adverse life experiences (Capaldi & Patterson, 1991; Kitson & Morgan, 1990; Patterson & Dishion, 1988; Simons, Johnson, & Lorenz, 1996). Adults with psychological problems such as depression or antisocial behavior often select partners who also experience psychological difficulties (Merikangas, Prusoff, & Weissman, 1988), thereby increasing their risk for marital problems and dissolution. This is called the marital selectivity hypothesis. In addition, some children have attributes that increase their vulnerability or protect them from deleterious consequences of stresses associated with their parents' marital transitions (Amato & Keith, 1991a; Emery & Forehand, 1994; Hetherington, 1989, 1991b).

Family Composition

It is commonly assumed that two biological parents provide the optimal family environment for healthy child development and that any deviation from this family structure, such as single-parent families or stepfamilies, is problematic for children (Amato & Keith, 1991a; Kitson & Holmes, 1992; Simons, 1996). Much of the early theorizing about divorce and family structure focused on father absence.

Stress and Socioeconomic Disadvantage

This perspective emphasizes that marital transitions trigger a series of negative social and economic changes, stresses, and practical problems that can interfere with the well-being of parents and children. For custodial mothers and their children, divorce is related to a notable economic decline that is associated with living conditions that make raising children more difficult (McLanahan & Sandefur, 1994), whereas remarriage is associated with an increase in household income for single mothers. Although much of the research on stress has focused on economic stresses, both divorced and remarried families encounter other stresses related to changing family roles and relationships (Cherlin & Furstenberg, 1994; Hetherington & Stanley Hagen, 1995; Simons, 1996).

Parental Distress

This perspective suggests that stressful life experiences, including economic decline and adaptive challenges associated with divorce and remarriage, lead to parental strain, distress, and diminished well-being, which are reflected in psychological problems such as depression, anxiety, irritability, and antisocial behaviors, as well as stress-related health problems (Capaldi & Patterson, 1991; Forgatch, Patterson, & Ray, 1995; Hetherington, 1989, 1991b; Kiecolt-Glaser et al., 1987; Lorenz, Simons, & Chao, 1996; Simons & Johnson, 1996). There is great individual variability in response to negative life changes; some parents cope with such changes with apparent equanimity, whereas others exhibit marked affective disruption and distress.

Family Process

Finally, many researchers have emphasized that differences between nondivorced families and divorced and remarried families on process variables such as conflict, control, expression of positive and negative affect, and problem solving largely explain the effects of divorce and remarriage. It is argued that more proximal variables, such as discipline and child-rearing practices, are most important in affecting children's adjustment.

Although these perspectives often are presented as competing with each other, empirical support can be found for each, suggesting that they may best be considered as complementary hypotheses (Amato & Keith, 1991a; Simons, 1996). In this article, research on the five perspectives is reviewed, and the direct and indirect effects of the five factors on the adjustment of children and parents in divorced and remarried families are examined. Finally, a transactional model of marital transitions involving relationships among the factors is presented.

Adjustment of Children in Divorced and Remarried Families

There is general agreement among researchers that children, adolescents, and adults from divorced and remarried families, in comparison with those from two-parent, nondivorced families, are at increased risk for developing problems in adjustment (for meta-analyses, see Amato & Keith, 1991a, 1991b) and that those who have undergone multiple divorces are at a greater risk (Capaldi & Patterson, 1991; Kurdek, Fine, & Sinclair, 1995). For the most part, the adjustment of children from divorced and remarried families is similar (Amato & Keith, 1991a; Cherlin & Furstenberg, 1994). Children from divorced and remarried families are more likely than children from nondivorced families to have academic problems, to exhibit externalizing behaviors and internalizing disorders, to be less socially responsible and competent, and to have lower self-esteem (Amato & Keith, 1991a; Cherlin & Furstenberg, 1994; Hetherington, 1989). They have problems in their relationships with parents, siblings, and peers (Amato & Keith, 1991b; Hetherington, 1997).

Normative developmental tasks of adolescence and young adulthood, such as attaining intimate relationships and increasing social and economic autonomy, seem to be especially difficult for youths from divorced and remarried families. Adolescents from divorced and remarried families exhibit some of the same behavior problems found in childhood and, in addition, are more likely to drop out of school, to be unemployed, to become sexually active at an earlier age, to have children out of wedlock, to be involved in delinquent activities and substance abuse, and to associate with antisocial peers (Amato & Keith, 1991a; Conger & Chao, 1996; Demo & Acock, 1996; Elder & Russell, 1996; Hetherington & Clingempeel, 1992; McLanahan & Sandefur, 1994; Simons & Chao, 1996; Whitbeck, Simons, & Goldberg, 1996). Increased rates of dropping out of high school and of low socioeconomic attainment in the offspring of divorced and remarried families extend across diverse ethnic groups (Amato & Keith, 1991b); however, the effect is stronger for females than for males (Hetherington, in press).

Adult offspring from divorced and remarried families continue to have more adjustment problems (Chase-Lansdale, Cherlin, & Kiernan, 1995; Hetherington, in press), are less satisfied with their lives, experience lower socioeconomic attainment, and are more likely to be on welfare (Amato & Keith, 1991b). Marital instability also is higher for adults from divorced and remarried families (Amato & Keith, 1991b; Glenn & Kramer, 1985; Hetherington, in press; McLanahan & Bumpass, 1988; Tzeng & Mare, 1995), in part because of the presence of a set of risk factors for divorce, including early sexual activity, adolescent childbearing and marriage, and cohabitation (Booth & Edwards, 1990; Hetherington, 1997). In addition, in comparison with young adults from nondivorced families, young adults from divorced and remarried families exhibit more reciprocated, escalating, negative exchanges, including denial, belligerence, criticism, and contempt, and less effective problem solving during their marital interactions (Hetherington, in press). This pattern is probably related to the intergenerational transmission of divorce, which is reported to be 70% higher in the first five years of marriage from adult women from divorced families than for those whose parents have remained married (Bumpass, Martin, & Sweet, 1991).

Although there is considerable consensus that, on average, offspring from divorced and remarried families exhibit more problems in adjustment than do those in nondivorced, two-parent families, there is less agreement on the size of these effects. Some researchers report that these effects are relatively modest, have become smaller as marital transitions have become more common (Amato & Keith, 1991a), and are considerably reduced when the adjustment of children preceding the marital transition is controlled (Block, Block, & Gjerde, 1986, 1988; Cherlin et al., 1991). However, others note that approximately 20%–25% of children in divorced and remarried families, in contrast to 10% of children in nondivorced families, have these problems, which is a notable twofold increase (Hetherington, 1989, 1991b; Hetherington & Clingempeel, 1992; Hetherington & Jodl, 1994; McLanahan & Sandefur, 1994; Simons & Associates, 1996; Zill, Morrison, & Coiro, 1993). Because these difficulties in adjustment tend to co-occur and appear as a single behavior-problem cluster (Jessor & Jessor, 1977; Mekos, Hetherington, & Reiss, 1996), the vast majority of children from divorced families and stepfamilies do not have these problems and eventually develop into reasonably competent individuals functioning within the normal range of adjustment (Emery & Forehand, 1994). This argument is not intended to minimize the importance of the increase in adjustment problems associated with divorce and remarriage nor to belittle the fact that children often report their parents' marital transitions to be their most painful life experience. It is intended to underscore the research evidence supporting the ability of most children to cope with their parents' divorce and remarriage and to counter the position that children are permanently blighted by their parents' marital transitions.

We turn now to an examination of some of the individual, social, economic, and family factors that contribute to the diversity in children's adjustment in divorced and remarried families. Each factor is discussed as it relates to the five perspectives on marital transitions.

Individual Risk and Vulnerability of Parents Associated With Divorce and Remarriage

Some adults have attributes that increase their probability not only of having dysfunctional marital relationships but also for having other problematic social relationships within and outside of the family, displaying inept parenting behaviors, encountering stressful life events, and having decreased psychological well-being (Amato & Booth, 1996; Block et al., 1986). Longitudinal studies have found that, in adults as well as in children, many of the problems attributed to divorce and remarriage and their concomitant life changes were present before these transitions occurred.

Although psychological distress and disorders may increase after divorce, parents who later divorce are more likely preceding divorce to be neurotic, depressed, antisocial, or alcoholic; to have economic problems (Amato, 1993; Capaldi & Patterson, 1991; Forgatch et al., 1995; Gotlib & McCabe, 1990); and to have dysfunctional beliefs about relationships (Baucom & Epstein, 1990; Kelly & Conley, 1987; Kurdek, 1993). In their marital interactions, they exhibit poor problem-solving and conflict resolution skills, thus escalating reciprocation of negative affect, contempt, denial, withdrawal, and stable, negative attributions about their spouses' behavior, which in turn significantly increase their risk for marital dissolution and multiple divorces (Bradbury & Fincham, 1990; Fincham, Bradbury, & Scott, 1990; Gottman, 1993, 1994; Gottman & Levenson, 1992; Matthews, Wickrama, & Conger, 1996). Sometimes these patterns are later found in the marital relationships of their adult offspring (Hetherington, in press). In relationships with their children, parents whose marriages will later be disrupted are more irritable, erratic, and nonauthoritative as much as 8–12 years prior to divorce (Amato & Booth, 1996; Block et al., 1988). These factors contribute to problems in children's adjustment and family relations in nondivorced families, single-parent families, and stepfamilies.

Children's Individual Risk, Vulnerability, and Resiliency Associated With Adjustment to Divorce and Remarriage

In accord with the individual risk perspective, characteristics of children may make them vulnerable or protect them from the adverse consequences or risks associated with their parents' divorce or remarriage. Some of these attributes influence the experiences and adjustment of children long before marital transitions occur.

Children's Adjustment Preceding Divorce and Remarriage

Children whose parents later divorce exhibit poorer adjustment before the breakup (Amato & Booth, 1996; Amato & Keith, 1991a; Block et al., 1986; Cherlin et al., 1991). When antecedent levels of problem behaviors are controlled, differences in problem behaviors between children from divorced and nondivorced families are greatly reduced (Cherlin et al., 1991; Guidubaldi, Perry, & Nastasi, 1987). Several alternative interpretations of these findings can be made. First, it is likely that maladapted parents, dysfunctional family relationships, and inept parenting already have taken their toll on children's adjustment before a divorce occurs. Second, divorce may be, in part, a result of having to deal with a difficult child. Third, personality problems in a parent, such as emotionality and lack of self-regulation, that lead to both divorce and inept socialization practices also may be genetically linked to behavior problems in children (Jockin, McGue, & Lykken, 1996; McGue & Lykken, 1992).

Children in stepfamilies also exhibit more behavior problems before remarriage occurs, and some researchers have speculated that the adaptive difficulties of stepchildren may be largely the result of experiences in divorced families (Furstenberg, 1988). This seems unlikely, because there is an increase in adjustment problems immediately after a marital transition, and because children in newly married families show more problems than those in stabilized, divorced, one-parent households (Hetherington & Clingempeel, 1992) or than those in longer remarried, stabilized stepfamilies (Hetherington & Jodl, 1994).

Personality and Temperament

Children who have easy temperaments; who are intelligent, socially mature, and responsible; and who exhibit few behavior problems are better able to cope with their parents' marital transitions. Stresses associated with divorce and remarriage are likely to exacerbate existing problems in children (Block et al., 1986; Elder, Caspi, & Van Nguyen, 1992; Hetherington, 1989, 1991b). In particular, children with difficult temperaments or behavior problems may elicit negative responses from their parents who are stressed in coping with their marital transitions. These children also may be less able to adapt to parental negativity when it occurs and may be less adept at gaining the support of people around them (Hetherington, 1989, 1991b; Rutter, 1987). Competent, adaptable children with social skills and attractive personal characteristics, such as an easy temperament and a sense of humor, are more likely to evoke positive responses and support and to maximize the use of available resources that help them negotiate stressful experiences (Hetherington, 1989; Werner, 1988).

Developmental Status

Developmental status and gender are the child characteristics most extensively researched in relation to adaptation to divorce and remarriage; however, the results of these studies have been inconsistent. Investigations of children's age at divorce must consider both age at the time of the marital transition and age at the time of assessment. In most studies, these variables are confounded with the length of time since the divorce or remarriage occurred. Some researchers have found that preschool-age children whose parents divorce are at greater risk for long-term problems in social and emotional development than are older children (Allison & Furstenberg, 1989; Zill et al., 1993). It has been suggested that younger children may be less able to appraise realistically the causes and consequences of divorce, may be more anxious about the possibility of total abandonment, may be more likely to blame themselves for the divorce, and may be less able to utilize extrafamilial protective resources (Hetherington, 1989). This greater vulnerability of young children to divorce has not been reported by other investigators (Amato & Keith, 1991a).

In contrast, early adolescence seems to be an especially difficult time in which to have a remarriage occur. Early adolescents are less able to adapt to parental remarriage than are younger children or late adolescents (Hetherington, 1993; Hetherington & Clingempeel, 1992), perhaps because the presence of a stepparent exacerbates normal early adolescent concerns about autonomy and sexuality. In addition, adolescence and young adulthood are periods in which problems in adjustment may emerge or increase, even when divorce or remarriage has occurred much earlier (Amato & Keith, 1991a, 1991b; Bray & Berger, 1993; Hetherington, 1993, in press; Hetherington & Clingempeel, 1992; Hetherington & Jodl, 1994).

Gender

Although earlier studies frequently reported gender differences in response to divorce and remarriage, with divorce being more deleterious for boys and remarriage for girls (Hetherington, 1989), more recent studies have found that gender differences in response to divorce are less pronounced and consistent than was previously believed (Amato & Keith, 1991a). Some of the inconsistencies may be attributable to the fact that fathers' custody, joint custody, and the involvement of noncustodial fathers are increasing and that involvement of fathers may be more important for boys than for girls (Amato & Keith, 1991a; Clarke-Stewart & Hayward, 1996; Lindner-Gunnoe, 1993; Zill, 1988).

Some research has shown that boys respond to divorce with increases in conduct disorders and girls with increases in depression (Emery, 1982); however, both male and female adolescents from divorced and remar-ried families show higher rates of conduct disorders and depression than do those from nondivorced families (Amato & Keith, 1991a; Hetherington, 1993; Hetherington & Clingempeel, 1992; Hetherington & Jodl, 1994). Female adolescents and young adults from divorced and remarried families are more likely than their male counterparts to drop out of high school and college. Male and female adolescents are similarly affected in the likelihood of becoming teenage parents; however, single parenthood has more adverse effects on the lives of female adolescents (McLanahan & Sandefur, 1994). Female young adults from divorced and remarried families are vulnerable to declining socioeconomic status because of the sequelae of adolescent childbearing and school dropout. These sequelae are compounded in stepdaughters by early home leaving, which they attribute to family conflict (Cherlin & Furstenberg, 1994; Hetherington, 1997, in press).

Some girls in divorced, mother-headed families emerge as exceptionally resilient individuals, enhanced by confronting the increases in challenges and responsibilities that follow divorce (Hetherington, 1989, 1991b; Werner, 1993). Such enhancement is not found for boys following marital transitions or for girls in stepfamilies (Hetherington, 1989, 1991b). Boys, especially preadolescent boys, are more likely than girls to benefit from being in stepfather families (Amato & Keith, 1991a; Hetherington, 1993). Close relationships with supportive stepfathers are more likely to reduce antisocial behavior and to enhance the achievement of stepsons than of stepdaughters (Amato & Keith, 1991a; Hetherington, 1993; Lindner-Gunnoe, 1993; Zimiles & Lee, 1991). Girls are at greater increased risk than are boys for poor adjustment and low achievement when they are in either stepfather or stepmother families rather than in nondivorced families (Lee, Burkam, Zimiles, & Ladewski, 1994; Zimiles & Lee, 1991).

Some research suggests that living in stepfamilies is more beneficial to Black adolescents than to White adolescents, although these effects vary by gender. In contrast to the findings for White youths, young Black women in stepfamilies have the same rate of teenage parenthood as do those in two-parent, nondivorced families, and young Black men in stepfamilies are at no greater risk to drop out of high school than are those in two-parent families (McLanahan & Sandefur, 1994). McLanahan and Sandefur proposed that the income, supervision, and role models provided by stepfathers may be more advantageous for Black children because they are more likely than White children to live in more disorganized neighborhoods with fewer resources and social controls.

Family Composition-Parental Absence and the Adjustment of Children

The family composition or parental absence perspective proposed that a deviation in structure from a family with two first-married parents, biologically related to their children, is associated with increases in problem behavior in children. Two parents can provide support to each other, especially in their child rearing, as well as multiple role models and increased resources, supervision, and involvement for their children (Amato, 1995; Demo & Acock, 1996; Dornbusch et al., 1985; Furstenberg, Morgan, & Allison, 1987; Lamb, 1997). If father unavailability or absence is a critical factor in divorce, father custody or contact with a noncustodial parent, stepfather, or father surrogate should enhance children's adjustment. Furthermore, children who experience loss of their fathers through divorce or death should exhibit similar adjustment problems. Less theorizing has focused on mother absence, although similar hypotheses might be proposed for mothers.

Children and adults from homes with an absent parent due to either divorce or death have more problems in adjustment than do those in nondivorced families; however, significantly more problems are found in academic achievement, socioeconomic attainment, and conduct disorders for offspring from divorced families (Amato & Keith, 1991a; Felner, Ginter, Boike, & Cowen, 1981; Felner, Stolberg, & Cowen, 1975; Hetherington, 1972). Although children of both divorced and widowed women suffer the loss of their fathers and economic declines, the finding suggests that other factors moderate the differences in their outcomes. One of these factors may be greater support and involvement with the extended family, especially that of the lost parent's family, following death but not divorce (Hetherington, 1972). Another may be the greater conflict in families preceding divorce but not the death of a parent (Amato & Keith, 1991a).

The parental absence hypothesis also suggests that contact with noncustodial parents or joint custody should promote children's well-being; however, contact with both noncustodial mothers and fathers diminishes rapidly following divorce. More than 20% of children have no contact with their noncustodial fathers or see them only a few times a year, and only about one quarter of children have weekly visits with their divorced fathers (Seltzer, 1991). Black noncustodial fathers have higher rates of both regular contact and no contact with their children than do non-Hispanic White fathers (McLanahan & Sandefur, 1994). Decreased paternal involvement is related to residential distance, low socioeconomic status, and parental remarriage (Seltzer, 1991). Seltzer and Brandreth (1994) noted that custodial mothers serve as "gatekeepers" (Ahrons, 1983), controlling noncustodial fathers' access to and the conditions of visits with their children. When conflict, resentment, and anger are high, the "gate" may be closed, and fathers may be discouraged or shut out. In contrast, when there is low conflict between divorced spouses, when mediation is used (Dillon & Emery, 1996), or when noncustodial fathers feel they have some control over decisions in their children's lives (Braver et al., 1993; Seltzer, 1991), paternal contact and child support payments are more likely to be maintained.

In contrast, noncustodial mothers are more likely than noncustodial fathers to sustain contact with their children and to rearrange their living situations to facilitate children's visits. They maintain approximately twice as much contact with their children as noncustodial fathers do and are less likely to completely drop out of their children's lives or to diminish contact when either parent remarries (Furstenberg & Nord, 1987; Furstenberg, Nord, Peterson, & Zill, 1983; Lindner-Gunnoe, 1993; Santrock, Sitterle, & Warshak, 1988; White, 1994; Zill, 1988). In addition, there is some evidence that noncustodial mothers, like noncustodial fathers, are more likely to maintain contact with sons than with daughters (Lindner-Gunnoe, 1993), although the preferential contact of fathers with sons is larger and more consistently obtained than that of mothers (Amato & Booth, 1991).

There is little support for the position that sheer frequency of contact facilitates positive adjustment in children (Amato & Keith, 1991a; King, 1994a, 1994b). However, as we discuss at greater length in the Family Process and the Adjustment to Divorce and Remarriage section, under conditions of low interparental conflict, contact with competent, supportive, authoritative noncustodial parents can have beneficial effects for children, and these effects are most marked for noncustodial parents and children of the same sex (Hetherington, 1989; Lindner-Gunnoe, 1993; Zill, 1988) Thus, it is the quality of contact, rather than the frequency, that is important (Amato, 1993; Emery, 1988; Furstenberg & Cherlin, 1991).

Research on custodial arrangements also has found few advantages of joint custody over sole residential custody. In a large study of custody in California, Maccoby and Mnookin (1992) found adolescents in the custody of their fathers had higher rates of delinquency, perhaps because of poorer monitoring by fathers. A meta-analysis of divorce by Amato and Keith (1991a), however, did not support the findings of poorer adjustment in children in families in which fathers have custody.

A corollary to the parental absence hypothesis would suggest that the addition of a stepparent might compensate for the loss of a parent. However, the family composition perspective implies that it is not only the presence of two parents but also biological relatedness to the parents that matter. Although divorce involves the exit of a family member, remarriage involves the restructuring of the family constellation with the entrance of a stepparent and sometimes stepsiblings. Predictions made about stepfamilies on the basis of the family composition hypothesis are unclear. On the one hand, the presence of a stepparent might compensate for the loss of the noncustodial parent by restoring a two-parent household. On the other hand, the child must confront an additional transition to another family with a nontraditional composition involving the addition of nonbiologically related family members to the household. In a family in which both divorced parents remarry, much more complex kin networks are created within and outside the household in a linked family system (Jacobson, 1982) or a binuclear family (Ahrons, 1979). A child's expanded kin networks may include stepsiblings, half siblings, and stepgrandparents, as well as stepparents and biologically related kin, and represent a marked deviation from the composition of the nondivorced nuclear family (Booth & Edwards, 1992; Bray, 1987, 1988; Bray, Berger, & Boethel, 1994; Burrell, 1995; Cherlin & Furstenberg, 1994; Giles-Sims, 1987).

Stress, Socioeconomic Disadvantage, and the Adjustment to Divorce and Remarriage

The stress perspective attributes problems in the adjustment of children from divorced and remarried families to the increased stresses experienced in these families. Parents and children living in divorced families encounter a diverse array of stressful life events (Hetherington, Cox, & Cox, 1985; Simons et al., 1996). Both custodial mothers and fathers complain of task overload and social isolation as they juggle household, child-care, and financial responsibilities that are usually dealt with by two parents (Hetherington & Stanley Hagan, 1997). Noncustodial parents express concerns associated with the establishment of new residences, social networks, and intimate relationships; loss of children; problems with visitation arrangements; and continued difficulties in relations with their ex-spouses (Hetherington, 1989, 1991b; Hetherington & Stanley Hagan, 1997; Hoffman, 1995; Minton & Pasley, 1996).

In spite of the diversity in stresses associated with divorce, most attention by sociologists and economists has focused on the marked decrement in the income of custodial mothers following marital dissolution and its accompanying risk factors. Those investigators who support a socioeconomic disadvantage perspective suggest that controlling for income will eliminate or greatly diminish the association between family structure and children's well-being (McLanahan & Sandefur, 1994). In addition, because custodial fathers do not encounter the financial decrements experienced by custodial mothers and because remarriage is the fastest way out of poverty for single mothers, it might be expected that children in father-custody families and stepfamilies will exhibit fewer behavior problems than those in divorced mother-custody households.

Because of increased enforcement of noncustodial fathers' child support payments and changes in the labor force for women, it has been speculated that custodial mothers and their children may no longer experience such drastic economic declines following divorce. A recent review (Bianchi, Subaiya, & Kahn, 1997) suggests, however, that custodial mothers still experience the loss of approximately one quarter to one half of their predivorce income in comparison to only 10% by custodial fathers following divorce (Arendell, 1986; Cherlin, 1992; Emery, 1994; McLanahan & Booth, 1989). For custodial mothers, this loss in income is accompanied by increased workloads; high rates of job instability; and residential moves to less desirable neighborhoods with poor schools, inadequate services, often high crime rates, and deviant peer populations (McLanahan & Booth, 1989; McLanahan & Sandefur, 1994).

Although father-only families have substantially higher incomes than do families with divorced custodial mothers, a significant number of father-only families (18%) live in poverty, and fathers rarely receive child support (Meyer & Garasky, 1993). However, most father-custody families have financial, housing, child-care, and educational resources not available to divorced custodial mothers. Custodial fathers report less child-rearing stress than do custodial mothers, and their children show fewer problems (Amato & Keith, 1991a; Clarke-Stewart & Hayward, 1996). This could be attributed to economic advantages in father-custody families; however, even with income controlled, children in father-custody families—especially boys—show greater well-being than those in mother-custody families (Clarke-Stewart & Hayward, 1996).

Newly repartnered parents and their children report higher levels of both positive and negative life changes than do those in never-divorced families (Forgatch et al., 1995; Hetherington et al., 1985). Although there is a marked increase in income for divorced mothers following remarriage, conflicts over finances, child rearing, and family relations remain potent problems in stepfamilies (Bray & Berger, 1993; Hetherington, 1993; Hetherington & Jodl, 1994). The economic improvement conferred by remarriage is not reflected in the improved adjustment of children in stepfamilies, and the new stresses associated with remarriage often counter the benefits associated with increased income (Amato & Booth, 1991; Bray & Berger, 1993; Cherlin & Furstenberg, 1994; Demo & Acock, 1996; Forgatch et al., 1995; Hetherington & Clingempeel, 1992; Hetherington & Jodl, 1994).

Parental Distress and the Adjustment to Divorce and Remarriage

Investigators taking the parental distress perspective propose that stressors affect children's adjustment through parental distress and diminished well-being (Bank, Duncan, Patterson, & Reid, 1993; Forgatch et al., 1995; Lorenz et al., 1996; Simons & Beaman, 1996; Simons, Beaman, Conger, & Chao, 1992; Simons & Johnson, 1996). In this view, it is the parents' response to stress, rather than the stress itself, that is most salient for children's adjustment.

Signs of diminished parental well-being and distress, including anger, anxiety, depression, loneliness, impulsivity, feelings of being externally controlled, and emotional liability, may emerge or increase in the immediate aftermath of divorce (Hetherington, 1989, 1993; Pearlin & Johnson, 1977). In addition, newly remarried parents are often depressed or preoccupied as they cope with the challenges of their new family life (Hetherington & Clingempeel, 1992; Hetherington & Jodl, 1994). The mental health of parents in divorced and remarried families is related to children's adjustment through diminished competence in their parenting (Clarke-Stewart & Hayward, 1996; Forgatch et al., 1995; Hetherington, 1993; Lorenz et al., 1996; Simons, 1996).

The stresses associated with marital transitions place both residential and nonresidential parents at risk not only for psychological disorders (Hetherington, 1989, 1991b; Kitson & Morgan, 1990; Stack, 1989; Travato & Lauris, 1989) but also for disruption in immune system functioning (Kiecolt-Glaser et al., 1988) and concomitant increased rates of illness and morbidity, which are notable in divorced adults, especially in men (Burman & Margolin, 1992; Hu & Goldman, 1990; Riessman & Gerstel, 1985). Nonresidential fathers engage in more health-compromising and impulsive behaviors, such as alcohol consumption, than do fathers in any other family type (Umberson, 1987; Umberson & Williams, 1993) and are overrepresented among suicides and homicides (Bloom, Asher, & White, 1978).

Although depression remains higher in divorced women than in nondivorced women, by two years after divorce, women show less depression and more psychological well-being than do those who remain in conflict-ridden marriages with husbands who undermine their discipline and feelings of competence. The well-being of both men and women increases after the formation of a mutually caring, intimate relationship, such as a remarriage (Hetherington, 1993). Most parents do adapt to their new marital situation, with concomitant decreases in psychological and physical problems. In support of the parental distress perspective, even temporary disruptions in parents' health, social, and psychological functioning may make it difficult to be competent in parenting children who may be confused, angry, and apprehensive about a divorce or remarriage, and this inept parenting adversely affects children's adjustment (Chase-Lansdale & Hetherington, 1990; Emery, 1988; Emery & Dillon, 1994; Hetherington, 1989; Hetherington & Stanley Hagan, 1995; Maccoby & Mnookin, 1992).

Family Process and the Adjustment to Divorce and Remarriage

Divorce and remarriage confront families with changes and challenges associated with pervasive alterations in family roles and functioning. The changes in family relationships can support or undermine the efforts of children to adapt to their new family situations. Proponents of the family process perspective argue that the impact of parental attributes, changes in family structure, socio-economic disadvantage, and parental distress on children's adjustment is largely mediated by disruptions in family relationships and interactions, such as those involved in discipline and child-rearing practices (Demo & Acock, 1996; Forgatch et al., 1995; Hetherington, 1993; Simons & Beaman, 1996; Simons & Johnson, 1996). Without disruptions in family functioning, the former risk factors are less likely to compromise children's adjustment.

Relationships Between Divorced Couples

Marital conflict is associated with a wide range of deleterious outcomes for children, including depression, poor social competence and academic performance, and conduct disorders (Amato & Keith, 1991a; Cowan & Cowan, 1990; Davies & Cummings, 1994; Forehand, Brody, Long, Slotkin, & Fauber, 1986; Gottman & Katz, 1989; Peterson & Zill, 1986). Conflict, contempt, anger, and acrimony often antecede divorce, and in the immediate aftermath of marital disruption, conflict may escalate. Consequently, one of the most frequently asked questions about divorce is whether parents should stay together in an unhappy, conflict-ridden marriage for the sake of the children.

The hypothesis that conflict is a major contributor to problems in divorced families is substantiated by evidence that children in high-conflict, nondivorced families have more problems in psychological adjustment and self-esteem than do those in divorced families or in low-conflict, nondivorced families (Amato & Keith, 1991a; Amato, Loomis, & Booth, 1995). In addition, longitudinal prospective studies of divorce indicate that divorce improves the adjustment of children removed from contentious marriages but is deleterious for children whose parents had less overtly conflictual relationships preceding divorce (Amato et al., 1995). When measures of marital dissatisfaction rather than conflict are used, the advantages of divorce over unhappy marital situations are less marked (Simons, 1996) because many couples in unsatisfying marriages may not exhibit overt conflict (Gottman, 1994).

Although contact and conflict between divorced couples diminish over time, they remain higher for couples with children as they attempt to negotiate coparenting relationships and economic responsibilities (Masheter, 1991). Despite the fact that cooperative, mutually supportive, and nonconfrontational coparenting relationships are advantageous to parents and children, only about one quarter of divorced parents attain such relationships and an approximately equal number maintain acrimonious relationships (Maccoby & Mnookin, 1992). Most coparenting relationships after divorce evolve into parallel coparenting relationships not only with little communication or coordination of parenting but also with lessened conflict because of the disengaged relationships. Cooperative coparenting is most likely to occur when family size is small and when there was little conflict at the time of divorce (Maccoby, Buchanan, Mnookin, & Dornbusch, 1993). With little conflict and cooperative coparenting, children adapt better not only to their parents' divorce but also to their parents' remarriages, and they tend to have more positive relations with their stepparents (Bray & Berger, 1993; Crosbie-Burnett, 1991).

The sheer frequency of conflict may not be as detrimental as the type of conflict. Conflicts in which children are caught in the middle while parents denigrate each other, precipitate loyalty conflicts, communicate through the children, or fight about the children are most destructive to children's well-being (Buchanan, Maccoby, & Dornbusch, 1991; Maccoby et al., 1993; Maccoby & Mnookin, 1992). Children in highly conflicted families not only are more distressed but also may learn to exploit and mislead their parents and to escape monitoring of their activities when they are older (Hetherington, Law, & O'Connor, 1992). Even when children are not directly involved in their parents' conflicts, the adverse effects of conflicts may be experienced through increased parental irritability and diminished monitoring, support, and involvement (Patterson, 1991).

Relationships of Custodial Mothers and Children

Children in both mother- and father-custody families show more problems than do children in nondivorced families; however, most offspring in both types of divorced families eventually are reasonably well-adjusted. Because approximately 84% of children reside with their mothers following divorce (Seltzer, 1994), most studies of parent-child relations following marital dissolution have involved custodial mothers. Close relationships with supportive, authoritative mothers who are warm but exert firm, consistent control and supervision are generally associated with positive adjustment in children and adolescents (Bray & Berger, 1993; Forehand, Thomas, Wierson, Brody, & Fauber, 1990; Hetherington, 1989, 1993; Hetherington & Clingempeel, 1992; Maccoby et al., 1993; Simons & Johnson, 1996). In the immediate aftermath of divorce, there is a period of disrupted parenting characterized by irritability and coercion and diminished communication, affection, consistency, control, and monitoring (Hetherington, 1991a, 1991b, 1993; Simons & Johnson, 1996).

The parenting of divorced mothers improves over the course of the two years following divorce but remains less authoritative than that of nondivorced mothers, and problems in control and coercive exchanges between divorced mothers and sons may remain high (Hetherington, 1991a). Even in adulthood, relationships between sons and divorced mothers are less close than those in nondivorced families, whereas differences in closeness are not found for daughters (Booth & Amato, 1994). Pre-

adolescent girls and their divorced mothers often have close, companionate, confiding relationships; however, in adolescence, there is a notable increase in conflict in these relationships (Hetherington, 1991a; Hetherington & Clingempeel, 1992). In comparison with adolescents in nondivorced, two-parent families, adolescents in divorced families and in stepfamilies experience the highest levels of mother-adolescent disagreements and the lowest levels of parental supervision (Demo & Acock, 1996). Both conflictive, negative parent-adolescent relationships and lack of monitoring are associated with involvement with antisocial peers—one of the most potent pathways to the development of delinquency, alcoholism, substance abuse, and teenage sexual activity and childbearing (Conger & Reuter, 1996; Hetherington, 1993; Simons & Chao, 1996; Whitbeck et al., 1996).

About one quarter to one third of adolescents in divorced and remarried families, in comparison with 10% of adolescents in nondivorced families, become disengaged from their families, spending as little time at home as possible and avoiding interactions, activities, and communication with family members (Hetherington, 1993; Hetherington & Jodl, 1994). This incidence is greater for boys in divorced families and for girls in stepfamilies. If disengagement is associated with lack of adult support and supervision and with involvement in a delinquent peer group, it leads to both antisocial behavior and academic problems in adolescents (Hetherington, 1993; Patterson, DeBaryshe, & Ramsey, 1989). However, if there is a caring adult involved with the adolescent outside of the home, such as the parent of a friend, a teacher, a neighbor, or a coach, disengagement may be a positive solution to a disrupted, conflictual family situation (Hetherington, 1993).

It has been noted that children in divorced families grow up faster, in part, because of early assignment of responsibilities (Weiss, 1979), more autonomous decision making (Dornbusch et al., 1985), and lack of adult supervision (Hetherington, 1991a; Thomson, McLanahan, & Curtin, 1992). Assignment of responsibility may be associated with resilience and unusual social competence in girls from divorced families; yet, if the task demands are beyond the children's capabilities, they also may be associated with low self-esteem, anxiety, and depression (Hetherington, 1989, in press). Furthermore, if adolescents perceive themselves as being unfairly burdened with responsibilities that interfere with their other activities, they may respond with resentment, rebellion, and noncompliance.

The restablilizing of family relations following a remarriage takes considerably longer than that following a divorce (Cherlin & Furstenberg, 1994). Whereas a new homeostasis is established in about two to three years following divorce, it has been estimated that the adjustment to remarriage may take as long as five to seven years (Cherlin & Furstenberg, 1994; Papernow, 1988; Visher & Visher, 1990). Because more than one quarter of remarriages are terminated within five years, with higher rates for families with children, restablization never occurs in many stepfamilies.

In the first year following a remarriage, custodial mothers engage in less affective involvement, less behavior control and monitoring, and more negativity than nondivorced mothers (Bray & Berger, 1993; Hetherington, 1993; Hetherington & Clingempeel, 1992). Negative mother-child interactions are related to more disengagement, dysfunctional family roles, poorer communication, and less cohesion in stepfamilies (Bray, 1990). However, in long-established remarriages, the parenting of custodial mothers with their biological offspring becomes increasingly similar to that in nondivorced families (Bray & Berger, 1993; Hetherington, 1993; Hetherington & Clingempeel, 1992; Hetherington & Jodl, 1994).

Relationships of Custodial Fathers and Children

Although children usually live with their mothers following the dissolution of their parents' marriage, father-headed families have tripled since 1974, making them the fastest growing family type in the United States (Meyer & Garasky, 1993). Arrangements about physical custody are often made on the basis of personal decisions by parents and not on judicial decree, and the preponderance of maternal physical custody, even when joint legal custody has been granted, may reflect concerns fathers have about assuming full-time parenting (Maccoby et al., 1993; Maccoby & Mnookin, 1992). Boys and older children are more likely to be placed in father-only custody, but some girls and young children do live with their fathers. In contrast to custodial mothers, custodial fathers are a very select group of fathers who may be more child-oriented than most fathers. Fathers who seek custody of their children are more involved and capable than those fathers who have custody thrust on them because the mothers were unwilling or incompetent to parent (Hanson, 1988; Mendes, 1976a, 1976b). Once their families have restabilized, custodial fathers report less child-rearing stress, better parent-child relations, and fewer behavior problems in their children than do custodial mothers (Amato & Keith, 1991a; Clarke-Stewart & Hayward, 1996; Furstenberg, 1988).

There are different strengths and weaknesses in the parenting of custodial mothers and fathers. Although custodial mothers and custodial fathers are perceived to be similarly warm and nurturing with younger children (Warshak, 1986), mothers have more problems with control and with assignment of household tasks, whereas fathers have more problems with communication, self-disclosure, and monitoring of their children's activities (Chase-Lansdale & Hetherington, 1990; Furstenberg, 1988; Warshak, 1986). Moreover, fathers have special difficulties with monitoring adolescents' behavior, espe-

cially that of daughters (Buchanan, Maccoby, & Dornbusch, 1992; Maccoby et al., 1993).

Recent evidence indicates that adolescent adjustment is more predictable from the parenting of a custodial parent of the same sex than one of the opposite sex (Lindner-Gunnoe, 1993). This evidence parallels findings of the greater salience of same-sex parents in the adjustment of adolescents in nondivorced families (Furman & Buhrmester, 1992; Kurdek & Fine, 1993). In spite of this greater influence of same-sex custodial parents, both sons and daughters report feeling closer to their custodial parent than their noncustodial parent, regardless of whether the parent is a mother or a father (Hetherington & Clingempeel, 1992; Maccoby et al., 1993; White, Brinkerhoff, & Booth, 1985).

As has been found with mothers, when custodial fathers remarry, there are disruptions in father-child relationships, especially with daughters (Clingempeel, Brand, & Ievoli, 1984). Fathers may alter their caretaking relationships more radically than mothers do because fathers are more likely to expect a stepmother to play a major role in household tasks and parenting (Hetherington & Stanley Hagen, 1995). However, in long-established stepfamilies, there are few differences in parent-child relations between remarried fathers and their residential biological children and those fathers and children in nondivorced families (Hetherington & Jodl, 1994).

Relationships of Noncustodial Mothers and Children

Although less is known about noncustodial mothers than noncustodial fathers, nonresidential mothers maintain more contact with their children than do nonresidential fathers. It is not only in the quantity but also in the quality of parent-child relationships that these mothers and fathers differ. Noncustodial mothers are less adept than custodial mothers in controlling and monitoring their children's behavior, but they are more effective in these parenting behaviors than are noncustodial fathers (Furstenberg & Nord, 1987; Lindner-Gunnoe, 1993). Children report that noncustodial mothers are more interested in and informed about their activities; are more supportive, sensitive, and responsive to their needs; and are more communicative than noncustodial fathers (Furstenberg & Nord, 1987; Lindner-Gunnoe, 1993; Santrock & Sitterle, 1987). Therefore, it is not surprising that children report talking more about their problems and activities and feeling closer to noncustodial mothers than to noncustodial fathers (Lindner-Gunnoe, 1993), nor that noncustodial mothers have more influence over their children's development, especially their daughters' adjustment, than do noncustodial fathers (Brand, Clingempeel, & Bowen-Woodward, 1988; Lindner-Gunnoe, 1993; Zill, 1988). Noncustodial mothers' warmth, support, and monitoring enhance their children's scholastic achievement and diminish antisocial, externalizing problems (Lindner-Gunnoe, 1993). In appraising some research findings that children have fewer problems in the custody of fathers than in the custody of mothers (Amato & Keith, 1991a; Clarke-Stewart & Hayward, 1996), it must be considered that part of this effect may be attributable to the more active involvement of noncustodial mothers.

When a custodial father remarries, closeness to the noncustodial mother can have some disadvantages because it is related to children's lack of acceptance of a stepmother. In contrast, there is no association between the relationship with a noncustodial father and building a close relationship with a stepfather (Hetherington, 1993; Hetherington & Jodl, 1994; White, 1994).

Relationships of Noncustodial Fathers and Children

In contrast to mothers' behavior, the postdivorce parenting behavior of fathers is less predictable from their predivorce behavior (Hetherington et al., 1985). Some previously attached and involved fathers find the enforced marginality and intermittent contact in being noncustodial fathers to be painful, and they drift away from their children. Other fathers, especially custodial fathers, rise to the occasion and increase their involvement and parenting competence. However, most nonresidential fathers have a friendly, egalitarian, companionate relationship rather than a traditional parental relationship with their children (Arendell, 1986; Furstenberg & Nord, 1987; Hetherington, Cox, & Cox, 1979; Munsch, Woodward, & Darling, 1995). They want their visits to be pleasant and entertaining and are hesitant to assume the role of disciplinarian or teacher. They are less likely than nondivorced fathers to criticize, control, and monitor their children's behavior or to help them with tasks such as homework (Bray & Berger, 1993; Furstenberg & Nord, 1987; Hetherington, 1991b).

Frequency of contact with noncustodial fathers and the adjustment of children are usually found to be unrelated (Amato & Keith, 1991a). Although obviously some degree of contact is essential, it seems to be the quality of the relationship and the circumstances of contact rather than frequency of visits that are most important (Amato, 1993; Emery, 1988; Furstenberg & Cherlin, 1991; Simons & Beaman, 1996). When noncustodial fathers are not just "tour guide" fathers but maintain more parent-like contact, participate in a variety of activities with their children, and spend holidays together, the well-being of children is promoted (Clarke-Stewart & Hayward, 1996). Under conditions of low conflict, the involvement of authoritative noncustodial fathers can enhance children's adjustment (Hetherington, 1989), especially that of boys (Lindner-Gunnoe, 1993). It can even, to some extent, protect the children from the adverse consequences of rejecting or incompetent noncustodial mothers (Hetherington, 1989). In contrast, under conditions of high conflict, frequent contact with noncustodial

parents may exacerbate children's problems (Kline, Johnston, & Tschann, 1991).

Relationships Between Stepparents and Stepchildren

Papernow (1998) commented that the typical starting point for a stepfamily involving "a weak couple subsystem, a tightly bonded parent-child alliance, and potential interference in family functioning from an outsider" (p. 56) would be considered problematic in a traditional nondivorced family. Clinicians have remarked that any stepfamily that uses a traditional nuclear family as its ideal is bound for disappointment (Visher & Visher, 1990). Similar patterns of relationships in traditional families and stepfamilies may lead to different outcomes. Patterns of functioning and family processes that undermine or promote positive adjustment may differ in the two types of families (Bray & Berger, 1993). The complex relationships between families following remarriage may require less rigid family boundaries and more open, less integrated relations among the family subsystems.

Although both stepfathers and stepmothers feel less close to stepchildren than do nondivorced parents to their children, they, if not the stepchildren, want the new marriage to be successful (Brand et al., 1988; Bray & Berger, 1993; Hetherington, 1993; Kurdek & Fine, 1993). In the early stages of a remarriage, stepfathers have been reported to be like polite strangers, trying to ingratiate themselves with their stepchildren by showing less negativity but also less control, monitoring, and affection than do fathers in nondivorced families (Bray & Berger, 1992; Hetherington & Clingempeel, 1992). In longer established stepfamilies, a distant, disengaged parenting style remains the predominant one for stepfathers, but conflict and negativity, especially between stepparents and stepdaughters, can remain high or increase, especially with adolescents (Brand et al., 1988; Bray & Berger, 1993; Hetherington, 1993; Hetherington & Jodl, 1994). Some of the conflict in stepfamilies is due to the negative rejecting behavior of stepchildren toward stepparents (Bray & Berger, 1993; Hetherington & Clingempeel, 1992; Hetherington & Jodl, 1994). Even stepparents with the best intentions may give up in the face of persistent hostile behavior by stepchildren.

Conflict between stepfathers and stepchildren is not necessarily precipitated by the children. In fact, rates of physical abuse perpetrated by stepfathers on their stepchildren are 7 times higher than those by fathers on their biological children, and homicide rates for stepfathers are 100 times higher than those for biological fathers (Daly & Wilson, 1996; Wilson, Daly, & Weghorst, 1980). These differential rates are most marked with infants and preschool-age children (Daly & Wilson, 1996).

Stepmothers have a more difficult time integrating themselves into stepfamilies than do stepfathers. Remarried fathers often expect that the stepmothers will participate in child rearing, forcing the stepmothers into more active, less distant, and more confrontational roles than those required of stepfathers (Brand et al., 1988). Support by the fathers for the stepmothers' parenting and parental agreement on child rearing are especially important in promoting effective parenting in stepmothers (Brand et al., 1988). The assumption of the dominant disciplinarian role is fraught with problems for stepparents (Brand et al., 1988; Bray & Berger, 1993; Hetherington, 1991a), and although authoritative parenting can have salutary effects on stepchildren's adjustment, especially with stepfathers and stepsons, authoritative parenting is not always a feasible option in stepfamilies (Bray & Berger, 1993). When custodial parents are authoritative and when stepparents are warm and involved and support the custodial parents' discipline rather than making independent control attempts, children can be responsive and adjust well (Bray & Berger, 1993; Hetherington, 1989).

It is not only parent-child relationships but also relationships between siblings that are more conflictual and less supportive in divorced families and stepfamilies than in nondivorced families (Hetherington, 1991a). These effects are more marked for biologically related siblings than for stepsiblings (Hetherington & Jodl, 1994). Less involved, harsher parenting is associated with rivalrous, aggressive, and unsupportive sibling relationships in divorced and remarried families (Conger & Conger, 1996; Hetherington, 1991a, 1993; Hetherington & Clingempeel, 1992), and, in turn, these negative sibling relations lead to low social competence and responsibility and to more behavior problems in children (Hetherington & Clingempeel, 1992).

Conclusion: What Matters? What Doesn't

In reviewing the five perspectives, it is clear that each may influence children's adjustment. The first perspective, the individual risk and vulnerability hypothesis, is supported by evidence suggesting that children and their parents have attributes that directly contribute to their experiencing marital transitions and to having more difficulties in adjusting to them. These problems may be transmitted genetically from parents to children, or the effect on children's adjustment may be indirect, due to parents' ineffective child-rearing strategies. However, individual vulnerability to the adverse outcomes of divorce and remarriage seems to involve a complex interaction among an array of individual attributes, including personality, age, gender, and ethnicity, and the effects of these interactions have been difficult to differentiate.

The family composition—parental absence hypothesis is not as well supported by the evidence. Generally, children in never-divorced families with two parents are more competent than children whose parents have divorced. However, this theory would suggest that chil-

dren's adjustment should benefit from the addition of a stepparent, yet there are few indications of lower levels of problems in children in stepfamilies as compared with children in divorced families. Furthermore, some studies indicate that especially in the early stages of a remarriage, stepchildren exhibit more difficulties than do children in stabilized, divorced, single-parent families (Amato & Keith, 1991a; Hetherington, 1993; Hetherington & Clingempeel, 1992; Hetherington & Jodl, 1994).

These comments must be qualified by findings indicating that the presence of a stepfather, especially with preadolescent boys, can attenuate problems in adjustment for stepsons, whereas the presence of either a stepmother or a stepfather may be associated with higher levels of problem behaviors for girls (Amato & Keith, 1991a; Hetherington, 1989; Hetherington & Jodl, 1994; Lee et al., 1994). These results, in conjunction with the somewhat inconsistent evidence that boys may also fare better in a father-custody family than in a mother-custody family (Amato & Keith, 1991a; Clarke-Stewart & Hayward, 1996; Zill, 1988), indicate that the presence of a father may have positive effects on the well-being of boys. Rather than rejecting the family composition-parental absence perspective, it should be concluded that there is not a simple main effect of family composition or parental absence but that it is modified by the reason for parental unavailability, the quality of family relationships, and the child's gender.

The findings thus far yield only modest support for marked direct effects of life stress and economic deprivation on children's adjustment. Even when income is controlled, children in divorced families show more problems than do those in nondivorced families (Amato & Keith, 1991a; Clarke-Stewart & Hayward, 1996; Demo & Acock, 1996; Guidubaldi et al., 1987; Hetherington, 1997, in press; Simons & Associates, 1996). In addition, although the income in stepfamilies is only slightly lower than that in nondivorced families, children in these families show a similar level of problem behavior to that in divorced mother-custody families (Amato & Keith, 1991a; Demo & Acock, 1996; Forgatch et al., 1995; Henderson, Hetherington, Mekos, & Reiss, 1996; Simons & Johnson, 1996). Thus, the effects of income do not seem to be primary and are largely indirect.

Some investigators using large-scale survey data report that as much as half of the effects of divorce on children's adjustment is attributable to economic factors (McLanahan & Sandefur, 1994); others find no direct effects of income but a major effect of the quality of family relationships that may alter children's adjustment (Demo & Acock, 1996). Furthermore, in studies in which income has been controlled, differences between offspring in divorced and nondivorced families remain (Amato & Keith, 1991a; Clarke-Stewart & Hayward, 1996; Demo & Acock, 1996; Guidubaldi et al., 1987; Hetherington, in press; Simons & Associates, 1996). Some of the inconsistencies in findings are due to methodological differences

Figure 1

A Transactional Model of the Predictors of Children's Adjustment Following Divorce and Remarriage

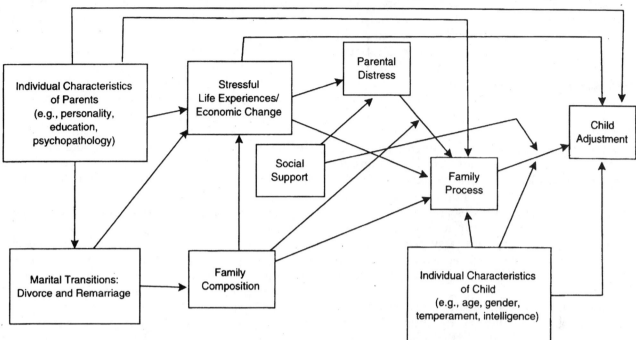

in studies. Surveys often have large representative samples but inadequate measures, sometimes involving only two or three items and single informants, to assess parental and family characteristics and family process variables. Studies using smaller, less representative samples but more reliable multimethod, multi-informant assessment, including observations, have found that much of the effects of family structure and economic stress are mediated by inept parenting (Forgatch et al., 1995; Simons & Johnson, 1996). Furthermore, there is some support in the research on stress, economic deprivation, and marital transitions for the individual risk position. As stated earlier, antisocial individuals are at greater risk not only for job instability, economic problems (Simons et al., 1992), and stressful life events but also for divorce (Capaldi & Patterson, 1991; Kitson & Holmes, 1992; Lahey et al., 1988), problems in successive marital relationships (Capaldi & Patterson, 1991), and incompetent parenting (Forgatch et al., 1995; Simons & Johnson, 1996).

Although it is true that parental distress increases in the aftermath of a divorce, research indicates that the effect of parents' well-being is largely mediated through their parenting. Even temporary disruptions in parents' physical and psychological functioning due to a marital transition interfere with their ability to offer support and supervision at a time when children need them most.

Although attributes of parents and children, family composition, stress and socioeconomic disadvantage, and parental distress impact children's adjustment, their effects may be mediated through the more proximal mechanism of family process. Dysfunctional family rela-

tionships, such as conflict, negativity, lack of support, and nonauthoritative parenting, exacerbate the effects of divorce and remarriage on children's adjustment. Certainly if divorced or remarried parents are authoritative and their families are harmonious, warm, and cohesive, the differences between the adjustment of children in these families and those in nondivorced families are reduced. However, marital transitions increase the probability that children will not find themselves in families with such functioning. Research on the relationships between family members in nondivorced families and stepfamilies supports the family process hypothesis, suggesting that, in large part, it is negative, conflictual, dysfunctional family relationships between parents, parents and children, and siblings that account for differences in children's adjustment.

It has become fashionable to attempt to estimate the relative contributions of individual attributes, family structure, stresses, parental distress, and family process to the adjustment of children in divorced and remarried families. These attempts have led to conflicting results, futile controversies, and misleading conclusions because the amount of variance explained by the factors differs from sample to sample and varies with the methods and the data analytic strategies used. Moreover, different risk and vulnerability factors are likely to come into play and to vary in salience at different points in the transitions from an unhappy marriage to divorce, to life in a single-parent household, through remarriage, and into subsequent marital transitions. These risk factors will be modified by shifting protective factors and resources.

A transactional model of risks associated with marital transitions is perhaps most appropriate (see Figure 1). Divorce and remarriage increase the probability of parents and children encountering a set of interrelated risks. These risks are linked, interact, and are mediated and moderated in complex ways. These effects are illustrated in the model in different ways. For example, parental distress (e.g., maternal depression) does not have a direct effect on children's adjustment, which is not to say it does not have an impact. Instead, its influence is mediated through its link to family process, specifically the depressed mothers' diminished ability to effectively parent. In contrast, some variables moderate the relationship between other variables, such that the relationship depends on the level of the moderator. For example, children with difficult temperaments are expected to be more adversely affected by disruptions in family functioning than are children with easy temperaments. Thus, individual variables such as temperament can moderate the effect of family process on children's adjustment.

All family members encounter stresses associated with marital transitions, and it may be the balance between risks and resources that determines the impact of stresses on divorced and remarried parents and their children. All five of the factors described at the beginning of this article are associated with divorce and remarriage and with adverse outcomes for children. Studies using path analyses (e.g., Conger & Conger, 1996; Forgatch et al., 1995; Simons & Associates, 1996) have helped illuminate the patterns of linkages among these risks and have suggested that many of the risk factors are mediated by proximal experiences such as disruptions in parent-child or sibling relationships. However, the fact that a path is indirect does not reduce its importance. Figure 1 presents the theoretical model describing the linkages among these factors. A set of individual attributes, such as antisocial behavior, is associated with an increased risk of divorce and an unsuccessful remarriage; problems in social relationships, including parent-child relationships; and stressful life events. All family members encounter stresses as they deal with the changes, challenges, and restructuring of the family associated with marital transitions, but these vary for different family members and for divorce and remarriage. Divorce usually leads to the loss or the diminished availability of a father and the economic, social, and emotional resources he can provide, which increases the probability of poverty and its concomitant environmental and experiential adversities for divorced custodial mothers and their children. Although some of the effects of stresses, such as living in neighborhoods with high crime rates, poor schools, antisocial peers, and few job opportunities or resources, may impact directly on children's adjustment and attainment, other effects of stress in divorced families may be indirect and mediated through parental psychological distress, inept or altered parenting, and disrupted family processes. Stresses associated with the changes and complexities in stepfamilies may also lead to distress and dysfunctional family functioning. Children, because of individual characteristics such as gender, temperament, personality, age, and intelligence, vary in their influence on family process and their vulnerability or resilience in dealing with their parents' divorce and remarriage and concomitant changes in family roles, relationships, and process. Thus, effects of the earlier risk factors on children's adjustment are mediated or moderated by associated transactional risk factors and often eventually by disruptions in family functioning. These indirect or mediated effects do not negate the importance of the earlier risk factors as a link in the transactional path of adversity leading to problems in child adjustment.

Static, cross-sectional slices out of the lives of parents and children in divorced or remarried families give a misleading picture of how risk and protective factors combine to influence the adjustment of children. An examination of the dynamic trajectories of interacting risk and protective factors associated with divorce and remarriage will yield a more valid and fruitful view of the multiple pathways associated with resiliency or adverse outcomes for children who have experienced their parents' marital transactions.

REFERENCES

Ahrons, C. R. (1979). The binuclear family: Two households, one family. *Alternative Lifestyles, 2*, 499–515.

Ahrons, C. R. (1983). Predictors of paternal involvement postdivorce: Mothers' and fathers' perceptions. *Journal of Divorce, 6*, 55–69.

Allison, P. D., & Furstenberg, F. F., Jr. (1989). How marital dissolution affects children: Variations by age and sex. *Developmental Psychology, 25*, 540–549.

Amato, P. R. (1993). Children's adjustment to divorce: Theories, hypotheses, and empirical support. *Journal of Marriage and the Family, 55*, 23–38.

Amato, P. R. (1995). Single-parent households as settings for children's development, well-being, and attainment: A social network/resources perspective. *Sociological Studies of Children, 7*, 19–47.

Amato, P. R., & Booth, A. (1991). Consequences of parental divorce and marital happiness for adult well-being. *Social Forces, 69*, 895–914.

Amato, P. R., & Booth, A. (1996). A prospective study of divorce and parent-child relationships. *Journal of Marriage and the Family, 58*, 356–365.

Amato, P. R. & Keith, B. (1991a). Parental divorce and adult well-being: A meta-analysis. *Journal of Marriage and the Family, 53*, 43–58.

Amato, P. R., & Keith, B. (1991b). Parental divorce and the well-being of children: A meta-analysis. *Psychological Bulletin, 110*, 26–46.

Amato, P. R., Loomis, L. S., & Booth, A. (1995). Parental divorce, marital conflict, and offspring well-being during early adulthood. *Social Forces, 73*, 895–915.

Arendell, T. (1986). *Mothers and divorce: Legal, economic, and social dilemmas.* Berkeley: University of California Press.

Bank, L., Duncan, T., Patterson, G. R., & Reid, J. (1993). Parent and teacher ratings in the assessment and prediction of antisocial and delinquent behaviors. *Journal of Personality, 61*, 693–709.

Baucom, D. H., & Epstein, N. (1990). *Cognitive-behavioral marital therapy.* New York: Brunner/Mazel.

Bianchi, S. M., Subaiya, L., & Kahn, J. (1997, March). *Economic well-being of husbands and wives after marital disruption.* Paper presented at the annual meeting of the Population Association of America, Washington, DC.

Block, J. H., Block, J., & Gjerde, P. F. (1986). The personality of children prior to divorce: A prospective study. *Child Development, 57*, 827–840.

Block, J. H., Block, J., & Gjerde, P. F. (1988). Parental functioning and the home environment in families of divorce: Prospective and concurrent analyses. *Journal of the American Academy of Child and Adolescent Psychiatry, 27*, 207–213.

Bloom, B. L., Asher, S. J., & White, S. W. (1978). Marital disruption as a stressor: A review and analysis. *Psychological Bulletin, 85*, 867–894.

Booth, A., & Amato, P. R. (1994). Parental marital quality, parental divorce, and relations with parents. *Journal of Marriage and the Family, 56*, 21–34.

Booth, A., & Edwards, J. N. (1990). Transmission of marital and family quality over the generations: The effects of parental divorce and unhappiness. *Journal of Divorce, 13*, 41–58.

Booth, A., & Edwards, J. N. (1992). Starting over: Why remarriages are more unstable. *Journal of Family Issues, 13*, 179–194.

Bradbury, T. N., & Fincham, F. D. (1990). Attributions in marriage: Review and critique. *Psychological Bulletin, 107*, 3–33.

Brand, E., Clingempeel, W. G., & Bowen-Woodward, K. (1988). Family relationships and children's psychosocial adjustment in stepmother and stepfather families. In E. M. Hetherington & J. D. Arasteh (Eds.), *Impact of divorce, single parenting, and stepparenting on children* (pp. 299–324). Hillsdale, NJ: Erlbaum.

Braver, S. L., Wolchik, S. A., Sandler, I. N., Sheets, V. L., Fogas, B., & Bay, R. C. (1993). A longitudinal study of noncustodial parents: Parents without children. *Journal of Family Psychology, 7*, 9–23.

Bray, J. H. (1987, August–September). *Becoming a stepfamily: Overview of The Developmental Issues in Stepfamilies Research Project.* Paper presented at the 95th Annual Convention of the American Psychological Association, New York.

Bray, J. H. (1988). Children's development during early remarriage. In E. M. Hetherington & J. D. Arasteh (Eds.), *Impact of divorce, single parenting, and stepparenting on children* (pp. 279–288). Hillsdale, NJ: Erlbaum.

Bray, J. H. (1990, August). *The developing stepfamily II: Overview and previous findings.* Paper presented at the 98th Annual Convention of the American Psychological Association, Boston.

Bray, J. H., & Berger, S. H. (1992). Nonresidential family-child relationships following divorce and remarriage. In C. E. Depner & J. H. Bray (Eds.), *Nonresidential parenting: New vistas in family living* (pp. 156–181). Newbury Park, CA: Sage.

Bray, J. H., & Berger, S. H. (1993). Developmental Issues in Stepfamilies Research Project: Family relationships and parent-child interactions. *Journal of Family Psychology, 7*, 76–90.

Bray, J. H., Berger, S. H., & Boethel, C. L. (1994). Role integration and marital adjustment in stepfather families. In K. Pasley & M. Ihinger-Tallman (Eds.), *Stepparenting: Issues in theory, research, and practice* (pp. 69–86). Westport, CT: Greenwood Press.

Buchanan, C. M., Maccoby, E. E., & Dornbusch, S. M. (1991). Caught between parents: Adolescents' experience in divorced homes. *Child Development, 62*, 1008–1029.

Buchanan, C. M., Maccoby, E. E., & Dornbusch, S. M. (1992). Adolescents and their families after divorce: Three residential arrangements compared. *Journal of Research on Adolescence, 2*, 261–291.

Bumpass, L. L., Martin, T. C., & Sweet, J. A. (1991). The impact of family background and early marital factors on marital disruption. *Journal of Family Issues, 12*, 22–42.

Bumpass, L. L., & Raley, R. K. (1995). Redefining single-parent families: Cohabitation and changing family reality. *Demography, 32*, 97–109.

Bumpass, L. L., & Sweet, J. A. (1989). *Children's experience in single-parent families: Implications of cohabitation and marital transitions* (National Study of Families and Households Working Paper No. 3). Madison: University of Wisconsin, Center for Demography and Ecology.

Bumpass, L. L., Sweet, J. A., & Castro-Martin, T. (1990). Changing patterns of remarriage. *Journal of Marriage and the Family, 52*, 747–756.

Bumpass, L. L., Sweet, J. A., & Cherlin, A. (1991). The role of cohabitation in declining rates of marriage. *Journal of Marriage and the Family, 53*, 913–927.

Burman, P., & Margolin, G. (1992). Analysis of the association between marital relationships and health problems: An interactional perspective. *Psychological Bulletin, 112*, 39–63.

Burrell, N. A. (1995). Communication patterns in stepfamilies: Redefining family roles, themes, and conflict styles. In M. A. Fitzpatrick & A. L. Vangelisti (Eds.), *Explaining family interactions* (pp. 290–309). Thousand Oaks, CA: Sage.

Capaldi, D. M., & Patterson, G. R. (1991). Relation of parental transitions to boys' adjustment problems: I. A linear hypothesis. II. Mothers at risk for transitions and unskilled parenting. *Developmental Psychology, 27*, 489–504.

Castro-Martin, T., & Bumpass, L. (1989). Recent trends and differentials in marital disruption. *Demography, 26*, 37–51.

Chase-Lansdale, P. L., Cherlin, A. J., & Kiernan, K. E. (1995). The long-term effects of parental divorce on the mental health of young adults: A developmental perspective. *Child Development, 66*, 1614–1634.

Chase-Lansdale, P. L., & Hetherington, E. M. (1990). The impact of divorce on life-span development: Short and long term effects. In P. B. Baltes, D. L. Featherman, & R. M. Lerner (Eds.), *Life-span development and behavior* (Vol. 10, pp. 105–150). Hillsdale, NJ: Erlbaum.

Cherlin, A. (1992). *Marriage, divorce, remarriage: Social trends in the U.S.* Cambridge, MA: Harvard University Press.

Cherlin, A. J., & Furstenberg, F. F. (1994). Stepfamilies in the United States: A reconsideration. In J. Blake & J. Hagen (Eds.), *Annual review of sociology* (pp. 359–381). Palo Alto, CA: Annual Reviews.

Cherlin, A. J., Furstenberg, F. F., Chase-Lansdale, P. L., Kiernan, K. E., Robins, P. K., Morrison, D. R., & Teitler, J. O. (1991). Longitudinal studies of effects of divorce in children in Great Britain and the United States. *Science, 252*, 1386–1389.

Clarke-Stewart, K. A., & Hayward, C. (1996). Advantages of father custody and contact for the psychological well-being of school-age children. *Journal of Applied Developmental Psychology, 17*, 239–270.

Clingempeel, W. G., Brand, E., & Ievoli, R. (1984). Stepparent-stepchild relationships in stepmother and stepfather families: A multimethod study. *Family Relations, 33*, 465–473.

Conger, R. D., & Chao, W. (1996). Adolescent depressed mood. In R. L. Simons & Associates (Eds.), *Understanding differences between divorced and intact families: Stress, interaction, and child outcome* (pp. 157–175). Thousand Oaks, CA: Sage.

Conger, R. D., & Conger, K. J. (1996). Sibling relationships. In R. L. Simons & Associates (Eds.), *Understanding differences between divorced and intact families: Stress, interaction, and child outcome* (pp. 104–124). Thousand Oaks, CA: Sage.

Conger, R. D., & Reuter, M. A. (1996). Siblings, parents, and peers: A longitudinal study of social influences in adolescent risk for alcohol use and abuse. In G. H. Brody (Ed.), *Sibling relationships: Their causes and consequences* (pp. 1–30). Norwood, NJ: Ablex.

Cowan, P. A., & Cowan, C. P. (1990). Becoming a family: Research and intervention. In I. Sigel & G. A. Brody (Eds.), *Family research* (pp. 246–279). Hillsdale, NJ: Erlbaum.

Crosbie-Burnett, M. (1991). Impact of joint versus sole custody and quality of the co-parental relationship on adjustment of adolescents in remarried families. *Behavioral Sciences and the Law, 9*, 439–449.

Daly, M., & Wilson, M. I. (1996). Violence against stepchildren. *Current Directions in Psychological Science, 5*, 77–81.

Davies, P. T., & Cummings, E. M. (1994). Marital conflict and child adjustment: An emotional security hypothesis. *Psychological Bulletin, 116*, 387–411.

Demo, D. H., & Acock, A. C. (1996). Family structure, family process, and adolescent well-being. *Journal of Research on Adolescence, 6*, 457–488.

Dillon, P. A., & Emery, R. E. (1996). Divorce mediation and resolution of child custody disputes: Long-term effects. *American Journal of Orthopsychiatry, 66*, 131–140.

Dornbusch, S. M., Carlsmith, J. M., Bushwall, S. J., Ritter, P. L., Liederman, H., Hastrof, A. H., & Gross, R. T. (1985). Single parents, extended households, and the control of adolescents. *Child Development, 56*, 326–341.

Elder, G., Caspi, A., & Van Nguyen, R. (1992). Resourceful and vulnerable children: Family influences in stressful times. In R. K. Silbereisen & K. Eyferth (Eds.), *Development in context: Integrative perspectives on youth development* (pp. 165–194). New York: Springer.

Elder, G. H., Jr., & Russell, S. T. (1996). Academic performance and future aspirations. In R. L. Simons & Associates (Eds.), *Understanding differences between divorced and intact families: Stress, interaction, and child outcome* (pp. 176–192). Thousand Oaks, CA: Sage.

Emery, R. E. (1982). Interpersonal conflict and the children of discord and divorce. *Psychological Bulletin, 92*, 310–330.

Emery, R. E. (1988). *Marriage, divorce, and children's adjustment.* Newbury Park, CA: Sage.

Emery, R. E. (1994). *Renegotiating family relationships.* New York: Guilford Press.

Emery, R. E., & Dillon, P. A. (1994). Conceptualizing the divorce process: Renegotiating boundaries of intimacy and power in the divorced family system. *Family Relations, 43,* 374–379.

Emery, R. E., & Forehand, R. (1994). Parental divorce and children's well-being: A focus on resilience. In R. J. Haggerty, L. R. Sherrod, N. Garmezy, & M. Rutter (Eds.), *Stress, risk, and resilience in children and adolescents* (pp. 64–99). Cambridge, England: Cambridge University Press.

Felner, R. D., Ginter, M. A., Boike, M. F., & Cowen, E. L. (1981). Parental death or divorce and the school adjustment of young children. *American Journal of Community Psychology, 9,* 181–191.

Felner, R. D., Stolberg, A., & Cowen, E. L. (1975). Crisis events and school mental health referral patterns of young children. *Journal of Consulting and Clinical Psychology, 43,* 305–310.

Fincham, F. D., Bradbury, T. N., & Scott, C. K. (1990). Cognition in marriage. In F. D. Fincham & T. N. Bradbury (Eds.), *The psychology of marriage* (pp. 118–149). New York: Guilford Press.

Forehand, R., Brody, G., Long, N., Slotkin, J., & Fauber, R. (1986). Divorce/divorce potential and interparental conflict: The relationship to early adolescent social and cognitive functioning. *Journal of Adolescent Research, 1,* 389–397.

Forehand, R., Thomas, A. M., Wierson, M., Brody, G., & Fauber, R. (1990). Role of maternal functioning and parenting skills in adolescent functioning following divorce. *Journal of Abnormal Psychology, 99,* 278–283.

Forgatch, M. S., Patterson, G. R., & Ray, J. A. (1995). Divorce and boys' adjustment problems: Two paths with a single model. In E. M. Hetherington & E. A. Blechman (Eds.), *Stress, coping, and resiliency in children and families* (pp. 67–105). Mahwah, NJ: Erlbaum.

Furman, W., & Buhrmester, D. (1992). Age and sex differences in perceptions of networks of personal relationships. *Child Development, 63,* 103–115.

Furstenberg, F. F., Jr. (1988). Child care after divorce and remarriage. In E. M. Hetherington & J. D. Arasteh (Eds.), *Impact of divorce, single parenting, and stepparenting on children* (pp. 245–261). Hillsdale, NJ: Erlbaum.

Furstenberg, F. F., Jr., & Cherlin, A. J. (1991). *Divided families: What happens to children when parents part.* Cambridge, MA: Harvard University Press.

Furstenberg, F. F., Jr., Morgan, S. P., & Allison, P. D. (1987). Paternal participation and children's well-being after marital dissolution. *American Sociological Review, 52,* 695–701.

Furstenberg, F. F., Jr., & Nord, C. W. (1987). Parenting apart: Patterns of childrearing after marital disruption. *Journal of Marriage and the Family, 47,* 893–904.

Furstenberg, F. F., Jr., Nord, C. W., Peterson, J. L., & Zill, N. (1983). The life course of children of divorce: Marital disruption and parental contact. *American Sociological Review, 48,* 656–668.

Ganong, L. H., & Coleman, M. (1994). *Remarried family relationships.* Thousand Oaks, CA: Sage.

Giles-Sims, J. (1987). Social exchange in remarried families. In K. Pasley & M. Ihinger-Tallman (Eds.), *Remarriage and stepparenting: Current research and theory* (pp. 141–163). New York: Guilford Press.

Glenn, N. D., & Kramer, K. B. (1985). The psychological well-being of adult children of divorce. *Journal of Marriage and the Family, 47,* 905–912.

Glick, P. C. (1989). Remarried families, stepfamilies, and stepchildren: A brief demographic profile. *Family Relations, 38,* 24–27.

Gotlib, I., & McCabe, S. B. (1990). Marriage and psychopathology. In F. D. Fincham & T. N. Bradbury (Eds.), *The psychology of marriage* (pp. 226–257). New York: Guilford Press.

Gottman, J. M. (1993). A theory of marital dissolution and stability. *Journal of Family Psychology, 7,* 57–75.

Gottman, J. M. (1994). *What predicts divorce?* Hillsdale, NJ: Erlbaum.

Gottman, J. M., & Katz, L. F. (1989). Effects of marital discord on young children's peer interaction and health. *Developmental Psychology, 25,* 373–381.

Gottman, J. M., & Levenson, R. W. (1992). Marital processes predictive of later dissolution: Behavior, physiology, and health. *Journal of Personality and Social Psychology, 63,* 221–233.

Guidubaldi, J., Perry, J. D., & Nastasi, B. K. (1987). Growing up in a divorced family: Initial and long-term perspectives on children's adjustment. In S. Oskamp (Ed.) *Applied social psychology annual: Vol. 7. Family processes and problems* (pp. 202–237). Newbury Park, CA: Sage.

Hanson, S. M. H. (1988). Single custodial fathers and the parent-child relationship. *Nursing Research, 30,* 202–204.

Henderson, S. H., Hetherington, E. M., Mekos, D., & Reiss, D. (1996). Stress, parenting, and adolescent psychopathology in nondivorced and stepfamilies: A within-family perspective. In E. M. Hetherington & E. H. Blechman (Eds.), *Stress, coping, and resiliency in children and families* (pp. 39–66). Mahwah, NJ: Erlbaum.

Hetherington, E. M. (1972). Effects of father absence on personality development in adolescent daughters. *Developmental Psychology, 7,* 313–326.

Hetherington, E. M. (1989). Coping with family transitions: Winners, losers, and survivors. *Child Development, 60,* 1–14.

Hetherington, E. M. (1991a). Families, lies, videotapes. *Journal of Research on Adolescence, 1,* 323–348.

Hetherington, E. M. (1991b). The role of individual differences in family relations in coping with divorce and remarriage. In P. Cowan & E. M. Hetherington (Eds.), *Advances in family research: Vol. 2, Family transitions* (pp. 165–194). Hillsdale, NJ: Erlbaum.

Hetherington, E. M. (1993). An overview of the Virginia Longitudinal Study of Divorce and Remarriage with a focus on early adolescence. *Journal of Family Psychology, 7,* 39–56.

Hetherington, E. M. (1997). Teenaged childbearing and divorce. In S. Luthar, J. A. Burack, D. Cicchetti, & J. Wiesz (Eds.), *Developmental psychopathology: Perspectives on adjustment, risk, and disorders* (pp. 350–373). Cambridge, England: Cambridge University Press.

Hetherington, E. M. (in press). Social capital and the development of youth from nondivorced, divorced, and remarried families. In A. Collins (Ed.), Relationships as developmental contexts: *The 29th Minnesota Symposium on Child Psychology.* Hillsdale, NJ: Erlbaum.

Hetherington, E. M., & Clingempeel, W. G. (1992). Coping with marital transitions: A family systems perspective. *Monographs of the Society for Research in Child Development, 57*(2–3, Serial No. 227).

Hetherington, E. M., Cox, M., & Cox, R. (1979). Family interaction and the social, emotional, and cognitive development of children following divorce. In V. Vaughn & T. Brazelton (Eds.), *The family: Setting priorities* (pp. 89–128). New York: Science and Medicine.

Hetherington, E. M. Cox, M., & Cox, R. (1985). Long-term effects of divorce and remarriage on the adjustment of children. *Journal of the American Academy of Child Psychiatry, 24,* 518–539.

Hetherington, E. M., & Jodl, K. M. (1994). Stepfamilies as settings for child development. In A. Booth & J. Dunn (Eds.), *Stepfamilies: Who benefits? Who does not?* (pp. 55–79). Hillsdale, NJ: Erlbaum.

Hetherington, E. M., Law, T. C., & O'Connor, T. G. (1992). Divorce: Challenges, changes, and new chances. In F. Walsh (Ed.), *Normal family processes* (2nd ed., pp. 219–246). New York: Guilford Press.

Hetherington, E. M., & Stanley Hagan, M. S. (1995). Parenting in divorced and remarried families. In M. Bornstein (Ed.), *Handbook of parenting* (pp. 233–255). Hillsdale, NJ: Erlbaum.

Hetherington, E. M., & Stanley Hagan, M. S. (1997). The effects of divorce on fathers and their children. In M. Bornstein (Ed.), *The role of the father in child development* (pp. 191–211). New York: Wiley.

Hoffman, C. D. (1995). Pre- and post-divorce father-child relationships and child adjustment: Noncustodial fathers' perspectives. *Journal of Divorce and Remarriage, 23,* 3–20.

Hu, Y., & Goldman, N. (1990). Mortality differentials by marital status: An international comparison. *Demography, 27,* 233–250.

Jacobson, D. S. (1982, August). *Family structure in the age of divorce.* Paper presented at the 90th Annual Convention of the American Psychological Association, Washington, DC.

Jessor, R., & Jessor, S. L. (1977). *Problem behavior and psycho-social development.* New York: Academic Press.

Jockin, V., McGue, M., & Lykken, D. T. (1996). Personality and divorce: A genetic analysis. *Journal of Personality and Social Psychology, 71,* 288–299.

Kelly, E. L., & Conley, J. J. (1987). Personality and compatibility: A prospective analysis of marital stability and marital satisfaction. *Journal of Personality and Social Psychology, 52,* 27–40.

Kiecolt-Glaser, J. K., Fisher, L. D., Ogrocki, P., Stout, J. C., Speicher, C. E., & Glaser, R. (1987). Marital quality, marital disruption, and immune function. *Psychosomatic Medicine, 49,* 13–34.

Kiecolt-Glaser, J. K., Kennedy, S., Malkoff, S., Fisher, L. D., Speicher, C. E., & Glaser, R. (1988). Marital discord and immunity in males. *Psychosomatic Medicine, 50,* 213–229.

King, V. (1994a). Nonresidential father involvement and child well-being: Can dads make a difference? *Journal of Family Issues, 15,* 78–96.

King, V. (1994b). Variation in the consequences of nonresidential father involvement for children's well-being. *Journal of Marriage and the Family, 56,* 964–972.

Kitson, G. C., & Holmes, W. M. (1992). *Portrait of divorce: Adjustment to marital breakdown.* New York: Guilford Press.

Kitson, G. C., & Morgan, L. A. (1990). The multiple consequences of divorce. *Journal of Marriage and the Family, 52,* 913–924.

Kline, M., Johnston, J. R., & Tschann, J. M. (1991). The long shadow of marital conflict: A model of children's post-divorce adjustment. *Journal of Marriage and the Family, 53,* 297–309.

Kurdek, L. A. (1993). Predicting marital dissolution: A 5-year prospective longitudinal study of newlywed couples. *Journal of Personality and Social Psychology, 64,* 221–242.

Kurdek, L. A., & Fine, M. A. (1993). Parent and nonparent residential family members as providers of warmth, support, and supervision to young adolescents. *Journal of Family Psychology, 7,* 245–249.

Kurdek, L. A., Fine, M. A., & Sinclair, R. J. (1995). School adjustment in sixth graders: Parenting transitions, family climate, and peer norm effects. *Child Development, 66,* 430–445.

Lahey, B. B., Hartdagen, S. E., Frick, P. J., McBurnett, K., Connor, R., & Hynd, G. W. (1988). Conduct disorder: Parsing the confounded relation to parental divorce and antisocial personality. *Journal of Abnormal Psychology, 97,* 334–337.

Lamb, M. E. (1997). Fathers and child development: An introductory overview and guide. In M. E. Lamb (Ed.), *The role of the father in child development* (pp. 1–18). New York: Wiley.

Lee, V. E., Burkam, D. T., Zimiles, H., & Ladewski, B. (1994). Family structure and its effect on behavioral and emotional problems in young adolescents. *Journal of Research on Adolescence, 4,* 405–437.

Lindner-Gunnoe, M. (1993). *Noncustodial mothers' and fathers' contributions to the adjustment of adolescent stepchildren.* Unpublished doctoral dissertation. University of Virginia.

Lorenz, F. O., Simons, R. L., & Chao, W. (1996). Family structure and mother's depression. In R. L. Simons & Associates (Eds.), *Understanding differences between divorced and intact families: Stress, interaction, and child outcome* (pp. 65–77). Thousand Oaks, CA: Sage.

Maccoby, E. E., Buchanan, C. M., Mnookin, R. H., & Dornbusch, S. M. (1993). Post-divorce roles of mothers and fathers in the lives of their children. *Journal of Family Psychology, 7,* 24–38.

Maccoby, E. E., & Mnookin, R. H. (1992). *Dividing the child: Social and legal dilemmas of custody.* Cambridge, MA: Harvard University Press.

Masheter, C. (1991). Post-divorce relationships between ex-spouses: The roles of attachment and interpersonal conflict. *Journal of Marriage and the Family, 53,* 101–110.

Matthews, L. S., Wickrama, K. A. S., & Conger, R. D. (1996). Predicting marital instability from spouse and observer reports of marital interaction. *Journal of Marriage and the Family, 58,* 641–655.

McGue, M., & Lykken, D. T. (1992). Genetic influence on risk of divorce. *Psychological Science, 6,* 368–373.

McLanahan, S. S., & Booth, K. (1989). Mother-only families: Problems, prospects, and politics. *Journal of Marriage and the Family, 51,* 557–580.

McLanahan, S. S., & Bumpass, L. (1988). Intergenerational consequences of family disruption. *American Journal of Sociology, 94,* 130–152.

McLanahan, S., & Sandefur, G. (1994). *Growing up with a single parent: What hurts, what helps?* Cambridge, MA: Harvard University Press.

Mekos, D., Hetherington, E. M., & Reiss, D. (1996). Sibling differences in problem behavior and parental treatment in nondivorced and remarried families. *Child Development, 67,* 2148–2165.

Mendes, H. A. (1976a). Single fatherhood. *Social Work, 21,* 308–312.

Mendes, H. A. (1976b). Single fathers. *Family Coordinator, 25,* 439–444.

Merikangas, K. R., Prusoff, B. A., & Weissman, M. M. (1988). Parental concordance for affective disorders: Psychopathology in offspring. *Journal of Affective Disorders, 15,* 279–290.

Meyer, D. R., & Garasky, S. (1993). Custodial fathers: Myths, realities, and child support policy. *Journal of Marriage and the Family, 55,* 73–89.

Minton, C., & Pasley, K. (1996). Fathers' parenting role identity and father involvement: A comparison of nondivorced and divorced, nonresident fathers. *Journal of Family Issues, 17,* 26–45.

Munsch, J., Woodward, J., & Darling, N. (1995). Children's perceptions of their relationships with coresiding and non-custodial fathers. *Journal of Divorce and Remarriage, 23,* 39–54.

National Center for Health Statistics. (1988). *Current estimates from the National Health Interview Survey: United States, 1987* (DHHS Publication No. 88–1594). Washington, DC: U.S. Government Printing Office.

Orbuch, T. L., Veroff, J., & Hunter, A. G. (in press). Black couples, White couples: The early years of marriage. In E. M. Hetherington (Ed.), *Coping with divorce, single-parenting, and remarriage: A risk and resiliency perspective.* Mahwah, NJ: Erlbaum.

Papernow, P. L. (1988). Stepparent role development: From outsider to intimate. In W. R. Beer (Ed.), *Relative strangers: Studies of stepfamily processes* (pp. 54–82). Totowa, NJ: Rowman & Littlefield.

Patterson, G. (1991, March). *Interaction of stress and family structure and their relation to child adjustment.* Paper presented at the biennial meetings of the Society for Research on Child Development, Seattle, WA.

Patterson, G., DeBaryshe, B., & Ramsey, E. (1989). A developmental perspective on antisocial behavior. *American Psychologist, 44,* 329–335.

Patterson, G., & Dishion, T. J. (1988). Multilevel family process models: Traits, interactions, and relationships. In R. Hinde & J. Stevenson-Hinde (Eds.), *Relationships within families: Mutual influences* (pp. 283–310). Oxford, England: Clarendon Press.

Pearlin, L. I., & Johnson, J. S. (1977). Marital status, life-stresses and depression. *American Sociological Review, 42,* 704–715.

Peterson, J. L., & Zill, N. (1986). Marital disruption, parent-child relationships, and behavior problems in children. *Journal of Marriage and the Family, 48,* 295–307.

Riessman, C. K., & Gerstel, N. (1985). Marital dissolution and health: Do males or females have greater risk? *Social Science and Medicine, 20,* 627–635.

Rutter, M. (1987). Psychosocial resilience and protective mechanisms. *American Journal of Orthopsychiatry, 57,* 316–331.

Santrock, J. W., & Sitterle, K. A. (1987). Parent-child relationships in stepmother families. In K. Pasley & M. Ihinger-Tallman (Eds.), *Remarriage and stepparenting: Current research and theory* (pp. 273–299). New York: Guilford Press.

Santrock, J. W., Sitterle, K. A., & Warshak, R. A. (1988). Parent-child relationships in stepfather families. In P. Bronstein & C. P. Cowan (Eds.), *Fatherhood today: Men's changing roles in the family* pp. 144–165). New York: Wiley.

Seltzer, J. A. (1991). Relationships between fathers and children who live apart: The father's role after separation. *Journal of Marriage and the Family, 53,* 79–101.

Seltzer, J. A. (1994). Consequences of marital dissolution for children. *Annual Review of Sociology, 20,* 235–266.

Seltzer, J. A., & Brandreth, Y. (1994). What fathers say about involvement with children after separation. *Journal of Family Issues, 15,* 49–77.

Simons, R. L. (1996). The effect of divorce on adult and child adjustment. In R. L. Simons & Associates (Eds.), Understanding differences between divorced and intact families: Stress, interaction, and child outcome *(pp. 3–20). Thousand Oaks, CA: Sage.*

Simons, R. L., & Associates. (Eds.. (1996). *Understanding differences between divorced and intact families: Stress, interaction, and child outcome.* Thousand Oaks, CA: Sage.

Simons, R. L., & Beaman, J. (1996). Father's parenting. In R. L. Simons & Associates (Eds.), *Understanding differences between divorced and intact families: Stress, interaction, and child outcome* (pp. 94–103). Thousand Oaks, CA: Sage.

Simons, R. L., Beaman, J., Conger, R. D., & Chao, W. (1992). Childhood experience, conceptions of parenting, and attitudes of spouse as determinants of parental behavior. *Journal of Marriage and the Family, 55,* 91–106.

Simons, R. L., & Chao, W. (1996). Conduct problems. In R. L. Simons & Associates (Eds.), *Understanding differences between divorced and intact families: Stress, interaction, and child outcome* (pp. 125–143). Thousand Oaks, CA: Sage.

Simons, R. L., & Johnson, C. (1996). Mother's parenting. In R. L. Simons & Associates (Eds.), *Understanding differences between divorced and intact families: Stress, interaction, and child outcome* (pp. 81–93). Thousand Oaks, CA: Sage.

Simons, R. L., Johnson, C., & Lorenz, F. O. (1996). Family structure differences in stress and behavioral predispositions. In R. L. Simons & Associates (Eds.), *Understanding differences between divorced and intact families: Stress, interaction, and child outcome* (pp. 45–63). Thousand Oaks, CA: Sage.

Stack, S. (1989). The impact of divorce on suicide in Norway, 1951–1980. *Journal of Marriage and the Family, 51,* 229–238.

Thomson, E., McLanahan, S. S., & Curtin, R. B. (1992). Family structure, gender, and parental separation. *Journal of Marriage and the Family, 54,* 368–378.

Travato, F., & Lauris, G. (1989). Marital status and mortality in Canada: 1951–81. *Journal of Marriage and the Family, 51,* 907–922.

Tzeng, J. M., & Mare, R. D. (1995). Labor market and socioeconomic effects on marital stability. *Social Science Research, 24,* 329–351.

Umberson, D. (1987). Family status and health behaviors: Social control as a dimension of social integration. *Journal of Health and Social Behavior, 28,* 306–319.

Umberson, D., & Williams, C. L. (1993). Divorced fathers: Parental role strain and psychological distress. *Journal of Family Issues, 14,* 378–400.

U.S. Bureau of the Census. (1992). *Marital status and living arrangements: March, 1992* (No. 468, Tables G & 5, Current Population Reports, Series P–20). Washington, DC: U.S. Government Printing Office.

Visher, E. B., & Visher, J. S. (1990). Dynamics of successful stepfamilies. *Journal of Divorce and Remarriage, 14,* 3–11.

Warshak, R. A. (1986). Father custody and child development: A review and analysis of psychological research. *Behavioral Sciences and the Law, 4,* 185–202.

Weiss, R. S. (1979). Growing up a little faster: The experience of growing up in a single-parent household. *Journal of Social Issues, 35,* 97–111.

Werner, E. E. (1988). Individual differences, universal needs: A 30-year study of resilient high-risk infants. *Zero to Three: Bulletin of National Center for Clinical Infant Programs, 8,* 1–15.

Werner, E. E. (1993). Risk, resilience, and recovery: Perspectives from the Kauaii Longitudinal Study. *Development and Psychopathology, 54,* 503–515.

Whitbeck, L. B., Simons, R. L., & Goldberg, E. (1996). Adolescent sexual intercourse. In R. L. Simons & Associates (Eds.), *Understanding differences between divorced and intact families: Stress, interaction, and child outcome* (pp. 144–156). Thousand Oaks, CA: Sage.

White, L. (1994). Stepfamilies over the life course: Social support. In A. Booth & J. Dunn (Eds.), *Stepfamilies: Who benefits? Who does not?* (pp. 109–137). Hillsdale, NJ: Erlbaum.

White, L. K., Brinkerhoff, D. B., & Booth, A. (1985). The effect of marital disruption on children's attachment to parents. *Journal of Family Issues, 6,* 5–22.

Wilson, M. I., Daly, M., & Weghorst, S. J. (1980). Household composition and the risk of child abuse and neglect. *Journal of Biosocial Science, 12,* 333–340.

Zill, N. (1988). Behavior, achievement, and health problems among children in stepfamilies. In E. M. Hetherington & J. D. Arasteh (Eds.), *Impact of divorce, single parenting, and stepparenting on children* (pp. 324–368). Hillsdale, NJ: Erlbaum.

Zill, N. Morrison, D. R., & Coiro, M. J. (1993). Long-term effects of parental divorce on parent-child relationships, adjustment, and achievement in young adulthood. *Journal of Family Psychology, 7,* 91–103.

Zimiles, H., & Lee, V. E. (1991). Adolescent family structure and educational progress. *Developmental Psychology, 27,* 314–320.

Boys will be Boys

Developmental research has been focused on girls; now it's their brothers' turn. Boys need help, too, but first they need to be understood.
BY BARBARA KANTROWITZ AND CLAUDIA KALB

IT WAS A CLASSIC MARS-VENUS ENCOUNTER. Only in this case, the woman was from Harvard and the man—well, boy—was a 4-year-old at a suburban Boston nursery school. Graduate student Judy Chu was in his classroom last fall to gather observations for her doctoral dissertation on human development. His greeting was startling: he held up his finger as if it were a gun and pretended to shoot her. "I felt bad," Chu recalls. "I felt as if he didn't like me." Months later and much more boy-savvy, Chu has a different interpretation: the gunplay wasn't hostile—it was just a way for him to say hello. "They don't mean it to have harsh consequences. It's a way for them to connect."

Researchers like Chu are discovering new meaning in lots of things boys have done for ages. In fact, they're dissecting just about every aspect of the developing male psyche and creating a hot new field of inquiry: the study of boys. They're also producing a slew of books with titles like "Real Boys: Rescuing Our Sons From the Myths of Boyhood" and "Raising Cain: Protecting the Emotional Life of Boys" that will hit the stores in the next few months.

What some researchers are finding is that boys and girls really are from two different planets. But since the two sexes have to live together here on Earth, they should be raised with special consideration for their distinct needs. Boys and girls have different "crisis points," experts say, stages in their emotional and social development where things can go very wrong. Until recently, girls got all the attention. But boys need help, too. They're much more likely than girls to have discipline problems at school and to be diagnosed with attention deficit disorder (ADD). Boys far outnumber girls in special-education classes. They're also more likely to commit violent crimes and end up in jail. Consider the headlines: Jonesboro, Ark.; Paducah, Ky.; Pearl, Miss. In all these school shootings, the perpetrators were young adolescent boys.

Even normal boy behavior has come to be considered pathological in the wake of the feminist movement. An abundance of physical energy and the urge to conquer— these are normal male characteristics, and in an earlier age they were good things, even essential to survival. "If Huck Finn or Tom Sawyer were alive today," says Michael Gurian, author of "The Wonder of Boys," "we'd say they had ADD or a conduct disorder." He says one of the new insights we're gaining about boys is a very old one: boys will be boys. "They are who they are," says Gurian, "and we need to love them for who they are. Let's not try to rewire them."

Indirectly, boys are benefiting from all the research done on girls, especially the landmark work by Harvard University's Carol Gilligan. Her 1982 book, "In a Different Voice: Psychological Theory and Women's Development," inspired Take Our Daughters to Work Day, along with best-selling spinoffs like Mary Pipher's "Reviving Ophelia." The traditional, unisex way of looking at child development was profoundly flawed, Gilligan says: "It was like having a one-dimensional perspective on a two-dimensional scene." At Harvard, where she chairs the gender-studies department, Gilligan is now supervising work on males, including Chu's project. Other researchers are studying mental illness and violence in boys.

While girls' horizons have been expanding, boys' have narrowed, confined to rigid ideas of acceptable male behavior no matter how hard their parents tried to avoid stereotypes. The macho ideal still rules. "We gave boys dolls and they used them as guns," says Gurian. "For 15 years, all we heard was that [gender differences] were all about socialization. Parents who raised their kids through that period said in the end, 'That's not true. Boys and girls can be awfully different.' I think we're awakening to the biological realities and the sociological realities."

But what exactly is the essential nature of boys? Even as infants, boys and girls behave differently. A recent study at Children's Hospital in Boston found that boy babies are more emotionally expressive; girls are more reflective. (That means boy babies tend to cry when they're unhappy; girl babies suck their thumbs.) This could indicate that girls are innately more able to control their emotions. Boys have higher levels of testosterone and lower levels of the neurotransmitter serotonin, which inhibits aggression and impulsivity. That may help explain why more males than females carry through with suicide, become alcoholics and are diagnosed with ADD.

The developmental research on the impact of these physiological differences is still in the embryonic stage, but psychologists are drawing some interesting comparisons between girls and boys (chart). For girls, the first crisis point often comes in early adolescence. Until then, Gilligan and others found, girls have an enormous capacity for establishing relationships and interpreting emotions. But in their early teens, girls clamp down, squash their emotions, blunt their insight. Their self-esteem plummets. The first crisis point for boys comes much earlier, researchers now say. "There's an outbreak of symptoms at age 5, 6, 7, just like you see in girls at 11, 12, 13," says Gilligan. Problems at this age include bed-wetting and separation anxiety. "They don't have the language or experience" to articulate it fully, she says, "but the feelings are no less intense." That's why Gilligan's student Chu is studying preschoolers. For girls at this age, Chu says, hugging a parent goodbye "is almost a nonissue." But little boys, who display a great deal of tenderness, soon begin to bury it with "big boy" behavior to avoid being called sissies. "When their parents drop them off, they want to be close and want to be held, but not in front of other people," says Chu. "Even as early as 4, they're already aware of those masculine stereotypes and are negotiating their way around them."

It's a phenomenon that parents, especially mothers, know well. One morning last month, Lori Dube, a 37-year-old mother of three from Evanston, Ill., visited her oldest son, Abe, almost 5, at his nursery school, where he was having lunch with his friends. She kissed him, prompting another boy to comment scornfully: "Do you know what your mom just did? She kissed you!" Dube acknowledges, with some sadness, that she'll have to be more sensitive to Abe's new reactions to future public displays of affection. "Even if he loves it, he's getting these messages that it's not good."

There's a struggle—a desire and need for warmth on the one hand and a pull toward independence on the other. Boys like Abe are going through what psychologists long ago declared an integral part of growing up: individualization and disconnection from parents, especially mothers. But now some researchers think that process is too abrupt. When boys repress normal feelings like love because of social pressure, says William Pollack, head of the Center for Men at Boston's McLean Hospital and author of the forthcoming "Real Boys," "they've lost contact with the genuine nature of who they are and what they feel. Boys are in a silent crisis. The only time we notice it is when they pull the trigger."

No one is saying that acting like Rambo in nursery school leads directly to tragedies like Jonesboro. But researchers do think that boys who are forced to shut down positive emotions are left with only one socially acceptable outlet: anger. The cultural ideals boys are exposed to in movies and on TV still emphasize traditional masculine roles—warrior, rogue, adventurer—with heavy doses of violence. For every Mr. Mom, there are a dozen Terminators. "The feminist movement has done a great job of convincing people that a woman can be nurturing and a mother and a tough trial lawyer at the same time," says Dan Kindlon, an assistant professor of psychiatry at Harvard Medical School. "But we haven't done that as much with men. We're afraid that if they're too soft, that's all they can be."

And the demands placed on boys in the early years of elementary school can increase their overall stress levels. Scientists have known for years that boys and girls develop physically and intellectually at very different rates (time-line). Boys' fine motor skills—the ability to hold a pencil, for example—are usually considerably behind

girls. They often learn to read later. At the same time, they're much more active—not the best combination for academic advancement. "Boys feel like school is a game rigged against them," says Michael Thompson, co-author with Kindlon of "Raising Cain." "The things at which they excel—gross motor skills, visual and spatial skills, their exuberance—do not find as good a reception in school" as the things girls excel at. Boys (and girls) are also in academic programs at much younger ages than they used to be, increasing the chances that males will be forced to sit still before they are ready. The result, for many boys, is frustration, says Thompson: "By fourth grade, they're saying the teachers like girls better."

A second crisis point for boys occurs around the same time their sisters are stumbling, in early adolescence. By then, say Thompson and Kindlon, boys go one step further in their drive to be "real guys." They partake in a "culture of cruelty," enforcing male stereotypes on one another. "Anything tender, anything compassionate or too artistic is labeled gay," says Thompson. "The homophobia of boys in the 11, 12, 13 range is a stronger force than gravity."

Boys who refuse to fit the mold suffer. Glo Wellman of the California Parenting Institute in Santa Rosa has three sons, 22, 19 and 12. One of her boys, she says, is a "nontypical boy: he's very sensitive and caring and creative and artistic." Not surprisingly, he had the most difficulty growing up, she says. "We've got a long way to go to help boys . . . to have a sense that they can be anything they want to be."

In later adolescence, the once affectionate toddler has been replaced by a sulky stranger who often acts as though torture would be preferable to a brief exchange of words with Mom or Dad. Parents have to try even harder to keep in touch. Boys want and need the attention, but often just don't know how to ask for it. In a recent national poll, teenagers named their parents as their No. 1 heroes. Researchers say a strong parental bond is the most important protection against everything from smoking to suicide.

For San Francisco Chronicle columnist Adair Lara, that message sank in when she

was traveling to New York a few years ago with her son, then 15. She sat next to a woman who told her that until recently she would have had to change seats because she would not have been able to bear the pain of seeing a teenage son and mother together. The woman's son was 17 when his girlfriend dumped him; he went into the garage and killed himself. "This story made me aware that with a boy especially, you have to keep talking because they don't come and talk to you," she says. Lara's son is now 17; she also has a 19-year-old daughter. "My daughter stalked me. She followed me from room to room. She was yelling, but she was in touch. Boys don't do that. They leave the room and you don't know what they're feeling." Her son is now 6 feet 3. "He's a man. There are barriers. You have to reach through that and remember to ruffle his hair."

With the high rate of divorce, many boys are growing up without any adult men in their lives at all. Don Elium, coauthor of the best-selling 1992 book "Raising a Son," says that with troubled boys, there's often a common theme: distant, uninvolved fathers, and mothers who have taken on more responsibility to fill the gap. That was the case with Raymundo Infante Jr., a 16-year-old high-school junior, who lives with his mother, Mildred, 38, a hospital administrative assistant in Chicago, and his sister, Vanessa, 19. His parents divorced when he was a baby and he had little contact with his father until a year ago. The hurt built up—in sixth grade, Raymundo was so depressed that he told a classmate he wanted to kill himself. The classmate told the teacher, who told a counselor, and Raymundo saw a psychiatrist for a year. "I felt that I just wasn't good enough, or he just didn't want me," Raymundo says. Last year Raymundo finally confronted his dad, who works two jobs—in an office and on a construction crew—and accused him of caring more about work than about his son. Now the two spend time together on weekends and sometimes go shopping, but there is still a huge gap of lost years.

Black boys are especially vulnerable, since they are more likely than whites to grow up in homes without fathers. They're often on their own much sooner than whites.

The Wonder (and Worry) Years

There may be no such thing as *child* development anymore. Instead, researchers are now studying each gender's development separately and discovering that boys and girls face very different sorts of challenges. Here is a rough guide to the major phases in their development.

Boys

0–3 years At birth, boys have brains that are 5% larger than girls' (size doesn't affect intelligence) and proportionately larger bodies—disparities that increase with age.

4–6 years The start of school is a tough time as boys must curb aggressive impulses. They lag behind girls in reading skills, and hyperactivity may be a problem.

| Age 1 | 2 | 3 | 4 | 5 | 6 | 7 |

Girls

0–3 years Girls are born with a higher proportion of nerve cells to process information. More brain regions are involved in language production and recognition.

4–6 years Girls are well suited to school. They are calm, get along with others, pick up on social cues, and reading and writing come easily to them.

Trouble Spots: Where Boys Run Into Problems

Not all boys are the same, of course, but most rebel in predictable patterns and with predictable weapons: underachievement, aggression and drug and alcohol use. While taking chances is an important aspect of the growth process, it can lead to real trouble.

When Johnny Can't Read
Girls have reading disorders nearly as often as boys, but are able to overcome them. Disability rates, as identified by:

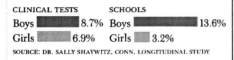

CLINICAL TESTS		SCHOOLS	
Boys	8.7%	Boys	13.6%
Girls	6.9%	Girls	3.2%

SOURCE: DR. SALLY SHAYWITZ, CONN. LONGITUDINAL STUDY

Suicidal Impulses
While girls are much more likely to try to kill themselves, boys are likelier to die from their attempts.

SUICIDE ATTEMPTS*		SUICIDE FATALITIES	
Boys	3,000	Boys	260
Girls	23,000	Girls	77

1995, AGES 5–14. *NEWSWEEK ESTIMATE. SOURCES: NCHS, CDC

Binge Drinking
Boys binge more on alcohol. Those who had five or more drinks in a row in the last two weeks:

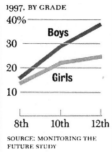

1997, BY GRADE

Boys

Girls

8th   10th   12th

SOURCE: MONITORING THE FUTURE STUDY

Aggression That Turns to Violence
Boys get arrested three times as often as girls, but for some nonviolent crimes the numbers are surprisingly even.

Arrests of 10- to 17-year-olds: ■ Boys ■ Girls

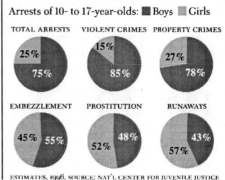

TOTAL ARRESTS	VIOLENT CRIMES	PROPERTY CRIMES
25% / 75%	15% / 85%	27% / 78%

EMBEZZLEMENT	PROSTITUTION	RUNAWAYS
45% / 55%	52% / 48%	43% / 57%

ESTIMATES, 1996. SOURCE: NAT'L CENTER FOR JUVENILE JUSTICE

Eating Disorders
Boys can also have eating disorders. Kids who used laxatives or vomited to lose weight:

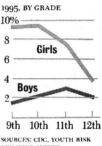

1995, BY GRADE

Girls

Boys

9th   10th   11th   12th

SOURCES: CDC, YOUTH RISK BEHAVIOR SURVEY

Black leaders are looking for alternatives. In Atlanta, the Rev. Tim McDonald's First Iconium Baptist Church just chartered a Boy Scout troop. "Gangs are so prevalent because guys want to belong to something," says McDonald. "We've got to give them something positive to belong to." Black educators like Chicagoan Jawanza Kunjufu think mentoring programs will overcome the bias against academic success as "too white." Some cities are also experimenting with all-boy classrooms in predominantly black schools.

Researchers hope that in the next few years, they'll come up with strategies that will help boys the way the work of Gilligan and others helped girls. In the meantime, experts say, there are some guidelines. Parents can channel their sons' energy into constructive activities, like team sports. They should also look for "teachable moments" to encourage qualities such as empathy. When Di-

ane Fisher, a Cincinnati-area psychologist, hears her 8- and 10-year-old boys talking about "finishing somebody," she knows she has mistakenly rented a violent videogame. She pulls the plug and tells them: "In our house, killing people is not entertainment, even if it's just pretend."

Parents can also teach by example. New Yorkers Dana and Frank Minaya say they've never disciplined their 16-year-old son Walter in anger. They insist on resolving all disputes calmly and reasonably, without yelling. If there is a problem, they call an official family meeting "and we never leave without a big hug," says Frank. Walter tries to be open with his parents. "I don't want to miss out on any advice," he says.

Most of all, wise parents of boys should go with the flow. Cindy Lang, 36, a full-time mother in Woodside, Calif., is continually amazed by the relentless energy of her sons, Roger Lloyd, 12, and Chris, 9. "You accept

the fact that they're going to involve themselves in risky behavior, like skateboarding down a flight of stairs. As a girl, I certainly wasn't skateboarding down a flight of stairs." Just last week, she got a phone call from school telling her that Roger Lloyd was in the emergency room because he had fallen backward while playing basketball and school officials thought he might have a concussion. He's fine now, but she's prepared for the next emergency: "I have a cell phone so I can be on alert." Boys will be boys. And we have to let them.

With KAREN SPRINGEN in Chicago, PATRICIA KING in San Francisco, PAT WINGERT in Washington, VERN E. SMITH in Atlanta and ELIZABETH ANGELL in New York

---

7–10 years While good at gross motor skills, boys trail girls in finer control. Many of the best students but also nearly all of the poorest ones are boys.

11–13 years A mixed bag. Dropout rates begin to climb, but good students start pulling ahead of girls in math skills and catching up some in verbal ones.

14–16 years Entering adolescence, boys hit another rough patch. Indulging in drugs, alcohol and aggressive behavior are common forms of rebellion.

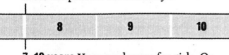

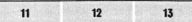

8	9	10

11	12	13

14	15	16

7–10 years Very good years for girls. On average, they outperform boys at school, excelling in verbal skills while holding their own in math.

11–13 years The start of puberty and girls' most vulnerable time. Many experience depression; as many as 15% may try to kill themselves.

14–16 years Eating disorders are a major concern. Although anorexia can manifest itself as early as 8, it typically afflicts girls starting at 11 or 12; bulimia at 15.

SOURCES: DR. MICHAEL THOMPSON, BARNEY BRAWER. RESEARCH BY BILL VOURVOULIAS — NEWSWEEK

Father Love and Child Development: History and Current Evidence

Abstract

Six types of studies show that father love sometimes explains as much or more of the variation in specific child and adult outcomes as does mother love. Sometimes, however, only father love is statistically associated with specific aspects of offsprings' development and adjustment, after controlling for the influence of mother love. Recognition of these facts was clouded historically by the cultural construction of fatherhood and fathering in America.

Keywords

father love; paternal acceptance; parental acceptance-rejection theory

Ronald P. Rohner[1]

Center for the Study of Parental Acceptance and Rejection, School of Family Studies, University of Connecticut, Storrs, Connecticut

Research in every major ethnic group of America (Rohner, 1998b), in dozens of nations internationally, and with several hundred societies in two major cross-cultural surveys (Rohner 1975, 1986, 1998c; Rohner & Chaki-Sircar, 1988) suggests that children and adults everywhere—regardless of differences in race, ethnicity, gender, or culture—tend to respond in essentially the same way when they experience themselves to be loved or unloved by their parents. The overwhelming bulk of research dealing with parental acceptance and rejection concentrates on mothers' behavior, however. Until recently, the possible influence of father love has been largely ignored. Here, I concentrate on evidence

showing the influence of fathers' love-related behaviors—or simply, *father love*—in relation to the social, emotional, and cognitive development and functioning of children, adolescents, and adult offspring. Moreover, I focus primarily, but not exclusively, on families for which information is available about both fathers and mothers—or about youths' perceptions of both their fathers' and mothers' parenting. My principal objective is to identify evidence about the relative contribution to offspring development of father love vis-à-vis mother love.

I define father love in terms of paternal acceptance and rejection as construed in parental acceptance-rejection theory (Rohner, 1986, in press). Paternal

acceptance includes such feelings and behaviors (or children's perceptions of such feelings and behaviors) as paternal nurturance, warmth, affection, support, comfort, and concern. Paternal rejection, on the other hand, is defined as the real or perceived absence or withdrawal of these feelings and behaviors. Rejection includes such feelings as coldness, indifference, and hostility toward the child. Paternal rejection may be expressed behaviorally as a lack of affection toward the child, as physical or verbal aggression, or as neglect. Paternal rejection may also be experienced in the form of undifferentiated rejection; that is, there may be situations in which individuals feel that their fathers (or significant male

From *Current Directions in Psychological Science,* October 1998, pp. 157-161. © 1998 by Ronald P. Rohner and the American Psychological Society. Reprinted by permission of Blackwell Publishers.

caregivers) do not really care about, want, or love them, even though there may not be observable behavioral indicators showing that the fathers are neglecting, unaffectionate, or aggressive toward them. Mother love (maternal acceptance-rejection) is defined in the same way.

FATHERHOOD AND MOTHERHOOD ARE CULTURAL CONSTRUCTIONS

The widely held cultural construction of fatherhood in America—especially prior to the 1970s—has two strands. Historically, the first strand asserted that fathers are ineffective, often incompetent, and maybe even biologically unsuited to the job of child-rearing. (The maternal counterpoint to this is that women are genetically endowed for child care.) The second strand asserted that fathers' influence on child development is unimportant, or at the very most peripheral or indirect. (The maternal counterpoint here is that mother love and competent maternal care provide everything that children need for normal, healthy development.) Because researchers internalized these cultural beliefs as their own personal beliefs, fathers were essentially ignored by mainstream behavioral science until late in the 20th century. The 1970s through the 1990s, however, have seen a revolution in recognizing fathers and the influence of their love on child development. Three interrelated lines of influence I have discussed elsewhere (Rohner, 1998a) seem to account for this revolution. The net effect of these influences has been to draw attention to the fact that father love sometimes explains a unique, independent portion of the variation in specific child outcomes, over and above the portion explained by mother love. In fact, a few recent studies suggest that father love is the sole significant predictor of specific outcomes, after removing the influence of mother love.

STUDIES SHOWING THE INFLUENCE OF FATHER LOVE

Six types of studies (discussed at greater length in Rohner, 1998a) demonstrate a strong association between father love and aspects of offspring development.

Studies Looking Exclusively at Variations in the Influence of Father Love

Many of the studies looking exclusively at the influence of variations in father love deal with one of two topics: gender role development, especially of sons, and father involvement. Studies of gender role development emerged prominently in the 1940s and continued through the 1970s. Commonly, researchers assessed the masculinity of fathers and of sons, and then correlated the two sets of scores. Many psychologists were surprised at first to discover that no consistent results emerged from this research. But when they examined the quality of the father-son relationship, they found that if the relationship between masculine fathers and their sons was warm and loving, the boys were indeed more masculine. Later, however, researchers found that the masculinity of fathers per se did not seem to make much difference because "boys seemed to conform to the sex-role standards of their culture when their relationships with their fathers were warm, regardless of how 'masculine' the fathers were" (Lamb, 1997, p. 9).

Paternal involvement is the second domain in which there has been a substantial amount of research on the influence of variations in father love. Many studies have concluded that children with highly involved fathers, in relation to children with less involved fathers, tend to be more cognitively and socially competent, less inclined toward gender stereotyping, more empathic, psychologically better adjusted, and the like. But "caring for" children is not necessarily the same thing as "caring about" them. And a closer examination of these studies suggests that it was not the simple fact of paternal engagement (i.e., direct interaction with the child), availability, or responsibility for child care that was associated with these positive outcomes. Rather, it appears that the quality of the father-child relationship—especially of father love—makes the greatest difference (Lamb, 1997; Veneziano & Rohner, 1998).

Father Love Is as Important as Mother Love

The great majority of studies in this category deal with one or a combination of the following four issues among children, adolescents, and young adults: (a) personality and psychological adjustment problems, including issues of self-concept and self-esteem, emotional

stability, and aggression; (b) conduct problems, especially in school; (c) cognitive and academic performance issues; and (d) psychopathology. Recent studies employing multivariate analyses have allowed researchers to conclude that fathers' and mothers' behaviors are sometimes each associated significantly and uniquely with these outcomes. The work of Young, Miller, Norton, and Hill (1995) is one of these studies. These authors employed a national sample of 640 12- to 16-year-olds living in two-parent families. They found that perceived paternal love and caring was as predictive of sons' and daughters' life satisfaction—including their sense of well-being—as was maternal love and caring.

Father Love Predicts Specific Outcomes Better Than Mother Love

As complex statistical procedures have become more commonplace in the 1980s and 1990s, it has also become more common to discover that the influence of father love explains a unique, independent portion of the variation in specific child and adult outcomes, over and above the portion of variation explained by mother love. Studies drawing this conclusion tend to deal with one or more of the following four issues among children, adolescents, and young adults: (a) personality and psychological adjustment problems, (b) conduct problems, (c) delinquency, and (d) psychopathology. For example, evidence is mounting that fathers may be especially salient in the development of such forms of psychopathology as substance abuse (drug and alcohol use and abuse), depression and depressed emotion, and behavior problems, including conduct disorder and externalizing behaviors (including aggression toward people and animals, property destruction, deceitfulness, and theft) (Rohner, 1998c). Fathers are also being increasingly implicated in the etiology of borderline personality disorder (a pervasive pattern of emotional and behavioral instability, especially in interpersonal relationships and in self-image) and borderline personality organization (a less severe form of borderline personality disorder) (Fowler, 1990; Rohner & Brothers, in press).

Father love appears to be uniquely associated not just with behavioral and psychological problems, however, but also with health and well-being. Amato (1994), for example, found in a national sample that perceived closeness to fathers made a significant contribution—over and above the contribution made by perceived closeness to mothers—to adult sons' and daughters' happiness, life satisfaction, and low psychological distress (i.e., to overall psychological well-being).

Father Love Is the Sole Significant Predictor of Specific Outcomes

In the 1990s, a handful of studies using a variety of multivariate statistics have concluded that father love is the sole significant predictor of specific child outcomes, after removing the influences of mother love. Most of these studies have dealt with psychological and behavioral problems of adolescents. For example, Cole and McPherson (1993) concluded that father-child conflict but not mother-child conflict (in each case, after the influence of the other was statistically controlled) was positively associated with depressive symptoms in adolescents. Moreover, father-adolescent cohesion was positively associated with the absence of depressive symptoms in adolescents. These results are consistent with Barrera and Garrison-Jones's (1992) conclusion that adolescents' satisfaction with fathers' support was related to a lowered incidence of depressive symptoms, whereas satisfaction with mothers' support was not. Barnett, Marshall, and Pleck (1992), too, found that when measures of the quality of both mother-son and father-son relationships were entered simultaneously into a regression equation, only the father-son relationship was related significantly to adult sons' psychological distress (a summed measure of anxiety and depression).

Father Love Moderates the Influence of Mother Love

A small but growing number of studies have concluded that fathers' behavior moderates and is moderated by (i.e., interacts with) other influences within the family. Apparently, however, only one study so far has addressed the issue of whether mother love has different effects on specific child outcomes depending on the level of father love. This study, by Forehand and Nousiainen (1993), found that when mothers were low in acceptance, fathers' acceptance scores had no significant impact on youths' cognitive competence. But when mothers were high in acceptance, fathers' acceptance scores made a dramatic difference: Fathers with low acceptance scores tended to have children with poorer cognitive competence, whereas highly accepting fathers tended to have children with substantially better cognitive competence.

Paternal Versus Maternal Parenting Is Sometimes Associated With Different Outcomes for Sons, Daughters, or Both

Many of the studies in this category were published in the 1950s and 1960s, and even earlier. Many of them may be criticized on methodological and conceptual grounds. Nonetheless, evidence suggests that serious research questions should be raised in the future about the possibility that associations between love-related parenting and child outcomes may depend on the gender of the parent and of the child. Three different kinds of studies tend to be found in this category.

First, some research shows that one pattern of paternal love-related behavior and a different pattern of maternal love-related behavior may be associated with a single outcome in sons, daughters, or both. For example, Barber and Thomas (1986) found that daughters' self-esteem was best predicted by their mothers' general support (e.g., praise and approval) but by their fathers' physical affection. Sons' self-esteem, however, was best predicted by their mothers' companionship (e.g., shared activities) and by their fathers' sustained contact (e.g., picking up the boys for safety or for fun).

Second, other research in this category shows that a single pattern of paternal love-related behavior may be associated with one outcome for sons and a different outcome for daughters. For example, Jordan, Radin, and Epstein (1975) found that paternal nurturance was positively associated with boys' but not girls' performance on an IQ test. Finally, the third type of research in this category shows that the influence of a single pattern of paternal love-related behaviors may be more strongly associated with a given outcome for one gender of offspring than for the other. For example, Eisman (1981) reported that fathers' love and acceptance correlated more highly with daughters' than with sons' self-concept.

DISCUSSION

The data reported here are but a minuscule part of a larger body of work showing that father love is heavily implicated not only in children's and adults' psychological well-being and health, but also in an array of psychological and behavioral problems. This evidence punctuates the need to include fathers (and other significant males, when appropriate) as well as mothers in future research, and then to analyze separately the data for possible father and mother effects. It is only by separating data in this way that behavioral scientists can discern when and under what conditions paternal and maternal factors have similar or different effects on specific outcomes for children. This recommendation explicitly contradicts a call sometimes seen in published research to merge data about fathers' and mothers' parenting behaviors.

Finally, it is important to note several problems and limitations in the existing research on father love. For example, even though it seems unmistakably clear that father love makes an important contribution to offsprings' development and psychological functioning, it is not at all clear what generative mechanisms produce these contributions. In particular, it is unclear why father love is sometimes more strongly associated with specific offspring outcomes than is mother love. And it is unclear why patterns of paternal versus maternal parenting may be associated with different outcomes for sons, daughters, or children of both genders. It remains for future research to inquire directly about these issues. Until then, we can know only that father love is often as influential as mother love—and sometimes more so.

Note

1. Address correspondence to Ronald P. Rohner, Center for the Study of Parental Acceptance and Rejection, School of Family Studies, University of Connecticut, Storrs, CT 06269–2058; e-mail: rohner@ uconnvm.uconn.edu or http://vm.uconn. edu/~rohner.

References

Amato, P. R. (1994). Father-child relations, mother-child relations and offspring psychological well-being in adulthood. *Journal of Marriage and the Family, 56,* 1031–1042.

Barber, B. & Thomas, D. (1986). Dimensions of fathers' and mothers' supportive behavior: A case for physical affection. *Journal of Marriage and the Family, 48,* 783–794.

Barnett, R. C., Marshall, N. L., & Pleck, J. H. (1992). Adult son-parent relationships and the associations with sons' psychological distress. *Journal of Family Issues, 13,* 505–525.

Barrera, M., Jr., & Garrison-Jones, C. (1992). Family and peer social support as specific correlates of adolescent depressive symptoms. *Journal of Abnormal Child Psychology, 20,* 1–16.

Cole, D., & McPherson, A. E. (1993). Relation of family subsystems to adolescent depression: Implementing a new family assessment strategy. *Journal of Family Psychology, 7,* 119–133.

Eisman, E. M. (1981). Sex-role characteristics of the parent, parental acceptance of the child and child self-concept. (Doctoral dissertation, California School of Professional Psychology at Los Angeles, 1981). *Dissertation Abstracts International, 24,* 2062.

Forehand, R., & Nousiainen, S. (1993). Maternal and paternal parenting: Critical dimensions in adolescent functioning. *Journal of Family Psychology, 7,* 213–221.

Fowler, S. D. (1990). *Paternal effects on severity of borderline psychopathology.* Unpublished doctoral dissertation, University of Texas, Austin.

Jordan, B., Radin, N., & Epstein, A. (1975). Paternal behavior and intellectual functioning in preschool boys and girls. *Developmental Psychology, 11,* 407–408.

Lamb, M. E. (1997). Fathers and child development: An introductory overview and guide. In M. E. Lamb (Ed.), *The role of the father in child development* (pp. 1–18). New York: John Wiley & Sons.

Rohner, R. P. (1975). *They love me, they love me not: A worldwide study of the effects of parental acceptance and rejection.* New Haven, CT: HRAF Press.

Rohner, R. P. (1986). *The warmth dimension: Foundations of parental acceptance-rejection theory.* Newbury Park, CA: SAGE.

Rohner, R. P. (1998a). *The importance of father love: History and contemporary evidence.* Manuscript submitted for publication.

Rohner, R. P. (1998b). *Parental acceptance-rejection bibliography* [On-line]. Available: http://vm.unconn.edu/~rohner

Rohner, R. P. (1998c). *Worldwide mental health correlates of parental acceptance-rejection: Review of cross-cultural and intracultural evidence.* Manuscript submitted for publication.

Rohner, R. P. (in press). Acceptance and rejection. In D. Levinson, J. Ponzetti, & P. Jorgensen (Eds.), *Encyclopedia of human emotions.* New York: MacMillan.

Rohner, R. P., & Brothers, S. A. (in press). Perceived parental rejection, psychological maladjustment, and borderline personality disorder. *Journal of Emotional Abuse.*

Rohner, R. P., & Chaki-Sircar, M. (1988). *Women and children in a Bengali village.* Hanover, NH: University Press of New England.

Veneziano, R. A., & Rohner, R. P. (1998). Perceived paternal warmth, paternal involvement, and youths' psychological adjustment in a rural, biracial southern community. *Journal of Marriage and the Family, 60,* 335–343.

Young, M. H., Miller, B. E., Norton, M. C., & Hill, J. E. (1995). The effect of parental supportive behaviors on life satisfaction of adolescent offspring. *Journal of Marriage and the Family, 57,* 813–822.

Recommended Reading

Biller, H. B. (1993). *Fathers and families: Paternal factors in child development.* Westport, CT: Auburn House.

Booth, A., & Crouter, A. C. (Eds.). (1998). *Men in families: When do they get involved? What difference does it make?* Mahwah, NJ: Erlbaum.

Lamb, M. E. (Ed.). (1997). *The role of the father in child development.* New York: John Wiley & Sons.

Rohner, R. P. (1986). (See References)

The Moral Development of Children

It is not enough for kids to tell right from wrong. They must develop a commitment to acting on their ideals. Enlightened parenting can help

by William Damon

With unsettling regularity, news reports tell us of children wreaking havoc on their schools and communities: attacking teachers and classmates, murdering parents, persecuting others out of viciousness, avarice or spite. We hear about feral gangs of children running drugs or numbers, about teenage date rape, about youthful vandalism, about epidemics of cheating even in academically elite schools. Not long ago a middle-class gang of youths terrorized an affluent California suburb through menacing threats and extortion, proudly awarding themselves points for each antisocial act. Such stories make *Lord of the Flies* seem eerily prophetic.

What many people forget in the face of this grim news is that most children most of the time do follow the rules of their society, act fairly, treat friends kindly, tell the truth and respect their elders. Many young-

sters do even more. A large portion of young Americans volunteer in community service—according to one survey, between 22 and 45 percent, depending on the location. Young people have also been leaders in social causes. Harvard University psychiatrist Robert Coles has written about children such as Ruby, an African-American girl who broke the color barrier in her school during the 1960s. Ruby's daily walk into the all-white school demonstrated a brave sense of moral purpose. When taunted by classmates, Ruby prayed for their redemption rather than cursing them. "Ruby," Coles observed, "had a will and used it to make an ethical choice; she demonstrated moral stamina; she possessed honor, courage."

All children are born with a running start on the path to moral development. A number of inborn responses predispose them to act in ethical ways. For example, empa-

thy—the capacity to experience another person's pleasure or pain vicariously—is part of our native endowment as humans. Newborns cry when they hear others cry and show signs of pleasure at happy sounds such as cooing and laughter. By the second year of life, children commonly console peers or parents in distress.

Sometimes, of course, they do not quite know what comfort to provide. Psychologist Martin L. Hoffman of New York University once saw a toddler offering his mother his security blanket when he perceived she was upset. Although the emotional disposition to help is present, the means of helping others effectively must be learned and refined through social experience. Moreover, in many people the capacity for empathy stagnates or even diminishes. People can act cruelly to those they refuse to empathize with. A New York police officer once asked a teenage thug how he could have crippled an 83-year-old woman during a mugging. The boy replied, "What do I care? I'm not her."

A scientific account of moral growth must explain both the good and the bad. Why do most children act in reasonably—sometimes exceptionally—moral ways, even when it flies in the face of their immediate self-interest? Why do some children depart from accepted standards, often to the great harm of themselves and others? How does a child acquire mores and develop a lifelong commitment to moral behavior, or not?

Psychologists do not have definitive answers to these questions, and often their studies seem merely to confirm parents' observations and intuition. But parents, like all people, can be led astray by subjective biases, incomplete information and media sensationalism. They may blame a relatively trivial event—say, a music concert—for a deep-seated problem such as drug dependency. They may incorrectly attribute their own problems to a strict upbringing and then try to compensate by raising their children in an overly permissive way. In such a hotly contested area as children's moral values, a systematic, scientific approach is the only way to avoid wild swings of emotional reaction that end up repeating the same mistakes.

The Genealogy of Morals

The study of moral development has become a lively growth industry within the social sciences. Journals are full of new findings and competing models. Some theories focus on natural biological forces; others stress social influence and experience; still others, the judgment that results from children's intellectual development. Although each theory has a different emphasis, all recognize that no single cause can account for either moral or immoral behavior. Watching violent videos or

The Six Stages of Moral Judgment

Growing up, children and young adults come to rely less on external discipline and more on deeply held beliefs. They go through as many as six stages (grouped into three levels) of moral reasoning, as first argued by psychologist Lawrence Kohlberg in the late 1950s (below). The evidence includes a long-term study of 58 young men interviewed periodically over two decades. Their moral maturity was judged by how they analyzed hypothetical dilemmas, such as whether a husband should steal a drug for his dying wife. Either yes or no was a valid answer; what mattered was how the men justified it. As they grew up, they passed through the stages in succession, albeit at different rates (bar graph). The sixth stage remained elusive. Despite the general success of this model for describing intellectual growth, it does not explain people's actual behavior. Two people at the same stage may act differently.   —W.D.

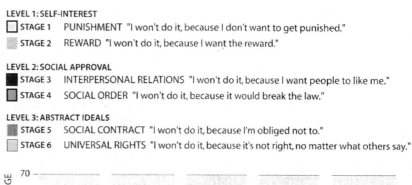

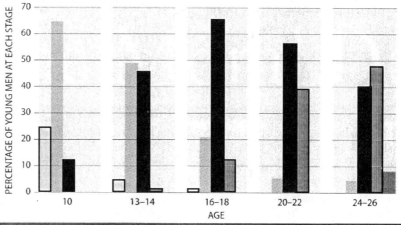

playing shoot-'em-up computer games may push some children over the edge and leave others unaffected. Conventional wisdom dwells on lone silver bullets, but scientific understanding must be built on an appreciation of the complexity and variety of children's lives.

Biologically oriented, or "nativist," theories maintain that human morality springs from emotional dispositions that are hardwired into our species. Hoffman, Colwyn Trevarthen of the University of Edinburgh and Nancy Eisenberg of Arizona State University have established

that babies can feel empathy as soon as they recognize the existence of others—sometimes in the first week after birth. Other moral emotions that make an early appearance include shame, guilt and indignation. As Harvard child psychologist Jerome S. Kagan has described, young children can be outraged by the violation of social expectations, such as a breach in the rules of a favorite game or rearranged buttons on a piece of familiar clothing.

Nearly everybody, in every culture, inherits these dispositions. Mary D. Ainsworth of the University of Virginia reported empathy among Ugandan and American infants; Norma Feshbach of the University of California at Los Angeles conducted a similar comparison of newborns in Europe, Israel and the U.S.; Millard C. Madsen of U.C.L.A. studied sharing by preschool children in nine cultures. As far as psychologists know, children everywhere start life with caring feelings toward those close to them and adverse reactions to inhumane or unjust behavior. Differences in how these reactions are triggered and expressed emerge only later, once children have been exposed to the particular value systems of their cultures.

In contrast, the learning theories concentrate on children's acquisition of behavioral norms and values through observation, imitation and reward. Research in this tradition has concluded that moral behavior is context-bound, varying from situation to situation almost independently of stated beliefs. Landmark studies in the 1920s, still frequently cited, include Hugh Hartshorne and Mark May's survey of how children reacted when given the chance to cheat. The children's behavior depended largely on whether they thought they would be caught. It could be predicted neither from their conduct in previous situations nor from their knowledge of common moral rules, such as the Ten Commandments and the Boy Scout's code.

Later reanalyses of Hartshorne and May's data, performed by Roger Burton of the State University of New York at Buffalo, discovered at least one general trend: younger children were more likely to cheat than adolescents. Perhaps socialization or mental growth can restrain dishonest behavior after all. But the effect was not a large one.

The third basic theory of moral development puts the emphasis on intellectual growth, arguing that virtue and vice are ultimately a matter of conscious choice. The best-known cognitive theories are those of psy-

"Could You Live with Yourself?"

In a distressed neighborhood in Camden, N.J., social psychologist Daniel Hart of Rutgers University interviewed an African-American teenager who was active in community service:

How would you describe yourself?
I am the kind of person who wants to get involved, who believes in getting involved. I just had this complex, I call it, where people think of Camden as being a bad place, which bothered me. Every city has its own bad places, you know. I just want to work with people, work to change that image that people have of Camden. You can't start with adults, because they don't change. But if you can get into the minds of young children, show them what's wrong and let them know that you don't want them to be this way, then it could work, because they're more persuadable.

Is there really one correct solution to moral problems like this one?
Basically, it's like I said before.You're supposed to try to help save a life.

How do you know?
Well, it's just—how could you live with yourself? Say that I could help save this person's life—could I just let that person die? I mean, I couldn't live with myself if that happened. A few years ago my sister was killed, and . . . the night she was killed I was over at her house, earlier that day. Maybe if I had spent the night at her house that day, maybe this wouldn't have happened.

You said that you're not a bad influence on others. Why is that important?
Well, I try not to be a bad role model. All of us have bad qualities, of course; still, you have to be a role model even if you're a person walking down the street. You know, we have a society today where there are criminals and crooks. There are drug users. Kids look to those people. If they see a drug dealer with a lot of money, they want money, too, and then they're going to do drugs. So it's important that you try not to be a bad influence, because that can go a long way. Even if you say, oh, wow, you tell your little sister or brother to be quiet so Mom and Dad won't wake so you won't have to go to school. And they get in the habit of being quiet [laughs], you're not going to school, things like that. So when you're a bad influence, it always travels very far.

Why don't you want that to happen?
Because in today's society there's just really too much crime, too much violence. I mean everywhere. And I've even experienced violence, because my sister was murdered. You know, we need not to have that in future years, so we need to teach our children otherwise.

chologists Jean Piaget and Lawrence Kohlberg. Both described children's early moral beliefs as oriented toward power and authority. For young children, might makes right, literally. Over time they come to understand that social rules are made by people and thus can be renegotiated and that reciprocity in relationships is more fair than unilateral obedience. Kohlberg identified a six-stage sequence in the maturation of moral judgment [see box, "The Six Stages of Moral Judgment]." Several thousand studies have used it as a measure of how advanced a person's moral reasoning is.

Conscience versus Chocolate

Although the main parts of Kohlberg's sequence have been confirmed, notable exceptions stand out. Few if any people reach the sixth and most advanced stage, in which their moral view is based purely on abstract principles. As for the early stages in the sequence, many studies (including ones from my own laboratory) have found that young children have a far richer sense of positive morality than the model indicates. In other words, they do not act simply out of fear of punishment. When a playmate hogs a plate of cookies or refuses to relinquish a swing, the protest "That's not fair!" is common. At the same time, young children realize that they have an obligation to share with others—even when their parents say not to. Preschool children generally believe in an equal distribution of goods and back up their beliefs with reasons such as empathy ("I want my friend to feel nice"), reciprocity ("She shares her toys with me") and egalitarianism ("We should all get the same"). All this they figure out through confrontation with peers at play. Without fairness, they learn, there will be trouble.

In fact, none of the three traditional theories is sufficient to explain children's moral growth and behavior. None captures the most essential dimensions of moral life: character and commitment. Regardless of how children develop their initial system of values, the key question is: What makes them live up to their ideals or not? This issue is the focus of recent scientific thinking.

Like adults, children struggle with temptation. To see how this tug of war plays itself out in the world of small children, my colleagues and I (then at Clark University) devised

How Universal Are Values?

The observed importance of shared values in children's moral development raises some of the most hotly debated questions in philosophy and the social sciences today. Do values vary from place to place, or is there a set of universal values that guides moral development everywhere? Do children growing up in different cultures or at different times acquire fundamentally different mores?

Some light was shed on the cultural issue by Richard A. Shweder of the University of Chicago and his colleagues in a study of Hindu-Brahmin children in India and children from Judeo-Christian backgrounds in the U.S. The study revealed striking contrasts between the two groups. From an early age, the Indian children learned to maintain tradition, to respect defined rules of interpersonal relationships and to help people in need. American children, in comparison, were oriented toward autonomy, liberty and personal rights. The Indian children said that breaches of tradition, such as eating beef or addressing one's father by his first name, were particularly reprehensible. They saw nothing wrong with a man caning his errant son or a husband beating his wife when she went to the movies without his permission. The American children were appalled by all physically punitive behavior but indifferent to infractions such as eating forbidden foods or using improper forms of address.

Moreover, the Indians and Americans moved in opposite directions as they matured. Whereas Indian children restricted value judgments to situations with which they were directly familiar, Indian adults generalized their values to a broad range of social conditions. American children said that moral standards should apply to everyone always; American adults modified values in the face of changing circumstances. In short, the Indians began life as relativists and ended up an universalists, whereas the Americans went precisely the other way.

It would be overstating matters, however, to say that children from different cultures adopt completely different moral codes. In Schweder's study, both groups of children thought that deceitful acts (a father breaking a promise to a child) and uncharitable acts (ignoring a beggar with a sick child) were wrong. They also shared a repugnance toward theft, vandalism and harming innocent victims, although there was some disagreement on what constitutes inno-

cence. Among these judgments may be found a universal moral sense, based on common human aversions. It reflects core values—benevolence, fairness, honesty—that may be necessary for sustaining human relationships in all but the most dysfunctional societies.

A parallel line of research has studied gender differences, arguing that girls learn to emphasize caring, whereas boys incline toward rules and justice. Unlike the predictions made by culture theory, however, these gender claims have not held up. The original research that claimed to find gender differences lacked proper control groups. Well-designed studies of American children—for example, those by Lawrence Walker of the University of British Columbia—rarely detect differences between boys' and girls' ideals. Even for adults, when educational or occupational levels are controlled, the differences disappear. Female lawyers have almost the same moral orientations as their male counterparts; the same can be said for male and female nurses, homemakers, scientists, high school dropouts and so on. As cultural theorists point out, there is far more similarity between male and female moral orientations within any given culture than between male and female orientations across cultures.

Generational differences are also of interest, especially to people who bemoan what they see as declining morality. Such complaints, of course, are nothing new [see "Teenage Attitudes," by H. H. Remmers and D. H. Radler; SCIENTIFIC AMERICAN, June 1958; and "The Origins of Alienation," by Urie Bronfenbrenner; SCIENTIFIC AMERICAN, August 1974]. Nevertheless, there is some evidence that young people today are more likely to engage in antisocial behavior than those a generation ago were. According to a survey by Thomas M. Achenbach and Catherine T. Howell of the University of Vermont, parents and teachers reported more behavioral problems (lying, cheating) and other threats to healthy development (depression, withdrawal) in 1989 than in 1976 (above). (The researchers are now updating their survey.) But in the long sweep of human history, 13 years is merely an eye blink. The changes could reflect a passing problem, such as overly permissive fashions in child rearing, rather than a permanent trend.

—W.D.

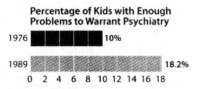

Percentage of Kids with Enough Problems to Warrant Psychiatry

1976   10%

1989   18.2%

0 2 4 6 8 10 12 14 16 18

KIDS THESE DAYS are likelier to need mental health services, judging from parents' reports of behavioral and emotional problems.

EDWARD BELL; SOURCE; THOMAS M. ACHENBACH AND CATHERINE T. HOWELL

the following experiment. We brought groups, each of four children, into our lab, gave them string and beads, and asked them to make bracelets and necklaces for us. We then thanked them profusely for their splendid work and rewarded them, as a group, with 10 candy bars. Then the real experiment began: we told each group that it would need to decide the best way to divide up the reward. We left the room and watched through a one-way mirror.

Before the experiment, we had interviewed participants about the concept of fairness. We were curious, of course, to find out whether the prospect of gobbling up real chocolate would overwhelm their abstract sense of right and wrong. To test this thoroughly, we gave one unfortunate control group an almost identical conundrum, using cardboard rectangles rather than real chocolate—a not so subtle way of defusing their self-interest. We observed groups of four-, six-, eight- and 10-year-old children to see whether the relationship between situational and hypothetical morality changed with age.

The children's ideals did make a difference but within limits circumscribed by narrow self-interest. Children given cardboard acted almost three times more generously toward one another than did children given chocolate. Yet moral beliefs still held some sway. For example, children who had earlier expressed a belief in merit-based solutions ("The one who did the best job should get more of the candy") were the ones most likely to advocate for merit in the real situation. But they did so most avidly when they themselves could claim to have done more than their peers. Without such a claim, they were easily persuaded to drop meritocracy for an equal division.

Even so, these children seldom abandoned fairness entirely. They may have switched from one idea of justice to another—say, from merit to equality—but they did not resort to egoistic justifications such as "I should get more because I'm big" or "Boys like candy more than girls, and I'm a boy." Such rationales generally came from children who had declared no belief in either equality or meritocracy. Older children were more likely to believe in fairness and to act accordingly, even when such action favored others. This finding was evidence for the reassuring proposition that ideals can have an increasing influence on conduct as a child matures.

Do the Right Thing

But this process is not automatic. A person must adopt those beliefs as a central part of his or her personal identity. When a person moves from saying "People should be honest" to "I want to be honest," he or she becomes more likely to tell the truth in everyday interactions. A person's use of moral principles to define the self is called the person's moral identity. Moral identity determines not merely what the person considers to be the right course of action but also why he or she would decide: "I myself must take this course." This distinction is crucial to understanding the variety of moral behavior. The same basic ideals are widely shared by even the youngest members of society; the difference is the resolve to act on those ideals.

Most children and adults will express the belief that it is wrong to allow others to suffer, but only a subset of them will conclude that they themselves must do something about, say, ethnic cleansing in Kosovo. Those are the ones who are most likely to donate money or fly to the Balkans to help. Their concerns about human suffering are central to the way they think about themselves and their life goals, and so they feel a responsibility to take action, even at great personal cost.

In a study of moral exemplars—people with long, publicly documented histories of charity and civil-rights work—psychologist Anne Colby of the Carnegie Foundation and I en- countered a high level of integration between self-identity and moral concerns. "People who define themselves in terms of their moral goals are likely to see moral problems in everyday events, and they are also likely to see themselves as necessarily implicated in these problems," we wrote. Yet the exemplars showed no signs of more insightful moral reasoning. Their ideals and Kohlberg levels were much the same as everyone else's.

Conversely, many people are equally aware of moral problems, but to them the issues seem remote from their own lives and their senses of self. Kosovo and Rwanda sound far away and insignificant; they are easily put out of mind. Even issues closer to home—say, a maniacal clique of peers who threaten a classmate—may seem like someone else's problem. For people who feel this way, inaction does not strike at their self-conception. Therefore, despite commonplace assumptions to the contrary, their moral knowledge will not be enough to impel moral action.

The development of a moral identity follows a general pattern. It normally takes shape in late childhood, when children acquire the capacity to analyze people—including themselves—in terms of stable character traits. In childhood, self-identifying traits usually consist of action-related skills and interests ("I'm smart" or "I love music"). With age, children start to use moral terms to define themselves. By the onset of puberty, they typically invoke adjectives such as "fairminded," "generous" and "honest."

Some adolescents go so far as to describe themselves primarily in terms of moral goals. They speak of noble purposes, such as caring for others or improving their communities, as missions that give meaning to their lives. Working in Camden, N.J., Daniel Hart and his colleagues at Rutgers University found that a high proportion of so-called care exemplars—teenagers identified by teachers and peers as highly committed to volunteering—had self-identities that were based on moral belief systems. Yet they scored no higher than their peers on the standard psychological tests of moral judgment. The study is noteworthy because it was conducted in an economically deprived urban setting among an adolescent population often stereotyped as high risk and criminally inclined [*see* box, "Could You Live with Yourself?"].

At the other end of the moral spectrum, further evidence indicates that moral identity drives behavior. Social psychologists Hazel Markus of Stanford University and Daphne Oyserman of the University of Michigan have observed that delinquent youths have immature senses of self, especially when talking about their future selves (a critical part of adolescent identity). These troubled teenagers do not imagine themselves as doctors, husbands, voting citizens, church members—any social role that embodies a positive value commitment.

How does a young person acquire, or not acquire, a moral identity? It is an incremental process, occurring gradually in thousands of small ways: feedback from others; observations of actions by others that either inspire or appall; reflections on one's own experience; cultural influences such as family, school, religious institutions and the mass media. The relative importance of these factors varies from child to child.

Teach Your Children Well

For most children, parents are the original source of moral guidance. Psychologists such as Diana Baumrind of the University of California at Berkeley have shown that "authoritative" parenting facilitates children's moral growth more surely than either "permissive" or "authoritarian" parenting. The authoritative mode establishes consistent family rules and firm limits but also en-courages open discussion and clear communication to explain and, when justified, revise the rules. In contrast, the permissive mode avoids rules entirely; the authoritarian mode irregularly enforces rules at the parent's whim—the "because I said so" approach.

Although permissive and authoritarian parenting seem like opposites, they actually tend to produce similar patterns of poor self-control and low social responsibility in children. Neither mode presents children with the realistic expectations and structured guidance that challenge them to expand their moral horizons. Both can foster habits—such as feeling that mores come from the outside—that could inhibit the development of a moral identity. In this way, moral or immoral conduct during adulthood often has roots in childhood experience.

As children grow, they are increasingly exposed to influences beyond the family. In most families, however, the parent-child relationship remains primary as long as the child lives at home. A parent's comment on a raunchy music lyric or a blood-drenched video usually will stick with a child long after the media experience has faded. In fact, if salacious or violent media programming opens the door to responsible parental feedback, the benefits can far outweigh the harm.

One of the most influential things parents can do is to encourage the right kinds of peer relations. Interactions with peers can spur moral growth by showing children the conflict between their preconceptions and social reality. During the debates about dividing the chocolate, some of our subjects seemed to pick up new—and more informed—ideas about justice. In a follow-up study, we confirmed that the peer debate had heightened their awareness of the rights of others. Children who participated actively in the debate, both expressing their opinions and listening to the viewpoints of others, were especially likely to benefit.

In adolescence, peer interactions are crucial in forging a self-identity. To be sure, this process often plays out in cliquish social behavior: as a means of defining and shoring up the sense of self, kids will seek out like-minded peers and spurn others who seem foreign. But when kept within reasonable bounds, the in-group clustering generally evolves into a more mature friendship pattern. What can parents do in the meantime to fortify a teenager who is bearing the brunt of isolation or persecution? The most important message they can give is that cruel behavior reveals something about the perpetrator rather than about the victim. If this advice helps the youngster resist taking the treatment personally, the period of persecution will pass without leaving any psychological scars.

Some psychologists, taking a sociological approach, are examining community-level variables, such as whether various moral influences—parents, teachers, mass media and so on—are consistent with one another. In a study of 311 adolescents from 10 American towns and cities, Francis A. J. Ianni of the Columbia University Teachers College noticed high degrees of altruistic behavior and low degrees of antisocial behavior among youngsters from communities where there was consensus in expectations for young people.

Everyone in these places agreed that honesty, for instance, is a fundamental value. Teachers did not tolerate cheating on exams, parents did not let their children lie and get away with it, sports coaches did not encourage teams to bend the rules for the sake of a win, and people of all ages expected openness from their friends. But many communities were divided along such lines. Coaches espoused winning above all else, and parents protested when teachers reprimanded their children for cheating or shoddy schoolwork. Under such circumstances, children learned not to take moral messages seriously.

Ianni named the set of shared standards in harmonious communities a "youth charter." Ethnicity, cultural diversity, socioeconomic status, geographic location and population size had nothing to do with whether a town offered its young people a steady moral compass. The notion of a youth charter is being explored in social interventions that foster communication among children, parents, teachers and other influential adults. Meanwhile other researchers have sought to understand whether the specific values depend on cultural, gender or generational background [see box, "How Universal Are Values?"].

Unfortunately, the concepts embodied in youth charters seem ever rarer in American society. Even when adults spot trouble, they may fail to step in. Parents are busy and often out of touch with the peer life of their children; they give kids more autonomy than ever before, and kids expect it—indeed, demand it. Teachers, for their part, feel that a child's nonacademic life is none of their business and that they could be censured, even sued, if they intervened in a student's personal or moral problem. And neighbors feel the same way: that they have no business interfering

with another family's business, even if they see a child headed for trouble.

Everything that psychologists know from the study of children's moral development indicates that moral identity—the key source of moral commitment throughout life—is fostered by multiple social influences that guide a child in the same general direction. Children must hear the message enough for it to stick. The challenge for pluralistic societies will be to find enough common ground to communicate the shared standards that the young need.

The Author

WILLIAM DAMON remembers being in an eighth-grade clique that tormented an unpopular kid. After describing his acts in the school newspaper, he was told by his English teacher, "I give you an A for the writing, but what you're doing is really shameful." That moral feedback has stayed with him. Damon is now director of the Center on Adolescence at Stanford University, an interdisciplinary program that specializes in what he has called "the least understood, the least trusted, the most feared and most neglected period of development." A developmental psychologist, he has studied intellectual and moral growth, educational methods, and peer and cultural influences on children. He is the author of numerous books and the father of three children, the youngest now in high school.

Further Reading

THE MEANING AND MEASUREMENT OF MORAL DEVELOPMENT. Lawrence Kohlberg. Clark University, Heinz Werner Institute, 1981.

THE EMERGENCE OF MORALITY IN YOUNG CHILDREN. Edited by Jerome Kagan and Sharon Lamb. University of Chicago Press, 1987.

THE MORAL CHILD: NURTURING CHILDREN'S NATURAL MORAL GROWTH. William Damon. Free Press, 1990.

ARE AMERICAN CHILDREN'S PROBLEMS GETTING WORSE? A 13-YEAR COMPARISON. Thomas M. Achenbach and Catherine T. Howell in *Journal of the American Academy of Child and Adolescent Psychiatry*, Vol. 32, No. 6, pages 1145–1154; November 1993.

SOME DO CARE: CONTEMPORARY LIVES OF MORAL COMMITMENT. Anne Colby. Free Press, 1994.

THE YOUTH CHARTER: HOW COMMUNITIES CAN WORK TOGETHER TO RAISE STANDARDS FOR ALL OUR CHILDREN. William Damon. Free Press, 1997.

Playing With God

by Tracy Cochran

The mother of an eight-year-old thinks religion only becomes meaningful when its meaning is discovered by her child. The child declares she does not believe in religion or God, but believes in nature and science. With the exception to Christmas, the parents admit they rarely take their daughter to church. When they do, she complains they are ruining her Christmas. The parents are told they cannot impart their understanding of religion onto their daughter and that their daughter subconsciously understands spirituality.

RELIGION ISN'T FOR ME," announced my eight-year-old daughter, Alexandra, as we ate dinner together one January night. "I think of it like an old spider on the wall. I know that it's there but I try to ignore it."

Alexandra took a bite of pasta and studied my reaction.

"When I pray it's usually just for ordinary things, like 'Please, please, let me get an A on this test,' " she added.

Since Christmas, Alexandra had been making provocative statements about religion and prayer.

"I don't believe in God, I believe in Nature," my daughter continued. "Everything comes from Nature. We are Nature, Mommy. Church makes everything seem boring. Even a nice song like 'Jingle Bells' sounds really slow in church." "Jiiiinnnnglllle Bellllls. . . . "Alexandra lowered her voice and sang a kind of funeral dirge to underline her point.

On Christmas Day, my husband and I had taken Alexandra to Mass at St. Patrick's Cathedral. We rarely took Alexandra to church, but we had wanted her to see thousands of people from around the world praying together and solemnly rejoicing about the appearance of the miraculous on earth. I was trying to delicately engineer an impression that would lead her to suspect there is a finer intelligence or reality behind the world of appearances. But Alexandra hated the ca-

thedral that day. She found it crowded and cold, and wailed that we were ruining Christmas for her by bringing her there.

A wise man once said that trying to impart your understanding to others by talking is like trying to fill them up with bread by looking at them. Since Christmas, Alexandra had been struggling to give me bread. She has reminded me that kids know how to touch this finer world inside themselves although they rarely call this intimate connection prayer.

That January night I asked Alexandra if she ever thought about where the universe came from, big questions like that.

"Of course, but that's science!" she exclaimed. "I love science so much I would rather go to school naked than not be able to study it."

It is becoming clear to me that "science" to my little daughter isn't a strictly intellectual discipline but a license to explore with all her senses and imagination. The "scientific" ideas and questions that catch fire for her—"Is every atom made up of matter?" "What if you could make a machine that could look into a dog's brain? Would it even be worth it?"—are fresh and generative. Shot through with a sense of wonder at creation, Alexandra's "science" is akin to our most ancient way of being spiritual. Like other children who speak but aren't yet too adept at arguing for their own feelings and beliefs, my daughter has been inhabiting her body and the natural world with a sense of deep connection and curiosity. In his collection of essays, Living By Wonder, the educator Richard Lewis describes this childhood state as the time of "the incandescent virtues of 'why?' "

AT THE CHRISTMAS Mass, a big, stern-looking priest, one of many serving Communion that day, came and stood in the aisle a few feet from our pew. The faithful flowed forward, including Alexandra's grandmother, who had accompanied us. A young Mexican wearing a red hooded sweatshirt over a battered leather jacket followed Alexandra's grandmother. He was followed by a willowy matron in a fur coat, who was in turn followed by a tiny old woman dressed in black.

"The Body of Christ, the Body of Christ," the priest repeated as he held up the Communion wafers. Some people reached out with cupped hands like small children. Others opened their mouths to be fed in the traditional infant-like pose of surrender to a greater power. Alexandra slumped at the end of the pew and sighed and glowered. "It's just that I don't really feel comfortable anywhere there aren't plants and animals," she explained to me later. After the Mass, I took her up to inspect the life-size creche near the altar. I told her the Christmas story again, picturing it as a kind of time-release capsule of higher truth that would take effect in the future. I was providing Alexandra with a cosmic vision, with food for prayer. She asked me how the wise men picked Jesus to be this "big deal baby." I told her the wise men followed an unusual star that shone over the manger.

"I know about the star," said Alexandra. "But a star is as big as the sun, so that's like saying the sun is over your house. It's not really over your house, it's over the whole earth."

As we walked up an aisle toward the cathedral's main entrance, my husband pointed to a gaunt, haunted portrait of Christ above an altar tiered with flickering candles. He explained to Alexandra that this face was based on marks that were left on the Shroud of Turin.

"Excuse me?" asked Alexandra. "Has anybody seriously looked at this man? Like, maybe he could use a shave or something?"

I knew Alexandra was trying to provoke me, but there was a visceral question under her words that galvanized my attention. I wondered how any child could feel a connection to this tortured-looking man who lived two thousand years ago.

I thought of telling her that Jesus loved children, or that she could try to feel a connection by saying his name in her heart. But these answers felt cheap. Alexandra regarded me with a calm, grave expression. She

looked very small and very present in this cold, cavernous, crowded place.

"They kept calling Jesus 'the king,' " Alexandra continued. "How can one baby be the king of the whole world?"

"He didn't call himself a king," I said. "He called himself the son of man. He wanted to show us that we can all be like him."

"Then why did he want to be worshipped in a huge, fancy place like this?"

"I'm not sure he would have wanted to be worshipped like this," I replied.

"Then what are we doing here?"

Brought to a full stop, I asked Alexandra where she would like to celebrate Christmas.

"In the African savannah surrounded by animals," she said. "Only I wouldn't make the animals celebrate. They should be what they are and I would observe them."

Alexandra lit up as she spoke of this. It occurred to me that I had been too busy trying to teach Alexandra to stop and listen to her. As she talked, I remembered that the heart of prayer was the experience of being seen and heard by a loving, boundlessly accepting attention.

MONTHS BEFORE Christmas, while spending a weekend at the wooded upstate New York community of the Omega Institute, I had watched from a distance as a young camp counselor led Alexandra and a group of other children through the woods blindfolded. They were identifying different kinds of trees by hugging them and smelling them. When Alexandra took her turn she looked so radiant, so deeply engaged in the life around her that I knew, as I had the first moment I laid eyes on my daughter, that she was already part of that other world that I was trying so hard to lead her to. She knew innately how to feel her way into the heart of things.

In Living By Wonder, Lewis describes how children are able to "fuse with the object of their play." According to him, children innately seek to understand the world around them by drawing on their own sensations and feelings, their own bodily understanding of growth and change. Imagination in children, according to Lewis, is their ability to project their inner images and experience on to the world as a way of sympathetically knowing.

"Did the tree hug you back?" I had asked Alexandra.

"I don't like it when you talk that way," she'd answered, although she knows that I've caught her saying hello to things as if they were alive.

In The Spell of the Sensuous, philosopher David Abram describes the way indigenous people have preserved our innate "carnal, sensorial empathy" with the natural world. More in touch with their bodies and "animal senses" than modern city dwellers, indigenous people are more aware that the natural world around us is awake and speaking. I have seen that children also have this capacity to listen to the world around them with their "animal bodies," and they don't stop at the natural world. They fuse their sensations with their earliest feelings of well-being (and fear of abandonment) to know the One behind the world.

Although Alexandra would never use these words, there's a chance that when she was hugging trees she was finding God in the flesh of life. I know this because once I was a kid and risked playing at prayer.

When I was a little girl, there was a game I played when I couldn't sleep. Although I never thought of it as a prayer or used these words, it was my way of seeking God. I would peel off my blankets and slip down to the cold hardwood floor (I remember doing this mostly in the winter). The first few moments on the floor were my leap of faith. Freezing and feeling utterly exposed and alone, I thought of all the people and other beings who had no beds, no blankets, no shelter at all. These thoughts were a ritual that always made me feel gratitude or a stab of empathy. They made me feel connected to the rest of the world. I would also feel brave in a special way, as if I were daring to venture out on my own. I was not only dipping into dangerously big subjects, I was risking being seen by the unknown.

As I lay there a shift always took place. The labels I had about "cold" and "hard" gave way. I noticed that the polished hardwood was soft in its own way, more giving than stone or steel. As I listened to the wind blowing outside my bedroom window (the winter temperatures in Watertown, New York, often hit twenty and even thirty below zero), I imagined what it was like outside, and truly valued that I was in a warm, life-saving shelter. As I broke through the isolation of my thoughts and sank into the experience of my body, I began to sense that everything in the world had emerged from a mystery. Why was there a world and not nothing? As a child I couldn't help but ask the question with my whole being, and as I asked it I felt vibrantly alive and present in a living world.

I would scramble back up to my bed and experience its incredible softness, wondering how I could

have been numb to it before. I would pull up the sheet, savoring its smoothness. I would pull up the blankets and quilt one at a time, feeling unimaginably rich and relaxed and provided for. Even the air that touched my face was luxurious. I felt cradled in a benevolent, listening silence, and I knew without words that I had drawn closer to God by going deep within myself. It was a state that I would recapture many years later in moments of meditation and prayer.

Not all imaginary play expresses an impulse to prayer, of course. I played another game in which I was a deadly, superintelligent black panther named Striker. Striker liked to crouch in trees and stalk the other kids who came to play in my backyard. Like a fairy tale, this game let me play with some of my wildest energies. My prayer game, on the other hand, harbored the wish to see and be seen by a finer, larger intelligence.

Recently, Alexandra and I heard Kaddish recited for the first time. The prayer was so exalted, so utterly above sentimental condolence that it occurred to me that, as tradition says, it really may have been given to man by the angels. I resolved to read Alexandra the Beatitudes and the Psalms, and to teach her the Lord's Prayer.

I still have to restrain myself, in other words, from the impulse to drag Alexandra to the threshold of sacred truth. Yet on a deeper level I know that I have to let her find her own way. I try to remember now that what becomes truly meaningful to any one of us are those truths which we have discovered inside ourselves.

Still, there is a reciprocal exchange between Alexandra and me. A few nights ago, there was a new development. I found Alexandra curled up in bed with a book of Bible stories.

"I'm not religious, you know," she said, studying me over the top of the book. "But could you just let me read for five more minutes?"

TRACY COCHRAN is co-author of Tranformations: Awakening to the Sacred in Ourselves (Bell Tower Books) and a contributing editor of Tricycle: The Buddhist Review.

Unit 5

Unit Selections

Social Issues
28. **Buried Alive,** David Denby
29. **It's 4:00 p.m. Do You Know Where Your Children Are?** Jonathan Alter
30. **Of Power Rangers and V-Chips,** Chris J. Boyatzis

Special Challenges
31. **The Effects of Poverty on Children,** Jeanne Brooks-Gunn and Greg J. Duncan
32. **Victimization of Children,** David Finkelhor and Jennifer Dziuba-Leatherman
33. **Resilience in Development,** Emmy E. Werner
34. **Creating False Memories,** Elizabeth F. Loftus
35. **Escaping from the Darkness,** Howard Chua-Eoan

Key Points to Consider

❖ Do you know what it's like to be a latchkey child? If you were a working parent confronted with inadequate child care for your school-age children, what arrangements would you be prepared to make for your children? How could you help children to be active and responsible participants in their own care?

❖ Due to changes in family structure, many American children are at risk and living in poverty. What should our nation do to help children? If family breakdown is related to numerous problems for children, should public policy be designed to help reduce the enormous number of children living in poverty in our country?

❖ What is the role of television in child development? How might television contribute to many of children's and society's problems? What advantages does television have for children's development? What can parents and schools do to help children become more "media literate" to protect them from negative influences in television and advertising? How do you balance our First Amendment rights to free speech with the data showing a correlation between media violence and murder rates in this country?

❖ As a child, did you ever suffer from some form of victimization or exploitation? What were the responses of the adults and peers around you? What suggestions would you have to prevent what appears to be a very high incidence of childhood victimization? Why do you think some children make it against all odds and go on to thrive despite acute victimization?

❖ Have you ever had a childhood memory that you felt sure happened, which you later learned was completely false or untrue? If false childhood memories of sexual abuse can be created, how can the courts and the accused be protected? How can actual victims of childhood sexual abuse be vindicated? What can or should therapists do in balancing these two concerns when working with "victim" patients?

❖ Depression is a serious clinical psychological condition. Have you experienced or known of others who have suffered from depression? If so, did medication help to improve the condition? Why might you be more concerned about medicating a child than an adult for depression? Even if there are risks associated with medication, is it better to take the risk than to withhold drugs from these children? What would you do if your child was diagnosed with depression that required drug therapy?

 **Links** **www.dushkin.com/online/**

27. **Ask NOAH About: Mental Health**
http://www.noah.cuny.edu/illness/mentalhealth/mental.html

28. **Association to Benefit Children (ABC)**
http://www.a-b-c.org

29. **Children Now**
http://www.childrennow.org

30. **Council for Exceptional Children**
http://www.cec.sped.org

31. **National Black Child Development Institute**
http://www.nbcdi.org

32. **Prevent Child Abuse America**
http://www.preventchildabuse.org/fs.html

These sites are annotated on pages 4 and 5.

Social scientists and developmental psychologists have come to realize that children are influenced by a multitude of social forces that surround them. In this unit we present articles to illuminate how American children are influenced by broad factors such as economics, culture, politics, and the media. These influences also affect the family, which is a major context of child development, and many children are now faced with more family challenges than ever. In addition, analysis of exceptional or atypical children gives the reader a more comprehensive account of child development. Thus, articles are presented on special challenges of development, such as poverty, violence, sexual abuse, and learning disabilities.

"Buried Alive" raises difficult and provocative issues about how American children today are faced with the challenge of unprecedented levels of change in the family, society, and larger popular culture. For example, the connection between broader societal values and the concomitant pressures exerted on educational practices has placed more demands on schools. At the same time, while we may espouse the need to hold onto certain core societal values, our popular culture often appears to directly contradict these core values. This essay helps us to take stock of the complex ways in which our society sometimes sends conflicting messages to our unsuspecting children.

Another influence on children is television, the "electronic family member." Nearly all American homes have a television set, and two-thirds of them own at least two sets. In fact, more families in the United States have a television set than a telephone. Given that by the time children graduate from high school they will have spent more time watching television than attending school, their exposure to television is likely to affect many aspects of development. "Of Power Rangers and V-Chips" discusses legislative changes regarding violent programming and the potentially negative and dangerous effects of television violence on children's development.

Some children all around the world are faced with challenges such as attention deficit disorder, autism, sexual abuse, and other forms of exploitation. These children are often misunderstood

and mistreated and pose special challenges to parents, teachers, and society. Are schools and families prepared to deal with such children? Teachers and parents need information to be better able to identify and deal with these children. These issues are discussed in "The Effects of Poverty on Children," "Victimization of Children," and "Resilience in Development."

False memories of childhood is a heated topic in many courtrooms when it comes to allegations of child sexual abuse. Elizabeth Loftus, a prominent scientist on the study of memory, describes this research in "Creating False Memories" and discusses how suggestion and imagination can lead to the creation of childhood memories that never occurred.

Depression is a psychological condition most people do not associate with children. Today, however, almost 1 million children in America suffer from this disorder and take medication. "Escaping from the Darkness" reports on this trend and reports on the risks of medication and what parents and teachers should know about depression in children.

Cultural and Societal Influences

BURIED ALIVE

Our children and the avalanche of crud.

DAVID DENBY

MAX, my older son, who just turned thirteen, once had a thick green carpet in his room, a tufted and matted shag that my wife and I inherited from the previous owners of our West End Avenue apartment, in New York. When Max was six or seven, we spent a good deal of time kneeling in the carpet, cleaning up his toys, and down there in the green we got to thinking about the moral nature of his education. Pennies, rubber bands, paper clips, marbles, peanut shells, dirty socks, toy soldiers, wooden blocks, G. I. Joes, crayons, dollops of synthetic slime—a sort of kiddies' bouillabaisse, a thickening brew of plastic and metallic stuff—gathered in the shag. It was the landscape of the American child.

One day, the carpet was covered with hundreds of pieces of plastic, and I sat among them, overwhelmed. A friend of Max's had just been over, and the boys had dumped boxes of toys on the floor. There were Legos, of course—the plugged and stamped modular pieces that fit together in innumerable combinations—but also the mobile olivegreen figures of the Teenage Mutant Ninja Turtles, along with He-Man and Skeletor, and odd figures from "Sesame Street" and two or three toy groups I couldn't identify. On the floor was the plastic detritus of half a dozen . . . what? Not toys, exactly, but toy systems, many of which were also available as a television show or a movie, or

both, with links to computer games, video-arcade games, comic books, regular children's books, clothes, and cereal boxes. Each part of the toy system sold another part, and so Max was encased in fantasy props—*stuff*—virtually to the limits of his horizon.

Idly, I extracted one of the superheroes from the carpet and broke off its arm.

TO my surprise, I find myself welcoming, or at least not opposing, the advent of the V-chip—the little device that is to be installed in new television sets sold from 1998 on and that will allow parents to block out programs they don't want their children to see. Many parents I know have similar feelings, and quite a few are surprised by the depths of their ambivalence and in some cases misery on the subject of the plastic on the carpet—upset by the way pop culture in all its forms has invaded their homes, and the habits, manners, and souls of their children. My friends are drawn from a small circle of well-educated New Yorkers; we are a fairly compact and no doubt privileged group. Yet our anguish about bringing up children is, I believe, widely shared by parents of all kinds. Child-rearing is at once the most prosaic and the most mesmerizing subject in the world. The nagging, repetitive tasks it requires—and the wrenching obsessions—reach across regional, class,

and political lines. "Married . . . with Children" and the computer game Doom are the same in Montana and in Manhattan.

No one I know expects that the V-chip will make much difference. The chip is no more than a finger in a dike that has already sprung a thousand leaks. In the past two decades or so, pop has triumphed, defeating all but a few pockets of resistance, absorbing or marginalizing the older, "high" arts, humbling the schools, setting the tone for an entire society. The children live in it, but, of course, their parents also live in it, and this is part of the confusion. How can you fight what you enjoy yourself? I am a film critic and I see more than a hundred movies every year, which puts me in the worst possible position when I berate my children for watching too many movies. My wife, a novelist, loves the new crop of girl rockers. In our family, "The Simpsons" is a source of wonder and "The Empire Strikes Back" and endlessly repeated pleasure.

Even parents who enjoy their share of pop are feeling wary and sore, as if someone has made fools of them. And a few parents I know have given themselves over to bitter rage and are locked in an unwinnable struggle to shut out pop culture and the life of the streets—the two are now indistinguishable—from their children's experience. Acting out of fear and love, and perhaps out of spiritual ambition, too, they have turned themselves into

 From *The New Yorker*, July 15, 1996, pp. 48–54, 56–58.

authoritarians, banning television, banning many kinds of "unsuitable" movies. There is so much to forbid—perhaps a whole culture to forbid! And in so doing, these parents risk making the forbidden glamorous and dangerous; they risk cutting the children off from their friends and bringing them up as alienated strangers in the electronic world of the future.

I don't want to be like them, but I understand their absolutism. We are all in the same boat, afloat in the boundless sea. For both relaxed and authoritarian parents, the real issue is much larger than bad TV shows and movies. (There are always some good ones.) We all believe in "choice," but our children, to our chagrin, may no longer have the choice *not* to live in pop. For many of them, pop has become not just a piece of reality—a mass of diversions, either good or bad, brilliant or cruddy—but the very ground of reality. The danger is not mere exposure to occasional violent or prurient images but the acceptance of a degraded environment that devalues everything—a shadow world in which our kids are breathing an awful lot of poison without knowing that there's clean air and sunshine elsewhere. They are shaped by the media as consumers before they've had a chance to develop their souls.

The usual response to such complaints is a sigh or a shrug or, alternatively, exhortations like "Get tough with them. Take control of what they see, what they read and listen to." Parents who think of themselves as conservatives often say this, and their assumptions give them a tactical advantage: they don't have to make so many choices; they are more likely to establish inflexible general principles for what their children can see and do and to insist on parental authority regardless of any contrary evidence or argument. If sex is something children should not see in movies, that's the end of the discussion. Yet the issue is not so simple, especially for parents like me and my wife, who are not eager

to stand over the children, guiding their progress all day long like missionaries leading the savages to light. To assume control over their habits and attitudes, we would have to become bullies.

In fact, our two boys are far from addicted to television, but like many American children they consider themselves entitled to a certain amount of TV and to video games and movies as well. As far as they are concerned, such pleasures come with the territory: consuming media, they think, is part of what children do. No doubt I should have been tougher with them; I should have made it clear when they were younger that watching TV was not an entitlement but a privilege. (The awful word makes me wince, but I'm sorry now that I didn't say it.) At this point, we are stuck with the usual compromise, which the children accept in principle: We establish limits—only so much TV, only certain movies, and so on. But there are always arguments, discussions, trades, and other negotiations, and we have come to realize that asserting control over the boys' tastes is no longer possible beyond a certain point. How can you control what they breathe?

MANDATED as part of the Telecommunications Act (signed earlier this year), the V-chip is an attempt to give parents more control (or, realists would say, the illusion of control). At this moment, the Motion Picture Association of America, which has administered the movie ratings since 1968, is hoping to get a workable system in place by next January, a year before the V-chipped sets come out. Just like movies, television shows will be rated according to their suitability for children. Parents at home, using a secret code and a remote control, will set their new TVs at whatever ratings level they are comfortable with. Any show rated above that level will automatically be shut off.

But how do you rate an endless sea? There are broadcast network and broadcast local shows, network cable and local cable shows, and public television, too: perhaps a thousand hours or more a day of programming. It is less a series of discrete shows than a nation's shared environment—our communal glop, our feed, our ether, our *medium*. Movies are currently rated by a group of thirteen Los Angeles-area citizens with experience as parents, but no group of ten, twenty, or fifty citizens, not even one chained to the spot like the inhabitants of Plato's cave, can sit and rate all the shows. What to do? Jack Valenti, who is the head of the M.P.A.A., and an industry advisory board have decided that the distributors of programming—networks, stations, cable operators—perhaps in consultation with the writers and producers of the shows, will assign the ratings to themselves.

Can the producers and distributors rate themselves? It seems a dubious procedure. In any case, the sheer amount of stuff overwhelms any rational attempt to assess it. Such criteria as intelligence, dramatic interest, and style will not play much of a role in the ratings. A few shows that I might want my older son to see are likely to receive the equivalent of an R—for instance, the occasional PBS series "Prime Suspect," made by England's Granada Television, and starring Helen Mirren as the London police detective Jane Tennison. One recent episode, "The Scent of Darkness," detailed with grim intensity and admirable British levelheadedness the pursuit and capture of a serial killer. Most of Tennison's colleagues doubt her judgment in the case, and the true subject of the episode—and of Mirren's performance—is the moral gallantry of a woman fighting the coldness of male contempt. Burrowing deep within its peculiar, mazelike world, the drama was so convincing and intelligent that when my older son drifted in, my wife and I let him watch. (We shooed away Thomas, who is nine.) Mirren's fierce, driving anger, here sense that she has an obligation not only to the job but to herself—an obligation not to betray herself—is the essence of modern heroism, and Max, who has seen his share of thoughtlessly violent movies and TV shows, was impressed. Afterward, we talked it over. He wanted to go deeper into the plot and the characters, to understand everyone's motives. With the V-chip in place, however, viewers unfamiliar with the special qualities of "Prime Suspect" will probably not let their thirteen-year-olds see it.

POP culture hardly takes up all of my sons' lives. Their school gives them plenty of work. They read, though not as much as we'd like. (We also read to them and tell them stories and bits of history constantly.) They play basketball, go snowboarding, collect things, make friends everywhere; Max blades and rides, and Thomas plays the piano. If we put on Toscanini's recording of Beethoven's Seventh, they twirl and jump around the living room and carom off the furniture. They seem busier and more active than I was at nine or thirteen. Nevertheless, their absorption in pop is very intense.

When Max is at home on a Saturday, or on vacation, he may hit the computer as soon as he gets up, ignoring repeated entreaties to eat breakfast, and finally ignoring bowls of cereal placed under his nose as he plays one of the war-strategy games that he currently loves—Caesar II, say, set in ancient Rome, or Warcraft II, in which the player, in charge of the Humans, builds forts, towns, farms, and mills, all for the purpose of defeating the unspeakable Orcs, ardent little creatures who attack from many sides and emit anguished groans as they are hacked, maced, and cannonaded into the world below. (Children with a taste for perversity can take the side of the Orcs, or two kids can play against each other.) Warcraft is a big advance in complexity over the

point-and-shoot games like Wolfenstein 3-D or Doom, in which the player passes through three-dimensional corridors and mows down endless assailants. (In Wolfenstein, after killing all the S. S. guards, one finally kills Hitler; I have played the game myself with a certain amount of pleasure.) In Warcraft, having won a particular battle, the player graduates to a more difficult level, and is greeted there by the game's narrator, who speaks the medieval fustian that seems to have spread from the Emperor in the "Star Wars" trilogy to many areas of the kiddie culture. "A great host of Orcs have reconstructed the Dark Portal and now lay siege to the land of Nethergarde," the narrator says. The voice rings out in the house like some lugubrious fake who won't go home after a dinner party.

Max may then meet some friends and go for some lunch at the nearest Burger King, where he will eat a Double Whopper and drink a Coke and sternly ignore (I hope) the free dolls and other promotional appeals for "The Hunchback of Notre Dame." Afterward, the group of boys may drift to a violent special-effects debauch like "Mission: Impossible." Later, they may play some basketball in the park (baseball is not the game of choice for media kids), or just hang out at home and (if we let them) watch TV or a rented movie. As the kids sit watching, we shove plates of raw vegetables and roast chicken in their faces, which they sample, all the while demanding chips, Fritos, and Pop-Tarts. And so on, into the night. We intervene, pulling Max away from his friends, but on these occasions when we're at work and can't intervene, he's spent his whole day in media junk, including the food—a day of pleasure, companionship, and maybe heightened alertness, but little else.

Crashing into the kitchen, my sons talk in the private languages they've worked up from exposure to the shows, movies, computer games, rap music, and basketball players that matter to them. Children have

always spoken in tongues, living inside their jokes and insults—my friends and I did it forty years ago—but in recent years the talk has grown quicker, more jangled and allusive, shifting at near-electronic speeds from, say, imitations of Apu, the Kwik-E-Mart manager in "The Simpsons," to Darth Vader, then to Snoop Doggy Dogg and on to jaw-jutting taunts from "Ace Ventura" and other Jim Carrey movies. The children channel-surf their own minds. They can talk logically and soberly, but they seem at their happiest bopping through the apartment, like Robin Williams on a roll, the older one with his high, serious forehead and dark-brown hair parted in the middle, like a German scientist from 1912, and the younger one singing and crowing and then tumbling over his own lines.

"Whooha! Whooha! It is *you*, young Skywalker, who are mistaken. Alrightee then! Power and the money, money and the power. Minute after minute, hour after hour. Thank you, come again!"

SOMEONE is bound to say, "It was ever thus," meaning that, as far as their elders are concerned, every generation of children is immersed in something that's no good for them. New York kids in the eighteen-sixties grew up in a rough city with gangs, street violence, and prostitutes, and most of them were no doubt familiar with such raucous and unenlightening entertainments as cockfighting and bare-knuckle boxing. It was ever thus. After all, many of us watched a good bit of TV as children, yet we wound up O.K., didn't we? What has changed? In a famous essay from 1954, "Paul, the Horror Comics, and Dr. Wertham," the cultural critic Robert Warshow deplored the violence and nihilistic goofiness of such pulp as "The Vault of Horror" and "Crime SuspenStories," but concluded that parents were worrying too much about horror comics. Children, like his son Paul, were resilient; most of them would outgrow comic books and would pass on to more complex narratives.

In the nineties, a great deal more than horror comics is jabbing at children, but we can agree with Warshow that the kids stay interested in nothing for very long. The computer games and TV shows, for instance, mark and cut the path of their own extinction, quickly creating a restlessness that causes the child to turn against the games and the shows themselves. Children go from one craving to another, discarding—I don't know—"Looney Tunes" for "Superman," and "Superman" for "MacGyver," and "MacGyver" for "The Wonder Years," and "The Wonder Years" for Wolfenstein, and Wolfenstein for Sim City, and Sim City for Myst, and Myst for Doom, and Doom for Doom II. Nothing lasts. The restlessness produced by each station on this Via Dolorosa annihilates any chance for real devotion, and the child passes on. Finally the child passes *out*: he emerges at the other end of the media tunnel—though perhaps still ungratified.

My boys, after all, do not seem to be in dire trouble. They can be determinedly earnest on moral questions; they stand up for their friends and for powerless people. They are not, I think, likely to behave violently or commit crimes (the rewards for staying straight are too obvious), and if they screw up they will, like most white upper-middle-class children, be given a second chance, and a third, and they will probably do all right—they will probably come through.

But with what internal injuries along the way? It is a miserable question. Social scientists, looking for quantifiable results, have devised clinical experiments that measure the different effects of violence on children. These effects, which are apparently greater on boys, can be placed in three categories: direct imitation, which is rare, and the more frequent effects of desensitization (acceptance of violence as the way of the world) and a generalized fear-

fulness, a learned distrust and wariness. But as I write these words, I realize that the test results, however disturbing, are not the point. No social scientist need prove a direct effect on children's behavior for some of us to hate the bullying, conformist shabbiness of the worst pop and the way it consumes our children. If children are living in pop culture, and a good part of it is ugly and stupid, that is effect enough; the sheer cruddiness is an affront.

Individually, the games or shows may have little effect—or, at least, no effect that can't be overcome. But collectively, I'm not so sure. Even if the child's character is not formed by a single TV show, movie, video game, or computer game, the endless electronic assault obviously leaves its marks all over him. The children grow up, but they become ironists—ironists of waste. They know that everything in the media is disposable. Everything on television is just for the moment—it's just television—and the kids pick up this devaluing tone, the sense that nothing matters. Sold a bill of goods from the time they are infants, many of today's children, I suspect, will never develop the equipment to fight off the system of flattery and propitiation which soothes their insecurities and pumps their egos. By the time they are five or six, they've been pulled into the marketplace. They're on their way to becoming not citizens but consumers.

It was not ever thus. Our reality has changed. The media have become three-dimensional, inescapable, omnivorous, and self-referring—a closed system that seems, for many of the kids, to answer all their questions. The older children teach the younger ones the games and movie references, so they have something to talk about when they're alone. I've just run into a three-year-old girl who knew the names of the characters in "Hunchback" before the movie opened. Disney has already claimed her. Pop has also absorbed the oppositional energies that used to be associated with the

avant-garde and with minority cultures, making once brave gestures empty gestures, commodifying discontent, inbreeding it with the edgy, in-your-face tone that teen-agers adopt as the sound of independence. That jeering tone has spread like a rash through the whole culture. It's awesome. It sucks.

When my older boy lets fly a stream of epithets in the rancorous tones of an inner-city black teenager, I know that the joke is on me—the white liberal. But the joke is not on me alone, of course: rap is very popular in the suburbs. One of the most remarkable social transactions of our time is the widespread assumption by white middle-class boys of the attitudes of a genuinely dispossessed class of young black men. Commodification of rage plays strange tricks. When the triumphal or despairing rant leaves its source, where it serves as a passionate expression of survival and protest, and goes into the heads of middle-class white children, it serves very different needs, fuelling the emotional demands of pre-teens and teens who may be afraid of women and of the adult world in general. The kids know that the profane rap lyrics are a violation; they speak the words with an almost ecstatic sense of release. Their parents, however, experience those words as an angry assault, and they can either roll with the punches, in which case they feel they've become teen-agers themselves, or sternly disapprove, like the squares in a fifties teen-rebel movie. "Make a stand," I tell myself as I disapprove and forbid, but dignity is not much to fall back on.

Some sort of commercialized aggression is always putting parents on the defensive—Jim Carrey with ketchup coming out of his ears in movie after movie, or Sylvester Stallone machine-gunning the population of Cleveland, or video arcades with so many shooting games that the noise level exceeds that of the Battle of the Somme. "Beavis and Butt-head" is a clever show—it mocks the cruddy teen culture even as it sells it to teens. The show brilliantly sends itself up. Still, it's hard to take. You have to listen to that warthog snort-giggle-snort, so reminiscent of advanced lunacy, as well as the frequent butthole-buttwipe exchanges. Hip parents may appreciate the wryness of B. & B.'s self-extinction, but it's dismaying that everything on teen TV—even irony —is a commodity.

The kids in the dating-game programs treat each other as commodities, the girls swinging their shoulders and smiling as they show themselves off, the audience whooping as the boys pull off their shirts and reveal their pecs and tattoos. Hardly the end of Western civilization, I admit, but the way the shows force teens to stereotype one another is awful. Children don't understand vulgarity as a concept, and the makers of commercial culture would be happy if they never understood it. Parents have to teach them what vulgarity is somehow. When I have the energy, I argue, I satirize, I get the boys to agree that the shows are stupid. Yet I don't turn off the set, because doing that would only cause them to turn it back on when I'm not there. I want *them* to turn it off.

Whether the sets are off or on, the cruddy tone is in the air and on the streets. The kids pick it up and repeat it, and every week there are moments when I feel a spasm of fury that surges back and forth between resentment and self-contempt. In those moments, I don't like the way my boys talk—I don't like the way they think. The crude, bottom-line attitudes they've picked up, the nutty obsessive profanity, the echo chamber of voices and attitudes, set my teeth on edge. The stuff fits, and they wear it. What American parent hasn't felt that spasm? Your kid is rude and surly and sees everything in terms of winning or losing or popularity and becomes insanely interested in clothes and seems far, far from courage and selfhood.

Aided by armies of psychologists and market researchers, the culture industries reach my children at every stage of their desires and their inevitable discontent. What's lost is the old dream that parents and teachers will nurture the organic development of the child's own interests, the child's own nature. That dream is largely dead. In this country, people possessed solely by the desire to sell have become far more powerful than parents tortuously working out the contradictions of authority, freedom, education, and soul-making.

IN "The Republic" Plato declares that the young should hear nothing—not even a few discordant lines from Homer—that would form their characters improperly. Plato can mischievous, but he appears to be saying that young people will adopt only the behavior that they have heard about. Today, fundamentalists have taken up this concept of education like a cudgel. Salman Rushdie's impressionistic, dream-filled novel "The Satanic Verses," in which the narrator makes fun of Muhammad, is an attack on all Islam. Kill the novelist! An American commercial movie—say, "Sleeping with the Enemy"—that has a bad marriage in it is seen not as the dramatization of a single, fictional marriage but as an attack on the institution of marriage itself. Save the institution of marriage! Well-educated American conservatives who vilify popular culture for political ends appear to want entertainment that is didactic, improving, hygienic.

In a true liberal-arts education, however, children are exposed to many stories, from many sources. They hear about all sorts of behavior—wickedness and goodness and the many fascinating varieties in between—and are taught what a narrative is and what its moral relation to life might be. Narratives give many pleasures, one of which, surely, is the working out of the story's moral significance, either simple and redundant or complex, layered, and exploratory. Parents and teachers still hope that a complicated narrative will serve as a prelude, preparing children for the complexities of life. They will learn good by studying evil as well as good.

Thinking back to my own lazy days at thirteen, I remember noodling around the house and eating my way through boxes chocolate-chip cookies and watching old movies on TV—thirties comedies and musicals, forties thrillers and war movies, the narrative achievements of a studio system that, whatever else it did wrong, invariably managed to tell stories that pulled the viewer in. I was more passive, and certainly more isolated, than Max, but I was luckier in my movies: the movies were still a narrative medium.

The computer games, I suppose, offer a kind of narrative, but one that yields without resistance to the child's desire for instant gratification. Affording a momentary—and spurious—feeling of power, the summer's new big-budget action movies like "Mission: Impossible" and "The Rock" (and last year's "Batman Forever") offer larger versions of the same thing—increasingly jangled and incoherent narratives that also yield instantly to pleasure. I believe in pleasure, but I hate the way my boys are jacked up by the new movies without ever being drawn into the more enveloping and transforming enchantments of a beautifully worked-out story. They get used to feeling nothing but excitement. ("I don't like *drama*," I once heard one of Max's friends say with considerable exasperation.) An American adventure movie is now simply a violent movie—and, increasingly, an impersonally violent movie whose thrills refer almost entirely to earlier movie images. The Hollywood studios need to top last year's explosions, so they keep the children bucking on a roller-coaster ride to nowhere.

I wouldn't mind the boys' seeing a certain amount of violence in movies or on TV if the violence were dramatized as serious or tragic, or even playful—anything more than an electric prod to their already overstimulated nerves. Children need secrets and hidden places, they need to tempt the forbidden. And they can really learn from tasting temptation. The thrill of danger is good for them: many of the classic stories and movies for children are about danger. But in the big new action movies, no one humanly vulnerable—no one children could identify with—is placed in jeopardy, so there's actually little sense of danger.

Because they haven't been touched or shaken, children think that having seen one violent film justifies seeing another. A parent who vetoes a movie is likely to be told, "I've seen much more violent things than this," by which he means "and yet I've survived." The kid wants to test himself against the movie, as if it were a wild ride at an amusement park, and the parent who doesn't utter an immediate and final "no" either argues endlessly, or allows himself to be dragged along with a heavy heart.

Film critics who are parents have a particularly rough time of it. A friend of mine who is also a film critic was confronted by her older son holding the videotape of a horror movie.

"Can I look at this?"

"No, you cannot."

"Why not?"

"Because it's scary, I didn't like it, and I don't want you to see it."

At that point, the child turned over the box and read aloud a rave quote from his mother's review.

My own personal calvary: Without my permission, Max saw "Pulp Fiction" on tape at a friend's house a few months ago, and enjoyed it as a bizarre collection of wicked thrills. I told him I wished he hadn't seen it, but I suppose that in one way I should have been relieved. He wasn't yet far enough along in his education in media irony to see how funny the movie was. "Pulp Fiction" is play, a mocking commentary on old genres, a celebration of pulp flagrancy and violation as pleasure—the sport of a declining movie

culture in which sincerity is the only unforgivable sin. Habitual moviegoers savor the fizz in the drink, including the S & M scene, which is deliberately absurd. But I didn't explain this to Max. I saw no reason to expand a twelve-year-old's interest in "Pulp Fiction."

But then, having seen "Pulp Fiction," he wanted to leverage himself into seeing Quentin Tarantino's earlier and much nastier (and more pointless) "Reservoir Dogs." No, I said. But why not? he asked. After all, his friends had seen it. I told him I couldn't stop him from seeing it at someone else's house, but I would prefer that he not. In such exchanges, Max is saying to me (in effect), "If I'm not old enough to see the movie, how come I'm old enough to understand the reasons I'm not supposed to see it?" That is the ultimate question posed to the parents of a media child.

Sometimes we win, but often we give in, because there are moments when my wife and I want to talk to each other or to a friend on the telephone, or read, or work. A hundred dollars for a moment of peace! It's the eternal parental cry. And in those moments and hours I let the kids watch what's on TV or play some inane point-and-shoot computer game. I am grateful that the boys have something that bottles them up for a time. The media have suffused the children with pleasure and their parents with guilt.

CONSERVATIVE critics attack the media easily and comfortably. But do they acknowledge any culpability for allowing pop culture and consumerism to become such an overwhelming force in our country's habits of child-rearing? Conservatives would like to believe that capitalism and its extraordinary executive tool, the marketplace, are not only productive and efficient but *good*. Thus they may criticize the "excesses" of a company like Time Warner; they may even criticize "greed," as if greed were some bi-

zarre aberration normally unknown to capitalism. But they can rarely bring themselves to admit that capitalism in its routine, healthy, rejuvenating rampage through our towns, cities, and farmlands forces parents to work at multiple jobs, substitutes malls for small-city commercial streets and neighborhoods, and dumps formerly employed groups (like blacks in the inner cities) onto the street or into dead-end jobs. Or that these developments loosen parental control, and help create the very nihilism and anomie—the rootlessness of nowhere men—that find release in junk movies, rap, pornography, and the rest.

When it comes to pop culture, conservatives are the last innocents. Surely there's something pathetic about Bob Dole's calling for restraint from Time Warner, when it's precisely the unrestrained nature of capitalism that conservatives have always celebrated. Conservatives would make a lot more sense on the subject of popular culture if they admitted that the unregulated marketplace, in its abundant energy, is amoral, that it inspires envy and greediness, that it shreds "values" and offers little space or encouragement for what William Bennett calls "virtues." Parents deserve better than such ideologically motivated hypocrisies.

Nearly every parent, consciously or not, cherishes a kind of idealized time-table that proposes a mood—a state of readiness—in which a child can best be introduced to a new experience. Children's first responses—to nature, to death, to sex, to violence, to the arts, to the news that this world is often a dark and dirty place—obsess parents almost as much as providing proper food and education. In hoping to maintain a reasonable schedule, parents do not necessarily want to protect children's innocence. The schedule, after all, is a way of regulating the *loss* of innocence—opening up the world to children in a way that makes sense.

Parents can still control some of the schedule, but a large part of it has been wrenched out of their hands by pop culture. Is this a calamity? Not really. Middle-class parents are often squeamish and overprotective. Some children may be better off if they escape their parents' grip, healthier if they grow up wild and free and sort things out on their own. Still, the schedule is a lovely idea—one of the enduring talismans of middle-class family life. And parents, however discouraged they may have become, will always try to impose it. They consider imposing it their right. For parents, the early responses are central to the poetry and moral charm of childhood. And to have those intimate moments and pleasures preëmpted by someone's marketing scheme is like receiving a blow to the chest.

If conservatives are going to oppose any sort of government regulation of the marketplace, they can't be surprised that the market overwhelms parents, and that parents then complain that they have lost control. When toys, movies, books, and television shows are all devoted to the same product or performer and are marketed by different branches of the same company, can we rationally speak of free choice in the marketplace? The producers and the distributors may be free, but are the children?

LIBERALS, too, have an accounting to make. There is a strain of opinion regarding the arts which has reigned during the last few decades in most of the bourgeois democracies—in the United States, Australia, Great Britain, France, Germany, and the rest of Western Europe. Let us call it cultural libertarianism (its god is John Stuart Mill). Cultural libertarianism insists on the paramount importance of free expression. Therefore, cultural libertarianism, when it has to, defends, as a corollary, the right of artists to use violence and sex in their work. That exploiters will use violence and sex, too, is exasperating, but such is the price of freedom. There is no way *in law* of

curtailing exploiters without also curtailing artists. The market is tawdry, corrupt, and corrupting; it is also exhilarating. In a free society, art and schlock come joined together like ship and barnacle. The way to separate the two is with education and criticism.

Any other approach, cultural libertarians will argue, leads to censorship or (just as bad) self-censorship. In any case, politicized criticism of the media, whether from the left or the right, is often a form of self-righteous hysteria that inflames people against imaginary or relatively harmless dangers while diverting them from genuine social problems. In the United States, we should be less obsessed with popular culture than with the unequal distribution of goods and opportunities in an increasingly stratified society. Anyone can bring pressure on Time Warner, but how do you change an inner-city neighborhood?

So goes the orthodoxy of enlightenment practiced for decades by many people (including me). Many cultural libertarians would agree, of course, that a different set of rules should be brought into play when we are talking about children. The children should be protected; they don't have the right to see and hear everything. But *can* they be protected anymore? Has our social reality changed so much that the automatic celebration of freedom in itself puts children at risk? Cultural libertarians are now faced with a number of unnerving challenges to their self-esteem.

For one thing, the tone of our common culture has coarsened in the last couple of decades. Everyone has said so, and everyone is right. The boasting polygamists on trash TV, the rap lyrics, the rancorous and openly racist talk-radio shows—these are just the most obvious examples. We left-wing types popularized rudeness and slangy candor as a style of public discourse thirty years ago—our language, we thought, would discredit the official hypocrisies—and now everyone is going in

for it. With depressing effect: even those who love profanity may be dismayed to hear a former mayor of New York calling someone a "schmuck" on the radio. It is not the words that matter so much as the ravaging lack of dignity. The rout of gentility, which cultural libertarians sparked, has now been followed by the rout of self-respect. On ragged and exhausted nights, the wised-up tone of everything wears one down. As I go to sleep in our second-floor bedroom, I can hear couples dully cursing one another on the street, the words landing like blows. (That women now give as much as they get makes the sound no less melancholy.) When the clock radio clicks on in the morning, giggles and hoots accompany anyone trying to talk about a subject more serious than the weather. In the nineties, sarcasm is no longer a resistance to the marketplace; it *is* the marketplace. The constant atmosphere of selling creates a common ironic consciousness, the derisiveness of people in the know. And what do they know? That everyone is out for himself, that greed is what drives life forward. Derision has become the spirit of the jammed, crazy, relentless talk, the needling spritz of radio, of late-night TV, of kids teasing and threatening on the street. In these worlds, in our common world, no other kind of talk takes hold. If you aren't derisive, you're out of it. You're not in the market.

Adults learn to screen a lot of this out, but children don't necessarily do so. They enjoy it. They imitate it—and who can blame them? The media and the streets are far more exciting than school, where virtue so often comes packaged as learning.

Then there's the problem of pop growth: the huge increases in the formidability and quantity of mass culture—the new Fox network, the local and national cable operators, the Sony PlayStation and Sega and Nintendo systems, the innumerable computer games, and the rest. The problem is not simply that the stuff comes flooding in on children from all sides. The problem is that easy entertainment and self-serving communication of one sort or another (political speech, commercial messages, infotainment, advertorials, ego rants, self-promoting "confessions") increasingly push everything else to the margins. If you click through the channels, including the zillion cable channels, at different times of day, you will discover that serious communication of any sort is a tiny portion of what's available. One of the comedies of intellectual life in recent years has been the spectacle of the cultural left in the universities complaining that the words of women or minorities have been suppressed, when the exponential growth of mass communication has swamped just about anything of real consequence.

Cultural libertarians have been too complacently self-regarding in their defense of free expression. It's a noble position, a necessary position, never to be relinquished, but at this point it isn't enough. How valuable is the latest constitutional victory for freedom of speech if the general level of speech continues to be degraded? Moreover, some of the cultural libertarians, including me, have a minor crime to answer for—the too-easy use of such loaded words as "subversive" and "transgressive" to praise movies and rock albums that offer a little more sex and violence than other good movies and albums. A few years ago, liberal-minded cultural critics, terrified of standing with the squares, got bullied out of any sort of principled public resistance to pop. They took themselves out of the game, and left the field open for William Bennett's iron moralism.

THOMAS becomes annoyed when I question him about the Saturday morning kiddies' shows, in which, it seems, the world is always being saved by uniformed teens from some basso-voiced monster and his wicked female companion. Whatever I may think about the ho-mogenized nature of these shows, however, Thomas sees important differences among them. What he loved six months ago, for instance, he now regards as beyond the pale. The market has moved him along and made him contemptuous of what he has discarded. He's a very easygoing child, but, as far as he's concerned, his entertainment choices are not our business. Shyly, like suitors with hat in hand, we question his tastes and try to introduce him to the older arts, to the things we love. It may be ridiculous, but parents suffer a narcissistic wound when their children don't care about their favorite pictures, their books and music. Five years ago, we heard, on the car radio, Chuck Berry singing "Johnny B. Goode," and Max, who was then in the depth of his Billy Joel phase, said he liked it. We were absurdly happy. He likes Chuck Berry! When Tommy popped out of bed at eleven o'clock recently and, half asleep, asked me if we could listen immediately to all nine of the Beethoven symphonies, I began playing the "Eroica," and he fell back to sleep on the couch, a warrior at rest, as the music swirled over him.

Choice! It has to mean more for parents than an endless opening to the market. An active and engaged liberalism, while rejecting censorship, would encourage the breaking up of such vertically integrated culture monoliths as Disney, Sony, and Time Warner. It would ask for more regulation. (The V-chip is only the beginning.) It would, for instance, support the attempt of Reed Hundt, the reform-minded F.C.C. chairman, to require broadcasters to put on three hours of educational television a week. (Which might mean three fewer hours of trash.) And it would go far beyond the mere celebration of choice. It would insist on discrimination—not in the racial sense but in the cultural arena, where liberals, so eager to appreciate everyone's point of view, are often milky and weak. If parents are not to feel defeated by the media and pop culture, they must get over their reluctance to make choices that are based on clear assertions of moral values. They cannot leave to the "virtuecrats" the defense of religion, high culture, the meritocracy, the Western literary classics, or anything else that implies a hierarchy of taste. They have to join the discourse and make it aesthetically and morally alive.

ON vacation, away from Media City, without a television or a movie threatre in sight, I read to Max the novel that begins, "My father's family name being Pirrip, and my Christian name Philip, my infant tongue could make of both names nothing longer or more explicit than Pip. So I called myself Pip, and came to be called Pip." The same novel was read to me at the same age—not by my father but by an elderly teacher who entertained her students after lunch by reciting both "Oliver Twist" and "Great Expectations" in a Mid-westerner's gentle version of a thick Cockney accent. On vacation, Max became completely absorbed in the book, his eyes turning dreamy and inward-looking, and we read a great deal, for ninety minutes at a time. I was happy, too, because I was not on the carpet anymore, down there in the plastic rubble.

But then we returned to the metropolis. TV sets and computers, as well as school and friends, pressed in on all sides, and the reading slowly petered out. We read less every night, and after a while Dickens, who only weeks earlier had enchanted so tenderly, now seemed slow, laborious, convoluted, even boring. We've picked the book up a few times since, and my son is slowly climbing back into it—that he enjoys it, I have no doubt—but I don't know if we'll ever finish it. I would like to, and so would he, but Dickens's long, rolling sentences require peace and time, and the air is just too charged around here.

It's 4:00 p.m.
Do You Know Where Your Children Are?

The most dangerous time of day for kids isn't late at night. It's from 2 p.m. to 8 p.m., when children are out of school and their parents are still working. This can be crime time, and prime time to get them on the right path.

BY JONATHAN ALTER

IT'S 4 P.M., AND SGT. MIKE GWYNES of the Jacksonville, Fla., police department is maneuvering his squad car past Jack Horner and Goldilocks toward Cinderella Street, where some teens are hanging out at a bus stop. Down in the Sweetwater section of town, the streets have fairy-tale names, but it's the kids who risk turning into pumpkins. And not at midnight. "The problem's 3 p.m. till about 8 p.m., when they go home unsupervised and get in with the wrong crowd," Gwynes says, making a sharp left. Over on Bo Peep, a few teenagers are playing some rough basketball in a driveway; on Tinkerbell, the activity looks a bit more suspicious. Drugs are a big problem here.

Up on Wilson Boulevard sits a big solution. An old National Guard armory restored by the Jacksonville Children's Commission now serves as an innovative charter school, a police substation and a Boys & Girls Club all rolled into one. At 4 p.m. the 5- to 9-year-olds are playing kickball, the 10- to 12-year-olds are playing board games or finishing up "Power Hour" homework help and the older kids are in the teen center, playing pool and flirting, under adult supervision. Cursing risks a fine (25 cents) and boomboxes aren't allowed, which means some kids won't show up. But plenty of others do, including some just out of juvenile detention. Youth crime in the area has plummeted.

It doesn't take a Ph.D. to figure out that young people need some place positive to go after school to stay off the streets and out

Jacob Inlong
CALIFORNIA

SEVEN-YEAR-OLD JACOB was worried about the rain. For the first half of the school year, the second grader had to hang around the playground of his school for two hours every afternoon until his folks could pick him up. His working parents hated leaving him without activities, but had to spend their child-care resources on Jacob's 2-year-old brother. After months on a waiting list, Jacob was admitted to one of his city's best after-school programs—one inside the school, 40 yards from his playground.

of their empty homes. If they end up in jail, in drug treatment or pregnant, we all pay. And even if they're good kids from good neighborhoods, we're anxious. A NEWSWEEK Poll shows that the number of Americans who worry "a lot" that their kids will get involved with troublemakers or use drugs or alcohol was up by a full one third since 1990. With 17 million American parents scrambling to find care for their school-age children during work hours, the problem keeps growing.

More than a decade after the media discovered "latchkey kids," the answers are still elusive. When budgets get tight, after-school programs—wrongly dismissed as "frills"—

are often cut first. When talk turns to society's worst problems, it's easy to shrug off concerns about kids home alone watching afternoon television or hanging with friends. After all, many of their parents did the same, and turned out just fine.

BUT TIMES HAVE CHANGED, and not just because "Jerry Springer" has replaced Jerry Mathers (the star of "Leave It to Beaver") as the TV babysitter. Among cops, social-service types and policymakers, there's a new awareness that structured activity during out-of-school hours is absolutely critical to confronting many of the country's most vexing social problems. For years, local TV-station public-service announcements sternly intoned: "It's 10 p.m. Do you know where your children are?" It was the wrong question. The answer was usually yes; relatively few kids are allowed to roam freely at that hour. Only one seventh of all juvenile crime is committed in the late night and early morning. But substitute "4 p.m." and millions of parents would have to answer no.

If idle hands are the Devil's workshop, the hellish consequences are being felt in the American heartland. Crime is down in metropolitan areas, but up in hundreds of small communities, especially among kids. Drug use in suburban middle schools is surging. Many rural counties now report teen-pregnancy rates equal to those in big cities. Sixty percent of the cases of sexually transmitted diseases are contracted by teens. The absence of parents from the home in the after-

Jeremy Reese
ALABAMA

JEREMY (PEEWEE) REESE has a wide choice of after-school programs in and around the Metropolitan Gardens housing project—he just doesn't always feel like joining in. The sixth grader sometimes drops by an inner-city athletic club for a little basketball or pool, but the volunteers won't hesitate to kick him out if he gets out of line. When that happens, he heads over to Marconi Park, even though he says two Disciples gang members approached him there last summer. "I told them 'I don't want to'," says Peewee, who lives with his grandmother. "They'll get you in trouble." He doesn't want to be in a gang, but he says he's not interested in the homework teachers assign him for the afternoons, and he doesn't often feel like following the rules. What does he want? "If I can't be a ballplayer, I want to be a judge. I want to be the one that makes the decisions."

noon has made it much more convenient to get into trouble. More than three quarters of first-time sexual encounters occur at someone's house (usually the boy's). "We had to use Chevys," says criminologist James Alan Fox of Northeastern University. "Now kids don't need cars. When the cat's away, the mice will have sex."

And commit crimes, both petty and serious. Juvenile crime *triples* starting at 3 p.m. In fact, the 2 p.m. to 8 p.m. period—"Crime Time"—now accounts for more than 50 percent of all youth offenses. Not your kid, you say? Well, he or she might be a victim; they outnumber perpetrators of crime by 10 to 1. Juvenile homicide, which has doubled in a decade, is usually connected to after-school fights, not late-night crime. But even for those who don't worry about a potential Jonesboro massacre in their neighborhood, everyday teen problems of all kinds get worse when the last school bell rings.

The research confirms common sense. According to one University of Southern California study, eighth graders looking after themselves were more likely to smoke, drink and use marijuana than those who have some supervision after school. Another study of sixth graders showed those in "self care" were more likely to get poor grades or behave badly.

Good youth-development programs not only keep kids safe, they often change their lives. Finally, social policymakers are getting the message. Last week Vice President Al Gore stumped for the administration's after-school initiative and foundations funded by

Charles Stewart Mott and George Soros planted some seed money. Organizations like Save the Children (which until recently concentrated its efforts overseas) are also turning to this issue. So is Colin Powell's America's Promise, an umbrella group for hundreds of nonprofits and corporations that's working to secure millions more "safe places" for kids (sidebar).

The struggle starts in the schools, which in many places still close in midafternoon. Even wealthy communities are beginning to recognize the folly of locking buildings for large chunks of the day when they're needed for recreation, tutoring and arts. Some districts embrace change: for years, Murfreesboro, Tenn., has kept schools open from 6 a.m. to 6 p.m. Others are actually moving in the wrong direction. Recently, Atlanta horrified child-development experts by canceling recess on the theory that there wasn't "enough time" for a break between classes. But the school day extends only until 2:30 p.m. Why? The current school schedule—six hours a day, nine months a year—was invented when the United States was an agrarian nation and children were needed in the fields.

Today, three out of four mothers of school-age children work outside the home. So it's not so surprising that by the time they are 12 years old, nearly 35 percent of American children are regularly left on their own. For the rest—the lucky ones—parents work by remote control to pull together a patchwork of supervised activities: soccer on Tuesdays, Scouts on Wednesday. Some child-care programs provide terrific enrichment; others amount to little more than warehousing. TV and videogames usually fill the gap. The average American child spends 900 hours a year in school—and 1,500 hours a year watching television.

For the working poor, having their kids watch TV at home is often the *best* option—far better than the streets. But the child-care arrangements can be alarming. According to a study sponsored by Wellesley College, more than 15 percent of low-income parents reported that their 4- to 7-year-old children regularly spent time all by themselves, or in the care of a sibling under the age of 12. Neighbors—who for generations helped out absent parents by shushing the kids—are no longer around much, either.

The schools that poor children attend are unlikely to have after-care. Currently only 30 percent of American schools offer after-hours supervision, and the vast majority of them charge fees. The average cost to parents is $45 a week per child, or more than $2,000 a year, which is too much for many who need it most. The YMCA, the largest provider of after-school activities, serves half a million kids a day from all backgrounds. But even Y's cost an average of $36 a week. The equation is straightforward: "If parents are well off, they purchase after-school care.

Anthony Scimeca
Kelsey Kordas
ILLINOIS

"NO HUGGING!" SHOUTS ONE of a dozen teenagers at Vanessa Swanson's suburban house, and everyone laughs. "I guess it's reasonable that we can't hug at school," says Anthony, 12—but here there are fewer rules for him and his buddy (not girlfriend, they insist) Kelsey, 13, to follow. The kids know to call in and tell their folks where they are and what they are doing. This usually amounts to playing Nintendo 64, jumping on the trampoline and blasting dance music. "If I didn't come here, I'd probably be at the mall," says another 13-year-old. "But it's a cool place to hang out." Vanessa's working mom, Victoria, thinks it's worth investing in a case of soda a day to give the group a place to go. "At first I had some concerns," she says. "But at least I know where my kids are."

If they're poor, [the kids] often get nothing," says Indianapolis Mayor Stephen Goldsmith, one of many mayors now trying to find new solutions.

Among the biggest backers of after-school programs are the nation's police chiefs, who argue that recent reductions in crime, while gratifying, are temporary. "We've come to the realization that we're not going to arrest our way out of this problem," says Salt Lake City Police Chief Ruben Ortega, who heads an association of big-city police chiefs. "If we don't change our strategy, we'll be complaining in five or 10 years about how bad crime has gotten again."

Los Angeles is a good object lesson. Until Proposition 13 in 1978, all L.A. schools offered after-school enrichment programs. By 1992, when riots broke out in the wake of the Rodney King verdict, not one public high school had anything after school except interscholastic sports. The riots erupted in mid-afternoon. Would as many kids have been on the streets to join in if they had had somewhere else to go? Would the city's gang problem have gotten so out of hand? A program called L.A.'s Best is now trying to bring back after-school programs in a few schools. The waiting lists are long.

This is not touchy-feely do-gooder territory. A survey of 548 police chiefs showed them favoring prevention programs by an astonishing four-to-one margin over tougher sentencing and more cops on the street. But their lobbying often falls short in Washington and state capitals. When it comes to crime, "politicians believe in the three R's: Retribution, Revenge and Retaliation, which they think takes them to the fourth R—Re-Election," says Fox.

There are signs that the politics of prevention might be changing. Gore, for example, has seen how the after-school issue resonates, and he's grabbing it. After a town meeting in New Orleans last week, he held a teleconference with local officials from Atlanta to Anchorage, Alaska, who are working on answers. One common worry: the organizational headaches involved in bringing schools, churches, parents, nonprofits, corporations and different levels of government together. That takes a new breed of leader at the local level.

In Washington, Republican attacks on "midnight basketball" as liberal waste helped sink prevention programs in 1994. But the stigma is wearing off. As part of its child-care plan, the Clinton administration wants to spend $200 million a year for after-school programs. The idea is to get schools and community nonprofits working together to serve an additional 500,000 kids a year on school grounds. At best, however, even with matching contributions from nonprofits, that's only one tenth of the 5 million "latchkey" kids.

'I Wasn't Left to Myself'

When I was a kid, the safety net protected me. Here's how to put it back in place.
BY GEN. COLIN POWELL

WHEN I WAS growing up in the South Bronx, I was as liable to be led astray by the temptations of the street as any other inner-city youth, then or now. Left to myself, I could have ended up on Rikers Island rather than chairman of the Joint Chiefs of Staff.

But I wasn't left to myself. The tough neighborhood of Banana Kelly where I grew up had a heart: people cared about kids. I was surrounded by family, church and a wonderful public-school system. And when I set off to school each morning, I had an aunt in every other house, stationed at the window with eyes peeled, ready to spot the slightest misbehavior on my part and report it back to my parents. The instant communication of today's Internet pales in comparison to the "Aunt-Net" I remember from my childhood.

My relations weren't the only caring adults who took an interest in my welfare. I think of Jay Sickser, the kindly merchant who gave me my first job—helping out at his store after school. Or the folks at the Young Men's Hebrew Association who provided me with a place where I could spend time in a secure environment. Given a safety net with a mesh that fine, it took *work* for even the most rambunctious kid to get into real trouble.

Fast-forward several decades. Today our society is materially richer, but it is easier than ever for kids to go wrong—in the suburbs as in the cities. Because many of the social structures that once kept our kids secure have broken down, we have today's appalling data on juvenile crime, gangs, drug abuse, pregnancy and dropouts. We know juvenile crime and other pathologies are at their worst in the hours immediately after school lets out. It is just common sense that if we don't provide young people with some kind of sanctuary —I call them "safe places"— and give kids something constructive to do once the last bell rings, they are going to be easy marks for drug dealers, gang recruiters and other predators.

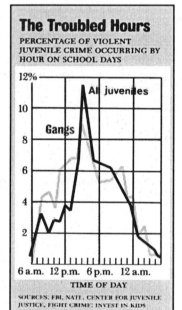

The Troubled Hours
PERCENTAGE OF VIOLENT JUVENILE CRIME OCCURRING BY HOUR ON SCHOOL DAYS

TIME OF DAY

SOURCES: FBI, NAT'L CENTER FOR JUVENILE JUSTICE, FIGHT CRIME: INVEST IN KIDS

A safe place can be a YMCA, a Boys & Girls Club, a rec room at a house of faith, a playground or a school. Ronald McDonald House Charities has donated $4 million to keep a hundred Chicago schools open after hours so that children can have a safe place until their parents pick them up. Not long ago I visited St. Elizabeth's Hospital in Beaumont, Texas. St. Elizabeth's is part of a program called Health Adventures, in which hospital staff members mentor needy youngsters. While I was there, one young man proudly told me about the medical skills he had acquired by learning to suture an orange. He might just grow up to be a brain surgeon.

Safe places do not have to cost a lot of money. In many instances, the building or location already exists; all you need are volunteers to donate their time. A few dollars contributed to a local youth service organization—or a few hours invested in being a mentor—can make a safer world for kids today and a better world for all of us tomorrow.

POWELL is chairman of America's Promise—The Alliance for Youth. Those interested in volunteering should call 888-55-YOUTH.

In the NEWSWEEK Poll, **64%** of parents worry at least a little about their children's getting hurt or into trouble if a parent can't be with them after school

FOR THIS NEWSWEEK POLL, PRINCETON SURVEY RESEARCH ASSOCIATES INTERVIEWED 500 PARENTS OF CHILDREN AGE 6–17 JAN. 16–26. THE MARGIN OF ERROR IS +/- 5 PERCENTAGE POINTS. THE NEWSWEEK POLL © 1998 BY NEWSWEEK, INC.

Benny Morales
OREGON

WHEN 8-YEAR-OLD Benny gets home from school, it's not his mom but his brother Cesar who is waiting at the door to their mobile home. Cesar, 16, does his best to keep both Benny and Eloy, 13, occupied until their mother comes home from her waitressing job around 9 p.m. "I feel safe with my brothers," says Benny. "All you do at day care is play Legos, and I don't like Legos." Twice a week, Eloy walks the second grader to T-Ball practice, but most afternoons in this economically depressed rural town are extremely quiet. When it starts to get dark, the boys sit down in the kitchen to do homework and help Benny with his school projects, dishing up dinner from a pot their mother Edith Sanchez has left bubbling on the stove whenever they get hungry. Cesar says he doesn't mind the way things are. How long will he be the caretaker? "As long as it takes."

THE REPUBLICAN LEADERSHIP in Congress opposes the Clinton plan, but doesn't want to go into the November midterm elections with no after-school program in hand. As a result, Congress is giving $20 million a year directly to the Boys & Girls Clubs of America. That's better than nothing, but the money will build only a few new clubs a year—and address one hundredth of the after-school problem. Unlike many social challenges, this one is not hugely expensive; $2 billion or $3 billion a year would go a long way toward solving it.

Skeptics say that even the best programs can't attract tougher kids who prefer life on the streets. Maybe so. Gang members very rarely quit their gangs. But predators can be made less dangerous. In Ft. Worth, Texas, 1,000 gang members go to "Coming Up" programs at eight Boys & Girls Clubs for late-night recreation and counseling. The police, at first dubious, are now pleased with the decline in gang-related violence.

But programs to reach out to the estimated 650,000 gang members across the country are still scarce. The key: when programs are established, they must be well run—or risk driving gang members away for good. "We need to make sure positive things will happen for the kids who are there, or they'll leave," says Sanford Newman of a Washington, D.C., group called Fight Crime/Invest in Kids.

The stakes couldn't be higher, and not just for the kids themselves. The larger society has a huge financial interest in confronting this problem. Juvenile crime surges at 14 and drops off at 18. Experts agree that if kids can get through this four-year period, the chances are good they will stay out of serious trouble. If they don't, the aggregate fiscal consequences are astronomical. Combining jail costs and lost taxes, career criminals cost taxpayers an estimated $1 million each during their lives. The United States now has 15 million at-risk children, several million of whom are in danger of going off track in the next 10 years. According to Ray Chambers, a financier and chair of America's Promise (which grew out of last year's Presidents' Summit in Philadelphia), that sends the stakes in this crisis into the hundreds of billions of dollars.

Back at the converted armory in Jacksonville, it's nearly 5 p.m. Some cops are talking about taking a few kids to a Go Kart track, or maybe to play some pinball. Navy Lt. Cmdr. Robert Sanders, who helped start the youth center, is reflecting back on his own life. "I think back to the kids I grew up

Stephen Ruggs
MASSACHUSETTS

ASK STEPHEN RUGGS WHERE he would be without the Rev. Eugene Rivers's after-school program, and he doesn't hesitate. "I'd be at the park somewhere, where people beat up on other people just for looking at them." Or worse—the 14-year-old had a friend who he says was killed over a $2 I.O.U. Instead, Stephen is bent over a table at the Ella J. Baker House, a renovated Victorian building in the rough Boston neighborhood of Dorchester, working hard at an anti-smoking campaign he and his friends in the program will be presenting to younger children. Stephen's grandparents, both of whom work for the city transit authority and have raised him since he was a baby, see Baker House as "a haven," and the boy agrees. "The kids here are the lucky ones," he says.

with who are not dead or in jail. What did we have in common? Those who succeeded had some kind of structure that let us go to the next level. A few years ago, the big thing was to say that kids had to have food in their stomachs to think. But that's not enough. We have 8-year-olds raising 3-year-olds and they're supposed to grow up to compete in the world economy? Our whole future, our national security, depends on what kids can do tomorrow." And that depends on what they do this afternoon.

With T. TRENT GEGAX, CLAUDIA KALB, DEBRA GWARTNEY *and* ADRIAN MAHER

46% of parents say it is very important that schools stay open all day; **43%** think after-school activities should be a high priority despite limited education budgets

Of *Power Rangers* and V-Chips

Chris J. Boyatzis

These are exciting times for people who care about children and what they watch on television. The latest wave of public and political debate about television has generated some encouraging outcomes. A major legal and political change is the Telecommunications Act of 1996, part of which calls for more educational programming for children, ratings for TV shows, and, beginning in early 1998, the inclusion in new television sets of the V-chip—a device that will allow parents to electronically block certain programs.

A major scientific change is the undertaking of the largest study ever on the effects of TV, the National Television Violence Study (NTVS), begun in 1994. The project is being conducted at four major universities across the country and is supervised by a council or representatives from 17 national organizations concerned about television. Their findings are informing public and political discussion about chil-

Chris J. Boyatzis, Ph.D., is assistant professor of psychology at Bucknell University. Chris has conducted research on the effects of television on children. At home he has two young children and two old TVs.

dren and television (Federman 1997).

I have been particularly interested in these changes ever since coworkers and I conducted an experiment several years ago on *The Mighty Morphin Power Rangers,* the most popular children's program of the mid-90s. In our study (Boyatzis, Matillo, & Nesbitt 1995), children in an elementary after-school program were randomly assigned to one of two groups. One group of children was shown, on one day during their after-school program, one episode of *Power Rangers.* Following this viewing we observed the children at play with their peers and recorded the number of aggressive acts. On another day we observed the other group of children, who were not shown the program, in normal, ongoing play and recorded the number of aggressive acts toward their peers. We found that after viewing just one episode, children—especially boys—committed aggressive acts seven times more often than did control children who did not see the show. Children who viewed *Power Rangers* typically used karate chops and flying kicks against their peers in direct and obvious imitation of the Power Rangers' actions.

Given the popularity of *Power Rangers,* our study is important because it was, as far as we can tell,

the first systematic assessment of the show's impact on children. The mix of the show's popularity and our findings—it made children aggressive—attracted extensive media attention for nearly two years.

When our findings were distributed through the media, we received many calls and letters from the public. A veteran kindergarten teacher in California lamented, "I can hardly do any teaching because of the time I spend on *Power Rangers* discipline problems." A grandfather from Michigan called to express worry about his two grandchildren who, after watching the show, were uncharacteristically hostile in their play. A mother wrote to say that after watching the show, her daughter kicked her in the legs, saying, "The Power Rangers do it."

The anecdotal testimony echoed the large majority (86%) of parents in a massive national survey who observed changes in their children's behavior after the children had watched a violent program (Levine 1994). But there were also defenders of *Power Rangers,* such as the mother who said the show offered heroic role models to children. Others claimed the show was merely the latest harmless fad for children. Some argued that the prior TV rage—*Teenage Mutant Ninja Turtles*—didn't inspire kids to kill each other;

older critics charged that their countless childhood hours watching Superman and the Lone Ranger beating up bad guys didn't make them violent criminals. Finally, the producers of the program and the Fox network, which airs it, defended the show as a source of positive role models and prosocial messages (Weinstein 1994).

Recently *The Mighty Morphin Power Rangers* has undergone changes, mostly cosmetic (it is now titled *Power Rangers Turbo*, there is a new villainess, etc.). Concerns remain, however, about this and other violent shows. I offer some below, putting them into an empirical context from the social science research. Although I focus on this program, the criticisms apply to many other children's programs as well.

Why worry about Power Rangers *and violent TV?*

1. **The show is extremely violent, and it makes children aggressive.**

In fact, according to the National Coalition on Television Violence, a nonprofit organization that has analyzed the content of children's programs since 1980, it is the most violent children's program ever (Kiesewetter 1993). The average Saturday morning cartoon has 20 to 25 violent acts per hour; *Ninja Turtles* had more than 90 violent acts an hour. Where did the original *Power Rangers* fit into this hierarchy of gratuitous violence? At the top, with 211 violent acts per hours. As recently as the 1995–96 season, the show was classified by one group in the NTVS project in the "sinister combat violence" category (Cole 1996).

Our first study (Boyatzis, Matillo, & Nesbitt 1995) provided direct evidence that children become more aggressive after watching *Power Rangers*. We then conducted a second study (Boyatzis, Matillo, Nesbitt, & Cathey 1995), surveying 263 parents of school children about their children's viewing habits and the par-

ents' beliefs about *Power Rangers*. We also had children's teachers rate the children's aggressiveness and altruism. We found that the more girls watch the show, the more aggressive they become; for boys the correlations were in the expected direction but not significant.

Although this study was correlational and hence cannot prove causality, it suggests that *Power Rangers* is associated with aggression. Did parents notice an effect on their children? Across the four different schools in this study, 70–80% of the parents said that after watching the show their children acted more aggressively toward friends, siblings, and even the parents themselves.

Our findings are not surprising. Scientific research from the past 30 years has demonstrated that viewing TV violence increases real-life aggression in children and youth (for reviews see Stein & Freidrich 1975; Heller & Polsky 1976; Hearold 1986; Huesmann & Eron 1986; Liebert & Sprafkin 1988; Paik & Comstock 1994). However, our studies were important for demonstrating for the first time a strong link between *Power Rangers* viewing and children's aggression.

Despite these findings, I must offer two important qualifications and rejoinders to them. First, *not all children are influenced in the same way by TV violence.* Indeed, our first study (Boyatzis, Matillo, & Nesbitt 1995) found that boys but not girls became much more aggressive after viewing *Power Rangers;* further, not all boys showed heightened aggression.

But let us remember that research rarely, if ever, offers guaranteed deterministic relationships between variables (such as that violent TV makes *all* children aggressive). Instead, research provides probabilistic relations: rather than black-and-white absolutes, we get odds and expectations.

Research over three decades shows unequivocally that the odds are that watching violent TV *increases the likelihood* that children will be more aggressive. This statement is as true as saying, for example, that

smoking cigarettes strongly increases the risk of serious health problems, even though smoking doesn't guarantee that all smokers will suffer them. Of course there are exceptions to the rule because individuals differ and other factors influence outcomes, but the general rule is clear: watching TV violence increases the risk for real-life aggression.

Second, *TV violence is not the only cause of aggression.* There are many causes, from societal to family factors (e.g., corporal punishment) to children's temperaments (see Eron 1987; Singer, Singer, & Rapaczynski 1989). Nevertheless, aggression is largely a learned behavior, and television is one of the teachers. Given that children watch so much TV—more than 25 hours a week on average—it is a pervasive and potent teacher.

How does viewing violent TV make children more aggressive? By watching others be aggressive, children learn new forms of hostile and dangerous behavior. This is *observational learning,* and it is perhaps the most long-confirmed mechanism for increased aggression (Brandura, Ross, & Ross 1961, 1963; Bandura 1965). Also, by watching others be aggressive, children become desensitized toward violence and more tolerant of real-life aggression (see Drabman & Thomas 1974; Thomas et al. 1977). Finally, watching violent TV promotes the internalization of aggressive scripts that can guide children's behavior (see Huesmann & Eron 1984; Eron 1987). These mental scripts are correlated with children's actual aggression (Huesmann & Guerra 1997), and they promote the use of some behaviors (e.g., hitting others to resolve conflicts) and inhibit the use of nonviolent alternatives.

2. **The show's violence is unrealistic.**

Despite violence that should leave the characters bloodied, immobile, or even dead, the Power Rangers seem immune to injury. This is typical for children's programs—consequences of violence are rarely

What Can Parents and Teachers Do?

Because our work received wide media attention—segments on *20/20, Entertainment Tonight,* and many local news stations; radio spots; extensive newspaper coverage—I would like to believe that our research on *The Mighty Morphin Power Rangers* contributed to the latest surge of public debate about television and children. For the sake of individual teachers and parents who feel they have little voice in this national discussion, I must note that the media attention was instigated by a single brief letter we wrote to the *Los Angeles Times* criticizing *Power Rangers.* Perhaps there's a moral here about "the power of one."

One concrete outcome of this public debate is the Telecommunications Act of 1996, which calls for, among other things, producers to provide more educational programming for children and ratings for their programs, and for TV manufacturers to build in V-chips. The 1996 act provides steps toward greater personal control of the medium in the home, in contrast to previous, less explicit telecommunications acts. The breadth of these legal actions reflects the complex ecology of factors in the role of TV in children's lives, which has been addressed by a number of researchers (e.g., Anderson & Bryant 1983; Pino, Huston, & Wright 1989; Truglio et al. 1996; Cantor, Harrison, & Nathanson 1997).

Taking action

There are several ways that parents concerned about their children might mitigate the aggression-inducing impact of *Power Rangers* and other violent or undesirable programs. The most effective step would be to unplug or remove the family TV. However, this may not be possible or even desirable since much of the educational programming for children has proven benefits. Presuming we keep the TV in the house, we need to strive for better TV management. At the very least, parents should not put television sets in children's bedrooms, where viewing time and programs are most difficult to monitor or discuss.

In the home, parents could "just say no" to programs that are offensive or unacceptable. While this can be jus-

tified in light of research on TV violence, it may not be feasible. For example, *Power Rangers* airs daily in many markets, which may make it more difficult to monitor. And exacerbating this problem is the fact that children frequently watch TV by themselves. In our survey study, 75% of parents said they do not watch *Power Rangers* with their children, a level of unmonitored children's viewing found by others for television in general (St. Peters et al. 1991).

Leave it to the V-chip?

Of course, the proposed V-chip technology, due in early 1998, should facilitate parents' prohibition of unwanted programs. But we can anticipate V-chip complications. Besides the obvious one—parents' difficulty in figuring out how to program the V-chip—there are other, more serious issues. For example, what percentage of parents will buy a new TV equipped with the chip? Will it be enough to make a difference? Further, how will we determine if the chip has the positive impact its proponents anticipate? I presume (and hope) researchers will study families to learn about family dynamics and child behavior before and after the chip. Such research will be necessary to demonstrate any positive change in children and, at a broader level, in society due to greater parental control over children's TV consumption. If such changes do not materialize, the television industry and other defenders to the medium will wag an "I-told-you-so" finger and repeat their standard line: societal problems are due to many things, but what children and adults watch on TV isn't one of them.

I also foresee problems stemming from V-chip technology. Producers might use the availability of the technology as a defense for abdicating their own responsibility for programming, placing the burden fully on parents. The industry could take the position that if parents don't want their children to view a program because it's too violent, sexual, or adult, they can use the V-chip to block it. Thus, the television industry may use the existence of the V-chip as justifica-

tion for producing programming that is more offensive than the current fare in terms of violence or sex. This could make the full spectrum of television programs worse and be especially problematic for those families without a chip-equipped TV. Finally, I worry that parents may come to rely on the technology as an easy fix, thereby reducing parent-child discussion about what is appropriate for children to watch and what isn't. If these scenarios are played out, the V-chip will be a solution that exacerbates the problem it was designed to remedy.

Another issue in banning unwanted shows—whether via V-chip or parental fiat—is that such action may create a forbidden-fruit syndrome: children will want even more to watch the programs because they are banned. Current research on the use of ratings for television programs supports this presumption. The television industry now applies the ratings of the Motion Picture Association of America (MPAA). These ratings (G, PG, PG-13, R) give guidance only on the age-appropriateness of programs. The National Television Violence Study found that the more restrictive ratings ("PG-13: Parents strongly cautioned" and "R: Restricted") increase a show's attractiveness to 10- to 15-year-olds, whereas the rating of "G: General audiences" lowers interest in it (Cantor, Harrison, & Nathanson 1997; Federman 1997). Banning a program is not as simple or even as desirable as it may seem.

Strategies for parents

Parents can try several strategies for managing their children's TV viewing. One approach is to *put children on a "reduced Power Rangers diet"*: if children are watching *Power Rangers* four times a week, reduce their viewing to once or twice a week. Parents might also want to share responsibility with children by giving older school children a "TV ration" that allots a specific number of hours per week for viewing, leaving it primarily to the children to choose the programs.

I know several sets of *parents and children who have struck a deal*—the children can watch *Power Rangers* (or any other violent show) as long as they don't imitate its violence—leading to kids happy to watch the show and parents pleased that their children aren't behaving aggressively.

Another tactic is to *watch TV with your child and discuss the programs*. This approach probably enhances children's critical-viewing skills. In fact, Cantor and Harrison (1996) found that children whose parents watch and discuss programs with them are less interested in programs that carry restrictive warnings or ratings, perhaps because the discussions promote the child's internalization of the parents' standards.

In addition to discussing the programs, *parents can draw on their ingenuity*. To help her child recognize the level of violence in *Power Rangers*, one mother had her son count the number of aggressive acts in a 10-minute segment. The child became exasperated, unable to keep track of the fighting. In another case, a creative father allowed his child to watch *Ninja Turtles* only if the child imagined an additional turtle named Gandhi who would settle conflicts with nonviolent means (Levine 1994).

I tried some of these tactics myself. When I first saw *Power Rangers*, its violence led me to ban it from my then-7-year-old's viewing options. After taking this just-say-no stance, I realized the discussing the show with her might be more beneficial. We watched several episodes together and generated nonviolent solutions for the Power Rangers' problems. We also discussed how unrealistic it was for them to emerge unscathed after so much fighting. Finally, watching the program together allowed me to highlight and reinforce the show's prosocial messages.

Such shared viewing and analysis might help children develop a form of TV literacy that will serve them as future viewers. Given the pervasiveness and influence of TV, media literacy should be part of the curriculum beginning in elementary school. And schools concerned about violence might also implement a violence-prevention curriculum for children (see Grossman et al. 1997).

Strategies for schools

At school, teachers, administrators, and parent-teacher organizations should consider taking a stance on offensive programs. One elementary school nurse, to ensure that parents were aware of *Power Rangers'* violent content, sent a letter to parents asking them to sign it to confirm that they had watched the show. Schools (teachers, school nurse) might record accidents and injuries related to *Power Rangers* or other action shows. Parents and schools may be more motivated to confront the program's effects if they discover that many injuries or fights are related to the program.

A course of action for all

Finally, let your views be known. Parents, educators, and concerned citizens can write to local television stations, advertisers, politicians, and media to express concern. The new telecommunications act (Telecommunications Act of 1996) facilitates contacting TV stations because it requires stations to make available a staff person as liaison with viewers who want to comment on children's programs.

Just months after the current ratings system for TV programs was implemented, the television industry and child advocacy groups engaged in heated argument, moderated by the Federal Communications Commission, about revising the ratings to include specific information about a show's content (e.g., sex, violence, offensive language). This change is due largely to the outcry from parents and child advocacy groups for improvements in the ratings system.

Guidelines based on content will be better not only because they give parents more information about programs, but because content advisories such as "mild violence" or "graphic violence" actually reduce five- to nine-year-olds' interest in those programs (Cantor, Harrison, & Nathanson 1997).

Finally, parents and educators can stay informed on other TV-management approaches by reading available resources, such as *The Smart Parent's Guide to Kids' TV* (Chen 1994).

shown (Potts & Henderson 1991)—and troubling, as exposure to unrealistic depiction of violence and injury-free action increases children's risk-taking and injurious behavior (Potts, Doppler, & Hernandez 1994).

3. The show has high visibility.

For two solid years *Power Rangers* was the most popular children's TV program in the country for two- to eleven-year-olds. In many TV markets the show airs daily. This high visibility is reason to worry because, as many studies have shown, the more children are exposed to TV violence, the more likely they are to imitate it.

4. The Power Rangers are actually people, not cartoon characters.

Part of the show's appeal may be that the characters are played by real actors who "morph" into Power Rangers. This is unfortunate because children are more likely to imitate the behavior of real people than that of animated cartoon characters (Bandura, Ross, & Ross 1963).

5. The Power Rangers are heroes.

The Power Rangers are "the good guys," exalted for their violent tactics against their enemies. Even when the characters are their normal, nonmorphed teenage selves, they are admired by other characters (often for their expertise in martial arts). Such high status is reason to worry because the more a character is rewarded for performing an aggressive act, the more likely children are to imitate it (Bandura & Walters 1963).

6. The Power Rangers are mostly male role models.

The majority of the Power Rangers are male, and their action is highlighted in most episodes. Our first study found that boys who viewed *Power Rangers* were much more aggressive than were any of the other children, perhaps because of the surfeit of male role models to identify with and emulate.

7. The show offers unfavorable representation of females and minorities.

The source of evil in the show's first several seasons was a shrill and dastardly Asian female, Rita Repulsa, whereas the Power Rangers' leader was a more dignified White male. (Though no longer Asian, the current villain is still a female and is dressed in revealing clothes.) Such images may perpetuate racist and sexist notions and reinforce the idea that it is normal or even wise to distrust and suspect people who are different (Carlsson-Paige & Levin 1990; Levin & Carlsson-Paige 1994).

8. The Power Rangers' prosocial messages are lost amidst the violence.

A redeeming feature of the show is that the characters often state positive messages (e.g., "Express your anger responsibly," "Fight only in self-defense"). Some anecdotal evidence suggests that these messages might be working. A second-grade teacher wrote to say that some of her students endorsed the show because the characters "tell you good things, like not to pollute." A child remarked that the characters tell children, "Don't go on the evil side."

Unfortunately, research has found that children do not understand prosocial messages when the messages are embedded in violence. Instead, they attend to the fighting, which is troubling because "visual presentations of aggressive acts, independent of plot and dialogue, may be sufficient to engender aggression" (Huesmann et al. 1984, 771).

In our survey study we asked teachers to rate children's altruism. If *Power Rangers* is associated with altruistic, prosocial qualities, we would expect to find a positive correlation between viewing the show

and children's altruism ratings. Instead, we found that the more children watched the show, the lower their altruism scores.

In addition, the large majority of parents we surveyed did not think their children learned anything positive from the show. The show's excessive violence squanders an opportunity to teach children appropriate means for conflict resolution.

When we surveyed parents regarding what they thought about the program, about 60% wrote comments to the effect that the show was too violent. This finding is all the more striking, given that the words "violent" and "violence" did not appear anywhere on the survey we gave parents. Thus we did not cue them to express this concern. In sum, if the show has any prosocial benefit for children, we have yet to find it in our research and the television industry has yet to offer a shred of evidence.

Conclusions

Recent developments, such as program ratings and V-chip technology, will surely evolve, and other unanticipated changes will come. It is unlikely, however, that a marked reduction in TV violence or even a significant decline in TV viewing by children will result from these developments. With the spread of cable, the growing number of stations, and the ubiquity of VCRs, the viewing options are greater than ever. Thus, it is all the more important that parents and teachers find ways to manage and use television so that it is a positive influence on children, not a negative one.

We cannot expect the television industry to do this, nor should we expect, or even want, the government to do so. But as both government and the industry itself take some encouraging legal and technological steps, let us put our own house in order. The harmful impact of *The Mighty Morphin Power Rangers* and other offensive programs may be mitigated by the types of action

suggested here, which are likely to be effective only when undertaken in earnest. Assuming that the TV will continue to bring violence and other unwelcomed fare into our homes, our children deserve at least these efforts from us.

References

Anderson, D. R., & J. Bryant. 1983. Research on children's television viewing: The state of the art. In *Children's understanding of television*, eds. J. Bryant & D. R. Anderson, 331–53. New York: Academic.

Bandura, A. 1965. Influence of models' reinforcement contingencies on the acquisition of imitative responses. *Journal of Personality and Social Psychology* 1: 589–95.

Bandura, A., D. Ross, & S. A. Ross. 1961. Transmission of aggression through imitation of aggressive models. *Journal of Abnormal and Social Psychology* 63: 575–82.

Bandura, A., D. Ross, & S. A. Ross. 1963. Imitation of film-mediated aggressive models. *Journal of Abnormal and Social Psychology* 66: 3–11.

Bandura, A., & R. H. Walters. 1963. *Social learning and personality development*. New York: Holt, Rinehart & Winston.

Boyatzis, C. J., G. Matillo, & K. Nesbitt, 1995. Effects of *The Mighty Morphin Power Rangers* on children's aggression with peers. *Child Study Journal* 25: 45–55.

Boyatzis, C. J., G. Matillo, K. Nesbitt, & G. Cathey. 1995. Effects of *The Mighty Morphin Power Rangers* on children's aggressive and prosocial behavior. Paper presented at the meeting of the Society for Research in Child Development, March, Indianapolis, Indiana.

Cantor, J., & K. Harrison. 1996. Ratings and advisories for television programming. In *National Television Violence Study*, vol. 1, ed. D. Kunkel, 361–410. Thousand Oaks, CA: Sage.

Cantor, J., K. Harrison, & A. Nathanson. 1997. Ratings and advisories for television programming. In *National Television Violence Study*, vol. 2, ed. B. Wilson, 267–322. Thousand Oaks, CA: Sage.

Carlsson-Paige, N., & D. E. Levin. 1990. *Who's calling the shots? How to respond effectively to children's fascination with war play and war toys*. Philadelphia: New Society.

Chen, M. 1994. *The smart parent's guide to kids' TV*. San Francisco: KQED Books.

Cole, J. 1996. *UCLA television violence report: 1996*. Los Angeles: UCLA Center for communication Policy.

Drabman, R., & M. Thomas. 1974. Does media violence increase children's toleration of real-life aggression? *Developmental Psychology* 10: 418–21.

Eron, L. D. 1987. The development of aggressive behavior from the perspective of a developing behaviorism. *American Psychologist* 42: 435–42.

Federman, J., ed. 1997. *National television violence study, vol. 2: Executive summary*. Santa Barbara: University of California, Center for Communication & Social Policy.

Grossman, D. C., H. J. Neckerman, T. D. Koepsell, P.-Y. Liu, K. N. Asher, D. Beland, K. Frey, & F. P. Rivara. 1997. Effectiveness of a violence prevention curriculum among children in elementary school. *Journal of the American Medical Association* 277: 1605–11.

Hearold, S. 1986. A synthesis of 1,043 effects of television on social behavior. In *Public communications and behavior*, vol. 1, ed. G. Comstock, 65–133. New York: Academic.

Heller, M. S., & S. Polsky. 1976. *Studies in violence and television*. New York: American Broadcasting Companies.

Huesmann, L. R., & L. D. Eron. 1984. Cognitive processes and the persistence of aggressive behavior. *Aggressive Behavior* 10: 243–51.

Huesmann, L. R., & L. D. Eron, eds. 1986. *Television and the aggressive child: A cross-national comparison*. Hillsdale, NJ: Erlbaum.

Huesmann, L. R., & L. D. Eron, M. M. Lefkowitz, & L. O. Walder. 1984. Stability of aggression over time and generations. *Developmental Psychology* 20: 1120–34.

Huesmann, L. R., & N. G. Guerra. 1997. Children's normative beliefs about aggression and aggressive behavior, *Journal of Personality and Social Psychology* 72: 408–19.

Kiesewetter, J. 1993. Top kids' show also ranks as most violent. *Cincinnati Enquirer*, 17 December, A1.

Levin, D. E., & N. Carlsson-Paige. 1994. Developmentally appropriate television: Putting children first. *Young Children* 49 (5): 38–44.

Levine, S. B. 1994. Caution: Children watching. *Ms.* July/August, 23–25.

Liebert, R., & J. Sprafkin. 1988. *The early window: Effects of television on children and youth*. New York: Pergamon.

Paik, H., & G. A. Comstock. 1994. The effects of television violence on antisocial behavior: A meta-analysis. *Communication Research* 21: 516–46.

Pinon, M. F., A. C. Huston, & J. C. Wright. 1989. Family ecology and child characteristics that predict young children's educational television viewing. *Child Development* 60: 846–56.

Potts, R., M. Doppler, & M. Hernandez. 1994. Effects of television content on physical risk-taking in children. *Journal of Experimental Child Psychology* 58: 321–31.

Potts, R., & J. Henderson. 1991. The dangerous world of television: A content analysis of physical injuries in children's television programming. *Children's Environments Quarterly* 8: 7–14.

Singer, J. L., D. G. Singer, & W. S. Rapaczynski. 1989. Family patterns and television viewing as predictors of children's beliefs and aggression. *Journal of Communication* 34: 73–89.

St. Peters, M., M. Fitch, A. C. Huston, J. C. Wright, & D. J. Eakins. 1991. Television and families: What do young children watch with their parents? *Child Development* 62: 1409–23.

Stein, A. H., & L. K. Freidrich, 1975. *Impact of television on children and youth*. Chicago: University of Chicago Press.

Telecommunications Act of 1996. U.S. Public Law 104, 105th Cong., 1st sess., 8 February 1996.

Thomas, M. H., R. W. Horton, E. C. Lippincott, & R. S. Drabman. 1977. Desensitization to portrayals of real-life aggression as a function of exposure to television violence. *Journal of Personality and Social Psychology* 35: 450–58.

Truglio, R. T., K. C. Murphy, S. Oppenheimer, A. C. Huston, & J. C. Wright. 1996. Predictors of children's entertainment television viewing: Why are they tuning in? *Journal of Applied Developmental Psychology* 17: 475–93.

Weinstein, S. 1994. Morphin mania: How—and why? *Los Angeles Times*, 26 February.

The Effects of Poverty on Children

Jeanne Brooks-Gunn
Greg J. Duncan

Jeanne Brooks-Gunn, Ph.D., is Virginia and Leonard Marx professor of child development and education, and is director of the Center for Young Children and Families at Teachers College, Columbia University.

Greg J. Duncan, Ph.D., is a professor of education and social policy, and is a faculty associate at the Institute for Policy Research, Northwestern University.

Abstract

Although hundreds of studies have documented the association between family poverty and children's health, achievement, and behavior, few measure the effects of the timing, depth, and duration of poverty on children, and many fail to adjust for other family characteristics (for example, female headship, mother's age, and schooling) that may account for much of the observed correlation between poverty and child outcomes. This article focuses on a recent set of studies that explore the relationship between poverty and child outcomes in depth. By and large, this research supports the conclusion that family income has selective but, in some instances, quite substantial effects on child and adolescent well-being. Family income appears to be more strongly related to children's ability and achievement than to their emotional outcomes. Children who live in extreme poverty and who live below the poverty line for multiple years appear, all other things being equal, to suffer the worst outcomes. The timing of poverty also seems to be important for certain child outcomes. Children who experience poverty during their preschool and early school years have lower rates of school completion than children and adolescents who experience poverty only in later years. Although more research is needed on the significance of the timing of poverty on child outcomes, findings to date suggest that interventions during early childhood may be most important in reducing poverty's impact on children.

In recent years, about one in five American children—some 12 to 14 million—have lived in families in which cash income failed to exceed official poverty thresholds. Another one-fifth lived in families whose incomes were no more than twice the poverty threshold.[1,2] For a small minority of children—4.8% of all children and 15% of children who ever became poor—childhood poverty lasted 10 years or more.[3]

Income poverty is the condition of not having enough income to meet basic needs for food, clothing, and shelter. Because children are dependent on others, they enter or avoid poverty by virtue of their family's economic circumstances. Children cannot alter family conditions by themselves, at least until they approach adulthood. Government programs, such as those described by Devaney, Ellwood, and Love in this journal issue, have been developed to increase the likelihood that poor children are provided basic necessities. But even with these programs, poor children do not fare as well as those whose families are not poor.[4]

What does poverty mean for children? How does the relative lack of income influence children's day-to-day lives? Is it through inadequate nutrition; fewer learning experiences; instability of residence; lower quality of schools; exposure to environmental toxins, family violence, and homelessness; dangerous streets; or less access to friends, services, and, for adolescents, jobs? This article reviews recent research that used longitudinal data to examine the relationship between low-income poverty and child outcomes in several domains.

Hundreds of studies, books, and reports have examined the detrimental effects of poverty on the well-being of children. Many have been summarized in recent reports such as *Wasting America's Future* from the Children's Defense Fund and *Alive and Well?* from the National Center for Children in Poverty.[5] However, while the literature on the effects of poverty on children is large, many studies lack the precision necessary to allow researchers to disentangle the effects on children of the array of factors associated with poverty. Understanding of these relationships is key to designing effective policies to ameliorate these problems for children.

This article examines these relationships and the consequences for children of growing up poor. It begins with a long, but by no means exhaustive, list of child outcomes (see Table 1) that have been found to be associated with poverty in several large, nationally representative, cross-sectional surveys. This list makes clear the broad range of effects poverty can have on children. It does little, however, to inform the discussion of the causal effects of income poverty on children because the studies from which this list is derived did not control for other variables associated with poverty. For example, poor families are more likely to be headed by a parent who is single, has low educational attainment, is unemployed, has low earning potential and is young. These parental attributes, separately or in combination, might

account for some of the observed negative consequences of poverty on children. Nor do the relationships identified in the table capture the critical factors of the timing, depth, and duration of childhood poverty on children.[6,7]

This article focuses on studies that used national longitudinal data sets to estimate the effects of family income on children's lives, independent of other family conditions that might be related to growing up in a low-income household. These studies attempt to isolate the effect of family income by taking into account, statistically, the effects of maternal age at the child's birth, maternal education, marital status, ethnicity, and other factors on child outcomes.[2,8] Many used data on family income over several years and at different stages of development to estimate the differential effects of the timing and duration of poverty on child outcomes. The data sets analyzed include the Panel Study of Income Dynamics (PSID), the National Longitudinal Survey of Youth (NLSY), Children of the NLSY (the follow-up of the children born to the women in the original NLSY cohort), the National Survey of Families and Households (NSFH), the National Health and Nutrition Examination Survey (NHANES), and the Infant Health and Development Program (IHDP). These rich data sets include multiple measures of child outcomes and family and child characteristics.

This article is divided into four sections. The first focuses on the consequences of poverty across five child outcomes. If income does, in fact, affect child outcomes, then it is important not only to identify these outcomes but also to describe the pathways through which income operates. Accordingly, in the second section, five pathways through which poverty might operate are described. The third section focuses on whether the links between poverty and outcomes can reasonably be attributed to income rather than other family characteristics. The concluding section considers policy implications of the research reviewed.

Effects of Income on Child Outcomes

Measures of Child Well-Being

As illustrated in Table 1, poor children suffer higher incidences of adverse health, developmental, and other outcomes than non-poor children. The specific dimensions of the well-being of children and youths considered in some detail in this article include (1) physical health (low birth weight, growth stunting, and lead poisoning), (2) cognitive ability (intelligence, verbal ability, and achievement test scores), (3) school achievement

Table 1

Selected Population-Based Indicators of Well-Being for Poor and Nonpoor Children in the United States

Indicator	Percentage of Poor Children (unless noted)	Percentage of Nonpoor Children (unless noted)	Ratio of Poor to Nonpoor Children
Physical Health Outcomes (for children between 0 and 17 years unless noted)			
Reported to be in excellent health[a]	37.4	55.2	0.7
Reported to be in fair to poor health[a]	11.7	6.5	1.8
Experienced an accident, poisoning, or injury in the past year that required medical attention[a]	11.8	14.7	0.8
Chronic asthma[a]	4.4	4.3	1.0
Low birth weight (less than 2,500 grams)[b]	1.0	0.6	1.7
Lead poisoning (blood lead levels 10u/dl or greater)[c]	16.3	4.7	3.5
Infant mortality[b]	1.4 deaths per 100 live births	0.8 death per 100 live births	1.7
Deaths During Childhood (0 to 14 years)[d]	1.2	0.8	1.5
Stunting (being in the fifth percentile for height for age for 2 to 17 years)[e]	10.0	5.0	2.0
Number of days spent in bed in past year[a]	5.3 days	3.8 days	1.4
Number of short-stay hospital episodes in past year per 1,000 children[a]	81.3 stays	41.2 stays	2.0
Cognitive Outcomes			
Developmental delay (includes both limited and long-term developmental deficits) (0 to 17 years)[a]	5.0	3.8	1.3
Learning disability (defined as having exceptional difficulty in learning to read, write, and do arithmetic) (3 to 17 years)[a]	8.3	6.1	1.4
School Achievement Outcomes (5 to 17 years)			
Grade repetition (reported to have ever repeated a grade)[a]	28.8	14.1	2.0
Ever expelled or suspended[a]	11.9	6.1	2.0
High school dropout (percentage 16- to 24-year olds who were not in school or did not finish high school in 1994)[f]	21.0	9.6	2.2
Emotional or Behavioral Outcomes (3 to 17 years unless noted)			
Parent reports child has ever had an emotional or behavioral problem that lasted three months or more[g]	16.4	12.7	1.3
Parent reports child ever being treated for an emotional problem or behavioral problem[a]	2.5	4.5	0.6
Parent reports child has experienced one or more of a list of typical child behavioral problems in the last three months[h] (5 to 17 years)	57.4	57.3	1.0
Other			
Female teens who had an out-of-wedlock birth[i]	11.0	3.6	3.1
Economically inactive at age 24 (not employed or in school)[j]	15.9	8.3	1.9
Experienced hunger (food insufficiency) at least once in past year[k]	15.9	1.6	9.9
Reported cases of child abuse and neglect[l]	5.4	0.8	6.8
Violent crimes (experienced by poor families and nonpoor families)[m]	5.4	2.6	2.1

(years of schooling, high school completion), (4) emotional and behavioral outcomes, and (5) teenage out-of-wedlock childbearing. Other outcomes are not addressed owing to a scarcity of available research, a lack of space, and because they overlap with included outcomes.

While this review is organized around specific outcomes, it could also have been organized around the various ages of childhood.[9-11] Five age groups are often distinguished—prenatal to 2 years, early childhood (ages 3 to 6), late childhood (ages 7 to 10), early adolescence (ages 11

Indicator	Percentage of Poor Children (unless noted)	Percentage of Nonpoor Children (unless noted)	Ratio of Poor to Nonpoor Children
Afraid to go out (percentage of family heads in poor and nonpoor families who report they are afraid to go out in their neighborhood)[n]	19.5	8.7	2.2

Note: This list of child outcomes reflects findings from large, nationally representative surveys that collect data on child outcomes and family income. While most data comes from the 1988 National Health Interview Survey Child Health Supplement, data from other nationally representative surveys are included. The rates presented are from simple cross-tabulations. In most cases, the data do not reflect factors that might be important to child outcomes other than poverty status at the time of data collection. The ratios reflect rounding.

[a] Data from the 1988 National Health Interview Survey Child Health Supplement (NHS-CHS), a nationwide household interview survey. Children's health status was reported by the adult household member who knew the most about the sample child's health, usually the child's mother. Figures calculated from Dawson, D.A. *Family structure and children's health: United States, 1988.* Vital Health and Statistics, Series 10, no. 178. Hyattsville, MD: U.S. Department of Health and Human Services, Public Health Service, June 1991; and Coiro, M.J., Zill, n., and Bloom, B. *Health of our nation's children.* Vital Health and Statistics, Series 10, no. 191. Hyattsville, MD: U.S. Department of Health and Human Services, Public Health Service, December 1994.

[b] Data from the National Maternal and Infant Health Survey, data collected in 1989 and 1990, with 1988 as the reference period. Percentages were calculated from the number of deaths and number of low birth weight births per 1,000 live births as reported in Federman, M., Garner, T., Short, K., et al. What does it mean to be poor in America? *Monthly Labor Review* (May 1996) 119, 5:10.

[c] Data from the NHANES III, 1988–1991. Poor children who lived in families with incomes less than 130% of the poverty threshold are classified as poor. All other children are classified as nonpoor.

[d] Percentages include only black and white youths. Percentages calculated from Table 7 in Rogot, E. *A mortality study of 1.3 million persons by demographic, social and economic factors: 1979–1985 follow-up.* Rockville, MD: National Institutes of Health, July 1992.

[e] Data from NHANES II, 1976–1980. For more discussion, see the Child Indicators article in this journal issue.

[f] National Center for Education Statistics. *Dropout rates in the United States: 1994.* Table 7, Status dropout rate, ages 16–24, by income and race ethnicity: October 1994. Available online at: http://www.ed.gov/NCES/pubs/r9410†07.html.

[g] Data from the NHIS-CHS. The question was meant to identify children with common psychological disorders such as attention deficit disorder or depression, as well as more severe problems such as autism.

[h] Data from the NHIS-CHS. Parents responded "sometimes true," "often true," or "not true" to a list of 32 statements typical of children's behaviors. Each statement corresponded to one of six individual behavior problems—antisocial behavior, anxiety, peer conflict/social withdrawal, dependency, hyperactivity, and headstrong behavior. Statements included behaviors such as cheating or lying, being disobedient in the home, being secretive, and demanding a lot of attention. For a more complete description, see Section P-11 of the NHIS-CHS questionnaire.

[i] Data from the Panel Study of Income Dynamics (PSID). Based on 1,705 children ages 0 to 6 in 1968; outcomes measured at ages 21 to 27. Haveman, R., and Wolfe, B. *Succeeding generations: On the effect of investments in children.* New York: Russell Sage Foundation, 1994, p. 108, Table 4, 10c.

[j] Data from the PSID. Based on 1,705 children ages 0 to 6 in 1968; outcomes measured at ages 21 to 27. In Succeeding generations: On the effect of investments in children. Haveman, R., and Wolfe, B. New York: Russell Sage Foundation, 1994, p. 108, Table 4, 10d. Economically inactive is defined as not being a full-time student, working 1,000 hours or more per year; attending school part time and working 500 hours; a mother of an infant or mother of two or more children less than five years old; a part-time student and the mother of a child less than five years old.

[k] Data from NHANES III, 1988–1991. Figures reflect food insufficiency, the term used in government hunger-related survey questions. For a more in-depth discussion, see Lewit, E.M., and Kerrebrock, N. Child indicators: Childhood hunger. *The Future of Children* (Spring 1997) 7, 1:128–37.

[l] Data from Study of National Incidence and Prevalence of Child Abuse and Neglect: 1988. In *Wasting America's future.* Children's Defense Fund. Boston: Beacon Press, 1994, pp. 5–29, 87, Tables 5–6. Poor families are those with annual incomes below $15,000.

[m] Data from the National Crime Victimization Interview Survey. Results are for households or persons living in households. Data were collected between January 1992 and June 1993 with 1992 as the reference period. Percentages are calculated from number of violent crimes per 1,000 people per year. Reported in Federman, M., Garner, T., Short, K., et al. What does it mean to be poor in America? *Monthly Labor Review* (May 1996) 119,5:9.

[n] Data from the Survey of Income and Program Participation. Participation data collection and reference periods are September through December 1992. Reported in Federman, M., Garner, T., Short, K., et al. What does it mean to be poor in America? *Monthly Labor Review* (May 1996) 119, 5:9.

to 15), and late adolescence (ages 16 to 19). Each age group covers one or two major transitions in a child's life, such as school entrances or exits, biological maturation, possible cognitive changes, role changes, or some combination of these. These periods are characterized by relatively uni-versal developmental challenges that require new modes of adaptation to biological, psychological, or social changes.[10]

Somewhat different indicators of child and youth well-being are associated with each period. For example, grade retention is more salient in the late childhood years than in adolescence (since most schools do not hold students back once they reach eighth grade[12]). Furthermore, low income might influence each indicator differently. As an illustration, income has stronger effects on cognitive and verbal ability test scores than it has on indices of emotional health in the childhood years.

Poverty status had a statistically significant effect on both low birth weight and the neonatal mortality rate for whites but not for blacks.

Physical Health

Compared with nonpoor children, poor children in the United States experience diminished physical health as measured by a number of indicators of health status and outcomes (see Table 1). In the 1988 National Health Interview Survey; parents reported that poor children were only two-thirds as likely to be in excellent health and almost twice as likely to be in fair or poor health as nonpoor children. These large differences in health status between poor and nonpoor children do not reflect adjustment for potentially confounding factors (factors, other than income, that may be associated with living in poverty) nor do they distinguish between long- or short-term poverty or the timing of poverty. This section reviews research on the relationship of poverty to several key measures of child health, low birth weight and infant mortality, growth stunting, and lead poisoning. For the most part, the focus is on research that attempts to adjust for important confounding factors and/or to address the effect of the duration of poverty on child health outcomes.

Birth Outcomes

Low birth weight (2,500 grams or less) and infant mortality are important indicators of child health. Low birth weight is associated with an increased likelihood of subsequent physical health and cognitive and emotional problems that can persist through childhood and adolescence. Serious physical disabilities, grade repetition, and learning disabilities are more prevalent among children who were low birth weight as infants, as are lower

levels of intelligence and of math and reading achievement. Low birth weight is also the key risk factor for infant mortality (especially death within the first 28 days of life), which is a widely accepted indicator of the health and well-being of children.[13]

Estimating the effects of poverty alone on birth outcomes is complicated by the fact that adverse birth outcomes are more prevalent for unmarried women, those with low levels of education, and black mothers—all groups with high poverty rates. One study that used data from the NLSY to examine the relationship between family income and low birth weight did find, however, that among whites, women with family income below the federal poverty level in the year of birth were 80% more likely to have a low birth weight baby as compared with women whose family incomes were above the poverty level (this study statistically controlled for mothers' age, education, marital status, and smoking status). Further analysis also showed that the duration of poverty had an important effect; if a white woman was poor both at the time when she entered the longitudinal NLSY sample and at the time of her pregnancy (5 to 10 years later), she was more than three times more likely to deliver a low birth weight infant than a white woman who was not poor at both times. For black women in this sample, although the odds of having a low birth weight baby were twice the odds for white mothers, the probability of having a low birth weight baby was not related to family poverty status.[14]

Other studies that used county level data to examine the effects of income or poverty status and a number of pregnancy-related health services on birth outcomes for white and black women also found that income or poverty status had a statistically significant effect on both low birth weight and the neonatal mortality rate for whites but not for blacks.[15,16]

Growth Stunting

Although overt malnutrition and starvation are rare among poor children in the United States, deficits in children's nutritional status are associated with poverty. As described more fully in the Child Indicators article in this journal issue, stunting (low height for age), a measure of nutritional status, is more prevalent among poor than nonpoor children. Studies using data from the NLSY show that differentials in height for age between poor and nonpoor children are greater when long-term rather than single-year measures of poverty are used in models to predict stunting. These differentials by poverty status are large even in models that statistically control for many other family and child characteristics associated with poverty.[17]

Lead Poisoning

Harmful effects of lead have been documented even at low levels of exposure. Health problems vary with length of exposure, intensity of lead in the environment, and the developmental stage of the child—with risks beginning prior to birth. At very young ages, lead exposure is linked to stunted growth,[18] hearing loss,[19] vitamin D metabolism damage, impaired blood production, and toxic effects on the kidneys.[20] Additionally, even a small increase in blood lead above the Centers for Disease Control and Prevention (CDC) current intervention threshold (10 μg/dL) is associated with a decrease in intelligence quotient (IQ).[21]

Today, deteriorating lead-based house paint remains the primary source of lead for young children. Infants and toddlers in old housing eat the sweet-tasting paint chips and breathe the lead dust from deteriorating paint. Four to five million children reside in homes with lead levels exceeding the accepted threshold for safety,[22] and more than 1.5 million children under six years of age have elevated blood lead levels.[23]

Using data from NHANES III (1988–1991), one study found that children's blood lead levels declined as family income increased.[23] All other things being equal, mean blood lead levels were 9% lower for one- to five-year-olds in families with incomes twice the poverty level than for those who were poor. Overall blood levels were highest among one- to five-year-olds who were non-Hispanic blacks from low-income families in large central cities. The mean blood lead level for this group, 9.7 μg/dL, was just under the CDC's threshold for intervention and almost three times the mean for all one- to five-year-olds.

Cognitive Abilities

As reported in Table 1, children living below the poverty threshold are 1.3 times as likely as non-poor children to experience learning disabilities and developmental delays. Reliable measures of cognitive ability and school achievement for young children in the Children of the NLSY and IHDP data sets have been used in a number of studies to examine the relationship between cognitive ability and poverty in detail.[6,24–26] This article reports on several studies that control for a number of potentially important family characteristics and attempts to distinguish between the effects of long- and short-term poverty.

A recent study using data from the Children of the NLSY and the IHDP compared children in families with incomes less than half of the poverty

threshold to children in families with incomes between 1.5 and twice the poverty threshold. The poorer children scored between 6 and 13 points lower on various standardized tests of IQ, verbal ability, and achievement.[25] These differences are very large from an educational perspective and were present even after controlling for maternal age, marital status, education, and ethnicity. A 6- to 13-point difference might mean, for example, the difference between being placed in a special education class or not. Children in families with incomes closer to, but still below, the poverty line also did worse than children in higher-income families, but the differences were smaller. The smallest differences appeared for the earliest (age two) measure of cognitive ability; however, the sizes of the effects were similar for children from three to eight. These findings suggest that the effects of poverty on children's cognitive development occur early.

> *The effects of long-term poverty on measures of children's cognitive ability were significantly greater than the effects of short-term poverty.*

The study also found that duration of poverty was an important factor in the lower scores of poor children on measures of cognitive ability. Children who lived in persistently poor families (defined in this study as poor over a four-year span) had scores on the various assessments six to nine points lower than children who were never poor.[25] Another analysis of the NLSY that controlled for a number of important maternal and child health characteristics showed that the effects of long-term poverty (based on family income averaged over 13 years prior to testing of the child) on measures of children's cognitive ability were significantly greater than the effects of short-term poverty (measured by income in the year of observation).[26]

A few studies link long-term family income to cognitive ability and achievement measured during the school years. Research on children's test scores at ages seven and eight found that the effects of income on these scores were similar in size to those reported for three-year-olds.[25] But research relating family income measured during adolescence on cognitive ability finds relatively smaller effects.[27] As summarized in the next section, these modest effects of income on cognitive ability are consistent with literature showing modest effects of income on schooling attainment, but both sets of studies may be biased by the fact that their measurement of parental income is restricted to the child's adolescent years. It is not yet possible to make conclusive statements regarding the size of the effects of poverty on children's long-term cognitive development.

For low-income children, a $10,000 increase in mean family income between birth and age 5 was associated with nearly a full-year increase in completed schooling.

School Achievement Outcomes

Educational attainment is well recognized as a powerful predictor of experiences in later life. A comprehensive review of the relationship between parental income and school attainment, published in 1994, concluded that poverty limited school achievement but that the effect of income on the number of school years completed was small.[28] In general, the studies suggested that a 10% increase in family income is associated with a 0.2% to 2% increase in the number of school years completed.[28]

Several more recent studies using different longitudinal data sets (the PSID, the NLSY and Children of the NLSY) also find that poverty status has a small negative impact on high school graduation and years of schooling obtained. Much of the observed relationship between income and schooling appears to be related to a number of confounding factors such as parental education, family structure, and neighborhood characteristics.[28-30] Some of these studies suggest that the components of income (for example, AFDC) and the way income is measured (number of years in poverty versus annual family income or the ratio of income to the poverty threshold) may lead to somewhat different conclusions. But all the studies suggest that, after controlling for many appropriate confounding variables, the effects of poverty

per se on school achievement are likely to be statistically significant, yet small. Based on the results of one study, the authors estimated that, if poverty were eliminated for all children, mean years of schooling for all children would increase by only 0.3% (less than half a month).[30]

Why do not the apparently strong effects of parental income on cognitive abilities and school achievement in the early childhood years translate into larger effects on completed schooling? One possible reason is that extrafamilial environments (for example, schools and neighborhoods) begin to matter as much or more for children than family conditions once children reach school age. A second possible reason is that school-related achievement depends on both ability and behavior. As is discussed in the Emotional and Behavioral Outcomes section, children's behavioral problems, measured either before or after the transition into school, are not very sensitive to parental income differences.

A third, and potentially crucial, reason concerns the timing of economic deprivation. Few studies measure income from early childhood to adolescence, so there is no way to know whether poverty early in childhood has noteworthy effects on later outcomes such as school completion. Because family income varies over time,[31] income measured during adolescence, or even middle childhood, may not reflect income in early childhood. A recent study that attempted to evaluate how the timing of income might affect completed schooling found that family income averaged from birth to age 5 had a much more powerful effect on the number of school years a child completes than does family income measured either between ages 5 and 10 or between ages 11 and 15.[7] For low-income children, a $10,000 increase in mean family income between birth and age 5 was associated with nearly a full-year increase in completed schooling. Similar increments to family income later in childhood had no significant impact, suggesting that income may indeed be an important determinant of completed schooling but that only income during the early childhood years matters.

Emotional and Behavioral Outcomes

Poor children suffer from emotional and behavioral problems more frequently than do nonpoor children (see Table 1). Emotional outcomes are often grouped along two dimensions: externalizing behaviors including aggression, fighting, and acting out, and internalizing behaviors such as anxiety, social withdrawal, and depression. Data regarding emotional outcomes are based on parental and teacher reports. This section reviews studies that distinguish between the effects of long- and short-term poverty on emotional outcomes of children at different ages.

One study of low birth weight five-year-olds using the IHDP data set found that children in persistently poor families had more internalizing and externalizing behavior problems than children who had never been poor. The analysis controlled for maternal education and family structure and defined long-term poverty as income below the poverty threshold for each of four consecutive years. Short-term poverty (defined as poor in at least one of four years) was also associated with more behavioral problems, though the effects were not as large as those for persistent poverty.[6]

Two different studies using the NLSY report findings consistent with those of the IHDP study. Both found persistent poverty to be a significant predictor of some behavioral problems.[26,32] One study used data from the 1986 NLSY and found that for four- to eight-year-olds persistent poverty (defined as a specific percentage of years of life during which the child lived below the poverty level) was positively related to the presence of internalizing symptoms (such as dependence, anxiety, and unhappiness) even after controlling for current poverty status, mother's age, education, and marital status. In contrast, current poverty (defined by current family income below the poverty line) but not persistent poverty was associated with more externalizing problems (such as hyperactivity, peer conflict, and headstrong behavior).[32]

The second study used NLSY data from 1978–1991 and analyzed children ages 3 to 11. On average children living in long-term poverty (defined by the ratio of family income to the poverty level averaged over 13 years) ranked three to seven percentile points higher (indicating more problems) on a behavior problem index than children with incomes above the poverty line. After controlling for a range of factors including mother's characteristics, nutrition, and infant health behaviors, the difference remained though it dropped in magnitude. This study also found that children who experienced one year of poverty had more behavioral problems than children who had lived in long-term poverty.[26]

The above studies demonstrate that problematic emotional outcomes are associated with family poverty. However, it is important to note that the effects of poverty on emotional outcomes are not as large as those found in cognitive outcomes. Also these studies do not show that children in long-term poverty experience emotional problems with greater frequency or of the same type as children who experience only short-term poverty. These studies analyzed data for young children. Few studies have examined the link between emotional

outcomes and poverty for adolescents. One small study of 7th- to 10th-graders in the rural Midwest did not find a statistically significant relationship between poverty and emotional problems, either internalizing or externalizing.[33] Self-reporting by the adolescents rather than maternal reporting, as used in the data sets on younger children, may account for the differences found in the effects of

> *Problematic emotional outcomes are associated with family poverty; however, the effects of poverty on emotional outcomes are not as large as its effects on cognitive outcomes.*

income on emotional outcomes in this study as compared with the previously reviewed research. It may also be that younger children are more affected by poverty than older children.

These findings point to the need for further research to improve understanding of the link between income and children's emotional outcomes.

Teenage Out-of-Wedlock Childbearing

The negative consequences for both mothers and children associated with births to unwed teen mothers make it a source of policy concern.[34] Although the rate of out-of-wedlock births among poor teens is almost three times as high as the rate among those from nonpoor families (see Table 1), the literature on linkages between family income and out-of-wedlock childbearing is not conclusive. A recent review of the evidence put it this way: "[P]arental income is negative and usually, but not always, significant. . . . The few reports of the quantitative effects of simulated changes in variables suggest that decreases in parental income . . . will lead to small increases in the probability that teen girls will experience a nonmarital birth."[28]

A recent study, which used data from the PSID to investigate factors in teen out-of-wedlock births, found that variations in income around the poverty threshold were not predictive of a teenage birth but that the probability of a teenager's having an out-of-wedlock birth declined significantly at family income levels above twice the poverty threshold.[35] The duration and timing of poverty had no effect on the probability of a teen out-of-wedlock birth. These findings are somewhat dif-

A child's home environment accounts for a substantial portion of the effects of family income on cognitive outcomes in young children.

ferent from those reported for cognitive outcomes and school achievement. In the case of cognitive outcomes for young children, the variation in income mattered most to children at very low levels of income; for school achievement, the timing and duration of poverty seemed to have important differential effects on outcomes.

Why should poverty status matter more for schooling than for childbearing? This difference is consistent with the more general result that parental income appears more strongly linked with ability and achievement than with behavior. The factors influencing teenage out-of-wedlock childbearing are less well understood than the factors influencing schooling completion: interventions have generally been much less successful in altering teen birthrates than in keeping teens in school.[36,37]

Pathways Through Which Poverty Operates

The research reviewed thus far suggests that living in poverty exacts a heavy toll on children. How-

ever, it does not shed light on the pathways or mechanisms by which low income exerts its effects on children. As the term is used in this discussion, a "pathway" is a mechanism through which poverty or income can influence a child outcome. By implication, this definition implies that a pathway should be causally related to both income and at least one child outcome. Exploration of these pathways is important for a more complete understanding of the effects of poverty on children; moreover, exploration of pathways can lead to the identification of leverage points that may be amenable to policy intervention and remediation in the absence of a change in family income.

Research on the size and strength of the pathways through which income might influence child health and development is still scanty. In this section, five potential pathways are discussed: (1) health and nutrition, (2) the home environment, (3) parental interactions with children, (4) parental mental health, and (5) neighborhood conditions. Space limitations preclude a discussion of other potential pathways such as access to and use of prenatal care, access to pediatric care, exposure to environmental toxins, household stability, provision of learning experiences outside the home, quality of school attended, and peer groups. Further, few studies have tested pathway models using these variables.

Health and Nutrition

Although health is itself an outcome, it can also be viewed as a pathway by which poverty influences other child outcomes, such as cognitive

© Steven Rubin

ability and school achievement. As discussed previously poor children experience increased rates of low birth weight and elevated blood lead levels when compared with nonpoor children. These conditions have, in turn, been associated with reduced IQ and other measures of cognitive functioning in young children and, in the case of low birth weight, with increased rates of learning disabilities, grade retention, and school dropout in older children and youths.

A 1990 analysis indicated that the poverty-related health factors such as low birth weight, elevated blood lead levels, anemia,[38] and recurrent ear infections and hearing loss contributed to the differential in IQ scores between poor and nonpoor four-year-olds.[39] The findings suggest that the cumulative health disadvantage experienced by poor children on these four health measures may have accounted for as much as 13% to 20% of the difference in IQ between the poor and nonpoor four-year-olds during the 1970s and 1980s.[39]

As discussed in the Child Indicators article in this journal issue, malnutrition in childhood (as measured by anthropometric indicators) is associated with lower scores on tests of cognitive development. Deficits in these anthropometric measures are associated with poverty among children in the United States, and the effects can be substantial. One recent study found that the effect of stunting on short-term memory was equivalent to the difference in short-term memory between children in families that had experienced poverty for 13 years and children in families with incomes at least three times the poverty level.[26]

Home Environment

A number of studies have found that a child's home environment—opportunities for learning, warmth of mother-child interactions, and the physical condition of the home—accounts for a substantial portion of the effects of family income on cognitive outcomes in young children. Some large longitudinal data sets use the HOME scale as a measure of the home environment. The HOME scale is made up of items that measure household resources, such as reading materials and toys, and parental practices, such as discipline methods. The HOME scale has been shown to be correlated with family income and poverty, with higher levels of income associated with improved home environments as measured by the scale.[7,40]

Several studies have found that differences in the home environment of higher- and lower-income children, as measured by the HOME scale, account for a substantial portion of the effect of income on the cognitive development of pre-

school children and on the achievement scores of elementary school children.[6,26,37] In one study, differences in the home environment also seemed to account for some of the effects of poverty status on behavioral problems. In addition, the provisions of learning experiences in the home (measured by specific subscales of the HOME scale) have been shown to account for up to half of the effect of poverty status on the IQ scores of five-year-olds.[37,41]

Parents who are poor are likely to be less healthy, both emotionally and physically, than those who are not poor.

Parental Interactions with Children

A number of studies have attempted to go beyond documentation of activities and materials in the home to capture the effects of parent-child interactions on child outcomes. Much of the work is based on small and/or community-based samples. That work suggests that child adjustment and achievement are facilitated by certain parental practices. There is also some evidence that poverty is linked to lower-quality parent-child interaction and to increased use of harsh punishment. This research suggests that parental practices may be an important pathway between economic resources and child outcomes.

Evidence of such a parental-practice pathway from research using large national data sets of the kind reviewed in this article is less consistent. One NLSY-based study found that currently poor mothers spanked their children more often than nonpoor mothers and that this harsh behavior was an important component of the effect of poverty on children's mental health.[32] Mothers' parenting behavior was not, however, found to be an important pathway by which persistent poverty affected children's mental health. A more recent study using the National Survey of Families and Households found that the level of household income was only weakly related to effective parenting and that differences in parent practices did not account for much of the association between poverty and child well-being.[42]

Among adolescents, family economic pressure may lead to conflict with parents, resulting in lower school grades, reduced emotional health, and impaired social relationships.[33,43] Other work suggests that it may be income loss or economic uncertainty due to unemployment, underemployment, and unstable work conditions, rather than poverty or low income per se, that is a source for conflict between parents and teens leading to emotional and school problems.[33,44]

Parental Mental Health

Parents who are poor are likely to be less healthy, both emotionally and physically, than those who are not poor.[45] And parental irritability and depressive symptoms are associated with more conflicted interactions with adolescents, leading to less satisfactory emotional, social, and cognitive development.[43,46,47] Some studies have established that parental mental health accounts for some of the effect of economic circumstances on child health and behavior. Additionally, poor parental mental health is associated with impaired parent-child interactions and less provision of learning experiences in the home.[33,41,48]

Low income may lead to residence in extremely poor neighborhoods characterized by social disorganization and few resources for child development.

Neighborhood Conditions

Another possible pathway through which family income operates has to do with the neighborhoods in which poor families reside. Poor parents are constrained in their choice of neighborhoods and schools. Low income may lead to residence in extremely poor neighborhoods characterized by social disorganization (crime, many unemployed adults, neighbors not monitoring the behavior of adolescents) and few resources for child development (playgrounds, child care, health care facilities, parks, after-school programs).[49,50] The affluence of neighborhoods is associated with child and adolescent outcomes (intelligence test scores at ages 3 and 5 and high school graduation rates by age 20) over and above family poverty.[37,51]

Neighborhood residence also seems to be associated with parenting practices, over and above family income and education.[52] Neighborhood effects on intelligence scores are in part mediated by the learning environment in the home.[52,53] Living in neighborhoods with high concentrations of poor people is associated with less provision of learning experiences in the homes of preschoolers, over and above the links seen between family income and learning experiences.

A key issue that has not been fully explored is the extent to which neighborhood effects may be overestimated because neighborhood characteristics also reflect the choices of neighborhood residents. One study that examined the effects of peer groups (as measured by the socioeconomic status of students in a respondent's school) on teenage pregnancy and school dropout behavior found that while student body socioeconomic status seemed to be an important predictor of both dropout and teen pregnancy rates, it did not appear to be related to those outcomes in statistical models that treated this peer characteristic as a matter of family choice.[54]

How Much Does Income Cause Child Outcomes?

It may seem odd to raise this question after summarizing evidence indicating that family income does matter—across the childhood and adolescent years and for a number of indicators of well-being. However, these associations have been demonstrated when a relatively small set of family characteristics are controlled through statistical analyses. It is possible, therefore, that other important family characteristics have not been controlled for and that, as a result of this omission, the effects of income are estimated incorrectly. . . . Distinguishing between the effects on children of poverty and its related events and conditions is crucial for public policy formulation. Programs that alter family income may not have intended benefits for children if the importance of family income has been mismeasured.

Despite the evidence reviewed in this article and elsewhere, there is an important segment of the population who believes that income per se may not appreciably affect child outcomes. This viewpoint sees parental income mainly as a proxy for other charateristics such as character (a strong work ethic) or genetic endowment that influence both children and parents. A recent book by Susan Mayer, *What Money Can't Buy: The Effect of Parental Income on Children's Outcomes,*[55] presents a series of tests to examine explicitly the effects of income on a set of child outcomes. In one test, measures of income *after* the occurrence of an outcome are added to statistical models of the effects of income and other characteristics on a child outcome. The idea behind this test is that unanticipated future income can capture unmeasured parental characteristics but cannot have caused the child outcome. The inclusion of future income frequently produced a large reduction in the estimated impact of prior parent income. Mayer also tries to estimate the effects on children of components of income (for example, asset income) that are independent of the actions of the family. Although these tests provide some support for the hypothesis that family income may not matter much for child outcomes, even Mayer admits that these statistical procedures are not without their problems. For example, prior income and future income are highly correlated, and if parents take reasonable expectations of future income into consideration in making decisions regarding the well-being of children, then the assumption that child outcomes are independent of future income, which underlies the first test, is violated.

A second approach to the problem that omitted variables may bias the estimation of the effects of income and poverty on children looks at siblings within families. Siblings reared in the same family share many of the same unmeasured family characteristics. Thus, comparing children at the same age within families makes it possible to look at the income of the family at different time points (for example, if a firstborn was five years of age in 1985 and the second child was five years of age in 1988, it is possible to look at their achievement levels at this age and the average family income between 1980 and 1985 for the firstborn and between 1983 and 1988 for the second child). One study that used this approach found that sibling differences in income were associated with sibling differences in completed schooling, which gave support to the notion that family income matters.[7]

Perhaps the most convincing demonstration of the effects of income is to provide poor families with income in the context of a randomized trial. In four Income Maintenance/Negative Income Tax Experiments in the 1960s and 1970s, experimental treatment families received a guaranteed minimum income. (These experiments are discussed in more detail in the article by Janet Currie in this journal issue.) Substantial benefits resulting from increased income effects were found for child nutrition, early school achievement, and high school completion in some sites but not in others. These results might be viewed as inconclusive; however, since the site with the largest effects for younger children (North Carolina) was also the poorest, one interpretation of the results is that income effects are most important for the very poorest families.[56,57]

Conclusion

The evidence reviewed in this article supports the conclusion that family income can substantially influence child and adolescent well-being. However, the associations between income and child outcomes are more complex and varied than suggested by the simple associations presented in Table 1. Family income seems to be more strongly related to children's ability and achievement-related outcomes than to emotional outcomes. In addition, the effects are particularly pronounced for children who live below the poverty line for multiple years and for children who live in extreme poverty (that is, 50% or less of the poverty threshold). These income effects are probably not due to some unmeasured characteristics of low-income families: family income, in and of itself, does appear to matter.

The timing of poverty is also important, although this conclusion is based on only a small number of studies. Low income during the preschool and early school years exhibits the strongest correlation with low rates of high school completion, as compared with low income during the childhood and adolescent years.[7,58] Poor-quality schooling, which is correlated with high neighborhood poverty, may exacerbate this effect.[59] These findings suggest that early childhood interventions may be critical in reducing the impact of low income on children's lives.

The pathways through which low income influences children also suggest some general recommendations. Nutrition programs, especially if they target the most undernourished poor, may have beneficial effects on both physical and cognitive outcomes. Lead abatement and parental education programs may improve cognitive outcomes in poor children residing in inner-city neighborhoods where lead is still an important hazard.

Because about one-half of the effect of family income on cognitive ability is mediated by the home environment, including learning experiences in the home, interventions might profitably focus on working with parents. An example is the Learningames curriculum in which parents are provided instruction, materials, and role playing in learning experiences.[60] Other effective learning-oriented programs might also be pursued.[61-63]

Finally, income policies (as discussed by Robert Plotnick in this journal issue) and in-kind support programs (as discussed by Devaney, Ellwood, and Love in this journal issue) can have immediate impact on the number or children living in poverty and on the circumstances in which they live. Most important, based on this review, would be efforts to eliminate deep and persistent poverty especially during a child's early years. Support to families with older children may be desirable on other grounds, but the available research suggests that it will probably not have the same impact on child outcomes as programs focused on younger children.

The authors would like to thank the National Institute of Child Health and Human Development Research Network on Child and Family Well-being for supporting the writing of this article. The Russell Sage Foundation's contribution is also appreciated as is that of the William T. Grant Foundation, and the Canadian Institute for Advanced Research. The authors are also grateful for the feedback provided by Linda Baker, Pamela K. Klebanov, and Judith Smith and would like to thank Phyllis Gyamfi for her editorial assistance.

1. Hernandez, D.J. *America's children: Resources from family government and the economy.* New York: Russell Sage Foundation, 1993.
2. Duncan, G.J., and Brooks-Gunn, J., eds. *Consequences of growing up poor.* New York: Russell Sage Foundation, 1997.
3. Duncan, G.J., and Rodgers, W.L. Longitudinal aspects of childhood poverty. *Journal of Marriage and the Family* (November 1988) 50,4:1007–21.
4. Chase-Lansdale, P.L., and Brooks-Gunn, J., eds. *Escape from poverty: What makes a difference for children?* New York: Cambridge University Press, 1995.
5. Children's Defense Fund. *Wasting America's future.* Boston: Beacon Press, 1994; Klerman, L. *Alive and well?* New York: National Center for Children in Poverty, Columbia University, 1991.
6. Duncan, G.J., Brooks-Gunn, J., and Klebanov, P.K. Economic deprivation and early-childhood development. *Child Development* (1994) 65,2:296–318.
7. Duncan, G.J., Yeung, W., Brooks-Gunn, J., and Smith, J.R. How much does childhood poverty affect the life chances of children? *American Sociological Review,* in press.
8. Hauser, R., Brown, B., and Prosser W. *Indicators of children's well-being.* New York: Russell Sage Foundation, in press.
9. Brooks-Gunn, J., Guo, G., and Furstenberg, F.F., Jr. Who drops out of and who continues beyond high school?: A 20-year study of black youth. *Journal of Research in Adolescence* (1993) 37,3:271–94.
10. Graber, J.A., and Brooks-Gunn, J. Transitions and turning points: Navigating the passage from childhood through adolescence. *Developmental Psychology* (1996) 32,4:768–76.
11. Rutter, M. Beyond longitudinal data: Causes, consequences, changes and continuity. *Journal of Counseling and Clinical Psychology* (1994) 62,5:928–90.
12. Guo, G., Brooks-Gunn, J., and Harris, K.M. Parents' labor-force attachment and grade retention among urban black children. *Sociology of Education* (1996) 69,3:217–36.
13. For a review of the causes and consequences of low birth weight in the United States, see Shiono, P., ed. Low Birth Weight. *The Future of Children* (Spring 1995) 5,1:4–231.
14. Starfield, B., Shapiro, S., Weiss, J., et al. Race, family income, and low birth weight. *American Journal of Epidemiology* (1991) 134,10:1167–74.
15. Corman, H., and Grossman, M. Determinants of neonatal mortality rates in the U.S.: A reduced form model. *Journal of Health Economics* (1985) 4,3:213–36.
16. Frank, R., Strobino, D., Salkever, D., and Jackson, C. Updated estimates of the impact of prenatal care on birthweight outcomes by race. *Journal of Human Resources* (1992) 27,4:629–42.
17. Miller, J., and Korenman, S. Poverty and children's nutritional status in the United States. *American Journal of Epidemiology* (1994) 140,3:233–43.
18. Schwartz, J., Angle, C., and Pitcher, H. Relationship between childhood blood lead levels and stature. *Pediatrics* (1986) 77,3:281–88.
19. Schwartz, J., and Otto, D. Lead and minor hearing impairment. *Archives of Environmental Health* (1991) 46,5:300–05.
20. Agency for Toxic Substances and Disease Registry. *The nature and extent of lead poisoning in the US.: A report to Congress.* Washington, DC: U.S. Department of Health and Human Services, 1988, Section II, p. 7.
21. Schwartz, J. Low level lead exposure and children's IQ: A meta-analysis and search for threshold. *Environmental Research* (1994) 65,1:42–55.
22. Ronald Morony, Deputy Director, U.S. Department of Housing and Urban Development, Office of Lead Based Paint Abatement and Poisoning Prevention, Washington, DC. Personal communication, November 20, 1996.
23. Brody, D.J., Pirkle, L., Kramer, R., et al. Blood lead levels in the U.S. population. *Journal of the American Medical Association* (1994) 272,4:277–81.
24. Brooks-Gunn, J., McCarton, C.M., Casey, P.H., et al. Early intervention in low birth weight premature infants: Results through age 5 years from the Infant Health and Development Program. *Journal of the American Medical Association* (1994) 272,16: 1257–62.
25. Smith, J.R., Brooks-Gunn, J., and Klebanov, P. The consequences of living in poverty for young children's cognitive and verbal ability and early school achievement. In *Consequences of growing up poor.* G.J. Duncan and J. Brooks-Gunn, eds. New York: Russell Sage Foundation, 1997.
26. Korenman, S., Miller, J.E., and Sjaastad, J.E. Long-term poverty and child development in the United States: Results from the National Longitudinal Survey of Youth. *Children and Youth Services Review* (1995)17,1/2:127–51.
27. Peters. E., and Mullis, N. The role of the family and source of income in adolescent achievement.

In *Consequences of growing up poor:* G. Duncan and J. Brooks-Gunn, eds. New York: Russell Sage Foundation, 1997.

28. Haveman, R., and Wolfe, B. The determinants of children's attainments: A review of methods and findings. *Journal of Economic Literature* (1995) 33,3:1829–78.

29. Teachman, J., Paasch, K.M., Day, R., and Carver, K.P. Poverty during adolescence and subsequent educational attainment. In *Consequences of growing up poor:* G. Duncan and J. Brooks-Gunn, eds. New York: Russell Sage Foundation, 1997.

30. Haveman, R., and Wolfe, B. *Succeeding generations: On the effect of investments in children.* New York: Russell Sage Foundation, 1994.

31. Duncan, G.J. Volatility of family income over the life course. In *Life-span development and behavior.* Vol. 9. P. Baltes, D. Featherman, and R.M. Lerner, eds. Hillsdale, NJ: Erlbaum, 1988, pp. 317–58.

32. McLeod, J.D., and Shanahan, M.J. Poverty, parenting and children's mental health. *American Sociological Review* (June 1993) 58,3:351–66.

33. Conger, R.D., Conger, K.J., and Elder, G.H. Family economic hardship and adolescent adjustment: Mediating and moderating processes. In *Consequences of growing up poor:* G. Duncan and J. Brooks-Gunn, eds. New York: Russell Sage Foundation, 1997.

34. Hotz, V.J., McElroy, S.W., and Sanders, S.G. Costs and consequences of teenage childbearing. *Chicago Policy Review.* Internet: http://www.spc.uchicago.edu/cpr/Teenage_Child.htm.

35. Haveman, R., Wolfe, B., and Wilson, K. Childhood poverty and adolescent schooling and fertility outcomes: Reduced form and structural estimates. In *Consequences of growing up poor.* G.J. Duncan and J. Brooks-Gunn, eds. New York: Russell Sage Foundation, 1997.

36. U.S. Department of Health and Human Services. *Report to Congress on out-of-wedlock childbearing.* PHS-95-1257. Hyattsville, MD: DHHS, September 1995.

37. Brooks-Gunn, J., Duncan, G.J., Klebanov, P.K., and Sealand, N. Do neighborhoods influence child and adolescent behavior? *American Journal of Sociology* (1993) 99,2:335–95.

38. Iron-deficiency anemia is an important health problem that was traditionally identified with child poverty. Iron-deficiency anemia has been associated with impaired exercise capacity, increased susceptibility to lead absorption, and developmental and behavioral problems; see Oski, F. Iron deficiency in infancy and childhood. *The New England Journal of Medicine.* (July 15, 1993) 329,3:190–93. The importance of iron-deficiency anemia and its sequelae among poor children in the United States today is unclear. Increased use of iron-fortified foods and infant formulas along with their provision through public nutrition programs such as the Special Supplemental Food Program for Women, Infants, and Children (see the article by Devaney, Ellwood, and Love in this journal issue) have contributed to a dramatic decline in anemia; see Yip, R., Binkin, N.J., Fleshood, L., and Trowbridge, F.L. Declining prevalence of anemia among low-income children in the U.S. *Journal of American Medical Association* (1987) 258,12:1623. Between 1980 and 1991, the prevalence of ane-

mia among infants and children through age five declined from 7% to 3%. Still, low-income children participating in public health programs have a higher-than-average prevalence of anemia; see Yip, R., Parvanta, I., Scanlon, K., et al. Pediatric Nutrition Surveillance System—United States, 1980–1991. *Morbidity and Mortality Weekly Report* (November 1992) 41,SS-7:1–24. In part, this is because risk of anemia is a criterion for enrollment in these programs and also because these low-income children have low iron levels.

39. Goldstein, N. *Explaining socioeconomic differences in children's cognitive test scores.* Working Paper No. H-90-1. Cambridge, MA: Malcolm Wiener Center for Social Policy, John F. Kennedy School of Government, Harvard University, 1990.

40. Garrett, P., Ng'andu, N., and Ferron, J. Poverty experience of young children and the quality of their home environments. *Child Development* (1994) 65,2:331–45.

41. Bradley, R.H. Home environment and parenting. In *Handbook of parenting:* M. Bornstein, ed. Hillsdale, NJ: Erlbaum, 1995.

42. Hanson, T., McLanahan, S., and Thomson, E. Economic resources, parental practices, and child well-being. In *Consequences of growing up poor:* G.J. Duncan and J. Brooks-Gunn, eds. New York: Russell Sage Foundation, 1997.

43. Conger, R.D., Ge, S., Elder, G.H., Jr., et al. Economic stress, coercive family process and developmental problems of adolescents. *Child Development* (1994) 65,2:541–61.

44. McLoyd, V.C. The impact of economic hardship on black families and children: Psychological distress, parenting, and socioemotional development. *Child Development* (1990) 61,2:311–46.

45. Adler, N.E., Boyce, T., Chesney, M.A., et al. Socioeconomic inequalities in health: No easy solution. *Journal of the American Medical Association* (1993) 269:3140–45.

46. Liaw, F.R., and Brooks-Gunn, J. Cumulative familial risks and low birth weight children's cognitive and behavioral development. *Journal of Clinical Child Psychology* (1995) 23,4:360–72.

47. McLoyd, V.C., Jayaratne, T.E., Ceballo, R., and Borquez, J. Unemployment and work interruption among African American single mothers. Effects on parenting and adolescent socioemotional functioning. *Child Development* (1994) 65,2:562–89.

48. Brooks-Gunn, J., Klebanov, P.K., and Liaw, F. The learning, physical, and emotional environment of the home in the context of poverty: The Infant Health and Development Program. *Children and Youth Services Review* (1995)17,1/2.251–76.

49. Wilson, W.J. *The truly disadvantaged. The inner city, the underclass, and public policy.* Chicago: University of Chicago Press, 1987.

50. Sampson, R., and Morenoff, J. Ecological perspectives on the neighborhood context of urban poverty: Past and present. In *Neighborhood poverty: Conceptual, methodological, and policy approaches to studying neighborhoods.* Vol. 2. J. Brooks-Gunn, G. Duncan, and J.L. Aber, eds. New York: Russell Sage Foundation, in press.

51. Brooks-Gunn, J., Duncan, G.J., and Aber, J.L., eds. *Neighborhood poverty: Context and consequences for*

children. Vol. 1. New York: Russell Sage Foundation, in press.

52. Klebanov, P.K., Brooks-Gunn, J., and Duncan, G.J. Does neighborhood and family poverty affect mother's parenting, mental health and social support? *Journal of Marriage and Family* (1994) 56,2:441–55.

53. Klebanov, P.K., Brooks-Gunn, J., Chase-Lansdale, L., and Gordon, R. The intersection of the neighborhood and home environment and its influence on young children. In *Neighborhood poverty: Context and consequences for children.* Vol. 1. J. Brooks-Gunn, G.J. Duncan, and J.L. Aber, eds. New York: Russell Sage Foundation, in press.

54. Evans, W.N., Oates, W.E., and Schwab, R.M. Measuring peer group effects: A study of teenage behavior. *Journal of Practical Economy* (1992) 100,5:966–91.

55. Mayer S.E. *What money can't buy: The effect of parental income on children's outcomes.* Cambridge, MA: Harvard University Press, 1997.

56. Kershwa, D., and Fair, J. *The New Jersey income maintenance experiment.* Vol. I. New York: Academic Press, 1976.

57. Salkind, N.J., and Haskins, R. Negative income tax: The impact on children from low-income families. *Journal of Family Issues* (1982) 3,2:165–80.

58. Baydar, N., Brooks-Gunn, J., and Furstenberg, E.F., Jr. Early warning signs of functional illiteracy: Predictors in childhood and adolescence. *Child Development* (1993) 64,3:815–29.

59. Alexander, K.L., and Entwisle, D.R. Achievement in the first 2 years of school: Patterns and processes. *Monographs of the Society for Research in Child Development* (1988) 53,2:1–153.

60. Sparling, J.J., and Lewis, J. *Partner for learning.* Lewisville, NC: Kaplan, 1984.

61. Olds, D.L., and Kitzman, H. Review of research on home visiting for pregnant women and parents of young children. *The Future of Children* (Winter 1993) 3,3:53–92.

62. Brooks-Gunn, J., Denner, J., and Klebanov, P.K. Families and neighborhoods as contexts for education. In *Changing populations, changing schools: Ninety-fourth yearbook of the National Society for the Study of Education, Part II.* E. Flaxman and A. H. Passow, eds. Chicago, IL: National Society for the Study of Education, 1995, pp. 233–52.

63. Brooks-Gunn, J. Strategies for altering the outcomes of poor children and their families. In *Escape from poverty: What makes a difference for children?* P.L. Chase-Lansdale and J. Brooks-Gunn, eds. New York: Cambridge University Press, 1996.

Victimization of Children

Children suffer more victimizations than do adults, including more conventional crimes, more family violence, and some forms virtually unique to children, such as family abduction. On the basis of national statistics, these victimizations can be grouped into three broad categories: the pandemic, *such as sibling assault, affecting most children; the* acute, *such as physical abuse, affecting a fractional but significant percentage; and the* extraordinary, *such as homicide, affecting a very small group. They can also be differentiated by the degree to which they result from the unique dependency status of children. A field called the victimology of childhood should be defined that adopts a developmental approach to understanding children's vulnerability to different types of victimizations and their different effects.*

David Finkelhor and Jennifer Dziuba-Leatherman

Although the issue of child victimization has elicited considerable attention from professionals and the public, the interest has largely been fragmented. Writers and advocates have tended to confine themselves to certain specific topics, such as child abuse, child molestation, or stranger abduction, and few have considered the larger whole (for exceptions, see Best, 1990; Christoffel, 1990; McDermott, Stanley, & Zimmerman-McKinney, 1982; Morgan & Zedner, 1992). Unfortunately, this fragmentation has inhibited the recognition and development of what should be a very important field: the general victimology of childhood. Such a general victimology would highlight more clearly the true vulnerability of children to victimization, the overlap and co-occurrence of different types of victimization, and the common risk factors and effects. It is our goal to assemble disparate statistics and knowledge about the victimization and maltreatment of children in order to define such a field. We will review findings on the incidence, risk factors, and effects of child victimization and suggest integrative concepts.

Children Are More Victimized Than Adults

One reality, not widely recognized, is that children are more prone to victimization than adults are. For example, according to the 1990 National Crime Survey (NCS; Bureau of Justice Statistics, 1991), the rates of assault, rape, and robbery against those aged 12–19 years are two to three times higher than for the adult population as a whole (Table 1). Homicide is the only violent crime category for which teens are somewhat less vulnerable than adults.[1]

This disproportionate victimization of children is also confirmed in studies that gather information from adults on their lifetime experience with crime. For example, in the first national survey to ask adult women about their lifetime experiences of forcible rape, 61% of the rapes occurred before the age of 18 (Kilpatrick, 1992). This translates roughly into a fivefold higher rape risk for children.

The disproportionate victimization of children would be even more evident if the NCS and other studies were not so deficient in their counting of incidents of family violence (Garbarino, 1989), to which children are enormously more vulnerable than adults. For example, in the National Family Violence Survey (Straus, Gelles, & Steinmetz, 1980), adults reported that they inflicted almost twice as much severe violence (which includes beating up, kicking, hitting with a fist or object) against a child in their household than they did against their adult partner (Table 2). When to family violence we add the frequent occurrence of peer and sibling assaults against younger children—experiences that have virtually no equivalent among adults (Pagelow, 1989)—evidence strongly suggests that children are more victimized than adults are.

---

[1] Unfortunately, this contrast is muddied by the fact that the NCS does not have rates on children under 12 years of age, and, although they are usually classified as young adults, 18- and 19-year-olds—a very high-risk group—are treated as children. Even if one reclassifies 18- and 19-year-olds as adults and assumes no victimizations at all for children younger than 12, the overall rate for children, based on NCS data, would still be higher than the overall rate for adults.

From *American Psychologist*, March 1994, pp. 173–183. © 1994 by the American Psychological Association. Reprinted by permission.

Statistics on Child Victimization

To illustrate the spectrum of child victimization, we have arrayed the national statistics gleaned from more than a dozen sources in Table 3 in rough order of magnitude. (See Appendix for list of sources.) We limited our notion of victimization to crimes, interpersonal violence (acts carried out with the intention or perceived intention of physically hurting another person, Gelles & Straus, 1979), child abuse, and certain related acts, such as abduction, that have been highlighted in the current wave of interest in child victimization. We included only forms of victimization for which there were scientifically defensible national estimates.

One of the interesting features of child victimology is that children suffer from certain types of violence that have been largely excluded from traditional criminologic concern. The first is assaults against young children by other children, including violent attacks by siblings. Prevailing ideology has tended to treat these as relatively inconsequential.[2] But from the point of view of the child, it is not clear, for example, why being beaten up by a peer would be any less traumatic or violative than it would be for an adult (Greenbaum, 1989).

An even more problematic type of noncriminalized violence toward children is spanking and other forms of corporal punishment. There are signs that a normative transformation is in progress regarding corporal punishment (Greven, 1990). A majority of states have banned it in schools, and several Scandinavian countries have outlawed its use even by parents. Some social scientists have begun to study it as a form of victimization with short- and long-term negative consequences (Daro & Gelles, 1991; Hyman, 1990; Straus, in press).

This is far from an exhaustive inventory of all the victimizations children could be said to suffer. For example, bullying and emotional abuse by peers have received some deserved attention (Olweus, 1978). Moreover, children have been plausibly described as victims when

Table 1

Crime Victimization Rate per 1,000: Adolescents Versus Adults

Crime	Age in years	
	12–19	20+
Assault[a]	58.45	17.85
Robbery[a]	11.53	4.73
Rape[a]	1.60	0.50
Homicide[b]	0.09[c]	0.10

Note. Some figures shown in this table did not appear in original source but were derived from data presented therein.
[a]National Crime Survey, 1900 (Bureau of Justice Statistics, 1992).
[b]Uniform Crime Report, 1991 (Federal Bureau of Investigation, 1992).
[c]Rate is for ages 10–19.

Table 2

Family Violence Victimization Rate per 1,000: Children Versus Adults, 1985

Perpetrator-victim relationship	Any violence	Severe violence[a]
Spouse to spouse	158	58
Parent to child	620	107

Note. Source: National Family Violence Resurvey, 1985 (Straus & Gelles, 1990).
[a]Includes kicking, biting, hitting with fist or object, beating up, using or threatening to use knife or gun.

crimes are committed against other members of their household (Morgan & Zedner, 1992). Finally, there are many types of criminal victimizations, such as involvement in child prostitution, for which we could identify no reliable national statistics.

Typology of Child Victimizations

Examining the figures in Table 3 and recognizing their methodological limitations, definitional imprecision, and variability, we nonetheless suggest that the types of child victimization reflected there should be broken into three broad categories according to their order of magnitude (Figure 1). First, there are the pandemic victimizations that occur to a majority of children in the course of growing up. At a minimum these include assault by siblings, physical punishment by parents, and theft, and probably also peer assault, vandalism, and robbery. Second, there are what might be called acute victimizations. These are less frequent—occurring to a minority, although perhaps a sizable minority, of children—but may be of generally greater severity. Among these we would include physical abuse, neglect, and family abduction. Finally, there are the extraordinary victimizations that occur to a very small number of children but that attract a great deal of attention. These include homicide, child abuse homicide, and nonfamily abduction.

Several observations follow from this typology. First, there has been much more public and professional attention paid to the extraordinary and acute victimizations

[2] The following quote in a discussion of the meaning of the NCS statistics on adolescents is an example: "A student who is coerced into surrendering the Twinkies in his or her lunchbox to a school bully is, by strict definition, a victim of robbery. These events, although unpleasant and perhaps frightening, are not as alarming as suggested by the labels 'assault' and 'robbery' " (Garofalo, Siegel, & Laub, 1987, p. 331). This is common stereotypy of peer victimizations, even though the kind of chronic bullying, terrorizing, and intimidation that characterizes the lives of many children in school and in their neighborhood has almost no equivalent for adults, except perhaps in the case of battered wives (Greenbaum, 1989). There is also a tendency to see violence among children, particularly young children, as fighting and not as victimization. It is important to point out that this is not a distinction made in any of the statistics regarding adult victimization. That is, an adult who is assaulted in a fight he or she may have "started" (according to some observers) will nonetheless be counted as a victim in the NCS.

Table 3

Rate and Incidence of Various Childhood Victimization

Type of violence/age in years	Rate per 1,000	No. victimized	Year	Source	Report type[a]
Sibling assault					
3–17	800.0	50,400,000[b]	1975	NFVS-1	C
3–17	530.0	33,300,000[c]	1975	NFVS-1	C
Physical punishment					
0–17	498.6	31,401,329[d]	1985	NFVS-2	C
Theft					
11–17	497.0	—	1978	NYS	S
12–15	89.2	—	1990	NCS90	S
Assault					
11–17	310.6	—	1978	NYS	S
Grade 8	172.0	—	1988	NASHS	S
12–15	53.3	—	1990	NCS90	S
Vandalism					
11–17	257.6	—	1978	NYS	S
Robbery					
11–17	245.8	—	1978	NYS	S
Grade 8	160.9	—	1988	NASHS	S
12–15	13.6	—	1990	NCS90	S
Rape					
Grade 8	118.0	—	1988	NASHS	S
11–17	78.0	—[e]	1978	NYS78	S
12–15	1.8	—	1990	NCS90	S
Physical abuse					
0–17	23.5	1,480,007	1985	NFVS-2	C
0–17	10.5	673,500	1991	50-SS	A
0–17	4.9	311,500	1986	NIS-2	A
Neglect					
0–17	20.2	1,293,120	1991	50-SS	A
0–17	11.3	710,700[f]	1986	NIS-2	A
Sexual abuse					
0–17	6.3	404,100	1991	50-SS	A
0–17	2.1	133,600	1986	NIS-2	A
Family abduction					
0–17	5.6	354,100[g]	1988	NISMART	C
0–17	2.6	163,200[h]	1988	NISMART	C
Psychological maltreatment					
0–17	3.0	188,100	1986	NIS-2	A
0–17	2.5	161,640	1991	50-SS	A
Nonfamily adbuction					
0–17	0.05–0.07	3200–4600[i]	1988	NISMART	A
0–17	0.003–0.005	200–300[j]	1988	NISMART	A
Homicide					
0–17	0.035	2,233	1991	UCR91	A
Abduction homicide					
0–17	0.001–0.002	43–147	1988	NISMART	A

Note. Some figures shown did not appear in original source but were derived from data presented therein. Dash = Unable to compute for entire population (0–17). NFVS-1 = National Family Violence Survey, 1975 (Straus & Gelles, 1990); NFVS-2 = National Family Violence Resurvey, 1985 (Straus & Gelles, 1990); NYS = National Youth Survey (Lauritsen, Sampson, and Laub, 1991); NCS90 = National Crime Survey, 1990 (Bureau of Justice Statistics, 1992); NASHS = National Adolescent Student Health survey (American School Health Association, 1985); NYS78 = National Youth Survey, 1978 (Ageton, 1983); 50-SS = Annual Fifty State Survey, 1990 (Daro & McCurdy, 1991); NIS-2 = National Study of the Incidence and Severity of Child Abuse and Neglect, 1988 (Sedlak, 1991); NISMART = National Incidence Study of Missing, Abducted, Runaway and Thrownaway Children, 1990 (Finkelhor, Hotaling, & Sedlak, 1990); UCR91 = Uniform Crime Reports, 1991 (Federal Bureau of Investigation, 1992). Categories listed are not necessarily distinct and mutually exclusive. Under some victimization categories, estimates of several studies have been listed, sometimes showing widely divergent numbers. These differences stem from two factors in particular: the source of the report and the definition of the activity. Of the three main sources of reports—children themselves, caretakers knowledgeable about children's experiences, and agencies such as police and child protection services—children and caretakers are quite likely to provide many more accounts than are available from agencies alone. Estimates also diverge because some studies used more careful or restrictive definitions.
[a]Report type: A = agency; C = caretaker; S = self-report. [b]Any violence. [c]Severe violence. [d]Excludes corporal punishment in schools. [e]Girls only. [f]Physical and emotional neglect. [g]Broad scope. [h]Policy focal. [i]Legal definition. [j]Stereotypical kidnapping.

Figure 1
Typology of Child Victimization

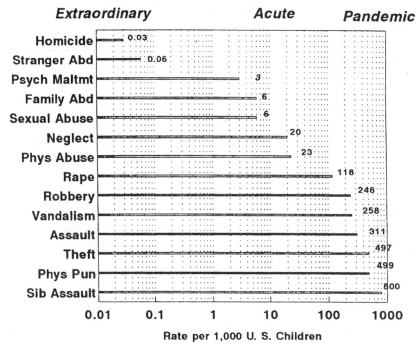

Note. Abd = abduction. Psych Maltmt = psychological maltreatment. Phys = physical. Pun = punishment. Sib = sibling.

than to the pandemic ones. For example, sibling violence, the most frequent victimization, is conspicuous for how little it has been studied in proportion to how often it occurs. This neglect of pandemic victimizations needs to be rectified. For one thing, it fails to reflect the concerns of children themselves. In a recent survey of 2,000 children aged 10–16 years, three times as many were concerned about the likelihood of being beaten up by peers as were concerned about being sexually abused (Finkelhor & Dziuba-Leatherman, in press-b). The pandemic victimizations deserve greater attention, if only because of their alarming frequency and the influence they have on children's everyday existence.

Second, this typology can be useful in developing theory and methodology concerning child victimization. For example, different types of victimization may require different conceptual frameworks. Because they are nearly normative occurrences, the impact of pandemic victimizations may be very different from extraordinary ones, which children experience in relative isolation.

Finally, the typology helps illustrate the diversity and frequency of children's victimization. Although homicide and child abuse have been widely studied, they are notable for how inadequately they convey the variety and true extent of the other victimizations that children suffer. Almost all the figures in Table 3 have been promoted in isolation at one time or another. Viewed together, they are just part of a total environment of various victimization dangers with which children live.

Why Is the Victimization of Children So Common?

When the victimization of children is considered as a whole and its scope and variety more fully appreciated, it prompts a number of interesting and important theoretical questions. The first concerns why the victimization of children is so common. Obviously this is a complex question; a complete answer will undoubtedly require the explanation of elevated risks for different categories of children for different kinds of victimization. However, some generalizations may apply. Certainly the weakness and small physical stature of many children and their dependency status put them at greater risk. They cannot retaliate or deter victimization as effectively as can those with more strength and power. The social toleration of child victimization also plays a role. Society has an influential set of institutions, the police and criminal justice system, to enforce its relatively strong prohibitions against many kinds of crime, but much of the victimization of children is considered outside the purview of this system.

Another important generalization about why children are at high risk for victimization is that children have comparatively little choice over whom they associate with, less choice perhaps than any segment of the population besides prisoners. This can put them in more involuntary contact with high-risk offenders and thus at greater jeopardy for victimization. For example, when children live in families that mistreat them, they are not free or able to leave. When they live in dangerous neighborhoods, they cannot choose on their own to move. If they attend a school with many hostile and delinquent peers, they cannot simply change schools or quit. The absence of choice over people and environments affects children's vulnerability to both intimate victimization and street crime. Although some adults, like battered women and the poor, suffer similar limitations, many adults are able to seek divorce or change their residences in reaction to dangerous conditions. Adults also have more ready access to cars and sometimes have the option to live and work alone. Children are obliged to live with other people, to travel collectively, and to work in high density, heterogenous environments, which is what schools are. In short, children have difficulty gaining access to the structures and mechanisms in society that help segregate people from dangerous associates and environments.

Differential Character of Child Victimization

A second interesting theoretical question concerns how the victimization of children differs from the victimization of adults. Children, of course, suffer from all the victimizations that adults do (including economic crimes like extortion and fraud), but they also suffer from some that are particular to their status. The main status characteristic of childhood is its condition of dependency, which is a function, at least in part, of social and psychological immaturity. The violation of this dependency status results in forms of victimization, like physical neglect, that are not suffered by most adults (with the exception of those, like the elderly and sick, who also become dependent).

The dependency of children creates a spectrum of vulnerability for victimizations. Interestingly, the victimization categories that we have identified in Table 3 can be arrayed on a continuum, according to the degree to which they involve violations of children's dependency status (Figure 2). At one extreme is physical neglect, which has practically no meaning as a victimization except in the case of a person who is dependent and needs to be cared for by others. Similarly, family abduction is a dependency-specific victimization because it is the unlawful removal of a child from the person who is supposed to be caring for him or her. Psychological maltreatment happens to both adults and children, but the sensitive psychological vulnerability of children in their dependent relationship to their caretakers renders such parental behavior a major threat to normal child development (Claussen & Crittenden, 1991; Hart & Brassard, 1987). This is why society considers psychological maltreatment of children a form of victimization that warrants an institutional response.

At the other end of the continuum are forms of victimization that are defined without reference to dependency and which exist in similar forms for both children and adults. Stranger abduction is prototypical in this instance because both children and adults are taken against their will and imprisoned for ransom or sexual purposes. Homicide is similar; the dependency status of the victim does little to define the victimization. In some cases, to be sure, children's deaths result from extreme and willful cases of neglect, but there are parallel instances of adult deaths resulting from extreme and willful negligence.

Finally, there are forms of child victimization that should be located along the midsection of the dependency continuum. Sexual abuse falls here, for example, because it encompasses at least two different situations, one dependency related, one not. Some sexual abuse entails activities, ordinarily acceptable between adults, that are deemed victimizing in the case of children because of their immaturity and dependency. But other sexual abuse involves violence and coercion that would be victimizing even with a nondependent adult.

In the case of physical abuse, there is also some mixture. Although most of the violent acts in this category would be considered victimizing even between adults,

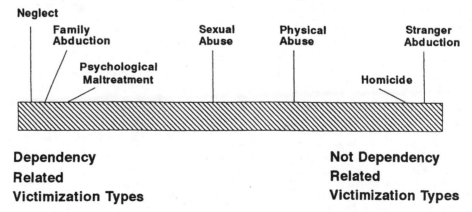

Figure 2
Dependency Continuum for Child Victimization Types

Neglect

Family Abduction

Psychological Maltreatment

Sexual Abuse

Physical Abuse

Homicide

Stranger Abduction

Dependency Related Victimization Types

Not Dependency Related Victimization Types

some of them, like the shaken baby syndrome, develop almost exclusively in a caretaking relationship in which there is an enormous differential in size and physical control.

The dependency continuum is a useful concept in thinking about some of the unique features of children's victimizations. It is also helpful in generating hypotheses about the expected correlates of different types of victimization, such as variations according to age.

Developmental Victimology

Childhood is such an extremely heterogenous category—4-year-olds and 17-year-olds having little in common—that it is inherently misleading to discuss child victimization in general without reference to age. We would expect the nature, quantity, and impact of victimization to vary across childhood with the different capabilities, activities, and environments that are characteristic of different stages of development. A good term for this might be *developmental victimology*. Unfortunately, we do not have good studies of the different types of victimization across all the ages of childhood with which to examine such changes.

There are two plausible propositions about age and child victimization that could be a starting place for developmental victimology. One is that victimizations stemming from the dependent status of children should be most common among the most dependent, hence the youngest, children. A corollary is that as children grow older, their victimization profile should more and more resemble that of adults.

One can examine such propositions in a crude way with the data that are available. In fact, it is apparent (Table 4) that the types of victimization that are most concentrated in the under-12 age group are the dependency related ones (see the dependency continuum in Figure 2), particularly family abduction and physical neglect. Victimizations such as homicide and stranger abduction, which we grouped at the nondependency end of the continuum, involve a greater percentage of teenagers. However, not everything falls neatly into place; sexual abuse seems anomalously concentrated among teenagers, too. We believe this to be an artifact of the National Incidence Study (NIS) data on sexual abuse (National Center on Child Abuse and Neglect, 1981), which was based only on reported cases and thus undercounted sexual abuse of young children.[3] When the incidence of sexual abuse is based on data from retrospective self-reports, 64% of victimizations occur before age 12 (Finkelhor, Hotaling, Lewis, & Smith, 1990), a pattern more consistent with

---

[3] The undercount stems from two problems: (a) Most sexual abuse reports, unlike other forms of child maltreatment, start from children's own disclosures, which are more difficult for younger children to make. (b) Much sexual abuse goes on for extended periods of time before being disclosed, and the age data in the NIS are based on age at the time of report, not age at onset.

Table 4

Victimization of Younger Children

Type of victimization	% of victims under 12 years of age	Source
Family abduction	81[a]	NISMART (R)
Physical neglect	70	NIS-2C
Psychological maltreatment	58[b]	NIS-2C, NSCANR
Physical abuse	56	NIS-2C
Sexual abuse	40	NIS-2C
Stranger abduction	27	NISMART (R)
Homicide	21[c]	UCR91

Note. Some figures shown in this table did not appear in original source but were derived from data presented therein. NISMART (R) = National Incidence Study of Missing, Abducted, Runaway and Thrownaway Children, 1990 (Authors' reanalysis of published data; Finkelhor, Hotaling, & Sedlak, 1990); NIS-2C = National Study of the Incidence and Severity of Child Abuse and Neglect, 1988 (Powers & Eckenrode, 1992); NSCANR = National Study on Child Abuse and Neglect Reporting, 1983 (American Association for Protecting Children, 1985); UCR91 = Uniform Crime Reports, 1991 (Federal Bureau of Investigation, 1992). [a]Broad scope. [b]Reflects midpoint of two divergent estimates. [c]Age group for this category is under 10.

---

the hypothesis and the place of sexual abuse on the dependency continuum.

For additional insights about development and victimization, one can look also at child homicide, the type of victimization to which a developmental analysis has been most extensively applied (Christoffel, 1990; Crittenden & Craig, 1990; Jason, 1983). Child homicide has a conspicuous bimodal frequency, with high rates for the very youngest and oldest children (Figure 3). But the two peaks represent very different phenomena. The homicides of young children are primarily committed by parents, most often using their hands—so-called "personal weapons." In contrast, the homicides of older children are committed mostly by peers and acquaintances, most often with the use of firearms.

Although the analysts do not agree entirely on the number and age span of the specific developmental categories for child homicides, a number of propositions are clear. There is a distinct group of neonaticides, or children killed on the first day or within the first few weeks of life. Homicide at this age is generally considered to include many isolated mothers dealing with unwanted children. After the neonatal period, there follows a period in which homicides are still primarily committed by caretakers using personal weapons, but the motives and circumstances are thought to be somewhat different. These appear to be mostly cases of fatal child abuse that occur as a result of parents' attempts to control child behavior (Christoffel, 1990; Crittenden & Craig, 1990). As children become of school age and older, the nature of

Figure 3
Relationship of Child Homicide Victims to Perpetrators

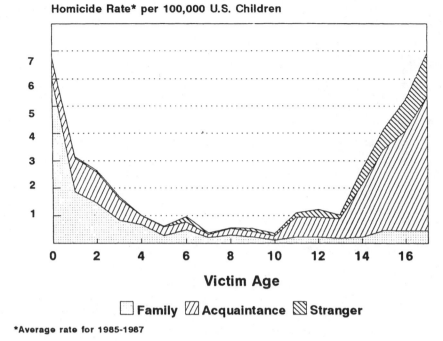

Homicide Rate* per 100,000 U.S. Children

Victim Age

☐ Family ▨ Acquaintance ▧ Stranger

*Average rate for 1985-1987

child homicide becomes incrementally more like adult homicide. Killings by parents and caretakers decline, and those by peers and acquaintances rise. Firearms become the predominant method.

These trends clearly suggest that the types of homicide suffered by children are related to the nature of their dependency and to the level of their integration into the adult world. These trends provide a good case for the importance and utility of a developmental perspective on child victimizations and a model of how such an approach could be applied to other types of victimization.

Intrafamily Victimization

Unlike many adults, children do not live alone; most live in families. Thus, another plausible principle of developmental victimology is that more of the victimization of children occurs at the hands of relatives. We illustrated this in Table 2 and also Table 3, showing the sheer quantity of victimization by relatives apparent in the elevated figures on sibling assault (Table 3), which outstrip any other kind of victimization.

The findings on homicide also suggest a developmental trend: Younger children have a greater proportion of their victimizations at the hands of intimates and correspondingly fewer at the hands of strangers. They live more sheltered lives, spend more time in the home and around family, and have less wealth and fewer valuable possessions that might make them attractive targets for strangers.

An additional possible principle is that the identity of perpetrators may vary according to the type of victimization and its place on the dependency continuum (Figure 2). Victimizations that are more dependency related should involve more perpetrators who are parents and family members. Accordingly, parents are 100% of the perpetrators of neglect and psychological maltreatment (Sedlak, 1991), the most dependency-related victimizations. However, they represent only 51% of the perpetrators of sexual abuse (Sedlak) and 28% of the perpetrators of homicide (Jason, Gilliand, & Taylor, 1983). This pattern occurs because the responsibilities created by children's dependency status fall primarily on parents and family members. They are the main individuals in a position to violate those responsibilities in a way that would create victimization. Thus, when a sick child fails to get available medical attention, it is the parents who are charged with neglecting the child, even if the neighbors also did nothing.

Gender and Victimization

Developmental victimology needs to take account of gender as well. On the basis of the conventional crime statistics available from the NCS and Uniform Crime Reports (UCR), boys would appear to suffer more homicide (2.3:1), more assault (1.7:1), and more robbery (2.0:1) than girls, whereas girls suffer vastly more rape (8.1:1). But this primarily pertains to the experience of adolescents and does not consider age and gender variations.

Figure 4
Gender Differences in Victimization Rates

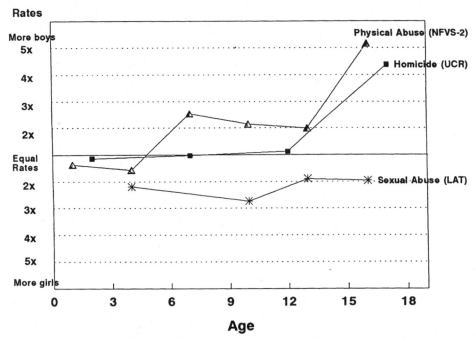

Note. NFVS-2 = National Family Violence Resurvey, 1985 (Straus & Gelles, 1990); UCR = UCR91, Uniform Crime Report (Federal Bureau of Investigation, 1992). LAT = *Los Angeles Times* Poll (Finkelhor, Hotaling, Lewis, & Smith, 1990).

Because gender differentiation increases as children grow older, a developmental hypothesis might predict that the pattern of victimization would be less gender-specific for younger children. That is, because younger boys and girls are more similar in their activities and physical characteristics, there might be less difference between sexes in the rate of victimization.

This pattern does indeed appear to be the case at last for homicide, the type of victimization for which we have the best data (Figure 4). Rates of homicide are quite similar for younger boys and girls, even up to age 14, after which point the vulnerability of boys increases dramatically.

However, this increased differentiation with age is less apparent for other types of victimization. In contrast to homicide, for example, for sexual abuse we might expect that it would be girls who would become increasingly vulnerable as they age. However, the national data do not show this. They show girls at roughly twice the risk of boys throughout childhood, with no increase during adolescence.

So it looks as though a developmental pattern in gender differentiation may apply to some forms of victimization but not others. This mixed picture in regard to gender and age merits more study. Some victimization

Table 5

Rate of Physical Injury Due to Childhood Victimization

Type of victimization	Rate of injury per 1,000 children	% of all victims sustaining injury	Source	Age in years
Assault	19.23	33	NCS90	12–19
Physical abuse	3.59	84	NIS-2	0–17
Robbery	2.71	24	NCS90-2	12–19
Physical neglect	1.39	52	NIS-2	0–17
Family abduction	0.22	04	NISMART	0–17
Sexual abuse	0.09	05	NIS-2	0–17
Stranger abduction	0.007–0.015	14–21	NISMART	0–17

Note. Some figures shown in this table did not appear in original source but were derived from data presented therein. NCS90 = National Crime Survey, 1990 (Bureau of Justice Statistics, 1992); NIS-2 = National Study of the Incidence and Severity of Child Abuse and Neglect, 1988 (Sedlak, 1991); NISMART = National Incidence Study of Missing, Abducted, Runaway and Thrownaway Children, 1990 (Finkelhor, Hotaling, & Sedlak, 1990).

types may have unique gender patterns reflecting their particular dynamics. However, we may also be suffering from inadequate data that are clouding the true situation.

Effects of Child Victimization

Homicide is currently one of the five leading causes of child mortality in the United States (Goetting, 1990). In addition to the more than 2,000 homicide deaths that occur each year (FBI, 1992), one needs to add a sizable proportion of 1,200 child abuse and neglect fatalities, an estimated two thirds of which are not often counted in the homicide statistics (Ewigman, Kivlahan, & Land, 1993). Victimization also results in a substantial toll of nonfatal injuries that are more difficult to count accurately. The NIS estimated that 317,700 children suffered serious or moderate physical injuries in one year (Table 5) as a result of physical abuse or neglect or sexual abuse, that is, injuries for which observable symptoms, such as bruises, lasted at least 48 hours. From the NCS, one can estimate that approximately 523,300 twelve- to 19-year-olds sustained physical injury due to an assault in 1990, and approximately 132,900 received hospital care as a result of any kind of violent crime. A Massachusetts study suggested that each year 1 in every 42 teenage boys receives hospital treatment for an assault-related injury (Guyer, Lescohier, Gallagher, Hausman, & Azzara, 1989).

Children's level of development undoubtedly influences the nature and severity of injuries resulting from victimization, although few analyses have taken such a developmental approach. An obvious example is the greater vulnerability of small children to death and serious harm as a result of inflicted blows. Another obvious example is the higher likelihood of older children to contract sexual-abuse-related HIV infection, because older children suffer more penetrative abuse (Kerns & Ritter, 1991).

In addition to physical injury, there is a growing literature documenting that victimization has grave short- and long-term effects on children's mental health. For example, sexually victimized children appear to be at a nearly fourfold increased lifetime risk for any psychiatric disorder and at a threefold risk for substance abuse (Saunders, Villeponteaux, Lipovsky, Kilpatrick, & Veronen, 1992 ; Scott, 1992). Scott estimated that approximately 8% of all psychiatric cases within the population at large can be attributed to childhood sexual assault.

Although they do not involve such specific epidemiological assessments, other studies have also demonstrated increased rates of mental health morbidity for other types of childhood victimization, including physical abuse (Kolko, 1992), psychological maltreatment (Briere & Runtz, 1990), and physical punishment (Straus, in press).

In addition to general mental health impairments, a proposition that has been established across various types of victimization is that a history of such victimi-

zation increases the likelihood that someone will become a perpetrator of crime, violence, or abuse. Although this popular shibboleth has been criticized and qualified (Kaufman & Ziegler, 1987), evidence to support it comes from a wide variety of methodologies, such as longitudinal follow-ups (McCord, 1983; Widom, 1989a), studies of offender populations (Hanson & Slater, 1988), and surveys of the general population (Straus et al., 1980) and concerns a wide variety of perpetrations, including violent crime, property crime, child abuse, wife abuse, and sexual assaults (for review, see Widom, 1989b). An important qualification is that victims are not necessarily prone to repeat their own form of victimization. But the proposition that childhood victims are more likely to grow up to victimize others is firmly established.

Theory about posttraumatic stress disorder (PTSD) is being applied to, and may be a unifying concept for, understanding common psychological effects of a wide variety of child victimizations (Eth & Pynoos, 1985), including abuse in schools (Hyman, Zelikoff, & Clarke, 1988). Terr (1990) has made some effort to cast PTSD in a more developmental framework, but its application is mostly anecdotal.

Sexual abuse is the only area in which a developmental approach to the psychological impact of victimization has advanced on the basis of empirical studies (Kendall-Tackett, Williams, & Finkelhor, 1993). For example, in reaction to sexual abuse, symptoms of sexualization seem to appear more frequently among preschool than among school-age girls, who seem more aware of appropriate and inappropriate sexual conduct (Friedrich et al., 1992). This is the direction the whole area of child victimization needs to take.

Research Needs

The research needs in this field of child victimization are vast and urgent, given the size of the problem and the seriousness of its impact, and they range from studies of risk factors to studies of treatment efficacy. In the limited space of this review, we mention only three important points.

First, if we are to take child victimization seriously, we need much better statistics to document and analyze its scope, nature, and trends. We need comprehensive, yearly, national and state figures on all officially reported crimes against children and forms of child abuse. These need to be supplemented by regular national studies (one is currently in progress; Finkelhor & Dziuba-Leatherman, in press-a) to assess the vast quantity of unreported victimization, including family violence and child-to-child and indirect victimizations. Currently, the NCS records crime victimizations only down to age 12. The UCR in the past has made no age information available about crimes, with the exception of homicide. Because the national data collection system for child abuse fails to include all states and has severe methodological limitations, the information cannot be aggregated nationally or compared across states (National Center on Child Abuse and Neglect, 1992).

Second, we need theory and research that cuts across and integrates the various forms of child victimization. One example is the research illustrating how forms of victimization occur together (Claussen & Crittenden, 1991) or create vulnerability for one another (Russell, 1984). Another good example is the work on PTSD in children, which has been applied to the effects of various victimizations: sexual abuse, corporal punishment-related abuse in schools, stranger abduction, and the witnessing of homicide (Eth & Pynoos, 1985; Hyman et al., 1988; Terr, 1990). Similar cross-cutting research could be done on other subjects, such as what makes children vulnerable to victimization or how responses by family members buffer or exacerbate the impact of victimization. To be truly synthetic, this research needs to study the pandemic victimizations, not just the acute and the extraordinary, which have been the main foci in the past.

Finally, the field needs a more developmental perspective on child victimization. This would start with an understanding of the mix of victimization threats that face children of different ages. It would include the kinds of factors that place children at risk, including ecological factors, and the strategies for victimization avoidance that are appropriate at different stages of development. It would also differentiate how children, with all their individual differences, react and cope at different stages with the challenges posed by victimization. It is only through this more differentiated approach that we can understand how victimization leaves its mark on children's lives.

REFERENCES

Ageton, S. S. (1983). *Sexual assault among adolescents.* Lexington, MA: Lexington Books.

American Association for Protecting Children. (1985). *Highlights of official child neglect and abuse reporting. 1983.* Denver, CO: American Humane Association.

American School Health Association. (1985). *The national adolescent student health survey: A report on the health of America's youth.* Kent, OH: Author.

Best, J. (1990). *Threatened children: Rhetoric and concern about child-victims.* Chicago: University of Chicago Press.

Briere, J., & Runtz, M. (1990). Differential adult symptomatology associated with three types of child abuse histories. *Child Abuse and Neglect, 14,* 357–364.

Bureau of Justice Statistics. (1991). *Teenage victims: A national crime survey report* (NCJ-128129). Washington, DC: U.S. Department of Justice.

Bureau of Justice Statistics. (1992). *Criminal victimization in the United States, 1990: A national crime victimization survey report* (NCJ-134126). Washington, DC: U.S. Department of Justice.

Christoffel, K. K. (1990). Violent death and injury in U.S. children and adolescents. *American Journal of Diseases of Children, 144,* 697–706.

Claussen, A. I. E., & Crittenden, P. M. (1991). Physical and psychological maltreatment: Relations among types of maltreatment. *Child Abuse and Neglect, 15,* 5–18.

Crittenden, P. A., & Craig, S. E. (1990). Developmental trends in the nature of child homicide. *Journal of Interpersonal Violence, 5,* 202–216.

Daro, D., & Gelles, R. (1991). *Public attitudes and behaviors with respect to child abuse prevention 1987–1991* (Working paper No. 840). Chicago: National Center on Child Abuse Prevention Research, National Committee for Prevention of Child Abuse.

Daro, D., & McCurdy, K. (1991). *Current trends in child abuse reporting and fatalities: The results of the 1990 annual fifty state survey* (Working paper No. 808). Chicago: National Center on Child Abuse Prevention Research, National Committee for Prevention of Child Abuse.

Eth, S., & Pynoos, R. S. (1985). *Post-traumatic stress disorder in children.* Washington, DC: American Psychiatric Press.

Ewigman, B., Kivlahan, C., & Land, G. (1993). The Missouri Child Fatality Study: Underreporting of maltreatment fatalities among children younger than five years of age: 1983 through 1996. *Pediatrics, 91,* 330–337.

Federal Bureau of Investigation. (1992). *Crime in the United States, 1991: Uniform crime reports.* Washington, DC: U.S. Department of Justice.

Finkelhor, D., & Dziuba-Leatherman, J. (in press-a). Children as victims of violence: A national survey. *Pediatrics.*

Finkelhor, D., & Dziuba-Leatherman, J. (in press-b). Victimization prevention programs: A national survey of children's exposure and reactions. *Child Abuse and Neglect.*

Finkelhor, D., Hotaling, G. T., Lewis, I. A., & Smith, C. (1990). Sexual abuse in a national survey of adult men and women: Prevalence, characteristics, and risk factors. *Child Abuse and Neglect, 14,* 19–28.

Finkelhor, D., Hotaling, G. T., & Sedlak, A. (1990). *Missing, abducted, runaway, and thrownaway children in America: First report.* Washington, DC: Juvenile Justice Clearinghouse.

Friedrich, W. N., Grambsch, P., Damon, L., Hewitt, S. K., Koverola, C., Wolfe, V., Lang, R. A., & Broughton, D. (1992). Child Sexual Behavior Inventory: Normative and clinical comparisons. *Psychological Assessment, 4,* 303–311.

Garbarino, J. (1989). The incidence and prevalence of child maltreatment. In L. Ohlin & M. Tonry (Eds.), *Family violence* (pp. 219–261). Chicago: University of Chicago Press.

Garofalo, J., Siegel, L., & Laub, J. (1987). School-related victimizations among adolescents: An analysis of National Crime Survey narratives. *Journal of Quantitative Criminology, 3,* 321–338.

Gelles, R. J., & Straus, M. A. (1979). Determinants of violence in the family: Towards a theoretical integration. In W. R. Burr, R. Hill, F. I. Nye, & I. L. Reiss (Eds.), *Contemporary theories about the family* (Vol. 1). New York: Free Press.

Goetting, A. (1990). Child victims of homicide: A portrait of their killers and the circumstances of their deaths. *Violence and Victims, 5,* 287–296.

Greenbaum, S. (1989). *School bullying and victimization* (NSSC resource paper). Malibu, CA: National School Safety Center.

Greven, P. (1990). *Spare the child: The religious roots of punishment and the psychological impact of physical abuse.* New York: Knopf.

Guyer, B., Lescohier, I., Gallagher, S. S., Hausman, A., & Azzara, C. V. (1989). Intentional injuries among children and adolescents in Massachusetts. *The New England Journal of Medicine, 321,* 1584–1589.

Hanson, R. L., & Slater, S. (1988). Sexual victimization in the history of sexual abusers: A review. *Annals of Sex Research, 4,* 485–499.

Hart, S. N., & Brassard, M. R. (1987). A major threat to children's mental health: Psychological maltreatment. *American Psychologist, 42,* 160–165.

Hyman, I. A. (1990). *Reading, writing and the hickory stick: The appalling story of physical and psychological abuse in American schools.* Lexington, MA: Lexington Books.

Hyman, I. A., Zelikoff, W., & Clarke, J. (1988). Psychological and physical abuse in the schools: A paradigm for understanding post-traumatic stress disorder in children and youths. *Journal of Traumatic Stress, 1,* 243–267.

Jason, J. (1983). Child homicide spectrum. *American Journal of Diseases of Children, 137,* 578–581.

Jason, J., Gilliand, J. C., & Taylor, C. W. (1983). Homicide as a cause of pediatric mortality in the United States. *Pediatrics, 72,* 191–197.

Kaufman, J., & Ziegler, E. (1987). Do abused children become abusive parents? *American Journal of Orthopsychiatry, 57,* 186–192.

Kendall-Tackett, K. A., Williams, L. M., & Finkelhor, D. (1993). Impact of sexual abuse on children: A review and synthesis of recent empirical studies. *Psychological Bulletin, 113,* 164–180.

Kerns, D. L., & Ritter, M. L. (1991, September). *Data analysis of the medical evaluation of 1,800 suspected child sexual abuse victims.* Paper presented at the Ninth National Conference on Child Abuse and Neglect, Denver, CO.

Kilpatrick, D. (1992). *Rape in America: A report to the nation.* Charleston, SC: Crime Victims Research Center.

Kolko, D. J. (1992). Characteristics of child victims of physical violence: Research findings and clinical implications. *Journal of Interpersonal Violence, 7,* 244–276.

Lauritsen, J. L., Sampson, R. J., & Laub, J. H. (1991). The link between offending and victimization among adolescents. *Criminology, 29,* 265–292.

McCord, J. (1983). A forty year perspective on effects of child abuse and neglect. *Child Abuse and Neglect, 7,* 265–270.

McDermott, M. J., Stanley, J. E., & Zimmerman-McKinney, M. A. (1982). The victimization of children and youths. *Victimology, 7,* 162–177.

Morgan, J., & Zedner, L. (1992). *Child victims: Crime, impact, and criminal justice.* Oxford, England: Clarendon Press.

National Center on Child Abuse and Neglect. (1981). *Study findings, National Study of the Incidence and Severity of Child Abuse and Neglect* (OHDS Publication No. 81-30325). Washington, DC: Department of Health and Human Services.

National Center on Child Abuse and Neglect. (1992). *National child abuse and neglect data system* (Working paper No. 1): *1990 summary data component* (DHHS Publication No. ACF 92-30361). Washington, DC: Department of Health and Human Services.

Olweus, D. (1978). *Aggression in the schools: Bullies and whipping boys.* Washington, DC: Hemisphere.

Pagelow, M. D. (1989). The incidence and prevalence of criminal abuse of other family members. In L. Ohlin & M. Tonry (Eds.), *Family violence* (pp. 263–314). Chicago: University of Chicago Press.

Powers, J., & Eckenrode, J. (1992, March). *The epidemiology of adolescent maltreatment.* Paper presented at the Fourth Biennial Meeting of the Society for Research on Adolescence, Washington, DC.

Russell, D. (1984). *Sexual exploitation: Rape, child sexual abuse, and work-place harassment.* Beverly Hills, CA: Sage.

Saunders, B. E., Villeponteaux, L. A., Lipovsky, J. A., Kilpatrick, D. G., & Veronen, L. J. (1992). Child sexual assault as a risk factor for mental disorders among women: A community survey. *Journal of Interpersonal Violence, 7,* 189–204.

Scott, K. D. (1992). Childhood sexual abuse: Impact on a community's mental health status. *Child Abuse and Neglect, 16,* 285–295.

Sedlak, A. J. (1991). *Supplementary analyses of data on the national incidence of child abuse and neglect.* Rockville, MD: Westat.

Straus, M. A. (in press). Corporal punishment of children and depression and suicide in adulthood. In J. McCord (Ed.), *Coercion and punishment in long-term perspective.* Cambridge, England: Cambridge University Press.

Straus, M. A., & Gelles, R. J. (1990). *Physical violence in American families: Risk factors and adaptations to violence in 8,145 families.* New Brunswick, NJ: Transaction.

Straus, M., Gelles, R., & Steinmetz, S. K. (1980). *Behind closed doors: Violence in the American family.* Garden City, NY: Anchor Press.

Terr, L. (1990). *Too scared to cry.* New York: Harper/Collins.

Widom, C. S. (1989a). The cycle of violence. *Science, 244,* 160–166.

Widom, C. S. (1989b). Does violence beget violence? A critical examination of the literature. *Psychological Bulletin, 106,* 3–28.

David Finkelhor and Jennifer Dziuba-Leatherman, Family Research Laboratory, University of New Hampshire.

Nadine M. Lambert served as action editor for this article.

We thank the Boy Scouts of America for financial support. We would also like to thank Kyle Ruonala for help in preparing the manuscript and Lucy Berliner, David Chadwick, Kathy Kaufer Christoffel, James Collins, Pat Crittenden, Howard Davidson, James Garbarino, Malcolm Gordon, Elizabeth Kandel, Kathy Kendall-Tackett, David Kerns, Ben Saunders, Murray Straus, James Tucker, members of the Family Violence Research Seminar, and several anonymous reviewers for helpful comments on the article.

Correspondence concerning this article should be addressed to David Finkelhor, Family Research Laboratory, University of New Hampshire, 126 Horton Social Science Center, Durham, NH 03824.

APPENDIX

Sources of Data

Acronym	Survey
50-SS	Annual Fifty State Survey, 1990 (Daro & McCurdy, 1991).
LAECA	Los Angeles Epiemiologic Catchment Area data (Scott, 1992).
LAT	*Los Angeles Times* Poll (Finkelhor, Hotaling, Lewis, & Smith, 1990).
NASHS	National Adolescent Student Health Survey (American School Health Association, 1985).
NCS90	National Crime Survey, 1990 (Bureau of Justice Statistics, 1992).
NCSTEEN	National Crime Survey, 1979–1988 (as presented in Bureau of Justice Statistics, 1991).
NFVS-1	National Family Violence Survey, 1975 (Straus & Gelles, 1990).
NFVS-2	National Family Villence Resurvey, 1985 (Straus & Gelles, 1990).
NISMART	National Incidence Study of Missing, Abducted, Runaway and Thownaway Children, 1990 (Finkelhor, Hotaling, & Sedlak, 1990).
NSCANR	National Study on Child Abuse and Neglect Reporting, 1983 (American Association for Protecting Children, 1985).
NIS-1	National Study of the Incidence and Severity of Child Abuse and Neglect, 1981 (National Center on Child Abuse and Neglect, 1981).
NIS-2	National Study of the Incidence and Severity of Child Abuse and Neglect, 1988 (Sedlak, 1991).
NIS-2C	National Study of the Incidence and Severity of Child Abuse and Neglect, 1988 (as presented in Powers & Eckenrode, 1992).
NYS	National Youth Survey (Lauritsen, Sampson, & Laub, 1991).
NYS78	National Youth Survey, 1978 (Ageton, 1983).
UCR91	Uniform Crime Reports, 1991 (Federal Bureau of Investigation, 1992).

Resilience in Development

Emmy E. Werner

Emmy E. Werner is Professor of Human Development at the University of California, Davis. Address correspondence to Emmy E. Werner, Department of Applied Behavioral Sciences, University of California, Davis, 2321 Hart Hall, Davis, CA 95616.

During the past decade, a number of investigators from different disciplines—child development, psychology, psychiatry, and sociology—have focused on the study of children and youths who overcame great odds. These researchers have used the term resilience to describe three kinds of phenomena: good developmental outcomes despite high-risk status, sustained competence under stress, and recovery from trauma. Under each of these conditions, behavioral scientists have focused their attention on protective factors, or mechanisms that moderate (ameliorate) a person's reaction to a stressful situation or chronic adversity so that his or her adaptation is more successful than would be the case if the protective factors were not present.[1]

So far, only a relatively small number of studies have focused on children who were exposed to biological insults. More numerous in the current research literature are studies of resilient children who grew up in chronic poverty, were exposed to parental psychopathology, or experienced the breakup of their family or serious caregiving deficits. There has also been a growing body of literature on resilience in children who have endured the horrors of contemporary wars.

Despite the heterogeneity of all these studies, one can begin to discern a common core of individual dispositions and sources of support that contribute to resilience in development. These protective buffers appear to transcend ethnic, social-class, and geographic boundaries. They also appear to make a more profound impact on the life course of individuals who grow up in adversity than do specific risk factors or stressful life events.

Most studies of individual resilience and protective factors in children have been short-term, focusing on middle childhood and adolescence. An exception is the Kauai Longitudinal Study, with which I have been associated during the past three decades.[2] This study has involved a team of pediatricians, psychologists, and public-health and social workers who have monitored the impact of a variety of biological and psychosocial risk factors, stressful life events, and protective factors on the development of a multiethnic cohort of 698 children born in 1955 on the "Garden Island" in the Hawaiian chain. These individuals were followed, with relatively little attrition, from the prenatal period through birth to ages 1, 2, 10, 18, and 32.

Some 30% of the survivors in this study population were considered high-risk children because they were born in chronic poverty, had experienced perinatal stress, and lived in family environments troubled by chronic discord, divorce, or parental psychopathology. Two thirds of the children who had experienced four or more such risk factors by age 2 developed serious learning or behavior problems by age 10 or had delinquency records, mental health problems, or pregnancies by age 18. But one third of the children who had experienced four or more such risk factors developed instead into competent, confident, and caring adults.

PROTECTIVE FACTORS WITHIN THE INDIVIDUAL

Infancy and Early Childhood

Our findings with these resilient children are consistent with the results of several other longitudinal studies which have reported that young children with good coping abilities under adverse conditions have temperamental characteristics that elicit positive responses from a wide range of caregivers. The resilient boys and girls in the Kauai study were consistently characterized by their mothers as active, affectionate, cuddly, good-natured, and easy to deal with. Egeland and his associates observed similar dispositions among securely attached infants of abusing mothers in the Minnesota Mother-Child Interaction Project,[3] and Moriarty found the same qualities among infants with congenital defects at the Menninger Foundation.[4] Such infants were alert, easy to soothe, and able to elicit support from a nurturant family member. An "easy" temperament and the ability to actively recruit competent adult caregivers were also observed by Elder and his associates[5] in the resourceful children of the Great Depression.

By the time they reach preschool age, resilient children appear to have developed a coping pattern that combines autonomy with an ability to ask for help when needed. These characteristics are also predictive of resilience in later years.

Middle Childhood and Adolescence

When the resilient children in the Kauai Longitudinal Study were in elementary school, their teachers were favorably impressed by their communication and problem-solving skills. Although these children were not particularly gifted, they used whatever talents they had effectively. Usually they had a special interest or a hobby they could share with a friend, and that gave them a sense of pride. These interests and activities were not narrowly sex typed. But the boys and the girls grew into adolescents who were outgoing and autonomous, but also nurturant and emotionally sensitive.

Similar findings have been reported by Anthony, who studied the resilient offspring of mentally ill parents in St. Louis;[6] by Felsman and Vaillant, who followed successful boys from a high-crime neighborhood in Boston into adulthood;[7] and by Rutter and Quinton, who studied the lives of British girls who had been institutionalized in childhood, but managed to become well-functioning adults and caring mothers.[8]

Most studies of resilient children and youths report that intelligence and scholastic competence are positively associated with the ability to overcome great odds. It stands to reason that youngsters who are better able to appraise stressful life events correctly are also better able to figure out strategies for coping with adversity, either through their own efforts or by actively reaching out to other people for help. This finding has been replicated in studies of Asian-American,

Caucasian, and African-American children.[2,9,10]

Other salient protective factors that operated in the lives of the resilient youths on Kauai were a belief in their own effectiveness (an internal locus of control) and a positive self-concept. Such characteristics were also found by Farrington among successful and law-abiding British youngsters who grew up in high-crime neighborhoods in London,[11] and by Wallerstein and her associates among American children who coped effectively with the breakup of their parents' marriages.[12]

PROTECTIVE FACTORS WITHIN THE FAMILY

Despite the burden of chronic poverty, family discord, or parental psychopathology, a child identified as resilient usually has had the opportunity to establish a close bond with at least one competent and emotionally stable person who is attuned to his or her needs. The stress-resistant children in the Kauai Longitudinal Study, the well-functioning offspring of child abusers in the Minnesota Mother-Child Interaction Project, the resilient children of psychotic parents studied by Anthony in St. Louis, and the youngsters who coped effectively with the breakup of their parents' marriages in Wallerstein's studies of divorce all had received enough good nurturing to establish a basic sense of trust.[2,3,6,12]

Much of this nurturing came from substitute caregivers within the extended family, such as grandparents and older siblings. Resilient children seem to be especially adept at recruiting such surrogate parents. In turn, they themselves are often called upon to take care of younger siblings and to practice acts of "required helpfulness" for members of their family who are ill or incapacitated.[2]

Both the Kauai Longitudinal Study and Block and Gjerde's studies of ego-resilient children[9] found characteristic child-rearing orientations that appear to promote resiliency differentially in boys and girls. Resilient boys tend to come from households with structure and rules, where a male serves as a model of identification (father, grandfather, or older brother), and where there is some encouragement of emotional expressiveness. Resilient girls, in contrast, tend to come from households that combine an emphasis on risk taking and independence with reliable support from a female caregiver, whether mother, grandmother, or older sister. The example of a mother who is gainfully and steadily employed appears to be an especially powerful model of identification for resilient girls.[2] A number of studies of resilient children from a wide variety of socioeconomic and ethnic backgrounds have also noted that the families of these children held religious beliefs that provided stability and meaning in times of hardship and adversity.[2,6,10]

PROTECTIVE FACTORS IN THE COMMUNITY

The Kauai Longitudinal Study and a number of other prospective studies in the United States have shown that resilient youngsters tend to rely on peers and elders in the community as sources of emotional support and seek them out for counsel and comfort in times of crisis.[2,6]

Favorite teachers are often positive role models. All of the resilient high-risk children in the Kauai study could point to at least one teacher who was an important source of support. These teachers listened to the children, challenged them, and rooted for them—whether in grade school, high school, or community college. Similar findings have been reported by Wallerstein and her associates from their long-term observations of youngsters who coped effectively with their parents' divorces[12] and by Rutter and his associates from their studies of inner-city schools in London.[13]

Finally, in the Kauai study, we found that the opening of opportunities at major life transitions enabled the majority of the high-risk children who had a troubled adolescence to rebound in their 20s and early 30s. Among the most potent second chances for such youths were adult education programs in community colleges, voluntary military service, active participation in a church community, and a supportive friend or marital partner. These protective buffers were also observed by Elder in the adult lives of the children of the Great Depression,[14] by Furstenberg and his associates in the later lives of black teenage mothers,[15] and by Farrington[11] and Felsman and Vaillant[7] in the adult lives of young men who had grown up in high-crime neighborhoods in London and Boston.

PROTECTIVE FACTORS: A SUMMARY

Several clusters of protective factors have emerged as recurrent themes in the lives of children who overcome great odds. Some protective factors are characteristics of the individual: Resilient children are engaging to other people, adults and peers alike; they have good communication and problem-solving skills, including the ability to recruit substitute caregivers; they have a talent or hobby that is valued by their elders or peers; and they have faith that their own actions can make a positive difference in their lives.

Another factor that enhances resilience in development is having affectional ties that encourage trust, autonomy, and initiative. These ties are often provided by members of the extended family. There are also support systems in the community that reinforce and reward the competencies of resilient children and provide them with positive role models: caring neighbors, teachers, elder mentors, youth workers, and peers.

LINKS BETWEEN PROTECTIVE FACTORS AND SUCCESSFUL ADAPTATION IN HIGH-RISK CHILDREN AND YOUTHS

In the Kauai study, when we examined the links between protective factors within the individual and outside sources of support, we noted a certain continuity in the life course of the high-risk individuals who successfully overcame a variety of childhood adversities. Their individual dispositions led them to select or construct environments that, in turn, reinforced and sustained their active approach to life and rewarded their special competencies.

Although the sources of support available to the individuals in their childhood homes were modestly linked to the quality of the individuals' adaptation as adults, their competencies, temperament, and self-esteem had a greater impact. Many resilient high-risk youths on Kauai left the adverse conditions of their childhood homes after high school and sought environments they found more compatible. In short, they picked their own niches.

Our findings lend some empirical support to Scarr and McCartney's theory[16] about how people make their own environment. Scarr and McCartney proposed three types of effects of people's genes on their environment: passive, evocative, and active. Because parents provide both children's genes and their rearing environments, children's genes are necessarily correlated with their own environments. This is the passive type of genotype-environment effect. The evocative type refers to the fact that a person's partially heritable characteristics, such as intelligence, personality, and physical attractiveness, evoke certain responses from other people. Finally, a person's interests, talents, and personality (genetically variable traits) may lead him or her to select or create particular environments;

this is called an active genotype-environment effect. In line with this theory, there was a shift from passive to active effects as the youths and young adults in the Kauai study left stressful home environments and sought extrafamilial environments (at school, at work, in the military) that they found more compatible and stimulating. Genotype-environment effects of the evocative sort tended to persist throughout the different life stages we studied, as individuals' physical characteristics, temperament, and intelligence elicited differential responses from other people (parents, teachers, peers).

IMPLICATIONS

So far, most studies of resilience have focused on children and youths who have "pulled themselves up by their bootstraps," with informal support by kith and kin, not on recipients of intervention services. Yet there are some lessons such children can teach society about effective intervention: If we want to help vulnerable youngsters become more resilient, we need to decrease their exposure to potent risk factors and increase their competencies and self-esteem, as well as the sources of support they can draw upon.

In *Within Our Reach,* Schorr has isolated a set of common characteristics of social programs that have successfully prevented poor outcomes for children who grew up in high-risk families.[17] Such programs typically offer a broad spectrum of health, education, and family support services, cross professional boundaries, and view the child in the context of the family, and the family in the context of the community. They provide children with sustained access to competent and caring adults, both professionals and volunteers, who teach them problem-solving skills, enhance their communication skills and self-esteem, and provide positive role models for them.

There is an urgent need for more systematic evaluations of such programs to illuminate the process by which we can forge a chain of protective factors that enables vulnerable children to become competent, confident, and caring individuals, despite the odds of chronic poverty or a medical or social disability. Future research on risk and resiliency needs to acquire a cross-cultural perspective as well. We need to know more about individual dispositions and sources of support that transcend cultural boundaries and operate effectively in a variety of high-risk contexts.

Notes

1. A. S. Masten, K. M. Best, and N. Garmezy, Resilience and development: Contributions from the study of children who overcame adversity, *Development and Psychopathology, 2,* 425–444 (1991).

2. All results from this study that are discussed in this review were reported in E. E. Werner, Risk resilience, and recovery: Perspectives from the Kauai Longitudinal Study, *Development and Psychopathology, 5,* 503–515 (1993).

3. B. Egeland, D. Jacobvitz, and L. A. Stroufe, Breaking the cycle of child abuse, *Child Development, 59,* 1080–1088 (1988).

4. A Moriarty, John, a boy who acquired resilience, in *The Invulnerable Child,* E. J. Anthony and B. J. Cohler, Eds. (Guilford Press, New York, 1987).

5. G. H. Elder, K. Liker, and C. E. Cross, Parent-child behavior in the Great Depression, in *Life Span Development and Behavior,* Vol. 6, T. B. Baltes and O. G. Brim, Jr., Eds. (Academic Press, New York, 1984).

6. E. J. Anthony, Children at risk for psychosis growing up successfully, in *The Invulnerable Child,* E. J. Anthony and B. J. Cohler, Eds. (Guilford Press, New York, 1987).

7. J. K. Felsman and G. E. Vaillant, Resilient children as adults: A 40 year study in *The Invulnerable Child,* E. J. Cohler, Eds. (Guilford Press, New York, 1987).

8. M. Rutter and D. Quinton, Long term follow-up of women institutionalized in childhood: Factors promoting good functioning in adult life, *British Journal of Developmental Psychology, 18,* 225–234 (1984).

9. J. Block and P. F. Gjerde, *Early antecedents of ego resiliency in late adolescence,* paper presented at the annual meeting of the American Psychological Association, Washington, DC (August 1986).

10. R. M. Clark, *Family Life and School Achievement: Why Poor Black Children Succeed or Fail* (University of Chicago Press, Chicago, 1983).

11. D. P. Farrington, *Protective Factors in the Development of Juvenile Delinquency and Adult Crime* (Institute of Criminology, Cambridge University, Cambridge, England, 1993).

12. J. S. Wallerstein and S. Blakeslee, *Second Chances: Men, Women and Children a Decade After Divorce* (Ticknor and Fields, New York, 1989).

13. M. Rutter, B. Maughan, P. Mortimore, and J. Ousten, *Fifteen Thousand Hours: Secondary Schools and Their Effects on Children* (Harvard University Press, Cambridge, MA, 1979).

14. G. H. Elder, Military times and turning points in men's lives, *Developmental Psychology, 22,* 233–245 (1986).

15. F. F. Furstenberg, J. Brooks-Gunn, and S. P. Morgan, *Adolescent Mothers in Later Life* (Cambridge University Press, New York, 1987).

16. S. Scarr and K. McCartney, How people make their own environments: A theory of genotype-environment effects, *Child Development, 54,* 424–435 (1983).

17. L. Schorr, *Within Our Reach: Breaking the Cycle of Disadvantage* (Anchor Press, New York, 1988).

Recommended Reading

Haggerty, R., Garmezy, N., Rutter, M., and Sherrod, L., Eds. (1994). *Stress, Risk, and Resilience in Childhood and Adolescence* (Cambridge University Press, New York).

Luthar, S., and Zigler, E. (1991). Vulnerability and competence: A review of research on resilience in childhood. *American Journal of Orthopsychiatry, 61,* 6–22.

Werner, E. E., and Smith, R. S. (1992). *Overcoming the Odds: High Risk Children From Birth to Adulthood* (Cornell University Press, Ithaca, NY).

Creating False Memories

*Researchers are showing how suggestion and imagination can
create "memories" of events that did not actually occur*

by Elizabeth F. Loftus

In 1986 Nadean Cool, a nurse's aide in Wisconsin, sought therapy from a psychiatrist to help her cope with her reaction to a traumatic event experienced by her daughter. During therapy, the psychiatrist used hypnosis and other suggestive techniques to dig out buried memories of abuse that Cool herself had allegedly experienced. In the process, Cool became convinced that she had repressed memories of having been in a satanic cult, of eating babies, of being raped, of having sex with animals and of being forced to watch the murder of her eight-year-old friend. She came to believe that she had more than 120 personalities—children, adults, angels and even a duck—all because, Cool was told, she had experienced severe childhood sexual and physical abuse. The psychiatrist also performed exorcisms on her, one of which lasted for five hours and included the sprinkling of holy water and screams for Satan to leave Cool's body.

When Cool finally realized that false memories had been planted, she sued the psychiatrist for malpractice. In March 1997, after five weeks of trial, her case was settled out of court for $2.4 million.

Nadean Cool is not the only patient to develop false memories as a result of questionable therapy. In Missouri in 1992 a church counselor helped Beth Rutherford to remember during therapy that her father, a clergyman, had regularly raped her between the ages of seven and 14 and that her mother sometimes helped him by holding her down. Under her therapist's guidance, Rutherford developed memories of her father twice impregnating her and forcing her to abort the fetus herself with a coat hanger. The father had to resign from his post as a clergyman when the allegations were made public. Later medical examination of the daughter revealed, however, that she was still a virgin at age 22 and had never been pregnant. The daughter sued the therapist and received a $1-million settlement in 1996.

About a year earlier two juries returned verdicts against a Minnesota psychiatrist accused of planting false memories by former patients Vynnette Hamanne and Elizabeth Carlson, who under hypnosis and

FALSE MEMORIES are often created by combining actual memories with suggestions received from others. The memory of a happy childhood outing to the beach with father and grandfather, for instance, can be distorted by a suggestion, perhaps from a relative, into a memory of being afraid or lost. False memories also can be induced when a person is encouraged to imagine experiencing specific events without worrying about whether they really happened or not.

sodium amytal, and after being fed misinformation about the workings of memory, had come to remember horrific abuse by family members. The juries awarded Hammane $2.67 million and Carlson $2.5 million for their ordeals.

In all four cases, the women developed memories about childhood

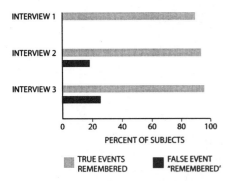

INTERVIEW 1
INTERVIEW 2
INTERVIEW 3

PERCENT OF SUBJECTS

TRUE EVENTS REMEMBERED   FALSE EVENT "REMEMBERED"

abuse in therapy and then later denied their authenticity. How can we determine if memories of childhood abuse are true or false? Without corroboration, it is very difficult to differentiate between false memories and true ones. Also, in these cases, some memories were contrary to physical evidence, such as explicit and detailed recollections of rape and abortion when medical examination confirmed virginity. How is it possible for people to acquire elaborate and confident false memories? A growing number of investigations demonstrate that under the right circumstances false memories can be instilled rather easily in some people.

My own research into memory distortion goes back to the early 1970s, when I began studies of the "misinformation effect." These studies show that when people who witness an event are later exposed to new and misleading information about it, their recollections often become distorted. In one example, participants viewed a simulated automobile accident at an intersection with a stop sign. After the viewing, half the participants received a suggestion that the traffic sign was a yield sign. When asked later what traffic sign they remembered seeing at the intersection, those who had

been given the suggestion tended to claim that they had seen a yield sign. Those who had not received the phony information were much more accurate in their recollection of the traffic sign.

My students and I have now conducted more than 200 experiments involving over 20,000 individuals that document how exposure to misinformation induces memory distortion. In these studies, people "recalled" a conspicuous barn in a bucolic scene that contained no buildings at all, broken glass and tape recorders that were not in the scenes they viewed, a white instead of a blue vehicle in a crime scene, and Minnie Mouse when they actually saw Mickey Mouse. Taken together, these studies show that misinformation can change an individual's recollection in predictable and sometimes very powerful ways.

Misinformation has the potential for invading our memories when we talk to other people, when we are suggestively interrogated or when we read or view media coverage about some event that we may have expe-

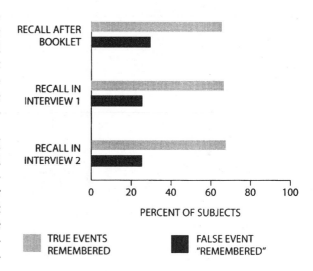

RECALL AFTER BOOKLET
RECALL IN INTERVIEW 1
RECALL IN INTERVIEW 2

PERCENT OF SUBJECTS

TRUE EVENTS REMEMBERED   FALSE EVENT "REMEMBERED"

rienced ourselves. After more than two decades of exploring the power of misinformation, researchers have learned a great deal about the conditions that make people susceptible to memory modification. Memories are more easily modified, for instance, when the passage of time allows the original memory to fade.

False Childhood Memories

It is one thing to change a detail or two in an otherwise intact memory but quite another to plant a false memory of an event that never hap-

RECALL OF PLANTED CHILDHOOD EVENTS in this study appears to increase slightly after the details become familiar to the subject and the source of the information is forgotten. Ira Hyman and his colleagues at Western Washington University presented subjects with true events provided by relatives along with a false event—such as spilling a punch bowl on the parents of the bride at a wedding. None of the participants remembered the false event when first told about it, but in two follow-up interviews, initially 18 percent and later 25 percent of the subjects said they remembered something about the incident.

pened. To study false memory, my students and I first had to find a way to plant a pseudomemory that would not cause our subjects undue emotional stress, either in the process of creating the false memory or when we revealed that they had been intentionally deceived. Yet we wanted to try to plant a memory that would be at least mildly traumatic, had the experience actually happened.

My research associate, Jacqueline E. Pickrell, and I settled on trying to plant a specific memory of being lost in a shopping mall or large department store at about the age of five. Here's how we did it. We asked our subjects, 24 individuals ranging in age from 18 to 53, to try to remember childhood events that had been recounted to us by a parent, an older sibling or another close relative. We prepared a booklet for each participant containing one-paragraph stories about three events that had actually happened to him or her and one that had not. We constructed the false event using information about a plausible shopping trip provided by a relative, who also verified that the participant had not in fact been lost at about the age of five. The lost-in-the-mall scenario included the following elements: lost for an extended period, crying, aid and comfort by an elderly woman and, finally, reunion with the family.

After reading each story in the booklet, the participants wrote what they remembered about the event. If they did not remember it, they were instructed to write, "I do not remember this." In two follow-up interviews, we told the participants that we were interested in examining how much detail they could remember and how their memories compared with those of their relative. The event paragraphs were not read to them verbatim, but rather parts were provided as retrieval cues. The participants recalled something about 49 of the 72 true events (68 percent) immediately after the initial reading of the booklet and also in each of the two follow-up inter-

views. After reading the booklet, seven of the 24 participants (29 percent) remembered either partially or fully the false event constructed for them, and in the two follow-up interviews six participants (25 percent) continued to claim that they remembered the fictitious event. Statistically, there were some differences between the true memories and the false ones: participants used more words to describe the true memories, and they rated the true memories as being somewhat more clear. But if an onlooker were to observe many of our participants describe an event, it would be difficult indeed to tell whether the account was of a true or a false memory.

Of course, being lost, however frightening, is not the same as being abused. But the lost-in-the-mall study is not about real experiences of being lost; it is about planting false memories of being lost. The paradigm shows a way of instilling false memories and takes a step toward allowing us to understand how this might happen in real-world settings. Moreover, the study provides evidence that people can be led to remember their past in different ways, and they can even be coaxed into "remembering" entire events that never happened.

Studies in other laboratories using a similar experimental proce-

dure have produced similar results. For instance, Ira Hyman, Troy H. Husband and F. James Billing of Western Washington University asked college students to recall childhood experiences that had been recounted by their parents. The researchers told the students that the study was about how people remember shared experiences differently. In addition to actual events reported by parents, each participant was given one false event—either an overnight hospitalization for a high fever and a possible ear infection, or a birthday party with pizza and a clown—that supposedly happened at about the age of five. The parents confirmed that neither of these events actually took place.

Hyman found that students fully or partially recalled 84 percent of the true events in the first interview and 88 percent in the second interview. None of the participants recalled the false event during the first interview, but 20 percent said they remembered something about the false event in the second interview. One participant who had been exposed to the emergency hospitalization story later remembered a male doctor, a female nurse and a friend from church who came to visit at the hospital.

In another study, along with true events Hyman presented different

FALSE MEMORY TOOK ROOT in roughly 25 percent of the subjects in this study by the author and her co-workers. The study was designed to create a false recollection of being lost at age five on a shopping trip. A booklet prepared for each participant included the false event and three events that he or she had actually experienced. After reading the scenarios, 29 percent of the subjects "recalled" something about being lost in the mall. Follow-up interviews showed there was little variation over time in recalling both the false and true events.

false events, such as accidentally spilling a bowl of punch on the parents of the bride at a wedding reception or having to evacuate a grocery store when the overhead sprinkler systems erroneously activated. Again, none of the participants recalled the false event during the first interview, but 18 percent remembered something about it in the second interview and 25 percent in the third interview. For example,

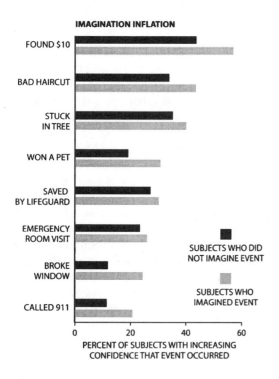

IMAGINATION INFLATION

FOUND $10

BAD HAIRCUT

STUCK IN TREE

WON A PET

SAVED BY LIFEGUARD

EMERGENCY ROOM VISIT

BROKE WINDOW

CALLED 911

■ SUBJECTS WHO DID NOT IMAGINE EVENT

▨ SUBJECTS WHO IMAGINED EVENT

0   20   40   60
PERCENT OF SUBJECTS WITH INCREASING CONFIDENCE THAT EVENT OCCURRED

during the first interview, one participant, when asked about the fictitious wedding event, stated, "I have no clue. I have never heard that one before." In the second interview, the participant said, "It was an outdoor wedding, and I think we were running around and knocked something over like the punch bowl or something and made a big mess and of course got yelled at for it."

Imagination Inflation

The finding that an external suggestion can lead to the construction of false childhood memories helps us understand the process by which false memories arise. It is natural to wonder whether this research is applicable in real situations such as being interrogated by law officers or in psychotherapy. Although strong suggestion may not routinely occur in police questioning or therapy, suggestion in the form of an imagination exercise sometimes does. For instance, when trying to obtain a confession, law officers may ask a suspect to imagine having participated in a criminal act. Some mental health professionals encourage patients to imagine childhood events as a way of recovering supposedly hidden memories.

Surveys of clinical psychologists reveal that 11 percent instruct their clients to "let the imagination run wild," and 22 percent tell their clients to "give free rein to the imagination." Therapist Wendy Maltz, author of a popular book on childhood sexual abuse, advocates telling the parent: "Spend time imagining that you were sexually abused, without worrying about accuracy, proving anything, or having your ideas make sense.... Ask yourself ... these questions: What time of day is it? Where are you? Indoors or outdoors? What kind of things are happening? Is there one or more person with you?" Maltz further recommends that therapists continue to ask questions such as "Who would have been likely perpetrators? When were you most vulnerable to sexual abuse in your life?"

The increasing use of such imagination exercises led me and several colleagues to wonder about their consequences. What happens when people imagine childhood experiences that did not happen to them? Does imagining a childhood event increase confidence that it occurred? To explore this, we designed a three-stage procedure. We first asked individuals to indicate the likelihood that certain events happened to them during their childhood. The list contains 40 events, each rated on a scale ranging from "definitely did not happen" to "definitely did happen." Two weeks later we asked the participants to imagine that they had experienced some of these events. Different subjects were asked to imagine different events. Sometime later the participants again were asked to respond to the original list of 40 childhood events, indicating how likely it was that these events actually happened to them.

Consider one of the imagination exercises. Participants are told to

IMAGINING AN EVENT can increase a person's belief that the fictitious event actually happened. To study the "imagination inflation" effect, the author and her colleagues asked participants to indicate on a scale the likelihood that each of 40 events occurred during their childhood. Two weeks later they were given guidance in imagining some of the events they said had not taken place and then were asked to rate the original 40 events again. Whereas all participants showed increased confidence that the events had occurred, those who took part in actively imagining the events reported an even greater increase.

imagine playing inside at home after school, hearing a strange noise outside, running toward the window, tripping, falling, reaching out and breaking the window with their hand. In addition, we asked participants questions such as "What did you trip on? How did you feel?"

In one study 24 percent of the participants who imagined the broken-window scenario later reported an increase in confidence that the event had occurred, whereas only 12 percent of those who were not asked to imagine the incident reported an increase in the likelihood that it had taken place. We found this "imagination inflation" effect in each of the eight events that participants were asked to imagine. A number of possible explanations come to mind. An obvious one is that an act of imagination simply makes the event seem more familiar and that familiarity is mistakenly related to childhood memories rather than to the act of imagination. Such source confusion—when a person does not remember the source of information—can be especially acute for the distant experiences of childhood.

Studies by Lyn Goff and Henry L. Roediger III of Washington University of recent rather than childhood experiences more directly connect imagined actions to the construction of false memory. During the initial session, the researchers instructed participants to perform the stated action, imagine doing it or just listen to the statement and do nothing else. The actions were simple ones: knock on the table, lift the stapler, break the toothpick, cross your fingers, roll your eyes. During the second session, the participants were asked to imagine some of the actions that they had not previously performed. During the final session, they answered questions about what actions they actually performed during the initial session. The investigators found that the more times participants imagined an unperformed action, the more likely they were to remember having performed it.

MEMORIES OF INFANCY—such as a mobile hanging over a crib—can be induced even though it is highly unlikely that events from the first year of life can be recalled. In a study by the late Nicholas Spanos and his colleagues at Carleton University, "impossible" memories of the first day of life were planted using either hypnosis or a guided mnemonic restructuring procedure. The mobile was "remembered" by 46 percent of the hypnotized group and by 56 percent of the guided group.

Impossible Memories

It is highly unlikely that an adult can recall genuine episodic memories from the first year of life, in part because the hippocampus, which plays a key role in the creation of memories, has not matured enough to form and store longlasting memories that can be retrieved in adulthood. A procedure for planting "impossible" memories about experiences that occur shortly after birth has been developed by the late Nicholas Spanos and his collaborators at Carleton University. Individuals are led to believe that they have well-coordinated eye movements and visual exploration skills probably because they were born in hospitals that hung swinging, colored mobiles over infant cribs. To confirm whether they had such an experience, half the participants are hypnotized, age-regressed to the day after birth and asked what they remembered. The other half of the group participates in a "guided mnemonic restructuring" procedure that uses age regression as well as active encouragement to re-create the infant experiences by imagining them.

Spanos and his co-workers found that the vast majority of their subjects were susceptible to these memory-planting procedures. Both the hypnotic and guided participants reported infant memories. Surprisingly, the guided group did so somewhat more (95 versus 70 percent). Both groups remembered the colored mobile at a relatively high rate (56 percent of the guided group and 46 percent of the hypnotic subjects). Many participants who did not remember the mobile did recall other things, such as doctors, nurses, bright lights, cribs and masks. Also, in both groups, of those who reported memories of infancy, 49 percent felt that they were real memories, as opposed to 16 percent who claimed that they were merely fantasies. These findings confirm earlier studies that many individuals can be led to construct complex, vivid and detailed false memories via a rather simple procedure. Hypnosis clearly is not necessary.

How False Memories Form

In the lost-in-the-mall study, implantation of false memory occurred when another person, usually a family member, claimed that the incident happened. Corroboration of an event by another person can be a powerful technique for instilling a false memory. In fact, merely claiming to have seen a person do something can lead that person to make a false confession of wrongdoing.

This effect was demonstrated in a study by Saul M. Kassin and his colleagues at Williams College, who investigated the reactions of individuals falsely accused of damaging a computer by pressing the wrong key. The innocent participants initially denied the charge, but when a confederate said that she had seen them perform the action, many participants signed a confession, internalized guilt for the act and went on to confabulate details that were consistent with that belief. These findings show that false incriminating evidence can induce people to accept guilt for a crime they did not commit and even to develop memories to support their guilty feelings.

Research is beginning to give us an understanding of how false memories of complete, emotional and self-participatory experiences are created in adults. First, there are social demands on individuals to remember; for instance, researchers exert some pressure on participants in a study to come up with memories. Second, memory construction by imagining events can be explicitly encouraged when people are having trouble remembering. And, finally, individuals can be encouraged not to think about whether their constructions are real or not. Creation of false memories is most likely to occur when these external factors are present, whether in an experimental setting, in a therapeutic setting or during everyday activities.

False memories are constructed by combining actual memories with the content of suggestions received from others. During the process, individuals may forget the source of the information. This is a classic example of source confusion, in which the content and the source become dissociated.

Of course, because we can implant false childhood memories in some individuals in no way implies that all memories that arise after suggestion are necessarily false. Put another way, although experimental work on the creation of false memories may raise doubt about the validity of long-buried memories, such as repeated trauma, it in no way disproves them. Without corroboration, there is little that can be done to help even the most experienced evaluator to differentiate true memories from ones that were suggestively planted.

The precise mechanisms by which such false memories are constructed await further research. We still have much to learn about the degree of confidence and the characteristics of false memories created in these ways, and we need to discover what types of individuals are particularly susceptible to these forms of suggestion and who is resistant.

As we continue this work, it is important to heed the cautionary tale in the data we have already obtained: mental health professionals and others must be aware of how greatly they can influence the recollection of events and of the urgent need for maintaining restraint in situations in which imagination is used as an aid in recovering presumably lost memories.

The Author

ELIZABETH F. LOFTUS is professor of psychology and adjunct professor of law at the University of Washington. She received her Ph.D. in psychology from Stanford University in 1970. Her research has focused on human memory, eyewitness testimony and courtroom procedure. Loftus has published 18 books and more than 250 scientific articles and has served as an expert witness or consultant in hundreds of trials, including the McMartin preschool molestation case. Her book Eyewitness Testimony won a National Media Award from the American Psychological Foundation. She has received honorary doctorates from Miami University, Leiden University and John Jay College of Criminal Justice. Loftus was recently elected president of the American Psychological Society.

Further Reading

THE MYTH OF REPRESSED MEMORY. Elizabeth F. Loftus and Katherine Ketcham. St. Martin's Press, 1994.

THE SOCIAL PSYCHOLOGY OF FALSE CONFESSIONS: COMPLIANCE, INTERNALIZATION, AND CONFABULATION. Saul M. Kassin and Katherine L. Kiechel in *Psychological Science*, Vol. 7, No. 3, pages 125–128; May 1996.

IMAGINATION INFLATION: IMAGINING A CHILDHOOD EVENT INFLATES CONFIDENCE THAT IT OCCURRED. Maryanne Garry, Charles G. Manning, Elizabeth F. Loftus and Steven J. Sherman in *Psychonomic Bulletin and Review*, Vol. 3, No. 2, pages 208–214; June 1996.

REMEMBERING OUR PAST: STUDIES IN AUTOBIOGRAPHICAL MEMORY. Edited by David C. Rubin. Cambridge University Press, 1996.

SEARCHING FOR MEMORY: THE BRAIN, THE MIND, AND THE PAST. Daniel L. Schacter. BasicBooks, 1996.

ESCAPING FROM THE DARKNESS

Drugs like Prozac, Paxil and Luvox can work wonders for clinically depressed kids. But what about the long-term consequences?

By HOWARD CHUA-EOAN

MEGAN KELLAR IS BUBBLY AND bouncing and lip-synching to the Backstreet Boys. *Get down, get down and move it all around!* The sixth-grader is dancing to the synthesized bubble-gum beat at a talent show at the John Muir Elementary School in Parma, Ohio. *Get down, get down and move it all around!* There is nothing down about Megan, even as she gets down in front of the audience. Her mother remembers a similar effervescence half a dozen years ago. "She'd be singing to herself and making up songs all the time," says Linda Kellar. And sure enough, that part of her is still there. "Megan's such a happy child," the mother of a girl on Megan's baseball team remarked to Linda. Yes, Linda agreed, but there's something you ought to know. Megan is clinically depressed and on the antidepressant Paxil. Says Linda: "She couldn't believe it."

Six years ago, Linda wouldn't have believed that her daughter was clinically depressed either. But shortly after her parents separated, Megan stopped singing. When other kids came over to play, she would lie down in the yard and just watch. At Christmas she wouldn't decorate the tree. Linda thought her daughter was simply melancholy over her parents' split and took her to see a counselor. That seemed to help for a while. Then for about eight months, when Megan was 10, she cried constantly and wouldn't go to school. She lost her appetite and got so weak that at one point she couldn't get out of bed. When a doctor recommended Paxil in conjunction with therapy, Linda recoiled. "I did not want to put my baby on an antidepressant," she says. Then she relented because, she says, "Megan wasn't living her childhood." Linda noticed changes in just two weeks. Soon Megan was singing again. "She's not drugged or doped," says Linda. "She still cries when she sees *Old Yeller* and still has moody days." But, as Megan says, "I'm back to normal, like I used to be."

Megan Kellar shares her kind of normality with hundreds of thousands of other American kids. Each year an estimated 500,000 to 1 million prescriptions for antidepressants are written for children and teens. On the one hand, the benefits are apparent and important. Experts estimate that as many as 1 in 20 American preteens and adolescents suffer from clinical depression. It is something they cannot outgrow. Depression cycles over and over again throughout a lifetime, peaking during episodes of emotional distress, subsiding only to well up again at the next crisis. And as research increasingly shows, depression is often a marker for other disorders, including the syndrome that used to be called manic depression and is now known as bipolar disorder. If undetected and untreated in preteens, depressive episodes can lead to severe anxiety or manic outbursts not only in adulthood but as early as adolescence.

On the other hand, come the questions. How do we tell which kids are at risk? Has science fully apprised us of the effects on kids of medication designed for an adult brain? Have we set out on a path that will produce a generation that escapes the pain only to lose the character-building properties of angst?

TO MEDICATE OR NOT TO MEDICATE? THE DIlemma can be traced back to 1987, when the FDA approved Prozac as the first of a new class of antidepressants known as selective serotonin reuptake inhibitors (SSRIs). Prozac had none of the more serious side effects and risks of the earlier antidepressants and worked faster to control depressive symptoms. Prozac and the other SSRIs (they now include Zoloft, Paxil, Luvox and Celexa) had one other advantage over the older, tricyclic antidepressants: children responded to them. One of the few recent studies on the subject showed that among depressed children ages 8 to 18, 56% improved while on Prozac, in contrast to 33% on a placebo. Says Dr. David Fassler, chair of the American Psychiatric Association's Council on Adolescents and Their Families: "Physicians have a lot of experience using the medications with adult patients with good results, and recent research increases their general level of comfort in using them with children and adolescents."

But which kids?

Not so long ago, many psychiatrists argued that children and young teens could not get depressed because they were not mature enough to internalize their anger. Today, says Fassler, "we realize that depression does occur in childhood and adolescence and that it occurs more often in children than we previously realized."

Still, depression is slightly harder to diagnose in adolescents than in adults, and not because teens are expected to be moodier and more withdrawn. They are less likely to realize that they are depressed and thus less likely to seek help. "Younger kids also have more difficulty expressing their feelings in words," says Dr. Boris Birmaher, a child psychiatrist at the University of Pittsburgh. "When kids become depressed, they become irritable, act out, have temper tantrums and other behavioral problems. It's hard to ascertain that these are the symptoms of depression unless you ask them questions in a language they can understand."

Furthermore, the very definition of being a child—what makes him survive and grow—is being able to move up and down

> "I would have sold my house . . . to get Nick taken care of."
> —SUSAN DUBUQUE, author and mother

emotionally, having a basic elasticity. Says Dr. Peter Jensen, child and adolescent psychiatrist at the National Institute of Mental Health: "A child is more fluid and plastic than an adult. A child may look depressed one day because his dog died but seem O.K. three days later."

But if parents live in a world of family mood swings, that doesn't mean they are prepared to put their own child on mind-altering drugs. That prospect can lead to major soul searching: Will they be thought less of as parents? And if they do agree to antidepressants, will the child still be the one they know?

Donna Mitchell was told her daughter, eight-year-old Sawateos, had attention-deficit hyperactivity disorder, but she also showed signs of serious depression and anxiety, which are often found in combination. Mitchell's first reaction was, "I can pray this away. I thought, Listen, nobody in my family is going on drugs. That's an insult. I figured all we needed was family talks." But two years after the diagnosis, Mitchell has agreed to put her child on the ADHD drug Ritalin. She still resists the idea of antidepressants. It's her preteen daughter who's making the

case for doing it. "Mama, it's in our genes," Sawateos tells her.

All this may help explain why it is so hard for the people closest to children to detect that anything is really wrong. Studies show that parents consistently miss the signs of depression. In one survey by researchers at Ball State and Columbia universities, 57% of teens who had attempted suicide were found to be suffering from major depression. But only 13% of the parents of suicides believed their child was depressed.

Diagnosis is critical because depressed children tend to develop increasingly severe mental disorders and in some cases psychosis as teens and adults. Three studies on children who were depressed before puberty show that as adults they had a higher rate of antisocial behavior, anxiety and major depression than those who experienced their first depressive episode as teens. "Prepubertal depression does occur, and those who get it are more susceptible to [the] mania [of bipolar disorder] later," says Dr. John March, director of the program on pediatric psychopharmacology at Duke University. "The earlier you get it, the more likely you will develop chronic depressive and anxiety symptoms."

So how do psychiatrists pick out kids who are depressed from those who are simply moody? In his book *"Help Me, I'm Sad,"* Fassler lists a number of physical symptoms in three age groups—preschoolers, young school-age children and adolescents. Among preschoolers, the signs include frequent, unexplained stomachaches, headaches and fatigue. Depressed school-age children frequently weigh 10 lbs. less than their peers, may have dramatic changes in sleep patterns and may start speaking in an affectless monotone. Adolescents go through eating disorders, dramatic weight gains or losses, promiscuity, drug abuse, excessive picking at acne, and fingernail biting to the point of bleeding.

Fassler cautions that none of these symptoms may ever be present and a whole con-

stellation of more subjective manifestations must be considered. Adults and adolescents share many of the same warning signs—low self-esteem, tearfulness, withdrawal and a morbid obsession with death and dying. Among adolescents, however, depression is often accompanied by episodes of irritability that, unlike mood swings, stretch for weeks rather than days.

Dr. Elizabeth Weller, professor of psychiatry and pediatrics at the University of Pennsylvania, has developed techniques for detecting depression in kids. First she establishes a rapport with a child. Then she asks, for example, whether he still has fun playing softball or whether it is taking him longer to finish his homework—both of which are ways to figure out whether the child has lost motivation and concentration. Crying is another marker for depression, but Weller says boys rarely admit to it. So she asks them how often they *feel* like crying.

She then quizzes parents and teachers for other signs. Parents can tell her if a child no

> "Depression occurs in children more often than we realized."
> —DAVID FASSLER, psychiatrist

longer cares about his appearance and has lost interest in bathing or getting new clothes. Teachers can tell her whether a child who used to be alert and active has turned to daydreaming or has lost a certain verve. As Weller puts it, "Has the bubble gone out of the face?"

There are several other complicating factors. Some psychiatrists believe depression

WHAT KIDS ARE TAKING

The most commonly prescribed antidepressants for children are not approved in the U.S. for those under 18, but anecdotal reports show that they appear to be safe and work well for this group. Some manufacturers of these drugs are currently conducting studies of their effect on depressed children.

	Prozac	Zoloft	Paxil	Luvox	Celexa
Approved for adults with	■ Depression ■ Bulimia ■ Obsessive-Compulsive Disorder	■ Depression ■ Obsessive-Compulsive Disorder ■ Panic Disorder	■ Depression ■ Obsessive-Compulsive Disorder ■ Panic Disorder ■ Social Phobia (approval pending)	■ Obsessive-Compulsive Disorder	■ Depression
Characteristics	Remains in body for at least two weeks. Makes some patients agitated, anxious	Remains in body for one week	Has sedating effect on many patients	Also approved for use in children with OCD	Produces fewer adverse reactions with other drugs

in younger children often appears in conjunction with other disorders. "Many depressed kids," notes Fassler, "are initially diagnosed with ADHD or learning disabilities. We need to separate out the conditions and treat both problems." But there's a chicken-and-egg problem here: antisocial behavior or a learning disability can lead a child to become isolated and alienated from peers and thus can trigger depression. And depression can further interfere with learning or bring on antisocial behavior.

But does a diagnosis of depression in a child require medication? Consider Nancy Allee's 10-month journey with SSRIs and other drugs. At 12, she was as bubbly as Megan Kellar is now. She soon developed "a five-month-long headache" and started having nightmares. After about a year in counseling, things seemed to be going better and, her mother Judith says, "we terminated it so as not to make it a way of life." A few months later, Nancy became hostile and rebellious but nothing that Judith considered "out of the bounds for a normal teenager." Then, "without any warning, she [took an] overdose" of her migraine medication, was hospitalized and depression was diagnosed. While Judith thought the overdose was out of the blue, Nancy says, "I'd had depression for a long time. If I'd had bad thoughts, I'd always had them and kind of grew up with them. I was always very bubbly, even when I was depressed. A lot of people didn't notice it. To me, suicide had always been an option."

Nancy was put on Zoloft. When that didn't work, the doctor added Paxil and then several other drugs. But there was a panoply of side effects: her hands would shake, she would bang her head against the wall. A voracious reader, she became too withdrawn and listless to pick up a book. There were times she couldn't sleep, but on one occasion she slept 72 hours straight.

"I was seeing five different doctors, and it was overkill," says Nancy. "At one point, I was taking 15 pills in the morning and 15 in the evening. I wound up burying my medication in the backyard. I didn't want to take it anymore." Then Nancy was tested for allergies, a process that required her to be medication free. "It was like the sky was blue again," says Nancy, who at 18 is still off drugs but sees a counselor occasionally. "The colors came back. It was a total change from the medication stupor. Everything wasn't peachy, but I was able to appreciate doing things again."

Most psychiatrists, despite their enthusiasm for the new antidepressants, write prescriptions for only six months to a year and taper the dosage toward the end. Even Fassler admits, "We try to use medication for the minimum amount of time possible. And with a younger child, we're more cautious about using medication because we have less research concerning both the effectiveness and the long-term consequences and

side effects." Says Michael Faenza, president of the National Mental Health Association: "I feel very strongly that no child should be receiving medication without counseling. Medication is just one spoke in the wheel."

HOW TO SPOT A DEPRESSED CHILD

The key thing to watch for is drastic changes in teen behavior. Other red flags to consider:

■ **DIFFICULTY MAINTAINING RELATIONSHIPS** May become antisocial, reject friends or refuse to take part in school and family events

■ **REDUCED PHYSICAL ACTIVITY** May suffer from lethargy or appear to drag self around

■ **MORBID OR SUICIDAL THOUGHTS** May seek out games, music, art or books with death-related themes

■ **LOW SELF-ESTEEM** May feel that they are worthless and that their peers, teachers and family disapprove of them

■ **SELF-DESTRUCTIVE BEHAVIOR** May harm their body by, for example, biting fingernails to the point of bleeding

■ **PROBLEMS AT SCHOOL** Grades may drop or classroom troublemaking rise

■ **CHANGES IN SLEEP PATTERNS** May either have restless nights or sleep away the day

Preschoolers

■ Frequent unexplained stomachaches, headaches, or fatigue

■ Overactivity or excessive restlessness

■ A sad appearance

■ Low tolerance for frustration

■ Irritability

■ Loss of pleasure in activities

■ Tendency to portray the world as bleak

The lack of science about the effects of these drugs on childhood development is the reason the FDA has required all manufacturers of SSRIs that treat depression to conduct studies on the subject. Says Dr. Peter Kramer, professor of psychiatry at Brown University and author of *Listening to Prozac:*

"Anyone who thinks about this problem is worried about what it means to substantially change neurotransmission in a developing brain. We don't know if these kids would compensate on their own over time and if by giving them these medicines we are interfering with that compensatory mechanism."

Until we know more, some argue, the risks of such medication are just too great, if only because of the message it sends to children. Says Dr. Sidney Wolfe, director of Public Citizen's Health Research Group: "We are moving into an era where any quirk of a personality is fair game for a drug. On one hand, we are telling kids to just say no to drugs, but on the other hand, their pediatricians are saying, 'Take this. You'll feel good.' "

Teen rebellion can put a twist on even that, however. One New York couple, becalmed by antidepressants themselves and openly concerned about the depression of their 18-year-old, were castigated by their son for their "weakness" and dependence on Prozac. His argument: your drugs change who you really are. In place of their drugs, the young man argued for his "natural" remedy: marijuana.

Indeed, pot and alcohol are common forms of self-medication among depressed teens. Weller estimates that about 30% of her teen patients have used pot or alcohol after a depressive episode, most of them at the urging of friends who said smoking and drinking would make them feel better. A high school social worker in Minnesota decided to look into the case of a troubled girl who was still a freshman at 17. The girl admitted she smoked pot as a constant habit but did not understand why she craved it so much. A psychological evaluation found the girl was suffering from clinical depression as well as ADHD. She was prescribed an antidepressant, which had striking results. It not only elevated her mood and helped her focus but also reduced her desire for pot and tobacco.

"IT USED TO BE SAID THAT ADOLESCENCE IS the most common form of psychosis," says Kramer, the man who helped make Prozac famous. Then he turns serious. "But if a child has a prolonged period of depressive moods, he needs to be evaluated for depression." Even if little is known about the long-term effects of SSRIs on young bodies, most doctors in the field argue that the drugs are a blessing to kids in pain. Says Duke's March, who is doing a comparative study of the benefits of Prozac and cognitive-behavior therapy: "My clinical experience is that it's worse to risk a major mental illness as a child than to be on medication. If you weigh the risks against the benefits, the benefits are probably going to win."

Susan Dubuque of Richmond, Va., is convinced of the benefits. Her son Nick went through "seven years of testing hell." At seven, ADHD was diagnosed and he was put

The Danger of Suppressing Sadness

What if Holden Caulfield had been taking Prozac?

CONSIDERING HIS WEALTH OF SYMPTOMS—lethargy, forgetfulness, loss of interest in friends and studies—can there be any doubt that Holden Caulfield, the dropout hero of J.D. Salinger's 1950s masterpiece *The Catcher in the Rye,* would be on Luvox, Prozac or a similar drug if he were a teenager today? No doubt whatsoever. A textbook teen depressive by current standards, Caulfield would be a natural candidate for pharmaceutical intervention, joining a rising number of adolescents whose moodiness, anxiety, and rebelliousness are being interpreted as warning signs of chemical imbalances. Indeed, if Caulfield had been a '90s teen, his incessant griping about "phonies" and general hostility toward mainstream society might have been nipped in the neurological bud. The cultural consequence? Incalculable.

With the stroke of countless pens on thousands of prescription pads, the American coming-of-age experience—the stuff of endless novels, movies and pop songs—could gradually be rendered unrecognizable. Goodbye Salinger, Elvis and Bob Dylan; hello psychopharmacology. "The kids in my school traded Zoloft and Prozac pills the way kids used to trade baseball cards," says Stephen Morris, an Episcopal priest and former chaplain at a Texas parochial school. Of course, this school experience doesn't prove that schoolyards everywhere have turned into bustling prescription-drug bazaars. But Morris, who headed a schoolwide committee called Addressing Behaviors of Concern, recalls that "the problems we focused on were not dramatically different from my own youthful experiences." At least three-quarters of the time, says Morris, the kids in question were placed on medication in what he saw as the beginning of a vicious cycle that frequently worsened the original problem. "Challenges that teachers used to handle are being handed over to psychiatrists. Instead of dealing with kids inside the classroom, they yank them out, put them on drugs and stick them back in with glazed eyes a few days later. No wonder the kids end up as outcasts."

Such outcasts may someday form their own majority, if this trend continues. The pain and confusion of growing up, once considered the proper subject of gloomy poetry read under the blankets and angry rock songs rehearsed in the garage, can now mean a quick ticket to the doctor's office. And it doesn't take a lot of acting up for a restless teenager to attract professional attention. On a website sponsored by Channel One, a television network for school-age youth, a recent posting written with the help of the National Association for Mental Illness classified the following behaviors as possible symptoms of manic depression in teens: "increased talking—the adolescent talks too much," "distractibility," unrealistic highs in self-esteem—for example, a teenager who feels specially connected to God."

That last one is a doozy. And heartbreaking. Could it be that Cassie Bernal, who bravely professed her religious faith while staring down the barrel of a gun at the height of the Columbine massacre, was not so much a hero and a martyr as an untreated candidate for lithium? For the education establishment to go on red alert at the first sign of spirituality in their students would be a devastating development.

What is happening here? For better or worse, an institutional drug culture has sprung up in the hallways of All-American High, mimicking the one already established among depressed adults. As was pointed out in the May issue of *Harper's* magazine, the line between illicit, feel-good drugs such as marijuana and amphetamines and legal mood-altering substances such as Luvox, Wellbutrin, and Effexor is a blurry one. Many of the same optimistic claims—enhanced concentration, decreased anxiety, a renewed capacity for feeling pleasure—are made for both types of magic bullet, whether they are bought on the street or in a pharmacy. A profoundly mixed message is being sent to teens when certain substances are demonized for promoting the same subjective states touted on the labels of other compounds. Adolescents, who are famously alert to hypocrisy among their elders, will surely be the first to catch this irony.

At least one hopes so. Teenage skepticism—Holden Caulfield's bitter gift for discerning inconsistencies in the solemn pronouncements of adults—may be one of the troubling traits on the medicators' target list. A pill that tones down youthful b.s. detectors would certainly be a boon to parents and teachers, but how would it enrich the lives of teenagers? Even if such a pill improved their moods—helping them to stick to their studies, say, and compete in a world with close to zero tolerance for unproductive monkeying around—would it not rob them (and the rest of us) of a potent source of social criticism, political idealism and cultural change? The trials and tribulations of growing up yield wisdom for all involved, both kids and parents. The young pose a constant challenge to the old, often an uncomfortable one, almost always an unexpected one, but meeting that challenge with hastily filled prescriptions may be bad medicine for everybody.

For teens who need medication just to function or lessen the real dangers they might pose to others or themselves, the new medications may truly be miraculous. I know from my own experience with clinical depression (contracted as an adult and treated with a combination of therapy and drugs) that such diseases are real and formidable, impossible to wish away. But for kids in the murky emotional borderlands described in books like *The Catcher in the Rye,* antidepressants, stimulants and sedatives aren't a substitute for books and records, heroes and antiheroes. "I get bored sometimes," Holden Caulfield says, "when people tell me to act my age. Sometimes I act a lot older than I am—I really do—but people never notice it. People never notice anything."

Maybe if people start noticing first and medicating second, more of today's confused young Caulfields will stand a chance of maturing into Salingers.

---

on Ritalin. "When he was 10 years old, he didn't want a birthday party because he just couldn't deal with it," she recalls. Then, his mother says, Nick "bottomed out and became suicidal, and one day I found him in a closet with a toy gun pointed at his head, and he said, 'If this was real, I'd use it.'" The next day she saw a psychologist who had recently evaluated Nick and was told, "If you don't get him help, next time he'll be successful." Nick was found to be suffering from clinical depression and took a series of antidepressants. "I was worried about my son's killing himself," says Susan, who was called by clinicians a "histrionic mother" and a "therapy junkie," as she spent $4,000 on drugs and therapy for her son. "I would have sold my house if that was what it would have taken."

Nick is better now, and has co-authored a book with his mom: *Kid Power Tactics for Dealing with Depression.* Susan is happy to have her son back safe—even though there is some stress. "It's so much fun to have an obnoxious 15-year-old," she says, "and I mean *normal* obnoxious."

Reported by Jodie Morse/New York, Alice Park/Washington and James Wilwerth/ Los Angeles

A

abduction, and victimization of children, 201–211
Ablow, Keith Russell, 10
Abram, David, 164
Accelerated Schools, 73, 76
affiliation, superhero play and, 104
age-held-constant research design, 83
after-school supervision, of children, 176–179
aggression, superhero play and, 102–105, 180–185
Ainsworth, Mary D., 157
alcoholism, genes and, 8–12
Allen, Garland, 11
American Academy of Pediatrics (AAP), 40, 41, 45
Anderson, W. French, 14
antidepressants, 221–224
anxiety, 93–94, 222
appearance-reality distinction, categorization and, 49–50
Aristotle, 93
Asia, methods of teaching mathematics in, 59–71
Aslin, Richard, 36
assault, and victimization of children, 201–211
attention deficit disorder (ADD), 149
attention-deficit hyperactivity disorder (ADHD), 57, 58, 222, 223
authoritative parenting, 161
autism, 21, 23
awake characteristics, of infants, 42–43
axons, 21, 22

B

Baumrind, Diana, 161
Bellugi, Ursula, 34–35, 38
Bennett, William, 173, 175
bipolar disorder. See manic depression
Birmaher, Boris, 221
bonding, parent-infant, 86–89
Boylston, Karen, 96
boys, developmental research on, 149–151
brain: bonding and, 86–89; growth of child's, 20–24, 26, 33–39; natural proclivities of, 26; research on, 25–28
Breakefield, Xandra, 9
breastfeeding, cosleeping and, 122, 123, 128
Bronfenbrenner, Urie, 12
Bruner, Jerome, 48
Bush, George, 25

C

Campbell, David, 96
Campbell, John, 15
Capecchi, Mario, 15
Catcher in the Rye, The (Salinger), 224

categories, development of, in young children's thinking, 47–53
censorship, media, and children, 168–175, 180–185
centralization, of public school systems, 73–79
cerebral cortex, 27
charter schools, 72
Chasnoff, Ira, 16
Cherlin, Andrew, 90
children: adoption of gender roles by, 29; development of, and father love, 152–155; divorce and, 131–148; grief and, 90–91; moral development of, 156–162; religion and, 163–165; unsupervised, 176–179; victimization of, 201–211
Chomsky, Noam, 33–34, 36–37
Chu, Judy, 149
Chugani, Harry, 21, 27
classroom organization, of mathematics lessons in Asia, 62–63
clinical depression, among children, 221–224
Clinton, Bill, 72, 73
cocaine, effects of prenatal exposures to, 16–17
cognitive categorization theory, 114–115
coherence, of mathematics lessons in Asia, 61
Cohler, Bert, 95
Coles, Robert, 156
concrete representations, in math lessons, 66
conduct disorder, 149
conflict: between toddlers and caregivers, 106–111; definition of, 107; intervention strategies of, 109–111; prevention strategies of, 109–110; process of, 107–108
cognitive skills, and effect of poverty on children, 186–199
"cootie phenomenon," 112–119
cosleeping, among Hispanic-American children, 128–129 CREB gene, 22
criminality, genes and, 8–12
cross-cultural evidence, 122, 123
cross-sequential lag research design, 83
cross-sex contact, 113, 116
cultural construction, of fatherhood, 153
cultural influences, development of, in sex differences, 31–32
cultural libertarianism, media censorship and, 174–175

D

Damasio, Antonio, 93
Darwin, Charles, 29
Dawson, Geraldine, 23
death, children's reactions to, 90, 91
"Decade of the Brain," 25
dendrites, 21
depression, 87, 88–89, 150, 221–224; warning signs of, 223

developmental victimization, 206–207
Diamond, Marian, 26, 27
Diaz, Rafael M., 55, 56
direct socialization, gender segregation and, among children, 113
diversity, handling of academic, in math lessons, 63–65
divorce, effect of, on children, 131–148
Dole, Bob, 173
dominance, superhero play and, 104
dopamine, 10
dropouts, school, 98–99

E

eating disorders, 151
education: childhood friendships and, 97–101; effect of poverty on children and, 186–199; gender issues and, 103; lack of after school parental supervision and, 176–179; mathematics, Asian methods of, 59–71; in New York City, 73–74; for poor children, 72–79; superhero play and, 102–105
Eisenberg, Nancy, 157
Elium, Don, 150
Emotional Brain, The (LeDoux), 25, 28
emotional intelligence, 28, 92–96
Emotional Intelligence (Goleman), 28
emotions: and development of wariness, 82–85; and effect of poverty on children, 186–199; genes and, 8–12
empathy, 95, 151, 156, 157
environment versus heredity: bonding and, 86–89; personality and, 8–12
epilepsy, 21
errors, use of, in math lessons, 67–68
eugenics, 9, 11
evolution: and development of sex differences, 29–32; framework of, 29; principles of, 29
external suggestion, and false childhood memories, 218

F

false memories, 215–220; implantation of, 219–220
family composition-parental absence hypothesis, and children of divorce, 135–137, 142
Fassler, David, 221, 223
fast mapping, 37–38
father love, 152–155
female-female competition, 29–30
feminism, 149
Fernald, Anne, 23, 37–38
fertility drugs, multiple births and, 13
first-time parents, cosleeping and, 127–128
Fisher, Diane, 151
Fitzpatrick, Susan, 25

Flynn, Laurie, 8
Fox, James Alan, 177
Freud, Sigmund, 9
Friedman, Dennis, 90
friendship, children and, 97–101
functional brain imaging, 35

G

gender: developmental research on
   boys and, 149–151; parents' marital transitions and, 135; play
   and, 103; victimization of children and, 207–209
gender segregation: among children,
   112–119; developmental consequences of, 112–113; reduction
   of, 116–119; salience of, 117–
   118
gene therapy, 14
generalizations, categorization and, 50
genes: brain development and, 21–
   22; personality and, 8–12
Gerken, LouAnn, 37
Gilligan, Carol, 149, 151
glial cells, 20
Goff, Lyn, 219
Goleman, Daniel, 28, 92–96
Goodman, Corey, 21, 22
Goodwin, Frederick, 9
Gore, Al, 177
grammar, language learning and, 33–39
Greenough, William, 12, 24
Greenspan, Stanley, 21, 23
grief, children and, 90–91
Grollman, Earl, 90
growth cone, 22
Gunnar, Megan, 87–88, 89
Gurian, Michael, 148

H

Hamer, Dean, 11
Hare, Robert, 95
Harlow, Harry, 87
Harris, Maxine, 90
health risks, of poverty, 186–199
hedgehog gene, 21
heredity. See genes
heroes, Power Rangers and, 180–185
Heyl, Peter, 13
Hillman, Catherine, 90
Hoffman, Martin L., 156, 157
Homer, 172
homicide, and victimization of chil-
   dren, 201–211
homosexuality, genes and, 8–12
Howell, Catherine T., 159
Human Genome Project, 15
Hundt, Reed, 175
Huttenlocher, Janellen, 39
Huttenlocher, Peter, 22
Hyman, Stephen, 12
hypnosis, 215

I

Ianni, Francis A., 161, 162
in vitro fertilization, 13, 14–15
individual risk and vulnerability hypothesis, and children of divorce,
   134–135, 142
inner-city schools, 74–79
Inside the Brain (Kotulak), 26
intelligence, emotional, 28, 92–96

J

James, William, 47
Jensen, Peter, 222
Jusczyk, Peter, 33, 36

K

Kagan, Jerome S., 88, 93, 157
Kamin, Leon, 8
Kandel, Eric, 22
Kegl, Judy, 38, 39
Kitcher, Philip, 11
Klima, Edward, 38
Kohlberg, Lawerence, 55, 56, 157, 158
Kotulak, Ronald, 26
Kramer, Peter, 222
Kranzler, Elliot, 91
Krimsky, Sheldon, 14, 15
Kruskal-Wallis test, 42
Kuhl, Patricia, 23

L

language, categorization and, 50–51
Lara, Adnir, 150
"latchkey kids," parental supervision
   and, 176–179
lead poisoning, 191
LeDoux, Joseph, 25, 28, 93
LeVay, Simon, 10–11
limbic system, 88, 89, 93
linear regression analysis, 42
locomotor experience, and development of wariness of heights, 82–
   85
Loftus, Elizabeth F., 215–220
logistic regression analysis, 45
love, bonding and, 86–89

M

Macklin, Ruth, 15
made-to-order genes, 14–15
male-male competition, 29–30, 32
Maltz, Wendy, 218
manic depression, 9–10, 221, 222
marital transitions, effect of, on children, 131, 148
Markus, Hazel, 161
math, Asian methods of teaching, 59–71
Mayer, John, 92
McGaugh, James, 28
McHugh, Paul, 92, 93, 96

McKenna, J. J., 122–130
media, influence of, on children, 168–
   175, 180–185
Melmed, Matthew, 24
memory, 88
memory distortion, 216
mental illness, as brain disease, 8–12
mental retardation, 21, 88
metamood, 93
Mills, Debra, 38
Mitchell, Walter, 96
"misinformation effect," 216
moral development, of children, 156–
   162
moral identity, development of, 160–161
moral judgement, 157
motor milestones, of infants, 40–46
Mott, Charles Stewart, 177
mourning, children and, 90–91
multiple births, 13
multiple solutions, use of, in math lessons, 66–67

N

National Assessment of Educational
   Progress, 72
national school designs, 72–73
nature versus nurture, brain development and, 21–22
neglect, and victimization of children,
   201–211
neocortex, 93
neural networks, 37
neural tube, 21
neuroscience, 25–28
Newman, Frank, 21
Newport, Elissa, 34, 36, 39

O

observational learning, 181
Ortega, Ruben, 177
out-of-wedlock births, 193–194
Oyserman, Daphne, 161

P

pandemic, victimization of children
   as, 202
parantese, 23
parent-infant cosleeping, 122–130;
   physiological changes in, 122–123
patchwork systems, 73
paternal acceptance, 152–155
paternal acceptance-rejection theory,
   152–155
Paxil. See antidepressants
Peele, Stanton, 10
peer interactions, self-identity and,
   among adolescents, 161
peer nomination, as measure of acceptance, 97
Perry, Bruce, 23, 88

personality, effect of children's and parents' marital transitions on, 134–135; genes and, 8–12
Phelps, Michael, 27
phonemes, 35
physical abuse, and victimization of children, 201–211
Piaget, Jean, 47, 50, 54–55, 109, 158
Pickerel, Jacqueline E., 217
Pinker, Steven, 33–34, 38
Pipher, Mary, 149
Plato, 172
play patterns, development of, and sex differences, 30–31
play, superhero, 102–105, 180–185
play-style hypothesis, 114
Pollack, William, 150
Positron Emission Tomography (PET) scans, 27
Poussaint, Alvin, 96
poverty, effect of, on children, 186–199
Powell, Colin, 177, 178
Power Rangers, 180–185
prematurity, multiple births and, 13
presidents, emotional intelligence of, 95
private speech, and cognitive development of children, 54–58
probabilistic epigenesis, 83
prone sleeping, children and, 40–46
prospective study design, 124–127
protective factors, resilient children and, 212–214
proximal processes, 12
Prozac. See antidepressants
public education, 72, 73
public policy, and, biological aspects of personality, 8–12

Rakic, Pasko, 21, 24
Ramey, Craig, 26
Rando, Therese, 91
rape, and victimization of children, 201–211
rating scales, as measure of acceptance, 97–98
Reading Recovery, 75
real-world problems and objects, use of, in math lessons, 65–66
registration review, 73
religion, children and, 163–165
remarriage, effect of, on children, 131–148
resilient children, 134, 212–214
Ritalin, 222, 224

robbery, and victimization of children, 201–211
Roediger, Henry L., 219
Rosenthal, Robert, 94–95
rough-and-tumble play, superhero play and, 102–105

Saffran, Jenny, 36
Salinger, J. D., 224
Salovey, Peter, 92, 96
schizophrenia, 8, 21
School Development Program, 73, 76
Seidenberg, Mark, 37
selective serotonin reuptake inhibitors (SSRIs), 221
Seligman, Martin, 94
sex differences, evolution and development of, 29–32; in play style, among children, 113–114
sex-typed toy hypothesis, 114
sexual abuse, and victimization of children, 201–211
Shatz, Carla, 20, 21
Shields, Donald, 22
Shweder, Richard A., 159
single-parent families, effect of, on children, 131–148
Slavin, Robert E., 75,76
sleep arousal, cosleeping and, 122, 123
sleep characteristics, of infants, 42
sleep position, effects of, on infant motor development, 40–46
Smolensky, Paul, 38
social communication, 56
social groups, impact of, 115–116
social psychiatry, 9
social skills: friendships and, 97–101; superhero play and, 102–107
socialization, interactions of, 106–111
Soros, George, 177
speech, egocentric, 54, 55, 56
stepfamilies, effect of, on children, 131–148
Stock, Gregory, 14
Stott, Fran, 95
stress, 23; parental divorce and, 137; resilient children and, 212–214
Stryker, Michael, 22
Success for All, 73–79
sudden infant death syndrome (SIDS), 40, 54, 122, 123
Suomi, Stephen, 86, 87
superhero play, 102–107, 180–185

supervision, lack of parental, after school, 176–179
supine sleeping, children and, 40–46

T

taxonomic grouping, categorization and, 48
Taylor, Frederick Winslow, 76
Tees, Richard, 35
Telecommunications Act of 1996, 180, 182
temperament, effect of children's and parents' marital transitions on, 134–135
Thatcher, Robert, 89
theft, and victimization of children, 201–211
thematic grouping, categorization and, 48
Thompson, Michael, 150
Title I program, 75, 79
toddlers and caregivers, conflict resolutions of, 106–111
toy preferences, and gender segregation of children, 113
Trevarthen, Colwyn, 157
trochees, use of, by parents, 36

V

Valenti, Jack, 169
V-chip, media censorship and, 168–175, 180–185
victimization, of children, 201–211
violence, Power Rangers and, 180–185
vouchers, 72
Vygotsky, Lev S., 54–58

W

Walker, Lawrence, 159
Warchow, Robert, 170, 171
Watson, James, 14
Weller, Elizabeth, 222, 223
Wellman, Glo, 50
Werker, Janet, 35
Williams syndrome, 34–35
"windows of opportunity," 27

W

Zinn, David, 90
Zoloft. See antidepressants

AE Article Review Form

We encourage you to photocopy and use this page as a tool to assess how the articles in **Annual Editions** expand on the information in your textbook. By reflecting on the articles you will gain enhanced text information. You can also access this useful form on a product's book support Web site at **http://www.dushkin.com/ online/.**

NAME: DATE:

_____

TITLE AND NUMBER OF ARTICLE:

_____

BRIEFLY STATE THE MAIN IDEA OF THIS ARTICLE:

_____

LIST THREE IMPORTANT FACTS THAT THE AUTHOR USES TO SUPPORT THE MAIN IDEA:

_____

WHAT INFORMATION OR IDEAS DISCUSSED IN THIS ARTICLE ARE ALSO DISCUSSED IN YOUR TEXTBOOK OR OTHER READINGS THAT YOU HAVE DONE? LIST THE TEXTBOOK CHAPTERS AND PAGE NUMBERS:

_____

LIST ANY EXAMPLES OF BIAS OR FAULTY REASONING THAT YOU FOUND IN THE ARTICLE:

_____

LIST ANY NEW TERMS/CONCEPTS THAT WERE DISCUSSED IN THE ARTICLE, AND WRITE A SHORT DEFINITION:

_____

ANNUAL EDITIONS revisions depend on two major opinion sources: one is our Advisory Board, listed in the front of this volume, which works with us in scanning the thousands of articles published in the public press each year; the other is you—the person actually using the book. Please help us and the users of the next edition by completing the prepaid article rating form on this page and returning it to us. Thank you for your help!

ANNUAL EDITIONS: Child Growth and Development 00/01

ARTICLE RATING FORM

Here is an opportunity for you to have direct input into the next revision of this volume. We would like you to rate each of the 35 articles listed below, using the following scale:

1. Excellent: should definitely be retained
2. Above average: should probably be retained
3. Below average: should probably be deleted
4. Poor: should definitely be deleted

Your ratings will play a vital part in the next revision.
So please mail this prepaid form to us just as soon as you complete it.
Thanks for your help!

RATING

ARTICLE

1. Politics of Biology
2. Multiplying the Risks
3. Designer Babies
4. Hope for 'Snow Babies'
5. Fertile Minds
6. What Do We Know from Brain Research?
7. Evolution and Developmental Sex Differences
8. Baby Talk
9. Effects of Sleep Position on Infant Motor Development
10. Categories in Young Children's Thinking
11. Why Children Talk to Themselves
12. How Asian Teachers Polish Each Lesson to Perfection
13. "Ready, READ!"
14. Early Experience and Emotional Development: The Emergence of Wariness of Heights
15. Babies, Bonds, and Brains
16. How Kids Mourn
17. The EQ Factor
18. Children without Friends
19. Teacher Response to Superhero Play: To Ban or Not to Ban?

RATING

ARTICLE

20. Assisting Toddlers & Caregivers During Conflict Resolutions: Interactions That Promote Socialization
21. Gender Segregation among Children: Understanding the "Cootie Phenomenon"
22. Where Will the Baby Sleep? Attitudes and Practices of New and Experienced Parents Regarding Cosleeping with Their Newborn Infants
23. What Matters? What Does Not? Five Perspectives on the Association between Marital Transitions and Children's Adjustment
24. Boys Will Be Boys
25. Father Love and Child Development: History and Current Evidence
26. The Moral Development of Children
27. Playing with God
28. Buried Alive
29. It's 4:00 p.m. Do You Know Where Your Children Are?
30. Of Power Rangers and V-Chips
31. The Effects of Poverty on Children
32. Victimization of Children
33. Resilience in Development
34. Creating False Memories
35. Escaping from the Darkness

(Continued on next page)

NO POSTAGE
NECESSARY
IF MAILED
IN THE
UNITED STATES

BUSINESS REPLY MAIL
FIRST-CLASS MAIL PERMIT NO. 84 GUILFORD CT

POSTAGE WILL BE PAID BY ADDRESSEE

Dushkin/McGraw-Hill
Sluice Dock
Guilford, CT 06437-9989

ABOUT YOU

Name _____   Date _____

Are you a teacher? ☐   A student? ☐
Your school's name _____

Department _____

Address _____ City _____ State ____ Zip ____

School telephone # _____

YOUR COMMENTS ARE IMPORTANT TO US !

Please fill in the following information:
For which course did you use this book?
_____

Did you use a text with this *ANNUAL EDITION*? ☐ yes ☐ no
What was the title of the text?
_____

What are your general reactions to the *Annual Editions* concept?
_____

Have you read any particular articles recently that you think should be included in the next edition?
_____

Are there any articles you feel should be replaced in the next edition? Why?
_____

Are there any World Wide Web sites you feel should be included in the next edition? Please annotate.
_____

May we contact you for editorial input? ☐ yes ☐ no
May we quote your comments? ☐ yes ☐ no